Gentleman Boss

Gentleman Boss

The Life and Times of Chester Alan Arthur

By

THOMAS C. REEVES

Published by American Political Biography Press

Newtown, CT

Grateful acknowledgment is made to the following
for permission to reprint privately owned material:

The New York Public Library:
For the Silas Burt Papers, Levi P. Morton Papers,
and Roscoe Conkling Letters from the Manuscripts and Archives Division,
Astor, Lenox and Tilden Foundations.

Chicago Historical Society: For quotes from David Davis letter to
Walter Q. Gresham, June 25, 1884.

New York State Library, Albany: For quotes from the Edwin D. Morgan Papers.

The Historical Society of Wisconsin: For quotations from the
Timothy O. Howe Papers.

The Rutherford B. Hayes Library: For quotations from the Hayes Papers.

Henry E. Huntington Library and Art Gallery, San Marino, California:
For Letter from Roscoe Conkling to Benjamin Perley Poore: HM 23742.

Charles Pinkerton Jr. and Peyton R. H. Pinkerton:
For material from the Charles Pinkerton Collection.

George F. Howe: For quotations from the William Arthur Jr. Papers.

New Hampshire Historical Society: For quotations from the following letters:
Chester A. Arthur to E. D. Morgan, 7–12–72;
George W. Marston to Chandler, 9–15–80;
James G. Blaine to Chandler, 1–12–82;
and Chester A. Arthur to Chandler, 10–4–86.

The New-York Historical Society: For quotes from the Chester A. Arthur,
George Bliss, Silas Burt, and Augustus Porter Greene collections.

Anne Eustis Emmet and Margaret Eustis Finley: For quotations
from three letters from and to Levi P. Morton:
William E. Curtis to Levi P. Morton, 7–20–80;
Roscoe Conkling to Levi P. Morton, 8–1–80;
and Levi P. Morton to Roscoe Conkling, 3–2–81.

What Arthur was in the New–York Custom–house
he is to-day in the President's chair. . . .
the boss system is a degradation;
it goes from the gutter to the White House.
—WAYNE MACVEAGH
April 13, 1882

He was wise in statesmanship and firm and effective
in administration. Honesty in national finance,
purity and effectiveness in the civil service,
the promotion of commerce,
the re-creation of the American navy,
reconciliation between North and South
and honorable friendship with foreign nations
received his active support. Good causes
found in him a friend and bad measures
met in him an unyielding opponent.
—ELIHU ROOT
June 13, 1899

Contents

Contents • xii

Illustrations

(following page 300)

THE POLITICS of late nineteenth-century America have attracted few historians in recent years. Polemicists of the Progressive Era and the Great Depression, amplifying the shrill condemnations and oversimplifications of such contemporary critics as Henry Adams and Lord Bryce, were profoundly influential in persuading succeeding generations of scholars that the Gilded Age required little study. Scores of major political figures of the period lack competent, up-to-date biographies, and much work remains to be done on party structures, campaign financing, voter behavior, and so on. Even the Presidents of the era have been generally ignored and forgotten. Chester A. Arthur? The name brings smiles. One might as well consider Rutherford B. Hayes or Benjamin Harrison, other supposedly nondescript, undistinguished, bland, bearded politicos of serious interest surely to no one in a swiftly changing era that has long known powerful Chief Executives, multibillion-dollar budgets, and a stupendous array of national and international responsibilities.

Disinterest alone does not account for Arthur's obscurity, for he scrupulously attempted to keep aloof from the press during his years in politics and ordered the great bulk of his personal and official papers destroyed shortly before his death. Many of his closest associates took similar steps to protect themselves from historians. Until now only a single scholarly biography of perhaps our least-known President has appeared, published in 1934, and fewer than a half-dozen articles. One leading encyclopedia carries an account of Arthur's life that contains twenty-one factual errors.

In December 1967, a graduate student of mine at the University of

Colorado, who doubled as an attorney, broached the possibility of studying some documents owned by a client. He was unsure of the origin of
the papers and could say only that they had something to do with President Arthur. I smiled and said I would like to see them. Several months
later I undertook their examination and discovered that they were
Arthur's personal letterbooks from the campaign of 1880—a contest in
which the New Yorker was both the vice-presidential candidate of the
Republican Party and chairman of the New York Republican State Committee. The Arthur I encountered was decidedly not the mildly bumbling,
ineffectual, pristine dandy common to traditional biographical accounts.

My curiosity aroused, I began to pursue other Arthur materials that
had come to light in recent years. Library research disclosed relevant
collections at the New York Historical Society and the Library of Congress, and Arthur letters were scattered in archives all across the country.
Papers of Cabinet members and close friends had also surfaced, and it was
not long before I realized that I was faced with a fascinating, intensely
human, and significant story. A biography was inevitable. The search led
to the former President's grandson, who owned boxes bulging with
family documents and photographs, and had many stories to share of his
father's life in the White House. President Arthur's son-in-law soon
turned up, alert and witty at ninety-nine, and he too possessed important
historical materials. Portions of Arthur's Civil War correspondence were
found in Cheyenne, Wyoming. His family Bible and White House scrapbooks were in New York City. A rare and valuable collection of newspaper clippings once belonging to Arthur's nieces was discovered lying
open to the public in the tiny replica of the Arthur birthplace in Fairfield,
Vermont. And so it went. Knowledge usually dissolves indifference, and
in this case the experience was exceptionally rewarding.

I am deeply indebted to the late Chester A. Arthur III and the late
Mr. Charles Pinkerton of Mt. Kisco, New York, for their many kind-
nesses. Special thanks go to Mrs. John Grathwol, Mr. Charles Morrissey
of the Vermont Historical Society, Mrs. Harriet S. Lacy of the New
Hampshire State Historical Society, Miss Betty Monkman of the White
House, Mrs. Warren J. Broderick and Mr. Warren F. Broderick of Lansingburgh, New York, Dr. George F. Howe of Washington, D.C., Mr.
Vernon B. Hampton of Staten Island, New York, Mrs. Cary I. Crockett
of Seven Mile Ford, Virginia, Mr. and Mrs. Charles Spicka of Cheyenne,
Wyoming, Mr. Arthur M. Crocker of New York City, Dr. John Broderick
and Dr. Oliver Orr of the Library of Congress, and the excellent library
staff at the University of Wisconsin, Parkside. Professors Louis G.
Geiger of Iowa State University and Vincent P. De Santis of the University of Notre Dame, and Dean Harry J. Sievers, S.J., of Fordham

University have provided stimulation and wisdom. Mr. Angus Cameron of Alfred A. Knopf is an inspiration as well as a first-rate editor.

This book was assisted by grants from the El Pomar Investment Company of Colorado Springs, Colorado, the American Philosophical Society, and the University of Wisconsin.

Gentleman Boss

Zack

O<small>N A STEAMY</small> July day in 1881, Americans were stunned by the news that the President of the United States had been gunned down in the Washington railway depot and was on the threshold of death. The assassin, captured moments after firing two shots into James A. Garfield, proudly announced that his deed had been undertaken for the purpose of placing the Vice-President in the White House.

Many bewildered Americans could barely recall the Vice-President's name. What was known of Chester A. Arthur by observers of national events was far from flattering. Only a few years earlier the Hayes Administration had forced him from the New York Customhouse amid charges of corruption, inefficiency, and excessive political partisanship. His elevation to the national GOP ticket in 1880 was understood to be a sop to the worst element in the party. It was generally agreed that he had disgraced the office of the Vice-President not only by remaining loyal to a number of notorious spoilsmen but by actively participating in a vigorous political attack against his former running mate. And now a self-proclaimed confidant of Arthur's had attempted to murder the President, perhaps on Arthur's behalf. Careful readers of the press also recalled a widely circulated rumor that the Vice-President had been born in Canada, rather than in Vermont as he claimed, and was thus constitutionally ineligible to become the Chief Executive. Suddenly millions of Americans were eager to find out who and what Chester A. Arthur really was.

Chester Alan Arthur was one of three first-generation Americans to become President of the United States. On his father's side he was Scotch-

Irish; his great-grandmother, Jane Campbell, was said to have come from Scotland to Ulster, where she married Gavin Arthur in 1720. (While the family Bible mentions only three generations preceding Chester's birth, one genealogist has the Arthurs descending from the "MacArthurs" of Scotland, whose history can be traced to the fifteenth century and Clan Campbell.) Their son, Alan, married Eliza McHarg, and William Arthur, Chester's father, was born in 1796 in the townland of Dreen, across the bridge from the village of Cullybackey, in County Antrim.[1]

A brick wall collapsed on one of William's feet as a boy, leaving him with a limp, and at his family's suggestion he channeled his considerable energy away from the normal farm chores and into his schoolwork. At about eighteen, he graduated from Belfast College and soon, probably in 1818 or 1819, he emigrated to Quebec in search of the prosperity that was rapidly disappearing in Ulster. One of his first jobs was teaching at the Free School of Royal Foundation in Dunham, fifteen miles north of the Vermont border.[2] Shortly, he eloped with an eighteen-year-old Vermonter, Malvina Stone, and the two were married in 1821.[3]

The Stones were of English descent. In 1763, Malvina's grandfather, Uriah Stone, built a log cabin in Piermont, New Hampshire, for his young wife, the former Hephzibah Hadley, and this part of the Connecticut River valley remained their home for nearly half a century. Uriah fought for the Continental army during the Revolution and named the seventh of his thirteen children, born January 22, 1777, George Washington Stone. This son was educated at Dartmouth and in about 1800 moved with four of his brothers to Berkshire, Vermont, to farm. He was soon married to Judith Stevens of Newbury, and their first child, Malvina, arrived on April 24, 1802. (Arthur family tradition says that Judith Stevens was part Indian, but this was a matter the twenty-first President chose never to discuss publicly.)[4]

Mrs. William Arthur was dubiously blessed with fertility, and her husband was hard-pressed to keep his growing family housed and fed. The first child, Regina, was born at Dunham in 1822. By March of 1824, when their next child, Jane, was born, the Arthurs were in Burlington, Vermont, where William studied law and taught school. They then moved to Jericho, Vermont, where the third daughter, Almeda, was born in December 1825. From there, in 1827, the Arthurs traveled to Waterville, Vermont, where their fourth daughter, Ann Eliza, was born on the first day of 1828.[5]

While living in Waterville, William attended a revival in Burlington and was converted to the Free Will Baptist persuasion. The Arthurs had been Presbyterians in Ireland, and William and Malvina were married in an Episcopal church. But the impact of the religious experience in Burlington was apparently such that William decided to join the Baptist clergy, and in 1827 he was licensed to preach. The following year he switched to the larger "regular" or "close communion" sect, underwent a formal clerical examination, and was ordained May 8, 1828. His first call came within the month from Fairfield, Vermont, a few miles northwest of Waterville, and the Arthurs moved their simple belongings to the town where their first son would be born.[6]

Fairfield was a farming community in the northwest corner of Vermont with a population of just over 2,200. Nevertheless, no fewer than twenty-one Baptist congregations were scattered in and around its borders.[7] It was not prosperous country, and William was forced to teach school and preach in other towns in the state and in Canada to supplement his meager annual salary of $250. The forty-six members of the congregation in North Fairfield were building a parsonage on a rather poor piece of land about a half-mile from the church when the Arthurs arrived, and for over a year all six members of the family were obliged to live in a small log cabin. A colleague remembered visiting William Arthur one stormy night in mid-winter: "He expressed to me some of the trials he had when out of bread, and out of wood, and himself a cripple. His temper would rise; and he would almost resolve to quit the ministry. Then the cloud would break; and a good meeting, with a sympathizing friend, would set all right again."[8]

It was within the crude surroundings of the temporary parsonage that, on October 5, 1829, Malvina Arthur gave birth to her fifth child. (The traditional date 1830 is incorrect. Arthur made himself a year younger, no doubt out of simple vanity, some time between 1870 and 1880. This slight measure of duplicity caused the state of Vermont in 1954 to place a replica of Arthur's birthplace on the wrong spot; the tiny house commemorates the new parsonage, completed in 1830.)[9] She was assisted by Dr. Chester Abell, one of William's close friends, and the nine-pound infant was named Chester for the physician, and Alan (pronounced Alán) after William's father.[10] Over a half century later a neighbor of the Arthurs' recalled:

> One day, early in October, my grandmother and mother were away all day, and were not home when it was time for me to go to bed. The next morning my mother told me that they had a little boy over at the Arthurs'. My grandmother came over from the Arthurs' soon afterward, and said she had been dressing the boy.
>
> "And think of it," she said to my father in a reproachful voice; "when I announced the boy to Elder Arthur he danced up and down the room."[11]

"Elder" Arthur, as William was called, not infrequently shocked and irritated his parishioners. "He was of medium size, and dark hair, with a keen, penetrating eye," a colleague recalled, an articulate, witty, passionate man whose "sarcasms, when used, were cutting." His thick Irish accent, hot temper, and argumentative spirit left indelible impressions wherever he went.[12] William Arthur did not suffer fools or sinners well; his students often lived in terror of him, and more than once a lengthy sermon was interrupted by a pointed reminder to one of his flock to wake up and/or pay attention. A friend would recall:

> Rev. William Arthur was a man of ability and originality of character, who formed his opinions without much reference to the views of others, and was most persistent and vigorous in asserting and maintaining them. A recalcitrant deacon or trustee in a church over which he was pastor had by no means a life of peace and his own way; the best thing such a malcontent could do was to maintain an armed neutrality while Mr. Arthur was at the head of affairs.[13]

Compounding his difficulties with deacons and trustees was the fact that Elder Arthur was an abolitionist. The Reverend Orson S. Murray, who converted him to the highly unpopular cause in the 1830s, recalled a half-century later: "He clung to his pulpit and preached the doctrines of Christianity, but was ever ready to extend the right hand of fellowship to me and, for that matter, any other anti-slavery lecturer in the country." Murray himself was mobbed seven times (or so he said) while preaching abolitionism in the Green Mountains, and it seems likely that at least a portion of Arthur's combativeness toward his parishioners stemmed from his hatred of slavery. At least two accounts of his life contend that he was a co-founder of the New-York Anti-Slavery Society in 1835. The congregation Arthur served near Greenwich, New York, from 1839 to 1844 "took [a] very strong and decided position regarding intemperance and slavery, a position that at times aroused hostility and even active opposition . . ."[14]

Predictably, the Arthurs moved often: between 1828 and 1864, when William retired, they served eleven different parishes. From Fairfield, in 1832, they went to Williston, Vermont, where William doubled as the principal of the Williston Academy. A year later they were in Hinesburg, Vermont, where their second son was born. From there, in April 1835, they traveled into western New York State, living in Perry, in Wyoming County, until September 1837, and then moving to York, in Livingston County, where they stayed until late 1839. William found a new job in November at the Bottskill Baptist Church in Union Village (now Greenwich) that paid the munificent sum of $500 a year, and remained until

July 30, 1844 (perhaps because the salary was increased to $550). He then accepted a position with the First Particular Baptist Church and Society of Gibbonsville and West Troy at Schenectady, where he stayed until September 1846. Other churches served were in Lansingburgh (1846–49), Hoosick (1849–53), West Troy [now Watervliet] (1853–55), and Albany (1855–64).[15]

In the mid-1840s, William Arthur had at last sufficient time and financial security to devote a portion of his week to scholarly and literary pursuits. Moreover, Union College was nearby and he must have been stimulated by its faculty and its famous President Eliphalet Nott. (In 1845, the college awarded Arthur an honorary Master of Arts.) In Schenectady he began the four-year task of editing *The Antiquarian and General Review*, a magazine of popular knowledge, covering history, philology, religion, and science. Arthur did much of the writing himself, and revealed a broad range of interests. Dr. Nott was a contributor, and some materials were borrowed from other magazines and journals. A part of a table of contents to one of the bound volumes read:

> Family Names, Import History and Heraldry of . . .
> Fish tamed by a child . . .
> Fight between a Frog and a Robin . . .
> Forty-seven years in the Bastille . . .
> First Watch . . .
> First discovery of Salt . . .

The magazine was not the vessel of higher learning it has sometimes been made out to be; its standards of historical and scientific inquiry were not unlike those of a great many periodicals of the time that found their way into the homes of rural New Yorkers. For example, Arthur apparently believed the story of a 370-year-old man who had "changed his hair and recovered his teeth four times," and who "in the course of his life . . . had 700 wives, some of whom died, and the rest he had put away."[16]

Of course, entertainment and education were not the primary goals of the magazine, and every issue contained its share of morality tales designed to portray the truths of God and the wisdom of the righteous. In the June 1848 issue readers encountered on the first page "The Defaulter—A True Tale," a treacly short story about a deceptive wife whose evil deeds drove her to suicide. Its author was "C.A.A." and more than a few people in the area of Schenectady and Lansingburgh (where the third and fourth volumes were published) knew that these were the initials of Elder Arthur's eighteen-year-old son.[17]

After a no-doubt-rigorous introduction to education by his father,

Chester first attended school at the academy in Union Village. Shortly after the family moved to Schenectady he was placed for the winter in the Lyceum to prepare for entrance to Union College. A teacher would recall: "His eyes were dark and brilliant, and his physical system finely formed. He was frank and open in his manners, and genial in his disposition."[18] An able and intelligent student, "Chet," as his classmates knew him, took time away from the heavily classical curriculum to co-edit *The Lyceum Review*, a school newspaper that featured short sermons (e.g., "Reflections on the Grave"), poetry, and campus news.[19] As a further diversion, in the fall of 1844 he joined a number of young Whigs who built an "ash pole" to testify to their support of Henry Clay, and took part in a brawl with another group of adolescents who objected. Years later, as President, Arthur thought back to this bruising struggle and chuckled, "I have been in many a political battle since then, but none livelier, or that more thoroughly enlisted me."[20]

Arthur entered Union College in September 1845 as a sophomore. Union could trace its traditions to 1795 and was a growing, prosperous part of the old Dutch town of Schenectady. Its respectable academic reputation and financial solvency were products of the indefatigable Dr. Eliphalet Nott, then in his fifth decade as the school's president. Students had always liked "Old Prex," as they called him, and he in turn revealed great warmth and admiration for the 250 young men in his charge. He had admitted so many boys to Union who had been expelled from other schools that the college was called "Botany Bay" in some quarters, a reference to the place of penal exile. Besides being an innovative educator, Nott was a well-known inventor who had patented thirty different kinds of stoves and devised an ingenious steamship boiler. Almost all of his energy and personal fortune went into the college he would head for sixty-two years, and students often smiled approvingly in 1845 as the seventy-two-year-old clergyman rode by in his custom-made three-wheeled carriage.[21]

Though the college offered a large number of science courses and a new program in civil engineering, Chester Arthur chose to pursue the traditional classical curriculum. This decision was undoubtedly influenced by Elder Arthur, who spoke Latin, Greek, and Hebrew.[22] The school records do not reveal exactly what he studied but it is known that he took French along with the traditional portions of the likes of Livy, Horace, Xenophon, Herodotus, Thucydides, Cicero, Demosthenes, Tacitus, Juvenal, Homer, and Hesiod. A friend remembered him as a tall, good-looking, slender youth with fashionably long hair and clear brown eyes. In his senior year he wore a green coat occasionally to show his sympathy for the Fennian movement. "In disposition," the friend recalled, "he was genial and very sociable and he had a good relative standing in his class though not a very diligent student." Arthur managed to be elected to Phi Beta Kappa as a senior, along with the top third of the seventy-nine-member graduating class.[23]

In an era of virtual laissez-faire on campus, the daily schedule of a Union College student in the late 1840s sounds more than a little tedious. It began at 6:30 A.M. with breakfast and prayers, ground through a number of study sessions and recitations, and concluded with a final period of study that began at 7:00 P.M. Few escaped, for almost all juniors and seniors (including Arthur) were compelled to live on campus and forbidden to leave without permission. Nevertheless, ways were found by the young men to lighten the load, a favorite being a trip to the nearby railroad station to jump on and off of slow-moving trains. Chet Arthur paid several fines for skipping chapel and breaking small objects in the course of pranks; he once threw the West College bell into the Erie Canal, and he carved his name at least twice on the somber college buildings. But he was distinguished from his classmates in such pursuits in no special way, and found time to join a social fraternity and serve as president of a debating society. During his two winter vacations he taught school at nearby Schaghticoke to help pay his expenses.[24]

Three of Arthur's writings from this period have survived, and they shed some light into the character and training of Elder Arthur's first son. One is a humorous sketch, created shortly after he entered college, modestly titled "A brief Universal history from the Deluge to the present time."

> Moses being the only man that survived the distruction [*sic*] of earth's inhabitants by water, after living some length of time in the open air, set his son Nebudchadnezzar to build Solomon's temple. In the course of which happened the confusion of languages, and this was the cause why the temple was left unfinished. About this period Alexander the Great after a siege of some months, took the tower of Babel by storm, and put all the inhabitants to the sword. But soon after he was attacked with vertigo, and fell into the bullrushes, where he was found by Pharaoh's daughter, and taken care of.

The second is a portion of an acceptance speech delivered before the debating society in 1847, stressing the delight of being surrounded by "*Gentlemen.*" The third, from the same year, is a serious, reflective paper that reveals a fervent distaste for the institution of slavery.

> Labour is the only source of support for a nation, and that nation which has the greatest amount of available employed labour, is, or bids fair to become the richest nation. It is with reference to this

important fact, that the disastrous effects of slavery become plainly visible. Labour being performed chiefly by slaves, it soon becomes entirely so, and the atmosphere almost becomes tainted with the paralyzing opinion that labour is disgraceful. Such a political pestilence having spread itself over the South, every southern breeze bears to the North the seeds of this ruinous disease and political death follows in its wake. The mild northern breezes coming in contact with the putrified air of the South are soon tainted, & the whole vast continent bids fair to fall under the blighting effects of the opinion that labour is disgraceful.[25]

Elder Arthur must have been proud.

Following the graduation exercises in July 1848, the eighteen-year-old returned to Schaghticoke to resume his teaching, possibly for the same $15 per month he had been paid earlier. Visions of a more rewarding life appeared soon, and Arthur traveled to Ballston Spa the following year to begin a legal education, probably at the newly opened State and National Law School. Several months later he returned to the family home at Hoosick and continued his studies.[26]

There were six other youngesters in the parsonage and it was obvious that Chester would soon have to become self-supporting. Elder Arthur preached a few times at a new church in nearby North Pownal, Vermont, and in 1851 he secured a job for his son as a principal of an academy that met in the church's basement. No doubt he taught educational rudiments to pupils of a variety of ages, and the evidence suggests they were all boys. Years later Arthur was remembered as a popular, if somewhat stern, instructor. His approach to teaching probably came in large part from his father, still bringing student-lodgers into the already crowded parsonage to supplement his income.

One eight-year-old, Asa G. Stillman, had an encounter with his teacher at North Pownal that he never forgot. Arthur required his students to recite a bit of verse on examination days before an assemblage of parents who came to measure the progress of their children's learning. Stillman sought exemption, pleading acute bashfulness. He was also under the mistaken impression that students were supposed to compose the poetry they spouted and claimed an inability to write anything worth memorizing. The excuses worked for a time, but one day, before an examination, Stillman was asked to stay after school. He dutifully reported, expecting to receive the full benefit of a birch rod. Instead, Arthur said smilingly to the quaking boy:

"Don't you think you can speak a piece tomorrow?"

"I haven't one," was the answer.

"Will you learn one if I write it down for you?"

"I'd try, but I can't read writing well enough," said the boy, anxious to be excused.

"Then I'll print it for you," said the persistent tutor. "Will you learn it if I do?"

"I'll do my best."

Arthur sat down and carefully put on paper a poem composed by Thaddeus Mason Harris, which began:

> Pray, how shall I a little lad
> In speaking make a figure?
> You are but jesting, I'm afraid,
> Do wait till I get bigger.
> But since you wish to hear my part,
> And urge me to begin it,
> I'll strive for praise with all my art,
> Though small my chance to win it.

The next day the trembling lad managed to execute his performance successfully and received the praise of his teacher, parents, and a number of visitors.

In 1883, when his former teacher was President of the United States, Stillman, a New York physician, told his story to a reporter and offered to show him the poem in Arthur's hand. He also mentioned proudly that some years earlier he had named his son Chester Arthur Stillman.[27]

As fate would have it, three years after Arthur left North Pownal, a student at Williams College named James A. Garfield came to the academy to teach penmanship. The little school in the church basement in the southwest corner of Vermont had hosted the future leaders of the Republican national ticket of 1880—the twentieth and twenty-first Presidents.

On November 8, 1852, Chester became the principal of the academy at Cohoes, where a sister, Malvina, was a teacher. He studied law in his spare time and tried to save enough of his $35-per-month salary to travel to New York City and serve in a law office in preparation for admission to the bar.

The students and faculty at the High Department of the District School in Cohoes were known to be rather unfriendly; there had been four teachers in the room during the past year and the last had remained only a week. Arthur said he would "conquer the school or forfeit his reputation." At nine o'clock on the first day he faced his unruly charges. In the words of one of those students:

He said that he knew about the past problems, but that with the proper respect for each other's rights teachers and students could live together in harmony. He said he did not threaten but would demand that the students obey him, and that he would try to win the good will of all present. Some of the leaders smiled a bit. A lad of 13 sent a marble shooting across the floor. The teacher walked to the lad and said "Get up, Sir." He said it a second time, and then took him by the collar, as if to raise him. The lad knew what he was up against, and got up. He was asked to follow Arthur toward the hall. The lad trembled. . . . Arthur took the boy into the primary room, and said "I have a pupil for you." He sat him down and told him to mind his teacher. Other troublemakers came in. The other students did not know what had happened to the boys, and Arthur showed no emotion upon returning to the room. At recess, everyone learned what had happened to the three troublemakers. They remained there in the primary room during recess. After school Arthur confronted the three. He talked kindly and gave good advice. He dismissed them, told them to go home, and upon returning to school to be good boys. In two weeks time there was not a scholar in the room who would not do anything the teacher asked.

The author of this recollection, the first boy led from the room, remembered that when Arthur left the school to pursue his legal career, his pupils presented him with an elegant volume of poetry; "many had tears in their eyes."[28]

While Arthur taught school and studied law he struck up an intensely personal friendship with a young man named Campbell Allen. James Masten, who would marry Chester's sister Almeda, made it a trio, and the three comrades enjoyed boisterous evenings and journeys together. Arthur and Allen, roommates briefly, used nicknames when addressing each other; Arthur was "Zack" and Allen was "John." Allen developed what appears to have been tuberculosis in 1850, and Arthur's effusive letters to him, twelve of which have been preserved, provide us with interesting glimpses into this phase of his life. On December 11, 1850, he wrote to his ailing friend:

What a life we did lead last winter! you and I particularly—sitting up like owls till two or three in the morning with our pipes, over the warm fire—quite satisfied with our little world within and philosophically discussing the world without—laying bare to each other our mutual plans, hopes & fears, adventures, and *experiences* & so cosily chatting & smoking—& then tumbling into bed in the "wee sma hours" & falling soundly asleep in each others arms . . .

Later, from New York, Arthur wrote to wish Allen a happy New Year:

You called my attention to our observance of New Years eve not to forget the hour of eight. James alluded to the same thing and I had reminded him of it in my letter to him. So you see our hearts turned towards it "true as the needle to the pole."

Need I tell you that the hour was sacredly observed and dear to me was the cup of *crystal water* in which I honored the cherished aspiration "To the Triangle."

Allen's illness worsened.

But I would like *so* much to see you, John. I look back to some of those hours which I have spent with you, in the open-hearted, confiding sympathizing fellowship which has always existed between us as among the happiest of my life. I know *you* often think of them too & can not help contrasting them with the dark hours now, yet the remembrance of them brings joy-for-

> "Let fate do her worst there are moments
>   of you,—
> Bright dreams of the past which she cannot
>   destroy,
> Which come in the night time of sorrow &
>   care,
> And bring back the features that joy used
>   to wear.
> Long long be *my heart* with such memories
>   filled."

A few weeks later he wrote:

Oh dear John, how I desire to be with you! You can imagine what my feelings are for I know that yours would be the same were our situations changed!

You *know* that the most earnest & continual wishes & prayers of poor Zack, are for you & with you, his *dearest friend*. I have thought of nothing else since the sad intelligence of your relapse.

I must see you dear John & I shall endeavor to do so before long.

James will keep me advised of your situation & should you grow worse I shall go up there [Saratoga County] at once.

But it *can* not, *must* not be so! It must be I shall yet see you *well my dear John, again*.[29]

Careful observers should not overlook this little-known side of Arthur's personality—his sensitivity, sentimentality, his penchant for forging strong and emotional friendships—for it would have significant effect upon his political career, including his role as President. Though he made a considerable effort to conceal the fact, Arthur was always to retain much of the romanticism of his early twenties.

In New York City, Chester entered a law office headed by E. D. Culver, whom the Arthurs had met during their stay at Union Village a decade earlier. Culver shared Elder Arthur's abolitionist persuasion, and it was later rumored that his firm had risked an association with the "underground railroad," by which fugitive slaves found their way into Canada.[30] Arthur served as a clerk and studied in the firm's office for over a year, and in May 1854 was admitted to the bar and made a partner in what now was called Culver, Parker and Arthur.[31]

The following year Culver was elected city judge of Brooklyn and young Arthur was compelled to pursue many of the senior attorney's cases. He wrote to his mother in March: "This change gives me much more to do than before as I have to take his place, to a great extent, as well as I can in the trial and argument of causes in the Courts. It comes rather hard at first but it will do me a great deal of good." Life seemed rather bleak for the new attorney. He suffered acutely from homesickness, occasionally attended a theater, and spent long hours chatting with his roommate, a fledgling lawyer named Henry D. Gardiner. He called on young ladies "just often enough to keep my name on the books."

Had he tried harder, Arthur might have been more successful with the opposite sex, for he was a strikingly good-looking young man, well dressed, polished, educated, with a highly promising future. He was remembered in Cohoes as being "slender as a maypole and six feet high in his stockings . . ." In fact, he was six foot two. The Arthurs were tall: Chester's great-grandfather, Gavin, was said to be six foot six; Elder Arthur was six foot, as was his son William; Chester's son would be six foot four and his grandson six foot two.[32] Chester wore his hair long, as was the fashion, fastidiously arranging it to reveal merely the lobes of his ears; he complemented this with a light beard that covered his cheeks and chin. His hair was dark brown and his eyes black. He was powerfully built, and from photographs of the period appears to have weighed about 180. And yet, going on twenty-six, he had experienced no serious relationship with any woman; he confided to a sister: "I am yet heart-whole and bid fair, I fear, to become an old bachelor."[33] The major problem seemed to be that so much of his time and energy was spent on his legal chores. One case in particular came to his attention during this period which would long be associated with his name.

In 1852, Jonathon Lemmon and his wife brought eight slaves into New York City from Virginia and lodged them temporarily at a boarding house while awaiting transportation to Texas. When their presence was discovered, a free Negro named Louis Napoleon appealed to Judge Elijah Paine of the Superior Court to issue a writ of *habeas corpus*, as state law permitted no human being to be held in bondage. Abolitionists quickly took up the cudgel, and E. D. Culver was hired, along with John Jay, to represent the petitioner. Attorneys for the Lemmons argued that the slaves were merely passing through New York, were not residents of a free state, and that their ownership was in no way affected by their travel. Despite the merits of the argument, the writ was granted.

This unprecedented decision provoked outrage in the South. The governor of Georgia thought it a "just cause of war," reprisals against the port of New York were threatened, and there was talk again of disunion. It was bad enough that northern extremists violated the new Fugitive Slave Law by frustrating attempts to capture runaway slaves; now they had the audacity, with the sanction of a court, to "liberate" slaves who were merely in transit across northern soil.

Of course, few northerners were abolitionists, and many New Yorkers, especially the businessmen who profited handsomely from their commercial ties with the South, were less than enthusiastic about Judge Paine's decision. The conservative *Courier and Journal* warned, "It will do more to separate the North and South than any other event which has happened since the birth of our confederation, and will open at once the gaping breach which has but now with so much solicitude been closed."[34] Even though the businessmen quickly raised $5,280 to compensate the Lemmons for their "property" loss, the Virginia legislature ordered the state's attorney general to employ counsel and file suit. In 1855 the New York legislature responded, appointing three attorneys to the case, one of whom was E. D. Culver.

The Lemmon Slave Case was argued before the Supreme Court of New York in December 1857 and in the Court of Appeals in early 1860. In both instances Judge Paine's decision was upheld, and the matter was closed soon afterward by the firing on Fort Sumter. Victory over the Virginia slaveholders in the courts was in large part a personal triumph for William M. Evarts, one of the nation's most talented trial lawyers and gifted orators. Evarts had been added to New York's legal team in 1856 after the death of one of the original appointees, and his eloquence was such before the Court of Appeals that the Albany *Evening Journal* was moved to declare that a "more finished argument has seldom if ever been presented to any Court."[35]

Twenty years later, when Chester Arthur was nominated for the vice-presidency, *The New York Times* carried a story contending that he and Evarts had won the Lemmon verdict together in the Supreme Court of the United States. This was altered shortly in a campaign biography by E. L. Murlin to read that Arthur had single-handedly lobbied in Albany to secure the joint resolution of the New York legislature that requested the governor to appoint counsel in the Lemmon Case.[36] Other versions of alleged contributions appeared at the time and after his death.[37]

Arthur's precise role in the matter is uncertain, but his active participation is beyond question. He may indeed have been sent to the State Capitol, despite his youth, to exercise his persuasive abilities before members of the legislature. In March 1858 he wrote to his father, "I have been expecting to go home for a long time and hope now to be able to do so within ten days, as I wish to be in Albany before the Legislature adjourns."[38] When the case came before the Court of Appeals, Arthur was listed as "attorney for the People," and he was rewarded with a one-third share of his firm's legal fees.[39]

Another example of Arthur's direct involvement in the prewar struggle for Negro rights was a test case that led to the integration of New York City's streetcar system. On July 16, 1854, Elizabeth Jennings, a Negro public school teacher, was roughed up by a streetcar conductor after refusing to leave a Third Avenue car reserved for whites. New York Negro leaders expressed outrage over the incident in a public meeting held shortly after the attack, and Miss Jennings consulted Culver, Parker and Arthur. The last was assigned the case. When the suit came to trial, Arthur called the attention of the presiding judge to a recently enacted section of the Revised Statutes, and the jury was instructed that common carriers were liable for the acts of their agents, and that "colored persons, if sober, well-behaved, and free from disease" could not be arbitrarily expelled from a common carrier. From that point on, the Third Avenue Railroad Company had no case, and Miss Jennings and Arthur won the suit. They had sought $500 in damages, but after a discussion among the jurors about "colored peoples' rights" she received $225, to which the court added another $25 and costs. Shortly, all New York City railroad companies integrated their cars, and for years the Colored Peoples' Legal Rights Association celebrated the anniversary of the day on which the Jennings verdict was rendered.[40]

In 1856, Arthur and his friend Henry D. Gardiner formed a law partnership, and in the following year the two traveled west to purchase land and perhaps settle permanently. Their destination was Kansas Territory, and along the way they stopped in Milwaukee and Omaha. The train deposited them in St. Joseph, where they took a steamer down the Missouri River. While in St. Joseph, Arthur wrote a letter to a young lady who had recently become his fiancée, telling her of plans to visit Leavenworth, Lawrence, and Lecompton, and of his eagerness "to learn as much as I can about the affairs and conditions of Kansas . . ."[41]

The territory was boiling with violence following the Kansas–

Nebraska Act, as Arthur well knew. Free state and slave state forces were stopping at nothing to claim the area. In 1855 Henry Ward Beecher, the famous pastor of Brooklyn's Plymouth Congregational Church, had urged the purchase of Sharps rifles for antislavery Kansas settlers, and several "soldiers" from New York's Emigrant Aid Society left for the territory equipped with "Beecher's Bibles." John Brown's bloody foray at Pottawatamie Creek a year later symbolized the ferocity of the struggle. In the New York election campaign of 1856 the young Republican orator George William Curtis declared: "And yet no victim of those [Revolutionary] days, sleeping under the green sod, is more truly a martyr of Liberty than every murdered man whose bones lie bleeding in this summer sun upon the silent plains of Kansas." The Republican Party's twin themes for the national election were "Bleeding Sumner" and "Bleeding Kansas." But rumor had it that great fortunes could be made in the area, that new towns would spring up, and that great populations would inhabit the fertile prairies. There was no want of speculators or settlers in the territory, and Arthur and Gardiner were among many who chose to brave the danger for the possibility of wealth.

The tense atmosphere in Kansas became evident soon after the two men arrived; a political meeting they attended in Leavenworth was broken up by an outburst of gunfire. After purchasing some two hundred or three hundred lots, Arthur took a stagecoach to Lawrence, passing over a road so treacherous that the coach overturned several times, causing the passengers, riding outside, to leap for their lives. In Lawrence he spoke at length with General James H. Lane and Sheriff Sam Walker, and then set out with them on horseback for Lecompton. On the way, two men mysteriously appeared, saw Lane, and quickly rode off toward Lecompton. Lane was sure they were scouts sent out by pro-slavery men and that he was riding into a trap. To his amazement he learned that Arthur was unarmed, and quickly loaned him a pistol, an indispensable implement in the raw frontier that lay ahead.

Shortly after arriving, Lane thought it wise to leave in haste, and Arthur strolled over to the crude structure that served temporarily as the territory's capitol building. He enjoyed a long talk with Governor Robert J. Walker, who had been sent by President Buchanan in March to create some sort of peace between the warring factions. Walker explained the many complex difficulties that clouded the territory's future and then invited his visitor to dinner.

That evening, in the dining room of a local hotel, Arthur was startled when the man seated on his left at the table was suddenly dragged from his chair by a deputy sheriff to answer a charge of murder. At the man's emphatic insistence, Arthur accompanied him to the magistrate's office.

Over in the corner of the room sat the sheriff, guarding a number of prisoners the rickety jail could not hold. Years later Arthur remembered seeing in the group a little red-headed boy of about sixteen who had been arrested for killing a cousin during a quarrel over a game of cards.[42]

Arthur and Gardiner remained in Kansas Territory about three or four months before deciding to return to New York. The immediate reason for leaving, in Arthur's case, was news of the tragic death of his fiancée's father.[43] But it may be that Governor Walker's discouraging comments and the growing economic plight caused by the Depression of 1857 also influenced the decision.

Once home the two men resumed their law practice and continued their busy lives within the relative calm of the great metropolis. But it seems likely that they could not soon forget the violence and hatred they had seen and heard about in Bleeding Kansas, and that they wondered if it might one day spread and engulf the entire nation.

Arthur not only resumed the practice of law in New York City but also his participation in politics. He had thought himself a Whig as far back as 1844; in 1852 he cast his first presidential vote for Winfield Scott. Two years later he and E. D. Culver attended a meeting of free soilers in Saratoga that would prove instrumental in creating a Republican Party in New York.[44] He served as an inspector of elections at a polling place on Broadway and Twenty-third Street for a time, and in 1856 he was on the executive committee of the Eighteenth Ward Young Men's Fremont Vigilance Committee.[45]

These were the years when Thurlow Weed dominated the politics of New York. Many young Whigs, including Arthur, had ample opportunity to study how "the Dictator" grasped and held on to power; more than one would learn the lessons well and be prepared to profit handsomely during the Gilded Age. In an interview of 1880 Arthur shared his impressions of Weed's prewar machine with a reporter from the Boston *Herald*:

> The Whig party was at one time under the absolute rule, in this State, of Mr. Thurlow Weed. The Whig Convention did nothing but give voice to his previously expressed wishes. His programmes extended to the smallest details, and were carried out to the letter. . . . Political leaders then had organized gangs of ruffians at their command, and could compel obedience at caucuses. The tactics were simple and effective. If their opponents were as superior in numbers as in respectability, it was customary to station "heelers" in the lines of voters, and these fellows would at a signal break up the lines. On one occasion these ruffians were provided with awls, which they prodded into the

flesh of the majority, thus dispersing them. Ballot boxes were stuffed almost openly.[46]

Weed also was a staunch defender of the spoils system. Rotation in office was fair and democratic, he argued; but more to the point, his machine had to have government jobs to offer the faithful, even if it meant an unstable, inefficient, ignorant, and corrupt civil service. The "voluntary contributions" of these officeholders, which were in fact party assessments on their salaries, were essential to the continuation of Weed's authority. Weed was "honest," in the sense that he was never caught taking a bribe: Weed was not Tweed. But his manipulation of public offices for political gain and his stifling of the democratic process at the party level and at the ballot box made him something less than an ideal leader of the nation's most populous state.[47]

The new Republican Party offered a great many opportunities for a young lawyer like Chester Arthur; the impact of Thurlow Weed on Elder Arthur's son remained to be seen.

One of Weed's staunchest supporters was a wealthy New York merchant named Edwin D. Morgan. Morgan had long been associated with politics: as a grocer in Connecticut he had served on the Hartford City Council, and in New York he had been an alderman, state senator, commissioner of immigration, and chairman of the Republican National Committee. In 1858 Weed rewarded him with the Republican nomination for governor and assisted him in the victorious campaign. Shortly after Morgan's reelection in 1860 he selected a new general staff, and on the first day of 1861 commissioned Chester Arthur engineer-in-chief.[48]

Arthur had joined the state militia after returning from Kansas, and was commissioned judge advocate of the Second Brigade. Young attorneys frequently belonged to a variety of similar organizations to gain clients and forge political ties. Through the influence of friends, and upon the recommendation of Thurlow Weed, Arthur became part of the governor's staff, an unpaid social corps that attended the governor on all state occasions, displaying expensive, gaudy military uniforms. Morgan and Arthur had not met prior to the appointment but almost immediately became friends. At thirty, Chester Arthur found himself in the favor of a powerful governor and leader of the Republican Party.[49]

Politics and law were not all that occupied Arthur's mind at the time, for he had abandoned the West, at least in part, to assist the grief-stricken young woman he was shortly to marry. Arthur had been introduced to Ellen Lewis Herndon in 1856 by her cousin, a young medical student named Dabney Herndon. She and her mother were paying a visit to their relative in the Bancroft House, where Arthur, Gardiner, and

Herndon had rooms and often shared meals and conversation. Nell, as she was called, was a rather small, frail, brown-haired girl of nineteen with a gay disposition and a beautiful contralto singing voice. Although she had spent most of her life in Washington, D.C., she was born at Culpeper Court House, Virginia, and could trace her ancestry in that state to the seventeenth century. (Her great-great-grandfather was General Hugh Mercer, who raised the first Virginia regiment in the American Revolution.) Her mother was the former Elizabeth Frances Hansbrough, a somewhat haughty, domineering southern aristocrat who played a prominent role in Washington society. Nell's father, Captain William Lewis Herndon, had won national attention a few years earlier as the leader of an expedition that explored the Amazon River from its headwaters to its mouth.[50]

By the time Arthur left for Kansas, he and Nell were deeply in love. From St. Joseph he wrote her: "I know you are thinking of me now. I feel the pulses of your love answering to mine. If I were with you now, you would go & sing for me 'Robin Adair' then you would come & sit by me—you would put your arms around my neck and press your soft sweet lips over my eyes. I can feel them now."[51]

At about the same time that Arthur was having dinner with Governor Walker in Lecompton, Nell's father, Captain Herndon, lost his life in one of American naval history's most widely noted disasters. He was in command of the *Central America,* a steamship carrying gold, mail, and passengers from Aspinwall to New York, when it was hit by a furious gale off Cape Hatteras and sprang a leak. Herndon bravely ordered the evacuation of as many people as possible, saving all of the women and children. And when the churning waters made further escape impossible, he calmly stood at his post upon the wheel-house in full uniform and went down with his ship, creating a legend that was soon commemorated in Annapolis by the erection of a Herndon monument.[52]

Nell was an only child, and her reasons for wiring her fiancé for help are understandable. On his return, Arthur assumed the responsibility of handling all of Mrs. Herndon's legal and financial matters.[53]

In late February 1858, Arthur made a two-week visit to Fredericksburg to meet members of the Herndon and Hansbrough families. It was his first trip to the South and he must have nervously pondered the impression he would make upon Nell's slaveholder relatives. (Mrs. Herndon and her daughter were frequently served by at least one family slave, so that Arthur, unlike his father, had obviously learned the art of compromise.)[54] The young man who presented himself to Dr. Brodie Herndon, Dabney's father, was large, handsomely dressed, soft-spoken, quick with a smile and a humorous story; he was fond of quoting long passages from Burns, and knew enough Latin and Greek to converse at ease with gentlemen. Moreover, he was an established attorney and had been entrusted with Mrs. Herndon's weighty bookkeeping. Even though Chester Arthur was the son of a humble Irish preacher, Nell's family took to him immediately, and Dr. Herndon wrote in his diary: "He is a fine looking man and we all like him very much."[55]

The Arthurs were married on October 25, 1859, in New York City's Calvary Episcopal Church.[56] They soon moved into Mrs. Herndon's home at 34 West Twenty-first Street and remained there until the newspapers one April day in 1861 exploded with the headlines announcing the Civil War.

CHAPTER TWO

Without Gold and Silver

THE SPIRIT of national patriotism was intense throughout New York following the assault upon Fort Sumter; flags were draped everywhere, "Yankee Doodle" and "Hail Columbia" evoked tears and trembling voices, and thousands of young men quickly offered to defend the Union with their lives. The rebellion was expected to last only a few months and provide a great many opportunities for demonstrations of valor. President Lincoln called on northern governors to raise 75,000 volunteers to quash what he called "combinations" of men who had taken over the South; the New York State legislature appropriated $3,000,000 to arm and equip up to 30,000 troops, and $500,000 for defense of the state. A board of top state officials, headed by the governor, was created to supervise New York's military preparedness, and the governor's general staff was called to active duty. Arthur's orders arrived the day after Beauregard's forces swarmed into Fort Sumter, and he soon found himself in an important military position in a key northern state.

As engineer-in-chief with the rank of brigadier general, Arthur was assigned the task of representing the Quartermaster General's office in New York City. It was up to him to help devise and implement methods by which thousands of enlisted men could be fed, housed, clothed, and properly equipped. His office bore similar responsibilities toward the militia regiments from New England and elsewhere that rapidly began converging on the city on their way to combat. There were no precedents to rely upon, and the young attorney had encountered no vaguely similar challenge. But by all accounts Arthur plunged into the task with vigor and carried it out with considerable effectiveness. Governor Morgan soon began to depend upon his judgment, and by April added "Acting Assistant Quartermaster General" to his title.[1]

In these early months of the war, General Arthur could be found virtually every day of the week in a large military storehouse at Number 51 Walker Street, a center of frantic activity. (By July 12, New York raised, equipped, and dispatched to the battlefield thirty-eight regiments; by December the state enrolled over 110,000 men.) From his office on the second floor Arthur handled the mountains of paperwork required by such complex duties as the awarding of contracts for military uniforms and the auditing of expenditures that would surpass the total spent by any other state. Great quantities of detail had to be mastered, and Arthur had to become an expert on stockings, blankets, ammunition, underwear, and rations. The smallest matters found their way to his desk. An aide later recalled:

> One Sunday it was reported that the outfit that was to be sent to a regiment in the country to enable it to move to the front the next day was short five dozen pairs of stockings. After consulting with Arthur I went to the church, got A. T. Stewart out and got him to go with me to his store and get out the stockings. Mr. Stewart used to tell with great glee how he was got out of church one Sunday to make fifteen cents.[2]

The acquisition of suitable housing for the swelling numbers of troops in New York City was a particularly acute problem. At first, local citizens were depended upon to volunteer buildings. But it soon became evident that the struggle was to last more than the thirty days some had predicted, and under Arthur's supervision temporary barracks were constructed on Long Island, Staten Island, Riker's Island, and in Central Park.

New York was able to meet these early challenges of the war successfully in part because of the enormous energy of its governor. Morgan was a whirlwind of activity and drove his staff without mercy. Arthur later told a biographer that for several months he had been permitted to sleep no more than three hours a night. A colonel recalled, "Governor Morgan had a powerful physical constitution and worked early and late; during his incumbency in the war times he seldom left the Capitol before midnight and he exacted from all his subordinates the utmost of their capacities." An adjutant general wrote many years later, "He was . . . unable to comprehend that because a robust man of fifty could work sixteen hours a day, it did not follow that a boy of twenty-three could labor nineteen or twenty."[3]

Morgan held Arthur in particular esteem, for he was willing to work hard, was personally and politically agreeable, and handled his assignments efficiently and honestly. In the opinion of a close aide, Arthur was "industrious, energetic and watchful," and "appeared to like his official duties."[4] Promotions came rapidly: on February 10, 1862, he was appointed inspector general, and on July 10 of the same year he was commissioned Quartermaster General.[5]

According to New York's constitution, officers in the militia were either elected or appointed by the governor. No examinations were necessary, and commissions were automatic upon designation. This method, altered only slightly during the war, did not at first produce many able officers; indeed, about two thirds of the men who received commissions by election failed to complete their two-year terms. As one colonel put it: "The good nature, sociable, easy manners, good-fellowship and other such traits as attract the great mass of mankind are generally incompatible with the power to enforce subordination and discipline."[6] A major reason Arthur stood out from among his peers was his ability to lead: to instill confidence in subordinates, to make quick decisions, to handle crises firmly and intelligently. Several incidents would later be recalled in which Arthur displayed qualities that might have led to a successful military career. (His brother was to be a career officer in the army.) One in particular earned him attention in early 1861.

After New York's initial thirty-eight regiments were recruited, all sorts of adventurers flocked to Washington to wangle commissions to raise troops. The War Department was desperate for manpower and frequently authorized prominent citizens to raise a regiment. Once permission was received, these gentlemen dubbed themselves high-ranking officers, set up headquarters, surrounded themselves with subordinates (who often purchased their commissions), passed out handbills, and began to recruit. At one point there were near a hundred such organizations in the state.

One such successful applicant was "Billy" Wilson, an alderman who represented one of New York City's most crime-ridden areas. Wilson recruited a gang of toughs from his district who proceeded to plunder local restaurants in full uniform. Police were unwilling to crack down on Wilson and his boys because of their great popularity in the vicinity. The harassed restaurant owners finally appealed to the state for relief, and Governor Morgan ordered Arthur to put a stop to Wilson's marauding.

Upon request, Billy appeared one day at Arthur's office and swaggered through the door in a colonel's uniform. When told of Arthur's objections to his recent activities, Wilson bellowed:

"Neither you nor the governor has anything to do with me. I am a colonel in the United States service, and you've got no right to order me."

"You are not a colonel," Arthur replied indignantly, "and you will not be until you have raised your regiment to its quota of men and received your commission."

"Well, I've got my shoulder-straps, anyway," said Wilson, "and as long as I wear them, I don't want no orders from any of you fellows."

At that, Arthur rose to his feet, ripped the straps from Wilson's shoulders, flung him into a chair, and had him put under arrest.[7]

A similar case involved an ex-confidence man named R. D. Goodwin, who became a colonel by raising volunteers for the President's Life-Guard. Officers of the Guard charged Goodwin with "Gross misrepresentations to the War Department in order to have a regiment accepted," and their evidence was apparently such that Arthur refused to provision and quarter Goodwin's men. Undaunted, Goodwin wangled temporary quarters in the Battery from the mayor. They were ordered off the premises by Arthur, but then took up residence at Camp Washington on Staten Island. This time Arthur told Goodwin that he and his men would be driven out of the area at the head of five hundred bayonets if they failed to leave immediately. The volunteers fled without even waiting to prepare dinner. To gain revenge, Goodwin printed broadsides charging that Arthur would not perform his duties "without fees and bribes in *gold and silver*."[8]

In the spring of 1861, Arthur confronted Colonel Elmer E. Ellsworth's "Fire Zouaves," a regiment recruited by a former aide to Abraham Lincoln and composed largely of New York City volunteer firemen. These troops fashioned themselves after the colorful French Zouaves, spending much of their time parading the streets in highly colorful uniforms and practicing daring acrobatic feats of dubious military utility. One day they refused to obey an order to unpack their muskets, and the frustrated colonel went to Arthur for help. Arthur collected several policemen, marched into the regiment's temporary quarters on Canal Street, and had the ringleaders among the 1,100 men pointed out. "Arrest that man, and that one, and that one," he commanded. The orders were obeyed and the regiment was soon more cooperative.

Ellsworth's regiment had been organized in an unorthodox way, and on April 29, 1861, the day of its scheduled departure for Annapolis, orders came from Washington canceling the trip until the regiment complied with army regulations. But when the directive arrived, the troops were already marching in full attire toward the steamer, escorted by 5,000 firemen and bearing a stand of colors sent by Mrs. John Jacob Astor Jr. General John E. Wool, commanding the Department of the

East, no doubt sensed the volatile consequences of Washington's demand and felt compelled to reverse the order and permit the ship to sail.

An hour later an officer strolled in to Arthur's office and said: "Well, the Fire Zouaves have got off at last."

"Got off!" said the astonished general, "that's not possible. Orders have been received from Washington forbidding them to leave, and there is not a pound of provisions of any sort on the troopship."

Arthur ran to a carriage, drove to an army contractor, and, by paying a higher price for rations, acquired a five-day supply in two hours. He then hired three tugs which caught up with the troopship, stopped it, and had the supplies transferred.

But Arthur was not yet free of the Fire Zouaves. Shortly after arriving in Washington the firemen proceeded to commit a series of pranks that aroused a good deal of indignation from the nervous citizens of the nation's capital. The Washington correspondent of the Philadelphia *Press* wrote at one point: "They have had two days of extensive, expensive and extreme fight, fun, and frolic. They have broken into taverns, terrified old ladies, ordered dinners and suppers which they had the impudence to request their victims to charge to the bankrupt concern, the Southern Confederacy, chased imaginary secessionists through the streets, and performed many other irreverent feats." The frolic soon developed into insubordination, and the regiment was returned to New York and quartered in tents on the Battery. There the men refused to obey orders and began to raid restaurants. Arthur, so the story goes, was directed to disband them, but instead, with the aid of police, arrested every member of the Zouaves found wandering in the streets and had them placed on board a transport ship. When four hundred were collected, the ship sailed for Hampton Roads. These highly independent troops were soon consolidated with another regiment, introduced to strict discipline, and eventually found their way back to the battlefields.[9]

The 139th Regiment, or "Ulster County Guards" as they called themselves, represented a much different breed of soldier. These volunteers had been recruited from the "finer" families of affluent Ulster County and had entered the war to get a taste of the fighting. On their way to Washington in 1861 they stopped temporarily at the barracks in Central Park, and soon received orders sending them home, as no more three-month recruits were needed. Outraged and disappointed, the guards appealed to Arthur, who immediately took a train for Albany to confer with Governor Morgan. Permission was granted to send the regiment into battle, and Arthur returned by special train with the news. He arrived at 1:00 A.M., and the barracks quickly erupted in celebration. The Guards named their temporary quarters "Camp Arthur," and later held annual reunions at which the friendship and assistance of the young officer were often recalled.[10]

Arthur's responsibilities increased and varied greatly from month to month as the demands upon New York shifted in response to developments in the war. He traveled to Washington with Morgan on several occasions, and in the autumn of 1861 was present when the governor obtained the rank of major general and won authority over all independent military organizations in the state. Shortly thereafter he contributed to the preparation of a new state militia law and advocated it before legislative committees in Albany.[11] And when war with England seemed likely, following an incident on the high seas in which a Union warship removed two Confederate emissaries from a British vessel, Arthur was charged with presiding over a committee of engineers summoned to devise a plan to defend New York's harbor.

The committee convened in Albany on December 22, 1861, and came up with the idea of building a temporary barrier across the harbor consisting of floats loaded with stone and connected and anchored with chain cables. Morgan ordered Arthur to purchase about 380,000 cubic feet of timber at a cost of approximately $80,000. (Several Arthur biographers would later claim, erroneously, that Arthur made the purchase on his own responsibility.) The threat from England soon waned, however, and the structure was not erected. Following criticisms in the state senate about the expenditure, Arthur was sent to Albany where he promoted an amendment to a military appropriations bill that provided for the sale of unused war materials. The timber was later sold at a profit to the state.[12]

It was also Arthur's responsibility to inspect forts and defenses throughout the state, and in late January 1862, with the assistance of the engineers, he submitted a detailed description of his findings and a number of rather large proposals for statewide defense. The recommendations were not to be carried out, but at the time Arthur's report drew several praises, and the New York *Herald* was moved to call it "one of the most important and valuable documents that has been this year presented to our Legislature."[13]

Two months later, the threat of an attack upon New York was revived when General McClellan sent a dispatch on March 8 warning that the ironclad Confederate steamer *Merrimac* had destroyed two Union frigates and might soon be in the vicinity. Arthur first heard the news from General Gustavus Loomis, an elderly infantry officer who stumbled into his office one Sunday morning out of breath and obviously exhausted. Arthur offered him a chair, asking:

"What in the world has happened, General?"

"The rebel ram *Merrimac*! The rebel ram *Merrimac*!" Loomis gasped.
"Well, what about her?"

"I have a dispatch from General McClellan that she has sunk two United States ships—that she is coming to New York to shell the city—may be expected at any moment—I'm so out of breath running to tell you the news I can hardly speak."

"Running to tell me the news!" said Arthur. "Why in heaven didn't you hire a carriage?"

"Hire a carriage!" Loomis replied, lifting his hands in amazement. "Hire a carriage! Why, that would cost me $2.50. I can't afford to spend so much out of my own pocket, and if I made such an expenditure on account of the government, it would take all the rest of my official life to explain why I did so."[14]

Word of the existence of the fearsome rebel weapon had reached the North earlier, and the New York legislature had pondered at length an effective defense. The best tactic the politicians could devise was a swarming of the vessel with every available steamship, ferry boat, and tug. As one observer remarked, "It was a barbaric project, like a thousand naked Indians overbearing a mailed knight . . ."[15]

McClellan had other plans, and Arthur was ordered to put his shore batteries in place and send vessels to the lower bay to watch for the appearance of the dreaded ship. Hopefully the ironclad could be lured within range of powerful guns and blasted from the water. For the rest of that day and all of the next Arthur and an assistant adjutant general named George Bliss rushed between the navy yard, Governor's Island, and Fort Hamilton attempting to carry out their instructions. Governor Morgan ordered all available militia companies into the harbor forts and arranged for a special train to take him to New York City. The mayor leaked the news to several prominent citizens, who promptly panicked, proposing that ships loaded with stones be sunk in the narrows to block the *Merrimac*'s approach—a plan that might have barricaded the port for years.

Fortunately, the day after the warning arrived, news came of the *Monitor*'s dramatic confrontation with the *Merrimac*; a short time later Arthur and Bliss were greatly relieved to learn of the *Merrimac*'s destruction.[16]

The closest Arthur ever came to battle was during the spring of 1862 when he traveled in the South to inspect New York troops. It may be, as one biographer has suggested, that he sought to enter the South in part to tend to the safety of his wife's family in Virginia; a cousin told an interviewer in 1932 that Arthur placed a guard around an uncle's home during the first Battle of Fredericksburg to prevent its destruction.[17]

From Fredericksburg he went to the Army of the Potomac on the Chickahominy River. The tour was interrupted by Governor Morgan in late June; Arthur received a cable ordering his return to New York as quickly as possible.

The Union effort was sagging badly by the summer of 1862; McClellan's "Peninsula campaign" was being throttled by Lee, recruiting for field regiments was falling off, desertions were increasing, and throughout the North there was grumbling about incompetence in high places. More manpower was obviously needed by the Union army but President Lincoln was keenly aware of the political dangers in asking for more troops; Governor Washburn of Maine had already warned him that the Republican Party was in danger of being overwhelmed at the polls. Secretary of State Seward was delegated to communicate confidentially with northern governors, asking them to request a new levy. In late June Seward met with Morgan, Weed, and Governor Curtin of Pennsylvania at the Astor House in New York; Arthur was given the honor of being the meeting's secretary. Telegrams were sent to governors by Seward and Morgan, and seventeen of them endorsed the appeal. Shortly, the President complied with the new "requests" and asked for 300,000 three-year volunteers and 300,000 militia for nine-month service. New York's quota was nearly 120,000 men, and on July 10 Chester Arthur was appointed Quartermaster General to supervise their enlistment and preparedness.[18]

Arthur established the headquarters of his department in New York City and pitched into the thorny bureaucratic task energetically. Though the order seems to have preceded his appointment, he later took credit for improving the enlistment procedure and treatment of recruits by establishing a camp in each of the thirty-two senatorial districts of the state. He recommended to the War Department that the executive officers of each regiment be mustered into the federal service, giving them sufficient authority to enforce military regulations. All new recruits were immediately put into uniform and introduced to discipline. Quartermasters were assigned to all regiments and required to come to New York City to receive instructions in the technicalities of their position. Over two hundred temporary barracks were constructed, whenever possible by enlisted men, at a low cost to the state. And by making special contracts with railroad companies to transport troops to the front, Arthur saved the federal government $43,174.13. By November Governor Morgan could announce that New York had sent a total of 219,000 men to the front.[19]

As the new Democratic governor was to assume office January 1, 1863, relieving Morgan and his staff of their responsibilities, Arthur spent the last month of 1862 completing unfinished business, serving on two important auditing boards, and compiling a summary of his achievements as Quartermaster General. The report noted that in the space of four months, from August 1 to December 1, ". . . there were completely clothed, uniformed, and equipped, supplied with camp and garrison equipage, and transported from this State to the seat of war, sixty-eight regiments of infantry, two battalions of cavalry, and four battalions and ten batteries of artillery." Arthur was quick to pay tribute to the clerks who had labored under his supervision. And he warmly acknowledged his gratitude to Governor Morgan: "In the discharge of the duties devolving upon me, which have been in this Department peculiarly grave and difficult, I have been always animated by the example given in the untiring zeal, exhaustless energy and unselfish devotion of your Excellency, in the public service."[20] No charge of corruption during the Civil War was ever to haunt a member of Morgan's staff.

Throughout his service on that staff, Chester Arthur earned the plaudits of those who observed his many activities. Slightly over two weeks after he became Quartermaster General, *The New York Times* noted "a great improvement" in his department, and called it "the scene of more bustle and activity than any other." A future critic who served under him later wrote: "As head of the quartermaster's department in New York, both acting and actual, he showed unusual executive ability both in routine and in occasional fields of business and under conditions very difficult and complex." In 1871, Governor Morgan would recall:

> During the first two years of the Rebellion he was my chief reliance in the duties of equipping and transporting troops and munitions of war. In the position of Quarter Master General he displayed not only great executive ability and unbending integrity, but great knowledge of Army Regulations. He can say No (which is important) without giving offence.[21]

Arthur's successor, General S. V. Talcott, wrote:

> I found, on entering on the discharge of my duties, a well organized system of labor and accountability, for which the State is chiefly indebted to my predecessor, General Chester A. Arthur, who, by his practical good sense and unremitting exertion, at a period when everything was in confusion, reduced the operations of this department to a matured plan, by which large amounts of money were saved to the government, and great economy of time secured in carrying out the details of the same.[22]

Although much of Arthur's success during his brief military career may be attributed to demands made by Governor Morgan and developments of the war, the young man revealed personal qualities that clearly earned the respect they were awarded. In retrospect, these two years were high points in Arthur's life, years distinguished by energy, integrity, determination, and selflessness. (Arthur's son, who knew a great deal about his father's political career, told an interviewer in 1931: "I think my father's greatest work was as Quartermaster General of New York State.")[23] The politics of postwar America would shatter a great many reputations forged in the service of either the Blue or the Gray.

When Morgan and his staff lost their commissions, Arthur failed to reenlist. Several writers later claimed that he had sought to serve in combat while working under Morgan but was restrained by the governor, who needed him in New York. The option to fight was open on the first day of 1863, of course, but Arthur chose to ignore it. The explanation for his decision is more complex than has been previously recognized by those eager to defend his personal courage. Foremost, no doubt, was the tension within his family engendered by his service in the Civil War.

Arthur's mother-in-law was openly sympathetic to the South during the conflict; fortunately, for Arthur, she spent most of the war years in Europe, but her sentiments were never doubted. Her daughter, Nell, was quietly but firmly of the same persuasion. This was, of course, quite understandable, for all of the Herndons, Hansbroughs, and Mercers were intensely loyal to the Confederacy once summoned to defend their native soil. Nell's uncle, Brodie Herndon, a Fredericksburg physician, wrote in his diary in June 1861:

> John & I have a serious talk what we shall do with our families in case the danger becomes more imminent. We must move them out of harm's way somewhere. I am almost without hope of keeping the enemy out of Fredericksburg.
> Their number & military power of all kinds is so great. We will have to retreat to the Hill Country and wage a guerilla war. Was there ever a more unrighteous invasion?[24]

Two years later one of his daughters wrote to a sister: "There are very few true men in the south who ever think of the possibility of our subjection. They are determined to be free, live under their own government or die defending it."[25]

Dr. Herndon and his two sons, Dabney (Arthur's close friend) and Brodie Jr., joined the Confederate army. Their home was partially destroyed by the second Battle of Fredericksburg, and both boys were captured and spent time in northern prison camps. Another of Nell's relatives was Matthew Fontaine Maury, the famous head of the Confederacy's coast, harbor, and river defenses. A cousin, Lieutenant John

Maury, was listed as missing in battle and never found. Still another cousin, Captain Henry Botts, was wounded.[26]

Quite expectedly, when Nell Arthur's husband became General Arthur, members of her family were shocked and embittered. Dr. Herndon recorded in his diary: "Mr. Arthur is an officer in Lincoln's army. How the people here do abuse him."[27] Their attitude softened somewhat when Arthur visited the Herndons while in Fredericksburg as inspector general in 1862. Brodie Herndon noted that Arthur "was very affectionate & kind. He thought we might be suffering and delicately proffered aid. We told him we forgot the General in the man."[28] Still, one cousin by marriage, whose house had been ransacked by Union soldiers, "tossed her head," upon seeing Arthur, "and with nose in air turned away from him . . . and walked away."[29]

During Arthur's stint in the militia, he and his family—there was now an infant son, born in late 1860—lived in a plushly furnished two-story family hotel near Twenty-second and Broadway. Callers were always charmed by Nell's graceful manners and elegant taste; she was an accomplished hostess, eager to be agreeable and pleasing. Nevertheless, friends were conscious of a private tension between the Arthurs, a subtle stiffness that Chester tried to make light of by laughingly referring to his "little rebel wife." One close friend, Adam Badeau, thought it remarkable that Arthur stayed in the militia as long as he did, given the prejudices of his wife and mother-in-law.[30]

With her husband's permission, Nell quietly visited Dabney Herndon several times while he was a prisoner of war at nearby David's Island. Nell and "Brother Dab" had been raised together: their fathers were brothers and their mothers sisters.[31] One can well imagine the mutual relief felt by the Arthurs when Chester decided to quit the war on the day Lincoln issued the Emancipation Proclamation.

Arthur also had a sister living in the South during the first two years of the war. Malvina Arthur had met Henry Haynesworth, a native of South Carolina, in 1854, shortly after journeying to the South to teach school. (Her brother William wrote that Malvina was "off for down South to locate herself among the niggars.")[32] In 1861 Haynesworth was a civil servant in the Confederacy, stationed in Petersburg, Virginia. Malvina elected to stay with him until the first month of 1863 when she returned alone for the duration of the conflict to the safety of her parents' home. A hypersensitive and neurotic woman in normal times, Malvina lived in constant anguish throughout 1864, fearing for her husband's safety. In July she wrote her brother William: "If Grant has got Petersburg *mined* and the papers [so] report, I hope you will contrive to let Henry know. I don't want him blown up." A few days later she pled,

"I don't care how soon you take Petersburg but *dont* [sic] *hurt Henry*."[33]

It may be too that Arthur became disenchanted with the North's shifting justifications for the continuation of the war. Conservative Republicans tended to be unsympathetic with the increasingly popular Radical position on slavery; they preferred to stress the preservation of the Union as the war's major goal. Thurlow Weed's relations with the President were often shaky. In a letter of May 19, 1864, William Arthur Jr. learned from a sister that Chester "was so down upon the administration that he was almost a copperhead," and that "he would not vote at all rather than vote for Lincoln for next President."[34] Moreover, the last year of Arthur's service had been a tragic year for the Union forces; military disasters, increasing debts, and the threat of a draft left many New Yorkers from the entire political spectrum cynical and disgusted.

Also to the point was the fact that with Morgan out of power Arthur was unable to secure a commission of as high a rank as the one he was forced to vacate. Democrats swept New York in the 1862 elections, as Morgan predicted they would, and the Lincoln Administration seemed in deep trouble. Rather than fight—an available option—Arthur chose to wait for a Republican resurgence and the possibility of obtaining a top military position. His opportunity came in the fall of 1864 when Reuben Fenton captured the governorship. Arthur applied for the position of inspector general, but Fenton, a Radical, denied the request. "Arthur was much disappointed," a friend recalled, "as it was the only staff position he would accept; it was in rank second to that of Adjutant General, it was a salaried position, permitted the incumbent to reside in New York and would not seriously interfere with his law practice, and with me as his assistant he said he would be safe and comfortable."[35]

Arthur had a strong desire for money. Morgan paid his generals the equivalent of what a major in the United States service would make.[36] This was still a comfortable sum, but Nell was ambitious, had to have servants, and expected to live in a fine home and play a role in high society. Moreover, as a top-ranking officer in the militia, Arthur assumed some expensive habits. A close observer later recalled:

> While at this time taking great interest in matters of dress and always neat and tasteful in his attire, he had an aversion to wearing any military costume; I think mainly because it was so general in those days. He loved the pleasures of the table and had an extraordinary power of digestion and could carry a great deal of wine and liquor without any manifest effect other than greater vivacity of speech.[37]

Arthur had built up a wide range of friends and contacts during his two years with Governor Morgan, he had studied military law, he knew a great deal about supplies and contracts, and on his trips to Washington he had undoubtedly heard of ways a young lawyer, who knew his way around, might earn fat fees.

Throughout the remainder of the war the firm of Arthur and Gardiner courted prosperity. Although Arthur was later known as strictly an office lawyer who avoided court appearances and public speaking, his specialty in the mid-1860s was the handling of war claims, frequently before the Board of Audit. He was often in the nation's capital, and in mid-1864 wrote his brother: "I have been here in Washington off and on, for four or five weeks having business before some of the Congressional Committees."[38] Arthur and Gardiner were soon gaining something of a reputation; in 1881 it was recalled: "This firm . . . became celebrated for the speed with which it could draft and put through legislative bills at Albany or Washington."[39] For one brief sojourn in the nation's capital in mid-1864 Arthur charged a client $500. And by then he had begun to collect fees from R. G. Dun, owner of the Mercantile Agency (forerunner of Dun and Bradstreet).[40]

Soon Arthur purchased a fine brownstone dwelling a short walk from Cyrus Field's stately home and hired Irish immigrants as servants—a fashionable step that may have seemed ironic to Elder Arthur.

Chester saw little of his parents during the war, but occasionally he stopped at the family home while on business in Albany.[41] The war years were hard for William and Malvina Arthur, both in their sixties; in 1864, Regina Caw, their eldest daughter, reported that their income had seriously declined—"no scholars, no salary, and two servants to pay." She added, "Chester knows this, for Mary told him, and *perhaps* he will volunteer to do something without being called upon."[42]

Chester and his brother William were both estranged from their parents to a degree by then because of their hostility to the faith that had consumed so much of the Arthurs' energy and passion over the past four decades. While Chester, on occasion, attended a local Episcopal church with Nell—a proper duty of proper people—he would never exhibit the personal commitment to the Gospel of Christ that would have pleased his father. Throughout the war, Malvina Arthur wrote long letters to her boys pleading with them to accept the Truth.

> Dear William I am very much interested in your welfare as you well know and I pray God every day and all the time to bless you and keep you from temtation [sic] for I know that many surround you, that drunkeness, licentiousness, profane swearing, and gambling are to be found in the Army as much or more than anywhere else, I pray God to keep you from all those sins, and you may hate them all as God

hates them. O that you would obey the commands of Christ to believe in him and be Baptized, for if you live or die, you will need religion more than all the world can give you. Dear Son, how long will you live in rebellion against God and refuse to obey his commandments. O that God would answer this my prayer, that before I am taken from life, you and Chester may come out publickly [sic], confess Christ, and be willing to be fools, for his sake. I know that he will lead you to everlasting life and glory if you are willing.[43]

Elder Arthur sent his youngest son his photograph, exhorting: "Pray daily for mercy, for you know not, when called to meet the enemy, you may fall in Battle. Do, my son, ask God, that whether you live or die [you] may be the Lord's.[44]

Death visited Chester Arthur and his young wife on July 8, 1863, taking their son William Lewis Herndon Arthur at the age of two and a half. Prostrated with grief, Chester wrote to his brother:

I have sad, sad news to tell you. We have lost our darling boy. He died yesterday morning at Englewood, N.J., where we were staying for a few weeks—from convulsions, brought on by some affection of the brain. It came upon us so unexpectedly and suddenly. Nell is broken hearted. I fear much for her health. You know how her heart was wrapped up in her dear boy.[45]

The Arthurs felt deep personal guilt about the death, believing that they had overtaxed the infant's brain with intellectual demands. Their second son, born in 1864, would be indulged lavishly to prevent a similar tragedy.[46]

In the summer of 1863, Arthur was called to the deathbed of his brother-in-law, forty-six-year-old William G. Caw. Caw, a merchant, community leader, and bank director in Cohoes, New York, had married Regina Arthur in 1848 and became a popular and respected member of the Arthur family. At his death, Malvina, Regina's sister, wrote: "It seems as if the great prop and standby of [the] family was gone, for he was in reality like an eldest son to Pa & Ma, and a brother to us all." Regina was deeply thankful for Chester's assistance. He was present throughout the crisis, made the funeral arrangements, and afterward remained several days to straighten out Mr. Caw's business affairs.[47] (The Arthur daughters were all deeply affected by the faith of their parents. Regina would remain a widow until her death in 1910, devoting her life to church work and the prohibition movement.)[48]

A month later Arthur learned that his brother had been seriously wounded in battle. William, a physician who never practiced medicine, joined the Fourth New York Artillery as a first lieutenant in early 1862;

a year later he became a captain, and was promoted to major in December 1863. He participated in seven bloody battles before being shot, while commanding a battalion of artillery, at Ream's Station, Virginia, on August 25, 1864.[49] Chester rushed to Washington, D.C., and found his brother at the Seminary Hospital in Georgetown.

> He is hit in the face, the ball entering the right side of the cheek just above the upper lip—passing straight through and coming out at the back of the head. I cannot see why it did not kill him outright but think it must have been a ball from a hunting rifle—the hole it made being very small. . . . He suffers greatly from the matter running from the wound internally which chokes him and makes him constantly uncomfortable.[50]

Soon after Chester escorted William to New York, he contacted Edwin D. Morgan, who was instrumental in securing a commission in the regular army for his friend's brother.[51]

Though there was nothing he could do about William's near total deafness or the jagged scar that marred his face, Chester could pull the necessary political strings to bolster his brother's future. The Civil War had opened a large number of political as well as financial opportunities, and politics was fast becoming Chester Arthur's consuming interest.

CHAPTER THREE

A Good Appointment

WHILE THE CIVIL WAR raged, Arthur began to construct a political career for himself. He had long been attracted to the Whigs; he had taken an early interest in the formation of the Republican Party, and had worked for the election of Fremont and Morgan. His appointment to Morgan's general staff was a political plum, and Arthur told friends at the time of his desire to become a politician.[1] During the busy years he served in the militia he found time to help political allies secure positions within the military. In October 1862, he was presented with a $250 assessment by the New York State Union Central Committee, signifying his arrival as a political figure of some importance.[2]

Arthur's political future was strengthened in early 1863 by the election of his patron, Edwin D. Morgan, to the United States Senate. Thurlow Weed was behind the victory, and if Arthur planned on attaching himself to the coattails of the new Senator, he would soon have to learn how to function smoothly and effectively within the political machinery fashioned by the New York boss.

Several lessons were administered by Thomas Murphy, a wealthy, ambitious, and unscrupulous New York hatter who had been accused of delivering inferior hats and caps to Union troops during the war. Murphy hired Arthur in 1864 to represent him in Washington (before a special commission on which sat Senator Morgan), and the two men quickly became close friends and partners in several real estate speculations.[3] They were both Republicans and eager to become involved in party affairs. For Arthur this was the beginning of a political career that would span more than two decades.

Arthur and Murphy were members of the Conservative wing of New York's Republican Party, dominated by Weed, Morgan, William Henry Seward, and Henry J. Raymond of *The New York Times.* Their opposition within the party were called Radicals, headed by the petulant and colorful Horace Greeley of the New York *Tribune.* While clashing personalities and greed for patronage accounted for much of the squabbling between the factions, they differed about the nature of the war and the peace, and about Negro civil rights. At the Union Republican Party's national convention in 1864, Republicans of all persuasions stifled their reservations about President Lincoln and supported his reelection. During the contest for the vice-presidential nomination, however, the New York factions resumed their feuding. It was generally recognized that the selection of a War Democrat would be advantageous to the party; Radicals, who dominated New York's delegation, supported Daniel S. Dickinson of their own state, while Conservatives, led by Raymond, cast their favor toward Andrew Johnson of Tennessee. Arthur and Murphy were present at the convention and later claimed to play a small role in Johnson's victory on the first ballot.

At one point Johnson won unexpected support from the New York delegation when a Radical, during a caucus meeting, delivered a particularly offensive diatribe against Seward. Arthur later described the subsequent events:

> Well, in the Convention next day, Simon Cameron, who favored Hannibal Hamlin, became convinced that Hamlin could not be nominated. So Cameron sent a messenger to the New York delegation to say that he and the other Pennsylvania delegates would unite on Dickinson. There was a dense crowd, and the messenger, after going a roundabout way, delivered his message to some of Seward's men, myself among the number. We at once sought Cameron, prevented him from uniting on Dickinson, and thus secured the nomination of Johnson.[4]

The campaign of 1864 marked the first time that assessments of government employees and contractors became an important source of party revenue. Senator Morgan headed the "Union Executive Committee," a party unit comprised of three Senators and three Congressmen that busied itself by levying assessments on postmasters and devising additional methods for raising money. Arthur and Murphy were employed to collect assessments and gather donations from their wealthy army contractor friends.[5] No doubt in appreciation of his efforts as well as in acknowledgment of his association with Morgan, Arthur and his wife attended Lincoln's inauguration ceremony.[6]

The following year, Murphy decided to run for State Senator in a predominantly Democratic district. He asked Arthur for assistance and the election was won. Almost twenty years later, Murphy's only comment about the race was that ". . . it cost me about $40,000."[7]

In early 1866 the Arthurs attended a reunion banquet of the Seventh Regiment National Guard, and brought along one of Mrs. Arthur's cousins from Fredericksburg and a young army officer named Silas Burt. Burt had attended Union College with Arthur, graduating a year after his friend, and in 1862 served him as assistant inspector general. The careers of these two men would cross repeatedly during the next twenty years, and many of the rarest and most perceptive insights about Arthur would come from the pen of the sensitive Mr. Burt.

After the festivities, Burt was invited to the Arthur home to stay overnight. The Arthurs had purchased a home at 123 Lexington Avenue in May of 1865 from a former state attorney general, a two-story brownstone that Nell had furnished with impeccable taste. Burt saw several servants in the home that evening, but it was much too late to greet the little boy his friend Chet took great pride in. Chester Alan Arthur II— he was called simply "Alan"—was born on July 25, 1864. His aunt Regina Caw proudly described him to a sister a few months earlier after a family reunion as "the most magnificent baby with the most splendid eyes I ever saw."[8]

Arthur and Burt sat up late chatting about politics, and Arthur told of his opposition to President Johnson's recent activities. This did not surprise Burt, for the Weed-Seward faction, which had busily pursued the new President's favor after Lincoln's assassination, was then alarmed by Johnson's obstinate and tactless behavior and by his veto of the Freedmen's Bureau Bill and the Civil Rights Bill. Senator Morgan had voted with the Radicals on the Civil Rights Bill, and Weed himself thought the President "bereft of judgment and reason."[9]

Like a great many workers within both major parties during this era, Arthur rarely if ever propounded political sympathies that contradicted positions held by the leaders of the faction to which he belonged. In 1866 and until his accidental ascension to the presidency, he was a dutiful functionary, a machine subordinate whose ideals rested upon the decisions of his superiors. His specialty was to be the science of gaining political office. To Silas Burt, Arthur was always "an excellent representative of the Whig element in the Republican party," and "an admirer of Mr. Thurlow Weed's political ideas and methods."[10]

By this time the Weed machine found itself unpopular within the state and the Republican Party. Radicals won the governor's office in 1864, and the incumbent, a clever businessman named Reuben E. Fenton, seemed destined for reelection. Weed's involvement with President Johnson had turned into disaster. Nevertheless, when the position of naval officer of the port of New York became available in early 1866, Chester Arthur believed he had the political influence to grab it. He asked Silas Burt to write letters and visit Senator Morgan on his behalf. "Arthur considered this the most desirable place in the Federal service," Burt recalled, "the perquisites then allowed by law to the three principal customs officers at this port amounted to at least twenty-five thousand dollars a year to each in addition to his salary. He also thought that an acceptance of this office would not prevent his keeping up his law connection." (Henry Gardiner had recently died and Arthur was operating the law firm independently.)

Burt sent letters to several influential politicians, including the powerful president of the State Senate, Charles J. Folger, and then traveled to Washington to labor on Arthur's behalf. Arthur wrote to Senator Morgan: "I am confident that my appointment to the place can be made very satisfactory to our friends here, & I need not say that *you* have no more faithful or attached friend than myself."[11] It was a bad time for Morgan to be asking the President for favors, and he could not give Burt a firm answer. Arthur then traveled to Washington, and Senator Morgan reported to an associate: "I have seen Gen'l Arthur, who is now here. It is impossible to say what the president wants to do about the Naval office. But many persons have tried to get it, & we shall know more about it today, or very soon. Mr. Weed is with the Pres. now."[12] The politics of the situation were such that Arthur failed to win the post, and, according to Burt, "he was much chagrined by the loss of such a prize."[13]

Later in the year Arthur participated in the Weed faction's desperate drive to defeat Fenton's renomination, but the effort was unsuccessful and the Conservatives were forced to wait until 1868 to rally their strength.[14] Perhaps a new presidential aspirant could be found who would deprive Radicals of their arrogance and restore power to the "true and faithful" Republicans.

In the mid-1860s Arthur could often be found at Tom Murphy's house on Thirty-ninth Street, a headquarters for New York's Conservative Republicans. As one frequent visitor later recalled: "Sooner or later, but always unfailing, was the well-known ring and footstep of General Arthur, as we used to call him. Always smiling and affectionate in his manner towards his friends, and apparently as attached to Mr. Murphy's family as though they were his nearest and dearest relatives . . ."[15] Arthur was learning how to ingratiate himself with the many other young political hopefuls and machine functionaries at Murphy's, and always seemed to be enjoying himself. He liked good cigars and whiskey, was invariably equipped with a humorous story or an apt limerick, and took pleasure in sitting up into the early hours of the morning talking politics. Silas Burt, plagued from birth with a sleepless conscience, noted sorrowfully that Arthur "expressed less interest in the principles then agitating parties than in the machinery and maneuvers of the managers. . . . He was absent from home on evenings almost continually, rising proportionably late in the mornings; and he frequently worked at his law business for two or three hours after midnight and for this purpose had an office in the front basement of his dwelling. He was also gaining in flesh and becoming more rubicund in countenance."[16]

Arthur made several valuable friends of the New Yorkers he encountered at Murphy's house during the early postwar years. Charles Folger was a moody, well-to-do Republican State Senator of strong Conservative views who often left his country house on Seneca Lake, near Geneva, to spend an entire weekend with the Murphys. One of his closest friends was Richard Crowley, a young attorney and State Senator from Lockport. General George H. Sharpe impressed those who enjoyed his company with his knowledge of foreign languages. Alonzo B. Cornell, son of the university founder, was a huge, crafty man, so quiet that he was called by the few who liked him "the Sphinx." George Bliss, an attorney, had been Edwin D. Morgan's private secretary in 1858 and had first become acquainted with Arthur while on the governor's staff during the war.

In 1867, Arthur was elected a member of New York's exclusive Century Club, and could now meet the likes of J. Pierpont Morgan, the actor Edwin Booth, the famous editors E. L. Godkin and George William Curtis, and the president of Cornell University, Andrew D. White. The selection undoubtedly involved Arthur's literary proficiency, but it mostly bore evidence of his increasing status within the Republican Party. (Adam Badeau said of the younger Arthur: ". . . he was good company; cheery and buoyant in spirit, full of talk and anecdote, though never brilliant and in no way intellectual . . .")[17] That same year he sat on the city executive committee as the representative of the Eighteenth Assembly District.

The Republican Party's organizational structure in New York City at the time was complex, the result of Tammany Hall's weight in local politics, Republican factionalism, and a rapidly expanding and shifting population. At the foundation lay some seven hundred election districts, from twenty-five to thirty-five of which constituted an assembly district, the basic unit of party organization. Each of the twenty-one assembly districts contained a Republican association comprised of a select group of party members with a full complement of officers. Here candidates were picked for party caucuses and meetings as well as public office, and members of the assembly districts were sworn to obedience and loyalty to the party by a series of oaths. On the next level was the Republican general city committee (or central committee), elected from the assembly districts. Its 159 members were charged with setting party policy and supervising the various activities of the assembly districts. In fact, this unwieldy body was dominated by its executive committee, which Arthur joined in 1867. At the top was the state central committee, chosen from representatives from the congressional districts at the annual state convention. Arthur would chair its executive committee in 1868.

Part of the attorney's rapid ascent through the maze of party machinery was no doubt the result of Senator Morgan's considerable influence. But his talents may also have won the attention of one of the rising stars of New York politics, a man who would soon dominate the Republican Party throughout the state and wield enormous influence over the next Republican President.

Roscoe Conkling's background bore a striking similarity to Arthur's. He was born in the same month and year, in Albany, had been an active New York Whig from the age of sixteen, had participated in the forming of the Republican Party in 1854, had worked for Fremont two years later, and had held abolitionist sympathies. His father was a graduate of Union College, but for some reason Roscoe bypassed college and went directly into law and then into politics. He had been introduced early to politics; his father had been a Congressman, a federal judge, and a powerful figure in the Whig Party, and such celebrated figures as Martin Van Buren, John Quincy Adams, James Kent, and Thurlow Weed visited the family home. After a brief stint as mayor of Utica, Conkling was elected to Congress in 1858. He won reelection in 1860, was defeated in his next bid, but was returned in 1864 and again in 1866.

No one ignored Roscoe Conkling, for he was one of the most handsome, eloquent, and controversial men of his era. He was six foot three inches tall, broad-shouldered, with wavy reddish blond hair, a meticulously trimmed beard, and flashing green eyes. His narcissistic personality was symbolized by a Hyperion curl carefully combed onto the middle of his broad forehead. At all times he paid great attention to his attire. One observer noted:

> He was dressed in faultless taste and looked as if he had just stepped out of a band-box. His polka-dot tie was fastened together with a plain gold pin. A checked kerchief was visible in the upper pocket of his cutaway coat. He wore English gaiters and pointed shoes that had been freshly polished. On his head was a high white hat, and his whiskers had been trimmed with great care. In his hand he carried a sun-

umbrella. He walked along with the air of a Prince, unmindful of the attention he attracted. His private secretary walked a few paces behind him, carrying a small satchel.[18]

Conkling had a fine mind and a highly retentive memory; he could (and often did) quote entire pages of the Bible and could match literary quotations and classical allusions with the most pedantic. He spent days and sometimes weeks writing and memorizing speeches that were delivered with an artful resonance and a studied forcefulness.

Above all, Roscoe Conkling was supremely and superbly arrogant. He demanded obedience, even reverence, from those who followed him, and he rarely forgave anyone who opposed his will. Andrew D. White, an admirer, would comment: "Conkling seemed to consider all men who differed with him as enemies of the human race."[19] He lacked a sense of humor, easily and quickly took offense, did not like to be touched or crowded, loathed tobacco and the use of it in his presence; he made no attempt to affect that style of self-deprecation which so many American politicians have honed to a science. (The Seventeenth Amendment would perhaps bar his likes from the United States Senate.) Horace Greeley once wrote: "If Moses' name had been Conkling when he descended from the Mount, and the Jews had asked him what he saw there, he would promptly have replied, 'Conkling.' "[20]

Conkling appeared to dislike James G. Blaine almost at sight. Senator Ingalls of Kansas recalled:

> They were rivals and foes from the start. Of about the same age, they both aspired to leadership, but in temperament and intellectual habits they had nothing in common. They were altogether the most striking personalities of their generation. They were enemies by instinct. Their hostility was automatic.[21]

Blaine was a Congressman from Maine, a strong, ambitious man of unusual ability who could not easily be bullied. In early 1866 he and Conkling clashed over the source of a literary allusion. (Blaine, whose memory was even superior to Conkling's, was correct.) In April they quarreled bitterly on the floor of the House over the Army Reorganization Bill. Soon their harsh words turned to insults, and when Blaine had taken enough of Conkling's caustic ridicule, he lashed out:

> As to the gentleman's cruel sarcasm, I hope he will not be too severe. The contempt of that large-minded gentleman is so wilting, his haughty disdain, his grandiloquent swell, his majestic, super-eminent, overpowering, turkey-gobbler strut has been so crushing to myself and to all the men of this House, that I know it was an act of the greatest temerity for me to venture upon a controversy with him.

George S. Boutwell once asked Conkling if he was ever going to forgive the Maine statesman for his stinging rebuke. Conkling's reply was unequivocal: "That attack was made without any provocation by me as against Mr. Blaine . . . and I shall never overlook it."[22] Throughout the remainder of their long and important political careers within the same party the two men failed to speak; Conkling refused even to acknowledge Blaine's presence.

Governor Reuben Fenton was another strong-willed politician; he desired to be the next Weed, and had his eye on Edwin D. Morgan's Senate seat, up for grabs in 1869. His position in New York was excellent in 1866; he had been reelected by a 13,000-vote majority, and Radicals had carried both branches of the legislature and elected twenty out of thirty-one Congressmen. Following the November balloting, however, he must have sensed trouble, for in the party caucus to fill the Senate seat held by Ira Harris, one of Weed's men, he attempted to scuttle the chances of Congressman Conkling. When Conkling was selected on the fifth ballot, in part because of his forensic ability, Fenton was quiet. Secretary of the Navy Gideon Welles wrote in his diary: "Conkling is vain, has ability with touches of spread-eagle eloquence, and a good deal of impetuous ardor. He may improve and he may not. At present he is an intense Radical. If he has real sense he will get the better of it with experience."[23] Fenton probably would have agreed, thinking that Conkling would learn to take orders. The New York *World* wrote reassuringly: ". . . he does not carry guns enough to be a party leader."[24]

But it was soon apparent that Conkling followed no man's instructions and had inordinate aspirations for personal power. His term in the Senate started with a flourish, and by late March the Washington *Chronicle* noted that "No new senator has ever made in so short a time such rapid strides to a commanding position in that body."[25] Moreover, it was observed that many of Weed's workers were beginning to side with the new Senator against the Fenton wing of the party. Conkling held no grudges against the Conservative flirtation with Andrew Johnson; he took an easy dislike to Horace Greeley, who chastised him for his independence and willingness to make public pronouncements. In September, Fenton supporters tried to deny Conkling the chairmanship of the Republican state convention, but were outmaneuvered. Few doubted that the division of New York Republicans into two warring camps was simply a matter of time.

Fenton's authority was weakened by the fall elections of 1867. There was a recession, and Republicans were tainted with canal frauds and open to charges of obstructing a state constitutional convention out of fear of submitting Negro suffrage to a vote. The Democratic majority at the polls was nearly 48,000; in every county in New York the Republican vote declined. While the tally undoubtedly revealed a lack of confidence in Republican leadership, Greeley also noted the strength of Boss Tweed, in 1867 on the verge of controlling the entire state.

William Marcy Tweed created the first effective big-city political organization, and his domination of New York politics from 1866 to 1871 marked the true beginning of boss rule in the United States. Tweed was talented—more in the way that Weed and Arthur were than Conkling. He excelled in the personal politics of the smoke-filled room: the jovial story, the pat on the back, the midnight supper, the personal pledge of loyalty, the quiet threat. He was a polished clubman and made influential friends easily, but also won the respect and admiration of his crudest henchman. He rarely made a public speech, avoided the press, worked in private. While on the surface a devoted parent, a philanthropist, and a man who abstained from liquor and tobacco, Tweed was also a tireless corruptor whose quenchless greed and ruthlessness have become legendary. The total amount stolen by the Tweed Ring has been estimated at between twenty and two hundred million dollars. No responsible guess can be made of the number of votes purchased, ballot boxes stuffed, or registrations illegally filed.

Of course, there was more to Tweed's success than his determination and cunning; between the Civil War and the New Deal every big city had a political machine at one time or another. The Tweed Ring fed upon a combination of historical conditions that formed the milieu in which machine rule thrived in America.

The postwar years were infected with corruption; the decay of standards seems to have been triggered by the cynicism that followed the crusade to end slavery and the emergence of Big Business. "Corruption" is not as difficult a word to define as a few modern historians would have us believe.[26] The Gilded Age was rife with thievery, bribery, fraud, and personal irresponsibility. This was widely recognized and condemned at the time, and the evidence to support the charges of such famous critics as E. L. Godkin, Henry Adams, and Lord Bryce is abundant, if often indirect. (Historians know well how carefully and often politicians and businessmen of the period culled their papers of incriminating materials. Conkling, Arthur, and Jay Gould are relevant examples.)

Moreover, population was increasing at a spectacular rate (in New York City from 300,000 in 1840 to almost 943,000 in 1870), and responsible city government virtually collapsed under the weight of such complex and overwhelming public problems as housing, sanitation, health, and employment. Little help came from rurally dominated state legislatures, obsessed with an agrarian dislike of cities. The way was opened for the boss, who, for a fee or a favor, could often get things done. At the primary level of machine authority, for example, an assembly district leader had many opportunities to serve his constituents, meeting some of the needs and providing some of the services city government could not or would not handle.

> If he wishes a strong following in his district he must be at the service day and night of his neighbors, who, in return for the services rendered them, are willing to attend primaries or vote at elections. A young man is arrested for fast driving; the district leader must visit a police justice and intercede for him. An old man wants to keep an apple-stand on a frequented corner: the district leader must see his Alderman and have a special ordinance passed over the Mayor's veto. A city ordinance has been violated, and the violator reported by the police to the Corporation Attorney: the district leader must see the Corporation Attorney and have the complaint pigeon-holed; or, if he fail in this, he must see the justice and have it dismissed when it is called for trial. If a laborer who can serve him is out of work, he must find something for him to do on the streets, or on the aqueduct, or in the parks. If a builder employing a number of men, or a lot-owner who is putting up a house, wants four or five feet of the city's property, free of cost, on which to build a "swell front" or a bay-window, the leader must see that the application runs through the board, with or without the Mayor's consent. If a corporation wants to dig a vault under the street to its very centre, he must lend a hand to put the matter through. If a liquor dealer is arrested for selling without a license, he must leave no stone unturned to secure his escape unpunished. Finally, if a poor devil is in want of a dollar, he must let him have it. He must attend all political meetings, go to club picnics, attend church fairs, not permit himself to be forgotten in the liquor stores and other places of frequent resort, and must hold himself generally in readiness to do whatever is required of him by the superior chiefs.[27]

Immigrants and working-class people have always been the mainstay of political machines: in New York City alone in 1870 there were some 400,000 immigrants. While Tammany Hall would never seriously come to grips with such issues as poverty, education, and housing (John A. Garraty has concluded that "Despite their welfare work and their admitted popularity with the masses, most bosses were essentially thieves."), it undoubtedly alleviated much of the misery immigrants suffered by offering friendship, charity, and jobs in exchange for votes. Tammany leaders after 1880 controlled an annual city payroll of $12,000,000, and 12,000 jobs—making them a larger employer than Carnegie Steel.

The old upper and middle classes of New York were by and large unsympathetic to the plight of immigrants, and increasingly abandoned politics as a worthy calling. As Alexander B. Callow Jr. put it:

> Seeing themselves as the guardians of Protestant, Anglo-Saxon standards, they regarded the immigrant as a threat to the purity of the Anglo-Saxon stock, its religion, its values of self-reliance and independence. Thus the immigrant was alienated and made more accessible to the professional Tammany politician who understood some of his problems. The old elite's genteel tradition in manners, education, and culture, gave it a marked distaste for personal contact with the masses. Its conception of the proper politician as a gentleman devoted to disinterested public service, made for a disdain that underestimated the wit and ability of a son of a saloonkeeper or livery stable owner turned politician. The middle- and upper-class view of politics as a means to moralize society committed them to the tactics of moral exhortation, and obscured the practical, concrete aspects of organized politics.[28]

As a result, political management fell into the hands of professional practitioners whose major interests were centered almost exclusively on the continuation of a machine's power; as Dennis Brogan once noted, "The true character of the machine is its political indifferentism. . . . It exists for itself."

The primary function of the boss was to organize, centralize, and utilize political power. He was selected for his ability to manage machine members and locate jobs for partisans, to strike bargains and alliances with opponents, to discover a man's price, to wring the last nickel of an assessment out of a federal judge or a rural postmaster. He was amiable, moderate, and kindly, a man of strong will and intelligence who was known to keep his word. His private life was usually impeccable, and he was frequently seen in church with his devoted family. But an honest machine was a contradiction in terms, as was a virtuous boss. For the boss must also have no hesitation about stuffing a ballot box, sending a group of "the boys" to threaten or rough up voters, about fixing a primary, bribing public officials, manipulating public funds, or removing battalions of political opponents from public office when profitable. He was essentially a businessman, a broker in the game of politics whose profit and loss sheet paid little heed to the values of democratic government. Moisei Ostrogorski wrote of the boss:

> He is incapable of grasping principles; his ideas in politics are hard to discover: he has none, and does not need them. This is not the compass he uses, it is the wind of circumstances and of personal conjunctures which steers the course of the boss. He is incapable of stating his views on the problems of the day. He is neither a writer, nor a speaker, nor even a good talker; on the stump he would cut a poor

figure. The stock of eloquence necessary for defending, by speech and by the pen, the name and style of the party under which the boss operates is supplied by others. He confines himself to turning their talents to account, just as he does those of the district leaders and other henchmen; he himself is invariably nothing more than a clever contractor.[29]

Due to its rapidly growing population, location, wealth, social differentiation, and near-even division of voters between the major parties, New York State had been prey to political absolutism from the early nineteenth century. The Federalist organization under DeWitt Clinton was the first, followed by the Democratic machine of Martin Van Buren and the Whig apparatus under the control of Thurlow Weed. By the close of the Civil War things were in flux on the state level, but from the creation of the Tweed Ring in 1866 Tammany Hall dominated the politics of New York City. Both Radical and Conservative Republicans feared that Democrats might sweep the state in 1868 and were delighted to discover a candidate with an enormous public following.

Ulysses S. Grant had received support for the presidential nomination from New York Conservatives as early as July 1867. Radicals were won over a month later when the normally taciturn general quarreled with President Johnson about the dismissal of Secretary of War Stanton. At a party convention in Syracuse in February 1868, Republicans endorsed Grant's candidacy by acclamation, setting the entire party aflame with the prospect of victory. Over objections from Weed and Conkling, the convention also voted to support New York's governor for the vice-presidency. Fenton failed to win a place on the national ticket, and in July saw his political supremacy slip a bit further when Horace Greeley failed to receive the nomination to become his successor.

During the campaign Conkling stumped the state for Grant, even though his brother-in-law, Horatio Seymour, was the general's Democratic opponent. Arthur served as chairman of the Central Grant Club of New York, toiled on the state committee, and was again employed collecting funds.[30] Thanks in part to some gigantic frauds by the Tweed Ring (perhaps more than 50,000 illegal votes were cast; one man registered to vote 127 times), Seymour carried New York State by 10,000 votes and his party won the governor's chair. Republicans took consolation in Grant's substantial national victory and in the fact that they held on to the state legislature. There was little time for relaxation after the ballots were counted, however, for shortly the two wings of the party in the Empire State were embroiled in a fierce struggle over the Senate seat held by Edwin D. Morgan.

To expand, perhaps even to conserve, their authority, Conservatives badly needed to defeat Fenton's long-awaited bid for the Senate. The wily governor was a formidable opponent: he had been an effective chief executive and had constructed an able machine through a careful distribution of patronage. It appeared that he would stop at nothing to control the Republican caucus when it voted in mid-January, for at stake was control of the party in the state and a potentially powerful voice in the new Republican administration.

Morgan's campaign began in the first week of the new year. Headquarters were established at Albany's Delavan Hotel, Chester Arthur and Tom Murphy were on hand, and the Senator himself appeared to lead his drive for reelection. Morgan produced letters of support from Conkling, Edwin Stanton, and Charles Sumner; charges of corruption were tossed around; an attempt was made (in which Murphy was a key figure) to link Fenton with a bribe. But these efforts fell flat. Morgan was hurt by the memory of his ties with President Johnson and by the absence of Thurlow Weed, on whom he had long relied in similar situations. For the time being, Fenton had the superior strength, and he was elected on the first ballot. Conservatives would simply have to bide their time until circumstances favored revenge.[31]

Arthur was especially dejected by his patron's failure to retain his Senate seat, for he had hoped to obtain a high-ranking position in the New York Customhouse under the Grant Administration and realized that Senator Fenton would resist such favors for Conservatives.[32] Prior to Morgan's defeat, Arthur had exercised influence in Customhouse appointments and had been active in building partisan strength in that venerable font of spoils politics. On October 12, 1868, for example, he sent a list of names to Senator Morgan, stating: "Please write to the Dept. at Washington to have the nominations confirmed. It is important they should be, without delay."[33]

While Arthur's political prospects seemed to be slumping temporarily, so too was his law practice. (An associate later recalled, with some exaggeration, "His law firm never did any business to speak of, and Arthur did not know any law.")[34] He continued to handle legal matters for R. G. Dun and Co., as well as for Tiffany and Co., and he even undertook some criminal cases.[35] But it was apparent that he would soon have to depend upon the business of politics to provide him with a handsome living.

At some point in 1869 Tom Murphy made an arrangement with Tweed, an acquaintance of more than a decade, to create the office of counsel to the New York City tax commission, a post that paid $10,000 a year. It was originally intended for Richard Crowley, but when he stepped aside, it went to Arthur. For many years, some Republicans in heavily Democratic New York City had chosen to work with Tammany Hall rather than be excluded from municipal jobs; by the time of Arthur's appointment it was virtually impossible to acquire, let alone create, such a well-paying position without Boss Tweed's approval. (In the fall elections of 1869 Democratic majorities were elected to both houses of the state legislature; they were slim, and Tweed was obliged to deal out $600,000 in bribes to Republican legislators. Tweed henchman John T. Hoffman was the figurehead governor; the dapper thief Oakey Hall was Tweed's mayor of New York City.) By 1870 at least eighty Republicans were employed at jobs attributable to Tammany.[36] Henry Smith, for example, was a member of the Republican general city committee (with Arthur) and at the same time a Tweed police commissioner and member of the Tweed Ring.[37] Arthur enjoyed his newly found salary until (according to his friend George Bliss) the summer of 1870, when he resigned.

Chester Arthur's role in the operations of the tax commission remains shrouded in secrecy. Tax levies, of course, were manipulated shamelessly by the Tweed Ring and were among the principal sources of its revenues; after Tweed's fall in 1871 few Republicans cared to be reminded of their dealings with him. Arthur would never utter a word about his position with the tax commission. His biographers invariably skim over the matter, brightening the picture somewhat with the assertion, made by Murphy and George Bliss in 1872, that Arthur resigned his office once Tammany threatened to exert influence over the commission. In fact, Arthur had to know from the beginning that the plush job came through Tweed, and it is doubtful, to say the least, that the Boss tied no strings to the favor. In June 1870, prior to Arthur's resignation, Horace Greeley was wailing, "Except in the agreement concerning the police and the Central Park, the republicans have no more power in local affairs than the Emperor of China. *Tammany has everything; her retainers fill all the offices.*"[38]

When Conkling rose to power several months later, he reorganized the New York City Republicans to exclude "Tammany Republicans" from power. By then Arthur had returned to his law practice and was awaiting his next opportunity. (His taxable income fell from $10,835 in 1870 to $4,019 in 1871.)[39] With such close friends as Tom Murphy the interval did not promise to be long.

While the first year of Grant's Administration brought prosperity to the Arthurs, they were also faced with death and near-tragedy. On January 16, Mrs. Malvina Arthur died in Newtonville, surrounded by three of the children who had long enjoyed her quiet strength. Chester arrived in the evening from New York City, and one of his sisters noted that "when he saw Mother he sat down and wept like a child."[40]

In May 1869, Arthur was summoned to Fredericksburg upon learning that his son, Alan, had been taken seriously ill with dysentery during a visit with his mother. He sped to the Brodie Herndon home and remained with his southern relatives for a week, until the danger had passed. Dr. Herndon recorded in his diary: "He was much affected by his little boy's extreme prostration and manifested a warmth [,] gratitude & affection for us all for our attention."[41]

Very soon afterward death struck William Arthur Jr.'s first child. William had married the former Alice Jackson in June 1867, and a son, William Arthur III, had been born a little more than a year later. Nothing was heard from Chester at first, but then came a letter.

> I cannot tell you how greatly grieved I was to hear that you had lost your darling boy. Regina was with me when the news came and I begged her to write for me as well as herself.
>
> I felt that I could say nothing to comfort you, for I cannot be reconciled or resigned when such trials come. It brought back to me so painfully the loss of my own first born!
>
> I have suffered, and I know how great the loss is, and the sorrow!
>
> I feel deeply for you both.
>
> Time will reconcile you to the bereavement—will lessen by degrees the bitterness of your grief until the memory of your lost darling will bring pleasure mingled with sorrow.[42]

Though few would have guessed it of this urbane politician, Arthur was a deeply emotional, even romantic person, capable of great loyalties and easily brought to tears. A close friend said of him at his death, "He was an extremely tender-hearted man."[43] Even the most cynical politicians were not immune to the effusive sentimentality of the Victorian era.[44] But Arthur's sensitivity to suffering and death was extraordinary, and it was later to affect his political career and be in part responsible for the tragic gloom that would haunt his presidency.

The inevitable struggle for supremacy in the Republican Party of New York occurred in July 1870 over the nomination of Tom Murphy as collector of the port of New York. President Grant had met Murphy a year earlier during his summer vacation at Long Branch (where Murphy and Arthur jointly owned property) and had been taken with his Irish humor and knowledge of horses. As their friendship blossomed, Grant, a notoriously poor judge of men, thought that Murphy would be useful to his administration. Complaints had come to the President's attention that the current collector, Moses Grinnell, a Grant appointee, had been insufficiently attentive to the demands of politicians, and had stressed economy and efficiency. Without consulting either Fenton or Conkling, Grant let it be known that Murphy was his choice to preside over the richest source of patronage in the country.[45]

Fenton had been treated fairly well by Grant to that point and was outraged at the news. Murphy was a Tammany Republican, a follower of Weed who sympathized with Andrew Johnson; he had worked against Fenton in the gubernatorial campaign of 1866 and at the national convention two years later; he was gathering endorsements from Edwin D. Morgan, Charles J. Folger, and other prominent New York Conservatives. Fenton boldly assured Secretary of the Treasury George Boutwell that Murphy could not get four votes in the Senate and that his confirmation was doomed from the start.[46]

Conkling was unsure of an appropriate response to Grant's whim at first; he told a friend, Senator William Stewart of Nevada, that Murphy would certainly not have been his first choice for the collector's office. Stewart convinced him to use the nomination as a device to overtake Fenton and win favor with the President. There were already several indications that Grant was growing weary of Fenton, and Conkling now had the opportunity to divide the two for his own profit. Shortly, Conkling and two of his followers, Surveyor of the Port Alonzo B. Cornell and Colonel Frank Howe, dined privately with the President and assured him of their loyal support. Apparently in return, Grant agreed to dismiss General Edwin A. Merritt, a Fentonite, from his post as naval officer at the Customhouse and replace him with the less dangerous Grinnell. On July 1, 1870, Murphy and Grinnell were publicly nominated for their respective positions, and the Fenton wing of New York's Republican Party knew it was suddenly in deep trouble.[47]

Reform-minded Republicans were also concerned by the turn of events, for the nominations appeared to confirm fears that the new administration was slipping under the control of spoilsmen. *The Nation* commented: "... in appointing Mr. Murphy, it may be fairly inferred that the President has cast aside all regard to the better aims and tendencies of the party, for Mr. Murphy is a politician of the politicians, has never been anywhere but 'inside politics,' is rich through Government contracts, and has that peculiar reputation which consists in being generally believed capable of participation in any job . . ."[48]

On July 11, the nominations came before the Senate, and few Republicans failed to realize that control of the party in the nation's most populous state depended on the result. The Senate met in executive session from 2:00 until 5:00 P.M., adjourned until 7:30, and continued well into the next morning. Fenton began his lengthy remarks during the afternoon by describing the lofty qualities a collector should possess, and then launched into a bitter tirade against Murphy. Affidavits and records were quoted documenting Murphy's alleged frauds during the war; collusion with Democrats was charged, and a certified copy of a deed was exhibited that revealed Murphy's co-ownership of New York property with leaders of the Tweed Ring. Fenton noted that Chester Arthur, present in Washington along with a horde of lobbyists supporting Murphy's nomination, had been given a lucrative job by Tweed, and claimed that the tax commission to which Arthur was counsel turned over assessments and tax collections to New York City Democrats.

After the adjournment Conkling took the floor, and every Senator was present in his seat. Stewart recalled: "Conkling immediately began an oration, every sentence of which was replete with logic, sarcasm, reason, and invective. Sometimes the Senators would rise to their feet, so great was its effect upon them." The speech lasted an hour, Conkling taking pains to show that Murphy had been exonerated of wartime charges by a government investigation, and citing his efforts on behalf of Grant's election. Toward the close of his address, Conkling walked down the aisle and stopped opposite Senator Fenton's seat. "It is true that Thomas Murphy is a mechanic, a hatter by trade; that he worked at his trade in Albany supporting an aged father and mother and a crippled brother. And while he was thus engaged there was another who visited Albany and played a different role . . ." He drew a court record from his pocket, pointed it toward Fenton, and concluded: ". . . the particulars of which I will not relate except at the special request of my colleague." Fenton's head dropped to his desk, "as if he had been struck down with a club." Years earlier Fenton had been hired to carry $12,000 from western New York to Albany, and reported the money lost. He was arrested and the money was found under his mattress. Fenton was cleared of charges but the incident left a cloud over his past. A large quantity of testimony was taken at the time of the investigation and Conkling had brought a copy of the proceedings into the Senate and thrust it in Fenton's face. It was a bold, stunningly effective move. (One colleague later told Conkling, "If you had spoken of me in that way I should have killed you." His reply was a smile.) The Senate moved 48 to 3 to confirm Murphy's nomination, and President Grant was pleased and grateful. There was little doubt any longer about who ruled the Republican Party in New York; at forty-one Roscoe Conkling was Thurlow Weed's successor, and his future seemed unlimited.[49]

But Fenton's powerful state machine still had to be dismantled, and the occasion was the state convention in Saratoga in September. Fenton arrived early at the famous spa, declaring that he desired to have his friend Charles Van Wyck made temporary chairman and himself permanent president. (Conkling also declared his intentions early: Collector Murphy and George Bliss tried unsuccessfully to bribe delegates from Horace Greeley's district to keep the editor out of the convention.)[50] Conkling and Murphy traveled to Saratoga together, the Senator bearing a letter from President Grant urging his attendance. Conkling cleverly nominated the reform-minded editor of *Harper's Weekly*, George William Curtis, as temporary chairman, and then proceeded to travel with Murphy to the hotel rooms of Fenton supporters to talk about the federal patronage the White House had entrusted to his supervision. These negotiations took time, and to delay convention proceedings a gang of Conkling supporters staged a brawl on the floor of the convention hall. When business resumed, Conkling's ability to make threats and promises concerning patronage had earned the votes necessary to elect Curtis, and the Senator found himself heading the important committee on resolutions. After a series of complex maneuvers that left Fenton and Greeley humiliated and enraged, General Stewart L. Woodford, Grant's choice for the governor's chair, won the nomination on the third ballot. Conkling was able to secure more than two thirds of the seats on the state committee and make Alonzo B. Cornell its chairman. Chester Arthur was one of those placed on the committee, and this relatively unknown attorney was now considered by observers, including members of the press, to be one of Roscoe Conkling's lieutenants—a man worth watching in the near future.[51]

A few months before the dramatic confrontation on the Senate floor between Conkling and Fenton, Silas Burt called at Arthur's law office. Through his old friend's intervention he had been appointed a special agent for New York City's internal revenue assessors, and from time to time he stopped by for a chat. Tom Murphy was just coming out of the office as Burt entered, and Burt later remembered him being "jubilantly sarcastic concerning the fate of Fenton and his followers." Arthur talked at length with Burt about the situation in the Customhouse and seemed to have a detailed knowledge of developments there. The trouble with Grinnell, he contended, was that he did not know how to dispense patronage. In his sixteen months in office he had fired 510 persons, more than half his subordinates, but had failed to please party bosses with his appointments. Had Arthur been collector, he told Burt, he would have taken the entire thousand positions and allotted them

> . . . to the several counties in the State in the rates of their Republican vote and would have asked the Committee of the party in each County

to name its selections for that county's quota. He would hold the several committees responsible for the integrity of their nominees and the several placemen responsible for the political fidelity of their nominators; with such sureties and hostages he would secure subordinates who would not dare to steal, while the whole party machinery could be consolidated, unified and concentrated for any purpose; this would prevent all the scandalous and injurious contests in primaries and conventions and make the party so compact and disciplined as to be practically invincible.

Arthur had apparently given his plan much thought, but conceded to Burt "that some expert officers would have to be retained and that some places would have to be reserved from the committees and put at the disposal of eminent men in the party."

Arthur's scheme resembled his proposal to streamline troop recruitments in New York during the war. Its sole purpose was to consolidate and strengthen the Republican Party. Burt too was a loyal Republican but had been flirting with the young civil service reform movement advocated by Congressman Jenckes of Rhode Island. He was becoming increasingly convinced that public offices should be held exclusively by qualified, honest, efficient personnel concerned solely with the public interest. Arthur's idea, he thought to himself sadly, was simply a variation of an increasingly familiar theme: "It was a very elaborate and ingenious plan for subordinating the public service to partisan ends and for suppressing or thwarting the popular will as presumptively expressed by political nominating conventions." It was out of a "political creed which favored the substitution of management and discipline for principles and convictions." Of course, the business (if not the practice) of politics had long depended upon the careful acquisition and dispensation of patronage, especially in New York. And one wonders what Burt expected from an ambitious party worker on his way up in a machine dominated by Conkling and Murphy. The idealistic and earnest Chet Arthur he had known in college and during two years in the militia seemed to bear only a faint resemblance to the portly, crafty political tactician seated across the desk mapping ways to manipulate federal jobs.[52]

The elections of 1870 went badly for Republicans: thirty seats in Congress were lost, the heavily populated states of New York and Indiana favored Democrats, and in Missouri a small but growing and potentially troublesome group of reformers who called themselves Liberal Republicans captured the governorship. Considerable publicity focused upon political assessments—the practice long employed by both parties of requiring civil servants, under the guise of "voluntary contributions," to return a percentage of their salaries for campaign purposes. Some reformers, such as E. L. Godkin of *The Nation* and the fiery journalist Carl Schurz, were already convinced that Grant should be replaced and that the party should begin to look for more enlightened leadership.

In December, President Grant divided reformers by unexpectedly speaking out in favor of civil service reform. "The present system," he said, "does not secure the best men, and often not even fit men, for public place." In March Congress reluctantly responded with a joint resolution empowering the President to appoint a commission to explore civil service rules. The commission met in June under the chairmanship of George William Curtis and quickly fell into bickering. Curtis favored open-competitive examinations for civil service positions, a formula adopted by the British in 1870 that would strip politicians of their patronage. Other members disagreed. One, a New Jersey banker secretly engaged in plundering the Navy Department, assured the commission that as a personal friend of the President he knew that Grant "was not a thorough believer in competitive examination" and was firmly opposed to any reduction in his power of removal.[53]

While the commission deliberated, the feud between New York's Senators continued to boil. With Conkling having the confidence of the President and control of the most lucrative sources of patronage in the country, Fenton turned civil service reformer. He instigated a congressional investigation of the New York Customhouse and introduced a Customhouse reform bill—which the administration curtly ignored. Conkling claimed to have no authority over Tom Murphy, going as far as to contend that he was merely a "disinterested and unbiased witness" of Customhouse affairs. Moreover, he denied that anyone had been dismissed from the Customhouse because of friendship for Fenton.[54]

In fact, Murphy carried out a zealous purge of Fenton supporters. (General Porter, Grant's private secretary, had written to Murphy shortly after his confirmation by the Senate: "I only hope you will distribute the patronage in such a manner as will help the Administration.")[55] Moses Grinnell had removed 510 employees to cleanse the Customhouse of Democrats, and Murphy proceeded to make 338 removals in order to extirpate "Fentonism." Silas Burt, a deputy collector in the Customhouse thanks to Arthur's political influence, commented later: "The removal of ninety-two percent of the employes within two years and nine months had rooted out every vestige of partisan heterodoxy and left nothing in the way of purification to be done." (When Grinnell took over the naval

office, Burt persuaded him to attempt an experiment in civil service reform: the grading of clerks by competitive examination. Grinnell was
quickly relieved of his position by the President and replaced with a
Conkling supporter. Burt was forced to appeal to Arthur to protect his
own job.)[56]

By the fall of 1871, bitterness between the two factions was intense.
Greeley had come out against Grant's renomination, and his New York
Tribune had earned Conkling's undying hatred for calling him the "Pet
of the petticoats," the "darling of the ladies' gallery" who "could look
hyacinthine in just thirty seconds after the appearence of a woman." The
Conkling-dominated state committee, with Grant's encouragement, had
taken steps to reorganize the party structure so as to deprive the Greeley-
Fenton forces of their authority in New York City.[57]

At the Republican state convention in September both Fenton and
Conkling were present to marshal their forces. At stake was not only
party leadership in the state but also representation at the national convention in 1872. Murphy's men lurked everywhere, a group of New York
City toughs seized the stage, fistfights broke out, the police were called.
One Fentonite later complained, "We have met in this Convention the
Collectors of ports, internal revenue officers all over the State. We have
met Postmasters in solid phalanx; the District Attorneys, the registers
in bankruptcy, and the bankrupts also." When it was all over, Conkling
totally dominated New York's Republican machinery and could lead a
solid delegation for Grant to the national convention. Fentonites bolted
the conclave in a rage; sealed off from spoils, they appeared headed
toward Liberal Republicanism.[58]

The *Tribune* attacked Tom Murphy furiously, resurrecting charges
of Civil War frauds and of collusion with recently deposed Boss Tweed.
Greeley lashed out: "This shoddy contractor, swollen with robberies from
our soldiers, and backed by all the power of an Administration that has
honestly trusted him, has had his clutch on the throat of the Republican
party in New York long enough."[59] *The Nation* claimed that Murphy
and members of the Tweed Ring were of

> . . . a class of greedy adventurers, without conscience, or honor, or
> shame, or decency, or patriotism, or fear of God or devil, or any strong
> spring of action, except love of money, and who go into politics and
> repeat the party war-cries for the same reason that other men pick
> locks and forge bills—to avoid honest labor, fill their bellies with
> rich food, and adorn their bodies with rich clothing. We hope the
> Republican press will see to it that the President gets no peace until
> this particular rascal is relegated to private life.[60]

The pressure increased, and Grant, with an eye toward the following year's nominating convention, accepted Murphy's resignation in November 1871.

An investigation of the Customhouse was inevitable, and to illustrate his virtue, Conkling initiated it, making sure that the Republican majority on the congressional committee was sympathetic. Nevertheless, the Democratic minority revealed Murphy to be one of the era's most ruthless spoilsmen. His removal of Fenton Republicans came to light, as did the fact that he had devoted almost all his time to politics, leaving the duties of the Customhouse to subordinates. Testimony showed that Murphy had organized delegations to the state convention of 1870, that he had offered city politicians Customhouse positions which they were invited to sell in exchange for Conkling delegations, and that he had paid money to a ward politician to defeat Greeley in his district and deny him a voice in the convention. The collection of party assessments was seen as a common practice in the Customhouse.

The investigation again brought to light Murphy's dealings in business and politics with the Tweed Ring. Murphy admitted having real estate holdings with Tweed, Peter B. Sweeney, Richard B. Connally, and Hugh Smith; he held a 20 percent share in properties close to burgeoning Central Park purchased for $542,500. (As Murphy's close friend and attorney, Arthur must have been privy to these entanglements; no doubt he lacked the financial resources to be offered a share.) At the time of his appointment as collector, Murphy was a member of a commission for the widening of Broadway, which had some $3,000,000 to dispense for the project. He was also a member of the city school board, which controlled appointments, purchases, and expenditures for the city school system. The commission and the board were products of Tammany Hall, and Murphy held his positions on them until about three months after being named collector.

Murphy was also involved with the activities of George Leet and Wilbur Stocking, two members of the motley cast of cronies and thieves that debauched the reputation of Grant's first administration. Leet had served on Grant's staff during the war, and in 1868 he presented a letter of recommendation from the President-elect to Moses Grinnell, shortly to be named collector. Grant said of Leet: "I cheerfully commend him as possessing all the qualities necessary to inspire confidence." Leet promptly demanded the general-order business of the Customhouse, and Grinnell, hardly in a position to do otherwise, granted him a percentage of it. The general-order warehouse system required merchants to take possession of their goods and pay taxes on them within forty-eight hours after a ship's entry into port or find their goods unloaded under a general order from the collector in a warehouse, where owners were forced to pay cartage and a minimum of a month's storage rate to secure their release. Leet farmed out his percentage of the system for $5,000 a year plus half of all profits over $10,000. He moved to Washington, where he roomed· with Grant's private secretaries—Generals Orville Babcock and Horace Porter—and enjoyed additional salaries from an army commission and a post in the War Department. Unsatisfied with the level of his income, Leet used his influence to threaten Grinnell with dismissal if he failed to receive a larger share of the general-order business. Grinnell's successor, Tom Murphy, gave Leet and his friend Wilbur Stocking the large North River general-order business, and with this monopoly the two raised rates on cartage and storage and devised an assortment of delays and inconveniences to plague merchants. Complaints were immediate and included a memorandum signed by one hundred New York importing firms. Responding to the clatter, Grant told Murphy in May 1871 to sever Leet's relations with the Customhouse. But the President did nothing once Murphy replied that attacks upon Leet and Stocking were unjustified. The exact value of the general-order plum was left uncertain by the Customhouse investigation; witnesses estimated the annual yield at between $60,000 and $200,000. One careful student of the matter has accepted the Democratic minority's estimate of $172,000 for 1871.

The investigation, followed closely by the press, also called attention to the moiety system. By a law of 1789 fines and forfeitures in customhouses were thus divided: one half (a moiety) went to the federal treasury, one quarter to the informer, and a quarter to the collector, naval officer, and surveyor. The system was designed to encourage diligence from customhouse employees, but the handsome profits in it frequently led to extralegal searches and hasty seizures; importers often complained bitterly about overzealous customs men who ransacked their books and their premises in search of evidence of fraud. Murphy was unsure about the exact amount he had made from moieties while collector. He recalled that his annual salary was $6,500 and could remember one case that brought him $10,000. When pushed a bit harder by specific questions, he said: ". . . I may have received $30,000, may have received $40,000 or $50,000."[61]

A large number of Conkling Republicans were sad to see Murphy leave the Customhouse; he had served his party faithfully and effectively. (Commented *The Nation*: "There can be no doubt that Murphy was appointed in order that he might do a certain kind of work in the Customhouse, and there is no doubt that he did it; but that work was not the prompt, careful, and honest collection of the revenue.") Right after Christmas, 1871, hundreds of friends and a hundred-piece band serenaded the ex-collector in front of his home on Thirty-ninth Street. Murphy's consolation was that the President had permitted him to choose his successor. The nod went to his "very close and very intimate" friend Chester A. Arthur.[62]

When Murphy's resignation had seemed imminent, the heart of the Conkling faction—including Richard Crowley, George Bliss, Alonzo B. Cornell, and Charles Folger—wrote to President Grant urging Arthur's appointment. The forty-two-year-old attorney had long sought a high-ranking post in the Customhouse and was a popular, experienced, and trustworthy party worker. When Murphy named Arthur, the matter was settled. Arthur feigned surprise when selected, and his biographers for the next century would accept his assertion that he assumed the collectorship with reluctance.[63]

The appointment elicited a mixed response. Arthur was by and large an unknown quantity and had to be judged by his political associations. Not unexpectedly, Horace Greeley wrote: ". . . the General will be in the Custom House a personal burlesque upon Civil Service Reform. He recently held a ten-thousand dollar Tammany office from which he was only driven by the Tribune's exposure; and he is a devoted servant of the Murphy clique; but he is not personally an objectionable man."[64] *The Nation* echoed this view:

> . . . we know of only two objections—that he is a lawyer and not a merchant, and that he is and has been a warm friend and supporter of Murphy, and an active politician of the same wing of the Republican party. Personally, he is a gentleman and a man of education, but the fact that he is a prominent member of the Customhouse faction forbids the hope that he will take the Customhouse out of politics or institute any real reform.[65]

On the other hand, the pro-Grant *New York Times* paid Arthur several compliments and assured its readers that the new collector "is well known to be in favor of those reforms upon which the people have wisely set their hearts."[66]

Thurlow Weed commented privately, "The appointment of General Arthur is a good one."[67]

CHAPTER FOUR

Those Derisive Smiles

THE SYSTEM of selecting public officials that had evolved since the ratification of the Constitution was based upon two unwritten but widely followed principles. The "spoils system" started with the Federalists, expanded with the rise of democracy, and was an established institution by the close of the Civil War, when it was dominated by Congress. Under it, civil servants were appointed for largely political reasons, with but the barest pretense of concern about capacity or qualification. After every turnover of party control, opponents holding government jobs were dismissed and the victors divided the spoils. "Rotation in office" was a Jacksonian embellishment which contended that when a party was in power over a protracted period, government employees should be removed at intervals to permit the largest possible number of citizens to share in the rewards and responsibilities of public office.

From their beginnings, political machines became dependent upon patronage dispersal. Bosses from both parties knew that local, state, and federal employees would exert time and money on behalf of their patrons' political efforts, and they could not envision American politics working any other way.

By 1865, the federal bureaucracy was a particularly rich source of patronage: it was subdivided into seven departments employing 53,000 workers who were paid some $30,000,000 a year. The Post Office Department accounted for more than half of all civil servants; nearly every village in the country had a postmaster who could be counted on for assessments and campaign assistance. The Treasury Department had a large office in Washington, customhouses in major port cities, and a body of internal revenue agents. The Interior Department contained land, patent, Indian, and pension bureaus. Less patronage was controlled by the War, Navy, State, and Justice departments. A few positions requiring technical competence—in the patent office, for example—remained relatively free from politics, while the others were frequently up for grabs. Under the Lincoln Administration 1,457 incumbents of the 1,639 presidential offices were removed, and many positions were filled by several different people between 1861 and 1865. A tally taken in December 1867 in the office of the United States Treasurer revealed that 219 of the 282 employees had been appointed within the preceding four years.

The New York Customhouse, which had jurisdiction over the sea waters and shores of New York State and over most of Hudson and Bergen counties in New Jersey, was of major significance to the country in the late nineteenth century. About 75 percent of the nation's customs receipts were collected here; by 1877 those receipts amounted to approximately $108,000,000. When Arthur took office, it was claimed that the Customhouse did an annual business five times greater than that of the largest business house in North America. As the largest single federal office in the nation, the Customhouse was also the greatest single source of patronage. Politicians from all parts of the country clamored to get jobs for their followers, and both Republicans and Democrats were eager to collect the rich assessments that could be culled regularly from its employees.

There were four chief offices of the New York Customhouse: the collector, surveyor, naval officer, and the appraiser. Each directed a principal department and was appointed for a four-year term.

The collector's department employed the largest number of clerks in the Customhouse. Among other duties, it received and recorded documents pertaining to the entry of ships, received revenues paid for duties, and was charged with the enforcement of the neutrality laws. Hypothetically the collector should have possessed considerable commercial and administrative experience, but in fact he was usually a politician in charge of dispensing spoils: the largest dispenser of federal patronage in the state and a power in his party's machinery. Pleasing a wide array of party chieftains was a delicate job, and few collectors lasted a full four years.

The naval office was relatively small and served as a check on the collector. It examined the collector's accounts and countersigned a large number of documents.

The surveyor was an important source of patronage, having charge of all work on the docks and vessels. Under him was a large staff of inspectors, weighers, measurers, and gaugers.

The appraiser's department also furnished many jobs, even though it had the complex task of deciding the market value of all imported commodities and determining an appropriate rate of duty for each item.

Directly under the four department heads were the deputy collectors; five of them in 1853 earned $2,500 a year apiece. Beneath them were the hundreds of employees whose loyalty to a party or faction had won them their low-paying and insecure jobs. The average employee was a native New Yorker (although most states were represented) of humble origin, with but a few years of schooling. Because his selection for a position in the Customhouse bore no relationship to his skill, intelligence, or experience, it should not have been surprising that he frequently exerted little effort and energy on behalf of his employer.

Over the entire operation stood the collector, as one scholar has described him, "the symbol of the Spoilsman, running a political machine, sacrificing the needs of the community as a whole to the selfish ends of factional politics."[1] The collector directed removals and appointments, subject only to the normally compliant supervision of the Secretary of the Treasury. He also guided the assessments of employees. By 1872 the Customhouse payroll was about $1,800,000 annually, and Republicans, by levying a 2 percent annual assessment, could count on $36,000 a year.

For his services the collector was handsomely rewarded; "Chet" Arthur, as his intimate friends addressed him, stepped into the highest paying job in the federal government. Moieties and an assortment of fees had brought an annual income of about $30,000 to collectors in the 1850s; by the early 1870s Arthur found that the position grossed more than $50,000 a year—which compared favorably (*after* the infamous "Salary Grab" of 1873) with the President's $50,000 salary, the $10,000 salaries of the Vice-President, Speaker, Cabinet members, and Supreme Court justices, and the $7,500 allotted members of Congress.[2]

Opposition to the spoils system grew rapidly after the war. By 1876, E. L. Godkin would contend that "the condition of the civil service includes almost every evil of which the American people have at this moment to complain. The seat of all the fraud and corruption and infidelity and inefficiency and negligence is to be found in it."[3] The civil service reform movement, one of the Gilded Age's most prominent crusades, was an effort to restore integrity and efficiency in the public service and to stem the threat to democratic government that resulted from the control of public servants by professional politicians. To insure the selection and retention of "good" men in positions of public-responsibility—moral, qualified men who placed community welfare over private greed—adherents of the movement desired a professionalization of the civil service. They wanted appointments based on competitive examinations, tenure of office, and promotions tied to a merit system. They also sought laws protecting salaries from political assessments. In short, they believed that taxpayers deserved an honest, efficient, inexpensive, nonpartisan civil service.[4]

"Nonpartisan" was an especially important word to reformers, for they believed that the spoils system was not only squandering taxpayers' money but—even more important—was also debasing and crippling democratic government. Officeholders, under the thumb of political bosses, constituted "an army of mercenaries" that consistently dominated party activities and frustrated the will of the people. Independent-minded candidates could not make their voices heard in nominating conventions over the organized clangor of civil servants engaged in partisan activity to protect their jobs. If public employees "were secure in their places as long as they did their duty honestly and faithfully," said *The New York Times* in 1876, "and if their only allegiance was paid to the department under which they served, the whip of the politician would be cracked over them in vain. They would take the same interest in politics as other citizens. They would attend the primaries, if they attended them at all, as independent citizens, not as henchmen of political chieftains." But what about the inevitable retort that the operation of the two-party system depended upon office-hopefuls? *The Times* continued:

> This is a low view of the case. If things have come to such a pass that the American people must be hired by the prospect of office to take an interest in the selection of their rulers and the administration of their Government, then they are no longer fit for self-government. And if any party has reached such a condition that it is held together "by the cohesive force of public plunder," and not by the power of its principles, it is time that its grave were dug, for it is plainly moribund. In truth, it is the interference of placemen and mercenaries that has driven honest and self-respecting citizens out of active politics.[5]

Reformers refused to believe that their goals were impractical or that their efforts conflicted in any way with the legitimate functions of political parties. To Dorman Eaton, a prominent leader of the movement, parties should be "convenient agencies for combining and expressing on a grand scale and with a true freedom the real views and interests of the people."[6] This did not require control of the public service.

Much has been written in recent years denigrating the motives of civil service reformers. Whereas scholars once described the likes of George William Curtis, E. L. Godkin, Carl Schurz, Charles Eliot Norton, Charles Francis Adams Jr., Charles J. Bonaparte, Horace White, and

Samuel Bowles as heroic figures—intelligent, cultured, responsible, high-minded men at war with a crass and corrupt era—several "revisionist" historians have labeled them ultraconservatives, antidemocratic elitists, impractical dreamers, and power-seekers. John G. Sproat, for example, has described at length their devotion to free trade, the gold dollar, and laissez-faire government, as well as their antipathy toward labor unions, immigrants, and Negroes. While admitting that "Certainly no other group of men had better intellectual and moral equipment to deal with the problems of the Gilded Age," Sproat condemned reformers of the Liberal Republican and Mugwump persuasion for an inability to grasp the most important issues of their period, and especially for their trust in "good breeding" and education.

> They wished to reform only in the sense of restoring certain conditions of the past or of mildly amending certain new and disturbing developments. There was nothing remotely revolutionary about them, for they had no quarrel with capitalism or the industrial revolution, and they were uncompromising defenders of private property. They wanted no fundamental changes in the nature of American government, beyond enjoining the "irresponsible" elements in society from exercising an undue or dominant influence in legislative affairs.[7]

Ari Hoogenboom, noting that many reformers came from older, once-wealthy New England families, suggested that they were suffering from status frustrations: "The post-Civil War political world was not what the 'outs' expected it to be. In their disappointment, they turned to reform."[8]

On the whole, these indictments seem exaggerated. Most are examples of "history by hindsight"—by which leaders (and even prophets) of every generation may stand condemned no matter what their purposes and actions. It is no doubt useful to point out that George William Curtis and his friends were self-righteous (what reformers are not?), that they were convinced of their own ability to dispense power wisely (who is not?), and that their trust in civil service reform as a sort of elixir for crime and corruption was unrealistic. But it is less interesting to berate men of the mid- and late-nineteenth century for failing to accept positions on race, economics, immigration, and government that were rejected by most educated Americans well beyond the Great Crash of 1929. Moreover, the once fashionable "status" theory of historical causation—the assumption that political activity results from social dislocation and the ensuing frustrations or tensions—has been all but totally discarded by the discipline of psychology. The abandonment of this always controversial concept, employed to explain such disparate movements as abolitionism, Progressivism, and McCarthyism, forces historians to reconsider the complexities underlying human motivation, and to weigh carefully the merits of activists' objectives.[9]

Judged by the highest values of their historical context—the most reasonable scholarly yardstick—the civil service reformers continue to seem to be among the most enlightened and attractive characters of the Gilded Age. John A. Garraty has rightly concluded of them, "their indignation was in the main disinterested, their objectives pure, although rather old-fashioned."[10] And it should not be overlooked that their case against the spoils system was a good one: the boss-ridden civil service in the postwar years *was* grossly inefficient, wasteful, and corrupt; government job-holders *did* tend to dominate party affairs during the period. If Curtis, Godkin, Burt, and the others were overly optimistic about the effects of divorcing politics from the public service and installing qualified, "good" men in positions of public responsibility, no superior solution to the problems they repeatedly documented seemed equally useful or practical at the time. No one argued against the desirability of seeking competent, intelligent public servants. (Professional politicians defended their hold over the civil service with extreme reluctance.) And few Americans have ever quarreled with the hypothetical link between knowledge (usually equated with education) and goodness.

The first forceful leader in Congress of civil service reform was Thomas A. Jenckes, a Rhode Island attorney who was elected to the House in 1862. Jenckes offered his first civil service bill in late 1865, but it was drowned out by the uproar surrounding President Johnson. Early in 1866, Johnson's Revenue Commission provided fuel for reform by declaring that corruption and inefficiency in the New York Customhouse was costing between $12,000,000 and $25,000,000 annually. With growing support, Jenckes proposed a second bill in December 1866; it was defeated a month later, but by the surprisingly close vote of 71 to 67. Widespread corruption within the Republican Party soon focused more attention on the movement. Certain business organizations began to urge Congress to consider reform in order to achieve fiscal reform and economy in government. In May 1868, a report of the Joint Select Committee on Retrenchment revealed strong support for reform within the government service. By early 1869 civil service reform counted among its declared adherents Secretary of the Treasury Hugh McColloch, Speaker of the House James G. Blaine, officials of the National Association of Manufacturers, the American Social Science Association, the Union League Club of New York, such important elements of the press as *The New York Times*, the New York *World*, the New York *Evening*

Post, and the Chicago *Tribune*, plus the influential journals *Harper's Weekly* and *The Nation*. Pressure was such that, as noted, the dying Forty-first Congress, on March 3, 1871, authorized the President to make rules and regulations for the civil service.

Most civil service reformers were Republicans, and they had been elated by the election of Ulysses S. Grant. During the war this quiet, shy, courteous little man had shown fierce determination and courage, and reformers felt him capable of great achievement. He was elected on a platform calling for "strictest economy" in the civil service and an end to the corruption that had flourished under Johnson, and he seemed willing to carry out this mandate. Reformers quickly became disenchanted with the President over his poor selection of Cabinet members and his willingness to reward Conkling and the fastidious spoilsman Ben Butler of Massachusetts with federal patronage. But they took heart at his support of a Civil Service Commission and were encouraged by the selection of George William Curtis, the scrupulous and activist editor of *Harper's Weekly*, as its chairman.

The commission submitted a number of civil service rules to the President in December 1871. Grant approved the recommendations by executive order and asked the commission to put them into effect. Under the rules, applicants were required to be American citizens, to be able to read, write, and speak English, and to provide satisfactory evidence about their character, health, and age. Departmental positions were grouped into uniform grades, and a board of examiners was created in each department to conduct competitive examinations within the lower ranks. A probationary period of six months was required of most appointees. Political assessments under any guise were strictly forbidden.

Although many of Grant's closest admirers in Congress were bitterly opposed to civil service reform, the President seemed pleased with his commission's work. In March 1872, he approved additional commission regulations, declaring that "honesty and efficiency, not political activity, will determine the tenure of office."[11] Senator Conkling wrote to an admirer, "I have no thought of doing anything to baffle a fair trial of the experiment. Moreover I am *for anything that will improve the matter of appointments to office.*"[12]

When Chester Arthur assumed his duties on December 1, 1871, he entered a mammoth structure of solid granite boasting huge bluish gray columns set on square blocks and a two-hundred-foot frontage on Wall Street. It was the old Merchants' Exchange building, leased by the government in 1863 and subsequently purchased for $1,000,000. Inside, a dome two hundred feet above the sidewalk looked down upon a circular rotunda with a large four-faced clock planted in its middle. Desks circled the clock manned by deputy collectors and clerks attempting to handle the business of a noisy throng of merchants and brokers who crowded the building between the hours of 10:00 A.M. and 3:00 P.M. To find the collector one traveled down a long corridor, passed a secretary in an anteroom, paid respects to the assistant collector seated in a reception room, and walked through yet another anteroom normally crowded with office-seekers to the collector's door.[13]

Arthur rapidly became one of the era's most popular Customhouse officials. In contrast with several of his predecessors, including Tom Murphy, Arthur worked amicably with the opulent and powerful businessmen of New York. The collector was tactful, sophisticated, dapper, and suave—a gentleman whose appearance, manners, education, and membership in the Union League Club marked him as a large cut above the political hacks with whom he frequently associated. His knowledge of law and commercial transactions, as well as his Whiggish, wholly orthodox views on fiscal conservatism, the tariff, and limited government were welcomed by businessmen. Arthur was a politician, of course— numerous merchants and bankers had first met him when approached for campaign funds. And it was generally assumed that he took orders from Roscoe Conkling—if only because it was unthinkable for one who enjoyed the lordly Senator's confidence to possess an independent mind. Nevertheless, Arthur was one servant of a machine who sought to accommodate and to please, one who seemed trustworthy and responsible to members of his class. In creating this impression, the collector played an important role in the Grant Administration's effort to secure valuable business support.[14]

To assure New York business and commercial interests of a new emphasis on fidelity at the Customhouse, Arthur, from the first month of his appointment, made public his correspondence with Cabinet members and merchants concerning the general-order business, which the President ordered reformed to prevent scandals of the Leet variety. Careful attention was paid to the language of the letters. Secretary of the Treasury George Boutwell wrote to Arthur in early 1872: "In the reorganization of the General Order business, political influences and personal interests should be set aside. Having first made the rights of the Government secure, it is the President's wish that the work shall be so arranged and conducted as to give the largest facilities to merchants with the least possible cost. The details of the organization must be left to your judgment."[15] When the plan was announced (storage rates were lowered by 35 to 40 percent), most of the laurels went to the collector. *The Evening Post* responded: "Collector Arthur promises to reform the whole vicious system of which the merchants have so long complained, and he invites the co-operation of the importers in his effort."[16]

The new collector also got along well with his subordinates, soon becoming known as a leader who, while demanding personal and party loyalty, cared about the welfare and happiness of the some 1,000 workers under his supervision. For example, he stubbornly resisted efforts to reduce salaries and personnel in the Customhouse (a stance that had political as well as paternalistic foundations). When a bill was introduced in Congress in 1874 to lower the salaries of gaugers, Arthur sent a two-man delegation to Washington to seek assistance from Senator Conkling. "Messrs. Williams and Babcock represent many of our most active and influential friends among the Gaugers and are themselves prominent and influential members of the party. I commend them to your friendly consideration, and shall feel greatly gratified if you can consistently favor their interests."[17] When several gaugers were let go, Arthur privately appealed their case to President Grant's private secretaries, Horace Porter and Orville Babcock. To the latter he complained: "The twenty gaugers dismissed are nearly all good men and very active and influential Republicans."[18] Later in the year, Benjamin Bristow, Grant's reform-minded Secretary of the Treasury, ordered cutbacks in the Customhouse when convinced that expenses incurred in collecting the revenue at the New York port were excessive. Arthur suggested some cuts, but Bristow found the proposal unsatisfactory. More than a few politicians were concerned that their own nominees might be fired, and Arthur confided to fellow Conkling lieutenant Tom Platt, "should the reduction affect any of the employees who are charged to Mr. Cornell and yourself, you will be duly advised of the fact."[19] He then wrote a sharp objection to Bristow: "Permit me to deprecate the wholesale reduction you propose as inexpedient, unjust and dangerous. Its effect would be pernicious, disastrous and demoralizing in the extreme, and the consequent loss of revenue would I am convinced, far exceed the additional saving effected."[20] Several years later, when an investigating commission caused a large reduction in the Customhouse work force, employees observed Arthur in tears.[21]

Favor was also won by a fortunate circumstance: Arthur was not obliged to terminate many subordinates for political reasons. In the five-year period prior to his appointment there had been 1,678 removals, more than were made among the officials serving in all the federal departments within the same period. Murphy had packed the Customhouse with partisans during his short career as collector, and during the Grant years there was little reason for turning them out. In over six years, only 392 men resigned, died, or were dismissed under Arthur's administration, and this figure included cutbacks ordered by Washington.[22] Later, biographers would cite the statistic out of its historical context, mistakenly alleging that Arthur valued efficiency over politics during his years in the Customhouse.

The collector's subordinates also appreciated his approach to the civil service reform movement. Arthur's views on the spoils system, in spite of pious statements to the contrary, were clearly those of his predecessors, fellow collectors, and political associates. His close friend and fellow New York Customhouse official George Bliss perhaps summarized them succinctly when he wrote in 1876: "I believe that an active interest in public affairs is and should be a recommendation to public office, just as I think inattention to them should be a disqualification."[23] On October 19, 1872, the Civil Service Commission's rules and regulations were applied to the New York Customhouse, and each of the four department heads selected a three-member examination board. Silas Burt was named chairman of the naval office board and chairman of a board of appeal, "because," he later wrote, "I was the only person in the service who had given any attention to the new principles of appointment." From the start he had no illusions about his old friend's attitudes on reform; Arthur was now a professional spoilsman, an administrator of patronage, an architect of party victory. The collector "had taken a merely perfunctory and languid interest in the new movement; it did not at all accord with his own views and threatened to destroy the springs of political action on which he had always depended. It was the law however and an Administration measure and could not be openly resisted." Throughout the Customhouse, Burt noted, reform was "treated with a jocular indulgence as the temporary essay of a few well-meaning visionaries with no practical sense of political needs."

Arthur appointed three good friends to the collector's board: Thomas L. James, John R. Lydecker, and James L. Benedict, all of them deputy collectors, party workers, and members of the Conkling faction. Out of interest, Burt attended the first two meetings of the board; shortly he was notified by Arthur, through the naval officer, that his presence at examinations was no longer welcome. In 1879 Burt came into possession of a portion of the board's records and discovered why he had been excluded from observing its activities. Benedict had been so bitterly opposed to reform that he took no part in the examinations. James was appointed postmaster of New York in early 1873 and told the collector that he would be unable to devote his time to the board. He was assured that none of it was needed, and he remained as the board's official chairman until the suspension of the civil service rules in March 1875. As a consequence, Deputy Collector Lydecker was the only active member of the board, assisted by a drunken clerk named Michael Murphy and a messenger named Alexander Powell (who would be President Arthur's personal valet). This trio prepared questions, conducted examinations, graded papers, and issued certificates of appointment in the collector's department. Their records revealed that applicants were limited to those Arthur desired appointed. Burt found one set of examinations used on November 18, 1874, and recognized them as part of a group he had prepared in 1872; they had apparently been used by the board for over two years, even though the answers to the questions were certainly well known. Only three candidates were permitted to take the test, and their responses were consistently, in Burt's words, "simply ridiculous." To the question "Into what three branches is the government of the United States divided?", Charles F. Meserole answered, "The army and navy." George M. Logan thought that the executive departments of the federal government were "Publick stores, Navy Yard." When asked "By what process is a statute of the United States enacted?", Logan read "statue". and wrote, "Never saw one *erected* and dont know the Process." The replies of the third man, Alexander Smyth, were lost, but since he was given the lowest grade of the three, Burt could well imagine their quality. All three men were employed; the certificate of capacity read:

> Charles F. Meserole 70
> George M. Logan 69.66
> Alexander Smyth 68.66

In fact, Smyth, a brother of one of Arthur's closest friends, John F. Smyth of Albany, was soon promoted to be an inspector of customs.

Was Arthur aware of this burlesque of civil service reform? Burt concluded that he had to be. "Knowing Arthur's arrogant demand from his subordinates of unqualified personal fealty to himself without regard to any other consideration, it cannot be questioned that he himself was privy to these proceedings. These men, Lydecker, Phillips and the mulatto, Powell, were his personal henchmen and would not have dared to violate the law in regard to their master's appointments, without his knowledge and support."[24] A few months prior to these appointments, Arthur's secretary wrote to a job applicant: "I am directed by the Collector to inform you that in compliance with the request of Hon. A. B. Cornell, T. C. Platt & other friends, he has appointed you an Asst. Weigher at a salary of $1400 per annum."[25]

Arthur was very popular among Republican politicians. His experienced special deputy surveyor would call him "probably the ablest politician that has ever filled the collector's chair." Veteran Republican leader Chauncey Depew would describe him as "one of the most rigid of organization and machine men in his days of local leadership."[26] Arthur had a better command of the details of his office than several of his predecessors; according to Burt he often gave excellent business advice to merchants and brokers. But most of his time was devoted to the duties and pleasures of machine politics. Symbolic of this was his habit of arriving at his office about 1:00 P.M.—three hours after the Customhouse opened. This was caused by a fondness for late hours: night after night Arthur sat up until two or three in the morning talking politics, smoking cigars, and eating and drinking with "the boys"—a number of friends and fellow Republican workers such as Johnny O'Brien, Steve French, Jake Hess, Barney Biglin, Mike Cregan, and Jake Patterson. Another intimate, Rufus Andrews, later recalled that "Arthur was always the last man to go to bed in any company and was fond of sitting down on his front steps at 3 A.M. and talking until anyone dared to stay."[27] Nell must have resented her husband's constant absence, but she dutifully chose not to criticize his behavior publicly and tolerated her neglect in silence. On occasion she was taken to the opera by an elderly friend, and there were summer vacations to look forward to. Years later Arthur's grandson was told by his father that Chester Arthur's nightly sessions had badly damaged his marriage, and that the couple was on the brink of separation when Mrs. Arthur died in 1880.[28]

Demands upon Arthur for Customhouse patronage were continuous, and emanated from all levels and factions within the party. Among others, requests were received from President Grant, Vice-President Schuyler Colfax, Secretary of State Hamilton Fish, Attorney General George Williams, Speaker of the House Blaine, Senators Conkling and Oliver P. Morton, banker Henry Clews, poet-editor William Cullen Bryant, party financier Levi P. Morton, and E. D. Morgan, who was named chairman of the Republican general committee in August 1871.[29] Arthur was compliant when he could be, of course, but now and then delayed or denied a petition by citing his adherence to the civil service rules. These occasions were predictable: when Blaine sought a promotion for a relative (his future biographer Edward Stanwood), Arthur primly replied: "I shall be most happy to comply with your request concerning his advancement to the position of Entry Clerk, so far as the Civil Service Rules will allow, and shall see that an opportunity is afforded him for examination whenever a vacancy occurs."[30]

Arthur was also pleased to perform a number of small favors for Republican leaders. For example, several of Orville Babcock's relatives received special attention at the Customhouse before departing by ship. And Arthur personally guided 205 cases of champagne through customs on their way to the President, Cabinet members, and Tom Murphy.[31]

In turn, the collector wielded his influence to find jobs and win favors for personal friends and relatives. He sought government positions for his brothers-in-law, Henry Haynesworth and James Masten, as well as for Dabney Herndon and Richard Crowley. He made sure of one law partner's reappointment as a notary public and no doubt assisted another to become a district attorney.[32] He also wrote to General Babcock about his brother's nomination as a regimental quartermaster in the army: "Will you be so kind as to look after the matter & see (if there be no objection) that the designation be approved by the Secretary of War."[33]

More often, Arthur's requests for government jobs had political overtones. Following a private letter to General Babcock, Steve French, one of Arthur's nighttime cronies and a member of the state committee, was made an internal revenue agent. (In 1876 he would become the Customhouse appraiser.) Undoubtedly with the collector's strong approval, President Grant, in December 1872, appointed George Bliss United States District Attorney in New York City. A few months later he named George Sharpe, another Murphy-Arthur confidant and a United States marshal, surveyor of the Customhouse—a move so blatantly partisan and opposed to the spirit of reform that George William Curtis resigned from the Civil Service Commission in protest. Yet another close friend of Arthur's, Alonzo Cornell, chairman of the Republican State Committee, became the naval officer of the Customhouse.[34]

Given the backing of the President and the control of statewide federal patronage, the Conkling machine was able to tighten its grip over the Republican Party in New York considerably during the early and mid-1870s. When reform was mentioned at the White House, Allan Nevins later commented, those with influence wore a derisive smile.[35]

Arthur was more than a collector in the traditional mold. As a member of New York's powerful state committee and as a leader in the Grant-Conkling wing of the party, he was intimately involved in the construction and development of Republican machinery on the municipal, state, and even national levels. Almost all of this activity was private and failed to reach the press, but professional politicians in both parties recognized him as one of Conkling's most effective lieutenants: a schemer with influence in the party's highest circles, and a spoilsman whose concern for power interested him in the smallest public job.

What remains of Arthur's correspondence during his years in the Customhouse shows that he recommended dozens of Republicans from a variety of states for federal positions; his knowledge of politics and politicians outside New York was extensive. At home, Silas Burt may have been exaggerating only slightly when he claimed that Arthur "conceived and perfected" a powerful state machine. In New York City especially the collector's hand was felt in the nominations and campaigns of hundreds of office-seekers. When necessary, bargains were struck with anti-Tammany Democrats against Tammany candidates; New York City was heavily Democratic, and Arthur would label such alliances the "corner-stone" upon which the party in the city was built.[36] According to Burt, Arthur was not, however, above indulging in an assortment of deals with Tammany Hall itself.[37] "Honest John" Kelly was Tweed's successor, and there is evidence that he and the collector were associated at times during the Grant years. *The New York Times* complained in 1877: "For the past four years Tammany Hall has never been able to elect its candidates for local offices, unless when it succeeded in making some corrupt bargain with Republicans."[38]

Unlike most state bosses of the period, Senator Conkling remained aloof from the day-to-day chores of running a successful political machine; they required skills in personal relations he made no pretense to possess or desire. Much of the tasks fell to Collector Arthur, and with the help of Cornell and with the increasing assistance of Platt, he kept a sensitive finger on the political pulse of his city and state. New York City aldermen, for example, received letters from the collector instructing them how to vote on nominations for police justices. In 1874 one alderman was told:

> The bill "authorizing the Judges of the Marine and General Sessions Courts in the City of New York to appoint Clerks," must not be allowed to pass. It is intended to oust some of our friends (republicans) who are now clerks in these courts.
>
> The Judges have the power now, to make these appointments, subject to *confirmation [by] the Board of Supervisors* which is as it should be as it gives our friends in the Board some control of the matter.

Several State Senators learned of Arthur's desire to delay the vote on a bill to regulate city ferries. A Senate committee chairman received this note from the collector: "I hope the Special Sessions Court Bill will not be reported from your committee today. Our friends here wish to advise with you in regard to it & will do so, if you are here on Saturday." Through a brother-in-law, Arthur attempted to influence the composition of the Republican general committee of Albany County. The collector of the port of New Haven, Connecticut, was informed: "If you can consistently with existing obligations nominate Captain Charles W. Darling of Port Jefferson as Keeper of Stratford Shoal Light Ship in place of Captain Jacob Willie resigned you will gratify me much and aid our political friends on Long Island at the coming election." In 1875 Arthur even sought to fill the position of principal of the Fifty-fourth Street School in the Twenty-second Ward.[39]

Every year during his tenure as collector, Arthur led a large contingent of Conklingites to the state party conventions. Symbolic of Conkling's authority, the meetings were held in the Senator's home town of Utica in 1872, 1873, and 1874; "the mountain must come to Mahomet," one reporter growled.[40] Arthur, Cornell, Sharpe, French, Patterson, and a number of other machine loyalists were present on August 20, 1872, when the annual session convened. Caucus headquarters were located in Arthur's vast suite of hotel rooms; on such occasions it was the collector's responsibility to provide the food, liquor, and cigars for the party hierarchy—an expense he was expected to bear because of his handsome income. One observer referred to Arthur and his associates as "the Custom-house party" and sensed that everything about the convention was "prearranged."[41] Indeed, with the exception of the gubernatorial candidate, the entire slate of nominees had been handpicked earlier. Conkling had apparently paid little attention to the governorship, being intent on reelecting Grant and winning a strong majority in the state legislature, charged with selecting a United States Senator in 1873. He at first looked to a rich friend, George Opdyke, as a possibility, but dropped the idea when banker Henry Clews reminded him that Opdyke had been a weak Democratic mayor of New York City during the draft riots of 1863 and a "shoddy" contractor during the war.[42] The convention settled for seventy-four-year-old John A. Dix, a former Secretary of the Treasury in Buchanan's Cabinet and a Union Democrat, who accepted the nomination with considerable reluctance.

Clews called Conkling's attention to Dix, he later wrote, out of a need to build strong support for the presidential contest. Grant had easily won renomination at the national convention in June, but many Republicans were keenly aware that he possessed a sorry record to present to voters. Grant's Reconstruction policies had earned intense hatred throughout the South, several of his appointments and removals had disappointed supporters, his fumbling association with the unscrupulous financiers Jay Gould and Jim Fisk had tarnished his image, his imperialistic schemes for San Domingo were unpopular, rumors of corruption were persistent, and the reform wing of the party was disgusted by his disposition to turn over patronage to a coterie of bosses who shamelessly manipulated public offices to their own advantage. Senators Oliver P. Morton of Indiana, Zachariah Chandler of Michigan, John A. Logan of Illinois, Simon Cameron of Pennsylvania, Matthew Carpenter of Wisconsin, and Conkling in the nation's most populous state: these were the bosses who, along with their cohorts, became known as the Stalwarts—professional spoilsmen whose power depended upon the compliant occupant of the White House. Their machines held nearly absolute control over elective and appointive offices within their state borders. Virtually every office had a price tag, and all public officials who owed their jobs to the bosses were expected to spend time and money on behalf of the party candidates under threat of dismissal.

Several disenchanted Republicans, led by Carl Schurz and a number of other reformers, bolted the party and under the banner of Liberal Republicanism invited all interested in honest government and civil service reform to unite behind their ticket. The movement was badly damaged when it presented the presidential nomination to eccentric Horace Greeley, but picked up slight hope when the hapless Democrats, still burdened with the stigma of secession, chose to support the New York editor.

To raise funds and to coordinate Grant's bid for a second term, regular Republicans selected Edwin D. Morgan as chairman and treasurer of the national committee. The committee's secretary, and Morgan's chief aide, was William E. Chandler, a wily and energetic attorney from New Hampshire. Businessmen contributed the bulk of the funds collected for the campaign (financier Jay Cooke gave at least $50,000), but officeholders, according to custom, also paid a large share of the bills. The Republican National Committee assessed the diplomatic corps while the congressional committee, another party organization created in 1868, assessed federal and some state officeholders. Carl Schurz declared that "the whole civil service of the country from the Cabinet minister down to the meanest postmaster, is converted into a vast political agency to secure the president's re-election."[43] He was exaggerating very little: the national committee alone raised approximately $200,000, while the congressional committee put government employees to work making speeches, collecting money, organizing political clubs, and writing for party newspapers.[44] The New York Customhouse, of course, was counted on by Republican officials as a major source of income and labor.

Several assessment circulars reached Customhouse employees in 1872, each requesting a "voluntary contribution" for a certain party committee. These demands for salary kickbacks had from their start been considered unethical by many, requiring spoilsmen to disguise them or deny their existence. But now for the first time—after October 10 in the Customhouse—they were illegal, according to the eleventh Civil Service Rule. This did not deter the collector. As Silas Burt saw the situation, "Arthur had been prominent in the large collections for the

Republican funds made in 1864 and 1868 and he was anxious that the Custom House should show under his reign no decline in productiveness."[45] The exact amount raised in the Customhouse is unknown. One study estimated that from 2 to 6 percent of all annual salaries was requested; Liberal Republicans claimed that a minimum of $25 was required of each employee.[46] The pro-Grant *New York Times*—which the Republican National Committee was distributing across the country— denied the existence of assessments entirely: "No such tax has been levied, directly or indirectly; none such would be permitted."[47]

Silas Burt had always contributed to campaign funds; he was a loyal Republican and understood that campaigns required money. But in 1872, out of his devotion to civil service reform and because of a personal determination to abide by the law, he decided to resist party assessments. Shortly after the naval officer learned of Burt's decision, the latter was summoned to the collector's office for a friendly discussion.

> Our interview opened in a pleasant and mild vein, but when I told him that under no circumstances could I give any money to the State Republican Committee he violently accused me of ingratitude to the party, asserting that my connection with the party had alone procured me my place. He said that every person who accepted a position under the government made a contract, as solemn in its implication as if plainly expressed, to give a part of his salary to sustain his party in power and that to repudiate such a contract was not only ingratitude but mean[n]ess. I denied that any such understanding was entertained by me when I accepted my place and that while I had hitherto freely contributed with others to the party funds, I was now firmly bound by the President's rule not to give any money. He passionately asked if I was going to make the rule a subterfuge and seeing that there could be no agreement between us as to my duty, I withdrew, much hurt by his inconsiderate and harsh expressions and by his apparent inability to appreciate my position. It was my first open variance with him and it proved to be the point of departure on courses ever divergent.

A few days later a personal friend of the naval officer, a chief clerk from his office, approached Burt with the proposition that $100 (4 percent of his annual salary) would be subscribed in his name for the Republican State Committee if he would make no objection. Burt angrily refused, stating that his objection to paying an assessment had nothing to do with penury. He remained firm—insulated from dismissal by his pronounced views on civil service reform (which the administration officially supported) and by what remained of his long friendship with Arthur. But most Customhouse employees enjoyed no such insurance, and only one, to Burt's knowledge, followed his course of action.[48]

On October 11, in response to a letter from the chairman of the Civil Service Commission, Arthur reluctantly acknowledged the existence of assessments in the Customhouse but claimed that until recently he had known nothing about them.

> I find that some months ago, one class of my subordinates wholly without my knowledge or communication with any other than their own members, voluntarily raised a sum of money to be devoted towards paying the legitimate expenses of the Republican Campaign Com., that more recently another class of employe[e]s have followed their example and further that persons not employed in the Custom House or under the Government, have solicited and received contributions from the clerks in the several departments of this office.
>
> Until after the receipt of your letter none of these facts were known to me. Since they became known, I have not thought it either my duty or my right to interfere with such contributions or solicitations, or the use which my subordinates voluntarily make of their own money.[49]

Arthur's interests in Republican campaigning extended beyond New York. In a letter to E. D. Morgan during the summer of 1872, he wrote: "I feel very anxious about N. Carolina. All the money should be sent there that can be used to advantage. The result in that state 1st Aug. will go far to make or mar us." The same document shows Morgan quietly passing funds to Senator Oliver P. Morton of Indiana through his friend the collector.[50]

Grant overwhelmed Greeley at the polls in November, enjoying a three quarters of a million majority and winning 286 out of 352 electoral votes. New York went for Grant by 53,000 votes, Dix captured the governor's chair with a majority of 55,000, and Republicans solidly controlled the legislature. The President's opposition throughout the country, especially within his own party, was humiliated and disorganized by the elections of 1872. Stalwart machines in New York, Pennsylvania, Indiana, and Illinois emerged triumphant and could count on at least another four years in which to consolidate and expand their power.

Roscoe Conkling was clearly the dominant political figure in New York. In January 1873, he easily won reelection to the Senate, and later in the year loftily declined Grant's offer to nominate him for Chief Justice of the United States Supreme Court. With the confidence of the President, firm control over party machinery, and command of the rich sources of patronage within the state, he and his organization looked to the future with assurance. The historian De Alva Alexander later observed: "About half a dozen able lieutenants, holding fat offices in the great patronage centres, revolved with the fidelity of planets, while in every custom-house and federal office in the State trained politicians performed the function of satellites. To harness the party more securely hundreds of young men, selected from the various counties because of their partisan zeal, filled the great departments at Washington."[51] When the state party convention met in 1873, the New York *Tribune* commented: "It was an old-fashioned machine caucus, held strictly in hand by its drivers, which made no pretense of independence or originality in any of its acts or utterances. None but the designated ones had anything to say. No debate was permitted upon the resolutions. The candidates selected by the managers were pushed through under whip and spur."[52] A year later the Conkling machine's brass was such that it selected Tom Murphy to represent the Eighteenth Assembly District at the convention (along with Arthur) and had him elected to the Committee on Permanent Organization.[53]

Civil service reformers suffered bitter disappointments during the second Grant Administration. As noted, the President violated the civil service rules in March 1873 by nominating Arthur's friend George Sharpe surveyor at the port of New York over more qualified rivals. In mid-1874, Congress refused to appropriate further funds for the Civil Service Commission, and competitive examinations were discontinued on March 9, 1875. A congressional act then went into effect that provided that future Treasury Department appointments be apportioned according to state populations. One of Ben Butler's henchmen, William Simmons, was appointed collector of the port of Boston. The spoilsmen reigned.

Grant's second term quickly degenerated into one of the most sordid periods in American political history, exacerbated by a severe depression that gripped the nation following a stock market panic in 1873. The "Salary Grab" was thought to be, as Allan Nevins later described it, a "shameless theft" which plunged the reputation of Congress to its lowest point since the days of slavery, and many observers deplored the President's willingness to permit his own salary to be doubled when the spirit of the Constitution disallowed it. The position of the carpetbag governments in the South continued to worsen: corruption flourished, federal troops were employed to intimidate Democrats, violence and murder were waged against Negroes. And charges of dishonesty in the federal government mounted to the point of national shock, staining the reputations of two Vice-Presidents, a Secretary of War, a Secretary of the Interior, an Attorney General, the President's private secretary, the Speaker of the House, a minister to Great Britain, and numerous others. Grant could barely comprehend what was going on about him. The cartoonist Thomas Nast, after a personal visit to the befuddled Chief Executive, thought: "The President was overwhelmed . . . wherever he turned some new dishonor lay concealed."[54]

One of the most dramatic swindles that besmirched the Grant Administrations concerned the Whiskey Ring, an organization formed by Grant Republicans in 1870 to raise funds against the Independent schism in Missouri and continued in a number of states for private as well as party profit. The scheme to evade the high internal revenue taxes on distilleries blossomed under the direction of General John A. McDonald, one of Grant's wartime cronies whom the President appointed supervisor of internal revenue in St. Louis over the objections of Carl Schurz and other Liberal Republicans. The conspiracy soon included the President's private secretary, Orville Babcock, the chief clerk of the Internal Revenue Office, an assortment of Treasury Department officials, numerous revenue collectors and politicians, and a St. Louis newspaper publisher. Distillers not privy to the frauds were often coerced into joining when entrapped by some technical violation of federal law and threatened with bankruptcy. The take was high: in 1874, St. Louis distillers alone defrauded the government out of $1,200,000 in revenue; two years later the total amount lost to the Treasury was conservatively estimated at $4,000,000. After many months of heroic effort, Secretary of the Treasury Benjamin Bristow managed to break the ring. Well over two hundred persons were indicted, about one hundred pleaded guilty, about twenty were finally convicted, and a dozen fled the country.

Orville Babcock, the President's private secretary and confidant, has been described by William Hesseltine as one who "had intimate contacts with most of the corrupt men of a corrupt decade. He fished for gold in every stinking cesspool, and served more than any other man to blacken the record of Grant's Administrations."[55] Babcock was just the sort to attract Tom Murphy, and the two men, admirers of George Leet, became good friends. In 1875 they convinced the President to appoint Murphy's bankrupt brother-in-law minister to Peru at a salary of $10,000 a year. And at Babcock's probable prod, Grant supported a bizarre scheme promoted by Murphy, Conkling, Jay Cooke, and others to raid the Treasury of $150,000, a plot foiled by Hamilton Fish, the capable Secretary of State.[56] Murphy may have remained entirely unaware of Babcock's important role in the Whiskey Ring, but considering the reputation of the two and the record of their mutual endeavors that seems unlikely.

It is just as possible that Collector Arthur knew about the ring in advance of its public exposure. Arthur often wrote private letters to Babcock asking favors and discussing patronage; and if Murphy was

aware of the ring, it seems reasonable to suggest that the matter might
have been discussed with his closest friend, attorney, and fellow machine
functionary. Moreover, as a Republican fund-raiser who kept an eye on
elections all over the country, Arthur may have known of some of the
many occasions at which Republican campaign committees demanded
funds from the ring. In the 1872 election drive, for example, the ring
contributed to the campaign of Stalwart Senator Oliver P. Morton of
Indiana. In the same contest, E. D. Morgan was in close touch with the
Senator, repeatedly sending him funds from the national committee
(more than $40,000 in all) and, as has been noted, privately channeling
money to the insatiable incumbent through Arthur.[57] To think that the
politically experienced collector and his veteran mentor were unaware
of all of the methods employed by their party to finance victory in
crucial campaigns is to ascribe to them an innocence and a naïveté exhibited by them at no other time.

Another link in the circumstantial evidence tying leaders of the
Conkling machine at least indirectly to the Whiskey Ring involves
George Bliss. As federal attorney in New York, Bliss sent a deputy west
to find evidence for the government's case against Babcock. By early
1876 the deputy came up with some relevant materials—and gave them
to Babcock! E. L. Godkin groaned: "In *bouffe* prosecutions, the Government always collects the evidence, and then hands it over to the
defense."[58]

Thanks largely to efforts by Grant, Babcock was acquitted of complicity with the ring, despite his obvious guilt. Shortly, a number of
Stalwarts started a fund to reimburse him for his legal expenses. Among
the contributors were Arthur intimates George Bliss and Clint Wheeler,
William E. Chandler (who had personally received a donation from the
ring in 1872), and Secretary of the Interior Zachariah Chandler, a Stalwart spoilsman from Michigan whose Cabinet post had been achieved
with Babcock's assistance. Senator Conkling, persistently emphatic in
his defense of Babcock's innocence, was reported to have blessed the
collection.[59] Within a few months, following heated attacks by such
Stalwarts as Conkling and Logan, Treasury Secretary Bristow was
obliged to leave Grant's Cabinet.

The New York Customhouse, under Arthur's leadership, also
played a role in blackening the reputation of Grant's two terms in the
White House.

The moiety system, by which Customhouse fines and forfeitures
were divided among the federal government, customs officials, and informers, had been under attack for two decades when Arthur became

collector. Some critics asserted that it encouraged extralegal searches and seizures, others contended that Customhouse employees should not be paid twice for performing their duties, while others objected to the sums turned over to the executive officers of the customs. Treasury Secretary George Boutwell condemned the system in 1870, and in the following year Senator Reuben Fenton, as part of his attack against Conkling, introduced a bill to abolish it. The final stimulus for the system's abolition came from the celebrated Phelps, Dodge case, a rather crude bit of extortion by the Conkling machine that came to light in early 1873 and aroused the fury of the entire northeastern mercantile community.

A former employee of Phelps, Dodge, and Company, fired for dishonesty, alleged that the old, highly respected importing firm had practiced undervaluations on the federal government through the use of duplicate invoices. Special Agent B. G. Jayne, whom economist David A. Wells called "the head detective, spy and informer of the Custom House," searched the company's books and determined that the charge was true. One of the firm's partners, copper magnate William E. Dodge, a past critic of Customhouse practices, was summoned to Jayne's office one day and impressed with the gravity of the case: the entire shipment in which the alleged frauds were discovered totaled $1,750,000, and legally that was the sum the government had the right to collect. To avoid publicity and a costly lawsuit, Dodge decided to settle for a payment of $271,017, the total of the portions of the invoices held to be undervalued. Company officials then discovered for the first time, from a letter written by United States District Attorney George Bliss, that the undervaluations totaled only $6,658.78, and that the duties involved amounted to a mere $1,664.68—a sum exceeded by the firm's errors of overvaluation. (The total amount of imports made by Phelps, Dodge during the five years covered by the records Jayne examined was $30,000,000.) Concluding quickly that they had been defrauded, Dodge and his colleagues angrily and loudly denounced their treatment at the hands of Customhouse officials, and this led to a congressional investigation of the matter.

During his testimony, Dodge complained about the way Jayne and his cohorts had bullied and tricked him into making payment.

> We paid the money in ignorance of the fact of the amount we owed to the Government. We never had a bill of specifications; we have not got one to-day; we have got simply the list of the vessels on which the goods were imported. We settled, and this has become the biggest case on record. It is known the world over. We look back upon it, and we think as you, gentlemen, think, no doubt, that we were fools.

Dodge, president of New York State's chamber of commerce, furthermore asserted: "The Government should have carefully prepared laws, and it should pay a salary to men sufficient to induce them to do their duty. It should have intelligent men, men of high character and standing in the custom-house, not having a custom-house simply and solely for the purpose of making places for men who know nothing about business, and have never had a particle of business experience." Of the $271,017 paid by Dodge, Collector Arthur, Naval Officer Lafflin, and Surveyor Cornell each received $21,906; Jayne got $61,718, out of which he had to pay the informer. Jayne had become proficient at this business: he took in $316,700 in moieties during the four-year period 1870–1873. In this case, the investigation brought out, a portion of his slice of the pie went to his attorney—Congressman Ben Butler of Massachusetts!

Arthur escaped public identification with the Phelps, Dodge fiasco by simply claiming to know nothing about it. Through George Bliss he stated a preference not to appear before the investigating committee, and his influence was apparently such that he was not summoned. But Bliss, who along with Jayne represented Customhouse officials at the inquiry, made it clear in his testimony that the collector was well aware of the details of the case. Moreover, when one Judge Noah Davis was called to the stand he described a meeting he had attended in the Customhouse with Arthur, Cornell, Lafflin, Jayne, and—of all people—Senator Conkling; a session devoted to a discussion of the Phelps, Dodge case. Both Conkling and Arthur, Davis said, favored a suit against the firm for the full $1,750,000, a sum that would have enormously increased the income of Conkling's Customhouse lieutenants. But Davis dissuaded them on the ground that a jury, learning of the true amount owed the government by the alleged undervaluations, "probably would not give a verdict for anything . . ." It was later learned that at that meeting the participants agreed to demand the figure of $271,017, most likely an arbitrary figure based on what it was assumed Dodge would pay.[60]

The Conkling machine's greed had clearly gotten the best of it, and the result was the acceleration of an effort designed to seal off a profitable source of income for professional politicians. Few could argue any longer that the major impetus behind the moiety system was the efficient collection of government revenue. Heeding much-publicized demands by merchants and reformers, the House Ways and Means Committee recommended abandonment of the system. When the appropriate bill reached the Senate, Conkling tried to kill and then to amend it, but he finally voted with the majority when he saw that his efforts were clearly futile. The Anti-Moiety Act of June 1874 repealed laws giving any shares of fines, penalties, or forfeitures to informers or customs officials, and curtailed "fishing expeditions" by requiring a court order for the production of corporate records. Intent to defraud had to be ascertained by a court or jury as a separate finding of fact prior to forfeiture.

The President was at first very reluctant to sign the act, even though it had passed the House unanimously and the Senate with only three dissenting votes. Hamilton Fish noted in his diary that three Stalwarts, including Tom Murphy, had been urging Grant for days to block passage of the bill.[61] The moiety system had been kind to Arthur and the Conkling machine, and its abolition was no doubt viewed with much regret. When the act became law, Arthur's annual income dropped from approximately $56,000 to a fixed salary of $12,000.[62]

On the day Arthur's selection as a collector was made public, November 21, 1871, a daughter was born into the family and named Ellen Herndon Arthur. Her brother, Alan, was then seven. While we do not know precisely how much of their father's income from the Customhouse had to be returned to the Republican Party, it is certain that the Arthurs enjoyed a comfortable upper-middle class life during the depression-ridden 1870s. There were as many as five servants in the home at one time, the children were privately educated (by 1875 Alan had a special French tutor), and the family took lengthy and expensive vacations (one five-week trip to Rhode Island in 1873 cost more than $600).

Nell, like her mother, was extremely conscious of society and its obligations. She and her husband spent lavishly on appearances, they were sometimes seen at an opera, recitals were given in their home for a select few, Nell sang at elite charity functions, they entertained at appropriate intervals, and attended a number of important social events including Nellie Grant's resplendent wedding in 1874.[63] Nell's address book was arranged by New York City streets and contained the names of most of those who were prominent in Republican circles during the period, from William Vanderbilt to Theodore Roosevelt, father of the future President.[64] One friend remembered: "Mrs. Arthur was a very ambitious woman. There was no happier woman in the country than she when her husband was made collector of the port of New York."[65] One of Arthur's political associates later mentioned her importance to her husband's career, calling her "one of the best specimens of the southern woman," and noting that she "visited and kept up his list of friends."[66] But Nell also won the admiration of those to whom it would have been easy to be haughty. On her birthday, August 30, the Arthurs ate dinner every year at a cottage in Cooperstown owned by a Mr. Thayer. In 1883 Thayer told a reporter that "the household, even to the servants, were always delighted with her coming, and when she good-naturedly sat down to sing at the piano, as she always did, they would open the kitchen doors to listen, and she had a smile and a kind word for all, remembering their names from one year to another, and saying something bright and merry to each."[67]

Nell's interests, beyond her social duties and a fondness for horseback riding, were almost completely domestic. The extent of her formal education is unknown but surely consisted of no more than a few years in a fashionable private school learning the rudiments of literacy and the intricacies of gracious living. Alan saved several dozen of her letters, and they reveal a woman Jane Austen would have understood: a cheery, proper person, deeply devoted to her husband and her children and whose world revolved largely around their needs and cares; a woman as helpless and as superficial as women of her rank were expected to be. Tom Murphy recalled in 1883: "I knew her very well, indeed, for years. To me she was almost like a sister. She was not a handsome woman, nor a large woman in size. She hardly weighed 125 pounds, but she had affection and great fine sense, and Arthur loved and appreciated her."[68]

At home Arthur was a stern and kindly pater familias whose word was law and who required his son to address him as "sir." He took great pride in Alan, kept him finely clothed, and saw to it that he became an accomplished horseman and sailor. During one family excursion to Cooperstown in 1878 a newspaperman reported Arthur watching his tall son play baseball for several hours.[69]

Of course, the major obstacle to happiness in the Arthur family was Chester's frequent absence. From the late 1860s on, Arthur's late-night eating and drinking caused him to put on weight with an uncomfortable facility, swelling at times to something over 225 pounds. When Brodie Herndon saw him in 1871 he wrote: "He looks fat & hearty."[70] As Silas Burt remembered him in 1873, "his figure was full and commanding but he was laced up as to conceal his tendency to corpulence; his face was high-colored but had not become so florid and puffy as in later years; he gave great attention to dress which was always in excellent taste and inconspicuous."[71] At a time when such politicians as Roscoe Conkling and Zach Chandler were famous for their flamboyant garb, Arthur's apparel was notable for its understated elegance. He enjoyed dressing in the latest English styles and sometimes had his Prince Albert coats, light trousers, and high hats imported from London. He wore a brown moustache and thin, carefully trimmed side whiskers. One observer in mid-1880 thought he had the appearance of a "well-fed Briton."[72] This affectation, of course, was highly expensive. Arthur bought dozens of pairs of trousers and vests annually; his bill for *hats* between February 13 and October 28, 1875, was $125.25.[73]

Often during the 1870s, Arthur fled politics and his family to join a number of friends, including R. G. Dun, Albany newspaper editor George Dawson, and Judge William Fullerton of New York, for fishing expeditions into Canada or along the coast of Maine. In 1876 Dawson wrote a book entitled *Pleasures of Angling with Rod and Reel for Trout and Salmon*, in which Arthur is portrayed, at the end of a day's recreation, delighting several Indian guides and farmpeople by reciting two works by Robert Burns. Arthur was an enthusiastic and accomplished angler; in the summer of 1873 when he and Dun spent a month fishing in New Brunswick, Dun reported that the catch was approximately a ton of salmon. In 1880 he would become a member of the Restigouche Salmon Club, an association of forty New York gentlemen, including William Vanderbilt, who constructed a private fishing and shooting preserve in the Acadian wilderness.[74]

In the fall of 1875, Arthur was summoned to the deathbed of his father. Elder Arthur had remained in Newtonville since his wife's death, cared for by daughters and attending to his literary pursuits. To the shock of his children, he remarried. The lady, mentioned in his will simply as Mary, locked her new husband in a barn shortly after the vows were said, and refused to live with him. She was totally shunned by members of the family, and her existence was ignored in the biographical accounts that appeared at William Arthur's death.[75]

When Elder Arthur's illness (perhaps stomach cancer) became severe, Chester and his sister Annie were sent for. Regina Caw recorded the scene of Chester's arrival for her younger brother:

> Chester came on Wednesday about twelve. I said to Pa, "Chester is here." "Who?" said he. "Chester." Oh, how his face brightened up as he tried to take his hand from under the bedclothes that he might shake hands with, and when Chester said, "You know me, don't you Pa?" he answered "Oh yes," and raised both arms and put them about Chester's neck. . . . From the time Chester came he seemed to rest on him, asking me once how long he was going to stay and giving such a satisfied look when I said "All night and all tomorrow and a long time."[76]

In fact, Chester soon returned to New York City, leaving memories of his youth behind in Newtonville—all the fiery sermons on frosty Sunday mornings, the tirades, the exhortations, the piety and privation; returned to the world of expensive Havana cigars, Tiffany silver, fine carriages, and grand balls; the "real" world where men manipulated, plotted, and stole for power and prestige and the riches that bought both; Tom Murphy's world. When Silas Burt called Arthur's attention to the corrupt activities of his special deputy, John Lydecker, the collector blurted out, "You are one of those goody-goody fellows who set up a high standard of morality that other people cannot reach."[77]

Elder Arthur gave instructions—always instructions—for his funeral and tombstone, and died peacefully on October 27, 1875, probably unaware of his eldest son's absence.

On December 10, 1875, Arthur's term as collector expired, leaving him with the distinction of being the first collector in a quarter century to serve a full four years. His survival was due in part to his popularity with businessmen, subordinates, and politicians: the President, Republican members of Congress, a great many merchants and importers, and the lowliest gaugers in the Customhouse believed they had a friend in the collector's office. Orders had been dutifully followed, party workers and friends had been given jobs, the civil service rules had been discreetly bypassed where possible, funds had been raised, favors had been shown, and scandals had been held to a minimum. Alonzo Cornell, supporting Arthur's reappointment, assured the President that the collector "has given the most complete satisfaction to the Republican party in this State . . ."[78] Moreover, the general-order reform had generated much favorable publicity, and most of the press had failed to link Arthur with the Phelps, Dodge case. (Commented the New York *Dispatch* at the time, "not one word has been uttered which connects the Collector of the Customs of the port of New York with the plundering raids of the spies and informers on our merchants . . .")[79] But the strength of Arthur's position and the inevitability of his reappointment depended even more upon the power of his political superior, Senator Conkling.

Following Grant's reelection, Conkling had become the most powerful figure in the Senate. Many lawmakers were attracted to him by his quick intellect and considerable talent in oratory. But more to the point was the fact that allegiance to the New York Senator reaped reward. With the President's ear and with the keys to the Customhouse, he was a man to be cultivated. Moreover, after 1873 the Stalwart faction usually dominated the Senate's committee on committees, and could name the membership of working committees. John P. Jones of Nevada, an early Conkling favorite, received a place on the finance committee almost immediately upon entering the Senate. Timothy Howe of Wisconsin, whose timid ways had earned him minor committee assignments since entering the Senate in 1862, revealed a great admiration for the Senator from New York and soon found himself on the railroad, judiciary, and finance committees. In 1875 Conkling won control of the commerce committee, a body that scrutinized the credentials of presidential appointees to port or harbor posts—and through which Arthur's renomination would be expected to pass.[80]

On December 14 *The New York Times*, still enamored of Grant, strongly endorsed Arthur's candidacy:

> Gen. Arthur has succeeded in the difficult task of performing his duty faithfully toward the Government, while retaining the entire confidence and respect of our merchants. It may literally be said that there has not been a single complaint made of his Administration. In politics, it is well known that he has interfered as little as possible, for he has devoted the whole of his time and attention to the proper duties of his office—the supervision of the great work of collecting the revenues of the Government at this port. It is not now a post of great emoluments, but even those who deem it incumbent upon them to assail the "Custom-house" as a part of the Federal Administration, have never suspected its present chief officers of making a cent beyond their assigned salaries. The heads of that department are universally admitted to be men of the strictest honor and integrity.

The editorial was quoted in several pro-administration newspapers throughout the state.[81]

On December 17, President Grant sent Arthur's nomination to the Senate, where it was immediately confirmed without a dissenting vote: a tribute to Arthur's tactful and at times clever management of a difficult job, but even more an awesome display of the power wielded by the Grant-Conkling forces. Quite naturally, Stalwart newspapers overlooked the latter consideration in their assessment of the victory. The Troy *Northern Budget* commented: "Gen. Arthur has brought so much suavity, good nature, skill, executive ability, and general fairness and uprightness into the discharge of his official duties that he has fully disarmed the shafts of all his political opponents."[82] Even liberals could be found who shared this view. With a bow to Arthur's membership in the "proper" class, George William Curtis wrote in *Harper's Weekly*: "The renomination of General Arthur for the Collectorship of the port of New York, and his immediate and unanimous Confirmation by the Senate, is a very high but quite deserved compliment to a gentleman who has won the esteem of the public, especially the mercantile portion of it, by the prompt, courteous, and intelligent discharge of his duties."[83]

Despite its authority in Washington, the Conkling machine found itself facing an eroding political base in New York during the second Grant Administration. The Democratic Party, rid of Tweed and riding a wave of protest against the severe depression and corruption in government, scored impressive victories at the polls over the Conkling machine's handpicked slates of nominees. In 1874, Samuel Tilden, the brilliant and popular foe of the Tweed Ring, defeated John A. Dix for the governorship, and his party carried the Assembly and won eighteen of the thirty-three congressional districts. A staunch Tilden supporter, Francis Kernan, was elected to the United States Senate, defeating Edwin D. Morgan, marking the first time in nearly three decades that state Democrats were represented in the upper house. With one exception, all of Tammany's candidates were elected. Democrats were victorious again in 1875 in the statewide contests, and with the governor noisily exposing a Canal Ring that had defrauded New York of millions of dollars, there was considerable discussion about a Tilden drive for the presidency.

Conkling also had cause to be concerned about the ranks of the reformers within his own party, clearly swelling during the mid-1870s despite the Greeley debacle. Mounting attacks against the Senator and his lieutenants came from local party units and influential representatives of the press. The Republican state convention of 1875 selected George William Curtis as its permanent chairman and passed an anti-third-term resolution.[84] The clamor for reform intensified when it became clear by late 1875 that Conkling had presidential aspirations. He and his cohorts had been hinting about a third term for Grant for over a year, but when public and party opinion made that course of action impossible, the Senator decided to insert himself into the race to be his chieftain's successor. Reform-minded Republicans feared that with his control over patronage and his ties to other Stalwart bosses, Conkling might well be able to stampede the national convention and grab the nomination.

The state convention to select delegates-at-large to the national conclave was set to meet at Syracuse in late March 1876, and for weeks rumors had flown that the Conkling machine was carefully planning to manipulate delegations to the Senator's advantage. On March 9, the Union League Club of New York, the aristocratic and somewhat liberal Republican organization, passed and released to the press a series of resolutions critical of the Grant Administration and its warmest supporters. They included:

> Second: That the exclusive management and control of the local affairs in the party of the State, and particularly in the City of New-York, by an organized machinery of office-holders, which suppresses and ignores the real voice of the voters of the party, is an intolerable grievance to which we refuse any longer to submit.

Claiming to represent "the sentiments of the Republican voters of the City of New York," the club called for the election of a state delegation to the national convention that was "wholly unpacked and unpledged."[85]

As *The Nation* interpreted the resolutions: "They meant to prevent, if possible, the selection of Mr. Roscoe Conkling as the candidate of the Republicans of New York for the Presidency, and to send to the National Convention at Cincinnati a delegation composed of able, honest, and patriotic men, who would work for the nomination of a vigorous reformer for the Presidency."[86]

Arthur and the other Conkling lieutenants who belonged to the Union League Club made no rejoinder, and allowed the resolutions to pass unanimously. They knew what had to be done, and upon leaving the meeting proceeded to do it; political power was their business, not sentimentality and oratory. Under the leadership of state committee chairman Alonzo B. Cornell and Arthur's friends George Bliss and George Sharpe, the Stalwarts found ways of selecting delegates from the assembly districts of New York City—Tom Murphy was one—who were, to a man, pledged to support Conkling's presidential nomination. (Asked *The New York Times*: "Of all the District Associations which sent sixty delegates from this City, how many are free from the dictation of Federal office-holders?")[87] Cornell sent a telegram to the Senator announcing completion of the task, adding: "This is the answer of the Republicans of New York to the impudent declarations of the Union League Club."[88]

When the state convention opened on March 22, some Conkling supporters predicted that as many as four fifths of the delegates would vote for a resolution endorsing the New York Senator for the presidential nomination. Supremely confident, Arthur and George Sharpe had arrived by train only the day before.[89] But the Stalwarts had badly underestimated the desire for reform within their party. Quarreling broke out almost as soon as Cornell called the meeting to order. Soon, George William Curtis was on his feet winning thunderous applause for a slashing attack upon the Grant Administration.

> . . . we, as Republicans, are yet conscious what we need at a time when every one of us knows, whether any of us are willing openly to confess it or not, that the party name that we cherish so sacredly has been stained with foul disgrace; the corruptions of administrations exposed in every direction and culminating at last in the self-confessed bribery of the Republican Secretary of War; the low tone of political honor and of political morality that has prevailed in official Republican service; the increasing disposition of the officers and agents of the administration of this country, to prostitute the party organization relentlessly and at all costs to personal ends, has everywhere aroused the friends of free government, and has startled and alarmed the honest masses of the Republican Party.

Conkling workers had initially attempted to push through a resolution supporting the unit rule, whereby the convention would appear to endorse a Conkling nomination unanimously. But sensing the degree of dissent at the meeting, they settled for a resolution simply calling for Conkling's name to be presented in Cincinnati. To everyone's surprise, only 251 of the 423 delegates voted in favor of the motion—113 supported a Curtis proposal to send an uninstructed delegation to Cincinnati, and 138 chose not to vote. It was a stunning setback for the New York Senator and seriously damaged his initial efforts to attain the nation's highest political honor. *The New York Times*, perhaps affected by two years of Republican defeat, changed its traditional stance toward Conkling considerably, and wrote of "the tyranny which has dominated the Republican Party for the last half dozen years." About the state convention, it commented: "This has been one of the most momentous days in the history of the Republican Party in the Empire-State, for it has shown that it is at last ready to cast off the shackles of self-appointed managers, and assert its own dignity."[90]

While reformers were jubilant over their ability to muster strength against the Conkling machine, they also realized that they had lost the battle at the state convention: the motion to present Conkling's name passed, albeit narrowly. Their struggle for clean, efficient government had just begun. To E. L. Godkin the local composition of the warring Republican factions was clear:

> Here we have, on the one side, in the leading commercial city of the Union, (the chief city, too, in a State which is very likely to hold the balance of power in the next election), the entire body of respectable Republicans, and the entire moral force of an active political club, whose leading members are looked to to supply a large amount of the sinews of war during the campaign—on the one hand, we have all these throwing their weight against the nomination for President of a man whose only local qualifications for the place are that he had been the bitter partisan defender and apologist of every abuse which has sapped the sources of the commercial prosperity of his own State, and whose only recommendation to the country at large is that he is the next friend of an Administration which has made itself an object of universal public contempt. On the other hand, we have a small body of office-holders, headed by obscure men of doubtful or worse than doubtful reputation, without a particle of public opinion behind them . . .[91]

"Chet" Arthur, "Clint" Wheeler, "Jakie" Patterson, and "Steve" French (the press frequently employed their nicknames) stepped off the train at Cincinnati on June 8, six days before the national convention was to open. They were not official delegates to the convention but neither were they to be mere spectators. Before them lay the opportunity of grasping the reins of the executive branch of the federal government —perhaps for another eight years, of holding on to and expanding Stalwart control over patronage at all levels of government, of turning back the self-righteous prigs whose impractical idealism threatened the futures of those who professed belief in the purity and wisdom of both Grant Administrations. Roscoe Conkling planned to make no appearance at Cincinnati—the presidential nomination was to appear to seek him. But his "boys" were to be there, marshaled by his experienced lieutenants Collector Arthur and naval officer Cornell, and no expense or effort was to be spared to pave the way for the proud Senator's entrance into the presidential mansion.

On the afternoon of the next day, "Tom" Platt, "Dick" Crowley, and a number of other leaders of the Conkling machine arrived. That evening a train pulled in from New York containing 150 additional Conkling supporters, including "Johnny" O'Brien and "Barney" Biglin. This large contingent had brought along its own band and a huge banner bearing Conkling's portrait, and all through western Pennsylvania and Ohio it had staged loud demonstrations for Conkling wherever the train stopped. At Cincinnati the train was met by Arthur, Wheeler, French, and Patterson. Although it was 9:00 P.M., the entire gathering—band playing and banners flying—staged a noisy parade to the Grand Hotel, which the New York delegation had rented and gaily decorated. This first public demonstration of the approaching convention served notice on rivals that the Conkling forces had come to win.[92]

By June 11, there were some 1,500 Conkling workers in Cincinnati, each wearing a blue badge bearing their candidate's name. At one point a large number of them marched to the Gibson House and pinned up a huge banner reading "For President, Roscoe Conkling"—immediately beneath the banner of the New York Reform Club. A *New York Times* reporter noted:

> All the hotels are filled with New-York men, the streets are lined with them, and, indeed, it seems almost as if they had captured the city and were occupying it to the exclusion of the delegates from the other States. Their confidence, or perhaps it would be better to say their assumed confidence, is quite as remarkable as is their drill and organization. The machine is in the very best working order, and represented only by its smooth-spoken, well-dressed, and presentable adherents. No others have been allowed to come to Cincinnati.

(This contrasted with the view of a Pennsylvania delegate who remarked, after observing the inhabitants of the Grand Hotel and the demonstrators, that "it was a mystery to him where the Custom-house got bail for all those fellows.")[93] A great many of the Conkling supporters undoubtedly were public employees. E. L. Godkin reported that at the convention "the platform and the floor were filled with postmasters, collectors, and supervisors; besides Federal office-holders, there were assessors, commissioners of charities, State and town officers in profusion." And their advance preparation was evident. Cornell had assigned a specific task to every prominent member of the drive; cards were prepared bearing instructions and names of persons to be visited. Even the "small fry" who led the cheering and the parades knew exactly when and where to perform. The *Times* reporter said of the Conkling forces: "They bring with them the most thorough organization and discipline, their every action is governed by a system, and they do nothing without the advice and knowledge of their leaders."[94]

Of course, they were not without opposition. The Reform Club of New York, organized by the "better part" of the Union League Club, sent a delegation of about sixty that arrived on June 10. New York reformers had organized at a conference in mid-May and were confident of their ability to influence the party's selection of a presidential candidate.[95] The Bristow Club of Cincinnati, boasting between 2,000 and 3,000 backers of the Treasury Secretary, were also on the scene, hiring a local opera house and a band for the week of the convention. On June 13 seventeen carloads of James G. Blaine supporters arrived from western New York, and by then the Blaine effort could even boast of its own campaign song. Supporters of Oliver P. Morton and Rutherford B. Hayes also had headquarters, flags, and banners.

On June 12, the seventy official delegates from New York met in caucus and voted 68–2 to support Conkling's presidential aspirations. A motion to give support to a mild species of civil service reform was introduced but got nowhere with the confident delegates.

That sort of smug intransigence illustrated the Conkling machine's failure to face reality: for all of its elaborate and expensive campaigning, it had again misread the strength of its opposition. The New York delegation in itself represented only one fifth of the votes needed to nominate a standard-bearer, and was forced to seek outside support. But where was it to come from?

The two most powerful factions within the party, beyond the Stalwarts, were the reformers, for the most part pushing the candidacy of Bristow, and the followers of Blaine. Deals, promises, threats, and parades could not convince the likes of George William Curtis to endorse a spoilsman who had persistently lauded the aims and tactics of the Grant Administrations. Liberal Republicans, united and determined, had served notice that they might again bolt the party unless a candidate was chosen "whose very name is . . . conclusive evidence of the most uncompromising determination of the American people to make this a pure government once more." Blaine strongly desired the nomination, and in spite of railroad scandals with which his name had been linked in recent months, he entered the convention the favorite. He had nothing to gain from bargains with Conkling lieutenants, and in any event was not likely to take steps that would promote the ambitions of his bitter enemy. In a famous interview with Judge Jeremiah Black in early May, Blaine had dismissed Conkling's presidential aspirations with one caustic sentence: "He cannot carry his own State in the convention or at the election, and his candidacy is an absurdity."

And little support might have been expected from the camps of other hopefuls. Senator Morton was a patronage-rich Stalwart chieftain who resented Conkling's opposition in the race. Rutherford B. Hayes, recently elected to an unprecedented third term as governor of Ohio, was considered by most party insiders as little more than a favorite-son candidate. So, where were the sources of Conkling's strength outside his native state? What was the efficacy of a marching band?

And despite the huge banner strung across the street in front of the Grand Hotel reading ROSCOE CONKLING'S NOMINATION ASSURES THE THIRTY-FIVE ELECTORAL VOTES OF NEW YORK, few delegates were unaware of the Senator's difficulties at his state convention. Just before the convention proceedings began, Theodore Roosevelt of New York made a biting speech against Conkling from the balcony of the Gibson House.

There was the remote chance that gains could be made with the carpetbag delegations controlled by Morton; a reporter observed on June 12 that Conkling men "have kindly seen that idle delegates from the South have had pleasant and enjoyable rides in the suburbs of the city without any expense."[96] But this tactic proved fruitless, as did efforts with the California and Pennsylvania delegations.

The failure of the Conkling campaign was due less to bungling by Arthur and Cornell (as has sometimes been claimed, without examples of the alleged errors) than to the nature of the historical setting in which the drive was begun. The likelihood of a Conkling nomination was taken lightly by most sophisticated observers from the start. Public opinion toward the Grant Administrations was such that the party was threatened with defeat for the first time since the Civil War, and Republicans realized that they dared not face voters in the fall with a ticket headed by an "Administration candidate." On the day the convention opened, *The New York Times* editorialized, "Whatever be the fate of Mr.

Blaine's candidature, that of Mr. Conkling appears to be substantially at an end."[97]

During the first afternoon of the proceedings in huge Exposition Hall, which Arthur observed from a reserved seat on stage, George William Curtis, representing New York's Reform Club, lashed out at the Conkling machine, calling it "an odious and intolerable oligarchy which menaces the very system of our Government." The New York delegation sat quietly through the speech, but "when the arraignment of the party managers in New-York for their conduct in making a close corporation of the party was read," a reporter noticed, "some of them did exchange sickly smiles."[98]

The next day the nominating speeches began. Sixteen speakers appeared on the platform, none making a greater impression than Robert J. Ingersoll of Illinois, whose oration extolling the virtues of Blaine became a classic. "Like an armed warrior, like a plumed knight, James G. Blaine marched down the halls of the American Congress and threw his shining lance full and fair against the brazen foreheads of the defamers of his country and the maligners of his honor." Shortly, Stewart L. Woodford of New York placed Conkling in nomination with a capable if somewhat flaccid speech. "Broad in culture, eloquent in debate, wise in council, fearless in leadership, and as true to the old Republican party as the needle to the pole—Roscoe Conkling needs no defense nor eulogy."

But in the end, oratory played no role in the convention's selection of a presidential nominee. Conkling's meager chances were revealed on the first ballot when he received a mere 99 votes, placing him well behind Blaine (with 285), Bristow (113), and Morton (124). His strength trailed off slowly, reaching 81 on the fifth ballot. On the next roll-call Conkling's candidacy was abandoned, and on the seventh ballot the nod went to Hayes, a largely unknown party regular from an important state who was offensive neither to reformers or machine operators. Most of the support the New York delegation had been able to win came from Hayes backers, hoping to pick up votes for their man later in the balloting. The strategy proved successful, for on the sixth and final tallies the New Yorkers went 61–9 for Hayes over Blaine.

Because of New York's assistance, and to balance the ticket geographically, Ohio men sought a vice-presidential candidate from the Empire State. After some bickering, the New York delegation decided to support Stewart Woodford; Tom Platt was selected to present his candidacy. But Blaine's supporters sought William A. Wheeler, a New Yorker who, according to George F. Hoar, "very much disliked Roscoe

Conkling, and all his ways." Wheeler's popularity and Blaine's strength were such that Woodford withdrew his name before the balloting reached New York.[99]

However despondent Arthur and his friends may have become, they realized that this was no time to agonize over losses; to maintain its hold over the state party and its influence in national circles the machine had to demonstrate both loyalty and energy on behalf of Hayes and Wheeler. At a ratification meeting following the selection of the national ticket Arthur was approached by the chairman of the Hayes delegation. "How is New York?" he asked. "All right," said Arthur, "all the time for Hayes." At that point a Hayes badge was presented to the collector, and he eagerly pinned it on. That same day *The New York Times* reported:

> Even the Conkling men are enthusiastic. They have all taken off their blue badges and covered them with the white one, which bears the inscription, Hayes and Wheeler, and to-night they are going through the streets crying with all their might that New-York will give Hayes 50,000 majority. Collector Arthur is one of Gov. Hayes' most enthusiastic supporters. He fought hard for Conkling, but he is now willing to accept the situation and glad to do everything in his power for the next President, Rutherford B. Hayes.

Cornell made public a telegram he received from Conkling: "Have just heard of the nomination of Gov. Hayes, and deem it good and wise."[100]

CHAPTER FIVE

Hand-Over Street

Rutherford B. Hayes was a powerfully built man of average height, quiet, intelligent, college-educated, a fifty-three-year-old native of Ohio who had spent much of his life as an attorney in his home state. He had seen battle in the Civil War, emerged from the conflict a major general, and then, like so many others of similar rank, turned to politics. After twice being elected to Congress, he became Ohio's governor in 1867 and was reelected in 1869. His two administrations were distinguished by caution and honesty, and featured a partial application of civil service reform as well as support for education, mental hospitals, and prisons. Hayes's idealism was tempered by ambition and a sense of political realism. He rocked no boats, made few enemies, remained loyal to Grant in 1872 (much as young Theodore Roosevelt would resist Mugwumpery in 1884), and earned the reputation among Republican workers of being "loyal" and "sound." Shortly after his inauguration as governor for a third term, in January 1876, he began quietly to angle for the presidential nomination, and was able to collect that honor from the faction-torn convention in Cincinnati largely because, as Donald B. Chidsey put it, "nobody had anything against him."

Despite Hayes's long association with civil service reform, both in word and deed, many reformers were disappointed by his selection. Henry Adams privately grumbled that the governor was "a third rate nonentity." E. L. Godkin wrote in *The Nation*:

> . . . to get rid of the master-evil of the Government in our day—that which has already degraded and paralyzed it, and threatens it with serious fundamental changes at no very remote date—the President must be a man of no ordinary tenacity and breadth of view, and must

be prepared to sacrifice personal ease and smoothness of administration, and party harmony and success, to higher and more important things. We do not believe, with our present knowledge, that Mr. Hayes is such a man.[1]

Reformers were pleased when the Democratic National Convention in St. Louis nominated Samuel Tilden. The sixty-three-year-old New York governor was among the most prominent members of his party, a wealthy, intellectually inclined, fastidious bachelor who was widely given credit for smashing the Canal Ring and the Tweed machine. Though a corporation lawyer of somewhat shady reputation himself, Tilden based his campaign on the theme "Throw the Rascals Out." But few reformers sought a Democratic President, and this emphasized the importance of convincing Hayes to come out boldly against everything "Grantism" stood for.[2]

The Republican platform made only an oblique reference to civil service reform, and reformers urged Hayes to take a strong position on the issue in his letter of acceptance. After consulting with George William Curtis and Carl Schurz, he complied fully. One half of the letter dated July 8 was devoted to the subject of the candidate's unequivocal desire to reform the civil service; even his dramatic announcement about seeking a single term centered upon his eagerness to be an effective and unselfish civil service reformer. The spoils system, Hayes wrote,

> . . . destroys the independence of the separate departments of the Government. It tends directly to extravagance and official incapacity; it is a temptation to dishonesty; it hinders and impairs that careful supervision and strict accountability by which alone faithful and efficient public service can be secured; it obstructs the prompt removal and sure punishment of the unworthy; in every way it degrades the civil service and the character of the Government.

The entire system ". . . ought to be abolished. The reform should be thorough, radical, and complete."[3]

Official reaction in Congress and in the nation's press was favorable. *The New York Times*, now strongly critical of the Conkling machine, commented: "The letter of Gen. Hayes accepting the Republican nomination leaves nothing to be desired."[4] The "bread and butter brigade," as New York Stalwarts were sometimes called, could no longer doubt the intentions of the man they were expected to assist in the forthcoming campaign.

Arthur made his first public appearance in the drive on July 12, when thousands of Republicans jammed the Cooper Union in New

York City to ratify the nominations of the Cincinnati convention. He sat quietly on the stage with George Sharpe, Jacob Patterson, John O'Brien, Hamilton Fish Jr., Thomas L. James, Frederick Douglass, and a number of other party reliables. A band played, speeches were made, banners were waved, and fireworks were set off outside the hall. It was all good fun. But the hard work lay ahead.[5]

The effectiveness of the campaign effort in New York was imperiled by trouble within the machine: after their feeble showing at Cincinnati, several Conkling lieutenants began to quarrel. The dissension centered around Alonzo B. Cornell's decision to run for governor. A few of his closest associates argued that he could not win the nomination, given the current state of public opinion and his own personal unpopularity, and that in trying to win it, he threatened party unity and a Republican victory in November. But Cornell would not listen, and energetically worked to build support for his candidacy in advance of the state convention, set for August 23.

Conkling apparently favored Cornell's bid at first. Knowing that Arthur and Cornell were not getting along well, he wrote to the collector inquiring about his willingness to assist a Cornell campaign. Arthur replied on July 11:

> Mr. Cornell, as a candidate for Governor, will receive the support of the delegations so far as my desires & influences to that end can secure it for him.
>
> I do not presume there is any special reason for your inquiry, but I had supposed that I was always to be counted as among those who could be relied on to stand by the friends who have for so long acted together.

Arthur said that he foresaw little danger of open schism within the machine. Conkling lieutenants ". . . are anxious only that a strong & wise nomination should be made."[6]

Cornell and several of his most ardent supporters appeared at Saratoga three days before the state convention was to open. They were certain that Senator Conkling would appear on their behalf and expressed confidence in a first-ballot victory. Other candidates included the reformers' choice, William M. Evarts, and Edwin D. Morgan, Arthur's elderly patron, who had come out for civil service reform in Cincinnati and had affected a curious independence of late. But to leaders of the Cornell drive the race was already decided. State Senator Tobey told a reporter: "Now never mind where the votes are coming from; we have them; and that's enough."

Arthur, Tom Murphy, George Bliss, Jacob Patterson, John J.

O'Brien, "and other worthies of like character from New York," arrived on August 21, and by then some two hundred of the expected four hundred delegates were on hand. That evening rumors began to spread that Conkling had decided against making an appearance at the convention. "Should he do so," reasoned one observer, "it is possible that he would be successful so far as the nomination of his friend went; but at the same time, in the opinion of the best-informed people here, he would kill himself politically. The general impression here is that Mr. Conkling is too shrewd a man to run so great a risk." Frantic telegrams were sent by Cornell supporters to the Senator, but to no avail. By midnight he had not arrived and it was widely believed that Cornell's defeat was certain. Rumor had it that Conkling was "unwell" and unable to leave home.

Apparently, within a few days of the opening of the convention, Conkling became convinced not to risk what remained of his party stature on Cornell's behalf. Few of the New York City delegates expressed enthusiasm for Cornell in Saratoga; George Bliss and George Sharpe were openly against his candidacy, and *The New York Times* reported that Arthur also opposed the bid.

> Gen. Arthur is quite willing that he should receive the complimentary vote of the New-York delegation on the first ballot. After that, however, there is good reason to believe that he will "put his hand out," as the saying goes, and take at least thirty votes away from him. The Collector is apparently a very quiet man, but anyone who believes that he lacks either determination or energy makes a mistake. He does not think it would be wise to nominate Mr. Cornell, and Mr. Cornell will not be nominated if he can prevent it.

Though Arthur has been criticized for "poor generalship" of the Cornell campaign on the floor of the convention, there is no evidence that he even played a role in it.[7]

The last-minute decision to abandon Cornell was, of course, costly to harmony within the Conkling ranks. *The Times* reported approvingly that ". . . 'the machine' is divided, broken up, and disorganized." Cornell bitterly resented his humiliation, and was persuaded to withdraw his name from the contest only about an hour before the balloting began. Nevertheless, Conkling was wise to stay out of Saratoga, for the delegates were clearly in no mood to run one of his lieutenants for governor.[8]

The nomination went to Morgan on the first ballot. (Perhaps Arthur, Bliss, and the others came to Saratoga with instructions to push for Morgan; the former governor won strong support from Conkling delegates. *The Nation* complained: "Mr. Morgan is an old politician, who has never by a single act given any one any reason to suppose that he dislikes the way in which politics are carried on, or disapproves of Messrs. Conkling, Bliss, Davenport, Murphy, and their ways, except in so far as their ways and his interfere."[9]) He was a compromise choice who, it was hoped, would unite the state party in the struggle against a ticket headed by the popular Tilden. The secretary of the Republican National Committee soon commented of Morgan's selection, "His nomination is received with great satisfaction and we think that the prospect of carrying this State is greatly improved." Cornell made a try at the nomination for lieutenant governor but it was awarded to a man favored by George William Curtis.

The winds of party sentiment were blowing in Curtis's direction in spite of Evarts's defeat. The convention endorsed Hayes's statement on civil service reform. And Liberal Republicans, also meeting in Saratoga, were invited to join the regular party delegates. "Many of them did so," a reporter noted, "and there was a great deal of hand-shaking and general good feeling. One well-known gentleman aptly described the scene by saying that it looked as if a band of long-lost brothers had returned to their homes."[10]

Even though the Conkling machine had shown symptoms of deterioration at Cincinnati and Saratoga, it was still a powerful force in the Republican Party. (Symbolic of this level of stature, Cornell was reelected chairman of the Republican State Committee and appointed chairman of the executive committee of the Republican National Committee.) It controlled the most important sources of patronage in the country, and had to be depended upon to assist in the effort to carry New York—a state many contended held the balance in the presidential election.

Democrats had good reason to be optimistic in 1876. Tilden was thought to be highly popular throughout the country, and it was estimated that he could win by carrying the South, New York, New Jersey, and Connecticut. The vice-presidential nominee, Senator Thomas A. Hendricks of Indiana, advocated "soft money" and was thought to neutralize much of Hayes's strength in the West. The party platform wrapped Democrats in the banner of reform. New York Democrats openly predicted victory. They had won the state the last two years, factional disputes had been buried, Tilden had an enormous following, and Tammany Hall, run by Honest John Kelly, was as potent a source of votes as ever.

The Republican Party stood in sharp contrast. Its presidential candidate was barely known outside of Ohio; party ranks were divided by factions headed by Conkling, Blaine, and the reformers; Reconstruction had sapped its strength in the South; the Depression of 1873 was causing uproar in the West; and "Grantism" was excoriated everywhere. Party orators were forced to "wave the bloody shirt," to warn Americans that the country would be unsafe in the hands of men stained with treason. Republican newspapers and magazines resorted to stories alleging that Tilden had once evaded income taxes.

Campaign funds were badly needed by Republicans in 1876, and predictably they turned to the New York Customhouse, where Collector Arthur was firmly determined to see that each party appointee paid every penny of his assigned "donation." Silas Burt recalled that ". . . the official enforcement of voluntary contributions to the State Republican Committee funds was more severe and ruthless than I ever have known it." The assessment for deputies was calculated at 4 percent of their annual salaries; it was 5 percent for weighers. Colonel Joseph J. Pinckney, a Republican alderman and a personal friend of the collector, was given a complete list of the names of persons employed in the Customhouse and their salaries. He opened an office on Hanover Street (which some called "Hand-Over" Street) directly across from the Customhouse, where employees were advised to report and pay their assessments. Burt recalled: "No place of want or distress could induce Col. Pinckney or his assistants to make any abatement from the sum set opposite any one's name. From the utter banality and insulting conduct of these political tax-gatherers I am certain that it was thought necessary by intimidation to crush out any spark of revolt." Since it was made clear that the collector, naval officer, and surveyor expected every subordinate to respond fully to the party's demands, no revolt occurred. Burt again refused to pay, but he remained alone in his course of action and was simply ignored.[11]

Burt estimated that Pinckney collected $50,000, but the sum may have been greater. During and slightly after the campaign, Arthur wrote checks to party leaders on the state and national levels totaling more than $72,000. John N. Knapp, treasurer of the Republican State Committee, received $34,821.50 from the collector. George H. Sharpe, chairman of the state committee's finance committee, received a check for $10,000 dated September 15. (The importance of these funds may be measured by the fact that the state committee spent about $25,000 during the contest to pay the expenses of some one hundred party speakers.) Henry Glidden, a national party figure, was given $1,600 in a check written on October 6. And Zachariah Chandler, chairman of the party's national committee, received checks from Arthur written between September 15 and November 6 totaling $26,000.[12] (Chandler's committee continued to function until March 1877, and Arthur's services continued to be in demand. Chandler prodded him for funds in late November, and he replied: "You know that as far as making every effort to raise this amt. of money is concerned, I will do it. But no one knows better than *you*, how exceedingly difficult it is to get any more money here." On January 4, 1877, Arthur wrote Chandler a check for $5,000, ". . . subject to your order, being contribution to the National Republican Committee as arranged between us." George Sharpe received $1,500 on January 24.)[13]

How much of the funds Arthur disbursed during the campaign came from his own pocket is uncertain. But when Edwin D. Morgan passed among his friends to collect money for the state committee he raised $47,750 in contributions of $1,000 or more, and among the angels was Arthur, who donated $1,000.[14]

Outside New York the exaction of funds from government workers was also carried out vigorously. Zachariah Chandler, Secretary of the Interior as well as chairman of the Republican National Committee, helped see to that. Chandler was an experienced spoilsman who had built a sizable machine in Michigan before becoming prominent in Washington as one of Grant's close advisers. His election in the summer to the national party position could hardly escape comment, for the incongruity of a Hayes campaign run by Chandler was painfully obvious to reformers. *The Nation* wrote of the Stalwart chieftain: "Now, Mr. Chandler is not only one of the most disreputable, coarse, and unscrupulous politicians in the party, but the most strenuous enemy of civil-service reform."[15] Carl Schurz protested to Hayes: "It is in the highest degree improper on principle that a man who wields the patronage and influence of one of the Departments of the Government, should also be the manager of a party in a campaign; and it seems utterly impossible that a member of General Grant's Administration, who is a notorious advocate of the vicious civil service system, which we want to abolish, should be the manager of a campaign in which the reform of the civil service is one of the principal issues."[16] Nevertheless, the party needed Stalwart support, and Hayes showed no inclination to remove Chandler. Postal employees and other federal workers outside Washington, D.C., received a circular from the national committee in early September. One postmaster protested the unfairness of his $150 assessment: "This, in view of the fact that *my whole time* is devoted to the labors of the canvass and all the responsibility of the same resting on my shoulders, and at an outlay, so far, from my own pocket of over $600.00." By October Postmaster General Payne of Milwaukee wrote, "The Federal officials have been bled until I am ashamed to ask for more."[17]

Another effective instrument for Republican victory was James N. Tyner, whom Grant had made Postmaster General after requesting the resignation of reform-minded Marshall Jewell. Under Tyner "voluntary contributions" were collected in Washington much as they were in the New York Customhouse. Carl Schurz reported that on pay day postal clerks were "requested by some official to step into a certain room where they found a gentleman connected with the party organization who told them they were expected to contribute 3 percent of their yearly salary to the campaign fund, and that the money was obtained from them."[18] Tyner was a protégé of Oliver P. Morton and during the campaign was sent to Indiana with money and instructions to do what he could to win the state. On November 1 he reported to Chairman Chandler:

> I have the apportionment of funds made out, & have selected my runners to all distant localities. I want to be cautious and discreet, and yet I believe *ten* more could be judiciously and profitably expended. I have telegraphed in cipher to Jay Gould asking him to consult you. . . . Not a dollar will go for anything but use next Tuesday [election day]. So far as it is now distributed, it is in the hands of men who don't steal. . . . I have adopted the plan of using most of the *funds* where we have the election boards; and a large floating population—In strong Democratic counties, we will use enough to insure a full pole [sic] of our vote and to pay broad-shouldered fellows to stand at the polls— and occasionally make conditional bargains with Democrats to give so much if the count is so and so.[19]

Of course, candidate Hayes knew a great deal about the nature of the efforts undertaken on his behalf. He was an intelligent and experienced politician who was aware of the methods commonly used by both parties to eke out victory in an era of closely balanced party strength. (One perceptive student of the period has suggested, "Surely many an election on every level was determined by who was in the best position for perpetrating frauds.")[20] Privately he condemned assessments and promised Schurz that ". . . if I ever have charge of an Administration this whole assessment business will go up, 'hook, line and sinker.' "[21] But he made no public protest against his party's campaign tactics. Indeed, as the race progressed, Hayes gave increasingly less attention to civil service reform and appeared more interested in banter about the "bloody shirt." On the last day of September *The New York Times* complained: "There is too much disposition shown by Republican writers and speakers to slight the question of civil service reform, as an issue in the pending canvass. Its intrinsic importance, no less than its prominence in the Republican platform and Gov. Hayes' letter of acceptance, entitles it to be treated as one of the chief issues of the campaign."[22] Reformers were disheartened but, with the notable exception of Charles Francis Adams, they continued to work hard for the Ohio governor and hope for the best. George William Curtis assured listeners in Schenectady in early October that Tilden had been in sympathy with the worst elements of the Democratic Party for sixty years (!), and that Hayes had always been on the side of the most enlightened Republicans.[23]

Roscoe Conkling took little part in the campaign personally. Hayes implored him to give speeches in Ohio and Indiana: "The more meetings you can address, the better, but if you speak only in two or three large cities in each of the States named, and at Chicago, and at Milwaukee, I shall feel that you have placed the country and all of us under great obligations." But the Senator claimed he was ill—perhaps he was—and limited his direct activity to a single address delivered in Utica on October 3. The question of health aside, it was no secret that Conkling was deeply affronted by his rebuff at Cincinnati and that he disliked Hayes and loathed Wheeler. It seemed natural that he might wish to participate as little as possible in an election drive dominated by do-gooders of the Curtis variety. Still, he could not afford to sulk for the duration of the campaign; party loyalty as well as his own future within a Hayes Administration demanded some effort on behalf of the Republican ticket.

At Utica, Conkling devoted much of his speech to a defense of the Grant Administration, calling attention to a shrinking national debt, and downplaying the issue of corruption. ("Did you ever know a case of official dishonesty brought to the knowledge of the President on which he did not lay prompt and unsparing hand? Show me such a case and you will show me something I never heard of.") He also felt obliged to call for the resumption of specie payment and to trot out the bloody shirt. ("The Democratic policy, North and South, brought on the rebellion, and every drop of blood, and every farthing it cost, is to be charged to Democratic account.") Noticeably absent from the rather tepid oration was any mention of civil service reform. Hayes was referred to only once, and then not by name; Wheeler was ignored entirely.[24]

Conkling's lieutenants, on the other hand, were hard at work throughout the contest. While Arthur raised funds in the Customhouse, Tom Platt was active as chairman of the Republican Congressional Committee and a member of the national committee, Alonzo Cornell, as noted, was chairman of the state committee and chairman of the national committee's executive committee, Jacob Patterson served as chairman of the Republican Central Committee of New York City, and George Sharpe and Richard Crowley made dozens of speeches and visits to party organizations throughout New York State.[25]

In late October, Arthur, Barney Biglin, and Clint Wheeler (now a New York City police commissioner) were elected delegates from the Eighteenth Assembly District to the county convention, a gathering of Republican leaders charged with nominating candidates for New York city and county offices. It became evident when the convention assembled on the 25th that Stalwarts continued to dominate party machinery in New York City. Arthur gave a brief speech cautioning delegates about the dangers of the upcoming elections, and then moved that the newly elected chairman, his law partner Benjamin K. Phelps, appoint a committee to create the slate of nominees. The motion passed and among the appointees were Arthur, Pierre Van Wyck, John J. O'Brien, George Bliss, and Frank Howe. Arthur was named chairman of the committee.[26]

Shortly, Arthur was approached by a leader of the Anti-Tammany Democrats, a local splinter group, to explore the possibility of affiliation. Arthur stated bluntly that he saw no chance for an alliance as long as the Anti-Tammanyites continued to support two individuals whom he named. Arthur's information had to come from spies, for the Anti-Tammany Party had publicly endorsed no one. Moreover, Arthur appeared to be speaking for the entire committee appointed at the Republican County Convention—as if he controlled it. Incensed, Anti-Tammanyites vowed to break off all further negotiations with Republicans and work independently. Arthur's unusual frankness had undoubtedly cost his party some valuable votes.[27]

When the county convention reconvened on October 31, Arthur's committee presented its list of nominees, which was promptly accepted. Stalwarts dominated the slate and Arthur's hand was clearly evident: one of the two candidates for alderman-at-large was General Joseph C. Pinckney, then busy at his office on "Hand-Over" Street; for county clerk the party chose to run Tom Murphy. On behalf of the latter nomination one speaker asserted lamely, ". . . that Republican that refuses to vote for Thomas Murphy does not deserve the name."[28]

Arthur appeared publicly with Edwin D. Morgan twice during the campaign. The first occasion was in early October when 1,200 veterans, members of the "Boys in Blue," serenaded the candidate in front of his home. On November 3, he again joined Morgan at his home to view a gigantic pre-election Republican parade.[29]

Several days later when the ballots were counted, New York Republicans found few reasons for festivity: Tilden ran ahead of Hayes in the state by almost 33,000 votes (his majority in New York City was almost 54,000), Morgan lost by a sizable margin to Lucius Robinson, and every candidate nominated by Arthur's committee and the county convention was defeated. Along with New York, Tilden carried New Jersey, Connecticut, Indiana, and all the "redeemed" southern states, enjoying a popular plurality nationally of approximately 250,000 votes. That he was ultimately denied the presidency was due to a number of Republican strategists, led by William Chandler, who employed carpetbag governments, federal troops, and fraud to see that Hayes won in the Electoral College by a single vote. It was a fitting climax to an election in which, as Harry Barnard put it, ". . . crime was conducted with more system, more organization and more unconcealed intent, than probably had been the case before."[30] Threats of violence and a congressional filibuster by Democrats were quelled by the famous Compromise of 1877, in reality a series of agreements in which ex-Whig southern Democrats and northern Republicans close to Hayes exchanged a peaceful ride to the inaugural ceremonies in exchange for home rule, internal improvements, and the promise of a southerner in Hayes's Cabinet.[31]

Though he made no public statement on the disputed election during the months in which it was being settled, Collector Arthur may have assisted Republican leaders in influencing the outcome. William Chandler, who was in a position to know, later wrote that ". . . Gen. Arthur's activity in connection with the contested countings in the southern states was of vital importance."[32] Probably his role was limited to fund-raising; the $5,000 check he wrote to Zachariah Chandler on January 4 might have greatly assisted the chairman of the national committee, who had passed out sums of money (including four $5,000 checks) to insure victory in the carpetbag states.[33] He may also have been instrumental in securing funds through the unscrupulous money baron Jay Gould, whose assistance had been requested (sometimes in code) throughout the campaign and who again contributed when the result of the presidential race was in doubt. In a guarded letter of December 4 marked "Private," Arthur wrote Gould: "I have seen several gentlemen in regard to the matter of which we talked when I last saw you, and expect to have, in the morning, some information as to the result. I am going to Washington at one o'clock tomorrow for a day or two, and will see you on my return."[34]

At the same time, however, Conkling decided quietly to throw in his lot with Tilden. No doubt he assumed that with Arthur assisting Republican moves to elect Hayes, he and his machine could make solid claims to perpetuity no matter which candidate won. (At any rate, an Arthur refusal to cooperate with party requests was unthinkable.) Conkling knew the New York governor and believed he could work with him; Hayes was surrounded by Schurz and Curtis, and there could be little hope for Stalwarts in such an administration. Democrats had told him that Hayes would take revenge for his lack of active campaign support and for the loss in New York. A friend, Albert D. Shaw, consul at Toronto, got nowhere with Hayes when he dropped hints that Conkling might welcome an invitation to be Secretary of State.

The New York Senator made no public statement on the matter, but his actions during the months of indecision bore an unmistakable pattern. While Conkling served as a member of a joint committee created to iron out charges by Democrats and Republicans, word leaked back to Hayes from John Sherman that the New Yorker would not favor Republican claims in two of the three disputed southern elections. Conkling led the fight in the Senate for an electoral commission, a proposal generally favored by Democrats and opposed by Republicans—including a number of Stalwarts. (*The New York Times* snarled, "This State supplies one-third of the Republicans voting in favor of the bill—a fact which may be explained in three words—Commerce, Cowardice, and Conkling.") He told several friends of his conviction that Tilden had won the election, and rumors scurried within Republican circles of Conkling's treachery. Matthew Quay of Pennsylvania wrote Hayes on January 20: "Conkling is undoubtedly faithless and Col. McClure of Philadelphia assures me he is in correspondence with Tilden."

Still, Conkling at no time publicly or in writing cut his ties with Hayes. After Hayes's election seemed certain, the Senator became unavailable for a rumored attempt to overturn the electoral commission's acceptance of a corrupt return from Louisiana. Democratic leader John Bigelow wrote: "Conkling has been trusted by our people to do something for Tilden: to at least enter his protest against giving a congressional sanction to the operations of the Louisiana returning board. Our friends have been fearfully deceived by him."[35]

The fruits of his cagy and ambiguous course were uncertain, but Conkling expected the worst. Once Hayes's victory was assured, he quickly ordered the removal of an appraiser in the New York Customhouse and several other federal officials in the state whose total loyalty had apparently fallen into doubt. The Senator was urgently strengthening his machine while there was time. The removals, of course, did not escape the attention of civil service reformers. *The New York Times* wrote: "They are an obvious infringement of the rights of the new Administration, and a rather insolent defiance of the principles and methods of appointment to the civil service to which that Administration stands committed."[36]

Ironically, Conkling seemed more convinced about Hayes's commitment to reform than several of the reformers. Early in the campaign the candidate had been eager to curse the spoils system, but as the race progressed, his enthusiasm seemed to wane and he appeared pleased to accept the funds and votes machine politicians delivered to him before and after November 5. In late January, Carl Schurz, one of several liberals who felt leery about the tactics used to secure the presidency, urged Hayes to stand fast and suggested that he insert a paragraph on civil service reform into his inaugural address.[37] But the doubt was unwarranted, for Hayes clearly had no intention of retreating from his earlier position. He did not feel compromised by the post-election machinations and was apparently convinced, as were most loyal partisans, that Republicans had carried all of the disputed states and that the uproar resulted from a typical Democratic conspiracy to thwart the will of the people.

Chester Arthur was present in the Senate chamber, along with Tom Murphy, Edwin D. Morgan, and five other New Yorkers, when the new lawmakers and the Vice-President were sworn in on March 5. He then became part of a crowd of 30,000 that viewed the inaugural ceremonies and the traditional address by the Chief Executive. The new administration, said Hayes, would follow the paths set out in his letter of acceptance: one term, hard money, and home rule in the South. Perhaps Arthur and Murphy exchanged solemn glances when Hayes reached the subject of civil service reform: "I ask attention of the public to the paramount necessity of reform in our civil service—a reform not merely as to certain abuses and practices of so-called official patronage which have come to have the sanction of usage, in the several departments of our Government, but a change in the system of appointment itself—a reform that shall be thorough, radical, and complete—a return to the principles and practices of the founders of the Government." The founders had wanted, he said, nonpartisan appointments and tenure for good behavior; moreover, they "neither expected nor desired from public office any partisan service." Since civil service reform had been endorsed by both party platforms in 1876, "It must be regarded as the expression of the united voice and will of the whole country . . . and both political parties are virtually pledged to give it their unreserved support."[38] Precisely how the President was to attack the entrenched patronage system was unclear, but Conkling had correctly assessed the attitude of a Hayes Administration toward the primary source of his power.

The Cabinet appointments pleased reformers. Carl Schurz replaced Zachariah Chandler in the Interior Department and William Evarts was made Secretary of State. There were a few qualms about John Sherman, the new Secretary of the Treasury, for he had flirted with inflationists and had taken no solid position on civil service reform. But Sherman had a reputation for party regularity and Hayes liked and trusted him; the two had been friends in Ohio, Sherman had fought for

Hayes's presidential nomination at Cincinnati, and he had been instrumental in securing Republican victory in Louisiana and in pacifying southern Democrats with the Compromise of 1877.[39]

Conkling's suggestion of Tom Platt as a member of the Cabinet went unexplored.

During the first weeks of the administration, reformers, eager for drastic changes, often expressed disappointment with the President's approach to the civil service. But Hayes's determination was firm. New Yorkers opened the *Daily Tribune* on April 9 to learn that the administration was planning a full-scale investigation of the nation's largest customhouse. The President had decided to launch a searching inquiry into the stronghold of the Conkling machine's power.[40]

CHAPTER SIX

Exciting the Whole Town

THE NEW PRESIDENT was indeed, in the words of T. Harry Williams, "a curious mixture of idealism and practicality." Hayes was an experienced politician when he entered the White House, a perceptive man thoroughly familiar with every technique employed by managers of both parties to win elections, including the manipulation of government officeholders. He knew what patronage meant to professional politicians, and carefully guided its dispensation before and after his presidential nomination for the benefit of partisan allies. And yet he sincerely harbored the ideal of a nonpartisan civil service, appointed reformers to his Cabinet, and confided to his diary repeatedly his desire to divorce politics from government employment. He did not, of course, seek to weaken the Republican Party by pursuing civil service reform; on the contrary, he was convinced that his party would be strengthened by adhering rigorously to the principles of honesty and efficiency as requirements for government service.[1]

The new Secretary of the Treasury differed from his long-time friend in both background and temperament. Whereas Hayes had always known relative affluence and was a graduate of Harvard Law School, John Sherman was a "self-made" man who, with little money and formal education, had constructed formidable legal and political careers by the opening of the Civil War. An ex-Whig, he won four elections to the House of Representatives under the banner of the Republican Party before ascending to the Senate in 1861. Sherman was shrewder and less ideologically inclined than Hayes; he felt obliged to adhere to few political visions beyond those simple conservative platitudes that Republicans of all factions professed. Power was his supreme desire (three times he would openly covet the presidency) and to get it he had learned early to depend upon conciliation and compromise; to accommodate himself, like Blaine, to temporary shifts in political winds when they were to his advantage. Did Sherman actually believe in civil service reform? Washington observers asked in 1877. Those who knew him best guessed correctly that whether he believed in it or not, he would take that path most likely to enhance his own political future. And in the opening weeks of the Hayes Administration markers along that path pointed in one direction.

In early April, Sherman was instrumental in creating, at the President's request, several commissions to investigate charges of political influence and corruption in the Philadelphia, Boston, Baltimore, San Francisco, New Orleans, and New York customhouses. The secretary had no personal quarrel with Conkling or Arthur and unquestionably respected their usefulness in securing funds, jobs, and votes. He advised Hayes against a confrontation with the Conkling machine on the ground of party unity, and opposed a query into the New York Customhouse. But Hayes selected Conkling's bailiwick as his primary target, doing so on grounds of principle and political expediency. On the one hand, a huge chunk of the nation's revenues emanated from its largest customhouse, and any sort of civil service reform would have to start there. On the other hand, the President still smarted over Conkling's campaign inactivity, his failure to carry New York, his flirtation with Tilden, and his sneering references to "Rutherfraud" B. Hayes. He sympathized with the reform wing in New York, led by Secretary of State Evarts, and hoped to lend it support by decreasing the influence of the Conkling machine. Sherman was obliged to set up the machinery necessary for the probe in spite of his personal misgivings.[2]

A few days after the *Tribune* leaked the news of an impending investigation of the New York Customhouse, Sherman summoned Arthur to Washington, that the collector might fully participate in the selection of members of the commission. While Hayes may not have shared his optimism, Sherman was hopeful that necessary reforms could be carried out in the Customhouse under its current leadership. If they could, Conkling might emerge from the investigation relatively unruffled, and both reformers and Stalwarts could claim satisfaction. With steps taken to implement civil service reform in the Customhouse, and with Conkling in retention of his control of the major source of patronage in the state, the result might be harmony at a time when Sherman himself had designs on the White House. But was it possible to placate both Silas Burt and Collector Arthur when their purposes and methods were so sharply divergent? To what degree were the principles of reform com-

patible with the claims of bossism? This was an issue Sherman had yet
to face.

Arthur arrived in Washington on April 14 for a conference with
Sherman where, according to the secretary, he "was fully advised on the
object of the investigation." Each of the customhouse commissions was
composed of three members, two private citizens and a government
official; Arthur and his colleagues were permitted to select one of the
citizens who would probe their official conduct. At Edwin D. Morgan's
suggestion, Arthur chose a prominent New York merchant, Lawrence
Turnure of Moses Taylor and Company. Sherman recommended ex-naval
officer John A. Dix to serve as chairman of the commission, but Dix
declined due to the serious illness of a son. Arthur then approached
Mr. Royal Phelps of New York, who also turned down the invitation.
With Arthur's concurrence, John Jay, grandson of the first Chief Justice
and president of the Union League Club, was selected. Sherman then
named Assistant Solicitor of the Treasury J. H. Robinson to be the third
member of what soon became known as the Jay Commission. Both
Sherman and Arthur seemed pleased with the commission's membership:
there was political balance—Turnure was a Whiggish Democrat, Jay a
Liberal Republican; Turnure and Jay were opulent businessmen of impeccable reputation; and Robinson was a veteran in the complex field of
customs management. Arthur's bitter complaints about the composition
of the commission would appear only after it issued its reports.[3]

A sizable number of rumors and charges surrounded the operations
of the New York Customhouse at the time. Treasury officials, according
to the *Tribune*, had received reports of lax administration, excessive expenditures, padding of salaries and employment rolls, bribe-taking, and
so on. Evidence was said to exist of frauds in the importation of silks.
Wire destined for a prominent Washington official was reported to have
passed through the port duty-free. Special Deputy-Collector John
Lydecker was singled out as guilty of several crimes. The din was such
that the New York State chamber of commerce had created a special
committee on customs revenue reform in October 1876, to conduct an
investigation. When word of an impending Customhouse commission
reached the press, *The New York Times* said that businessmen enthusiastically welcomed the probe, adding: "The Custom-house is, in
fact, the most complete and offensive example of the need of that reform
in the civil service which President Hayes had promised that could be
found in the country."[4]

Sherman's instructions to the commission were published in *The
Times* on April 18, while Arthur was still approaching prospective members. The body was charged with conducting "a thorough examination

into the conduct of business at the New-York Customhouse"; several categories for specific attention were listed that encompassed the traditional concerns of reformers and businessmen alike, such as the honesty and efficiency of the more than 1,000-member staff. The Jay Commission was formally constituted on April 23, and three days later it convened in the Customhouse to begin a lengthy series of hearings. Its first witness, who testified for six hours, was Chester A. Arthur.[5]

After the first two sessions, Sherman opened the hearings to the public, and for the next six weeks the New York press paid rather close attention to the proceedings. Twenty-four open sessions were conducted, while several others were held in private at the request of witnesses or members of the commission. Almost ninety witnesses testified during the public hearings, over half of them Customhouse employees, along with a number of committees of merchants and brokers appearing to bare grievances and provide information. Arthur appeared before the commission in public four times, Burt three times, and surveyor George Sharpe twice. Alonzo Cornell made his comments in private and in writing.[6]

The commission conducted its affairs with fairness, perspicacity, and thoroughness. A broad assortment of concerned citizens gave testimony. The collector and every other Customhouse officer—even Arthur's private secretary, Fred Phillips—were permitted to respond at length to all charges and allegations. Jay and his colleagues did not permit cross-examination of witnesses, but then they were gathering and weighing information rather than conducting a trial. Moreover, as Turnure told Sharpe, cross-examination would drag out the hearings for perhaps a year. With assistance from special agents of the Treasury Department, and with the cooperation of the collector, the commission compiled a massive quantity of detailed information about the operations of every facet of the Customhouse. On at least one occasion commission members visited an area of the Customhouse to observe firsthand the specific functions carried out by employees.

Testimony from the hearings augmented data to confirm the darkest suspicions of civil service reformers. In the first place, the Customhouse was grossly overstaffed. Burt contended that steps taken to increase efficiency could result in a 10 percent reduction, and that simplification of processes could mean a further 10 percent cut. A thirty-five-year veteran, chief of the auditor's department, said that "better men might be got if more money were given, if the tenure of office were rendered more certain, and if politics were made less potent in securing appointments," adding that these improvements could effect a reduction of from 10 to 20 percent. The chief of the Bureau of Statistics asserted that his staff could be reduced 10 percent. Paymaster Frederick G. Wentworth said that the annual appropriation for laborers could be reduced $105,000, and continued, "men are sometimes paid for walking around the district and doing nothing." The assistant collector of customs at Jersey City said simply that he had nothing to do. An assistant appraiser, a veteran of thirty-six years in the Customhouse, believed that about a third of the appointments in his department were due to politics, and recommended the abolition of the entire damage department. One assistant weigher claimed that if he could select his workers he could reduce his force by a third. A dozen more witnesses gave similar testimony.

Charges of inefficiency were commonplace during the public hearings. An assistant auditor complained that "men are frequently sent to me without brains enough to do the work." An assistant appraiser called several of his underlings "only fit to hold the plow or to hoe in the fields." The chief clerk of the invoice bureau told of instances "where fruit was classified as printing matter, soap as toothbrushes, cosmetics as silk in piece, and gils nails as jewelery." A general broker complained that employees in the damage allowance bureau were "totally incompetent." Accounting errors in the collector's office were said to amount to about a million and a half dollars a year. A clerk in the auditor's office reported that most clerks scrupulously avoided work. A deputation from the silk importers called for more efficiency in the appraiser's department. Twenty brokers signed a petition requesting a special order prohibiting clerks and officers in the Customhouse from earning outside incomes as notaries public during business hours.

Corruption appeared rampant throughout the Customhouse. A special deputy surveyor with twenty-four years' experience described the common acceptance of "hatchets," money received by inspectors from merchants to hold importations on the docks and out of a general-order warehouse, and "bones," bribes paid by passengers who wanted their baggage cleared rapidly and without investigation. Joseph S. Moore of the Treasury Department's Bureau of Statistics was of the opinion that between eight and ten million dollars a year worth of silk was brought duty-free into the country through smuggling and undervaluation; his charge was supported by testimony from several Customhouse employees. A former entry clerk told of colleagues accepting $400 to $500 a year in bribes. Representatives of Grantz, Jones and Company cited examples of corruption among weighers. The keeper of a bonded warehouse said he had been compelled to bribe a superintendent of warehouses. A former broker for a wholesale liquor company charged that the firm had paid up to $1,000 annually in bribes to gaugers, and had been obliged to provide free liquor for Customhouse employees and their friends on demand. A representative of the state chamber of commerce spoke of "gross outrages" to which merchants had to submit at the hands of appraisers. *The New York Times* reported on May 25: "Revelations of a private nature against Customs officers of every grade are crowding so thick and fast upon the Investigating Commission that it is compelled to be in secret session more than half the time before it can determine the value of the testimony voluntarily offered, and whether it would be proper to let it be given in public."

Several witnesses told of the influence of politics on employment practices at the Customhouse. A. B. Adams took a civil service examination in 1872 and made satisfactory scores on everything but "general aptitude," which, he said, meant political influence. James H. Roper testified that he was promised a place in the Customhouse by Arthur and Sharpe if he would name a political ally of theirs chairman of the inspectors of primary elections in his district; he did not accept the proposition and was not appointed. John E. Haggarty was assigned to the appraiser's department in 1872 because he was a Union veteran and a Republican, but was discharged three years later, he said, because he refused to follow the political dictates of his superiors. A paymaster testified that he had been removed from his job as customs inspector in 1875 for political reasons.

Some Customhouse employees were actively involved in partisan politics, testimony revealed. Arthur's good friend John J. O'Brien had acted as an election supervisor while on the payroll as a weigher. Another weigher had held a second job as supervisor of his town. Of course, this issue was not pursued at length for everyone knew that Cornell was a Republican official and that he, Arthur, and Sharpe appeared at dozens of party meetings and served on numerous party committees in the course of running the Conkling machine.

The Jay Commission also learned that party assessments were made regularly in the Customhouse. A much-experienced assistant appraiser said that the dun in 1876 had been 4 percent. A chief clerk told of being required to pay 2 percent. Bonded warehouse proprietors paid assessments directly to Customhouse employees; Henry R. Meyer had paid from $100 to $300 annually over the previous twelve years to Samuel P. Russell, superintendent of warehouses. Another proprietor said that Russell was seldom seen except when in pursuit of funds.

During the investigation, on May 14, Arthur and Sharpe, along with some three hundred other guests, attended a chamber of commerce banquet at Delmonico's, one of the city's most fashionable and expensive restaurants. The featured speaker was none other than Carl Schurz, who selected this time and place to deliver a fiery address on civil service reform. Perhaps a few furtive glances were cast in the direction of the collector as the Secretary of the Interior claimed that with reform, "You will have withdrawn their sustenance from that class of politicians whose power does not rest upon real ability and sound information, but upon a shrewd management and manipulation of the public plunder." A reporter observed that the speech drew "loud applause and cheers."

The next evening, Edwin D. Morgan held a reception at his Fifth Avenue mansion for the President and Mrs. Hayes, and Arthur, Tom Murphy, Sharpe, Thomas James, Thomas Acton, and Jacob Patterson were in attendance. Schurz, Evarts, John Jay, and Lawrence Turnure were also there—which probably accounted for Conkling's absence. Apparently the conversation was restricted to pleasantries, if only because of the presence of ladies. Surely Arthur was among those relieved that the awkwardness of the situation was not compounded by oratory.

As might be expected, Collector Arthur and the other leaders of the Customhouse were not inclined to suffer in silence as witnesses paraded before the commission. They not only testified in public and behind closed doors themselves but made sure that their protagonists among Customhouse employees were given an audience. A few machine witnesses, such as Lydecker, tended to deny all allegations—*The New York Times* called his testimony "rose-colored." But the chief officers took a more sophisticated approach, admitting the need for some changes in certain limited areas, defending themselves with data whenever possible, arguing all the while their persistent devotion to efficiency, economy, and fidelity.

Surveyor Sharpe and appraiser Dutcher both admitted that cuts could be made in personnel, though Fred Phillips said that he knew of no sinecures in the Customhouse. As for efficiency, Arthur considered it extremely high, and Sharpe said he did not feel that the Customhouse could be made more efficient than it then was.

Arthur was quick to tell of pressures upon him to find jobs for the friends of politicians and businessmen. But he argued that the role played by politics in actual appointments was no greater in New York than in other customhouses, and assured the commission that recommendations for appointments were carefully scrutinized and that no applicant was approved unless he was apparently qualified for the position sought. New appointments, he said, were almost invariably made to the lowest grade in the several divisions, and promotions were based on merit. He presented figures showing that he had removed a smaller annual percentage of employees than any previous collector.

Fred Phillips, however, admitted that Treasury Department rules were not generally carried out in regard to examinations. Sharpe contended that it was impossible to gauge a man's qualifications prior to his employment, and said that if he had the power "a very different class of men" would be appointed. Within the week, he told commission members, he had received a letter from "a very high official," who had previously paid him visits on the same matter, seeking reappointment of a man who had been fired three times from the Customhouse—on the last occasion for defrauding the revenue.

Questioned about assessments, Sharpe said that contributions were collected annually but that they were strictly voluntary. When Commissioner Turnure asked him about "Hand-Over" Street and the 4 percent assessment of 1876, the surveyor expressed doubt about their existence. Fred Phillips also stressed the voluntary nature of assessments, adding that he thought not more than a third of all Customhouse employees took an active part in politics.

At the commission's request, Arthur, Cornell, and Sharpe replied in writing to charges of Customhouse corruption. All three were evasive. While virtually admitting the presence of bribery and fraud in their departments, they claimed on the one hand that such practices were long established, and on the other that proof of their existence was not readily available. Cornell said that clerks who took "gratuities" "are but human." The officers thought that the careful selection of employees was the best way to improve Customhouse affairs—but avoided any reference to civil service reform.[7]

As he had earlier, Arthur resisted suggestions of cuts in personnel. No political machine could be expected to damage its authority voluntarily by reducing sources of patronage for the sake of efficiency. Still, concessions were clearly in order. In a private letter to John Jay, on May 21, Arthur said that his department could safely decrease its staff by forty-three—a reduction of less than 10 percent.[8] But he badly underestimated the commission's resolve.

The Jay Commission's first report was issued on May 24, and caused a flurry of comment in the press. It declared that appointments were made "generally at the request of politicians and political associations in this and other States, with little or no examination into the fitness of the appointees beyond the recommendations of their friends." It condemned the process as "unsound in principle, dangerous in practice, demoralizing in its influence on all connected with the customs service, and calculated to encourage and perpetuate the official ignorance, inefficiency, and corruption which, perverting the powers of Government to personal and party ends, have burdened the country with debt and taxes, and assisted to prostrate the trade and industry of the nation." Party assessments were seen to be "quietly permitted, if not openly sanctioned"; inefficiency and corruption were described as omnifarious and omnipresent.

The commission recommended a 20 percent reduction of the 1,038-man staff, the abolition of several positions, and an extension of the length of business hours. But it added that these were only palliatives: "the success of every effort through the customs service to relieve the national commerce and industry from the evils wrought by mismanagement and corruption, can be accomplished only by the emancipation of the service from partisan control."[9] What that implied, of course, was the ousting of Conkling's lieutenants from the Customhouse.

John Sherman was undoubtedly disturbed by the report, for it threatened to provoke a party-splintering confrontation between the administration and the New York machine. His peacemaking task was not made easier by the reactions of the Customhouse leaders to the report. Arthur said flatly that he could reduce personnel only to the 12 percent level. Sharpe objected strongly to the 20 percent proposal, promising only to effect "a large proportion" of the reduction soon and the remainder more gradually, "if approved by the Secretary of the Treasury." Cornell wrote a cold one-sentence reply, stating that he could fire only seven of his eighty-one men. Appraiser Silas Dutcher also stood in firm opposition to extensive employee dismissals.[10]

The President's response to the report was enthusiastic. In a letter to Sherman he wrote:

> I concur with the commission in their recommendations. It is my wish that the collection of the revenues should be free from partisan control, and organized on a strictly business basis, with the same guarantees for efficiency and fidelity in the selection of the chief and subordinate officers that would be required by a prudent merchant. Party leaders should have no more influence in appointments than other equally respectable citizens. No assessments for political purposes on officers or subordinates should be allowed. No useless officer or employe should be retained. No officer should be required or permitted to take part in the management of political organizations, caucuses, conventions, or election campaigns.

Sherman's formal response to the commission, however, bore a different tone. The secretary ordered the 20 percent reduction in personnel as well as the extension of business hours. But he said little about political influence, failed to mention assessments, and characterized

Arthur as an ardent supporter of the May 24 report. (It was difficult for Sherman to condemn the Customhouse leadership for playing politics with the customs service, since on several occasions, as recently as May 9, he had written private letters to the collector seeking to acquire or protect jobs for political friends.)[11] In an official letter to Arthur, Sherman assigned him the task of designating the some two hundred employees to be dismissed, again referring to him as a welcome participant in the crusade for better government. "If any have been appointed for purely political reasons, without regard to their efficiency, now is a good time to get rid of them." "After all, the success of this movement for reform of old abuses, which existed for many years before you became collector, will depend mainly upon your good sense and discretion."[12]

The special committee of the New York State chamber of commerce appointed in October to look into charges of inefficiency and corruption in the Customhouse thought the Jay Commission's first report disappointingly mild. On the basis of its own findings and a poll of some two hundred leading merchants, the committee recommended twenty-nine specific proposals, including the abolition of the entire naval department, by which the Customhouse would be thoroughly overhauled. Before the commission in a public hearing, committee members compared the high cost of collecting the customs in the United States with the much lower expenses incurred in Great Britain. They also cited examples of laxity, stupidity, and thievery in the customs service at New York. One merchant, Jackson S. Schultz, was sharply critical of Arthur, and at one point in his testimony expressed the wish to bring the collector to the stand and ask him why he retained incompetents in his department. The committee seemed clearly impatient with the idea that the Customhouse could be reformed under its current management.[13]

Obviously shaken by the prestigious committee's charges, Arthur told the Jay Commission the following day that he was preparing a written reply. He then belittled testimony given before the commission (excluding that of the chamber of commerce members) and repeated Sherman's erroneous contention that "nearly all" of the complaints and evidence against the management of the Customhouse referred to matters that occurred years earlier under former collectors. A few days later, in a private letter, he felt obliged to remind John Jay that he had personally relieved fewer men of their employment for political reasons than had his predecessors. The commission chairman fully understood how this claim could be made and remained unimpressed by it.[14]

Sherman gave Arthur until the end of June to make the necessary reductions in personnel stemming from the May 24 report and provided him with the commission's detailed recommendations for trimming his own department. On June 6 the collector appointed three veteran Customhouse workers to a committee charged with determining who among the hundreds of men in the department would be terminated; he asked Sharpe to set up a similar body.[15] Names were rapidly compiled and severances carried out. The entire personnel reduction cut the annual Customhouse payroll $235,298. Arthur played no personal role in his committee's distasteful work and made but a single revision in its list.[16] Among those severed, at the Jay Commission's recommendation, were eight deputy collectors. Arthur was particularly bitter about these dismissals, telling reporters that the men were competent, experienced, and, with one or two exceptions, apolitical.[17]

The machine's authority in New York was further threatened on June 22 when the President issued an order forbidding federal officeholders "to take part in the management of political organizations, caucuses, conventions, or election campaigns," and prohibiting assessments. To comply with this order the Conkling machine would virtually have to commit suicide; to defy it might mean a similar fate. Arthur, Cornell, and the hundreds of other Customhouse employees who were active party functionaries could take little comfort from the report that "Those who have conversed with the President upon this subject are convinced that he is determined to enforce the spirit of his letter, and that he will direct the removal of the first official reported for its violation."[18]

The second Jay Commission report, issued July 4, was again sharply critical of the chief officers of the Customhouse. Their selection of personnel fell under special censure; citing numerous examples of inefficiency and corruption among employees, the report declared: "The evidence shows a degree and extent of carelessness which we think should not be permitted to continue."[19]

By this time both Arthur and Sherman were fearful of a purge of Customhouse leadership. William Evarts was pressing for Arthur's removal, and a good many other reformers, including Charles Eliot Norton, thought it inevitable in light of the Jay Commission findings. To retain Arthur and Boston Collector Simmons in public office, Norton wrote to Hayes, politicians "long . . . identified with the 'machine' and its worst will," men who "have been among the chief corrupters of our political life," "would be to weaken greatly your own power of good" and cause the public to suspect "either your sincerity or your good sense . . ."[20]

On July 5, Sherman let Hayes know privately that he had met with the collector, and advised the President to give Arthur assurances that he would be permitted to retain his position. Sharpe's term of office was nearing its expiration, and to placate reformers, Sherman suggested, perhaps "some one agreeable to Mr. Evarts" might be appointed in his place.[21] But Hayes was not to reveal his intentions until Jay and his colleagues had completed their work.

On July 21, the third commission report appeared. It contained results of a detailed study of the business activities of weighers and gaugers, and made eleven recommendations leading to a complete reorganization of this branch of the service. The final principal statement by the commission, dated August 31, was a survey of the appraiser's office, calling for major changes. Underlying proposals in both reports was further evidence of the waste and illegality that seemed inextricably linked with machine control of the Customhouse.[22]

The possibility of accord between Hayes and the Conklingites was shattered in late August when Alonzo Cornell defied the President's order forbidding officeholders to participate in partisan political activities. He not only declined to resign his party positions but chaired a meeting of the state committee.[23] Reformers were convinced that Cornell was challenging the President's resolve, that this was a "test case" demanding Cornell's immediate dismissal. Tom Platt and another Stalwart were sent to the White House with rationalizations for the naval officer's action, but Hayes seemed unwilling to listen. He told a *New York Times* reporter that he continued to believe in the wisdom of his June 22 order. "I mean strictly to enforce it, and anybody who comes under it—anybody who violates it will be removed."[24] A few days later he privately informed Sherman of his decision to request the resignations of Cornell, Arthur, and Sharpe.

In his *Recollections* John Sherman recalled accurately that Hayes placed his decision to change the hierarchy of the Customhouse "upon the ground that he thought the public service would be best promoted by a general change, that new officers would be more likely to make the radical reforms required than those then in the customhouse." This seemed apparent to the President, for Arthur, Cornell, and Sharpe had tolerated and sometimes encouraged the partisan, unbusinesslike, and often illegal conduct the Jay Commission had disclosed; they had ridiculed what appeared to be highly significant testimony given during the hearings (a few witnesses complained of intimidation by the Customhouse leadership); they had executed the order to cut personnel with great reluctance and public complaint; and Cornell had openly violated a presidential order. The three officers might have been dealt with separately: Cornell could have been fired for his arrogance, Sharpe might have been permitted to retire, and Arthur given a stern warning. But the President decided that all three were as one in the overall conduct of their public offices and in their attitudes toward the Jay Commission and its findings. In requesting their resignations he confessed to the obvious, which he had probably known all along: Conkling politicians could not and would not be enthusiastic civil service reformers. Of course, there were also political considerations involved in the decision, but they were to be left unspoken. Hayes hoped that the transition in the Customhouse would be smoothly and swiftly accomplished to avoid personal conflict and minimize political disharmony.

On September 6, Sherman wrote a confidential letter to Arthur, informing him of the President's request and asking him to come to Washington for consultation. In another letter of that date to Assistant Secretary of the Treasury Richard C. McCormick, one of Arthur's close friends, he broke the same news and hinted at possible compensatory offers by the administration. But later in the day he inexplicably made the President's decision public. "After full consideration it has been determined by the President that the public interests would be better served by the appointment of new officers for the three leading positions in the New-York Custom-house." The story appeared in the press before Sherman's letters were delivered.[25]

Quite naturally, Arthur was offended by the secretary's mishandling of the delicate situation. He replied to Sherman, "I am in receipt of your communication of the 6th instant informing me officially of facts which had already come to my knowledge through the newspapers of this morning." He would come to Washington for a conference, but would be unavoidably detained (in part, no doubt, by his pride) for about a week. The same day McCormick reported to Sherman that he had just seen Arthur, "and his only regret is that he was not permitted to resign before there was any announcement of a determination to remove him."[26]

Shortly after Arthur was seated in the secretary's office, on September 17, Sherman offered him the consulship at Paris in exchange for his resignation. Though not part of the discussion at the time, the dimensions of the situation must have seemed apparent to Sherman. If Arthur accepted the position he might clear his name of any onus of personal guilt contained in the newspaper stories of a shakeup in the Customhouse and quash rumors of a serious split between Republican factions; the entire matter could be explained as an intra-administration readjustment of responsibility. Should he decline, he would have somehow to be driven from the collectorship, which would mean an end to Sherman's conciliatory efforts and the beginning of a struggle of potentially ruinous proportions for the party. Arthur said he was not inclined to accept the offer but would think it over.[27] From the secretary's viewpoint there was hope: George Sharpe had withdrawn his candidacy for reappointment to the surveyorship. Perhaps more evidence of the Conkling machine's intentions would surface at the New York state convention, scheduled for September 26.

On the 24th, Conkling and Cornell arrived together in Rochester, ready to do battle. Conkling had come in person to the convention, as he had in 1871, to demolish his opposition, to muster his minions in defense of his right to control Republicanism in the state. Newspapers reported plans by administration supporters to pass a resolution endorsing the President; Conkling interpreted the move as an effort by Evarts to assume control of party affairs, and he was determined to crush it. The time and place were at hand for the Senator not only to crack the whip at home but to show the administration what sort of resistance it could expect if it persisted in its effort to deprive him of his patronage. A large number of machine delegates were soon at hand to lend assistance: Tom Murphy, Tom Platt, Steve French, John Smyth, Lyman Tremain, Pierre Van Wyck, Jacob Patterson, Benjamin K. Phelps, Mike Cregan, John Knapp, and others. Arthur stayed home, unlike Cornell respecting the presidential order forbidding officeholders to attend.

From the turmoil of the two sessions Conkling emerged triumphant. He and his supporters organized the committees, drafted the platform, elected the permanent president (Platt), and created a committee to select candidates for state offices. The platform denounced the presidential order of June 22. Efforts by George William Curtis to secure an endorsement of the administration fell flat. While Cornell retired from the state committee, its new membership included Murphy, Platt, Patterson, Smyth, and Knapp.

Just before the convention assembled, Conklingites were boasting that the Senator "has it in his pocket." They were right.

Curtis and Conkling clashed repeatedly in the course of the proceedings, and at one point Conkling lashed out at his long-time foe in a well-prepared and memorized oration that has been quoted ever since to illustrate the Senator's fascinating capacity for invective and sarcasm. "Who are these men," Conkling roared, "who, in newspapers and elsewhere, are cracking their whips over Republicans and playing schoolmaster to the Republican party and its conscience and convictions?" Knowing that *Harper's* was currently publishing fashion articles,

Conkling sniggered at "the man-milliners, the dilletanti, and carpet-knights of politics . . . "

> Some of these worthies masquerade as reformers. Their vocation and ministry is to lament the sins of other people. Their stock in trade is rancid, canting self-righteousness. They are wolves in sheep's clothing. Their real object is office and plunder. When Dr. Johnson defined patriotism as the last refuge of a scoundrel, he was unconscious of the then undeveloped capabilities and uses of the word "Reform."

As a parting shot to illustrate his total contempt for Curtis and all those priggish reformers who had the President's ear, he snorted, "They forget that parties are not built up by deportment, or by ladies' magazines, or gush."[28]

When he had finished, Conkling employed parliamentary procedure to prevent a reply by Curtis. The editor later confided to Charles Eliot Norton, "It was the saddest sight I ever knew, that man glaring at me in a fury of hate, and storming his foolish blackguardism. I was all pity. I had not thought him great, but I had not suspected how small he was. His friends—the best—were confounded."[29]

Numerous Republican newspapers and journals expressed shock at the Senator's performance. *The New York Times* wrote: "He abused Mr. Curtis like a fish-wife, and was well hissed for his pains from first to last. He acted more like a maniac than a sensible man."[30] And yet the press, as well as the administration, had to face the reality of Conkling's power; oratory aside, he had effectively revealed at the convention his firm grip over party affairs in New York. He had, moreover, cast the gauntlet at "His Fraudulency" (one of several titles Conkling unceremoniously bestowed upon Hayes), informing him in no uncertain terms that he was not to sit meekly by while "dilletanti" dismantled his machine in the Customhouse. Shortly, Arthur informed Evarts of his decision to decline the free trip to Paris.[31]

When the decision to replace the Customhouse leadership was announced, administration sources said that successors had not been selected. A month later reporters learned that Theodore Roosevelt had been chosen to fill Arthur's chair and that Edwin A. Merritt would be asked to serve as surveyor.[32] The elderly, opulent Mr. Roosevelt had a successful business and administrative background, was a leader of the Union League Club and an advocate of civil service reform, and in 1876 had supported Bristow and vigorously opposed Conkling at the Cincinnati convention.[33] Merritt had been naval officer of the port of New York before Tom Murphy came to power; a former Fentonite, he had followed his mentor into the Liberal Republican camp in 1872, returning to the regular party two years later. After an almost two-week delay, the press reported that Le Baron Bradford Prince, a New York attorney, former state assemblyman, and one-time national party official, was chosen to be naval officer.[34]

All three men had histories of active political participation, but the administration was convinced that they were committed to removing the Customhouse from politics. It was also believed that their nominations could clear the Senate.[35] Conkling, of course, interpreted these selections as further evidence of the Hayes-Evarts-Schurz-Curtis design to destroy his influence in the party, and he was correct. A nonpartisan Customhouse concerned exclusively with the efficient handling of government business was indeed inimical to his interests.

A special session of Congress opened on October 15, and the administration was anxious to submit its nominations and have the Customhouse changes made promptly. Pressure was on Sherman to persuade Arthur to resign. Twice the secretary pled with him to reconsider his refusal, even suggesting that his resignation might be inferred from correspondence on file. But Arthur was firm, laying the responsibility for his decision squarely upon Sherman. "The treatment of the whole matter has been so unfortunate that I feel I cannot now resign. Before your letter of September sixth or any suggestion to me of a resignation, official & public announcement was made that I was to be removed. The general understanding that it is a removal cannot now be changed."[36] The administration would not get away with public inferences about misconduct in the Customhouse under the machine's reign—it would be forced to produce facts. Appointment of the likes of Theodore Roosevelt would be resisted. As Hayes might have expected after the Stalwart triumph at Rochester, Arthur and Cornell were determined to fight.

On October 24, the President sent the nominations of Roosevelt, Merritt, and Prince to the Senate. According to the Tenure of Office Act, an officer could retain his position for a full term until a successor was confirmed by the Senate, if in session. (If it was not in session, the President could suspend an officer and replace him, but if the Senate failed to confirm the successor within thirty days after the start of its next session, the suspended official would resume his office.) The administration knew that the confirmations would not be easily obtained. Conkling was chairman of the committee on commerce, through which the nominations would have to pass. And there was the custom of "courtesy of the Senate," whereby a Senator from the President's party was permitted to have the last word about offices in his own state. There was a slim Republican majority in the Senate, but it was not united behind the administration on several issues, including civil service reform.

Hayes sadly acknowledged the opposition he faced within his own party, but confided to his diary, "I am clear that I am right. I believe that a large majority of the best people are in full accord with me."[37]

The controversy also assumed another dimension—the authority of the presidency. Congress had dominated the Chief Executives since Lincoln's assassination, and Hayes was determined to restore a measure of balance to the branches of government by insisting on the right of the President to make his own appointments. When the Republican senatorial caucus sent a committee headed by George Edmunds to advise the President to cooperate more fully with the desires of party Senators, Hayes replied, "We must all co-operate in the interest of the country," and added, "We must not forget that I am President of the whole country, not of any party." Edmunds reported to his colleagues that Hayes's attitude toward "Senatorial courtesy" was one of "substantial defiance."[38]

Conkling fired his opening volley on November 15 when, as chairman of the commerce committee, he wrote a letter directly to the President (curtly ignoring Sherman) seeking all evidence surrounding "the question of removing Chester A. Arthur." He had been authorized, he said, to request:

1. Petitions or communications asking or advising the removal of the present Collector.
2. All communications asking or advising the retention of the present Collector; or remonstrating against his removal.
3. Any charges of personal or official misconduct against the present Collector.
4. Any communication to the present Collector from, or by direction of, the President, or the Secretary of the Treasury, wherein he has been censured, or notified that any act of his was disapproved; and also his answer thereto.
5. Any correspondence, telegraphic or otherwise, with the present incumbent, touching his vacation of the office of Collector.
6. The recommendations upon which Mr. Roosevelt was nominated.

And "If any oral charge has been made against Mr. Arthur, or if any reprehensible, or insubordinate act of his has been discovered, the committee ask to be fully apprised of it."[39]

Several years earlier the Tenure of Office Act had been amended to preclude demands upon a President to give reasons for the removal of federal officials, and the administration chose not to comply with Conkling's request. Hayes did not wish to convict Conkling's lieutenant of crimes, he merely wished to replace him with a reformer. Continuing to hope that a party wrangle could be avoided, Sherman replied to the

Senator in rather general terms, repeating the view that new Custom-house leaders would be more likely to effect reforms. But it was already too late for that sort of response. *The New York Times* expressed shock: "Specific charges of incompetency or neglect of duty are not made."[40]

Unknown to the press, and perhaps even to the President, the collector himself was managing a clandestine campaign to throttle the administration's efforts to alter the leadership of the New York Customhouse. He wrote to Conkling on November 24, "I have had many letters sent to Senators B, R, & others & will continue to do all I can in that direction." (Two days earlier R. G. Dun urged his son-in-law, Senator Zachariah Chandler, to use his influence with colleagues on Arthur's behalf.) Enclosed in the letter were page proofs of a lengthy reply to the Jay Commission reports and a request for suggestions.[41]

On the 27th, Arthur sent printed copies of the rebuttal to the Senator and apprised him of further developments. "We have brought everything to bear that we could think of upon Senator R." (The recipient of all this attention was undoubtedly Senator M. W. Ransom of North Carolina, a Democrat on the commerce committee, who was being persuaded to permit the nominations to slumber in committee.) Machine leaders often communicated with each other using code names; Cornell's, at the time, was "January," and Conkling was assured that the naval officer was on hand "trying to help us"—apparently by striking bargains with Democrats. "He had a conference here on Sunday with 'Jasper'-& their Chrbat [?] Com[mittee] & the Speaker [,] & they return to Washington fully impressed with January's views that the matter should be kept where it is. The Chm of the Nat[ional] Com[mittee] was to see Senator R particularly." Two men, ex-mayor Wickham and an attorney named Whitney, were being dispatched to Washington to apply further pressure. "I have told them to talk with Senator Eaton who would communicate with you. They will remain there only over Wednesday."[42]

In his published response, dated November 23, Arthur lashed out against the Jay Commission, charging that its membership was rigged and that it "did not pretend to investigate thoroughly any question, or to seek for evidence on both sides." (He chose not to mention his own role in the selection of Turnure or his appearances before the Commission.) An honest and objective study, he contended, would have concluded that his administration had been popular, efficient, and ever-mindful of the "essential elements" of reform. Arthur portrayed himself as a champion of civil service reform, one who believed in removals strictly for cause, promotion by merit, prompt and thorough investigation of all complaints, and equally prompt punishment. He pointed to the low annual rate of turnover during his almost six years in office and contended that promotions had consistently been made from lower ranks. In fact, wrote Arthur, "civil service reform has been more faithfully observed, and more thoroughly carried out in the New York Custom House, than in any other branch or Department of the Government, either under the present or any past national administration." He told of asking commission members to provide him with proof of misconduct on the part of a single subordinate, "but they wholly failed to communicate any evidence." In addition, he countered New York chamber of commerce data with statistics showing what he called the low cost of collecting the revenue at the Customhouse in recent years.

Most potent was Arthur's charge that he had made several reforms and suggestions for reforms in the Customhouse for which he had not received proper credit: ". . . of the fifteen recommendations made by the Commission, two are for the introduction of what already existed, eight are repetitions of my own previous recommendations, one only differs from my recommendation in carrying reductions to what I believe to be an unwise extent, and one other is both unwise and illegal."

Getting to the heart of the administration's case against him, he challenged anyone to reveal an unwillingness on his part to execute the recommendations of the commission. He effectively quoted from a letter written in late July by Sherman commending him for the "great care and impartiality" with which his departmental committee had designated those to be dismissed.[43]

It was a clever and impressive piece of writing, buttressed with three appendices. When George William Curtis read it, he was moved to write, "We do not need, we hope, to say that those who desire a real reform are not waging war upon Collector Arthur or Collector Simmons, but upon an evil system."[44] (Almost all of the historians who have discussed the Customhouse controversy in any detail have accepted this polemic at face value.) It may have reminded New Yorkers of Arthur's reputation as an efficient administrator during the war; E. D. Morgan continued to be a vocal admirer.[45] Whether or not the collector was equally famous as a Conkling lieutenant, his letter of November 23 demanded reply. Sherman's position in the matter was not strengthened by newspaper reports (no doubt accurate) of assessment circulars in the Treasury Department, raising funds to assist the fall campaigns.[46]

On November 28, the administration made public excerpts from the fifth Jay Commission report, which included further evidence of scandal in the Customhouse. But it was to no avail; two days later the commerce committee voted unanimously (three Democrats abstained) to reject the nominations. The special session ended December 3 and reassembled in regular session without recess. Conkling, of course, played a role in this unorthodox procedure, for without a recess the President was unable to suspend Arthur and Cornell and replace them with the administration's nominees.[47]

Many Republicans were anxious to end the clash between Conkling and the administration, and some hoped that the President would not resubmit the nominations. On December 6 two Congressmen presented Hayes with a petition signed by fifteen of New York's seventeen Congressmen asking him to drop his plans for the Customhouse. But the Cabinet had already met and determined to send the names to the Senate.[48]

Compromise was out of the question. Hayes firmly believed that the President should have the right to appoint those willing to perform government duties in accordance with what he considered the highest ideals. Defeat of the custom of "Senatorial courtesy," he wrote in his diary, "is the first and most important step in the effort to reform the Civil Service." And as for Conkling: his friends were spreading the story that he would have nothing to do with the administration until Evarts was ousted from the Cabinet![49]

Conkling now took a somewhat new approach in his attack upon the nominations, claiming in an executive session of the Senate that Hayes was violating his own pleas for reform by removing Arthur and Cornell without a statement of cause: it was the President who was guilty of profaning civil service principles. (The New York Times commented: "Mr. Conkling's own practice in dealing with the Federal appointments made in this State shortly before the close of President Grant's term gives a somewhat amusing aspect to his present theory about the rights of public officers.") He also appealed to his colleagues by objecting strongly to executive "encroachment" upon the independence of the Senate.[50]

Only one change had been made in the membership of the commerce committee since the last vote on the nominations had been taken—Senator Jones was replaced by pro-administration Senator Burnside (famous for his whiskers). On December 11 the committee voted to confirm the nomination of Merritt, with whom Conkling apparently believed he could work, and to reject Roosevelt and Prince. The next day the full Senate followed suit. Only six Republicans joined nineteen Democrats in support of the President's nominations for collector and naval officer; even Blaine voted with Conkling.[51]

Hayes was disappointed but privately far from ready to concede the issue. He wrote in his diary, "In the language of the press 'Senator Conkling has won a great victory over the Administration.' My N.Y.

nominations were rejected 31. to 25. But the end is not yet. I am right, and shall not give up the contest."[52]

Arthur, of course, was elated by news of the vote and thought the struggle concluded. He wrote to his chieftain, "I cannot tell you how gratified I am at the splendid victory you have won,—apart from & way beyond any personal considerations of my own. The whole town is excited by the event & the current of popular feeling is all with you."[53]

A few days before Christmas, the President, Mrs. Hayes, and William Evarts were guests at a reception held by the Union League Club in New York City. Mr. and Mrs. Arthur were present, and so were Acton, Phelps, Van Wyck, and a few other machine dependables. The collector, in fact, was a member of the reception committee, along with Theodore Roosevelt. Arthur no doubt regretted Conkling's absence; no one could gloat quite like the Senator.[54]

CHAPTER SEVEN

The Keys to the Customhouse

As the administration's first year wound to a close, many observers concluded that Hayes's loudly proclaimed drive for civil service reform was a failure. Numerous compromises had been made with state bosses, several objectionable appointments in the South were part of the record, and, above all, the Conkling machine seemed as firmly in control of the party in New York as ever. *The New York Times* commented, "The friends of reform are alternately disheartened and disgusted by performances that render the President's pretensions ridiculous, while its enemies chuckle over his inconsistencies, and point mockingly to his tortuous, hesitating course." Hayes was aware of his critics, and admitted to his diary, "In my anxiety to complete the great work of pacification I have neglected to give due attention to the Civil Service—to the appointments and removals. The result is some bad appointments have been made. Some removals have been mistakes. There have been delays in action. All this I must try now to correct."[1]

Those pleased with the course of events put considerable pressure on the President to discontinue his efforts in the Empire State and patch up his quarrel with its senior Senator. Among those advisers, reportedly, was John Sherman. Apparently convinced that the business of politics was to resume along its normal course, the Treasury Secretary, on several occasions throughout the first three months of 1878, sent personal letters to Arthur seeking Customhouse positions for friends and allies. "I have received the enclosed letter from Gen. Kilpatrick," Sherman wrote at one point, "and feel a strong desire, if possible, to oblige him. It so happened in the distribution of patronage that, although for political reasons he deserves much, he has received nothing." Arthur was no doubt pleased (and perhaps slightly amused) by the correspondence, seeing it as proof of the administration's unwillingness to resume the struggle. Hayes did not return to the Senate with further nominations in January, and reports were widespread of a desire on his part to forget the matter.[2]

The collector complied with one of Sherman's requests, awarding a clerkship to the son of Supreme Court Justice Bradley—the New Jersey Republican who had been a key figure on the electoral commission. But in another case he rejected a petition and reminded Sherman of the damage the administration had done to his reservoir of patronage:

> The vacancies that now occur here, are, as you may be aware, very few, and although it is, of course, my desire, to accede to your wishes in such matters so far as possible, it has not been without considerable difficulty and delay that I have been enabled to provide for one or two of the cases you have already brought to my attention.[3]

Conkling workers, inside and outside the Customhouse, continued their political rounds in early 1878 almost as though Hayes's hopes for reform did not exist. Cornell, for example, was reelected to the Republican Central Committee and was seen lobbying in Albany and elsewhere to win government positions for friends. Arthur, on the other hand, remained conspicuously absent from party affairs, no doubt being less trustful of the administration's docility than the naval officer.[4]

The machine ran into trouble in February when John F. Smyth, chairman of the Republican State Committee and State Superintendent of Insurance, was charged by Governor Robinson with "official misconduct" involving frauds totaling more than $24,000. A legal firm headed by ex-State Senator Tobey, a close friend of Cornell's, was involved in the swindle, and a *New York Times* reporter was moved to refer to "the political firm of 'Conkling, Cornell, Tobey, Platt & Co.' "

Smyth's trial before the State Senate was held the following month, and stories swirled around Albany of the presence of "Conkling politicians" engaged in striking bargains to prevent Smyth's removal. Tom Murphy and Jacob Patterson, among others, were, in fact, on hand, and Patterson later admitted that he had attempted to influence senatorial votes. An Albany newspaper editor, W. J. Hilton, privately informed President Hayes on March 6: "Collector Arthur has been here within the last four or five days and, as I am very reliably informed, for the purpose of influencing anti-Conkling Republican Senators voting against the removal of Superintendent Smyth. While here he kept very quiet and out of sight as much as possible."

When the Senate was polled, Smyth was acquitted 19 to 12, though he had admitted breaking the law. It was immediately noticed that the Tammany Senators had unanimously voted to acquit; charges by a *New York Times* reporter of a "fix," centering around Stalwart Representative Hamilton Fish Jr., led to an investigation by the House Committee on Privileges and Elections. George Bliss represented Fish, while Congressman Matthew Hale represented *The Times*. After several stormy sessions, which made it clear that Conklingites had indeed attempted to rescue Smyth, the matter was dropped. Arthur's alleged presence in Albany went unmentioned. But a few days later the President again heard privately from Hilton, who wrote: "Governor Robinson, in a conversation I had with him a day or so ago, distinctly charged without qualification that Smyth's acquittal was the result of Customhouse influence, that within a week previous to it Collector Arthur had wined, dined, and feasted Senators and the very ones who voted to acquit Smyth." Hayes may have winced as he read that the governor was convinced "the Senate of the State of New York had become the villainous football of the New York Customhouse."[5]

Conklingites were deeply irritated by the presidential order of June 22, 1877, forbidding assessments and prohibiting federal officeholders from participating in political organizations, caucuses, conventions, and election campaigns. They were not alone in this view, for spoilsmen from all of the party's factions feared the possible consequences. The depth of Stalwart feeling on the issue emerged in late March when Senator Timothy Howe of Wisconsin roasted the administration in a stinging two-hour address before the Senate, so bitter that it even recalled into question Hayes's title to the presidency. (Senator Conkling sat in the first row a few feet from the speaker, obviously pleased.) Howe singled out the June 22 order for special fire: "That is not reform; that is tyranny—tyranny which no predecessor of his ever attempted, and no successor will venture to imitate."[6]

Two weeks later, at a well-attended Republican congressional caucus in Washington, Stalwart Senator Sargent proclaimed that 90,000 Republican officeholders in the country felt bound by the President's order, and that as long as they did, Democrats stood a good chance of running the country. The caucus urged the President to avert the calamity by repealing his order. Shortly, the Republican Central Committee of New York City—on which sat Murphy, Pinckney, O'Brien, Patterson, Cregan, Hess, and Van Wyck—endorsed Howe's speech and joined in calling for an end to the June 22 order.[7]

While the President was unwilling to abandon his mandate, he was sufficiently flexible to permit party contributions from officeholders that were truly voluntary, carefully stipulating that no employee would suffer reprisals for refusing to donate. The administration also interpreted the presidential order to mean that federal employees might support a political candidate "in any way that will not interfere with the proper discharge of their official duties," reemphasizing the required abstention from active participation in party caucuses, primary meetings, and conventions. But these mild compromises pleased neither spoilsmen nor reformers. The latter were outraged to learn that the Republican congressional campaign committee was proceeding to distribute assessment circulars, assuring "those who happen to be in Federal employ that there will be no objection in any quarter to such voluntary contribution." It seemed apparent to reform leaders that if Hayes failed in some dramatic way to illustrate his firm commitment to the ideal of an apolitical civil service, Conkling, Blaine, and other professional politicians might be able to bury the entire effort. *The New York Times* glumly announced, "Of the famous civil service reform not a vestige now remains. Mr. Hayes has buried it, rags, bones, and all. The old regime is restored."[8]

The New York Customhouse was again in the news in late April when a special agent of the Treasury Department told the House Appropriations Committee of frauds amounting to more than $42,000 perpetrated by clerks in the auditor's department and naval office. The agent said he had called the facts to the collector's attention and that Arthur had ignored him. Of the clerks charged with the frauds, all had been retained, one had been promoted, and another had been recommended for promotion.[9]

On May 15, Arthur greeted an investigating committee headed by J. H. Meredith, general appraiser of the Baltimore Customhouse, and two treasury agents. The committee had been appointed by Sherman in March to look into charges against customs appraisers in eastern ports, and had held hearings in Chicago, St. Louis, Cincinnati, Boston, Portland, Philadelphia, and Baltimore before coming to New York. Complaints by western merchants about customhouse corruption focused upon the port of New York, and Arthur was asked to invite the city's major importers to appear before the committee. While the secret hearings were under way, a memorial, signed by many of New York's leading merchants, was sent to the President complaining of difficulties encountered in obtaining the passage of their goods through the Customhouse.[10]

The Meredith Committee made a confidential report to the administration on June 25 which charged that Chief Deputy Lydecker, in whom Arthur had expressed great trust, was guilty of neglect of duty and fraud. Administration leaders were undoubtedly apprised as well of the contents of a full committee report, officially dated July 17, documenting numerous Customhouse frauds, including undervaluations, false classifications, improper weights and measures, and illegal damage allowances. Meredith and his colleagues were particularly critical of the collector, condemning him for his habit of arriving at his office several hours late, for permitting Lydecker "to practically control the business management of the office," and for failing to take action against his chief deputy when informed of his misdeeds.

> We found that the more honest and intelligent officials at the Custom House had long had reason to distrust Mr. Lydecker's integrity, and that the influence exercised by him over the Collector had been for a long time the subject of comment among them. This matter, as well as the Collector's neglect of office hours, was repeatedly referred to in an unfavorable manner by the merchants who were associated with us in the early part of our investigation at this port.[11]

After two Customhouse investigations the case against Arthur and Cornell was firmly established; it was a quagmire of evidence out of which, it was thought, Conkling's lieutenants could neither swim nor leap. Carl Schurz observed, "The question is whether the President and the Secretary of the Treasury are to be permitted to correct crying evils long complained of and to secure an efficient management of the most important Customhouse in the country by the appointment of officers [who can] be depended upon for faithful performance of duty or whether the Administration is to be coerced to abandon necessary reforms by forcing upon for the most important places men who have proved unwilling or unable to give it the cooperation required." With Congress no longer in session, the President suspended Arthur and Cornell on July 11 and appointed Edwin A. Merritt collector (Roosevelt had died in February) and Silas Burt naval officer.[12]

While the announcement of this surprise move was awkwardly handled—Cornell's active participation in politics went unmentioned, and Sherman would shortly assure reporters of Arthur's absolute integrity —the strategy behind it was well conceived. Hayes knew, of course, that when Congress reconvened in December Conkling would be waiting with fire in his eyes. But by that time the appointees would have had several months in which to demonstrate the efficacy and necessity of reform. Moreover, it was assumed that the Senate would take at least a month to act on the nominations. Should Merritt and Burt be rejected, Arthur and Cornell could resume their positions only until March 4, when they could again be ousted with the expiration of the session. With the next Senate in the hands of Democrats, confirmation of the nominations seemed certain. The intensity of the coming struggle was revealed when Arthur and Cornell refused to resign and when someone leaked word to the press of Sherman's personal letters to Arthur requesting Customhouse jobs.[13]

Several observers believed that what was occurring was a mere factional fight, that Hayes was attempting to damage Conkling's chances for reelection in 1879 by constructing a pro-administration faction in New York out of ex-Fentonites. This suspicion was strengthened by the nomination of George K. Graham as surveyor, for Graham, like Merritt, was a former Fenton Republican. But in fact this was *both* a struggle between factions and an effort to effect genuine civil service reform. Of course Hayes sought to bolster pro-administration Republicans in New York: there was not only the senatorial election to think of but an important gubernatorial race in 1879 that could be of critical significance in the selection and election of a presidential candidate the following year. There were already strong indications that Conkling was plotting to win a third term for Grant. But the President also was serious about cleaning up the Customhouse and taking it out of politics. When Curtis expressed puzzlement over the selection of Graham, Hayes assured him, "I agree with you as to the error of removing one set of 'workers' to put in another," and added, "While I do not want to proscribe people who have been active in politics, I prefer to so act as not to be chargeable with the sins we condemn."[14] When Merritt was asked by a reporter what course he intended to follow as collector, he replied, "The customhouse will no longer be the headquarters of a political party, controlling primary meetings and conventions. I don't think, however, that a man should cease to be a working Republican when he becomes a government officer, and there are legitimate methods by which he can work for the achievement of the party; but the vast patronage of the custom-house will not be used as a part of the political machine." He was serious: for the first time in decades the Customhouse was to play no part in the fall campaigns.[15]

However the administration may have desired Conkling's political retirement, it was still forced to recognize his overwhelming authority in New York. When the state convention met in late September, it was estimated that at least 390 of the 454 delegates were under the Senator's influence. Conkling, affecting a desire for party harmony, was made temporary and permanent chairman of the convention; Cornell was appointed chairman of the state central committee; and the new state committee included Cornell, Murphy, Wheeler, Patterson, Sharpe, Smyth, Vrooman, Knapp, and Platt. Arthur headed the New York City delegation to the convention, and the announcement of his name was greeted with prolonged applause. The only reference to the civil service in the platform was an objection to Arthur's suspension: "We renew our declarations for the elevation of the public service on the basis of a secure tenure during the faithful performance of official duties for a fixed term . . ."[16]

There were no statewide races in 1878, and Arthur's duties in the canvass were restricted to local contests. He was elected, along with Tom Murphy and Barney Biglin, to the county convention, and, as chairman of the Republican conference committee, he directed negotiations with anti-Tammanyites, culminating in a common ticket. Edward Cooper, the venerable Peter Cooper's son, was supported for mayor, and Arthur's role in his campaign was such that the candidate would be labeled Arthur's puppet. Also on the slate were machine regulars Murphy, Biglin, Pinckney, Gedney, and Phelps.[17] While Chet Arthur and "the boys" toiled in their own bailiwick, Conkling, with an eye to his own reelection a few months away, stumped the state on behalf of party candidates.

When the votes were counted, Republicans carried the state for the first time since 1872, easily capturing the Assembly (thus virtually assuring Conkling of a third term) and 26 of the 33 congressional seats. In the city Cooper was elected mayor, Phelps was reelected district attorney, and Tom Murphy squeaked through by a margin of 357 votes out of 24,000 cast to become a State Senator. Three other Arthur intimates—Biglin, Pinckney, and Gedney—were not as fortunate, losing their bids to return as aldermen. In late October the three had been involved in a railroad fraud of rather impressive proportions and were forced to endure withering attacks from several New York newspapers. (Biglin's conduct was such that George Bliss supported his Democratic opponent. For that offense to party loyalty, Mike Cregan and other Conklingites had him expelled from the central committee.) Undaunted, Biglin joined Arthur and Murphy, a few weeks later, as a delegate to the central committee. It was business as usual.[18]

Congress convened on December 2 and the Customhouse nominations dominated conversations throughout the nation's capital. Since the suspensions in July, two more investigations of the New York Customhouse had been undertaken (one by the House Ways and Means Committee and another by an assistant secretary of the Treasury), several reforms had been enacted, and numerous employees had been discharged. But the odds were that Conkling had the votes to curb further administration tinkering and trimming and that Merritt, Burt, and Graham would soon be unemployed.[19]

John Sherman was now aware that the President did not contemplate either retreat or defeat. He would simply have to swallow his personal reservations about what Congressman James Garfield called the "dreamy doctrines" of civil service reform and go all out to secure passage of the administration's nominations. He later wrote in his autobiography, "I had definitely made up my mind that if the Senate again rejected them I would resign."[20]

The nominations were submitted on December 3 and were shortly turned over to the commerce committee. Even though membership on the committee had remained stable between sessions, and the chairman's position seemed as commanding as before, Conkling decided to delay matters until after the holidays. Hayes wrote in his diary:

> This is a test case. The Senators generally *prefer* to confirm Merritt and Graham. But many, perhaps a majority, will not oppose Conkling on the question. Senatorial courtesy, the Senatorial prerogative, and the fear of C's vengeance in future control them. He is like Butler, more powerful because he is vindictive and not restrained by conscience.[21]

Before the issue came to a head in the Senate, Arthur's intense hatred for his reform-minded antagonists boiled to the surface in remarks he made at a meeting of the Eighteenth Assembly District Association. They were prompted by a member who presented the association with a list of the names of 150 Liberal Republicans who sought admission to the organization. Angrily, Arthur rose to his feet and reminded fellow members that these same Republicans had bolted the association two years earlier to work against regular party candidates. He asked how long the association could be expected to welcome men who persisted in leaving its ranks whenever they found it convenient. If they were to be readmitted, Arthur insisted, each one of the 150 should be required to make a pledge to stand by the party's selections—no matter who they were, no matter what they believed. Some might call this the "machine" outlook, he conceded, but it was also the most desirable way to function politically.

Of course, Arthur had recently concluded a campaign in which he helped elect Democrats. But that was consistent with his remarks if one translated "party" into "machine," for Arthur's primary allegiance was to Conkling's political organization, the depository of "true Republicanism." New York Stalwarts operated by the politics of self-interest: what enhanced their power, prestige, and bank accounts was good for Republicans and the public. The ideological content of this approach to American government was virtually invisible. Support for Democrats sanctioned by the machine—sometimes Tammany, sometimes anti-Tammany—was acceptable; Liberal Republicanism was by definition anathema. Reformers were worse than Democrats because they not only threatened the machine's authority but they could not be bargained with or bought. Their idealism was their sin.

Arthur's assistance to the anti-Tammanyites was not overlooked at the association meeting. A resolution was introduced to sanction that action by the ex-collector, and it passed unanimously. As if to further symbolize the solidarity within this political unit, long dominated by Arthur and his friends, Barney Biglin's candidate was elected chairman of the association's executive committee.[22]

The opening salvo of the administration's drive to win confirmation of its nominees occurred on January 15 when a letter from Sherman was read at an executive session of the Senate spelling out the specific reasons for Arthur's removal. There was no legal requirement for this statement of cause, but the President feared that without it members of the Senate would blindly follow Conkling and his commerce committee. The timing of the letter's appearance was not accidental, for newspapers reported that the committee was set to vote on the nominations the next day.[23]

Sherman's lengthy statement was a straightforward summary of much of the evidence collected by the Jay Commission and the Meredith Committee, and amounted to an impressive indictment of machine control of the Customhouse. The secretary employed statistics to document effectively the high cost of collecting the customs revenue, discussed the full range of corruption revealed during the investigations, and, perhaps most damaging, documented resistance on the part of the former Customhouse official to effect reforms. Arthur opposed personnel reductions, Sherman wrote, as well as efforts to halt the widespread acceptance of bribes. He defended notorious irregularities conducted in the Department of Weighers and Gaugers and refused to dismiss John Lydecker (who, along with John J. O'Brien, quietly resigned when Arthur was removed). "I preferred to try to execute the reforms proposed with Mr. Arthur in office rather than a stranger," wrote Sherman. "The President acquiesced in this view; but gradually it became evident that neither Mr. Arthur nor Mr. Cornell was in sympathy with the recommendations of the Commission and could and did obstruct their fair execution." "A very brief experience proved," Sherman continued, "that any hope of carrying out any systematic reforms or changes in the mode of conducting the business would be abortive while the Collector held his position. The same system, the same persons, the same influences prevailed as before."

Sherman pointed to Edwin Merritt's qualifications to hold the office of collector and pointed to numerous reforms already made, demonstrating "a gain to the Government of $164,000,000 for a period covered being equal to $245,636.15 per annum, while the results obtained, by a higher condition of discipline and more rigid responsibility of weighers can not be estimated." The restoration of Arthur and Cornell, he concluded, would do serious damage to the public service.

> To require this business to be performed by persons in hostility to the general policy of the Administration would create discord and contention, where there ought to be unity and harmony. It would be unjust to the President and personally embarrassing to me in the discharge of my duties to have the office of Collector of Customs at New York held by one who will not perform his duties according to the general policy of the Department.[24]

What Sherman chose not to discuss in his erudite missive was the cornerstone of the case against Arthur and Cornell: the fact that under their leadership the Customhouse had been heavily engaged in partisan politics. Sherman clearly sensed a strong antipathy on the part of many Senators toward civil service reform and, moreover, no doubt wished to avoid the awkward matter of his own requests for Customhouse positions. By restricting the charges to the issues of efficiency and fiscal responsibility he hoped to sway that great majority of Senators who equated those crusty concepts with Holy Writ.

After the letter was read, according to reports, Conkling took the Senate floor and bitterly attacked the administration, calling its charges flimsy and unconvincing. Twisting facts conveniently, he contended that not a single piece of evidence against Arthur's administration of the Customhouse had come to light since the President had twice offered him responsible and important foreign missions. Conkling opposed the publication of Sherman's letter and asked for time to permit the construction of replies by Arthur and Cornell. On a motion by Senator Edmunds, the Senate voted to refer Sherman's charges to the commerce committee for investigation.[25]

That evening Conkling wrote a letter to Arthur—in Albany, no doubt continuing work on behalf of Conkling's impending reelection—informing him of the day's events and telling of his intention to forward a copy of Sherman's letter immediately. "Please show or tell this to Mr. Cornell."[26]

The commerce committee met on January 16 but decided to take no further action until its chairman had secured his reelection to the Senate.[27]

Four days later the Republican caucus gathered in the new assembly chamber in Albany. The floor and galleries were packed, and spectators were standing in the aisles; ladies had arrived two hours early to avoid the crush. Amid the sea of faces, illuminated by the steamy bright light of gas jets, could be seen Chester Arthur, Alonzo Cornell, John F. Smyth, Jacob Patterson, and Richard Crowley. They had done their work well: Conkling was the unanimous choice of the caucus. E. L. Godkin growled, "What his success proves is the enormous power which 'the machine' still possesses over the party, and the skill with which Mr. Conkling uses it."[28] Arthur and his colleagues had undoubtedly assured party leaders of Conkling's victory over the administration and of their own return to power; they had no history of pessimism. But the Senator still had to prove that he could successfully retain the keys to the Customhouse, for without them his forthcoming term, even perhaps his well-known desire to return Grant to the White House, might dissolve into mere frustration.

No time was wasted. The next day Conkling, Arthur, and John Lydecker were huddled together in New York City mapping strategy for the impending contest in the Senate; Cornell was expected shortly. That evening, at a gathering of the city's Republican Central Committee, Arthur and George Bliss were greeted with a wild demonstration in their honor by the 145 members in attendance. The machine was ready to fight back. "Granny Hayes," as Conkling contemptuously referred to the President, was about to learn where in the pantheon of power he properly belonged.[29]

The administration's direct appeal to the Senate, however, seemed to be having effect. Democrats were reported changing their minds, being unwilling to appear to condone neglect of public duty and inefficiency in the collection of public revenue for the sake of Senate custom. One Republican Senator was quoted as saying that if Conkling failed to answer Sherman's charges he would have to abandon his effort to scuttle the nominations.[30]

The machine was prepared. Arthur's formal reply to the Secretary of the Treasury was presented to the commerce committee by its chairman on January 23. With a vote to reject the administration's nominees in his pocket, Conkling went before the Senate on January 27 and had the ex-collector's rejoinder read aloud in executive session.

The letter, signed by Arthur but bearing more than a little trace of Conkling's pen, oozed with self-righteousness and conceded virtually nothing. It dripped with venom and held back little to convince readers of the administration's unprovoked villainy. It began:

> . . . my suspension was not only directly contrary to all the professions of the Administration, but was a violation of every principle of justice. When an Administration deliberately avows and constantly reiterates that removal from office is to take place only for cause, it is obvious,

no matter what may be said to the contrary, that a removal must, at least in the estimation of that portion of the public which has faith in the sincerity of the Administration, carry with it a stigma upon the character of the removed officer, and this stigma is not fully removed even if the first notice of intended removal is accompanied—as was the case with me—with an urgent offer of an important foreign appointment under another department of the Government.

Arthur repeated his claim that the Jay Commission had been handpicked to assassinate his character and that its methods were biased and unjust. Moreover, he condemned Sherman for "carefully and prudently" concealing the commission's evidence from public scrutiny. He chided the secretary for overlooking his claim to have authored a majority of the Jay Commission's recommendations, and demanded to know specifically how or in what ways he obstructed the implementation of the recommendations. He also questioned Sherman's rather obvious failure to discuss civil service reform. "The mode of appointment and removal, the terms of office, and the general civil service policy of my administration, which constituted the chief burden of one at least of the Jay reports, seems to have been so successfully defended by me that the Secretary abstained from any reference to it." The Meredith Committee was briskly and adroitly dismissed as irrelevant, for its report was dated July 17 and the collector had been suspended July 11. "It would have been at least prudent if Mr. Sherman had paid a little attention to these dates."

Sherman's allegations were "unfounded" and "insincere," Arthur wrote, and their author was guilty of "studied indefiniteness." He was a man who sent "Special Agents" to the Customhouse to "gather gossip and impute crime when they cannot detect it." "It should be borne in mind that the Collector can incur no new or increased expense, cannot appoint a single additional subordinate, or change the compensation of any one without the express and special authority of the Secretary of the Treasury." And Sherman should explain much of his own conduct, Arthur said, charging him with revoking the dismissal of a Customhouse employee who had taken bribes, "avowedly on the ground that prominent politicians requested it," and with abetting the continued distribution of illegal "free permits" which allowed imported goods to escape duties.

The former collector defended his opposition to personnel cuts and claimed that because of them merchants had suffered serious and costly delays. He added, in the artful language familiar to all attorneys, "I am informed, though I have not had time to verify the report, that the force has, since my suspension, been much increased by the appointment of other subordinates, temporary and permanent; and that the amount paid for salaries under the Acting Collector's administration during the latter half of 1878 is considerably larger than was paid under my administration during the first half of the same year." He also defended his tardiness in arriving at the Customhouse. "I can only say that I found it constantly necessary to work at my house, where I could escape interruption in the examination of voluminous papers, and perplexing questions constantly coming before me, but that I always made it a rule to finish the work of the day before I left the Custom-house, though that frequently required me to remain there far into the evening."

Arthur's self-image was that of a faithful, conscientious, innovative, reform-minded public servant who had fallen victim to the cynical persecution of an administration bent on purging the federal service of its opponents with or without cause. "When communicating to me my suspension, Mr. Sherman expressly informed me that from the outset there had been no wavering in the determination to remove me, but it had been delayed by accidental causes which he mentioned, among which he did not state the one he now impliedly admits, viz.: a desire to avoid the control of the Senate."

Cornell's response totaled a mere four sentences, as he had not been the object of Sherman's letter to the Senate. His official conduct was faultless, he wrote Conkling, and his suspension "undoubtedly had its origin in my refusal to surrender my personal and political rights"— which meant his unwillingness to obey the presidential order to abstain from the practice of political manipulation.[31]

Sherman let it be known immediately that he wished to reply to these letters, and the Senate, over Conkling's objections, postponed action for two days. It also decided to give Arthur the right to respond further should the secretary raise new allegations.[32]

Conkling then privately informed Arthur of the most recent events and told him of Stalwart Senator Stephen Dorsey's wish that he be present in Washington. He concluded, "The Albany petition of which I hear, bespeaks some strange misleading of our friends. I am sorry about it." The petition, signed by forty-one Republicans from the New York Assembly and forwarded to Washington, called for the confirmation of Merritt in the name of party harmony. It also desired to see the conflict settled before Democrats assumed the reins of the Senate on March 4.[33]

On January 31, a presidential secretary appeared at the doors of the Senate with what a reporter called "a wheelbarrow-load of documents." The Senate quickly suspended its normal fare of business and went into executive session in preparation for the resumption of the Customhouse battle. The documents, made available to all interested

Senators, were the papers of the Jay Commission, which Arthur said had been "carefully and prudently" concealed by Sherman. The administration was pulling out all the stops to win confirmation for its nominees, and had ready for distribution a printed sixteen-page pamphlet containing messages to the Senate by the President and the Secretary of the Treasury.

Hayes's brief message got to the point quickly. The New York Customhouse, he said, collected two thirds of the government's customs revenue and was of national significance. "The officers suspended by me are, and for several years have been, engaged in the active personal management of the party politics of the city and State of New York. The duties of the offices held by them have been regarded as of subordinate importance to their partisan work. Their offices have been conducted as part of the political machinery under their control. They have made the custom-house a centre of partisan political management." Cleverly alluding to Stalwart Thomas L. James's efficient handling of the New York City post office, Hayes argued that the Customhouse too could be made a nonpartisan business office instead of a machine headquarters. "But under the suspended officers the custom-house would be one of the principal political agencies in the State of New York. To change this, they profess to believe, would be, in the language of Mr. Cornell, in his response, 'to surrender their personal and political rights.'" The President pledged "to do all in my power to introduce into this great office the reforms which the country desires." "I regard it as my plain duty to suspend the officers in question, and to make the nominations now before the Senate, in order that this important office may be honestly and efficiently administered."

Sherman's political future appeared to hang on the outcome of this struggle, and the secretary's very lengthy letter to the Senate recounted virtually every major piece of evidence against Arthur, Cornell, and Lydecker collected over the past twenty-one months. To all but the blindest partisans it was an awesome defense of the President's message that left Arthur's pristine pretensions in ruins. And for anyone who wished to challenge or verify anything in the secretary's letter there was that "wheelbarrow-load of documents" awaiting inspection on the Vice-President's desk. Sherman wrote:

> If to secure the removal of an officer it is necessary to establish the actual commission of a crime, by proofs demanded in a court of justice, then it is clear that the case against Mr. Arthur is not made out, especially if his answer is held to be conclusive, without reference to the proofs on the public records, and tendered to the committee and the Senate.

But, if it is to be held that to procure the removal of Mr. Arthur it is sufficient to reasonably establish that gross abuses of administration have continued and increased during his incumbency; that many persons have been regularly paid on his rolls who rendered little or no service; that the expenses of his office have increased while collections have been diminishing; that bribes or gratuities in the nature of bribes have been received by his subordinates in several branches of the custom-house; that efforts to correct these abuses have not met his support, and that he has not given to the duties of the office the requisite diligence and attention, then it is submitted that the case is made out. This form of proof the Department is prepared to submit.[34]

When the messages had been read, Conkling rose from his seat, angrily spat out a string of denunciations, and then called for a vote on the nominations. When a motion was made to postpone the balloting over the weekend, Conkling objected. But the motion carried 36 to 26. It was a test vote, and sophisticated observers were convinced that the administration had all but won the contest.[35]

John Sherman, however, was taking no chances, for he knew that Conkling would stop at nothing to prevent the loss of *his* Customhouse. The secretary spent the weekend writing letters to prominent Senators and visiting their homes. He was quite blunt with Senator Aldrich: "If the restoration of Arthur is insisted upon, the whole liberal element will be against us and it will lose us tens of thousands of votes without doing a particle of good." "Arthur will not go back into the office. This contest will be continued, and the only result of all this foolish madness will be to compel a Republican administration to appeal to a Democratic Senate for confirmation of a collector at New York. It is a most fatal mistake."[36] That may not have echoed the President's ringing appeal for civil service reform, but it was a sound, practical argument for supporting the nominations.

Hayes eagerly awaited what he hoped would be the final clash with the Stalwarts. If he emerged victorious, he told his diary, he would "lay down the law to my New York offices according to the doctrines of the strictest sect of Civil Service reformers." "I shall say to Gen Merritt disregard all influence, all solicitation, all pressure—even if it come from me, or his immediate chief, the Secy of the Treasury."[37]

The President may have been anticipating Conkling's final ploy. For when the Senator took the floor on February 3, after reading a last, rather caustic reply from Arthur, he waved before his colleagues a packet of letters which contained, he proudly announced, John Sherman's private appeals for Customhouse patronage. The letters could only have come, of course, from Arthur; in revealing them to the Senate (and, indirectly, to the public) Conkling was openly acknowledging his authority over the former collector. Conkling read one of the letters aloud and described the contents of several others. He then launched into a ninety-minute oration, castigating Sherman and damning Hayes for his "petty, perverse spite."

The appearance of the letters, according to one report, "created a profound sensation," and perhaps caught Sherman by surprise. Gentlemen, let alone leaders of the same party, did not stoop to disclosure of private political correspondence. (Sherman later said he did not think Arthur's action "honorable.") Had Hayes known of the requests at the time they were written? Undoubtedly not. But he learned of them subsequently, at the latest when word of their existence was leaked to the press.

The administration was most forcefully supported during the tense, exhausting seven-hour executive session by Democratic Senator Thomas F. Bayard, who said that he looked at the issue from a nonpartisan point of view and argued that a President must have the right to select his subordinates. He was also quick to state that he felt there was sufficient cause for the removal of Chester Arthur.

When the final tally was taken, Conkling, Arthur, Cornell, and the entire machine went down to defeat. Merritt's nomination was confirmed 33 to 24, and Burt's carried 31 to 18; Surveyor Graham's nomination was confirmed handily four days later. In the Merritt vote thirteen Republicans joined twenty Democrats in supporting the administration. It seems certain that Bayard's argument was persuasive. There were also reports that Democrats had been offended by Conkling's disclosure of the Sherman letters and by his attack upon the President. But it was the switch of Republican votes that carried the day; only six Republicans had supported the nominations of Roosevelt and Prince.[38] The similarity of the final vote with the vote to postpone, taken before Conkling's display of temper on February 3, suggests that many Republican Senators were impressed by the administration's case against Arthur and Cornell, as well as by the reforms initiated under Merritt. Sherman's activities over the weekend no doubt also bore fruit.[39]

Messages of congratulation flooded the White House when news of the vote was learned. E. L. Godkin thought the event "an effective blow struck at what is worst in the present system." As for Conkling, "It will rob him of the allegiance and confidence of scores of 'henchmen,' and reduce him before long to the sorry plight of having to maintain himself in public life by useful industry and by application to serious public questions."[40]

Elated by the victory, Hayes confided to Curtis, "This ends the

Senatorial courtesy pretension." But he promptly added, "The ground we placed it on viz, that public offices ought not to be party machines adds also to the value of the result." Determined to fulfill his commitment to his diary, he wrote a letter to Merritt on February 4, which said in part: "My desire is that your office shall be conducted on strictly business principles, and according to the rules which were adopted on the recommendation of the civil service commission by the administration of General Grant. In making appointments and removals of subordinates you should be perfectly independent of mere influence. Neither my recommendation, nor Secretary Sherman's, nor that of any member of Congress, or other influential persons should be specially regarded." As an expression of this principle, but also as a gesture to heel the gaping wounds of intraparty strife, Hayes added, "Let no man be put out merely because he is Mr. Arthur's friend, and no man put in merely because he is our friend."[41]

CHAPTER EIGHT

On the Battlefield

ARTHUR RETURNED to the practice
of law when suspended from the collectorship and managed to secure
enough office work from his many friends and acquaintances to keep mod-
erately busy and affluent. He was not pressed for funds; his huge income
during the Customhouse years had enabled him to increase his investments
in land, and at the death of his mother-in-law in 1878 he and Nell inherited a modest sum of money. But law had not been Arthur's principle
interest since the Civil War, and it was now merely a sideline. His
absorbing concern continued to be machine politics, a field, unlike law,
in which he was considered a skilled practitioner.

Leaders of the Conkling machine, like Stalwarts throughout the
country, were anxiously awaiting the time when Hayes and his prissy,
pristine friends would politely remove themselves from Washington,
enabling "real" Republicans to make an all-out effort to return Ulysses
S. Grant to the White House. Since May 1877, the former President,
his wife, a son, and a reporter from the New York *Herald* had been
traveling across the world, enjoying lavish affairs of state that kept the
stolid little general's name continuously in the press. As early as the summer of 1878, support for a third term was swelling throughout the North,
and when Republicans lost control of the Senate as well as the House
that fall, political forecasters were saying that the "election means
Grant." In early April 1879, *The New York Times* published what is
called a nationwide poll of voters containing evidence of an overwhelming Republican desire for Grant.[1]

No one, of course, could surpass Roscoe Conkling and his lieutenants
in their devotion to the cause. In anticipation of the nominating con-

vention in June 1880, it was imperative, despite the loss of the Custom-house, to retain a firm grip on New York Republicanism: to make what-ever alliances were necessary, to win as many offices as possible, to crush opposition within the party wherever it appeared. The burden of this task fell in great part on the shoulders of the ex-collector; the large, im-peccably dressed, carefully coiffured, polished politician to whom several observers would soon refer as the "Gentleman Boss."

Arthur would later tell an interviewer that he first accurately measured his political influence when he left the Customhouse.[2] That is no doubt true, for without the burdens of government office and investigation he was able to devote almost all of his time to Conkling's interests. In February 1879, he became the permanent president of the Republican Central Committee, the ruling body of city Republicanism and the heart of the statewide machine. When conducted to the platform after the vote he said that the election in the fall of a governor would have an important bearing on the presidential contest in 1880, and he pledged his earnest and undivided zeal in both contests and requested the same of his listeners. He was among friends: Tom Murphy was the committee's treasurer, and Patterson, Bliss, Cregan, and Biglin sat on its executive committee.[3]

A few weeks later the Conkling organization was jolted by the news that Mayor Cooper had betrayed his political alliance with Republicans and had fired Joel Erhardt from the Board of Police Commissioners for neglect of duty and inefficiency. Erhardt and his friend De Witt C. Wheeler had been placed on the hypothetically nonpartisan board in an Arthur-Tilden deal of 1875 and were the body's only Republicans. After several weeks of bickering, Arthur and Cornell paid a visit to the mayor to persuade him to retain the lubricious Mr. Erhardt. Wheeler and George Sharpe traveled to Albany and pushed a bill through the As-sembly designed to prevent Cooper from tampering with machine patronage. *The New York Times* angrily editorialized: "the whole contest is a vulgar and selfish scramble for the spoils of office, rather than a struggle for any well-defined requirements of public interest."[4]

Pressure was such that the mayor capitulated, nominating Steve French to replace Erhardt, and naming two other machine workers, Cornelius Van Cott and Jake Hess, to other sinecures. The issue then passed to the Board of Aldermen, which had the authority to approve or reject the nominations. This board was composed of nine Tammany men, seven anti-Tammanyites, and six Republicans. Receiving no cooperation from the anti-Tammanyites, Arthur met with John Kelly and struck a bargain that resulted in passage of the nominations. Even a contract of sorts was involved. George Bliss wrote to Kelly, in a letter understandably marked "Personal," "The arrangement will be carried out. That there may be no mistake, I enclose a mem[orandum] of its terms. The last clause I added, as one that we did not speak about today, but which we arranged before." A New York Stalwart would later be quoted as saying, "Arthur and Kelly were both Irish, and rather fond of each other. Kelly had once started to become a priest and Arthur was a preacher's son. Through Tom Murphy and other Catholics, Kelly and Arthur had a very good understanding."[5]

When the central committee next met, members laughingly said that John Kelly had been called upon to preside and declared themselves part of the uptown branch of Tammany Hall. One former judge told a reporter, "It is no secret that Gen. Arthur has all the Republican Aldermen, except the one who voted against Mr. French, under such efficient discipline as to be able to direct their movements as absolutely as a skillful officer on the battle-field directs the movements of his men."[6]

The police commissioners soon returned to the news when Clint Wheeler was charged with having deficiencies in his official accounts of over $8,000. His case was not helped by the fact that he had declared personal bankruptcy a short time earlier. (His debts totaled $147,275; his annual salary was $2,500.) George Bliss and a young machine attorney named Elihu Root (who had defended Erhardt) quickly came to Wheeler's defense and, in a highly unusual move, obtained a writ preventing the commissioner's removal by the mayor. Matters were stalled for months, when finally Arthur was able to secure a safe replacement for Wheeler: Joseph C. Pinckney, formerly of "Hand-Over" Street.[7]

However effective his lieutenants were in maintaining the machine's authority in New York City, Roscoe Conkling suffered two serious blows to his political future in 1879. On the floor of the Senate in mid-June he got into a shouting match with Mississippi Senator Lucius Q. C. Lamar over an army appropriation bill. The language employed, described by *The New York Times* as "violent and offensive, beyond anything ever before heard in that body," suggested the certainty of a duel. At one point Conkling stormed at the former Confederate general:

> Let me be more specific, Mr. President. Should the member from Mississippi, except in the presence of the Senate, charge me, by intimation or otherwise, with falsehood, I would denounce him as a blackguard, as a coward, and a liar; and understanding what he said as I have, the rules and proprieties of the Senate are the only restraint upon me.

Lamar sternly replied: "Mr. President, I have only to say that the Senator from New York understood me correctly. I did mean to say just precisely the words, and all that they imported." But then, curiously, Conkling did nothing. He had prided himself for years on his athletic prowess and manliness; he was an amateur boxer; it was rumored that he always carried a pistol. He strutted, he preened, he commanded, and men were withered by his gaze. But now, suddenly, his masculine mystique, his cultivated air of swaggering bravado dissolved when put to the test; that enormous chip on his shoulder was struck to the ground and he could but sit in silence. David S. Berry recalled, "It was the beginning of his loss of prestige in the Senate and with the public." Senator John J. Ingalls of Kansas wrote, "Mr. Conkling never seemed quite the same afterward. His prestige was gone. His enemies—and they were many—exulted in his discomfiture." Blaine told a friend, "Oh, it was exceedingly rich! I don't think I ever saw Conkling's wattles quite so red."[8]

Two months later, newspapers all over the country contained stories of an awkward tangle between Conkling and the outraged husband of a famous woman. During the 1860s, Kate Chase had been the toast of Washington, where her father, Salmon P. Chase, served as Secretary of the Treasury and as Chief Justice of the Supreme Court. A tall, slender, auburn-haired beauty, she was the apogee of high fashion from Lincoln's Administration on, and was famous for her vivacity as well as her abilities as a hostess. In 1863 she married the tempestuous and alcoholic war governor and Senator from Rhode Island, William Sprague. It was largely a political alliance, doomed almost from the start, and Kate found solace in the strength of her father and the plenitude of her husband's wealth. With the death of Justice Chase and the collapse of the Sprague fortune in the Depression of 1873, Kate became enmeshed in an affair with the handsome Senator from New York, long estranged from his own wife. By 1875, Conkling and Mrs. Sprague made little effort to conceal their romance. They were seen together often, they met in Europe in 1877, and she frequently appeared in the Senate gallery to admire her lordly paramour. In fact, she was present when Conkling and Lamar had their bitter exchange, and the story circulated that she had almost fainted. When Kate's financial difficulties became acute, Conkling introduced legislation that exempted the Chase estate from taxation, a concession transparently based upon the distinguished record of the Chief Justice.

The affair became everybody's business in August 1879. Conkling was a guest at the Sprague home in Rhode Island during one of the former governor's many absences, when suddenly Sprague appeared at three o'clock in the morning carrying a shotgun. The first version of the story had it that a servant warned Conkling in advance, and he was able to flee through a window, leaving behind his belongings. At any rate, the next morning Conkling was again chased from the house by the armed husband, and later, at a nearby restaurant, there was an ugly scene between the two men that was observed by several fascinated bystanders.[9]

Few stories so captured the imaginations of Conkling's enemies as the tale of his escape through a bedroom window clutching his trousers. Politicians grinned, businessmen leered, women clucked at the haughty Senator's embarrassment. President Hayes wrote in his diary, "The Conkling scandal is the newspaper sensation of the time. This exposure of C's rottenness will do good in one direction. It will weaken his political power, which is bad and only bad."[10] Conkling, of course, refused to appear ruffled and made no official comment; he preferred to treat the matter as more twaddle spread by demented gossips and reformers. United States Senators were elected by politicians, not the public, and he felt perfectly capable of coping with officeholders.

The elections of 1879 were of particular importance to New Yorkers because for the first time all of their chief state officers were to be elected at one time. Arthur had been mentioned for the governor's chair but declined to run, no doubt because of his unwillingness to campaign for office and because of Cornell's intense desire for the position.[11] Alonzo Cornell was not a popular man (even Arthur did not care for him, reportedly finding him rather rude and vulgar); he held no credentials qualifying him as the chief executive of the nation's most populous state; in fact, he bore the stigma of removal from federal office. His very nomination would be a slap at the administration and a further threat to party unity. But what did Conkling care about qualifications or "Granny" Hayes? Cornell was a loyal and hard-working lieutenant; for that alone he deserved to be governor—Conkling's governor. The Senator desired the office and its patronage not only to enhance his local power but also to bolster his position at the nominating convention. Politicians all over the nation kept an eye on New York, for the outcome of its political contests would clearly influence the selection of a national ticket in 1880.

Conkling, Arthur, Tom Murphy, and numerous other Stalwarts worked for days behind the scenes in preparation for the state convention in Saratoga. *The New York Times* reported: "The tyranny of Conkling & Co. has been exercised to its fullest extent in the canvass for Cornell . . ." So many officeholders were soon on hand that Curtis was prompted to remind Hayes, "Should this conduct be disregarded by the Executive the same means will secure the State Presidential convention next year."[12] The meeting went smoothly. Arthur was appointed chairman of the Committee on Organization, and Conkling was elected temporary chairman. In a short speech, the Senator drew cheers with a reference to "the modest soldier who had crushed the rebellion." Cornell was nominated on the first ballot, and the other top slots—with one exception—also went to machine candidates. The new state committee included Arthur (soon named its chairman), Van Wyck, Wheeler, Patterson, Van Cott, Shook, Sharpe, Smyth, Johnson, Vrooman, Knapp, Platt, and Glidden—to a man sympathetic with Conkling's aspirations for "the modest soldier."

Still, careful observers noticed that Cornell had received only 234 of the 450 votes on the first ballot—a mere eight votes more than the required majority. Three years earlier, at Syracuse, the machine had defeated a move to free delegates from the requirement of voting for Conkling at the national convention by a vote of 251 to 113. Those statistics could be interpreted as revealing a 33 percent increase in opposition to the Stalwart manipulators.[13]

While most Republicans felt obligated to support their party, there was not great enthusiasm for the ticket. One young journalist named Richard Bowker went so far as to organize a campaign to persuade Republicans to vote for all members of the ticket except Cornell and Howard Soule, the unsavory nominee for state engineer. His slogan was "We propose not to bolt but to scratch!" and the "Scratchers" were able to raise over $5,000 for their drive and win editorial support from Godkin and Curtis. When Republicans criticized Curtis for his position, he resigned from his county convention, defiantly proclaiming the right to support honest men regardless of party.[14]

Whatever damage such independence threatened to Cornell's campaign was offset by John Kelly. The fiery boss of Tammany Hall had fallen out with Governor Lucius Robinson over patronage dispensation, and when the Tilden forces renominated Robinson, Kelly bolted, choosing to run for governor himself. He entered the race, he declared, for the purpose of defeating the regular Democratic ticket, and everyone knew that the defection would have precisely that result. But there may have been more to his move than mere hatred for Robinson and Tilden. In light of his alliance with Arthur, Kelly might well have assumed that he could more often have his way with the Conkling machine than with his traditional allies. One New York Stalwart later said flatly that Kelly's candidacy had been arranged by Arthur to insure Cornell's victory.[15] *The New York Times* editorialized at the time: "People can hardly be blamed for jumping to the conclusion that if John Kelly is to find his chief support among Republicans in New York City, he is not likely to be denied similar help at Albany." Arthur denied having any tie with Kelly, just as Conkling had denied his flirtation with Tilden during the months when his election to the presidency seemed certain.

Evarts passed the assurance on to Washington, where it was no doubt greeted with skepticism.[16]

As chairman of both the city's central committee and the state committee, Chester Arthur was in charge of the entire Republican campaign. Fifty years old, he had been participating in election drives most of his life, and had "studied" under such masters of campaign management as Weed and Morgan. He was now wholly in his element, and expressed relief at being freed from the "drudgery and constant assault" associated with the Customhouse. Many observers came away from the struggles of that fall deeply impressed by Arthur's ability to collect and administer party resources. *The New York Times*, while it occasionally censured him on other grounds, commented:

> The committees of both parties have worked . . . as committees seldom worked before. Gen. Chester A. Arthur, the Chairman of the Republican organization, has been most conspicuous in this respect. His unbounded energy and scrupulous attention to the most minute detail have astonished even those who knew him to be a man of much resource and executive ability. In all parts of the State his praises are sounded by county committeemen and others who have been associated with him in the conduct of the canvass.[17]

Among Arthur's tasks was the recruitment of speakers to perform at hundreds of meetings held in every city and village in the state. Sometimes the speechmakers were local officials or dignitaries, but Arthur also attempted to import some of the party's most prominent figures. Among those who received personal letters from the state committee chairman were Schurz, Evarts, and Sherman. The irony was obvious: here was the ex-collector requesting administration assistance to enhance the political fortunes of the ex-naval officer. As might be expected, Carl Schurz sent his regrets. But Evarts and Sherman consented to appear.[18]

Evarts, being a New Yorker with continuing political aspirations, had little choice. He spoke at the Cooper Institute on October 21, and his long talk was distinguished by its warning against Scratchers. Godkin was furious with him for his condescension, and called his speech "indecent." Curtis thought the Secretary of State "unspeakable."[19] (Vice-President Wheeler, in a similar political position, was obliged to tell one rural audience: "Mr. Cornell is a man of spotless integrity, of rare good judgment, and of high executive capacity.")[20]

John Jay was equally outraged at Sherman for his willingness to campaign for Cornell. He fired off a personal protest to the Treasury Secretary and followed it up with a public letter demanding that the gubernatorial candidate and his associates endorse the civil service clause of the 1876 Republican platform. Sherman's reply to Jay blandly stressed the need for Republican victory.[21] But beneath the platitudes, as Jay surely knew, was Sherman's burning desire for the presidential nomination. He could not get far without at least some of New York's votes, and if the drive for Grant somehow sputtered there was the chance of winning them all. It would be difficult to placate Cornell and Arthur after the events of recent months, but he could hardly afford not to try.

Sherman appeared at a huge rally in New York City on October 27, and was escorted to the stage by Arthur. Toward the close of a lengthy and rather dull address, he startled listeners by declaring: "I know of no objection to Mr. Cornell's personal character or his ability to discharge faithfully the duties of the high office for which he is nominated. I can say for the President that . . . he has openly expressed his desire for the success of the entire Republican ticket. As for myself, I regard the election of Mr. Cornell as of the highest national importance, and if I had a thousand votes and a thousand voices they would all be for him."[22]

Zachariah Chandler also answered Arthur's call, as did Blaine, Emory Storrs, William Woodin, Eugene Hale, and Benjamin Brewster of Pennsylvania. It was a time of dizzying activity, and Arthur rarely left the state committee's headquarters at the swank Fifth Avenue Hotel.

One evening, however, he and Clint Wheeler dropped in on a festive meeting conducted by Jake Patterson's Tenth Assembly District Association. The flag-draped platform was bordered by huge portraits of Grant and Cornell. The crowd sang "Marching Through Georgia," "Rally Round the Flag," and "John Brown's Body." Then Hamilton Ward, the party's candidate for Attorney General, gave a rousing speech in which he expressed hope that the state could be carried by a majority of 100,000 so that New York might be in the vanguard of those who would fight for the presidential nomination of "the great man before whom two continents stood uncovered."[23] Grant had landed at San Francisco a few days earlier, ending his worldwide travels. The Stalwart vision was lucent.

No one had to ask Roscoe Conkling to get to work. He feverishly crisscrossed the state giving speeches. Few could remember seeing him work quite as hard for a ticket. He told an audience in Canton, "by all I have learned by years of experience in public life, I believe that, with one possible exception, there has not been an election in a quarter of a century where it was more momentous that every vote should be cast for the right."[24] That "possible exception" was no doubt held in 1860.

The campaign in New York was financed in the traditional way. Arthur not only circulated among wealthy businessmen, as he had for almost twenty years, but also signed the state committee's assessment circulars, mailed to opulent party members.[25] Under the shelter of Hayes's inconsistent approval of "voluntary contributions" there was also activity in the Customhouse. According to Curtis, the state committee had complete lists of employees and their "contributions" over the past two years, and Arthur directed the distribution of assessment circulars accordingly. In addition, Joseph Pinckney reopened an office and sent small cards to Customhouse workers informing them of his presence. The assessment figure was 2 percent, and to exact the required sum the traditional threats of dismissals were purportedly made.[26]

The results of the election were mixed. Republicans won every state office but that of state engineer, and solidly controlled the state legislature—thus insuring the selection of a Republican Senator in 1881. Cornell drew 418,567 votes to Robinson's 375,000. But the governor's race was decided by Kelly, who won 77,566 votes, and the combined total of Democratic ballots made the state doubtful in the forthcoming presidential race. Moreover, Cornell ran far behind the rest of the Republican ticket, winning almost 20,000 fewer votes than the new controller, the only nominee lacking machine backing.[27]

Still, Conkling had the right to feel pleased. Despite his loss of the Customhouse and his humiliating confrontations with Senator Lamar and William Sprague, he emerged from the elections in full command of New York's Republican machinery. He controlled the governor's office and the state legislature, and wielded great influence in the city's operation. He would soon have a Republican colleague, and it was not long before he began to consider Chester Arthur for the position.

City Republicans held their own in the elections, and as long as they continued their alliance with Kelly could retain their authority.[28] But it was not simply the alliance that worried George Bliss, the only member of the machine disturbed by John Smyth's defalcation. For months he had pled with Arthur to root out the corruption within the city machine itself. Association membership lists were padded with names of Democrats and the deceased, they were kept secret in violation of the party constitution, and were employed to prevent recalcitrant Republicans from voting in party elections. Of the some 13,000 names on the rolls, Bliss claimed, less than 6,000 were legitimate. Arthur took no action, so in desperation his long-time friend wrote him a public letter, calling attention to "the rottenness of the organization," and begging him "as the very capable head of the Republican Party in the City" to enact reforms. "A word from you will do this." Bliss had tried to work for changes internally, he explained, but "I have accomplished little except to receive the sneers and slurs of those who glory in fraud because they profit in it, and whose approval is a disgrace to any honorable man."[29]

Bliss must have reminded Arthur of Silas Burt; it was irritating to see old acquaintances succumb to the feminine mushiness of "do-gooders." Party machinery in the city continued to function in its accustomed fashion.

Right after New Year's Day, 1880, Arthur and Police Commissioners French and Wheeler left for Albany to do their part in shaping the structure of the legislature. Within two days of their arrival George Sharpe was selected unanimously by the Republican caucus to be Assembly Speaker—the third of the former Customhouse officials to be "vindicated," as partisans put it. One of the Speaker's most important duties was the appointment of committees, and Arthur was assisting Sharpe with that task when he was suddenly called home by a telegram telling of the critical illness of his wife.[30]

Friends told reporters that Nell's attack of pneumonia was the result of nervous and physical exhaustion brought on by a trip to France to bring home the remains of her deceased mother, and this explanation has become standard.[31] In fact, Nell had left for France in April 1878, hoping to find her mother alive, and when she arrived too late, decided to remain abroad for a short time with her daughter and maid to shop and visit relatives. However rattled she may have been at the time, her return to New York had occurred some nineteen months before she contracted her fatal sickness. The bad cold which developed into pneumonia was caught on the evening of January 10 while waiting outdoors for a carriage following a concert.[32]

The only vehicle Arthur could take from Albany on a Sunday morning was a milk train that crept agonizingly downstate. He arrived late in the evening and rushed home to find Nell under the influence of morphine administered by her physician. She was never to regain consciousness. Arthur remained at her bedside for more than twenty-four hours until it was all over. She was only forty-two.[33]

Funeral services were held at the Church of the Heavenly Rest on Fifth Avenue, and the city machine turned out almost to a man. The State Assembly passed a resolution of sympathy and adjourned in Arthur's honor. A delegation from both houses of the legislature accompanied the governor to the Rural Cemetery in Albany where Nell was buried in the family plot.[34]

Arthur was shattered by the bereavement. R. G. Dun saw him the evening after the death and described him as "completely unnerved & prostrated." At home after the graveside service, he paced up and down Twenty-ninth Street between Third and Fifth avenues until two o'clock in the morning pouring out his grief to Tom Murphy. A month later a cousin thought him little improved.[35] He had deeply loved his wife, and over the more than twenty years of their marriage had showered her with luxuries. But he had permitted his almost total absorption with politics to usurp his home life. Unlike Mrs. Conkling, left in Utica to putter in her garden, Nell was not endowed with vast inner resources, and she chafed at the loneliness she was forced to bear by Arthur's late hours and frequent travels. He had been unwilling to amend his habits, and death had visited amidst his neglect. However easily he could rationalize his conduct in the political arena, he would find it impossible to overcome completely the remorse that was the price of his insensitivity.

Within the last seven years of Chester Arthur's life—years in which he would reach the pinnacle of political success and become among the most famous men of his generation—he would wistfully confide to friends on repeated occasions how very different it all would have been had Nell been there. "Honors to me now," he told Brodie Herndon, "are not what they once were."[36]

CHAPTER NINE

A Time to Do Battle

ULYSSES S. GRANT was probably the most popular man in the country when he arrived in San Francisco in September 1879. For many Americans the nearly two and a half years of his absence had left much to be desired. The most significant achievements of the Hayes Administration—the reform of the New York Customhouse, the return of self-government to the South, and the resumption of specie payment—had earned it a host of enemies within the Republican Party. Hard times persisted, labor troubles mounted, politics seemed adrift. Some looked to the former President as a source of strength, desiring the sort of iron will Grant's battlefield reputation brought to mind. There were also those convinced that he had been broadened and deepened by his sojourn, that he had absorbed knowledge and insight and was at last prepared to become the tower of enlightened statesmanship he had promised to be in 1868. After all, it was said, he had talked with kings and skilled diplomats, he had studied a variety of political systems, and had scrutinized mankind's highest cultural achievements. People were eager to forgive and forget the dismal record of his two previous administrations. He had then been an inexperienced and well-intentioned soldier whose innocence was exploited by thieves. A new decade was about to dawn, and a new Grant, transformed by his travels, could take a firm grip on the reins of national affairs and breathe new life into the quarrelsome and divided Republican Party.

But such enchantment was fabricated out of hope. Grant's limited background and intellect made him virtually impervious to the educational opportunities of his trip. He was bored and wearied by the public receptions, the groaning banquet tables, the unintelligible languages, the huge museums full of paintings and sculptures he knew and cared nothing about. In Berne he refused to be dragged to yet another cathedral; "Why should we waste our time on any more architecture?" While in Rome, Adam Badeau took him to see the equestrian Marcus Aurelius because "I thought he would like the horse." Grant took some interest in bridges, railroads, hotels, and sewer systems, but profited little from their hasty observation. He made a good many short speeches during the tour, expressing personal thanks and stressing goodwill between nations, but his only memorable comment was the suggestion that Venice might be more attractive if the streets were drained. The narrow, phlegmatic army officer who left the White House to see the world returned unimpaired by the experience.

Stalwarts understood Grant's limitations, and had carefully planned his sojourn and loudly trumpeted his every move in the hope of returning him to the White House. His arrival in America was considered premature; six months later and he might have been escorted triumphantly across the country right into the convention hall in Chicago. But Mrs. Grant was anxious to see the children, and her husband was eager to please. As expected, Grant was greeted with huge celebrations wherever he went. From city to city, bands played, people cheered, politicians orated, and veterans turned out by the thousands to see the symbol of their long, bloody struggle. In Philadelphia, where the overseas tour had started, 60,000 people applauded him in a procession twelve miles long. He was a living flag to the roaring crowds, the greatest general of them all.

The Grant boom swelled in every section. Southern Republicans, abandoned by Hayes, looked to the general to break up the Solid South. Easterners, terrified by the specter of free silver, saw him as a bulwark against unsound money. The Chicago *Tribune* was convinced that westerners were again ready to entrust their futures to the hero of Appomattox.

Was Grant himself interested in the presidency? As usual, he said little, but it seems apparent that he was receptive to the idea almost immediately after his return. His wife made it clear to him that she wished to be White House hostess again. Continuously beset with inner doubts and personal insecurity, he quietly coveted the unsurpassed honor a third term would bestow. Moreover, Grant needed money; to live in appropriate style he was required to have employment.[1] As his procession wended its way across the states his ambition became increasingly apparent.

Grant may not have realized how desperately Stalwarts were hoping for his return to Washington. All three of the leading Stalwart machines —in New York, Pennsylvania, and Illinois—were under severe attack by early 1880, and critics claimed that without assistance from the White House their rapid disintegration was inevitable.

Don Cameron, who inherited political muscle and a Senate seat from his father, had fallen out quickly with the Hayes Administration and had lost the state legislature in 1879. His machine in Pennsylvania was tarred with such gross scandal that it was compared with the Tweed Ring. To win support for Grant's political resurrection, Cameron assumed the chairmanship of the moribund Republican National Committee. He then proceeded to call a very early state convention at which he rammed through resolutions instructing the delegation to the national convention to vote as a unit for the former President. Cameron wrote to Timothy Howe: "I had a time in my own state and could not pay much attention to other questions but am now looking southward and expect good results from that quarter. Don't get despondent [,] we will win sure and by such a majority before the convention that it will ensure Grant's election."[2]

John Logan, the swarthy boss of Illinois Republicanism, had suffered defeat in his bid for reelection to the Senate in 1877 and won a seat two years later with great difficulty. Shortly before the national conclave of 1880 opened, he secured his state convention for Grant but was forced to resort to unorthodox parliamentary maneuvers which resulted in contested seats. (Smart enough to keep his options open, he told a Chicago *Daily News* reporter: "No man has heard me say a cruel or unjustifiable word about Mr. Blaine, Mr. Sherman, or indeed any of the gentlemen whose names have been mentioned as candidates.")[3]

Roscoe Conkling seemed stronger than either Cameron or Logan. He dominated the party's state committee and its city organization, and his new governor was busily appointing the likes of Platt and Smyth to state office.[4] When the state convention assembled on February 25 in Utica, the entire program was prearranged by Conkling and Arthur, and both men, along with Cornell and Buffalo journalist J. D. Warren, were scheduled to become delegates-at-large to Chicago. But the machine encountered stiff opposition during the convention proceedings and failed to bind New York's delegates as a unit for Grant. (One State Senator said he opposed "those who trained with John Kelly, Boss McLaughlin [of Brooklyn], and other disreputable Democrats.") The best Conkling could do was to push through a resolution stating that "the delegates this day assembled are called upon and instructed to use their most earnest and united efforts to secure his nomination." Even then, as the resolution was read aloud, one delegate shouted, "Hurrah for Blaine!"

and was rewarded with cheers. It was also noticed that the machine had lost power since 1876; a motion to free delegates of all instructions failed by only 217 to 180.[5]

As the nominating convention approached, the Grant tide perceptibly began to recede. The pageantry of Grant's return had started too early and was wearing thin. Sensing this, his managers had him pay a visit to Cuba and Mexico, to set the stage for yet another series of welcoming demonstrations. But from all over the country came indications that it would do little good. Newspapers were losing their enthusiasm, anti-third-term clubs were being formed, and several Liberal Republicans, including Carl Schurz, warned that they would abandon the Grand Old Party should Grant be nominated. No one doubted that the former President would be a formidable contender at Chicago, but by early spring other candidates and potential candidates captured the attention of the nation's Republicans.

James G. Blaine was thought by many to be the front-runner. His twelve years in the House and three years in the Senate had won him a great many admirers despite his barren legislative record and a scrape or two with corruption. He was a skilled parliamentarian, a brilliant speaker, an intelligent political strategist, and a party regular who rarely refused an invitation to campaign for others. His uncanny memory for names and faces and his often vivacious personality (marred by chronic hypochondria) contributed to his attractiveness. But the Plumed Knight had crossed swords with more than a few during his career and had a formidable array of enemies. Even his friends had reservations about him at times; he seemed a bit too expedient, a little shifty. James A. Garfield wrote in his journal in April 1880: "I like Blaine, always have, and yet there is an element in him which I distrust."[6]

By now Blaine's most avid partisans were called "Half-Breeds." No substantive issues divided them from the Stalwarts; Blaine, for example, was as opposed to civil service reform as Conkling, and voted against the nominations of Merritt and Burt. The two camps were distinguished largely by their allegiance to their leaders, two talented and intensely self-confident politicians who feuded mightily because each saw in the other a reflection of his own desire to dominate.[7]

William Chandler, Senators Hale and Frye, and Whitelaw Reid of the New York Tribune, among others, were eager for Blaine to jump into the contest for the presidential nomination. But the man from Maine held back, expressing reluctance to undertake the sort of two-fisted combat that had failed him in 1876. He would leave it to his friends: the nomination would be accepted if offered; if not, then he would work for an agreeable candidate. "Blaine for President" offices opened in Washington in February, but the Senator remained aloof. Though he wrote, "The nomination of Grant is the inevitable defeat of the Republican party and the triumph of Democracy with all its attending evils," he expressed an unwillingness to go to Chicago. As late as May 23, he told Garfield that Grant's nomination was "quite probable."[8] Nevertheless (that shiftiness again), he had a private telegraph line connected from his Washington home to the convention hall to enable him to be in touch with developments as they occurred.

John Sherman was the administration's candidate and thus enjoyed the advantage of federal patronage and influence among southern delegates. (Grant men sanctimoniously howled at what they reported were efforts by the Treasury Secretary to win convention votes through the activities of federal employees.) Many people gave him credit for the resumption of species payment which contributed to the gradual return of American prosperity, and several businessmen pledged financial assistance. But his candidacy was impaired by his frigid personality, his drabness on the podium, and by the assertion that he was pro-Catholic. Few Party leaders, including the President, were enthusiastically behind him, and no major newspaper offered its endorsement. A friend asked, "What is the use of being for Sherman when no one else is for him?"[9]

While the nation's press narrowed the probable selection to either Grant, Blaine, or Sherman, there were others thought to have at least an outside chance of winning the nomination. Many Liberal Republicans favored George Edmunds, the dour Vermont Senator whose enigmatic policies had earned him the title "the Stalwart Sweetheart of the Reformers." Grant's old friend, Elihu B. Washburne, was referred to as a dark horse. Senator William Windom of Minnesota threw his hat in the ring. And several politicians, including the cagy William Chandler, spoke of yet another possibility, the newly elected Senator from Ohio, James A. Garfield.

Garfield's personal history was well known in the Midwest and was a campaign manager's dream. Born in a log cabin and soon left fatherless, he split wood on the family farm in the Western Reserve, toiled on a canal barge, worked his way through Williams College in Massachusetts, served as a college president and lay missionary in Ohio, and in 1859, at the age of twenty-eight, was elected to the Ohio Senate. He obtained an army commission when the war broke out, distinguished himself in the clashes at Middle Creek, Kentucky, Shiloh, and Chickamauga, and rose to the rank of brigadier general. Elected to Congress in 1862, he served in the House until early 1880 when, with John Sherman's assistance, he advanced to the Senate. As Republican floor leader in the House he favorably impressed colleagues with his simplicity, tact, and eagerness to please. He was a party regular, a moderate, a pragmatist, a Hayes adviser who thought civil service reform overly idealistic. There was evidence that he had had a small hand in the Crédit Mobilier scandal, but he vigorously denied the charge, and no one considered him a dishonest man.

Hayes had long thought of Garfield as an attractive successor and so had others. By early 1880 the Senator-elect was receiving flocks of mail urging him to declare his candidacy. Garfield declared his loyalty to Ohio's official candidate and was tapped to be Sherman's chief spokesman at the nominating convention. Still, his name continued to be mentioned as a possible contender. The Norwalk *Reflector* published a straw vote of the Ohio state legislature that read: Grant 30, Garfield 30, Blaine 28, Sherman 7. On March 2 the Toledo *Commercial* remarked: "General Garfield is not a candidate but the number who wish to see him a candidate is increasing daily." Several newspapers outside the state picked up the idea, including *The New York Times*, the Duluth *Tribune*, and the Springfield *Republican*. Garfield stuck by his commitment to Sherman, and yet did not completely rule out the possibility of his nomination. He told Wharton Baker, "if anything happened to me in that connection it would only be in case the Convention at Chicago could not nominate either of the candidates . . . ." He would not seek the honor, and would not work for it. Nevertheless, he declined to take himself irrevocably out of the race.[10]

While Arthur eagerly anticipated what he assumed would be a fruitful journey to Chicago, he spent much of the spring directing an attempt to expand the machine's authority in the City of New York. With the legislature securely in Republican hands, Arthur and his colleagues planned to rewrite legislation covering public offices in the city to favor themselves. *The New York Times* would call the effort "a partisan grab for patronage and plunder" and refer to "petty tricks of the ward politician." Several commentators would be reminded of tactics employed by Tweed.

The target of the machine's dissatisfaction with city politics was still its one-time friend Edward Cooper. The independent mayor had on several occasions refused to nominate Conklingites for public positions; at the same time, the Board of Aldermen, dominated by men representing Arthur and Kelly, had refused to confirm unfriendly nominees. The result was a standoff—several public offices bearing good salaries and patronage power had remained vacant for months. Moreover, Clint Wheeler's replacement on the police commission was soon to be named, and machine leaders valued the post highly. To overcome Cooper's obstinance, Arthur sought legislation to transfer the power of nomination from the mayor to a board controlled by Republicans.

In late April, Arthur and Commissioners French and Wheeler journeyed to the state capital and issued an invitation to all Republican legislators to what later became known as the "champagne caucus." From 10:00 P.M. until after one in the morning Senators and Assemblymen soaked up free champagne at Albany's swank Delavan House while listening to the three Conkling lieutenants. The plan, of course, was phrased somewhat delicately: city Republicans needed control of the Bureau of Elections, for example, to insure an honest count of ballots. But the point was made, and a committee of four Senators and six Assemblymen was created to draft legislation. A few days later, members of the committee traveled to Arthur's New York City home where details of the bills were polished. To blunt protests by Cooper and *The New York Times*, it was decided to place the mayor on the new board along with the president of the Board of Aldermen and the president of the police department. This did little to placate Cooper, for he knew that machine Republicans held the two offices in question and would invariably outvote him. When the bills were formally presented to the party caucus in Albany on May 5 they were approved by voice vote. Reporters were ordered out of the room during the discussion but rumors of vigorous dissent floated through the halls.[11]

Only a handful of people understood at the time that there was not only rising Republican opposition throughout the state to the Conkling organization but that the machine itself was suffering severe internal division. The enmity between Arthur and Cornell had not diminished with the gubernatorial election. And Tom Platt felt deeply abused by Conkling's selection of Arthur to fill the soon-vacant Senate seat. On March 3, Platt wrote Cornell:

> Senator Conkling sneered and snubbed me at the Convention till I made up my mind I was an idiot or he was crazy—& that in either case I had better disavow all future claims to leadership. It seems to me that the more one tries to serve him & execute his purposes the more certain he is to tyrannise over him. I don't enjoy it. While bowing to his transcendent talents & powers I do not think he possesses all the practical common sense that the State has ever produced & I believe the opinions of pigmies, like myself, are entitled to respect. I have my own views & when I am satisfied I am right I am quite as tenacious as he.[12]

Cornell had also smarted at Conkling's sneers and commands, and determined to help Platt become the state's next Senator. He was governor now, not just another spear-carrier, and he saw no reason why he should be obligated to assist the ex-collector's rise to future fame and fortune. His first step was to oppose the bills presented in the Senate and Assembly to create a new appointing board in the City of New York. He based his objection on a technicality—the constitutionality of bestowing such authority on a police commissioner. But it became known among careful political observers that the governor was eager to deny Arthur further power and was, as well, anxious to tarnish his image as an effective party leader. Sensing a shift in the political wind, Arthur's longtime associate Jake Patterson quickly defected to the new alliance.

Arthur and Cornell had a private talk about the matter—some called it a quarrel—and the governor denied any personal affiliation with Platt. But when Arthur tried to push his bills through the legislature he found that his party support had swiftly deteriorated. A test vote in the Assembly failed 59 to 39, and the bills thereafter fell from sight. All was not completely lost, for Arthur managed to have Joel Mason chosen to succeed Wheeler on the Board of Aldermen. But it was painfully clear to the boss of the city machine that Cornell's course of action raised serious doubts about his ability to be named a United States Senator by the state legislature.[13]

The Conkling machine was confronted by another challenge on May 6, when William H. Robertson of Westchester, a delegate to the national convention, informed the Albany *Evening Journal* of his decision to support Blaine. Robertson was an ex-Fentonite and a long-time office-seeker who had never forgiven Conkling for thwarting his bid for the Republican gubernatorial nomination in 1872. Stalwarts expressed shock at Robertson's announcement, pretending that all state delegates were bound to Grant, but this did little to halt the bolt from machine dictate. State Senator William Woodin quickly followed Robertson into Blaine's camp, Senators Loren B. Sessions and John Birdsall declared their independence, and ex-Sheriff Albert Dagget came out for Sherman. As the convention approached, Conklingites feared that as many as twenty of New York's seventy delegates could not be counted on.[14]

New York City's fourteen-man delegation was untouched by the rebellion, as Arthur had chosen his men with care. Tom Murphy would be going to Chicago, as would Barney Biglin, Clint Wheeler, Steve French, Jake Patterson, John O'Brien, Joel Mason, Jake Hess, Charles Blackie, Levi P. Morton, Edwards Pierrepont, John D. Lawson, Edwin W. Stoughton, and Charles E. Cornell, the governor's young son.[15] (The governor sent his alternate.) John Smyth and Arthur's private secretary Fred Phillips were also to attend, as was Alexander Powell, brought along to poll the sentiments of southern Negroes.

Arthur arrived in the Windy City five days ahead of the convention's scheduled opening in the company of French, Smyth, Pierrepont, and Phillips. He began a busy round of Stalwart strategy sessions and meetings with out-of-state delegates and jauntily predicted a first-ballot victory for Grant. When Conkling made his appearance two days later he told reporters that he refused even to contemplate a second ballot.[16]

This was the first visit by Conkling and Arthur to Chicago and it marked the first time Conkling had attended a national convention. The two men took rooms in the elegant Grand Pacific Hotel, a few doors from James Garfield's suite, and welcomed a steady stream of fellow workers and well-wishers. Outside, over the front of the hotel, fluttered a huge banner reading "New York Solid For Grant."

Stalwart strategy was highly predictable. There were 756 convention delegates and 379 votes were required to nominate. Grant men estimated that they commanded about 360 votes, that Blaine had a little more than 200, and that Sherman possessed about 80. But those figures depended upon the convention's adoption of the unit rule, by which the vote of an entire state would be decided by a majority of its delegates. Without the rule Grant would be denied 63 critical votes owned by bolters from New York, Pennsylvania, and Illinois. In the preconvention skirmishing, managers for Blaine and Sherman determined to work together to insure each delegate an individual vote. On May 29 Garfield wrote to his wife: "I find the city boiling over with politics. Everything is in the vague of vastness and uncertainty. No definite thing appears on the face of this chaos except the fact that the unit rule will be the center of battle and to that I expect to address myself. Whatever fight is in me I will make on that point."[17]

The next morning Conkling, Arthur, Logan, Carpenter, Cameron, and a number of others huddled to iron out the details of their plan of action. It was Senator Cameron's responsibility, as chairman of the national committee, to call the convention to order and wield the gavel until a temporary chairman was elected. Should the national committee name an unsympathetic candidate for the post, Stalwarts planned to nominate one of their own from the floor. When the roll was called to determine the choice, Cameron would officially declare that the unit rule prevailed. This would not only elect a pro-Grant temporary chairman but would sanction employment of the unit rule. Cameron would refuse to entertain motions concerning the rules of the convention, and his successor would simply proceed with the business at hand assuming that such questions were settled. The result would be that no vote could be taken on the unit rule that was not based on the principle itself.

News of the clever plot leaked out, and when the national committee met on May 31, Cameron was bluntly asked if he intended to pursue the scheme. The imperious Senator would not answer. He then refused to recognize a motion made against the unit rule on the ground that the committee had no jurisdiction over the matter. Stalwart hopes were based on arrogance and fantasy; twenty-nine of the forty-seven men on the committee were anti-Grant, and amid the opposition were such astute tacticians as William Chandler and Garfield. Following considerable wrangling, Cameron was informed that he would be removed as chairman if he continued to defy the majority's wishes. The committee then adjourned until the next morning.

In desperation, Stalwarts quietly approached the newly appointed sergeant-at-arms, a Grant supporter from Illinois named Colonel William E. Strong, and asked if he would refuse to recognize anyone other than Cameron as the party official entitled to call the convention to order. They hoped he would agree, providing them with leverage for the next day's session. A move to deny the committee the right to elect a new chairman would destroy any semblance of party unity and set the stage for ferocious fighting on the convention floor, but Grant men were fighting for their political lives and were determined to have their way at any cost. Strong talked to Senator Philetus Sawyer of Wisconsin about the legality of the proposal, and he in turn consulted his former colleague Timothy Howe, an experienced attorney. As devoted to Conkling as Howe was, he advised against the scheme and it was dropped.

That evening leaders of the New York delegation summoned a caucus of all Grant delegates. Only 296 appeared, and despite brave talk of at least 60 more Grant supporters the dimensions of the upcoming struggle were apparent.[18]

The next day Grant men were forced to compromise. A previous suggestion by Garfield was reluctantly accepted, and Senator George F. Hoar, an Edmunds backer, was named temporary and permanent chairman. It was a significant setback for the Stalwarts, as Hoar's selection put an end to their hope of adopting the unit rule by proclamation. Garfield assured Sherman that the unit rule was dead, but Grant leaders were far from conceding the point.[19]

The New York delegation met on convention eve. A motion by George Sharpe to pledge all state delegates to the unit rule passed by only 45 to 23, and William Woodin told reporters that the bolters retained every intention of voting as they saw fit. Stalwarts held a Grant rally later in the evening and drew no more delegates than they had the night before. Conkling urged perseverance. John Logan talked of victory on the second ballot.[20]

The streets of downtown Chicago were choked with thousands of people who were drawn by the excitement of the approaching convention. Fireworks periodically lit up the streets, carriages crashed into one another, bands blared, veterans marched, partisans laden with buttons and badges shrieked the names of an assortment of politicians equipped to save the Republic from dire peril. At the Palmer House, where a large number of delegates stayed, the main staircase was boarded up and decorated with flags surrounding a huge portrait of Grant. The management, at the last minute, constructed an even larger portrait of the general on horseback and placed a legend in gas jets behind the clerk's desk reading "Let Us Have Peace." (Anti-third-term men retaliated by hoisting a gigantic transparency that said: "Nominate Grant and Lose the Election.") Crowds were even larger at the Grand Pacific. A reporter noted, "The din and confusion is indescribable, and unpleasant to guests who are not here on political business . . . there are seats in the Convention hall for less than 10,000 persons. One would guess that not less than 50,000 people expected to find the best places to-morrow . . ."[21]

Convention day, June 2, was bright and clear, and people were out in the streets early. Hawkers milled through the throngs with souvenirs and treats; "Here's your Blaine lemonade." Most of the delegates wandered into the convention hall in small groups, but New York's delegates and alternates assembled in front of the Grand Pacific and marched in a body along Clark and Adams streets to Michigan Avenue. As the 140 men tramped along, people cheered, fell back, made way. At the head of the formidable phalanx, striding arm in arm, were Roscoe Conkling and Chester Arthur. It was a time to do battle.[22]

Exposition Hall had been lavishly decorated to greet the delegates. Flags were draped everywhere—on stage, across the galleries, around the braces supporting the arched roof. Along the sides and at the rear of the auditorium hung portraits of party greats, and overhead was a huge painting of George Washington. The galleries were adorned with shields bearing the arms of individual states and busts of famous Americans. The main platform was filled with flowers and banners and boasted a large white statue of liberty.

Don Cameron was seated on the platform that first morning of the convention, as were other members of the national committee and several distinguished guests. About a thousand newspapermen were in the press gallery, and behind them sat the delegates. New York's large contingent was placed near the front; the first two seats of its first row, on the aisle, were occupied by Conkling and Arthur. The physical stature and elegant attire of these two Stalwart leaders attracted immediate attention. Conkling quickly learned that a late entrance would draw applause and create a stir among the several thousand spectators.[23]

The first session lasted only three hours. A few brief speeches were made, Hoar was elected temporary chairman, and the rest of the time was devoted to the formation of committees. Grant men fared poorly: William E. Chandler managed to become chairman of the credentials committee, and Garfield was selected to head the committee on rules.

When the committees met, Stalwarts suffered serious setbacks. The credentials committee voted to seat two Alabama bolters who had been replaced for defying their state convention's unit rule, a decision that predicted victory for Logan's opponents in Illinois.[24] In the rules committee an anti-Grant coalition led by Garfield voted to report against the unit rule. George Sharpe, Conkling's representative on the committee, could do little more than declare his intention to issue a minority report to the convention.

That evening several Stalwarts assembled at the Palmer House to assess their position. Conkling implored his colleagues not to lose hope, assuring them that if Grant could collect 300 votes on the first ballot the additional 79 would be forthcoming. That was a great many votes to be counting on: how were they to be won? Senator Preston Plumb of Kansas reported to his delegation that Conkling handed him a blank sheet of paper and asked him to fill in any political favor it would take to bring Kansas to Grant. He promised to sign it, along with Logan and Cameron, and have Grant affix his signature if necessary.[25]

On the next day, June 3, the convention met at 11:00 A.M. and elected Hoar permanent president. Little else could be achieved until the credentials committee was prepared to make a report, and Conkling moved to retire until 6:00 P.M. Half-Breed Eugene Hale of Maine objected and persuaded a majority to remain in session; Grant men could not even win a vote to adjourn. Conkling tasted defeat again when the convention voted 406 to 318 against a Stalwart motion concerning the credentials committee. *The New York Times* observed: "It is evident, in spite of the sanguine calculations reported from the Grant headquarters, that the Blaine and Sherman men united can control the Convention . . ."[26]

Shortly after the opening prayer on Friday, June 4, Conkling moved that it be the sense of the convention that all delegates were bound in honor to support the nominee whoever it may be, and that no one intending to do otherwise be permitted a seat. According to Platt, this was aimed at a number of Independents who had threatened to turn to a Democrat should Grant be nominated. The motion was simply a call for party unity and passed 716 to 3. But Conkling's passion for crushing his opposition drove him on: he next proposed that the three dissenters (from West Virginia) be expelled from the convention. It was a silly move, guaranteed to alienate delegates, and after some turmoil the Senator was forced to abandon the idea. The most appealing remarks against the proposal came from James Garfield, whose star had been rising for several days. Conkling thought Garfield was simply advertising his own availability by his opposition, and sent him a sarcastic note: "New York requests that Ohio's real candidate and dark horse come forward. We want him in our seats while we prepare our ballots."[27]

The convention then formally turned to the unit rule. The majority reports of both the credentials committee and the rules committee strongly opposed it, while minority reports from the committees just as firmly favored it. Battle lines were clearly drawn, and delegates, newsmen, and spectators understood that at stake, rhetoric aside, was a Stalwart tactic designed to insure Grant's speedy nomination. Debate on the matter lasted sixteen hours and continued on into the next day's session. Arthur sat quietly during the shouting and speech-making, voting when called upon with the orthodoxy expected of all machine regulars. When it was over, the majority reports of the committees were upheld and the unit rule was buried. Illinois bolters were seated and a minority resolution from the rules committee was crushed 479 to 276. Rutherford B. Hayes felt confident to write in his diary: "It now seems impossible to nominate Grant."[28] But Stalwarts were not prepared to admit defeat. The anti-Grant majority was fragmented, and as long as it remained that way there was hope. George F. Hoar later recalled: ". . . the Grant leaders were still confident. They felt sure that none of their original votes, numbering three hundred and more, would desert them, and it would be impossible for the rest of the convention, divided among so many candidates, to agree, and they would in the end get a majority."[29]

The next order of business on Saturday, June 5, was the presentation of the platform. The chairman of the committee on resolutions was Arthur's friend Edwards Pierrepont, who assured delegates that he and his colleagues on the committee had labored mightily to pursue harmony within the convention. The platform called on the federal government to aid public education "to the extent of its constitutional duty"; it called for a constitutional amendment forbidding states to appropriate public funds for all (not just Roman Catholic) sectarian schools; the tariff plank declared that "duties levied for the purpose of revenue should so discriminate as to favor American labor"; congressional improvement of seacoasts and harbors was encouraged; and opposition was expressed toward polygamy, unlimited Chinese immigration, and further grants of public lands to railroads and corporations. The Hayes Administration was lauded for its "efficient, just, and courteous discharge of the public business," but nowhere was there mention of civil service reform.

When the full document had been read, a Massachusetts delegate called for a plank asking Congress to pass "thorough, radical and complete" civil service legislation. Webster Flanagan, a Stalwart delegate-at-large from Texas, then arose to speak in opposition to the proposal. "Texas has had quite enough of the civil service," he bellowed. "There is one plank in the Democratic party that I have ever admired, and that is, 'To the victors belong the spoils.' After we have won the race as we will, we will give those who are entitled to positions office. What are we up here for? I mean that members of the Republican party are entitled to office, and if we are victorious we will have office." Laughter rippled through the hall, for the frank Texan had expressed a view with which a majority of the delegates was sympathetic. A civil service plank was inserted into the platform but it was more innocuous than that passed in 1876. A provision calling for removal from office solely for cause was rejected on the ground that it would promote lifetime tenure and an officeholding class.

At ten o'clock that evening tension mounted within the convention as the business of nominating candidates at last got under way. Detroit millionaire James F. Joy presented Blaine's name. His performance was inept and dull, and at one point he urged support for "James S. Blaine." (Angry partisans shouted, "G., you fool, G!") William Windom was nominated by a Minnesota delegate who took only a few minutes to describe the Senator's twenty-year record in Congress. Then Stalwarts had their opportunity, and John Logan placed Grant's name in nomination. His remarks were terse, for the main effort on behalf of the general was left to another. Every eye turned to the front row of New York's delegation.

While Grant men cheered, stamped their feet, and applauded wildly, Roscoe Conkling made his way forward to the press gallery and mounted a reporter's table, in full view of the 10,000 people in his audience. He waited until there was total silence and then began one of the most famous orations of the period:

> If asked what state he hails from
> Our sole reply shall be
> He hails from Appomattox
> And its famous apple tree!

This familiar verse by Miles O'Reilly (suggested the previous evening by Tom Murphy) evoked pandemonium, an uproar that lasted twenty minutes. Tom Platt recalled: "He was in magnificent voice. Those in the most distant corners of the great auditorium distinctly heard every word he uttered." As he stood there, poised and proud, six feet three inches tall, his left thumb hooked in a waistcoat pocket, his Hyperion curl carefully in place, Conkling could fully enjoy the adulation, for every word of his speech had been carefully polished and memorized; each re-arrangement of his feet and sweep of his hands had been thoroughly rehearsed.

When quiet was restored, the Senator lashed out at opponents of the unit rule: "In obedience to instructions I should never dare to dis-regard—expressing, also, my own firm convictions—I rise to propose a nomination with which the country, and the Republican party, can grandly win." The upcoming election, he continued:

> . . . is to be the Austerlitz of American politics. It will decide, for many years, whether the country shall be Republican or Cossack. . . . the need that presses upon this convention is of a candidate who can carry doubtful states both North and South. And believing that he, more surely than any other man, can carry New York against any opponent, and can carry not only the North, but several States of the South, New York is for Ulysses S. Grant. Never defeated in peace or in war, his name is the most illustrious borne by living man.

Conkling argued that Grant's travels enhanced his already superior qualifications for the nomination.

> He has studied the needs and defects of many systems of government, and he has returned a better American than ever, with a wealth of knowledge and experience added to the hard common sense which shone so conspicuously in all the fierce light that beat upon him during sixteen years, the most trying, the most portentous, the most perilous in the nation's history.

What of those who objected to the rupture of the two-term tradition established by the Founding Fathers? "There is no field of human activity, responsibility or reason in which rational beings object to an agent because he has been weighed in the balance and not found want-ing." "Who dares who dares to put fetters on that free choice and judgment, which is the birthright of the American people?"

Conkling could not forego the chance to ridicule his opposition. He obviously relished a blast at Blaine: with Grant as our leader, he said, "we shall have no defensive campaign. No! We shall have nothing to explain away. We shall have no apologies to make." One series of sentences crackled with invective as Sherman, Blaine, and the Inde-pendents were placed consecutively under fire.

> Can it be said that Grant has used official power and place to perpetuate his term? He has no place, and official power has not been used for

him. Without patronage and without emissaries, without committees, without bureaus, without telegraph wires running from his house to his convention, or running from his house anywhere else, this man is the candidate whose friends have never threatened to bolt unless this convention did as they said. He is a Republican who never wavers. He and his friends stand by the creed and the candidates of the Republican party.

Unwilling to leave the likes of George William Curtis without a parting shot, he said that Republicans were forced to fight not only Democrats but also "the charlatans, jay hawkers, tramps and guerillas—the men who deploy between the lines and forage now on one side and then on the other."

Even those lashed by Conkling's scorn were moved by the sheer power of his presence and the brilliance of his elocution. Applause thundered as his perfect phrases rolled over the huge audience; men thrilled at the portrayal of Grant as the very soul of the Union humbly offering his sword to the party of liberty. "Gentlemen, we have only to listen above the din, and look beyond the dust of an hour, to behold the Republican party, advancing with its ensigns resplendent with illustrious achievements, marching to certain and lasting victory with its greatest marshal at its head."

As the last words of exhortation echoed throughout the hall the galleries exploded. For fifteen minutes—or was it a half hour?—the noise was deafening. Observers claimed that nothing like it had ever occurred at a political convention. Grant men, one reporter wrote, "threw away the characteristics of age and became boys once more." John Logan was viewed shouting at the top of his lungs in the Illinois delegation; Tom Murphy and other New Yorkers were screaming; Johnny O'Brien stood atop his seat brandishing the state banner over his head as he cheered. Through it all, Conkling could be seen waving his handkerchief to cheer on his legions.[30]

When peace was restored it was almost midnight. If the exhausted delegates had been given the opportunity then and there to cast ballots, Conkling's cause might have been won. But others were scheduled to speak praises of other candidates, and as they did, the passion stirred by powerful oratory dissipated quickly. Indeed, many delegates had been turned into irreconcilable opponents of Grant's nomination by Conkling's stinging barbs against their own favorites. A member of the Illinois delegation said: "His sarcasm is all right in some places but out of place here." George Boutwell, a sympathetic observer, later wrote: "Whatever he said that was in support of his cause, affirmatively, was of the highest order of dramatic eloquence. When he dealt with his opponents, his speech was not advanced in quality and its influence was diminished."[31]

Shortly, James Garfield advanced to the stage to nominate John Sherman. While there is little evidence to confirm the charge that he was interested primarily in his own candidacy, Garfield curiously had neglected to prepare his speech before the convention assembled, and his brief remarks, heavily laden with classical allusions, did little to convince delegates of Sherman's higher qualities. "I do not present him as a better Republican or a better man than thousands of others we honor; but I present him for your deliberate and favorable consideration." And yet Garfield made a highly favorable impression on his listeners, for unlike Conkling, he stressed party unity and appealed for the healing of old wounds. "How shall we accomplish this great work? We cannot do it, my friends, by assailing our Republican brethren. . . . In order to win victory now we need the vote of every Republican—of every Grant Republican and every anti-Grant Republican in America,— of every Blaine man and every anti-Blaine man." At one point in his speech he asked, ". . . and now, Gentlemen of the Convention, what do we want?" A loud voice shot back: "We want Garfield."[32]

Edmunds and Washburne were then placed in nomination. Augustus Brandegee of Connecticut seconded Washburne's nomination, and midway through his speech noticed Conkling shaking his head at one of his points, as if to say that no one but Grant had a chance of victory. It was late and tempers were thin. Brandegee lashed out:

> The gentleman from New York shakes his head. He shakes his head magnificently. No man can shake it like him, nor shake such rhetoric and wisdom out of it. But let me tell the gentleman from New York he cannot sit down at the ear of every voter and give the argument that he has given tonight against the tradition of our fathers. He may, by the magic of his eloquence, take this Convention and the galleries off their feet, in his fervor; but even his great abilities, even his unmatched eloquence cannot go down to the fireside of every voter and persuade them that all the traditions of the fathers with reference to a third term are but humbug and masquerade. Does he not know that his candidate would be on the defensive, that even the magic name of Grant can hardly carry him in this Convention. Does he not know— no one knows so well as he—that the name of Grant would carry this Convention through by storm if there were not an invincible argument against his nomination?

For the Stalwart cause this was an unfortunate theme on which to conclude the critically important session.

No formal business was undertaken on Sunday, June 6, and delegates no doubt appreciated the respite. This seventh national Republican convention was already the longest on record, and indications were that several ballots would be required to name a new party leader. The anti-Grant coalition forged during the first days of the convention had quickly dissolved; Grant, Blaine, and Sherman forces were in no mood to give assistance to each other; while Windom, Edmunds, and Washburne supporters were prepared to hold fast in case of deadlock.

The balloting began on Monday morning, and when the roll call reached New York Conkling asked that his delegation be polled. Behind the request was typical Conkling spite: he would force each of the bolters to confess his treacherous apostasy in public—a few feet away from the withering glare of the state's senior Senator. John Birdsall, a one-time Conklingite, declared for Blaine in a barely audible voice and quickly sat down, his face flushed with embarrassment. Machine regulars hissed. When the polling reached William Robertson he planted his feet squarely and loudly proclaimed his choice, drawing several cheers from Blaine men throughout the hall. The vote in the delegation was Grant 51, Blaine 17, and Sherman 2.

On the first ballot Grant drew 304 votes, Blaine had 284, followed by Sherman's 93, Edmunds's 34, Washburne's 30, and Windom's 10. Grant and Blaine thus controlled 79 percent of the delegate strength, and as long as their lines held firm only Sherman could push either one over the top. Twenty-seven more ballots were taken that day with little fluctuation in the tally. Each time New York was called, Conkling announced the state's vote with a sneer to which no one quite became accustomed: "Two delegates are said to be for Sherman, seventeen are said to be for Blaine, and fifty-one *are* for Grant."[33]

As the weary delegates plodded to their hotels it was apparent that bargains would have to be struck to break the deadlock. But Stalwarts would have nothing to do with deals—Grant was the only acceptable candidate; only he could be fully trusted to reward his friends. Conkling, Arthur, Logan, Stephen Dorsey, and a number of other Grant men came together that evening to discuss the day's activity. To a man they swore to stick together at all cost, to win the nomination by simply waiting until the necessary votes came their way. Three hundred votes might have won a great many favors: Cabinet posts, ambassadorships, even customhouse appointments. But they were firm; as Tom Platt later put it: "We Grant men had sworn to die with our boots on."[34]

The break in the voting finally came early Tuesday afternoon on the thirty-fourth ballot when Wisconsin threw 16 votes to Garfield. The Senator-elect from Ohio protested slightly but Chairman Hoar ruled him out of order. The idea of Garfield as a compromise candidate swept the hall. On the thirty-fifth ballot he had 50 votes, and on the next ballot, state after state fell in line. When Maine went for Garfield, Senator Jones rushed up to Conkling and implored him to break the trend by throwing New York's Stalwart votes to Blaine. He angrily refused. The state's bolters went for Garfield when the roll call reached New York, and before long Garfield had 399 votes and the nomination.[35]

As delegates cheered hysterically and paraded around the auditorium Garfield stood quietly near his seat shaking hands and accepting congratulations. Grant men, stunned by their defeat, expressed little emotion. A reporter noted: "Senator Conkling . . . sat an unmoved spectator on the scene. Gen. Logan was calm, but his dark face was darker than usual, and in Senator Cameron's gray eye the cold, hard look was colder and harder."[36]

Stalwarts had stood fast to the end, casting 306 votes on the thirty-sixth ballot for Grant. Not long afterward a Missouri delegate, Chauncey I. Filley, ordered 306 medals struck bearing the words "The Old Guard." Grant men carried these symbols of loyalty to their peerless general with pride, and for decades they held reunions. One of them wrote in 1893: "We have nothing to regret, nothing to apologize for. Our chosen leader then, if he were alive, would be our chosen leader still."[37]

When the celebration in honor of the party's choice subsided, Conkling rose to move that Garfield's nomination be made unanimous. It was a formality, quickly accomplished, and the convention adjourned for three hours. In the late afternoon delegates would select a running mate to complete the Republican ticket.

It seemed obvious to a good many politicians that the vice-presidential nomination would go to a New Yorker, as it had in 1876, for the state was pivotal in a national election. That the nod would go to a Conklingite, especially should Grant fail to win first place on the ticket, was a reasonable guess; without assistance from the machine, chances of Republican victory in the Empire State were greatly diminished. Even before the convention assembled, Levi P. Morton, a Stalwart and business partner of George Bliss, discussed the position privately with Cornell; one campaign journal bore the names of "John Sherman of Ohio for President, and Levi P. Morton of New York for Vice-President."[38]

Minutes after the convention was adjourned, ex-Governor Dennison of Ohio elbowed his way through the crowd to the New York delegation. He thereupon offered Conkling the right to name Garfield's running mate, promising full support from Garfield and the entire Ohio delegation. The Senator replied that he had no one in mind but would call a caucus in half an hour and see what could be done. No formal attention had been given by the delegation to a possible vice-presidential candidate, as its leaders had devoted their energy exclusively to the drive for Grant. Lieutenant-Governor George Hoskins and District Attorney Stewart Woodford had expressed interest in the position that morning, but not within range of Conkling's hearing.

Steve French and Clint Wheeler overheard Dennison's overture and immediately went to Arthur, suggesting that he make a bid for the honor. Without question, Arthur, like Morton, Hoskins, and Woodford, had thought about his own course of action should the vice-presidential nomination be offered to New York; he was never known to overlook any political position or public office within his grasp. He had been smarting for months over his expulsion from the Customhouse and perhaps thought how much a place on the national ticket would serve as an answer to the charges of President Hayes. He undoubtedly took into consideration the alliance between Cornell and Platt which cast dark clouds over his future. Then, too, he may have considered Conkling's declining stature in the Senate and within the state and pondered what sort of crumbs might be cast his way by an administration led by anyone other than a Stalwart. Arthur had said nothing about the nomination, but now that the opportunity was here to win it, he would go all out. French and Wheeler, upon hearing Arthur's vigorous assent, scurried off to find other members of the city machine. There was not much time to organize—the caucus was called for 3:00 P.M. and it was already past 2:30. French ran into Tom Murphy and gasped, "We can get Arthur that nomination, and he wants it." Murphy quickly found a carriage, raced to the Grand Pacific Hotel, and began searching for colleagues.

Grant's defeat wounded Conkling deeply, and his first inclination was to strike back, to cripple the Republican campaign by withdrawing his machine's support. A cub reporter seated in the corner of a room adjoining the convention platform observed the Senator soon after the 306 had been overcome. "Conkling was plainly much perturbed. He walked up and down the long aisle with energetic steps, sometimes gesticulating vigorously as if giving emphasis to his thoughts and often muttering aloud." According to the reporter (writing thirty-one years later) Arthur soon entered by the door leading from the platform, and the two men met at the center of the room.

"I have been hunting everywhere for you, Senator," Arthur said.

"Well, sir," replied Conkling.

There was a moment of hesitation, as Arthur could see that Conkling was inwardly boiling.

"The Ohio men have offered me the vice-presidency." (The young eyewitness obviously did not take good notes during the confrontation. Instead, Arthur must have announced his intention to seek the nomination.)

"Well, sir," Conkling blustered, "you should drop it as you would a red hot shoe from the forge."

There was a flash of resentment in Arthur's eyes as he replied, "I sought you to consult, not—"

"What is there to consult about? This trickster of Mentor will be defeated before the country."

"There is something else to be said," remarked Arthur.

"What, sir, you think of accepting?" Conkling fairly shouted.

Again there was a moment of hesitation, and then Arthur said firmly: "The office of the Vice-President is a greater honor than I ever dreamed of attaining. A barren nomination would be a great honor. In a calmer moment you will look at this differently."

"If you wish for my favor and respect," Conkling fired back, "you will contemptuously decline it."

Arthur defiantly exclaimed: "Senator Conkling, I shall accept the nomination and I shall carry with me the majority of the delegation."

For a moment Conkling glared at his lieutenant. Then, abruptly, he turned his back on him and stalked out of the room.

A short time later Tom Murphy met Conkling at the hotel. The Senator was calmer now and was content to ask Murphy if he approved of Arthur's bid for the nomination. Murphy emphatically said that he did and proceeded to make a case for it. Conkling balked slightly; he did not seem to care for the idea. But he raised no serious objections and made no threats. The city machine was solidly behind its boss and further resistance would provoke needless animosity. Conkling thought the decision foolish, and he bitterly resented his old friend's unprecedented impertinence. But if Arthur really sought the glory of running for national office that was his affair; the Senator washed his hands of the matter.

After Dennison left the convention hall he went to Garfield's suite and told a number of people gathered there of his offer to Conkling. Garfield turned pale and asked Dennison if he had been authorized by the Ohio delegation to strike such a bargain with the Stalwart chieftain. No, the former governor said, he had taken action on his own without consulting anyone. Eugene Hale of Maine said sarcastically: "The friends of Mr. Blaine, who furnished the bulk of the vote for Mr. Garfield, might desire to be considered in the matter of Vice-President," and he and William Chandler bolted from the room. Garfield then startled

Dennison with the news that he had sent the chairman of the Ohio delegation, Governor Foster, to Levi P. Morton minutes after his nomination with the offer to be his running mate. Dennison would simply have to explain this turn of events to Conkling—somehow!

When Morton caught up with Conkling he told him of Foster's overture and asked for his advice.

"If you think the ticket will be elected," Conkling sighed, "if you think you will be happy in the association, accept."

Morton said, "I have more confidence in your judgment than my own."

Conkling suggested that he talk with George Boutwell, then governor of Massachusetts. Boutwell thought the idea unsound, and Morton agreed not to run. This relieved the tangle somewhat, but did not alter the fact that Conkling had been given assurances in Garfield's name. To weld any sort of bond between the presidential nominee and the New York machine Garfield would have to honor Dennison's commitment. Blaine men might feel cheated, but the party simply could not afford to alienate Stalwarts any further.

The New York caucus did not get under way until three thirty, and only forty-two delegates were present. (Arthur remained in his room, awaiting the result of their deliberations.) Conkling chaired the meeting, and right after he called it to order, Pierre Van Wyck proposed Arthur for the vice-presidential nomination. Morton then rose and said that he did not desire to be a candidate. One delegate presented the name of Vice-President Wheeler, and another spoke for Lieutenant-Governor Hoskins. Members of the Ohio delegation, headed by Foster and Dennison, then appeared and were invited to make a statement. Dennison said that Ohio would give substantial support to a candidate named by the caucus. Outside, the elderly politician sheepishly confessed to Conkling that he did not have the authority to pledge *every one* of his state's delegates as he had claimed over an hour earlier. Conkling said crisply: "Sir, I am not surprised at anything from Ohio."

The caucus lasted only a half hour. Stewart Woodford's name was also placed before the meeting, but Murphy had assembled most of the delegates present and it was clear that the machine was to have its way. Still, there was resistance: even after three seconding speeches on Arthur's behalf, the ex-collector had to be elected by voice vote.

Afterward certain members of the Ohio delegation expressed doubt about the wisdom of New York's choice. One delegate mentioned the Customhouse controversy and said that Arthur would hurt the ticket in Ohio. Others feared that certain newspapers and influences would not accept a man so closely connected with the Grant Administration. Murphy soon heard enough of this. "Gentlemen," he said imperiously, "if that is what you have to say, New York doesn't want the Vice-Presidency." The grumbling subsided as the convention assembled for its concluding session. Dennison sent his apologies to Hayes, assuring the President that he had meant no disrespect and that Arthur had not crossed his mind when he approached Conkling.[39]

New York bolters seethed when they learned of Arthur's good fortune. They had not been informed of Dennison's assurances, and most of them, apparently, had not been told of the caucus. Twenty-eight delegates were absent from the meeting; Murphy and his associates clearly felt no obligation to extend them personal invitations.[40] John Birdsall complained to a reporter, "It was Robertson who engineered the break for Garfield, but without consulting the men who did so much for the nomination, these Ohio men undertook to placate the Conkling men by giving the second place to a Conkling heeler."[41]

Conkling could not bring himself to attend the final session of the convention, and Arthur was officially placed in nomination by Stewart Woodford. (Some thought it fitting that the role be assigned to a federal officeholder.) Dennison and several others made seconding speeches; Emory Storrs of Illinois declared that the Old Guard demanded Arthur's selection. One delegate opposed the choice, reminding the convention of the party's civil service plank and pleading: "Let us not stultify ourselves before the country." Only one ballot was taken: Arthur won 468 of the 661 votes cast; his nearest competitor was Washburne, who polled 103. (Ohio went for Arthur 42–2; New York's delegates voted for him to a man.) The nomination was declared unanimous, and at seven twenty-five the long, exhausting convention adjourned for the last time.

Garfield and Arthur smilingly greeted each other at the Grand Pacific Hotel and walked to a large parlor where they stood side by side for two hours shaking hands with an endless stream of well-wishers. (Arthur's right hand became so swollen that a ring he had worn for years had later to be filed off.)[42] Garfield had removed his delegation's insignia, but for some reason Arthur kept his Grant badge pinned to a lapel. His height was such that delegates could not miss seeing the badge, and several took it as an act of defiance.[43]

Reactions to Arthur's nomination were predictable. Garfield, of course, publicly expressed great satisfaction. (Privately, he was sorry that Morton had not accepted his offer. A friend wrote Morton: "While he did not consider that the Vice Presidential candidate was ordinarily effective beyond personal popularity, he said your name upon the ticket would have placed New York out of the doubtful list.")[44] Governor Foster spoke of Arthur's honesty and popularity, and ascribed much of the Customhouse controversy to Cornell.[45] Old Thurlow Weed said that he was pleased: "Mr. Arthur is a gentleman with whom every one that is in the slightest degree acquainted . . . cannot but respect, and his long and faithful service as a leader entitles him to the recognition. I have known him for twenty-five years as Whig and Republican, and a more loyal party man and truer Republican cannot be found anywhere."[46] Young Henry Cabot Lodge wrote: "No one will abandon Garfield on account of Arthur," and the ticket would benefit from the "direction of the shrewdest political manager in the country."[47]

Republican journalists tended to speak kindly of Arthur when they said anything at all. Godkin wryly considered another side of the nomination: ". . . there is no place in which his powers of mischief will be so small as in the Vice Presidency, and it will remove him during a great part of the year from his own field of activity." The editor continued, with words that were to haunt him: "It is true General Garfield, if elected, may die during his term of office, but this is too unlikely a contingency to be worth making extraordinary provision for."[48]

John Sherman, understandably, was bitter, and wrote privately that Arthur's nomination was "a ridiculous burlesque." "The only reason for his nomination was that he was discharged from an office that he was unfit to fill."[49] Silas Burt consoled Hayes: "It is unfortunate that the presumed necessities of conciliation have brought this embarrassment but it cannot be misconstrued to your injury nor to the detriment of the reform movement."[50] The Democratic press lambasted the vice-presidential candidate from the start. The Louisville *Courier-Journal* published a picture of Arthur with the caption: "Nominated at Chicago for the Vice-Presidency. Suspended by President Hayes from the New York Collectorship, that the office might be honestly administered." The Concord (New Hampshire) *People and Patriot* contended that Arthur had been "kicked out of the Custom House by Hayes and Sherman for inefficiency and general corruption."[51] The New York *Herald* editorialized: "He has had a bitter quarrel, as is perfectly well known in his own State, with those machinists who control the State administration. . . . It is certain that he will get no help in his canvass from Governor Cornell, whom he did more than any other person, except Mr. Samuel J. Tilden, to elect. His nomination simply proves how entirely ignorant politicians may be of State politics in other States than their own."[52]

Arthur stepped aboard a train bound for New York accompanied by Senator Dorsey, Steve French, and several other friends. (Conkling, still in a huff, made separate travel reservations.) They arrived home on the evening of June 11 and were met by a cheering crowd. Later that night a reporter called at Arthur's home and was admitted. As he had a decade earlier when appointed collector, Arthur said that his selection had been a startling surprise. For several hours, he continued, he had pondered the responsibilities of the nomination before accepting it on the advice of friends.[53]

The next evening 2,500 city Republicans gathered with a band in front of the Fifth Avenue Hotel chanting "Arthur! Arthur!" When the general stepped out on one of the balconies, the band struck up "Hail to the Chief" and the crowd roared its approval. His remarks were customarily brief:

> I thank you, gentlemen, for your kind and enthusiastic greeting. I am glad to meet you tonight, and to see the familiar faces of my friends at the great City which has been my home for nearly 30 years. I am glad to meet the tired and faithful soldiers, "the Old Guard" of the Republican Party, with so many of whom I have been associated in its cause since its birth. I am glad to meet you here, in this spot, our headquarters through so many hard-fought campaigns, where so many glorious Republican victories have been announced and celebrated. The honor which has been conferred upon me, of which I am deeply sensible, is but a recognition of yourselves, gentlemen, and your fellow-Republicans of our great State.[54]

Seated in his study at the White House, Rutherford B. Hayes thoughtfully weighed the dramatic events of the past week and pondered what paths might be followed to pursue Republican victory. The convention defeat of the unit rule, he told his diary, "was an important achievement," and it was good that the push for a third term had been stopped. As for the party's choice to head the ticket, "Gen. Garfield's nomination at Chicago was the best that was possible." When his thoughts turned to Garfield's running mate, however, his mood abruptly changed. "The sop thrown to Conkling in the nomination of Arthur, only serves to emphasis [sic] the completeness of his defeat. He was so crushed that it was from sheer sympathy that this bone was thrown to him." What about the forthcoming campaign? Where were the necessary votes to come from? His own election drive had come perilously close to defeat, and in the intervening years his administration had seemed to create enemies no matter which way it turned. "But now how to win," he wrote. "The contest will be close and fierce. We may be beaten. . . . We must neglect no element of success."[55]

CHAPTER TEN

Pushing Things

THE BALANCE of political power during the Gilded Age was almost perfect and has been called "the most spectacular degree of equilibrium in American history." Party majorities in Congress fluctuated frequently and were often razor-thin. Democrats won control of the House of Representatives in 1874, lost it in 1880, won it again in 1882, lost it in 1888, and regained it in 1890; Republicans lost their hold over the Senate only once, between 1879 and 1881, but their majority between 1876 and 1890 was more than three for only two years. No President enjoyed a majority of his own party in both houses of Congress for his full term. Control of the White House shifted back and forth, and the contests were often extremely close. After Grant no President during the era won a majority of the popular votes; in two elections Democrats won pluralities of the popular vote only to be defeated in the Electoral College.

The fundamental division between the two major parties reflected the sectional cleavage that led to the Civil War. The South, by the end of Reconstruction, was solidly Democratic. New England was just as strongly Republican. Elsewhere the parties were fairly even in strength, though Republicans held a slight edge. Aside from the sectional consideration, party preferences seem to have had their roots in family tradition, religion, and local matters. As Robert Marcus has noted: "Questions that voters of the Gilded Age found salient revolved almost exclusively about local cultural conflicts: native versus immigrant, Protestant versus Catholic, evangelical temperance-oriented church groups versus liturgical tradition-oriented Lutherans." National politicians avoided such explosive matters and found it extraordinarily expedient to shun controversial questions altogether. Party platforms and speeches by presidential candidates and their partisans were filled with platitudes, personal attacks, appeals for party loyalty (straight-ticket voting was common), and the ever-dependable references to the Civil War. Indeed, it was difficult to identify a consistent Republican or Democratic position on any issue of the period.[1]

With the political equilibrium so delicate, the outcome of a presidential contest was usually determined in a small number of populous states: New York, Ohio, Indiana, and Illinois. In 1880 New York and Indiana seemed pivotal. If Democrats could capture the Empire State's 35 electoral votes and add them to the 138 from the Solid South they would be just 12 short of the required 185; Indiana's 15 would spell victory. Republicans knew they had to capture at least one of these two doubtful states or yield the White House to the opposition for the first time since 1856. Both Indiana and New York had gone for Tilden in 1876, but the margins were narrow—in Indiana a mere 5,000 votes. Republicans controlled most of New York's state offices as well as both houses of the legislature; Boss Kelly's contribution to that situation was widely acknowledged, however, and GOP politicians anticipated a fierce struggle.

The battle between John Kelly and the Tilden machine that had resulted in Cornell's election continued to rage during the months that followed. The two camps held separate state conventions in April 1880 —across the street from each other in Syracuse. At the regular Democratic conclave a unit rule was adopted that virtually pledged delegates to Tilden. Tammanyites selected their own slate of delegates, and Kelly declared that if it was not recognized by the national convention in Cincinnati he would again bolt the party. No one was sure of Tilden's precise intentions; it was consistent with his sphinxlike and devious character that he kept his closest followers in the dark right up to the eve of the convention. It was clear, however, that if he failed to make peace with Kelly his chances for another nomination were slight, for Democrats could not risk losing New York.

Kelly lost his bid for recognition at the national convention but not before he was able to tell the credentials committee of his unwillingness to support Tilden. From the balcony of a local hotel he informed a crowd that if Tilden were nominated he would back a third candidate or stay at home. But Kelly had little to fear from his rival. The ambiguity of Tilden's intentions convinced most partisans that he did not choose to run, and support for the New Yorker was faint. On the second ballot the convention named General Winfield Scott Hancock of Pennsylvania to run for President, and selected William H. English, a banker and former Congressman from Indiana, to be its vice-presidential candidate. Hancock had a solid record as a Union officer in the Civil War and it was hoped that his candidacy would win the votes of northern veterans and forever bury the "bloody shirt" indictment. He was attractive to the South because of his moderate administration of the Fifth Military District (Louisiana and Texas) during Reconstruction. He had strength in his home state and was thought to be able to unite northern Democrats. Without any political experience, he was without enemies. Kelly quickly pledged his full support: "Let past differences be banished from our midst forever." With the party's forces apparently united in New York and a native son from Indiana on the ticket, a great many Democrats were convinced they were in a superb position to gain revenge for "the fraud of 1876."

The Democratic platform was a hastily prepared document of little significance. It came out for "honest money," consisting of gold and silver, and paper convertible into coin on demand; it favored a "free ballot," but failed to mention Negroes; it sought restrictions on Chinese immigration; and it called for a "tariff for revenue only"—a slogan no one quite understood.[2]

The new sense of harmony enjoyed by Democrats contrasted sharply with the bitterness and division plaguing Republican ranks. New York's party organization was split in half, and there were rumors that Conkling intended to sit on his hands during the campaign despite Arthur's nomination. In Illinois and Pennsylvania the situation was similar, Stalwarts and their opponents eyeing each other with suspicion and jealousy. Garfield would have to find ways to mend these wounds or go down to defeat in November. He fully understood this and was ready to do what he could to restore unity. In fact, some of Garfield's intimates were afraid he might concede too much in his efforts to bring peace to the party. The presidential candidate was a congenial and attractive man, a skilled parliamentarian and a good orator. But he lacked firm convictions and was known to be easily swayed from one position to another. John Sherman said that "his will power was not equal to his personal magnetism. He easily changed his mind, and honestly veered from one impulse to another."[3] Shortly after Garfield's nomination his friend Whitelaw Reid wrote: "First of all, I beg of you to make no promises to anybody."[4]

On the very day the Republican convention adjourned in Chicago Senator Cameron called an impromptu meeting of the national committee, where Stalwarts planned to elect officers who would exact concessions from Garfield before the campaign began. Two Blaine men, William E. Chandler and William P. Frye, heard of the strategy and blocked it. With Cameron discredited and Blaine leaders adamantly opposed to his reelection, the party standard-bearer was asked to name his own choices for chairman and secretary. It was a touchy matter, for Stalwarts seemed disinterested in compromise and party harmony and saw anything less than capitulation as treachery.

Even before Garfield was able to submit his nominations the nation's capital buzzed with rumors of a widening breach within the GOP. Garfield had gone to Washington in mid-June to collect some personal papers, and while there visted Blaine and Schurz. His efforts to see Conkling and Arthur were stymied by circumstances. Predictably, Conkling was affronted by the candidate's conversations with his archenemies and did not keep his intense displeasure a secret.

On June 29, Garfield forwarded four names of men acceptable to him as chairman, adding his wish, to soothe Stalwart tempers, that Tom Platt be named secretary. The national committee met a few days later, and by then Grant men were demanding Platt's selection as chairman. After much heated debate, Marshall P. Jewell, a wealthy Connecticut manufacturer and a former Postmaster General in the Grant Administration, was elected to the top post. Jewell was a figurehead chairman, the favorite of William Chandler to ease the factional dispute. But Stalwarts were dissatisfied, and John Logan warned that he and his friends were ready to pull out of the campaign altogether. To prevent this, the committee permitted Logan to appoint Stephen W. Dorsey its secretary. Like Arthur, Dorsey was a sop to the Stalwarts; whether the titles awarded both men were sufficient to win Conkling's earnest support in the campaign remained in doubt. Garfield confided to Blaine: "In one quarter silence. The Oracles are dumb and seem not yet to have determinded whether it shall be peace or war."[5]

Garfield worked hard at his farm in Mentor to draft a letter of acceptance that would appeal to all factions of the party, and he solicited opinions and suggestions from an assortment of Republican leaders, including Arthur.[6] The cautiously worded letter, for the most part a bland amplification of the party platform, was published on July 12. It appeared to many observers as an obvious attempt to placate the "306" men. Garfield not only failed to endorse the Hayes Administration's general position on the civil service but deliberately omitted the word "reform." Consistent with his earlier pronouncements on the issue, he repudiated Hayes's order banning federal officeholders from politics and came out in favor of congressional control over public offices. Hopefully, Conkling would now be assured that a Republican victory in the fall would mean no disruption in the spoils system and that his advice would be seriously considered when appointments were made in New York.[7]

Reformers expressed shock and discouragement over the letter. Carl Schurz told Garfield that it was a disappointment to "very many great men who hailed your nomination with joy and hope." Horace White was convinced that it would drive Independents out of the campaign and hand New York to the Democrats, by which fact Conkling "would not be ill-pleased."[8]

Arthur's letter of acceptance, his first public statement ever on national issues, was published a week later. Not surprisingly, it contained positions on hard money, federal aid to sectarian schools, the tariff, and internal improvements that were consistent with the party platform. On the issue of civil service reform the letter raised some eyebrows. Arthur joined Garfield in his disapproval of the political restrictions on federal officeholders, and expressed some doubt about the wisdom of civil service examinations, "because they have seemed to exalt more educational and abstract tests above general business capacity, and even special fitness for the particular work in hand." Nevertheless, he expressed a strong belief in the necessity for honest and efficient public servants.

> Original appointments should be based upon ascertained fitness. The tenure of office should be stable. Positions of responsibility should, so far as practicable, be filled by the promotion of worthy and efficient officers. The investigation of all complaints, and the punishment of all official misconduct, should be prompt and thorough. These views, which I have long held, repeatedly declared, and uniformly applied when called upon to act, I find embodied in the [platform] resolution, which, of course, I approve.[9]

Although the paragraph contained a slap at President Hayes and those who supported him during the Customhouse controversy, it impressed several Republicans. *The New York Times* wrote: "Gen. Arthur's reference to the civil service reform resolution of the Republican platform is more satisfactory to the friends of the reform than Gen. Garfield's, because, while not expressing that complete attachment to the reform which they would be glad to see, it shows a more intelligent appreciation of its real aims and a clearer conception of its methods."[10] E. L. Godkin, who described Arthur as "if not exactly . . . the wicked partner [of the ticket], at least as the poor relation," thought that the vice-presidential candidate "must be surprised to find his character rising by simple contrast with his chief."[11] George William Curtis, on the other hand, smirked to Silas Burt: "Arthur's letter is very amusing to one who knows of some of his performances, as I do."[12]

The night Arthur returned from Chicago a national figure, Regina Caw wrote a letter to a cousin describing her brother's first few hours at home. During dinner eight-year-old Nell asked another aunt what she might do to congratulate her father and was told that she should bring him some flowers. "When they were brought on to the table and Chester called little Nell to him to kiss her he completely broke down and said 'there is nothing worth having now.'" Arthur's continuing grief over the loss of his wife, intensified by an honor she would have cherished, remained a secret to all but his family and intimate friends. Guests arrived shortly after dinner, and by then he had regained his composure and was every inch the cool, sophisticated New York politician.[13]

Among those who gained entrance to the Lexington Avenue home was a reporter from the Boston *Herald* who had obviously observed Arthur on other occasions. Arthur chose not to discuss the campaign at that time, pleading, "I am only a subordinate on the ticket, remember, and you cannot expect me to constitute myself its spokesman." In lieu of further direct quotations, the reporter sent his editor some perceptive impressions of his host. Arthur's physical bearing and fastidious apparel drew favorable comment, as did his courtesy toward callers. Friends were said to believe him an honest man; the reporter noted "that he will go to any length in serving a friend; that his word is as good as his bond, and that his air of geniality is unaffectedly genuine." His associates added "that in politics he is given to schemes that are the next thing to trickery, that he believes it right and honorable to use all means against political opponents, that he has no conception of raising politics above the aim of office-holding, and that he will unhesitatingly turn against his political companions, if a turn of affairs makes it desirable. In short, he is one of the many who act on the principle that all is fair in politics."

The reporter was fascinated by one of the sources of Arthur's popularity among political workers: though a gentleman himself with friendships among the most refined, Arthur "has the added gift of letting himself down on occasion to the mental and social level of all grades of politicians with whom he is brought in contact." Arthur was earlier observed drinking at the bar in the Fifth Avenue Hotel with an assortment of ward heelers, "and even consented to be button-holed by Theodore Allen, the gambler, dance house keeper, and Republican hard worker." But the reporter was convinced that Arthur did this out of political necessity. "In his new attitude of candidate for Vice President he will not fail in dignity of conduct."[14]

However angry Conkling may have been at Arthur over his desire to be on the national ticket, the two patched up their difficulties quickly. Up to this time Conkling was never known to forgive anyone for defying his will, but Arthur was a special friend whose absolute loyalty had been demonstrated hundreds of times for well over a decade. On July 15, the two friends, along with Stephen Dorsey, traveled to Canada for some salmon fishing. When Conkling arrived home in Utica on August 1, he wrote Levi P. Morton: "Every day & everything was enjoyable. Genl Arthur's constant effort was to make every body else happy. No wonder we all like him."[15]

Conkling was willing to participate actively in the campaign for Garfield and Arthur but demanded as the price concrete assurances from the presidential candidate that he would retain the authority to dispense patronage in New York. Without that power the Conkling machine would crumble even if Republicans won the election. Conklingites determined early in the campaign to bring Garfield east for a face-to-face encounter in order to gauge his intentions. As early as June 28, Arthur wired his running mate, asking him to meet in New York on July 1 with the Republican National Committee. Garfield declined the invitation and confided to Whitelaw Reid, "I have made all reasonable personal advances for harmonious action."[16]

Garfield thought that his acceptance letter would win Conkling's confidence, but it soon became clear that the New York Stalwarts persisted in their desire to have a confrontation with the party standard-bearer. Stephen Dorsey telegraphed Garfield in late July saying it was imperative that he go to New York. William Chandler had dinner with Conkling and several of his lieutenants and was impressed by their fear of again being attacked by a Republican President. Pondering the necessity of winning New York in November, Chandler advised Garfield that it would be worth while "to stoop a little to conquer much." Garfield resisted the idea for fear of further alienating Half-Breeds and Independents. In a reply to Chandler he suggested that Conkling visit Mentor, and that Blaine, and perhaps Grant and Sherman also, be in attendance at whatever talks might take place.

A few days later Garfield received a strongly worded ultimatum from Dorsey asserting that Stalwarts would be satisfied with nothing less than a personal conference. In Jewell's absence, he was calling together a huge meeting of Republican leaders in New York on August 5 to discuss the campaign. "I repeat with all the earnestness I have, that in my judgment it is a duty which you owe to yourself and to the Republican party to be here on the 5th of August regardless of what Mr. Jewell says or Mr. George William Curtis, or Mr. Anybody else." Why was it imperative that Garfield attend? Dorsey was blunt: Conklingites "want to know whether the Republicans of the State of New York are to be recognized . . . or whether the 'Scratchers' and

Independents and 'feather-heads' are to ride over the Republican party of this state as they have for the last four years." Reluctantly, Garfield agreed to come, but told Dorsey he wanted to avoid private meetings. He assured Curtis that he was traveling east only at the unanimous request of the national committee, and told Hayes that he was unwilling to make any deals with Conkling. To Blaine he wrote: "My dear friend, you must stand by me. Many of our friends who have written me think there are evidences that a few leaders in New York meditate treachery and say that the visit will either prevent it or so develop it that the country will understand it and place the responsibility where it belongs." Since Blaine would also be invited to attend the meeting, "I want you to find the exact situation, if possible before I arrive, I want to know how large a force C has behind him and just what the trouble is."[17] For all of his wavering and trembling, Garfield knew exactly what Conkling was prepared to demand, and he realized that to carry New York he would have to assent. The Conkling machine had done virtually nothing to this point; to activate it, a major concession was required. But how was Garfield to win over Conkling and at the same time retain the allegiance of his other major supporters in the campaign?

Garfield left Mentor for New York on August 3. At Buffalo he was greeted by a crowd of 50,000 and was welcomed by several party notables, including Marshall Jewell, Levi P. Morton, William Robertson, and Richard Crowley. (Two future Presidents, Benjamin Harrison and William McKinley, were also on hand.) The train made some twenty stops along the route, where the candidate shook scores of eager hands and made brief remarks. Arthur and Cornell joined the travelers in Albany. Dorsey, Platt, Biglin, and a crowd of 3,000 met the train at New York City when it arrived early in the evening on August 4, and at the Fifth Avenue Hotel Garfield was greeted by Blaine, Sherman, and scores of other prominent Republicans.[18]

Roscoe Conkling had checked into the Fifth Avenue Hotel two days earlier in anticipation of the meeting, which he was expected to address.[19] Before Garfield arrived, however, the Senator fled, leaving Arthur and his associates the awkward task of attempting to explain his absence. Garfield wrote in his journal: "I think his friends are showing zeal and enthusiasm and will work whether he does or not."[20] Garfield quickly learned that Conkling's lieutenants had the authority to bargain for their chieftain. Nevertheless, he was angered by the haughty Senator's flight. Platt later wrote: "Garfield came as arranged. But his chagrin, mortification, and indignation, which were manifested (only, of course, to the inner circle) when he found that Conkling was absent and would not be present, are left to the imagination."[21] There are various explanations for Conkling's action. Apologists unconvincingly depicted him as being above any sort of agreement with the presidential candidate.[22] More likely it was the thought of having to be near and talk to the likes of George William Curtis that prompted Conkling to pack his bags.[23]

The Fifth Avenue Hotel conference was a joint informal session of the Republican National Committee, the congressional committee, and other party leaders from across the country. With one hundred participants, it was the largest gathering of its kind ever held. It was also, in Platt's words, "a mere cover and a farce," for the meeting was actually convened to serve as a pretext for Garfield's encounter with the Conklingites. The conference opened at noon on August 5 with speeches by Sherman, Logan, Weed, and others, followed by lengthy discussions between members of the national committee and representatives from an assortment of states. Meanwhile, Garfield attended a private session with Arthur, Platt, Morton, and Crowley in Morton's hotel suite. That evening Arthur and the others reported complete agreement about the forthcoming race and said that no obstacle remained in the path of a zealous and vigorous campaign effort.[24]

What precisely happened during the session remains in dispute. According to Platt, writing in 1910, Garfield was told frankly that the Conkling machine wanted concrete assurances about the dispensation of patronage in New York before entering the fray. "We cannot afford to do the work, and let others reap the reward." In reply, Garfield expressed his disfavor with the Hayes Administration and disavowed any sympathy with civil service reform. He acknowledged the Conkling machine's strength in New York, adding that he could not be elected without its support. In reward for their help, Conklingites could have their way with the state's patronage: "in dispensing those favors, he would consult with our friends and do only what was approved by them. These assurances were oft repeated, and solemnly emphasized, and were accepted and agreed to by all those present."

After the session broke up, Platt recalled, Garfield and Morton retired to an inner room for a private conversation. Earlier, Morton had agreed to head a committee of wealthy New Yorkers engaged in creating a secret fund designed for use in New York and Indiana. Garfield had also asked Morton to direct the national committee's fundraising efforts. Morton did not intend to undertake the latter task without assurance of a prestigious position within the new administration. According to Platt, Garfield offered Morton, during the course of their confidential talk, the option of becoming Secretary of the Treasury, Ambassador to England, or the government's principal agent for funding the bonded debt.[25]

However inaccurate elsewhere, Platt's autobiography seems convincing on the events of August 5. Stalwart intentions were made clear to Garfield before he traveled to New York, and he knew the cost of the machine's assistance. Arthur and the other Conkling lieutenants were shrewd, experienced politicians who could be expected to state their demands clearly and accept only the most positive and unequivocal assurances from the presidential candidate. Moreover, once the conference adjourned, Conkling men went to work, and it is most unlikely that their sudden efforts were based on mere faith in Garfield's post-election benevolence.

Roscoe Conkling returned to the Fifth Avenue Hotel on August 9 and spent much of the evening with Arthur.[26] The Senator was left with no doubt about Garfield's stated intentions, and within a few days he announced his decision to campaign personally. Later he would recall the assurances Arthur described to him and comment bitterly: "How willing Garfield then was, when everything looked blue and certain defeat seemed to stare him in the face; how willing he was to concede anything and everything to the Stalwarts if they would only rush to the rescue and save the day!"[27]

Whatever Garfield said in New York, he returned to Mentor contending that he remained uncompromised. On August 9 he wrote in his diary: "No trades, no shackles, and as well fitted for defeat or victory as ever."[28] Garfield's apparent belief that he left the conference having resisted a bargain with the Conkling machine is difficult to explain. Perhaps, as T. C. Smith has suggested, Garfield was convinced that he had merely promised to "consult" Stalwarts on patronage, and that this did not mean he was pledged to accept their proposals. If he thought that, then he had deliberately or subconsciously played tricks with words at the expense of his auditors. Platt recalled that Garfield said he would not only consult but would "do only what was approved by" the Conkling machine. Just as likely, Garfield, in his desire to placate all factions of the party, simply refused to admit to Conkling's opponents that he had caved in on August 5 while face to face with four hardboiled Stalwarts who held the fate of the election in their hands.

The national committee, led officially by Jewell but in fact by Dorsey, determined early in the campaign to stress the "bloody shirt" issue, even though many Republicans thought that Hancock's nomination had eliminated the venerable tactic.[29] In handbills, flyers, pamphlets, placards, advertisements, oratory, and even in song, Democrats were pummeled with the crusty charges of treason and brigandage. The *Garfield and*

Arthur Campaign Song Book contained the "Conspirator's Song," which portrayed Democratic leaders warbling:

> Arouse! Confederate Brigadiers!
> Turn out your men in gray-aye!
> The Ku-Klux Klan and Rifle Clubs,
> Are ready for the fray-aye!
> Unfurl the stars and bars again,
> With Hancock we must win-in!
> For if defeated at the polls,
> We shall be counted in-Too thin![30]

At the same time, party polemicists churned out biographies of Garfield (at least six by late August), gushingly picturing him as a faultless "plow boy" who had served his country with valor in war and peace. Arthur merited short sketches in several of the volumes. His humble background and war record were described and his abolitionist sympathies as a young attorney were stressed—all with appropriate embellishment.[31]

Democrats responded similarly to the task of electing a President, choosing to sidestep significant issues while liberally employing black-and-white characterizations of the two parties and their standard-bearers. *The Democratic Campaign Text Book for 1880* portrayed Garfield as a political plunderer, the "supporter of every job, the defender of every steal, which by hook or crook got through Congress from 1863 to 1875." Among other things, it bore down hard on his acceptance of a $5,000 "legal fee" from a street-paving company seeking a government contract while he served as chairman of the House Appropriations Committee. It also devoted twenty-four pages to his role in the Crédit Mobilier, linking him directly with what it called "the monster fraud of the nineteenth century." This latter allegation offered especially appealing ammunition for Democrats. Congressional testimony surrounding the Crédit Mobilier was published, a damaging Nast cartoon from 1873 was circulated, and across the country Hancock men scrawled "$329" on sidewalks and fences to remind voters of the sum Garfield allegedly made from the stock.[32]

By and large, Republican strategists felt that silence was the wisest response to the charges. Garfield "ached" to reply to his attackers, but during the period it was considered undignified and unwise for presidential candidates to take the stump. "They dare not meet the issues raised," he wrote to Whitelaw Reid on September 2, ". . . but are seeking to draw us off into personal controversy." It would not work, he predicted. "I still think that the Democrats are feeling the force and presence of the tide that is now sweeping against them."[33]

When Maine went to the polls on September 13, Garfield was confident that Blaine could deliver a decisive win that would rally the faithful in the "October states," Ohio and Indiana, where other gubernatorial races would set the pace for the presidential election. Instead, Republicans were jolted by a Democratic-Greenback fusion ticket victory. An embarrassed Blaine quickly wired Mentor, contending that Democrats had sent from $75,000 to $100,000 into Maine four days before the balloting. Garfield analyzed the returns and sadly predicted: "This will make the contest close and bitter through the North."[34]

The shock of the defeat in Maine prompted Republicans to turn from the "bloody shirt" to the tariff as their major campaign theme. In fact, both parties had taken the same position on the issue, but "a tariff for revenue only" was vague enough to frighten some businessmen and provide Republicans with a weapon. Tons of posters and tracts poured from the presses bearing warnings of the dire consequences of "Democratic free trade as dictated by the South." Hancock, who understood little about the subject, gave an interview on October 7 in which he said: "The tariff question is a local question." This made even less sense than the platform statement, and Republicans rejoiced at the blunder. Thomas Nast drew a famous cartoon portraying Hancock whispering to a friend: "Who is Tariff and why is he for revenue only?" A large book was produced entitled *Record of the Statesmanship and Achievements of General Winfield Scott Hancock.* Its pages were blank.

Convinced of their "agreement" with Garfield, New York Stalwarts devoted their full energies to the election of the Republican ticket. With authority over all federal and state employees in New York they had a powerful arsenal of workers and funds. One of Garfield's lieutenants reported: "Cornell and Conkling control about 20,000 men, so I am told, on the canals and other state institutions."[35] Postmasters and Customhouse employees added several thousand more to the total.

The central figure in New York's Republican campaign was Arthur, who served the party not only as the vice-presidential candidate but as chairman of the state committee. His tasks as Garfield's running mate were minimal; this was a time in which state machinery dominated national campaigns. From his plush office at the Fifth Avenue Hotel Arthur was expected to coordinate the scores of rallies and meetings held throughout the state under the auspices of his committee, acquire and schedule a full slate of speechmakers, supervise the dispersal of the committee's assessment circulars, raise funds from businessmen, and handle a voluminous correspondence concerning details of local campaign management. In addition, he took personal charge of the travels of Conkling and Grant through the Midwest. It was a time-consuming and exhausting assignment requiring much political expertise. Arthur was in his element—the techniques of office-seeking had consumed most of his life for the past two decades—and he responded to the challenge with enthusiasm and determination.

It was thought important to have the party's most prominent orators at work in New York, and among those solicited by Arthur were Blaine, Schurz, Evarts, Benjamin Brewster, Hamilton Fish, Benjamin Harrison, clergyman Henry Ward Beecher, attorney Joseph H. Choate, Vermont Senator George F. Edmunds, and writer Mark Twain. Most complied willingly; Blaine was an exception, complaining of a curious, unusually severe, and long-lasting affliction of the throat.[36]

Conkling made his first platform appearance of the campaign on September 17 before a packed house at New York City's Academy of Music. Following the three-hour-and-forty-minute oration 6,000 veterans paraded, and a huge crowd broke into cheers when Arthur introduced the state's senior Senator from a hotel balcony.[37]

Arthur handled all the arrangements for the famous tour by Conkling and Grant into the key states of Ohio and Indiana. Correspondence concerning speaking dates, travel accommodations, the size of auditoriums, platform dignitaries, and the like was turned over to the vice-presidential candidate.

Garfield telegrammed Morton on September 10 suggesting that Conkling and Grant speak in Ohio. The matter was quickly turned over to Arthur, and four days later meetings were scheduled in Warren, Cleveland, and Cincinnati. Local Republicans urged Garfield to go to Warren to meet the Stalwart chieftains. Perhaps still smarting over Conkling's absence from the Fifth Avenue Hotel conference, Garfield thought it more satisfying to invite the Stalwarts to call upon him. On September 15 he wired Arthur: "Please arrange that General Grant-Senator Conkling & yourself spend the night of Sept[ember] twenty seventh at my house."[38]

A crowd of 35,000 attended the rally at Warren. The Senator spoke for more than four hours, while the former President managed to extend his remarks for only seven minutes. (Arthur chose to remain in New York throughout the campaign.) The meeting was meant to be a display of party unity as well as a bid for votes, but several Republicans promptly observed that neither Conkling nor Grant mentioned the presidential candidate's name in the course of their speeches. Garfield was angered by the slight and wrote a friend shortly: "Conkling is a singular com-

pound of a very brilliant man and an exceedingly petulant spoiled child.
. . . It has become apparent that he, and some of the men who are working with him, are more concerned in running Grant in 1884 than they
are for carrying the Republicans safely through the contest of 1880."[39]

The next evening Grant, Conkling, John Logan, Levi P. Morton,
and about fifteen Ohio Republicans spent an hour with Garfield at his
farm. Conkling later told Tom Platt that as he drove up in his carriage
Garfield rushed hatless into the rain, exclaiming "pathetically":
"Conkling, you have saved me. Whatever man can do for man that will
I do for you." Garfield also allegedly pledged once again to secure
Conkling's approval of all federal appointments in New York. The story
of the "Treaty of Mentor" seems artificial and has been discounted by
historians. Garfield's secretary, who was in Conkling's carriage and
present during the meeting, called it "a deliberate lie." Moreover,
Conkling was in Ohio, as Garfield knew, because of promises made on
August 5; further assurances were unnecessary. Even after the meeting
at Mentor the Senator continued to distrust the presidential candidate.
When Platt asked him if he had any faith in Garfield, "Conkling made
a wry face, sneered, and replied, 'Not much, but we will try him out.' "[40]

Details of the tour through Indiana were worked out by Arthur
with the assistance of Republican boss John C. New. Conkling gave
lengthy addresses in Richmond, Terre Haute, Indianapolis, and Lafayette.
This was his first campaign trip west and large crowds turned out to hear
him. According to his nephew, many weathered spectators thought
Conkling's oratory superior to Henry Clay's.[41]

Grant returned to New York on October 9 and was welcomed by
festivities staged by the state committee. A parade seven miles long
containing 60,000 people filed by a reviewing stand on which sat Grant
and Arthur. Some 800,000 spectators were said to make this the largest
rally in city history.[42]

When Conkling returned to New York two weeks later, Arthur
greeted him with a request for further activity. "I understand from the
military style of your telegram that you report for duty and so ask
whether I shall now make some appointments for you in this State."
Within a few days, under Arthur's direction, Conkling and Grant were
speaking their way across New York.[43]

Arthur's state committee pursued "voluntary contributions" from
government employees with a zeal rarely if ever before observed in
Empire State politics. New York was, of course, a fertile field for such
demands: the annual payroll of city officials alone was nearly $11,000,-
000; salaries at the city's post office and Customhouse amounted to over

$2,500,000 a year. The committee mailed twelve series of assessment circulars in the sixty-seven days leading up to the election. Letters reached every postmaster in the state, all workers in the area offices of the Internal Revenue Service, and all Customhouse employees. (Silas Burt collected several of the circulars and later wrote: "Never were the Committees as persistent and arrogant in their demands upon the Customs employes as in this year . . .")[44] Few public servants were spared: circulars were sent to federal judges, police chiefs, workers on the new capitol building at Albany (right down to the night watchmen), employees of the State Museum of Natural History, and lighthouse keepers. The committee used a list of those employed by the New York Quarantine Department (T. C. Platt, Commissioner) to exact funds from ship stewards and deck hands.

The standard assessment circular was a printed form letter bearing the amount expected filled in by hand. The routine request was 3 percent of an annual salary. Because of the furor over civil service reform, circulars were worded carefully to appear as appeals rather than threats. One dated October 15 described the national importance of a Republican victory, and continued:

> These important considerations have moved this Committee to make the Presidential Campaign in New York State one of unusual activity; and in order to meet the heavy legitimate expenses already incurred, for Speakers, Documents, Meetings, etc., throughout the State, money is greatly needed.
>
> The Republican State Committee, therefore, in view of the magnitude of the National interests involved in this Canvass, hope you may find it convenient to facilitate their Campaign-work by a generous contribution, at an early day.

Circulars sent to those who ignored the first appeal tended to lose their delicacy. Platt, chairman of the executive committee, signed one dated September 13 that requested the employee's "immediate attention to this matter . . . without further delay." Committee Treasurer John N. Knapp signed a similar reminder to those who had sent only a portion of their assigned sum: "As this matter seems to have been in part neglected, and in order that there may be no misunderstanding, please let me know, by return mail, if we shall hear from you further and when." Henry A. Glidden, the committee's secretary, later sent letters to the federal supervisory personnel in New York containing the names of noncontributing subordinates.

The national committee, the congressional campaign committee, and scores of local committees also sent circulars, prompting a chorus of complaints from harassed Republicans. The state committee received several hundred letters condemning the party's rapacity. One correspondent charged that 20 percent of his new salary had been taken by various assessments. An employee of the Collector's Office of the New York Customhouse at Jersey City objected to his assessment of $60 because of previous contributions:

National Com[mittee] $25.00
New Jersey State Com[mittee] $25.00
Hudson Co[unty] Ex[ecutive] Com[mittee] $25.00
Have also contributed to Boys in blue—and will have to contribute to the City Com[mittee] as well as numerous clubs. . . .

A few letters went further. One postmaster wrote:

You may and I presume you have the power to influence Government Employees through fear of loosing [sic] their positions, if they are base enough to sacrifice principle for supposed financial gains, but I deem the practice of taxing persons holding office under the Government or employed by the Government pernicious in its effects & one exercising a baneful influence in the politics of this country & a practice beneath the dignity of any great political party.

Arthur not only presided over the state committee's efforts to raise funds but was fully engaged in every phase of its assessment business. In two cases he made revisions in the wording of circulars. Hundreds of replies crossed his desk, and he passed them along through the proper channels, frequently making notations to assist the prompt collection of payments. One federal judge who had solicited funds from colleagues on the bench contacted Arthur directly: "Please let me know when and where to pay it over—I am ready at anytime—of course this letter is strictly personal." Arthur had his secretary write to another judge, asking "if you can not now make some report in regard to the matter of contributions for this Committee which was the subject of consultation between . . . you and the other judges." The committee request of the superintendent of construction at the capitol building in Albany for assessments totaling $945 came from Arthur, as did a confidential entreaty to officials of the Internal Revenue Service in New York asking for the names and salaries of all present employees. A similar list of state postmasters resulted from a request by Arthur to James N. Tyner, the Stalwart First Assistant Postmaster General.

The only circular actually signed by Arthur made no reference to funds and consisted of a general appeal for continued support.

Take heed that no feeling of security shall tempt you to abate your efforts. From now until the counting of the votes has ceased, *work*. Inspire your friends by your own activity. See to it that the canvass in your neighborhood is thorough and that every Republican ballot is polled and counted. *"Push things."*

Arthur left no record of the number of circulars mailed or their financial yield, but one student of assessments estimated that the state committee brought in between $90,000 and $125,000 by this method. Still, in mid-October Arthur could complain to a friend of his committee's relative poverty:

> The financial condition of the State Com[mittee] this year is different from what it generally is for the reason that the necessities of the October campaign in the West impelled this Com[mittee] to stand aside and let the National Com[mittee] and our friends here for them raise in this city the greater part of the money required for the expenses of the Western campaign.
>
> This is going to make it exceedingly difficult for us to raise money here even to cover the expenses already incurred by this Com[mittee].

He soon wrote to Levi P. Morton of the committee's immediate need for $27,000. "I am in serious trouble if something is not done at once."[45]

Shortly after the Fifth Avenue Hotel conference both Levi P. Morton and Arthur went to work raising money from New York businessmen for the secret fund aimed, in large part, at bringing victory in Indiana. A friend of Arthur's, in 1882, claimed that $350,000 was collected; a year later, Stephen Dorsey put the figure at over $400,000.[46] Indiana, one of two "October states," caused GOP leaders great concern: Democrats had carried it in 1876 and 1878, and there were rumors of Democratic plans to import professional voters and to intimidate Negroes.[47] Dorsey conducted an extensive poll of voters in the crucial state and concluded that money would have to be spent lavishly to win it. While the study was in progress, a party worker wrote to William Chandler: "Dorsey is all right, doubtless sounding the possibilities & probabilities in Indiana. And if he reports favorably, forward goes the 'boodle.' "[48] All or a large portion of the secret fund arrived by messenger in late September. Dorsey distributed much of the money to local committees in the form of crisp, new $2 bills. (Democrats soon charged that the Treasury Department printed the bills specifically for Republican use.) The currency was employed to buy the votes of "floaters," men whose ballots were for sale to the highest bidder.[49]

Many top party leaders were aware of Dorsey's tactics in Indiana. Garfield had been privy to the creation of the secret fund and was in close contact with those directing its expenditure. On September 27, Morton, Senator Allison, and old Simon Cameron came to Mentor to talk over campaign strategy. Garfield wrote in his diary: "Had a full conversation on the political situation in Indiana. Allison and Morton spent the night with us and the situation of the campaign was quite fully discussed." When his guests had departed, he wrote to Dorsey: "You will hear from them in time. Don't relax any grip anywhere." Allison wired Dorsey telling him that "all required" would be forwarded from New York "on Thursday night."[50] Within a few days the money raised by Morton and Arthur arrived in Indianapolis.

(Garfield also concerned himself with the success of assessments. He consulted with the notorious post office spoilsman James N. Tyner, on his way to Indiana to aid Dorsey. And at one point in the campaign he wrote to the chairman of the finance committee of the congressional campaign committee: "Please say to Brady that I hope he will give us all the assistance he can. I think he can help effectively. . . . Please tell me how the Departments generally are doing." Thomas J. Brady, Second Assistant Postmaster General, was then busily collecting funds from government officeholders.)[51]

Republicans carried both Indiana and Ohio on October 13, and their prospects for winning in November brightened sharply. One GOP worker, fresh from campaigning in Indiana, appeared the next day at the national committee's headquarters, praising Dorsey and exclaiming: "There was never anything like it before." On the following afternoon, Dorsey and New slipped into town and reported to Arthur at the Fifth Avenue Hotel.[52]

Arthur's contributions to the campaign were winning applause by this time from partisans in a position to observe him in action. *The New York Times* commented:

> He has worked for weeks with such application as few men are capable of standing, and has seen several men about him laid up with fatigue while he has been compelled to keep right on. It would inspire Republicans with enthusiasm to see with what industry and judgment he goes on attending to his duties as Chairman of the State Committee, perfecting his plans for making the result of the campaign in this State as glorious to the party as that of Indiana has been.[53]

As might be expected, Democrats referred to Arthur in their campaign literature with a sneer. He was the lowest sort of political hack, a prince of spoilsmen, a ballot-box stuffer whose every move had to be scrutinized by those interested in honest elections. Furthermore, Arthur's legal right to be on the Republican ticket was challenged. A New York attorney named Arthur P. Hinman was hired, apparently by Democrats, to explore rumors that Arthur had been born in a foreign country, was not a natural-born citizen of the United States, and was thus, by the Constitution, ineligible for the vice-presidency. By mid-August, Hinman was claiming that Arthur was born in Ireland and had been brought to the United States by his father when he was fourteen. Arthur denied the charge and said that his mother was a New Englander who had never left her native country—a statement every member of the Arthur family knew was untrue.[54] The Irish birthplace story was palpably false and was abandoned by Hinman as the campaign progressed. In its place he alleged that Arthur was born in Canada, just across the Vermont border where his mother often visited her parents. Little attention was paid to the charge during the campaign of 1880, for Garfield was a young, robust man who could easily be expected to fill one or two terms in the White House.

Less than a week after the Republican triumphs in Indiana and Ohio, Democrats took one last, rather desperate swipe at Garfield. On October 18, the editor of New York City's penny newspaper *Truth* found a letter on his desk, written on House of Representatives stationery and bearing the signature of James A. Garfield. In it Garfield appeared to oppose limitations upon Chinese immigration and defend the right of employers to hire labor as cheaply as possible. Democratic newspapers published the contents of the letter widely, especially in California, Oregon, and Nevada, where the Chinese issue was highly controversial. Republicans proved the letter to be a forgery a week before the election, but the extent to which the document damaged Garfield's popularity among workers and labor unions was unknown.[55]

In New York Democrats were cautiously optimistic. Funds had been raised with relative ease—Tilden and his friends alone were said to have produced almost $200,000.[56] And Tilden and John Kelly, after a considerable amount of squabbling, united behind a state ticket and a candidate for mayor of New York City. The mayoralty candidate was William R. Grace, a Roman Catholic who many Protestants feared might divert educational funds to parochial schools. (Hoping to profit by those fears, Republican newspapers ran such headlines as "Public Schools in Peril." Arthur's organization responded by nominating a sometime Democrat named William Dowd, a Protestant member of the Board of Education.)[57] There was concern among Democrats that Grace would jeopardize the national ticket, but Kelly was confident and predicted privately that New York would give Hancock and English a 30,000 majority and that New York City would be carried by 60,000.[58]

In the closing days of the campaign Arthur wrote checks to GOP workers all over the state, concentrating his attention on close associates in New York City. The day before the election, for example, John O'Brien and Mike Cregan each received $2,000, while Barney Biglin accepted $1,500. Arthur's neatly kept accounts attribute the expenditure of $40,446 merely to "campaign purposes," a term that undoubtedly harbored the purchase of "floating" votes and perhaps, as Democrats soon charged, the importation of voters.[59] When Stephen Dorsey was later asked about the campaign in New York he said that the sole chance for victory " 'lay in concentrating all our powers in New York and Kings Counties—that is, the two cities of New York and Brooklyn. Well, we did so. We cut down the Democratic majorities more than 75,000 and the State was carried by 20,000. You want to know how this was done?' He smiled and was silent."[60]

The largest percentage of qualified voters ever recorded in an American presidential election (78.4) turned out on November 2. The result was extremely close: with ten million ballots cast, Garfield and Arthur came out ahead by a margin of only 7,018. In the Electoral College the vote was 214 to 155. As predicted, New York was the pivotal state: if its 35 electoral votes had gone to Hancock, his total would have been 190, enough to win the election.[61]

A decrease in Democratic strength in New York City was the deciding factor in claiming the state for the GOP—555,544 to 534,511. William Grace was elected mayor by a slim margin, but several observers, including George Jones of *The New York Times* and James Gordon Bennett of the New York *Herald*, were convinced that his controversial candidacy cost Democrats the state and ultimately the entire national contest.[62]

More than a few Republicans recognized the role played in the victory by the man who would soon be Vice-President of the United States. George Jones wrote that Arthur's services were "of the highest importance to the Republican Party" and that his management of the campaign was distinguished by "ability and quiet strength."[63] For years New Yorkers would talk about the shrewdness and effectiveness with which Arthur led the state committee. In 1910 Tom Platt thought back to the campaign of 1880 in his home state and declared: "No equally exhaustive and 'red hot' canvass was ever before made."[64]

CHAPTER ELEVEN

With a Feather

O<small>N THE DAY</small> following the election, Chester Arthur relaxed at the Fifth Avenue Hotel, accepting congratulations from dozens of callers and acknowledging receipt of hundreds of telegrams. He charmed well-wishers with his modesty, but it was no secret that inwardly he glowed at the prospect of becoming the seventh New Yorker to serve as Vice-President.[1] A few months earlier he had felt himself disgraced before his family, his party, and the nation—the victim of a hypocritical President and a handful of priggish visionaries. Now he could enjoy great social prominence and a measure of national political influence in an office elevated beyond anything, until recently, he had even hoped to hold. He knew nothing about the task of presiding over the Senate, of course, but he would quickly learn. Besides, his consuming challenge would have little to do with the hoary legalities and formalities surrounding the routine business of the Senate. To Arthur, politics was a struggle for spoils, and he now stood ready as ever to do whatever he could to strengthen the Conkling machine. New York Stalwarts had debts to collect from the President-elect, and Arthur was no doubt anxious to get to the matter of parceling out government jobs to loyal partisans. The question of the Senate seat from New York had also to be resolved, and Arthur already had plans for landing that office for a friend.

Garfield enjoyed almost no opportunity for relaxation following his triumph of November 2, for immediately he was faced with the highly delicate assignment of selecting a Cabinet from among his party's quarrelsome factions. He knew that somehow the Stalwarts would have to be appeased without alienating Blaine men and the others, like Godkin and

Curtis, who urged him to extract politics from the selection process. How exactly this was to be achieved was anybody's guess.

Standing solidly in the path toward party unity were the agreements of August 5. Garfield and the Conklingites held clashing views of what was said at the Fifth Avenue Hotel, and unless either side yielded its claims, the future could hold only costly conflict. Garfield faced this problem on November 27 when he sent for Levi P. Morton to discuss rewards for the New Yorker's service in the campaign. Morton affably reminded the President-elect of his pledge and said that he now wished to become Secretary of the Treasury. Garfield appeared annoyed by this and told Morton that he could not appoint him to the Treasury because of his ties with Wall Street. Then, for the first time, he told a member of Conkling's faction flatly that he considered himself under no specific obligation to the New York machine. The two men met again the following day, and Garfield was blunt: "I will not tolerate nor act upon any understanding that anything has been pledged to any party, state, or person."[2]

However enraged Conkling may have become at the news of Garfield's hostile attitude, he determined, for lack of alternatives, to negotiate with the President-elect in the hope of persuading him to recognize Stalwart claims. On December 13, Governor Cornell, Richard Crowley, and Louis Payn arrived in Mentor to talk over the situation with Garfield. The delegation assured its host that Conkling wished to support the new administration and even work for a second term. Its members went on to say that Conkling would take nothing less for Morton than the Cabinet post he had been given the option of accepting in August. Garfield denied having made such a promise and said he thought Morton's appointment unwise. After three hours the defeated New Yorkers left for the railroad station.

Conkling then employed Stephen Dorsey, whom Garfield liked and admired, as an intermediary. Dorsey wrote a lengthy letter to Garfield on December 16 describing in detail an interview with Conkling. The Senator again expressed his earnest desire to cooperate with Garfield, Dorsey reported, and said that he recognized him as among the ablest men in the country. (Conkling was not above flattery if circumstances seemed to cry out for it.) He was even willing to have Morton rewarded with another Cabinet seat. "I must confess," Dorsey wrote, "that I was a good deal surprised at Mr. Conkling by his manner as well as by what he said." Garfield was pleased by the letter and came up with the idea of having Morton fill a vacancy as Secretary of the Navy, a post he might continue to hold in the new administration. Shortly, he wrote to Hayes and was informed that Stalwarts had declined the offer. Of what use was a largely decorative Cabinet post? Conklingites thought themselves entitled to more—much more. A New York *Tribune* dispatch of January 1 reported that Morton was interested solely in the Treasury Department.[3]

By this time word had leaked out of James G. Blaine's acceptance of the position of Secretary of State. It was reasonable that the Maine Senator would play a prominent role in the new administration: his supporters had furnished most of the votes that won the nomination for Garfield in Chicago, he was a powerful figure in the party, and he was one of the President-elect's close friends. Garfield had approached him with the offer on the very day he confronted Morton, but the proposal was made only after Blaine declared his disinterest in running for the presidency in 1884. (Very few trusted Blaine completely, even his most ardent admirers.) The Senator officially accepted in a letter of December 20, and within little more than a week the story was in the headlines.[4]

Conkling and his lieutenants thought they understood the flow of events only too well. Blaine was a power-hungry, ruthless, and very clever man who would dominate Garfield and turn the administration against the Stalwarts; he would overlook nothing to weaken Conkling's authority in New York and block his aspirations in Washington. Conkling feared that his opportunity for a rewarding arrangement with the President-elect was shattered; perhaps his struggles with the Hayes Administration were but a prelude to the conflicts ahead.

Evidence supporting this gloomy conclusion appeared quickly. On December 30, Blaine traveled to New York and, on his own authority, persuaded Vanderbilt attorney Chauncey Depew to run for the Senate as an administration supporter.[5] The following evening Blaine, Depew, Conkling's erstwhile enemy William H. Robertson, and a number of other Half-Breed partisans had dinner together at the home of New York *Tribune* editor Whitelaw Reid, where strategy was discussed for winning the upcoming senatorial contest. Reid then warned Garfield in a letter of the dangers presented by Conklingites: "They mean to confront you with the two Senators from the State, and to demand the entire patronage of the State. In a word they mean to be your masters, and when you submit they will like you well enough."[6] A few days later Blaine published an editorial in the *Tribune* that was a declaration of war against the Conkling machine. Saying he was "fully authorized" to speak for Garfield, he wrote:

> It is proper to say . . . that the incoming Administration will see to it that the men from New York and from other States, who had the courage at Chicago to obey the wishes of their districts in the balloting for President, and who thus finally voted for Garfield, shall not suffer

for it, nor lose by it. . . . Gentlemen at Albany, who are said to have been threatened with a different course at Washington, may reassure themselves. The Administration of President Garfield is to be an Administration for the whole Republican party. . . . it will not permit its friends to be persecuted for their friendship.

Garfield had not, indeed, authorized the editorial, but he took no exception to it when it appeared. He blandly commented to Reid: "The article is all right and may do good," and expressed a desire to remain personally aloof from the senatorial race.[7]

Conkling, of course, was infuriated by the editorial. "What was the meaning of that article," he asked, "but that the men who had voted faithfully for Grant need expect no quarter from the administration, while the men who had basely violated their pledges by abandoning Grant for Garfield were to be rewarded for their treachery?"[8] George Boutwell told Conkling he had heard Blaine say that New York Stalwarts would be treated fairly in the future. Conkling replied, "Do you believe one word of that?"

"Yes," Boutwell said, "I believe Mr. Blaine."

Conkling sneered, "I don't."[9]

The Senator had good reason to be cynical. The first thrust of an effort to undermine his power in New York opened with the new year and centered around George Sharpe's bid for reelection as Speaker of the Assembly. Sharpe had been a popular and effective leader and enjoyed the full support of the Conkling organization; his selection by the Republican caucus was considered certain. Nevertheless, Whitelaw Reid hurried to Albany on January 3, the day the caucus was to vote, to boost a Half-Breed named Skinner and assure Republicans that support for antimachine aspirants would in no way endanger opportunities for winning patronage from the new administration. Sharpe's strength was such that his opponent conceded shortly before the balloting, but the struggle to select a senatorial candidate promised to be more complex.[10]

Republicans dominated the state legislature, and Conkling had a safe majority in the GOP caucus. The Senator was in a position to name his next colleague. Before the Chicago convention it was clear that Arthur was being groomed for the seat held by Democrat Francis Kernan, but with his election to national office the Senate race was open. Conkling's choice was difficult, for he was faced not only with Blaine's new designs but with the fact that his machine was coming apart. The jealousy and animosity between Cornell and Arthur, smoldering at least since 1876, was boiling to the surface now that both held prominent positions, and Conklingites were being forced to take sides. As governor and keeper of the state's patronage, Cornell seemed able to offer more than Arthur, and he won the allegiance of Platt, Dutcher, Payn, and Patterson. But Arthur had well-established personal ties with a large number of the machine's dependables and could take credit for landing many of them government jobs. Moreover, the Vice-President-elect remained a prominent figure in the party and was not to be without a voice in the Garfield Administration. Arthur knew he could depend upon Bliss, Rollins, Murphy, Sharpe, Crowley, Smyth, Hess, Wheeler, Folger, and virtually all of the workers in the city machinery.

There was little Conkling felt himself able to do about the schism between his friends; it could not be healed either by appeal or command. Then, too, the Senator seemed to be slowly succumbing to bitterness. Friends noticed his growing inclination toward silence; something was gone from his strut. This sullenness, a sort of grim resignation that fate had been unkind, stemmed no doubt from his personal embarrassments of the past two years, his loss of the Customhouse, the jarring defeat of the "306," and most recently from what he considered the ultimate treachery—the appointment of Blaine. Each of the factions within his organization decided to run a candidate for the Senate seat; Conkling looked quietly on, determined to leave the matter to his lieutenants, hopeful that the Senator from Maine would not wind up the ultimate victor.

By New Year's Day there were five major candidates in the field. Richard Crowley was Arthur's favorite, Tom Platt was Cornell's choice, Levi P. Morton entered the race on his own, Chauncey Depew had been won over by Blaine, and Sherman S. Rogers had backing from Independents. From the beginning, experts picked either Crowley or Platt to win.

Crowley's qualifications for the office were above average. A forty-six-year-old Lockport attorney, he was a skilled orator and debater who had served four years in the State Senate, a term in Congress, and eight years as United States attorney in the Northern District of New York. Critics argued, however, that he was insufficiently wealthy to be honored with the position he sought; his Roman Catholicism was also considered a liability. Crowley was the first of the candidates to appear in Albany, and he campaigned intensively on his own behalf. Sharpe delayed announcement of his committee assignments until after the caucus convened, hoping to pressure members of the Assembly to support his friend. When even that failed to produce a comfortable margin of votes, the Vice-President-elect arrived in Albany.

Some observers were appalled at the impropriety of Arthur's appearance, feeling that his newly attained position placed him above direct involvement in such contests. But Arthur was determined to have his man in the Senate and cared nothing about offending those who failed to understand what he considered the realities of political warfare. Hess, Cregan, Smyth, French, Wheeler, and a number of other Arthur men were soon on the scene. A reporter commented: "The presence of Gen. Arthur here, and in Mr. Crowley's behalf, is felt to be a very powerful aid to him, for Gen. Arthur's ability as a manager was too well displayed in the Presidential campaign to be for a moment questioned now."[11]

Crowley's most formidable opponent, Tom Platt, had combined a successful business career with a strong desire for political power. Now forty-eight, he was president of the United States Express Company, the Tioga National Bank, the Tioga Manufacturing Company, and the Southern Central Railroad. He had first held office in 1859 as a county clerk, had twice been elected to Congress, and was currently a quarantine commissioner. A great many Republicans respected him for his labors in state and national campaigns. But for all of his wealth, experience, and contacts, and no matter how hard he electioneered, Platt was unable to pull away from Crowley in the polling that preceded the caucus vote. Cornell made no personal appearances for his candidate but sent dozens of state officials into the fray to buttonhole legislators. One observer wrote: "Never before was such a complete array of State officers seen in the Capital at one time."[12]

Gloom shadowed Levi P. Morton as he roamed the halls of the Delavan House reminding friends of his own candidacy. Conkling had talked him out of accepting the vice-presidential nomination, Garfield had denied him the Cabinet post he thought himself promised, and now he was faced with powerful opposition from within the machine while seeking an alternative honor. In desperation he turned to Conkling, sending him a private request that he take Platt out of the race. Conkling replied with a shrug: "I can see no right of mine to ask Mr. P. to withdraw, and on reflection I think you will agree to this."[13] Morton then called on Cornell to talk over the situation. The governor realized that the presence of three Stalwarts in the race was unproductive and proposed a plan to narrow the field: Crowley, Platt, and Morton should each select three representatives; these nine men would come together and hammer out the compromises necessary to select one of the aspirants as the machine's candidate. Morton agreed readily, and after much deliberation Arthur consented. But Platt delayed, saying he needed more time to think about the proposal.[14] In fact, he was seeking other arrangements.

On January 12, William Robertson attempted to strike an alliance with Arthur. If Crowley would promise not to resist efforts by the new administration to reward Half-Breeds with patronage, and if he would support Blaine's friends should they be attacked by Cornell and his associates, Depew would withdraw from the skirmish and hand over his

17 votes. The offer requested the betrayal of Conkling, and Arthur turned it down, according to a friend, "promptly and indignantly." Depew then went to Platt with the proposal and he accepted it. The deal elected Platt the next day on the caucus's first ballot; he received 54 votes to Crowley's 26.[15]

When Reid privately spelled out the terms of the agreement to Garfield he noted that Platt not only had agreed to aid Half-Breeds in their pursuit of patronage but also "would help in the prompt confirmation of your Cabinet—even in so extreme a case as the possibility of its containing the name of Judge Robertson—though much opposed to such a nomination." Platt furthermore pledged to "do all he could (not much, probably) to keep Conkling reasonable."[16]

After returning to New York City, Platt called on Reid to reaffirm their alliance. His parting words, according to the editor, were: "I am yours to command; draw on me at sight."[17]

Enough of the bargain reached the press to convince observers that Conkling was at the mercy of the President-elect. The Senator's machine was split in two, the state's second Senate seat had eluded his grasp, the chance for securing strong representation in the Cabinet seemed doomed, and Half-Breeds appeared certain to reap the spoils in New York. Dorsey wrote to Garfield: "I don't like to see it repeated in the newspapers, day after day, as coming from Mr. Blaine and his frends, that men who voted for Grant or for some other man at Chicago are especially selected to be ridden down under the wheels of Mr. Blaine's triumphal car."[18]

Reports of mounting Stalwart wrath reached Mentor daily. Morton sent a bitter letter blaming his loss in the senatorial contest on the widespread belief that he was to become the next Secretary of the Treasury.[19] When Mrs. Garfield heard from Reid that Morton was making angry statements about her husband she thought them indicative of an attitude shared by all Conklingites, and advised: "You will never have anything from those men but their assured contempt, until you fight them *dead.* You can put every one of them in his political grave if you are a mind to & that is the only place where they can be kept peaceable."[20]

Blaine, Reid, and Robertson hoped that Garfield would exclude Conkling men entirely from his Cabinet. The Senator from Maine stigmatized Grant supporters as "all the desperate bad men of the party," and counseled Garfield: "they must not be knocked down with bludgeons; they must have their throats cut with a feather."[21] But however Garfield may have disliked Conkling and his lieutenants, and however much he respected advice from his wife and his soon-to-be Secretary of State, he knew that it was extremely unwise politically to shun the entire

Grant wing of the party. He let Blaine know as early as December 19 that Stalwarts "must not be ignored or neglected." To Grant, on January 31, he wrote: "I have never thought for a moment of selecting from New York for a place in the cabinet, any one who is hostile to Senator Conkling."[22] The challenge of achieving party harmony that faced Garfield on the day of his election had yet to be met squarely; by mid-January he had named only one member of his Cabinet, and that selection had troubled Independents and infuriated Stalwarts. Garfield procrastinated, blew one way and then another; he spent almost the entire interim between November 3 and March 4 agonizing over Cabinet appointments.

On January 17, he thought of Thomas James for Postmaster General. He solicited advice from Blaine, Sherman, and Dorsey, and all three responded negatively, contending that James would be a tool of Conkling. Soon he was pondering the selection of Charles J. Folger for the Treasury. On January 29 Cornell and Platt arrived in Mentor to discuss the Cabinet, and Garfield raised the possibility of Folger's candidacy; he was not necessarily opposed to a New Yorker heading the Treasury, only a man from Wall Street. But Cornell and Platt asserted that Folger, New York's Chief Justice, "could not safely be spared," and again pushed for their friend Morton's selection. Garfield ruled that out of the question and then stunned his guests by suggesting that Conkling accept a Cabinet portfolio. The discussion got nowhere, and after three hours the New Yorkers left, shaking their heads.

Two days later Garfield invited Conkling to Mentor to talk over the situation. To Blaine he wrote: "what would you say to exchanging seats—you for the Treasury, he [Conkling] for State?" Horrified by the thought and rattled by Garfield's wavering, Blaine exploded: "His appointment would act like strychnine upon your administration—first, bring contortions and then followed by death."[23]

Conkling was badly shaken by recent events. At times he was the familiar firebrand of the Grant era, spatting out denunciations of his deceivers, shaking his fists at the thought of those who dared attempt to strip him of his authority. But as his future darkened he said increasingly less, retreating into the womb of self-pity; always an actor, he appeared to see himself as a noble warrior who had suffered betrayal—a Caesar whose trusted friends and colleagues had conspired to wound him mortally. In a private letter of January 19 to Timothy Howe he wrote: "I want nothing myself, and do not even feel aggrieved at being left in ignorance; my wish is very strong that Gen. G. may have a smooth & successful Administration, which is very simple & easy . . ."[24] Of course, Conkling desperately wanted something from Garfield: a patronage-rich Cabinet post for one of his men and, above all, power over the federal offices in New York. But how was he to proceed? What could be done to counteract Blaine now that he appeared to hold the reins of the new administration? The suggestion that he accept a Cabinet portfolio himself was silly; he and Blaine could never sit at the same White House table. And if Garfield was unprepared to honor the August 5 agreements, personal appointment to the Cabinet would be meaningless. While he might be, say, studying the political affairs of Cuba, Half-Breeds in New York could be casting Stalwarts out of post-masterships.

At one point Conkling's despair was such that he felt even Arthur, his most loyal lieutenant, had turned against him. Arthur was apprised of this by Kate Chase Sprague, whose affair with Conkling continued, albeit more privately than before. On January 18 she told of Conkling's purchase of two Arthur lithographs, one of which he placed in her home: "the Senator, *your friend*, never passes the table where the likeness stands, that he does not apostrophize it with some hearty expression of real affection, such as is rare in man to man & a tribute from this self-contained but noble & true nature that any man may feel fond to possess." Getting to the point, Mrs. Sprague observed: "Garfield & Sherman & Blaine (as it looks to private forecast) are to combine forces to overthrow & crush the power that saved them, but which they recognize only to fear & hate." "Surely," she wrote, "the Senator's friends, his tried friends & true will not cripple or soon embarrass the man to whom they owe so much?"[25]

Arthur had no intention of abandoning his close ties with Conkling and was no doubt saddened by his chieftain's doubts. Within a few weeks he was in Washington for political talks with the Senator and undoubtedly took the occasion to reassure him of his total fidelity.[26] Arthur was obviously persuasive, for when he first officially visited the Senate in February, Conkling personally escorted him through the chamber introducing him to his colleagues; shortly the two men were sharing a Washington apartment.[27] But there was plainly little Arthur could do to enhance Conkling's political fortunes. He did not have Garfield's ear, and he was anathema to Blaine. Moreover, his public image, stained by Democrats during the campaign and battered by his trip to Albany on behalf of Crowley, suffered a severe blow three weeks before the inauguration as the result of a curiously undiplomatic speech about GOP tactics in the recent presidential race.

On February 11, a dinner in honor of Stephen Dorsey was given by prominent members of the Union League Club at Delmonico's. Among the two hundred guests were John Jacob Astor, J. Pierpont Morgan, Jay Gould, Thurlow Weed, and most of the New York Stalwart leaders (excluding Conkling). Republicans came from Indiana, Missouri, and California to pay tribute to the national committee's secretary. Delmonico's was lavishly decorated with floral displays for the occasion; no one could overlook the huge coat of arms of the state of Indiana done in flowers, grasses, and moss, complete with a prairie, a rising sun, a buffalo, and a pioneer. Grant was seated at the place of honor at the President's table; on his right sat a beaming Dorsey, and on his left was Arthur.

After three hours of eating and drinking, cigars were lit and the gloating party members sat back to listen to the first of the evening's speeches, delivered, appropriately, by the former President. "We have assembled here this evening," Grant said, "to do honor to a gentleman who, we think, has contributed more than any other one man in bringing about the result that we all hoped for, and all now feel so grateful for, at the last Presidential election." The speaker drew cheers with a reference to Dorsey's activities in Indiana. "To his skill, his executive ability, we are largely, if not wholly, indebted for the result which was attained there."

Dorsey was then called upon to respond, and he thanked his many associates who assisted him in the campaign and singled out Arthur for special praise.

> I need not say a word in this presence in respect to the eminent man who sits beyond me, (looking at Gen. Arthur). You have most of you known him for a generation; but I can say that he is the only candidate that I know of or ever heard of who during a national campaign had a private character and public record so thoroughly intrenched that they were alike unassailed and unassailable.

This drew loud applause, and Dorsey continued:

> Those of us who were associated with him during the campaign and had intercourse with him nearly every day, know how to appreciate the work he did then. I have reason to believe that had it not been for his steady hand and clear head we would hardly be here to-night celebrating the victory of November last.

The audience thundered its approval.

It was then Arthur's turn. Perhaps he had enjoyed too much liquor by this time, or perhaps he was merely carried away by the enthusiasms of the evening. In any case his rambling remarks lacked the discretion that always characterized his public comments. Surrounded by old friends, veteran campaigners, party financiers, Arthur chose to allude playfully to methods employed to bring victory in the last election. Judging from accounts of the crowd's cheers, laughter, and applause, the speech was the high point of the evening. Following a few words of introduction, Arthur was saying:

> I don't think we had better go into the minute secrets of the campaign, so far as I know them, because I see the reporters are present, who are taking it all down; and, while there is no harm in talking about some things after the election is over you cannot tell what they may make of it, because the inauguration has not yet taken place, and while I don't mean to say anything about my birthplace, whether it was in Canada or elsewhere, still, if I should get to going about the secrets of the campaign, there is no saying what I might say to make trouble between now and the 4th of March.

After a squib at an absent Blaine for the loss of Maine in September, Arthur went on: "the first great business of the [national] committee was to carry Indiana, and Mr. Dorsey was selected as the leader of the forlorn hope to carry Indiana. That was a cheerful task." When the laughter subsided, Arthur continued: "Indiana was really, I suppose, a Democratic State. It had always been put down in the book as a State that might be carried by close and careful and perfect organization and a great deal of—" Here he paused for a moment, and there were cries from the audience of "soap"—a reference to purchased votes—followed by more laughter. "I see the reporters here," Arthur warned, "and therefore I will simply say that everybody showed a great deal of interest in the occasion, and distributed tracts and political documents all through the country." The audience thoroughly appreciated this. When it was again relatively quiet, Arthur added, "If it were not for the reporters I would tell you the truth, because I know you are intimate friends and devoted adherents to the Republican Party."

When it came time for Henry Ward Beecher to speak, he said that he was not present as a clergyman, and that it was well for some in the audience that he was not. The crowd roared in delight.[28]

Arthur's speech drew much attention from the press. E. L. Godkin, who had recently reminded his readers of Arthur's role in the Phelps, Dodge case, published portions of the remarks and commented: "The cynicism of this, coming from such a veteran Machinist as Mr. Arthur, was not surprising, but people were rather shocked—though we do not see why they should have been—when they remembered that it came from the lips not of Mr. Conkling's 'lieutenant' in this city, but of the Vice-President-elect of the United States."[29] Others pondered the purpose behind the banquet itself. Was it merely a celebration or an effort to remind Garfield of his indebtedness to New York Stalwarts? William Chandler told Garfield that the dinner was an attempt "to degrade and injure the party and the new administration by public proclamation that they hold power through the corrupt acts of corrupt men," and would lead to demands by Dorsey.[30] Blaine warned Garfield about Dorsey in stronger terms, predicting that his goal was "to enable him to make demands of the Administration which will in the end modestly center in the Second Assistant Postmaster-Generalship, through which channel, in my judgment, there are cunning preparations being made by a small cabal to steal half a million a year during your Administration."[31] There was more to this charge than mere hostility toward Stalwarts, for while New York GOP leaders were shouting his praises, Dorsey was, in fact, as a congressional investigation of 1878 had indicated, deeply involved in one of the era's more infamous frauds.

Throughout the western states and territories mail contracts were awarded to the lowest bidders who would pledge to carry the mail with "certainty, celerity, and security." These words were indicated on clerks' registers by three stars, and thus the routes became known as the star routes. Contracts were let for four-year periods, but the Post Office Department retained the right to alter rates of compensation stipulated in the contracts to effect improved service. Thomas J. Brady, Second Assistant Postmaster General, the Grant appointee Arthur turned to for lists of New York postmasters in the campaign of 1880, was in charge of changing the star route contracts. As the scheme was designed, friendly contractors would win star routes through impossibly low bids, they would "improve" their service, and Brady would grant them a huge increase in their payments. There were 135 routes affected by the frauds, and the graft totaled hundreds of thousands of dollars annually. A Dorsey route in Dakota and Montana was raised from $2,350 to $72,350 a year; another in New Mexico went up from $6,330 to $150,592. In January 1880, the House Committee on Appropriations publicized Brady's actions, and Dorsey's role in the affair was quickly ascertained. During the presidential campaign the former Arkansas carpetbagger was distrusted and feared by a good many Republicans; the *Democratic Campaign Text Book* referred to "the Forty Thieves" and "the Dorsey rake." Nevertheless, Stalwarts placed him on the national committee and he was assigned the critical task of carrying Indiana. Star route funds were undoubtedly an ingredient in the "soap" employed liberally throughout that state. Garfield was unsure about the meaning of the dinner at Delmonico's, but the warnings from Chandler and Blaine prompted him to discount Dorsey's future advice. Still, for the sake of party unity and a peaceful administration, some way had to be found to placate Dorsey's friends.

Conkling appeared at Mentor on February 16, and he and Garfield talked quietly and politely for six hours about Stalwart claims. There were no surprises: Conkling once more urged Morton's selection to the Treasury, and Garfield again declined; Garfield suggested Folger for a lesser spot in the Cabinet, and Conkling said that he was too valuable to the party in New York to be spared. Conkling made it clear that New York would rather be without representation in the Cabinet than be offered a minor post. He was assured that the Empire State would not be forgotten.

Immediately after the Senator departed, Garfield invited Charles Folger to Mentor and offered him the Attorney Generalship. Completely exasperated, Conkling asked a friend: "Was it only to make his indifference to my wishes more marked that he summoned Folger, whose character he had impugned, the moment my back was turned, to offer him an office less in dignity than I said New York was entitled to?" Blaine was furious with Garfield for his bid to Folger: "In New York, it is understood to be the original concoction of Dorsey, Tom Murphy, and a whole nest of unclean birds who wish to go in for loot and booty." On February 23, after a talk with Conkling, Folger declined. Ten days before the inauguration Garfield was back where he started.[32]

Continuing to hope that Conkling would be satisfied with a relatively insignificant Cabinet post, Garfield then offered the Navy Department to Morton. Desperate for any sort of high public office, Morton accepted by telegraph on February 28. When Conkling heard of this, he flew into a rage; as long as there was the chance of landing the Treasury Department he would accept nothing from Garfield. At one o'clock in the morning on March 2 Morton was routed out of bed by Stalwart Congressman John H. Starin and taken to the apartment shared by Conkling and Arthur. The "conversation" lasted the rest of the night. The next morning Morton wired his apologies to Garfield, revoking his earlier acceptance of the Navy Department. In order to come out of the fray with something, however, he accepted an offer to become minister to France. Morton informed Conkling of his action and reminded him that it was taken "solely in deference to the wishes of yourself & other friends . . ."[33]

Despite his disappointment over Morton's retreat and the proximity of the inauguration ceremony, Garfield continued to resist Stalwart demands for the Treasury Department. Several portfolios were claimed by this time: Blaine, of course, would be Secretary of State; to please John Logan, Robert Lincoln of Illinois would get the War Department; Independents would be satisfied with the selection of Wayne MacVeagh of Pennsylvania as Attorney General. But what was to be done about Conkling? Garfield was so angered by the Senator's treatment of Morton that he considered offering the Treasury to William Robertson. Mentioning this to his fiancée, Whitelaw Reid hastened to add: "But that will surely not be done."[34]

After a careful scrutiny of Conkling's lieutenants, Reid became convinced that yet another one of them, Thomas L. James, might be detached from the Senator by the lure of office. If James could be persuaded to pledge his allegiance to Garfield and accept the Postmaster Generalship the President-elect would be able to contend that he had rewarded New York Stalwarts for their campaign efforts. At the same time, of course, Conkling would be denied power over patronage. James was approached and seemed friendly to Reid's scheme. Blaine was won over and so was Garfield—at last, two days before his inauguration, determined to refuse Conkling any actual representation on his Cabinet.

James was sent for and arrived at Reid's front door at 8:00 A.M. on March 3. He won immediate entrance, for Reid had orders "to keep him out of harm's way, and particularly to keep him away from his old political associates." The two men got Blaine out of bed, and a few minutes later James was ushered into Garfield's hotel room and introduced to the President-elect. Determining that James was trustworthy, Reid contacted Platt, rushed him into Garfield's presence, and extracted his acceptance of the appointment. This concluded, Garfield instructed Reid "to keep James as quiet as possible and to get him out of town on the afternoon train." James departed, according to Reid, "profoundly grateful," pledging his loyalty to Garfield "in the strongest fashion, whether Conkling supports the administration or fights it . . ."[35]

Conkling and Arthur were having breakfast when Platt, apparently playing both sides to his own advantage, brought them the news of James's deal with Garfield. All three men marched immediately over to Garfield's hotel. For over an hour, according to an account probably derived from Arthur, Conkling stormed angrily up and down the room, castigating Garfield to his face for deceiving his friends and betraying the party. The man who was to be President of the United States the following day sat quietly on the edge of his bed listening patiently to the tirade. Finally conceding that he could not move Garfield to name a New Yorker to the Treasury, Conkling attempted to badger him into selecting reliable Timothy Howe of Wisconsin. Garfield took all of this in stride; when the Senator calmed down, he politely wished his guests a pleasant good morning. The matter of Conkling's representation on the Cabinet was settled to his satisfaction.[36]

(Though considered a Conkling man, Thomas James had earned a high reputation as an efficient and honest postmaster in New York City. When Stephen Dorsey learned of the decision to make him Postmaster

General, he panicked, pleading with Garfield: "I would no more speak of him or recognize him than I would the vilest wretch I ever knew or saw. I beg you not to do it."[37] Dorsey had good reason to fear his future prosecutor.)

Garfield then hastened to complete his Cabinet. On March 3, Senator William Allison of Iowa agreed to become the Treasury Secretary, but he backed down the following morning and the post went to Senator William Windom of Minnesota. Iowa Senator Samuel J. Kirkwood became Secretary of the Interior, and William H. Hunt, an obscure Louisiana claims court judge, was named Secretary of the Navy.

When Garfield sent the list of his Cabinet appointees to the Senate on March 5 he was rather pleased by the fruits of his long months of anguish. "The result is better than I expected," he wrote in his diary. "Though not an ideal cabinet, it is a good combination of *esse et videre*."[38] Similar sentiments were expressed by Blaine men and Independents.

New York Stalwarts, on the other hand, were grim-faced about the Cabinet and furious with Garfield for ignoring his campaign pledges to them. When Grant was informed of the Cabinet's composition, he wrote to Conkling, "I confess to much disappointment."[39] For all of the labors of Conklingites in the campaign, efforts they believed directly responsible for Garfield's victory, Arthur was to be their only reliable man in the higher circles of the new administration; and with Blaine apparently at the helm, the Vice-President's influence was guaranteed to approach the invisible. Surveying his current political position, Conkling had much cause to despair. His authority in New York now rested on the hope that Garfield would reward him with key federal posts in the state. Given the history of the past several months, the worst might be expected.

CHAPTER TWELVE

The Crisis of His Fate

At 10:00 a.m. on March 4, the colorfully uniformed Cleveland Mounted Troop rode up to the front door of the White House to escort Hayes, Garfield, and Arthur to the Capitol for the inauguration ceremonies. General Sherman, the chief marshal for the occasion, was close by, as were the governor's guards of Columbus, Ohio. Snow had fallen the night before and lay more than an inch deep on the ground, but the skies were now clear and thousands awaited the start of the procession. Two open carriages appeared, drawn by lavishly caparisoned teams of horses. Garfield stepped into the first, followed by President Hayes and Senators Thurman and Bayard, representing the Senate committee on arrangements. Arthur and Senator Pendleton then entered the Vice-President's carriage. A detachment of police led the way, followed by twelve artillery companies and six companies of Marines. The Ohio troops escorted the carriages, and behind them marched the Utica Veterans, the Utica Citizens' Corps, the Maryland Fifth, the Boston Fusiliers, the "Grand Army," a company of Pennsylvania volunteers, some naval cadets, local militia companies, the Signal Corps, and members of a Negro association. Hundreds of temporary balconies had been erected along Pennsylvania Avenue, and flags and banners were everywhere. The huge crowd cheered and shouted its approval as the carriages passed bearing the nation's most prominent political leaders.

The dignitaries arrived at the Capitol at eleven thirty, and a short time later entered the crowded Senate chambers. Arthur made a short formal address and was sworn into office. Members of the House filed in to observe Arthur administer the oath of office to new Senators, and then the assemblage adjourned to the outdoor platform. Some 50,000 people were gathered at the east front of the Capitol to see the presidency change hands. Arthur, dressed in light trousers, a blue Prince Albert coat, a colored necktie, and light gloves, stood next to former Vice-President Wheeler, and drew considerable attention. A reporter observed, "Gen. Arthur, strong, keen-eyed, and handsome as ever, and because of his commanding form and military bearing [was] a central attraction." Garfield's tepid inaugural address, hastily prepared and completed only hours earlier, was warmly applauded. Conkling stood close by and smiled quietly at a reference to the civil service. Chief Justice White then arose, and James A. Garfield was sworn in as the nation's twentieth Chief Executive.

The newly constructed National Museum Building was lit by electricity for the inauguration ball that evening. Guests were greeted in the central rotunda by a large statue of liberty holding a torch. President Garfield and his wife, escorted by the venerable historian George Bancroft, ex-President and Mrs. Hayes, Arthur, and Wheeler arrived just after 9:00 P.M. and shook hands with hundreds of admirers until almost midnight. Mrs. Garfield was gowned in light heliotrope satin, elaborately trimmed with lace, a cluster of pansies at her neck, and no jewelry; Mrs. Hayes was in a cream-colored satin dress trimmed with ermine. For refreshments a caterer provided 1,500 pounds of turkey, 100 gallons of oysters, 50 hams, 15,000 cakes, and an assortment of additional treats in similar proportion. The orchestra, the dancing, the bright lights, the handsome dresses, the rich food, the gay mood of all who attended prompted one observer to describe the evening as the "grandest ball night that Washington has ever seen."[1]

The next day the Senate convened and was called to order by the new Vice-President. The special session was expected to last ten or twelve days and to restrict its activities to the consideration of treaties and the confirmation of a large number of presidential nominations. The vote held by Arthur in the event of a tie was considered of unusual importance, for party strength in the upper chamber was practically even: 37 Republicans, 37 Democrats, one independent, David Davis of Illinois, and a Virginia Readjuster named William Mahone. When the session opened, there were four Republican vacancies: Matt Carpenter had died on February 24, and Blaine, Windom, and Kirkwood had entered the Cabinet. It would take a short time to seat their replacements. Attempting to profit by their temporary numerical advantage, Democrats challenged Republican claims to a majority and attempted to organize Senate committees in their favor, a move that touched off a series of partisan squabbles that kept Senators in Washington for eleven weeks.

On March 10, Senator Pendleton proposed a slate of committees complete with Democratic chairmen and Democratic majorities. The following day David Davis, elected in 1877 by a coalition of Democrats and Independents, announced his support of Pendleton's plan. This placed the balance of party power in the hands of William Mahone, a bantam-sized ex-Democrat who had won a Senate seat on a platform calling for readjustment of his state's debt. Republicans swallowed their dislike of "repudiation" and quietly struck a bargain with the former Confederate general. In return for his allegiance, Mahone was promised at least some control over his state's patronage and removal of the Republican ticket from future Virginia elections; Republicans agreed to make his friend George C. Gorham secretary of the Senate and his Virginia associate Harrison H. Riddleberger sergeant-at-arms; furthermore, Mahone was pledged five committee assignments—a sizeable number for a freshman Senator. On March 14, he cast his ballot for the first time with the GOP.[2] Arthur's vote would thus be decisive.

Events came to a head on March 18, with all of the Republican Senators present. Twice Arthur broke ties in favor of his party. He seemed extremely nervous in his new role; his hands trembled, and at one point he announced the result of a vote incorrectly. But the GOP gained control of the Senate committees with his ballot. Thirty-nine Republicans won chairmanships; Mahone was awarded the agriculture committee, and Conkling resumed his place as head of the commerce committee.[3]

In retaliation, Democrats launched a filibuster to prevent the confirmation of Gorham and Riddleberger. Republicans refused to go into executive session to consider the administration's nominations until these officers were appointed. From March 23 to May 4, the Senate was deadlocked. Finally, Republicans elected to abandon the effort and to proceed with their formal business. Several treaties were ratified and almost three hundred nominations approved. By this time a few of the President's selections for federal office had captured the entire nation's attention.[4]

In mid-March Conkling was summoned to the White House to talk over once again the role of the New York Stalwarts in the administration. Platt was sure this was a sign that Garfield was ready to honor his pledge of August 5. If Conkling did not share Platt's optimism he was nevertheless eager to see what specific positions might be won. Nothing worthwhile developed out of the two-and-one-half hour session on

March 20. Garfield seemed willing to reappoint several of Conkling's followers, adding that he also intended to recognize some of the New Yorkers who supported him in Chicago. Conkling suggested foreign assignments, but the President said they deserved reward in their home state. Perhaps slightly suspicious, Conkling inquired, "Mr. President, what do you propose about the collectorship of New York?" Garfield replied reassuringly, "We will leave that for another time."[5]

Two days later Garfield sent the names of five Conklingites to the Senate: Stewart Woodford was named to be U.S. Attorney for the Southern District in New York; Louis Payn, marshal for the Southern District of New York; Asa Tenney, U.S. Attorney for the Eastern District of New York; Clinton McDougall, marshal for the Northern District of New York; and John Tyler, customs collector at Buffalo. Leaders of the machine were ecstatic over the unexpected news. William Robertson, on the other hand, told reporters that he was surprised and chagrined; he had not anticipated the President's submission to Conkling. Complaints poured into the White House. *The New York Times*, Philadelphia *Inquirer*, and Boston *Herald* deplored what they interpreted as Garfield's surrender. Blaine spent several hours with the President that evening persuading him to reconsider his posture toward Stalwarts in the Empire State.[6]

The next day, in the Senate chamber, Arthur opened a list of nominations sent from the White House and was stunned to see the name of William Robertson for collector of the New York Customhouse. Collector Merritt was nominated consul general at London, replacing General Badeau, Grant's close friend, who was demoted to minister to Copenhagen. Arthur folded the list with Robertson's name uppermost and sent it to Conkling. The New York Stalwarts correctly saw the Secretary of State's hand in this coup and concluded that their worst fear had been realized: Garfield was Blaine's puppet. What hope was there now for peace within the party?[7]

Robertson, fifty-eight, had been active in politics most of his life. After admission to the bar in 1847 he served as a town supervisor, a county judge, an Assemblyman, State Senator, and Congressman. Currently he was a powerful State Senator and a member of the Republican State Committee.[8] It did not concern the administration that he lacked the business experience and commitment to honesty and efficiency a superior collector would find useful. (Any more than it concerned Grant when he appointed Murphy and Arthur.) Political power was at stake; Robertson would be a capable ally in the struggle to smash Conkling's authority and win control of the GOP in New York. Independents, proud of the achievements in civil service reform made under Merritt, looked on sadly. E. L. Godkin wrote, "It is said in some quarters that Mr. Robertson's appointment means 'war' on Conkling. Now we are in favor of 'war' on Conkling, but we do not think it ought to be carried on at the expense of the public business, or with Conkling's own weapons."[9]

News of Robertson's nomination created a sensation across the country. Jay Gould's New York *Herald* declared, "every wish and suggestion of Mr. Conkling has been denied and a sharp politician put at the head of the Customs House who will know how to work it for all it is worth against Conkling." The St. Louis *Globe Democrat* asked, "Was James A. Garfield elected President of the United States simply that he might become a willing instrument for the execution of James G. Blaine's private vengeance?" As expected, Whitelaw Reid's *Tribune* found the President's action admirable. "He has recognized every wing and faction of the party. He gave Mr. Conkling a devoted personal adherent in the Post Master-General, and an obedient follower in the District-Attorney. He gave Mr. Platt a warm friend in the United States Marshal; and Mr. Arthur and Mr. Crowley another in the Buffalo Collector. These offices in the State had been in the hands of what is known as the Conkling wing, and the President left them there. The Collectorship he did not find in their hands, and he has not put it there. What fair-minded man could have expected that he would?"[10]

The stage was set for what was obviously to be a bitter battle in the Senate over the confirmation of Robertson's appointment. Conkling chaired the commerce committee, through which the nomination would pass, and he was certain to exert determined opposition. Garfield anticipated this, of course. He wrote to a friend, "This brings on the contest at once and will settle the question whether the President is registering clerk of the Senate or the Executive of the United States."[11] Conkling had been through a similar struggle with Hayes; everyone remembered he lost.

On March 24, the State Senate in New York unexpectedly endorsed Robertson's nomination by unanimous vote and called for prompt confirmation. The Assembly quickly followed suit. Even though Speaker Sharpe was soon able to push through a motion to reconsider the Assembly resolution, the ballots by New York legislators revealed a striking degree of administration support in the state.[12] The President's position seemed popular outside New York as well. A tabulation of nationwide newspaper opinion on the Robertson nomination, published by the Albany *Evening Journal*, showed 125 editors in favor of confirmation and only 15 against.[13]

Thomas James and Wayne MacVeagh called on the President on

March 25 to protest the recent appointments. The new Postmaster General threatened to resign in order to prove to his friends that he had nothing to do with the Robertson nomination. The Attorney General was upset not only about Robertson but about the naming of shady William E. Chandler for Solicitor General. Both men had concluded that Blaine was behind the objectionable nominations and consequently agreed to see the President together. Garfield smiled, put an arm around each of his friends, and encouraged them to invite Conkling over that evening. The Cabinet would be on hand and no doubt everything could be ironed out! Conkling snubbed the invitation. He desired no more empty assurances from the President and was not about to have tea with Blaine. Moreover, he was disturbed by a wire from Cornell advising him not to oppose Robertson's appointment.[14]

The Senator's rage soon subsided and he went on the attack. Tom Platt called at the White House on March 28 to contend that he and Conkling were personally affronted when Robertson was nominated without their prior consultation. (Garfield privately admitted to his diary that perhaps he should have given the Senators advance warning, "But that would have made no difference in the result.") Later in the day Postmaster James appeared bearing a written protest signed by himself, the Vice-President, and both New York Senators. At the core of the complaint was the violation of senatorial courtesy. "We had only two days before this been informed from you that a change in the customs office at New York was not contemplated; and, quite ignorant of a purpose to take any action now, we had no opportunity, until after the nominations, to make the suggestion we now present." The "suggestion," of course, was the prompt withdrawal of Robertson's name.

Half-Breeds were uneasy about Garfield: to them, far from being a puppet, he appeared to be a weathervane, a timorous man likely to alter his course of action at any time if the pressure was sufficient. John Hay, temporarily editor of the *Tribune*, paid a call at the White House the same day Platt and James appeared. His purpose was to read a lengthy dispatch from Whitelaw Reid imploring the President to hold fast. "I wish to say to the President," Reid concluded, "that in my judgment this is the turning point of his whole Administration—the crisis of his Fate. If he surrenders now, Conkling is President for the rest of the term and Garfield becomes a laughing-stock. On the other hand he has only to stand firm to succeed. . . . In one word, there is no safe or honorable way out now but to go straight on. Robertson should be held firm. Boldness and tenacity now insure victory not merely for this year but for the whole term. The least wavering would be fatal."

Garfield listened attentively, obviously moved by the emotional appeal to his courage and honor. When Hay had finished, he set his jaw and declared, "They may take him out of the Senate head-first or feet-first: I will never withdraw him."[15]

On April 3, a number of prominent Stalwarts gathered at Arthur's home in New York to map future strategy. Governor Cornell and Postmaster General James were on hand, as were Tom Murphy, Clint Wheeler, John O'Brien, Steve French, Joel Mason, and several other veteran politicos. The meeting was supposed to be secret, but at least two newspapers learned of it.[16]

Two days later Platt proposed that all New York nominations be withdrawn and that Robertson be appointed district attorney in place of Woodford. John Logan then tried his hand at swaying the President.[17] With Reid's plea still ringing in his ears, Garfield would not budge.

The next weapons in the Stalwart arsenal were petitions distributed to New York import merchants criticizing Robertson's record in the state legislature and calling for the retention of Collector Merritt. Both Conkling and Arthur urged their friends and associates among the businessmen to sign. One newspaper editorialized, "Of course the bulldozed importers must sign the petitions or run the risk of being 'Boycotted' in a revenue way by Collector Merritt should he remain in office." Dozens of merchants complied. The documents were sent to the White House by the prestigious Board of Trade and Transportation.[18] A similar petition was circulated in the Assembly by Speaker Sharpe and signed by a majority of the Republican members.[19]

Arthur's role in these maneuvers was by this time drawing stiff criticism from the press. Independent newspapers and journals condemned him for his blatant partisanship and disloyalty to the President. Half-Breed editors hounded his every move, pouring invective upon him. Democrats, of course, took delight in flaying his character. The Chicago *Evening Journal* found Arthur's tactics on behalf of Conklingites "reprehensible and disgusting in the second officer of the Government." "The great Republican party of the Union," it editorialized, "did not elevate him to the high position he now holds in order that he might condescend to foment jealousies and to grease the New York machine, nor to play the boss at the back of Lord Roscoe, but to deport himself in a gentlemanly and respectable manner."[20] However Arthur may have resented such attacks, and he surely did, he would not permit them to influence his activities. He had been a Stalwart too long to surrender an inch—much less the war—to Blaine and those he controlled. If he could not be popular, at least he could be true to his friends; and if Conkling regained his political power there would soon be admirers enough.

On the evening of April 14, Arthur eluded reporters and slipped into the White House for a private conversation with the President. He implored Garfield to drop Robertson's nomination on the ground that its confirmation would badly fracture New York Republicanism and consign the party to certain defeat. Garfield politely refused to change his mind, and afterward wrote proudly to Reid: "Of course I deprecate war, but if it is brought to my door the bringer will find me at home."[21]

Despite Garfield's obstinacy, Conkling was optimistic about the chances of blocking Robertson's appointment. The Senate was prevented from considering nominations by its deadlock over the naming of Senate officers, and this gave Stalwarts badly needed time to persuade Republican Senators—if not the President—to quash the proposed change in the New York Customhouse. "No harm is done in our delaying confirmation," Conkling said. "The duties of the offices are performed by their present incumbents, and it would not cause much damage if some of the nominations were never confirmed."[22]

On April 27, Conkling appeared before a committee of Republican Senators created by the party caucus to consider nominations. For more than two hours he condemned the Robertson appointment with all the oratorical thunder at his command. He would use every effort, he stormed, to defeat confirmation, and nothing short of a withdrawal of Robertson's name would avert a struggle. He would fight the nomination in committee and in executive session; should it pass, he would publicly arraign the President on the floor of the Senate for his wanton breach of faith, pledged both at the August 5 conference in New York and at Mentor during the campaign. Conkling also claimed to have in his pocket a letter signed by the President, "which I pray God I may never be compelled in self-defense to make public; but if that time shall ever come, I declare to you, his friends, he shall bite the dust."

The Senators were deeply impressed and alarmed by what they witnessed. Henry Dawes of Massachusetts, chairman of the committee, later wrote that he had watched Conkling for twenty years, "but I had never heard anything which equalled his effort for flights of oratorical power—genuine eloquence, bitter denunciations, ridicule of the despised faction in New York and contempt for its leader." At the same time he and his colleagues could envision a potentially disastrous internecine war.[23]

The committee quickly called on the President and recommended the withdrawal of Robertson's nomination. Garfield calmly and firmly refused. He had acted, he said, in the best interests of the party and it was up to the Senate to confirm or reject his nominations. In his diary he hastily dismissed this conciliatory attempt. "The committee had been bull-dozed by Senator Conkling."[24]

Senator Dawes made several trips to the White House seeking accommodation, and at one point he inquired about the document Conkling claimed to possess that would force the President to "bite the dust." Garfield had heard of Conkling's threat and treated the matter lightly. "I know what it is," he said, "and have a copy of it." Dawes was shown a letter to Jay Hubbell, written during the campaign, asking indirectly about the progress of assessments in federal departments. One sentence referred to Thomas Brady, so presumably the letter would be used to link the President with the star route frauds. The Senator urged Garfield to forestall Conkling's attack by having the letter published. At that moment Blaine entered the room and was asked by the President for his advice. The Secretary of State recommended against publication—and no action was taken.

When Dawes ran into Conkling on the street he gently coaxed him to forgive and forget in the name of party unity. Conkling shook his head and said it was too late for that. "If I should take the course you suggest, I should myself go under and should be burned in effigy from Buffalo to Montauk Point, and could not be elected a delegate to a county convention in Oneida County."[25]

Dawes's committee finally recommended to the caucus that the party abandon its efforts to seat Mahone's friends and meet in executive session to vote on the President's nominations. Hundreds of appointments awaited confirmation, Garfield was demanding action, and further delay could be injurious to the work of the federal government. Sensing approval of the recommendation, Conkling frantically appealed to his colleagues to extract Robertson's nomination from the others and vote on it at the next session of Congress. The prospect of delaying a heated party conflict until after the fall elections appealed to the caucus, and it voted to consider "uncontested" nominations ahead of "contested" ones. The first lists of names could be disposed of swiftly; if cases within the second category produced excessive friction, several Republicans commented, the Senate might adjourn until December. Conkling and Platt now smilingly predicted their ability to postpone consideration of Robertson's appointment. The caucus decision was entirely unsatisfactory to the President, who realized that all of Conkling's men who had been nominated for federal positions could breeze into office under the "uncontested" banner, while the one New Yorker he most adamantly wished to reward might be ignored.[26]

The Senate met in executive session on May 4 and confirmed several nominations, including one belonging to a minor Conklingite. If this was insufficient to anger the President, Stalwarts published Garfield's letter to

Jay Hubbell, thereby charging the Chief Executive with complicity in the most notorious thievery of the period.[27]

The next day, at Blaine's urging, Garfield withdrew the five major New York Stalwart nominations. "This will bring the Robertson nomination to an issue," he wrote in his diary. "It may end in his defeat but it will protect me against being finessed out of a test." "My dear President," Blaine wrote, "Glory to God, Victory is yours, sure & Lasting."[28] Half-Breeds held a jubilee dinner in Albany.[29]

Garfield's bold step was the talk of the nation's capital. Republican Senators scurried to the White House to prevent further internal bloodshed; Democrats observed events with amusement. Some newspapers were critical of the move; *The New York Times* called it "an act of political and personal warfare, which is not only entirely unworthy of the Presidential office, but is for its own ends singularly ill-timed and ill-planned."[30] The New York *Sun*, the New York *Herald*, and the upstate Stalwart press made similar statements. Perhaps a great many more newspapers, however, were sympathetic. "At Last," the Baltimore *American* trumpeted, "President Garfield has answered the question 'Who is president?'" The Philadelphia *Inquirer* commented, "The President has at last hit the Bull's eye." The editor of the Chicago *Tribune* telegraphed: "Hold the fort. Better resign to his henchman Arthur and go back to Mentor than degrade the presidency by succumbing to the usurping boss." Garfield recorded in his diary, "The withdrawal of the New York appointments has brought me vigorous responses from many quarters and I think shows that the public do not desire the continuance of boss rule in the Senate."[31]

New York *Herald* editor J. L. Connery was summoned to Washington by Conkling and Arthur to lend a hand with the struggle against Garfield. Conkling poured out his case against the President, describing each of the occasions on which he and his colleagues had been promised control of New York's patronage and arguing that the purpose behind Robertson's nomination was his political destruction. He concluded with the assertion that the real battle was between him and Blaine. Arthur agreed. "It is a hard thing to say of a President," he stated, "but it is, unfortunately, only the truth. Garfield, spurred by Blaine, by whom he is easily led, has broke every pledge made to us; not only that, but he seems to have wished to do it in the most offensive way." Conkling would now be forced to lay the whole case before the public, Arthur said.[32]

When Connery returned to New York he published much of what he was told in Washington, discreetly refraining from quoting the Vice-President. Introduced into the story for the first time was the claim that Garfield had written a memorandum during the campaign containing his promise to follow Conkling's advice in matters of state patronage. No such document would ever be produced. Garfield rejected the article as "an ugly assault . . . evidently inspired by Conkling."[33]

Robertson's nomination was discussed fully in a five-hour Republican caucus meeting on May 9. Senator Edmunds moved to postpone action on it until December, and Conkling supported the proposal with a two-and-one-half-hour tirade. Republican Senators wished to respect the principle of senatorial courtesy and regretted Garfield's failure to recognize it when Robertson was appointed. But they were growing restive about an assault against their party standard-bearer in the opening months of his administration. The President would not be budged, and it made no political sense to defy him any longer. Half-Breed Senators were soon claiming that three fourths of their GOP colleagues would vote for Robertson. Democrats, mollified in the Mahone matter and eager to adjourn, were also going over to the President. Senator Vorhees of Indiana told a New York *Star* reporter: "The President has the right under the Constitution to select such persons as he sees fit for the public offices and send their names to the Senate. If in doing so factions arise in his own party, that is not my affair. . . . I can only look to the person nominated in the Senate. If he fills the Jeffersonian requirements, on what grounds can I vote to reject him?" Edmunds's motion was withdrawn the next day in the face of certain defeat. At another meeting a few days later it became apparent that most Republicans were ready to vote on Robertson, and Conkling stormed from the room, vowing never again to attend a party caucus.[34]

Several GOP leaders now predicted that Robertson would be approved within a week. "All idea of effecting an arrangement looking to his withdrawal has been abandoned," reported *The New York Times,* "and his confirmation is regarded as certain." Conkling was even without hope of blocking the nomination in his commerce committee; of the nine members, only three, including himself, were known to be opposed. A motion to discharge the nomination from the committee, should the chairman attempt to sit on it, was thought sure to pass.[35]

On May 14, Platt persuaded Conkling to join him in resigning from the Senate. The turn of events had placed Platt in an exceedingly awkward position. Whatever personal difficulties he had had with his long-time chieftain, he wished to remain Conkling's friend and ally. While seeking a Senate seat for himself a few months earlier, however, he had sworn to support Garfield's attempts to reward Half-Breeds. Apparently he had not envisioned so drastic a move as the appointment of

Robertson to the collectorship, and when that happened, like James, he threatened to resign his seat in protest. Conkling talked him out of it at the time, arguing that Garfield might be pressured into dropping the nomination. Now that Robertson's confirmation was imminent, Platt convinced Conkling that a joint resignation, followed by a triumphant reelection in the state legislature, would be an effective way to protest their treatment at the hands of the President and vindicate their position. Arthur, along with James, Cornell, and a number of other New Yorkers, opposed the plan, no doubt recalling the legislature's earlier endorsement of Robertson. But Conkling probably felt he had little to lose, for with the Secretary of State at the controls of the Customhouse his machine would be wrecked and his political voice reduced to a whimper. The alternative to accepting Platt's advice would be to suffer the wounds of Blaine's gloat.[36]

On Monday, May 16, the Vice-President entered the Senate chamber a few minutes late. During the services by the chaplain, observers noticed that he appeared flushed and nervous. As the lengthy prayer wound to a close, however, Arthur regained his composure and coolly directed the clerk to read the proceedings of the previous session. That completed, he handed the clerk Conkling's letter of resignation, which was read aloud. Some of the Senators were inattentive, while others gasped in disbelief. The clerk was requested to read the communication a second time. Then Arthur handed him Platt's resignation, and the Senate was soon in an uproar.

A joint letter of resignation sent to Cornell was published the same day, describing the events leading to the action, disclosing the petition to the President signed by Arthur, James, and both former Senators, and condemning Garfield and Robertson on numerous grounds. In one especially curious sentence the removal of Merritt from the Customhouse was objected to on the ground that it was a breach of sound civil service policy. "Although party service may be fairly considered in making selections of public officers, it can hardly be maintained that the Senate is bound to remove without cause incumbents merely to make places for those whom any individual, even the President or a member of his Cabinet, wishes to repay for being recreant to others or serviceable to him."[37] This sudden flurry of reform-mindedness was somewhat unusual for Grant men.

Reaction to the dramatic and unprecedented move was not what Platt expected. (First reports attributed the initiation of the resignations to Conkling. His colleague was ridiculed as "Me too!" Platt.) Nearly every member of the Senate was critical; Senator Vest said, "Conkling has made a fool of himself." Most of the nation's press heaped scorn upon the New Yorkers. *The New York Times* commented, "In this City the most common sentiment was impatience and disgust that the State should have been made the laughing-stock of the country by the childish display of temper on the part of its Senators." Old Thurlow Weed was shocked by the news. "Mr. Conkling has deliberately transferred his fight with the President from Washington to Albany, and in doing so he has insulted the Legislature, which represents the people of this State." Even so devout a Stalwart as Henry Ward Beecher condemned Conkling. "I am utterly opposed to his antagonizing the Administration. His conduct has been heedless, not to say wanton."[38]

When Garfield learned of the resignations he called them "a very weak attempt at the heroic" and vowed to persevere. "Having done all I fairly could to avoid a fight I will fight to the end."[39] A delighted John Hay wrote to Whitelaw Reid, "to speak of certainties, Roscoe is finished. That Olympian brow will never again garner up the thousands of yore."[40]

With Conkling and Platt out of the Senate, opposition to the Robertson nomination virtually disappeared. The commerce committee voted for the New York Half-Breed 7 to 1, and two days after the resignations his appointment sailed through the Senate. Merritt was confirmed to succeed Badeau in London, and Badeau's nomination was withdrawn at his request.[41]

Marshal Louis Payn and two other Conkling agents arrived in Albany even before the resignations were announced to lay the groundwork for the speedy reelection of their superiors. The law required vacant Senate seats to be filled by the second Tuesday after notice was officially given to the state legislature by the governor. The plan was to have Cornell issue the formal notice on the same Monday evening the resignations were read in Washington, the 16th, thereby forcing the legislature to make its selections on the 24th. Hopefully, this would prevent administration leaders from organizing effective opposition and obstruct their ability to decide upon popular alternative candidates.

Half-Breeds in the State Senate quickly gauged Stalwart strategy, however, and capitalized on a miscalculation by Cornell. Instead of sending two messengers to the legislature bearing documents of notification, one to each house, the governor sent his private secretary to inform both branches. The young man reached the Assembly, but ten minutes before he arrived at the Senate, Robertson men pushed through an adjournment. Both houses of the legislature were therefore not officially informed of the resignations, and the election was delayed until May 31. With two weeks in which to work, Half-Breeds believed Conkling and Platt could be sent into permanent retirement.

They probably did not need the extra time. Two days later a petition was circulated in the State Senate pledging opposition to any candidate hostile to the Garfield Administration. By noon more than thirty-five Republicans had signed. "The Conkling men are all at sea," *The New York Times* chortled, "losing strength every hour, partly through the absence of leaders, but more clearly because the Conkling men have no purpose except to re-elect the men who have resigned . . ."[42]

One Stalwart on the scene thought that the situation cried for Conkling's presence in Albany. "Why if he would only come here and walk through the hall of the Delavan he would make the half-breeds up stairs tremble."[43]

On May 21, Arthur slipped into the Fifth Avenue Hotel by a side entrance and conferred with Conkling until the small hours of the morning. The next afternoon, Conkling, Platt, Payn, Speaker Sharpe, State Senator Robert Strahan, Smyth, French, A. B. Johnson of Utica, and Senator Jones of Nevada held a lengthy strategy session at the Vice-President's home. (The meeting was intended to be secret, but reporters picked up the scent and greeted the politicians as they arrived. Three weeks later Arthur snapped at a newsman, "Cannot two men come into this house without it being reported from one end of the land to the other that a conference is being held in the Vice-President's house? . . . I tell you there were no conferences here.")[44] It was decided that Conkling, Platt, Arthur, and their top workers in the state should converge on Albany to ride herd on the legislature. Conkling was said to resist the idea at first, no doubt wishing to be the pursued rather than the pursuer, but after listening to a careful analysis of Half-Breed strength in the state capital, he was won over. George Bliss told a reporter the same day, "The Conkling men have got their breath now, and are doing good work, the effect of which will be seen next week."[45]

Stalwarts hoped to call a caucus on the 26th and bind all members of the GOP with a majority vote. The "vindication" Conkling and Platt sought was actually to be requested from a bare majority of the legislators. Predictably, Half-Breeds refused to enter a caucus, arguing that it was more democratic to place the issue before the full legislature. While both sides plotted schemes and counted heads, the entire leadership of the Conkling machine poured out of arriving trains. Blaine hurried to New York City and persuaded Chauncey Depew to reenter the Senate race.[46] The Secretary of State confided to a friend, "Everything possible or impossible must be done to beat those fellows at Albany."[47]

Albany quickly filled with politicians, newsmen, and spectators eagerly anticipating the head-on collision between the New York Stalwarts and the administration forces in the state. Conkling and Arthur arrived together on the afternoon of May 24. A band of loyalists at the railway station gave three cheers for the former Senator; both men lifted their hats obligingly and walked over to the Delavan House. Instead of ignoring the clerk at the desk, as was his custom, Conkling signed the hotel register in bold letters and stood grinning as a crowd cheered for Conkling, Platt, Grant, and the brave "306." As he made his way up the stairs to his rooms, he shook hands with everyone in reach. "Nothing could have been more gracious than his manner," said an awed reporter, "and no statesman ever wore a more winning smile." Conkling was prepared for the supreme fight of his political life.[48]

There were 106 Republicans in the state legislature; 72 of them had to agree to call a caucus. Stalwarts expressed extreme confidence in their ability to procure enough signatures, and scores of their workers swarmed over the city bearing petitions. But opposition to the effort was immediate. Forty lawmakers went on record as opposing a party conclave, including every member of the Senate caucus committee. Conklingites sputtered that such obduracy was unprecedented, outrageous, subversive of all party discipline. Robertson and his allies countered with a reminder of Conkling's declaration of hostility toward the caucus of United States Senators. "A rebel against caucus dictation at Washington," *The New York Times* agreed, "ought surely to have some tolerance for those who refuse to bow to the tyranny of the caucus at Albany."[49]

A story went the rounds of one legislator who was invited to the Vice-President's suite, confronted with a caucus petition, and requested to sign. When he balked, saying that his constituents very much opposed the reelection bid by Conkling and Platt, he was told that his signature would bind him to no specific candidate. Conkling, Arthur, and Platt each pled with the politician, but he resisted their overtures.[50]

Switching tactics, Conklingites invited Republicans to a "convention," an informal consultation on the upcoming election which would undoubtedly feature oratory by Roscoe Conkling. But the offer appealed to few and was soon dropped. With the senatorial election only a few days away, Stalwart leaders returned to New York City for the weekend, dejected but determined to persist.[51]

By this time Arthur's appearance in Albany in his traditional role as a Conkling lieutenant was drawing heated barbs from large segments of the nation's press. The New York *Tribune* declared, "If General Arthur does not desire four years of public contempt he would do well to desist from the business in which he is now engaged before his inexcusable indiscretion becomes a National scandal."[52] E. L. Godkin observed, "Mr. Arthur, the Vice-President, is exciting a great deal of indignation, not only in this state but all over the country, by his performances at Albany as a touter for votes for his friend, Mr. Conkling.

But we must say that much of this condemnation, certainly that part of it which comes from Republicans, seems to us unreasonable. Mr. Arthur was nominated by the Republican Convention and elected by the voters with a full knowledge of his character and antecedents . . ." Arthur was long known for "his great skill and energy in all subterranean politics." "The moral of his performances is that we must not expect to change a man's nature by electing him to the Vice-Presidency."[53] Thomas Nast drew a scathing cartoon portraying Arthur as a bootblack for Conkling and Platt; under it was the caption, "I did not engage you, Vice-President Arthur, to do this kind of work."[54]

Cornell's role in the struggle puzzled observers at first. The governor consulted with Stalwart leaders during their stay in Albany, but made no public statement and did not permit the state machinery to enter the contest. As everyone recalled, he had used his weight a few months earlier to help Platt win his Senate seat; now he remained curiously aloof, pleading that his administrative duties absorbed almost all of his time. The New York *Herald* reported Conkling angry with the governor for failing to come to his aid.[55]

On Monday, May 30, with Conkling, Arthur, and Platt back in Albany, Stalwarts revealed their desperation in a move that drew ridicule and scorn from their opposition. Speaker Sharpe and three other Assembly leaders, on their own and without the necessary signatures, called a caucus for that evening. Only thirty-five Republicans attended. Stalwarts gathered at the session in Arthur's home on May 22 had grossly miscalculated their strength in the legislature; too many Republicans refused to tangle with the new administration, and the presence in Albany of Conkling and his aides had made little difference. *The Times* commented, "The extraordinary imbecility of calling a caucus to demonstrate beyond the possibility of dispute the hopeless weakness of the Conkling cause is of a piece with most of the important moves made by the ex-Senator and his friends during this extraordinary struggle."[56]

The balloting to fill the vacant seats began the next day. By law, if the legislature could not elect on the first day, it was required to meet daily thereafter and to take at least one vote until the vacancies were filled. A stalemate was predictable from the start. Democrats had sworn in caucus to support one of their own, neither Republican faction could readily muster the majority needed to win, and the administration forces were unable to unite behind a pair of candidates. Twenty men were nominated on the first ballot. Among them were Cornell, Folger, Crowley, Dutcher, and Morton, aware of the futility of Conkling's quest and looking out for themselves. With 105 Republicans present, Conkling received 39 votes. (Garfield sneered, "And this is the 'vindication' he appealed for.") Platt got only 29. Neither man would again equal his first ballot strength.[57]

Conkling and Platt might have chosen to bow out of the race at this point, for the futility of their candidacies was obvious. Had either genuinely sought retirement, as several historians have surmised, they might have saved a little face by hurling epithets at appropriate targets and taking the first train home. But as in 1880 when the "306" stuck together to the bitter end, Conkling and those who remained loyal to him determined to fight to the last against Blaine and his cohorts, to remain in Albany the rest of the summer if necessary in hope of victory. And should the dispute fail to be resolved, the people of New York could decide matters in the fall election. "Mr. Conkling is a monomaniac on the subject of his own importance," Rutherford B. Hayes declared.[58] Arthur, of course, would remain at the former Senator's side.

The balloting continued, six days a week, for more than seven weeks. For a short time Conklingites held the largest single bloc of Republican votes, but other candidates from within the administration faction soon gained ground. By the seventh roll call Chauncey Depew forged ahead of Platt. (Two ballots later, a Stalwart claimed he had been bribed to vote for Depew by a leading Half-Breed. The charge seemed contrived from the start; a legislative investigation dismissed it.) On the sixteenth ballot former Vice-President Wheeler moved in front of Conkling. After the twenty-second ballot one exhausted participant moved to keep the legislature in session and on bread and water until two Senators were elected. To relieve the monotony, several Democrats soon challenged Stalwarts to a game of baseball.[59]

After the thirty-first ballot, conducted on July 1, Platt suddenly retired from the race. A few Half-Breeds on a stepladder had peered through an open transom into a hotel room spying him in bed with a woman decidedly not his wife. When the story began to spread throughout the city and leak into the press, Platt thought it appropriate to bow out.[60] Stalwart humiliation was now complete. But Conkling and Arthur would concede nothing.

On the morning of July 2, the day newspapers announced Platt's withdrawal, President Garfield entered the almost-empty Baltimore and Potomac Station in Washington arm in arm with Blaine. He was to catch a train that would take him to New York and then to New England to attend commencement exercises at his alma mater, Williams College; afterward he planned a vacation with his family. Four Cabinet members and their wives had preceded Garfield to the station and were seated in the train awaiting his arrival.

A small, shabbily dressed man with a dark brown beard and sallow complexion suddenly appeared behind the two men as they strode by, drew a revolver, pointed it at the President's back, and fired. He ran a few steps closer and fired again. Garfield fell to the floor. The assailant said nothing and fled toward an exit.

Officer Patrick Kearney of the District of Columbia police heard the shots and ran into the reception room in time to seize the gunman. "I must arrest you," the excited policeman gasped. "All right," came the quiet reply. "I did it and will go to jail for it. I am a Stalwart, and Arthur will be President."[61]

CHAPTER THIRTEEN

On the Annals of History

DURING THE IMBROGLIO over New York's Senate seats, Conkling, Platt, and Arthur returned to New York City on weekends to relax and take care of business matters. When the steamer from Albany landed on Saturday morning, July 2, Arthur and Conkling stepped onto the dock and learned for the first time of the shooting of the President. For two hours after the tragedy telegraphic reports declared Garfield dead, and that was no doubt Arthur's first impression. Later dispatches altered the story to describe his condition as grave and to predict a slight hope for recovery.[1]

A carriage sped the two men to the Fifth Avenue Hotel, where they spent more than an hour in private consultation. When Arthur arrived home, a telegram from Blaine was waiting describing the assassination attempt and expressing optimism for Garfield's recovery. Arthur replied, "I am profoundly shocked at the dreadful news. The hopes you express relieve somewhat the horror of the first announcement. I await further intelligence with the greatest anxiety. Express to the President and those about him my great grief and sympathy, in which the whole American people will join." Shortly, a somber wire arrived from the Secretary of State: "At this hour, Six O'clock the condition of the President is very alarming. He is losing his strength and the worst may be apprehended." When Arthur finally consented to see a reporter, he asked, "What can I say? What is there to be said by me? I am overwhelmed with grief over the awful news."[2]

At first, Arthur expressed an unwillingness to go to Washington until officially notified of Garfield's death. Twice during the evening he traveled to Conkling's hotel room to talk things over with a coterie of

Stalwarts. At 9:30 P.M. Navy Secretary Hunt and Postmaster James wired, "The President is no better, and we fear sinking." A telegram from Blaine soon arrived stating that the Cabinet wished Arthur to take the midnight train to Washington. Conkling, Senator Jones, and Steve French accompanied the Vice-President to the depot—Conkling carried his suitcases. As Arthur was about to enter his coach with Jones and a government detective, Conkling grasped his hand firmly and said, "God bless you, I'll see you on Thursday."[3]

By this time Garfield's physical condition was the primary public concern of the nation and much of the world. One bullet had only grazed his arm, but the other had entered his back and lodged near the spinal column, and its consequences were considered extremely serious. Garfield was returned to the White House and made as comfortable as possible. A battery of physicians and attendants watched over him, and bulletins describing his progress were released at thirty-minute intervals. Doctors thought the President's condition too grave to permit a probe for the bullet; most contented themselves with sticking their fingers into the wound. Garfield was alert throughout most of the crisis and tried valiantly to cheer those who approached his bedside. He asked only once about his assailant, and said, "He must have been crazy. None but an insane person could have done such a thing. What could he have wanted to shoot me for?"[4]

Few doubted Charles Guiteau's madness, for his irrationality was obvious from the moment of his capture. Subsequently it would be learned that his mother suffered from what would be called today a postpartum psychosis, that his father was at best unstable, and that Charles, forty-eight when he leaped into history, had long been considered insane by numerous observers.[5] Still, in the initial agony of those tense, fearful July days, many read of Guiteau's professed link with Arthur and the Stalwarts and wondered if there could be more to the attempted murder than was readily apparent.

A drifter, chiseler, and sometime attorney, theologian, and preacher, Guiteau had turned his energy toward politics in 1880 and become emotionally attached to the Stalwarts and their drive to win a third term for Grant. He readily announced his support of the Garfield-Arthur ticket and hung around the Fifth Avenue Hotel during the campaign, passing out copies of an incoherent speech he had written and pressing politicians for speaking engagements. He made little or no impression on GOP leaders but was permitted to give a speech at a rally marking the conclusion of the Fifth Avenue Hotel conference and another at a meeting of a dozen New York City Negroes.[6] After the election Guiteau was overjoyed, writing to Garfield, "We have cleaned them out, just as I expected. Thank God." The two men had not met, and the letter, like its author, was ignored.

Guiteau had designs on the ministry to Vienna, and wrote a letter to Garfield in October hinting at his availability for the post. He moved to Washington shortly after the inauguration to pursue the consul-general-ship to Paris and was a familiar figure in the corridors of the State Department. Before long the small, threadbare man from Illinois became something of a joke to Washingtonians, in the words of one, "a kind of butt, sent around from place to place, his own egotism sustaining him." He bombarded the President with letters and was soon forbidden entrance to the White House anterooms by weary secretaries. Blaine encountered him at the State Department in mid-May and snapped, "Never bother me again about the Paris consulship so long as you live." Unemployed, hungry, and depressed, Guiteau shortly determined that the President should be "removed." He borrowed money to purchase an elegant revolver (expecting to be caught, he wished the weapon to be impressive on display), target-practiced along the Potomac, and stalked Garfield for several weeks. On Thursday, June 30, he read a newspaper report that the President would be leaving Saturday morning at 9:30 A.M. from the Baltimore and Potomac depot.[7]

When Guiteau was captured, police found on him a letter dated July 2 that began, "The President's tragic death was a sad necessity, but it will unite the Republican Party and save the Republic." "I had no ill-will toward the President," Guiteau had written. "His death was a political necessity. . . . I am a Stalwart of the Stalwarts. I was with Gen. Grant and the rest of our men in New-York during the canvass." Among Guiteau's papers was a letter addressed to Arthur, informing him of the assassination and making recommendations for a new Cabinet. While under heavy guard at the District jail, Guiteau confided to a detective, "Gen. Sherman is coming down to take charge. Arthur and all those men are my friends, and I'll have you made Chief of Police."[8] This statement, along with Guiteau's letters, was immediately in the press.

A few believed that Guiteau was a hired killer and that Conkling and Arthur were his employers. But this view was not entertained seriously by major newspapers and journals or by the bulk of the public. On the other hand, the shooting was interpreted widely as representing more than the work of a single lunatic. Many influential citizens held the spoils system responsible for Guiteau's act. *The National Republican* editorialized, "This desperate deed of the assassin Guiteau was mainly, if not entirely, the promptings of a disappointed office-seeker. There is but little doubt that if Guiteau had not come here for the purpose of getting an office and had failed to do so he would not have attempted to shoot the President."[9] Rochester's *Sunday Morning Herald* stated, "The almost universal expression of public sentiment as voiced in the press of the country indicates that the attempt on the President's life, which it is universally agreed was simply an outgrowth of the pernicious spoils system now in vogue in this country, did not find the people ignorant or indifferent regarding the abuses of the civil service."[10] The New York *Evening Mail* speculated, "Guiteau's bullet did not do fatal injury to President Garfield, as there is daily increasing reason to hope, but it inflicted a wound upon the spoils system which is likely to prove fatal to that conspicuous curse of the country."[11]

In the eyes of a great many, of course, Chester A. Arthur was a supreme example of the political boss, a symbol of the worst traits of the spoils system. *The New York Times* declared bitterly, "Active politicians, uncompromising partisans, have held before now the office of Vice-President of the United States, but no holder of that office has ever made it so plainly subordinate to his self-interest as a politician and his narrowness as a partisan. . . . While his succession to the Presidency of the United States depends simply on the issue of a strong man's struggle with death, Gen. Arthur is about the last man who would be considered eligible to that position, did the choice depend on the voice either of a majority of his own party or of a majority of the people of the United States."[12] E. L. Godkin outlined Arthur's political career and concluded, "It is out of this mess of filth that Mr. Arthur will go to the Presidential chair in case of the President's death."[13] Andrew Dickson White later reported, "It was a common saying of that time among those who knew him best, ' "Chet" Arthur President of the United States. Good God.' "[14]

Many expressed the fear that an Arthur presidency would mean simply that the executive branch of the government belonged to Roscoe Conkling. New York business circles seemed especially vulnerable to this theory. Several administration leaders agreed, predicting the substitution of Conkling for Blaine and the dismissal of James, MacVeagh, and Robertson.[15] Rutherford B. Hayes wrote in his diary, "Arthur for President! Conkling the power behind the throne, superior to the throne!"[16]

It was immediately noticed, moreover, that there was currently no president *pro tem* of the United States Senate, no one to succeed Arthur in the event of Garfield's death. The responsibility for this now-crucial omission rested squarely upon the Vice-President. When Conkling and Platt had resigned, Democrats held a majority in the Senate. Fearing the selection of Democratic Senator Thomas Bayard, Arthur had refused to vacate his chair, and the Senate adjourned without a president *pro tem*. Here was yet another crime attributable to excessive partisanship and charged against the Vice-President's reputation. Bayard wrote to Carl Schurz, "May Heaven avert the contingency of Arthur's promotion."[17]

Arthur and Senator Jones arrived in Washington at 8:00 A.M. on July 3. Both men went directly to the Jones residence, a large granite house directly south of the Capitol, where Arthur remained in seclusion the rest of the day. That evening he called at the White House and visited briefly with Mrs. Garfield. Senator Benjamin Harrison was in the private secretary's office as Arthur came out. "He showed deep feeling and seemed to be overcome with the calamity," Harrison recalled a few years later.[18]

Everyone who saw Arthur as he awaited the call to assume the presidency recognized his agony. He had never coveted the office of Chief Executive, and was overwhelmed by the prospect of filling the highest office in the land; he was stunned by the cruel circumstances that brought him to Washington and crushed by the savage attacks in the nation's press. Old friends likened his condition to that suffered at the death of his wife. One reporter walked in on him during the second day of his residence at the Jones home and found him with his head bowed, looking vacantly through an open window. "Tears stood in his eyes, and the orbs themselves were bloodshot. On his face were the traces of recent weeping. He would trust himself to speak but little, and was evidently afraid of being overcome by his emotions."[19]

The next day another reporter called on the Vice-President and indelicately alluded to newspaper editorials linking him and Conkling with Guiteau. Arthur seemed deeply moved by the aspersion. "No one," he said, "deplores the calamity more than Senator Conkling and myself. These reports are so base and so unfounded that I cannot believe they will be credited." "If it were possible for me to be with the President," he continued, "I would not only offer him my sympathy, I would ask that I might remain by his bedside. All personal considerations and political views must be merged in the national sorrow. I am an American among millions of Americans grieving for their wounded chief."[20] When Blaine brought him encouraging news about Garfield's condition a few days later, Arthur replied with a smile, "As the President gets better I get better, too."[21]

The Secretary of State had also been severely jolted by the asassination attempt and was grieved not only by the suffering of a good friend and his family but by the prospect of losing the immense political influence Garfield had handed him. He was constantly at the White House plying physicians with questions and coming away either greatly exhilarated or severely depressed. At the President's death his course of action would be clear: he would resign. But suppose Garfield remained disabled for months or even years? And if the disability was sufficiently serious, would Arthur be asked to don presidential authority? Blaine anguished over such questions and told his wife that an administration with a sickbed for its center was not a pleasant thought.[22] However anxious he was over the President's health, and whatever his distaste for the Vice-President, Blaine extended every courtesy to Arthur during the crisis. He and other members of the Cabinet paid daily visits to the Jones residence during the first week of Arthur's stay in Washington.[23]

On July 13, Garfield's physicians expressed optimism about his full recovery. Even though the President was barely able to move and continued to receive morphine, his condition was more favorable than at any time since the shooting. This was welcome news to the millions who followed the hourly medical bulletins in their newspapers. Arthur returned to his home in New York City immensely relieved.[24] Close friends from the Conkling machine were soon at hand.

Despite all that had happened, Roscoe Conkling stubbornly continued to pursue his reelection to the Senate. He, like Arthur, had never met Charles Guiteau, and he saw no reason to absorb blame for the senseless deed of a madman. He was aware, of course, of the attacks in the press, but assured a friend that they would all "in due time rebound upon the assassins who fulminate them." His critics, he said, "have seized a dark and dangerous hour for what you call their 'devilish' machinations; but in the end reason and judgment will prevail."[25]

Conkling was soon forced to recognize, however, that the shooting had broken the long stalemate in Albany. Sixty-two Republicans signed a caucus petition and the meeting convened on July 8. Sensing the hostility of their colleagues, Conklingites completely reversed their position on the sacredness of a party caucus and elected to boycott the session. This was too much for Arthur, who told a reporter that his friends had made a serious mistake.[26] The caucus hammered out a compromise that gave one Senate seat to a Half-Breed and the other to a Stalwart. To replace Platt, the Republicans selected Half-Breed Congressman Warner Miller. Congressman Elbridge Lapham defected from the Conkling ranks and was chosen to fill the short term. The caucus had brought a measure of unity to the GOP, but everyone knew that it lacked the power itself to elect its candidates. Several votes from the Stalwart camp were needed to win a majority in the legislature, and Conkling men were clamoring for adjournment.[27]

On July 16, Assembly Speaker Sharpe conceded the futility of the struggle and assisted in Miller's election.[28] Conkling and those few who remained loyal to him resisted the inevitable until July 22 when Lapham was elected on the fifty-sixth ballot.[29]

Satisfied administration leaders in Albany spoke of Conkling shortly after his defeat with patronizing pity. Perhaps throughout this awful conflict, they said, he had simply been "misguided." More than a few professed to believe that his decision to resign from the Senate and pursue vindication in Albany had been based on advice from the Vice-President.[30]

Conkling received word of Lapham's election while in his suite at the Fifth Avenue Hotel. Dejected, weary, and overcome with bitterness, he took a short walk alone in the neighborhood to ponder what was certainly the conclusion of his career in politics. On returning to the hotel he sent a wire to a friendly Assemblyman that began, "The heroic constancy of the spartan band which so long has stood for principle and truth has my deepest gratitude and admiration."[31] Several observers expected the Vice-President to call on Conkling to express his condolence. But Arthur did not appear.[32]

Garfield's condition began to worsen in late July. Two operations were required to stem a persistent infection, and on August 15 vomiting began which reduced the President's health to its lowest ebb since the shooting. One physician described the situation as very critical, and thoughts turned again to the possibility of Arthur's succession.[33]

Throughout these hot summer days Arthur remained in virtual seclusion in his Lexington Avenue home.[34] When news of Garfield's setback appeared, Arthur told a friend he was averse to going to the nation's capital for fear of giving the impression that he eagerly awaited the vacant office. Plans had been made, it was revealed, for the oath to be taken in New York if the President died suddenly.[35]

On August 16, Arthur gathered around him several of his closest friends and advisers for a confidential discussion of his course of action should he soon inhabit the White House. Grant and Conkling were present, as were Senator Jones, George Bliss, Steve French, Thomas Acton, and John Lydecker.[36] If there was to be an Arthur Administration, few could doubt its initial leanings.

Garfield's health deteriorated rapidly as August came to a close. An inflamed gland, revealing serious infection, caused physicians virtually to give up hope. Blaine prepared a paper on the critical situation and presented it to the Cabinet. Since the Constitution contained no directions for replacing a disabled President, he argued, Arthur should be called to Washington immediately to assume the reins of the executive branch.

Only two Cabinet members agreed, but Thomas James was sent scurrying to New York on August 27 to obtain Arthur's view of the question. The Vice-President refused to assume the powers of office and continued to resist the suggestion that he travel to Washington.[37]

By now, Garfield's gallant struggle had transformed him in the public eye from a fumbling, indecisive politician into a powerful Chief Executive who stood solidly for the highest virtues of the land. Reformers labeled him a fearless crusader for civil service reform and repeatedly quoted from his earlier speeches and articles. The reputation of his certain successor, however, had barely risen nearly two months after the shooting. Newspapers and journals had tempered their hostility somewhat; Arthur was described as a gentleman, and his conduct during the crisis was considered unexceptionable. Still, he could not escape his past as easily as the wounded President. The aura of Grantism hovered over his name and was reinforced by reports of those he sought for counsel. His presidency was almost unanimously dreaded. There were those, however, who contended that Arthur would change dramatically once he found himself in the White House. Governor Foster of Ohio predicted, "The people and the politicians will find that Vice-President Arthur and President Arthur are different men."[38]

In late August, Arthur received a letter from someone who identified herself merely as Julia Sand. It began, "The hours of Garfield's life are numbered—before this meets your eye, you may be President. The people are bowed in grief; but—do you realize it?—not so much because he is dying, as because *you* are his successor." No doubt somewhat surprised by the bluntness of the lady's first two sentences, Arthur read further.

> What President ever entered office under circumstances so sad! The day he was shot, the thought rose in a thousand minds that *you* might be the instigator of the foul act. Is not that a humiliation which cuts deeper than any bullet can pierce? Your best friends said: "Arthur must resign—he cannot accept office, with such a suspicion resting upon him." And now your kindest opponents say: "Arthur will try to do right"—adding gloomily—"He won't succeed, though—making a man President cannot change him."

It became readily apparent that Julia Sand disagreed with that forecast. "Great emergencies awaken generous traits which have lain dormant half a life," she continued. "If there is a spark of true nobility in you, now is the occasion to let it shine."

> Faith in your better nature forces me to write to you—but not to beg you to resign. Do what is more difficult & more brave. Reform! It is not

the proof of highest goodness never to have done wrong—but it is a proof of it, sometime in one's career, to pause & ponder, to recognize the evil, to turn resolutely against it & devote the remainder of one's life to that only which is pure & exalted.

The author exhorted, "Rise to the emergency. Disappoint our fears. Force the nation to have faith in you. Show from the first that you have none but the purest aims. It may be difficult at once to inspire confidence, but persevere. In time—when you have given reason for it—the country will love & trust you." She urged Arthur to champion civil service reform and to refrain from appointing untrustworthy men to office. "Your name now is on the annals of history," she concluded. "You cannot slink back into obscurity, if you would. . . . It is for you to choose whether your record shall be written in black or in gold. For the sake of your country, for your own sake & for the sakes of all who have ever loved you, let it be pure & bright."

Arthur was touched by this earnest appeal and decided to check out its New York return address to identify the author. He discovered only that the residence was owned by a banker named Theodore V. Sand; Julia was perhaps his wife, sister, or daughter. Her vibrant letter was saved for future reference.[39]

On September 1, Arthur received a personal note from Wayne Mac-Veagh warning that Garfield was "in a most grave and critical condition." To escape Washington's heat, the President was moved to a cottage on the coast at Elberon, New Jersey, a few days later. "Thank God, it is good to be here," he said, on smelling the salt air. But his condition continued to deteriorate. MacVeagh confided to Arthur on September 10 that he held little hope.[40] An old friend of Arthur's visited Elberon and reported that the President's death was only a few days away. He later wrote of Arthur, "His manner when he met me was very quiet and dignified, and showed that he understood full well what the second official in the Nation should do under such circumstances."[41] When Chauncey Depew called on Arthur, he was told, "with a depth of feeling which no man could ever forget," that the greatest calamity that could happen to him personally would be Garfield's death. "The most frightful responsibility which ever devolved upon any one," said Arthur, "would be the casting of the Presidency upon me under the conditions which you and all my friends so well understand."[42]

On the morning of September 19, Arthur received a telegram from the Cabinet warning that Garfield's end was near. Newspapers were declaring the battle almost over and called for prayer. The rest of the day and most of the evening Arthur nervously paced the floor of his home awaiting further word. At 11:30 P.M. a messenger boy brought the news of the President's death. Numerous telegraphic dispatches poured in from Elberon confirming the story. Reporters rushed to the Arthur residence and asked the doorkeeper, Alec Powell, if the Vice-President would make a statement about his future plans. "I daren't ask him," Powell replied, "he is sitting alone in his room sobbing like a child, with his head on his desk and his face buried in his hands. I dare not disturb him."

About midnight Alan Arthur, a freshman at Columbia, drove up in a carriage to be with his father. At 12:25 the formal notification of the President's death signed by the Cabinet was received. Shortly after 1:00 A.M. Arthur sent a wire to Attorney General MacVeagh: "I have your telegram, and the intelligence fills me with profound sorrow. Express to Mrs. Garfield my deepest sympathy." A few minutes later three of Arthur's friends, who had been with him during the evening, were sent out to find a judge of the State Supreme Court. Elihu Root and Daniel Rollins appeared with Judge John R. Brady at 1:50, followed soon afterward by Steve French and Judge Charles Donohue. Judge Brady, being the first to arrive, administered the oath at 2:15. Arthur received a kiss from his son and shook hands with the others in the room. He was now the nation's twenty-first President. Except for the presence of a half dozen carriages and a few reporters, there was no visible evidence along Lexington Avenue of the historic event that had taken place behind the closed green blinds of number 123.[43]

While the nation mourned the passing of a Chief Executive, several thoughtful observers were deeply concerned about the absence of a successor to President Arthur. There was no Vice-President, president of the Senate, or Speaker of the House; no official stood between Arthur and an interregnum. Arthur recognized this problem early and quietly took steps to correct it. Before leaving his home to accompany Garfield's body to Washington, he wrote a proclamation summoning the Senate into immediate special session, during which it could elect a president *pro tem.* He mailed it to Washington, addressed to the White House. Should he live to call the Senate into session himself, the letter would be destroyed. If a Guiteau were to strike him down before he could reach the nation's capital—and the mood of the country was ugly in the extreme—a constitutional impasse would be prevented.[44]

Arthur waited a day for Blaine to arrive in New Jersey, and then set out for Elberon to participate in ceremonies honoring the late President. On the way to the station he quoted unpublished lines from Tennyson, sent to him earlier by an Englishman:

> Not he that breaks the dams; but he
> That, through the channels of the State,
> Convoys the people's wish, is great.
> His name is pure his fame is free.[45]

In Elberon Arthur called on Mrs. Garfield, lunched with members of the Cabinet, and sadly boarded the funeral train bearing Garfield's emaciated remains to Washington. Following an impressive ceremony, the coffin was placed on a catafalque in the rotunda of the Capitol, paying tribute to Garfield's many years in the House. Some 100,000 people filed past the body during the two days it lay in state. "It may be doubted," a sympathetic biographer later wrote, "if at any time in the history of the United States the human sympathies of the people had been worked up to such a pitch of intensity."[46] President Arthur's first official act was to issue a proclamation appointing Monday, September 26, the day Garfield was to be buried in Cleveland, a day of humiliation and mourning throughout the nation.[47]

Arthur repeated his oath of office before Chief Justice Waite in the Vice-President's room at the Capitol on September 22. About forty guests were present, including former Presidents Hayes and Grant, Associate Justices Harlan and Matthews, members of Garfield's Cabinet, seven Senators, six members of the House, ex-Vice-President Hannibal Hamlin, and New York Assembly Speaker George Sharpe.[48] With the oath administered, Arthur then read a brief inaugural address.

> For the fourth time in the history of the Republic its Chief Magistrate has been removed by death. All hearts are filled with grief and horror at the hideous crime which has darkened our land, and the memory of the murdered President, his protracted sufferings, his unyielding fortitude, the example and achievements of his life, and the pathos of his death will forever illumine the pages of our history. . . . Men may die, but the fabrics of our free institutions remain unshaken. No higher or more assuring proof could exist of the strength and permanence of popular government than the fact that though the chosen of the people be struck down his constitutional successor is peacefully installed without shock or strain except the sorrow which mourns the bereavement. All the noble aspirations of my lamented predecessor which found expression in his life, the measures devised and suggested during his brief Administration to correct abuses, to enforce economy, to advance prosperity, and to promote the general welfare, to ensure domestic security and maintain friendly and honorable relations with the nations of the earth, will be

garnered in the hearts of the people; and it will be my earnest endeavor to profit, and to see that the nation shall profit, by his example and experience.

Prosperity blesses our country, our fiscal policy is fixed by law, is well grounded and generally approved. No threatening issue mars our foreign intercourse, and the wisdom, integrity, and thrift of our people may be trusted to continue undisturbed the present assured career of peace, tranquillity, and welfare. The gloom and anxiety which have enshrouded the country must make repose especially welcome now. No demand for speedy legislation has been heard; no adequate occasion is apparent for an unusual session of Congress. The Constitution defines the functions and powers of the executive as clearly as those of either of the other two department of the Government, and he must answer for the just exercise of the discretion it permits and the performance of the duties it imposes. Summoned to these high duties and responsibilities and profoundly conscious of their magnitude and gravity, I assume the trust imposed by the Constitution, relying for aid on divine guidance and the virtue, patriotism, and intelligence of the American people.[49]

By this time Arthur's conduct throughout the agonizing weeks Garfield lay incapacitated had prompted a visible mellowing of public opinion toward the new President. Out of the rage vented against him during the first days of July was emerging a sense of hopefulness tinged with optimism. "He has effaced himself after a fashion as manly as it was statesmanlike," *The New York Times* commented. "No man ever assumed the Presidency of the United States under more trying circumstances; no President has needed more the generous appreciation, the indulgent forbearance of his fellow-citizens. . . . He is a much better and broader man than the majority of those with whom his recent political career has been identified."[50] The New York *Sun* declared: "While Mr. Arthur is not a man who would have entered anybody's mind as a direct candidate for the office, it is not at all certain that he will not make a successful administration. He is a gentleman in his manners, neither obsequious nor arrogant. His bearing is manly, and such as to prepossess in his favor all whom he meets. Truth in speech and fidelity to his friends and his engagements form a part of his character. He has tact and common sense."[51] The same Chicago *Tribune* that had recently called Arthur "a mere tool and whipper-in for Conkling" now editorialized, "The country is prepared to welcome and greet the new President for his personal worth and his personal ability; they are willing to grant him their confidence and support, and in doing this they do not expect or believe that he will hastily, or at any time, do violence to the policy of his illustrious predecessor, or do any act in his high office to disturb or destroy that peace and tranquility which prevail throughout the land by the revival of party strife, or the even more calamitous renewal of those domestic troubles in the matter of rewarding friends and punishing enemies."[52]

The President's inaugural address was welcomed enthusiastically. E. L. Godkin described it as "in all respects what the occasion called for. It was brief, because having declared with sufficient explicitness his intention to adopt the ideas, so far as practicable, of his predecessor, he had no policy to sketch, and his tribute to the memory of the deceased President was as respectful and sympathetic as anyone could desire. This, moreover, seems to have satisfied the spectators that he fully realizes the solemnity of the occasion, and is sensible of the limitations which the peculiar manner of his accession to the office, and the state of popular feeling, necessarily impose on him in the use he will make of his great powers and opportunities."[53]

Even Whitelaw Reid grudgingly wished the new President well. "Arthur's antecedents do not inspire confidence," he wrote to John Hay. "He is now, however, entitled to support, unless he forfeits it. No man can have either the support or the respect of the American people, who, succeeding Garfield, undoes Garfield's work."[54]

CHAPTER FOURTEEN

Encouraging Signs

THE OBSTACLES standing between Chester Arthur and a successful presidency were enormous. His political experience had been restricted almost exclusively to one state, and his knowledge of national and international affairs was limited to what any reasonably curious New Yorker might cull from local newspapers and journals. Unlike his three predecessors who succeeded to the presidency —John Tyler, Millard Fillmore, and Andrew Johnson—Arthur did not bring a positive national reputation to the White House. His nomination at Chicago had been entirely unexpected, and was commonly interpreted as a device for placating the most opprobrious forces within the GOP. Since then his public image had come largely from press reports describing the dinner at Delmonico's, the struggles to elect Crowley and reelect Conkling and Platt, an analysis by *The Nation* of charges leading to his removal from the Customhouse, and Guiteau's professions of intimate friendship. Moreover, the GOP was seriously divided, threatening stiff opposition no matter what the future course of action. Republican Congressmen were not likely to unite behind the new President. All members of Garfield's Cabinet were thought certain to resign. And Blaine, John Sherman, and perhaps a dozen other Republican leaders were soon expected to begin jockeying for the 1884 nomination. None of the other Vice-Presidents catapulted into the White House had been chosen to succeed themselves. And Hayes's weak performance had illustrated the handicaps imposed upon a Chief Executive by the likelihood of a single term.

On the other hand, Arthur was intelligent, had extensive administrative experience, and enjoyed a number of battle-worn friends, like former Governor Morgan, who might give useful counsel. Of late he had earned much public sympathy; a moratorium was in effect on critical inquiries into his past, and most Americans were eager for his success. Then too, the role of his office at the time was such that it was perhaps within Arthur's reach, despite the obstacles, to win the trust and affection of his countrymen. The theory of the presidency from Grant to McKinley was based firmly on Whig doctrine; the Chief Executive was responsible for the execution rather than the initiation of legislation. The impeachment of Andrew Johnson and the weakness of Grant had shifted a great deal of power from the executive to the legislative branch, and the Capitol rather than the White House was the hub of action in Washington. The close division of party strength prohibited Presidents from commanding majorities in both houses long enough to push through legislation had they so desired. Party organizations lacked coherence and were unable to discipline legislators. Many contemporaries were convinced that the Senate dominated the government. Senator George F. Hoar wrote that each of his colleagues, "kept his own orbit and shone in his own sphere, within which he tolerated no intrusion from the President or from anybody else."[1] Hayes and Garfield restored some of the influence of their office by challenging Conkling, but they rarely exercised initiative in legislative matters. To be an acceptable and perhaps even popular President, Arthur was required to be a dignified representative of the American people, as well as an honest and reasonably efficient administrator. He would have to walk fairly close to his predecessor's footsteps. And he would find it profitable to be prudent in the use of executive authority. Arthur's inaugural address revealed a keen sensitivity to these duties and restraints.

There were also several actions that would clearly bring severe censure upon the new President. Above all, he dared not give Roscoe Conkling a major seat in the Cabinet, for this would signal the haughty Stalwart's control of the administration and the intensification of political warfare. For a similar reason Arthur could not remove Collector Robertson from the New York Customhouse. Public opinion, since July 2, had taken a sharp turn in favor of civil service reform, and should Arthur so blatantly oppose the trend he would confirm the nation's blackest suspicions about his character and career. In addition, the President could not safely extend leniency toward Guiteau or prevent the prosecution, started under Garfield, of Brady, Dorsey, and several other friends for the star route frauds. The degree to which Arthur recognized these pitfalls remained to be seen.

In Washington Arthur once again resided at the Jones home, delaying his occupancy of the White House in anticipation of some interior redecorating. Office-seekers swarmed around the house, and the press was full of speculation about the scores of appointments to be made. When Arthur returned to New York briefly to take care of personal business, reporters noted visits from Senators Cameron and Logan, and numerous local Stalwarts. Senator Jones also came to call, directly from a parlay with Conkling. Restless Ohio Republicans warned publicly that if Arthur surrendered to the former New York Senator, 30,000 party members would boycott the polls on election day.[2]

On October 10, the Senate convened in special session at Arthur's request mainly to elect a president *pro tem*. Democrats had a temporary majority, for without a presiding officer of the body three new Republican Senators could not be sworn in. This authority was employed to elect Democrat Thomas F. Bayard to be next in succession to the presidency. The following day Warner Miller and Elbridge Lapham of New York, and Nelson W. Aldrich of Rhode Island took their oaths of office. Try as they might, GOP leaders were unable to replace Bayard with a Republican and had to settle for the selection of independent David B. Davis, the sixty-seven-year-old, 350-pound ex-Supreme Court Justice from Illinois. Committees were again organized with Republican majorities, and the Senate turned to other business.[3]

A week later, Arthur traveled to Yorktown for the celebration of the centennial anniversary of the Battle of Yorktown. Naval vessels had been ordered to Chesapeake Bay, many colorfully clad troops were on hand, markers had been placed on the spots where siege guns were used by Washington and Lafayette, and descendants of Lafayette, Rochambeau, DeGrasse, and Steuben were present. Arthur's first public speech was terse and eloquent. At the conclusion of the ceremonies, from the deck of a flagship, Arthur ordered a salute to the British flag. By all accounts the new President handled the assignment impressively.[4]

By this time many Americans were growing increasingly anxious to learn the direction the administration would take. John Hay wrote to Whitelaw Reid in London, "Everything is at sea about Arthur. Perhaps the cable will tell you in a day or two what he is up to. But at present the Cabinet knows nothing whatever of his intentions. The facts are: 1. He is living with Jones. 2. Jones has gone to Utica to confer with Conkling. 3. The Grant crowd seems happy."[5]

Even before Garfield's death, E. D. Morgan urged Arthur, in the event he was to become President, to retain Garfield's Cabinet for a suitable length of time to assure the nation of stability and continuity.[6] A week after Arthur took office, Julia Sand advised a similar course of action, adding, "What the nation needs most at present, is rest. We all are worn out with watching—& when people are very tired, they are apt to be irritable, unreasonable & ready to quarrel on small provocation. If a doctor could lay his finger on the public pulse, his prescription would be, perfect quiet."[7] In the past, Vice-Presidents who succeeded to the executive chair made almost complete changes in their Cabinets. Given the ill will between the major GOP factions, this was certain to happen again. But Arthur saw the wisdom in delaying the resignations of Garfield's advisers, and attempted to persuade each of them to continue in office at least until the full Congress convened in December.[8]

Treasury Secretary William Windom, who had voted for Arthur's removal from the Customhouse, resigned soon after the President's appeal and entered a Senate race, throwing open one of the administration's key positions. Grant suggested the appointment of John Jacob Astor.[9] But Arthur sought the services of his venerable patron Edwin D. Morgan. When Morgan declined the offer because of failing health, Arthur urged him to reconsider. "It will cause the greatest embarrassment to me to change the plan which I have made, and beyond that, I have a strong personal feeling about it, which I am sure you appreciate. I beg my dear Governor that you will come & help me at this time."[10] Thurlow Weed and Arthur's secretary, Fred Phillips, were dispatched to win Morgan over, but the offer was again declined.[11] Undeterred, Arthur submitted Morgan's nomination to the Senate, where it was confirmed. Still, the seventy-year-old former New York governor sorrowfully and firmly refused the honor.[12] On October 27, Arthur's long-time friend and fellow Conkling supporter Charles J. Folger, Chief Justice of the New York Supreme Court, was nominated and confirmed. The fervid desire of Stalwarts to control the Treasury Department was at last realized. *The Nation* commented, however, "his appointment is a safe one, and an honest and conservative view of all legal questions which may arise in the Department may be expected of him." Businessmen were said to be pleased with the selection.[13]

In late September newspapers carried stories of yet another Cabinet member who soon intended to resign. Attorney General Wayne Mac-Veagh was an Independent who had long favored civil service reform. He had also played a leading role in the prosecution of the star route suspects, and because of that had suffered considerable abuse from Stalwart newspapers. He could not picture himself as part of an Arthur Administration, and, as soon as Garfield died, informed the new President and the Associated Press of his decision to leave the Cabinet. Arthur quickly urged MacVeagh to reconsider but was turned down. On November 7, Arthur wrote a personal letter to the Pennsylvania attorney asking him to remain in office at least long enough to initiate the star route trials. "I greatly fear that your retirement from the control now, might seriously imperil their success." If his commitment was firm, Arthur inquired, would he accept a retainer as chief counsel in the cases?[14] MacVeagh replied at once, making it clear that he was not impressed by Arthur's professed interest in justice. He argued that in fact he knew little about the star route frauds, that the cases were now in competent hands, and that the administration should take all the credit for its efforts in the matter. A personal conference with the President in New York failed to shake MacVeagh's determination. His resignation followed a few days later.[15]

MacVeagh had already turned over the star route cases to two attorneys who were known to be close to the new President: George Bliss and Benjamin Harris Brewster of Pennsylvania. Brewster had been acquainted with Arthur for many years and had journeyed to New York often to make campaign speeches. He had defended Arthur publicly after Garfield was shot and had written a long, thoughtful letter to the President on November 1 describing the Attorney General's hostility.[16] Arthur thought that Brewster would make a fine replacement for MacVeagh. Don Cameron was agreeable though not enthusiastic, for while Brewster was commonly thought to be associated with his machine he was also reputed to be an advocate of civil service reform. Brewster's credentials were worthy of the Cabinet post. He was well educated, had been a commissioner to adjudicate Indian claims against the United States in 1846, had served as Pennsylvania's Attorney General from 1867 to 1869, and enjoyed a high reputation as a lawyer. His nomination was submitted in mid-December and promptly confirmed. *The New York Times* applauded: "The best testimony to the fitness of this appointment is to be found in the disgust it excites in star route circles."[17] Mrs. James G. Blaine, on the other hand, wrote to her daughter, "Brewster is made Attorney General. All the Stalwarts are going in, and though the mills of Arthur may seem to grind slow, they grind exceeding fine."[18]

The Secretary of State had agreed to stay in office until Congress convened, but by mid-October he was restless and asked to be relieved of his duties early.[19] Whitelaw Reid advised Blaine, "To remain in the Cabinet (beyond a reasonable time, for the selection of a successor) unless to be the real head and controller of it, would be a mistake. But with Folger in, and Grant at the elbow, you can't control it." It would be wiser to return to Maine, Reid wrote, to participate in political campaigns and build a solid organization. "You are the popular representative of Garfield's Administration, the residuary legatee of his popularity. You ought to be and can be chosen at the next election, as his sucessor."[20] By now this was conventional wisdom, for few insiders believed that Blaine would take orders from the new President, and many, including

Arthur, fully expected him to begin laying plans for the 1884 nomination. (Blaine, wrote Mrs. Henry Adams, "is a crafty old bird and will now pose as Garfield's immediate successor. No one knows that better than Arthur.")[21] Even as Garfield's health began to fail, rumors swirled through the streets of Washington about potential candidates for Blaine's Cabinet seat, and the name on most tongues was Roscoe Conkling.

According to a close friend, Conkling desired and fully expected to be invited to become Secretary of State.[22] Surely his trusted lieutenant would not deny him the pleasure of wrenching Blaine's portfolio from his hands to recreate an administration as glorious as Grant's. But Conkling and other Stalwarts underestimated the effect upon Chester Arthur of the events leading to his assumption of the presidency. Out of the shock and mortification brought about by Guiteau's deed and Garfield's suffering came the determination to avoid actions that would disgrace the high office he held or bring shame upon himself. Arthur had always prized personal loyalty; as Vice-President he had permitted it to dominate his conduct. ("I was at Albany," a friend would recall, "when he came up there to help re-elect Conkling and Platt, and the newspapers opened on the trio; and I give you my word that Chet Arthur went up to a room in the top of the Delavan House and hardly put his nose out of the door as long as he stayed there.")[23] He considered himself a Stalwart. He admired his long-time chieftain and earnestly desired his continued friendship and counsel. But Conkling's appointment to Blaine's post would be greeted throughout the nation by an explosion of outrage. It would be interpreted as a surrender of the presidency; it would stain the twenty-first Chief Executive's reputation permanently and confirm the mocking epithets of Godkin, Curtis, and Nast; it would condemn the new administration from its outset and probably result in future Republican losses at the polls. Arthur did not intend to cut himself off from his Stalwart friends or even to deny some of them positions when circumstances permitted. But he was determined to stave off charges that he was a mere ward heeler in the clutches of one of the least admired politicians in the country. When a few New York associates proposed that Conkling be named Secretary of State, shortly after Arthur took the oath of office, he flatly refused.

Kate Chase Sprague wrote a letter to a friend in early October—that found its way to the President—urging Arthur to appoint Conkling promptly to a position of eminence. A short time later, at Mrs. Sprague's urging, Conkling visited the White House to talk things over with his old friend. "When I saw him *afterwards*," Mrs. Sprague reported to Arthur, "& saw *how he was suffering*, I urged his quitting Washington without delay. Friends who have seen him within a day or two, report him as very ill."[24]

The search for a new Secretary of State was ended in mid-November with the selection of Frederick T. Frelinghuysen. Sixty-four-year-old Frelinghuysen came from a distinguished New Jersey family, was educated at Rutgers, became a well-known attorney, was appointed a delegate to the Peace Congress in 1861, served as Attorney General of his native state from 1861 to 1866, and had been a United States Senator between 1866 and 1869 and between 1871 and 1877. While in the Senate he sat on the naval affairs, judiciary, and claims committees, and was one of three Republicans appointed to the Electoral Commission to decide the disputed presidential election of 1876. He was a Stalwart and was recommended to Arthur by Grant.[25] Blaine delayed his resignation until December 12, when Frelinghuysen was nominated and confirmed. *Harper's Weekly* described the new secretary in glowing terms. The Washington *Post* thought him a pale reflection of Blaine: "A commonplace and routine management of the State Department, during his continuance in office, is all that the public will expect, and nobody is likely to meet with either agreeable or unhappy disappointments."[26]

Frelinghuysen advised Arthur privately to retain three members of Garfield's Cabinet to forestall the charge that Stalwarts were benefiting inordinately from the assassination. "There are abundant indications that the natural opponents of your administration are waiting for the opportunity on the ground indicated to incite hostility."[27] Arthur told friends that he held no grudges toward those who had opposed him in the past, but would employ only men committed to the success of his administration.[28] As he had with MacVeagh, the President made every effort to persuade Thomas James to retain his Cabinet seat. He publicly expressed confidence in the Postmaster General's ability and integrity, and on October 27 nominated him to be his own successor.[29] James, however, resigned on December 12, telling Arthur of an offer from a New York bank so lucrative it could not be resisted. [30]

Instead of heeding Frelinghuysen's counsel about a politically balanced Cabinet, Arthur selected a long-time friend and well-known Stalwart to take James's place. Timothy O. Howe, sixty-five, had emigrated in 1845 from Maine to Green Bay, Wisconsin, where he practiced law. From 1850 to 1855 he was a judge of the Circuit and Supreme Courts of Wisconsin, and from 1860 to 1879 he represented his state in the United States Senate. At the Chicago convention in 1880 he had been a Grant man to the end, and to placate Conklingites in the ensuing struggles for position, Garfield had appointed Howe a delegate to the International Monetary Conference in Paris.[31] To many reformers Howe was not in the same league with James as an administrator (in fact, he had never held an administrative office), and it was certain that he had no commitment to civil service reform. Even worse, it was learned that Howe's son-in-law was one of several attorneys for the star route defendants. (Arthur discovered this unfortunate coincidence shortly after selecting Howe to replace MacVeagh, and it prompted him to turn to Brewster.)[32] On his way to Washington, Howe told reporters that he had not followed newspaper reports of the star route frauds and was unfamiliar with the cases. He added that while in the Senate the postal department committee was one of the few important committees on which he had not served.[33]

Early in the fall, General Grant had vigorously urged Arthur to appoint his good friend General Edward Fitzgerald Beale Secretary of the Navy. When Arthur looked elsewhere, Grant grew sullen, never quite forgiving the President for his unwillingness to aid a crony.[34] Several months later Blaine hesitatingly approached Arthur to suggest William E. Chandler for the post. "I had a pleasant chat with him," Blaine reported, "& told him I had come to say that no possible appointment of his in any field could be so agreeable to me as to place you in his Cabinet . . ." Arthur had ignored several similar appeals by the man from Maine, but this time Blaine felt that his advice might be taken.[35] There was reason to think otherwise, for not only had Chandler championed Blaine at the Chicago convention in 1880, but Stalwarts had helped defeat his nomination for Solicitor General when it was sent to the Senate by Garfield. Nevertheless, Chandler was highly respected for his political guile, and his presence in the Cabinet would add much-needed factional balance. Arthur made numerous inquiries of Grant men, and finding little resistance, forwarded Chandler's nomination on April 6, 1882, moving William Hunt to the post of minister to Russia.

Chandler was a life-long resident of New Hampshire and a graduate of Harvard Law School. A small, wiry, shifty man of forty-seven, he had been a member of his state's Assembly during the war, Lincoln appointed him Solicitor and Judge Advocate General of the Navy Department, and President Johnson named him Assistant Secretary of the Treasury. After that he devoted his time to law, lobbying, and Republican campaigning. As a member of the Republican National Committee he assisted in the direction of presidential races from 1868 through 1880. Democrats never forgave him for the part he played in the Hayes-Tilden entanglement, and when his nomination as Naval Secretary reached the Senate floor not a single member of that party voted affirmatively.[36]

Samuel J. Kirkwood, Garfield's Secretary of the Interior, had voted for Arthur's removal from the Customhouse in 1879; he was elderly and ineffective, and was not expected to remain part of the new administration.[37] For several months Arthur considered ex-Senator Chaffee of Colorado (who had Grant's blessing) and ex-Senator Sargent of Wisconsin to fill the post. Finding public and party objections to these names, he settled on Senator Henry Teller of Colorado.

Teller was born in New York in 1830, later moved to Illinois to practice law, and in 1861 went to Central City, Colorado, where he continued to reside. During the Civil War he became one of the region's most wealthy and prominent citizens, and when Colorado entered the Union in 1876 he was elected to the Senate. Teller was a Stalwart, a member of the "306," and was known to be wholly unsympathetic to civil service reform. His appointment pleased Cameron, Logan, and Republican leaders of the Far West. But E. L. Godkin also thought highly of Teller, describing him as "a man of ability [who] brings to the discharge of his duties such an equipment as the experience of the Senate, of an active law practice in land and mining cases, and of Western life gives."[38]

Secretary of War Robert Lincoln was the sole Garfield Cabinet appointee to retain his portfolio. A colorless Stalwart, he contributed loyalty and his father's name to the administration.[39]

Reactions to Arthur's selections were generally favorable. The President's attempts to retain Garfield appointees were appreciated, and while their successors were Stalwarts, with the exception of Chandler, they were known to have individual strengths. Reformers were mildly dissatisfied, of course, but they had expected worse. Half-Breeds thought the Cabinet weak politically and could not understand how Arthur expected it to assist his reelection. Sheridan Shook of New York smirked, "Look at old Howe of Wisconsin. Why, he had not been able to be elected a delegate to the last three national conventions, and yet they gave him the postoffice department. Here is Frelinghuysen in New Jersey, who is a figurehead of mush."[40] Few overlooked the absence of a southerner.

Arthur was highly pleased with his new colleagues. Timothy Howe was a favorite. One evening in January 1882, after an elegant dinner with his Cabinet, the President asked Howe to remain for a private chat. The elderly Postmaster General later confided to his niece, "He said he did not often 'slop over' but said he, to-night I want to. He told me how 'solid' he felt when he saw Frelinghuysen, Folger and Brewster and myself about him—'Especially you and Frelinghuysen' he added."[41]

As the President distributed the vast patronage at his disposal, it was widely noted that he did virtually nothing for his old New York companions in the Conkling machine. Stalwart associates who observed Arthur during the months Garfield lay dying said sadly that "he assumed a totally different manner to his friends and former advisers," and that even before entering the White House he was "transformed completely."[42] Smyth, French, Hess, Lydecker, and the others called often at the White House and were invited to late-night suppers and bull sessions. But Arthur refused their pleas for favors and jobs, fully aware that he dared not do otherwise and hope for the success of his administration. Conklingites loudly protested their treatment. "We regard Arthur as our leader," said one, "and when he became President, knowing as he did the thankless tasks we have to do here, we expected that we would be appreciated—not to say rewarded. We thought he would throw in our direction enough of the patronage to make our work less onerous. On the contrary, he has done less for us than Garfield, or even Hayes."[43] Another complained, "I tell you it is pretty hard to see Murphy, who made Arthur, going around without a cent in his pocket, and Arthur running the whole United States, and too timorous to reward Tom Murphy with any position whatever."[44] John Smyth growled, "no one who had ever arisen to great power in this country ever caused so many wrecks to be scattered on the shore."[45]

Arthur also resisted repeated appeals to remove Collector Robertson. The Half-Breed's dismissal and the wholesale firing of his friends in the Customhouse would have done much to revivify the Conkling machine, slumping badly after defeats at the polls in the fall of 1881. Conkling strongly urged Arthur to sever Robertson, and when his request was denied, he told Mrs. Richard Crowley that his former lieutenant's "cowardice" disgusted him. Platt remembered Arthur saying that he was morally bound to continue Garfield's policy. "He isn't 'Chet' Arthur any more," John O'Brien said sadly, "he's the President."[46]

In late January 1882, a friendly New York newspaper editor confided to Arthur that Conkling seemed greatly depressed. "He talks as if his old friends had deserted him."[47] About the same time, the President told Timothy Howe that he would name Conkling to fill a vacancy on the United States Supreme Court left by Ward Hunt of New York.

Arthur's first appointment to the court was Judge Horace Gray, a distinguished jurist and legal scholar who held a seat on the Massachusetts Supreme Judicial Court.[48] Conkling's credentials stood in sharp contrast to Gray's. His formal legal training had been meager, his reputation as an attorney was unacclaimed (Jay Gould was his current employer), and his temperament was not exactly judicial. Even his record as a statesman was weak, for his many years in Congress were surprisingly barren of achievement. Arthur must have weighed the offer carefully, knowing the impact it would have on public opinion. Moreover, the nomination was far from what Conkling sought: salaries for members of the court were low and political influence was non-existent. Everyone remembered that Conkling had spurned a similar offer from Grant. Still, Arthur felt honor-bound to do something for his old colleague; if he could not give him power he might at least bestow a measure of dignity.

In the third week of February, Secretary Howe was quietly dispatched to Chief Justice Waite and several of his colleagues to discuss the possible nomination; Senator Jones was sent to Conkling to sound him out. Jones reported doubt that Conkling would accept a seat on the bench. After talking with Jones, Howe thought, "Conkling is terribly bruised and seems to be biting himself. . . . I don't know if he will consent to take up his bed and walk."[49] As he had with E. D. Morgan, Arthur proceeded to send the nomination to the Senate despite the uncertainty of an acceptance. It was confirmed on March 2, 39 to 12, with four Republicans voting negatively.[50] Predictably, much of the nation's press bellowed its derision. *The Nation* commented, "It was folly to suppose that after having worked in politics for twenty years under Mr. Conkling's leadership, and having supported him in the disastrous contest at Albany over the Senatorship last spring, Mr. Arthur would in consequence of anything that has happened, change his estimate of his friend's capacity and character."[51] In Ohio, former Garfield supporters were particularly bitter. The Youngstown *News Register* said, "Better for Conkling that he pass at least a decent probation in the seclusion of private life, and better for Arthur not to force under the nostrils of the American people an unsavory smelling object."[52]

On March 3, Conkling curtly rejected the nomination. He did not deign to make a public explanation, but friends told reporters he had already accepted huge retainers for his legal services. The affair damaged the administration's reputation and did little to heal the breach within the GOP. Within two weeks the Supreme Court seat was given to Samuel Blatchford of New York, an estimable judge with fifteen years service in the federal courts.[53]

Charles Guiteau was brought to trial for murder on November 14, 1881. Since that fateful day in July, he had been kept under tight security in the District of Columbia jail, enjoying the regular meals and glorying in his fame. Several attempts had been made on his life, and the mails brought scores of rumors and threats. But Guiteau was convinced that his freedom and future prosperity were inevitable. He could not be convicted for carrying out God's will; besides, his Stalwart friends would "fix" things. In an interview with Washington's district attorney, Colonel George Corkhill, Guiteau had slapped him on the knee and leaned forward to ask, "Colonel, you are a Stalwart?" At the affirmative reply, Guiteau straightened up and smiled.

The assassin's only hope was the plea of insanity, a highly controversial tactic that was popularly called the "insanity dodge." The legal rule governing the determination of criminal responsibility in England and throughout most American jurisdictions in 1881 made acquittal by this route difficult, for a defendant was to be considered responsible if he was aware of the nature and consequences of his deed at the time it was committeed and knew it to be illegal. The test was not that the accused was able to conform to prescribed conduct, merely that he had an understanding of it. By this simple standard the case against Guiteau was persuasive. Premeditation was beyond question, as was the defendant's awareness that Garfield's "removal" was against the law, and he clearly anticipated public reaction to the shooting. Motive might be established by pointing to his frustration at being denied a federal position and to his desire for notoriety. While many were willing to concede that Guiteau was eccentric—"mad" was dropped a few days after the shooting—few thought he should be declared legally insane. Americans were grimly determined to see him hang for the murder of their President. *The New York Times* declared, "Guiteau should have a fair trial. Everything that can be urged in his behalf should be patiently heard. It is the right of the meanest thing that bears a human form, but such a trial, such a hearing, in a community of intelligent beings can have but one result."[54]

While there was little likelihood that a jury would fail to convict, the prosecution went to great lengths to construct an iron-clad case against the defendant. Corkhill was assisted by Walter Davidge, a leader of the Washington bar, and Judge John K. Porter, a distinguished New York attorney. Stalwarts, of course, were eager for a guilty verdict in order to quash all memories of plots. Attorney General MacVeagh was authorized by Arthur to offer the services of Daniel G. Rollins, New York City's district attorney, "the President," he wrote, "being solicitous that no slip shall in reasonable possibility, occur in any matter connected with the trial of Guiteau."

The defense was penniless and without influence. Guiteau was to be represented by his brother-in-law, George Scoville, an attorney completely inexperienced in criminal practice, who told reporters in early October, "If I didn't think the unfortunate man was insane, I would not defend him at all. If he is not insane and cannot be clearly made to appear so, he ought to be hung." Appeals to the legal profession in general and to several prominent trial lawyers for assistance got nowhere. A young court-appointed attorney was found unsatisfactory by the defendant. Guiteau wrote his own formal plea, submitted to the court on October 22. In it he argued that the shooting was God's act, not his own; the Lord had stripped him of his free will, he wrote, and without it there could be no responsibility or criminal intent. He also charged that the President had died of malpractice rather than his bullet and that the court itself was without jurisdiction, since Garfield had died in New Jersey rather than the District of Columbia. Guiteau deluged his brother with appeals to contact Arthur. "See him at once," said one note, "and get what time we want. He is bound to help me, and he will help me if you stick to him."

The parade of witnesses and the arguments of attorneys lasted more than two months. To document the contention that Garfield's back wound was necessarily mortal, a portion of the late President's spine was submitted in evidence by the prosecution. Ladies wept, a reporter noted, "while even strong men trembled." A battery of experts testified about the defendant's mental state, illustrating a growing disagreement over the meaning of insanity. The judge decided to give almost complete latitude to the accused in the courtroom on the ground that since his mental condition was in question the jury might learn much by observation. Throughout the proceedings Guiteau leaped to his feet to ask questions, make comments, and shout objections. On a number of occasions guards were called to hold him in his seat, and reporters described him as almost "foaming at the mouth." His courtroom histrionics only more deeply embittered those who felt him fortunate to be given a trial at all. At one point Washington's *Evening Critic* commented, "A few more such scenes as have been witnessed during the past week will to a certainty nerve the hand of some honest man to kill him." A Maryland farmer took a shot at Guiteau through the bars of a prison van, putting a bullet hole in the prisoner's new coat. (A defense fund was quickly organized for the farmer.)

When Guiteau took the stand he talked for more than five days. Toward the conclusion of his performance he reached events leading directly to the assassination and claimed that he had been on close terms with all of the GOP's leaders during the campaign of 1880. "I used to go to General Arthur and talk just as freely with him as I would with anybody."

On January 14, 1882, Guiteau wrote a letter to the President asking him to tell John K. Porter confidentially to argue his case "lightly." "A word from you to Mr. Porter will let me down easily & the country will be satisfied with a verdict of acquittal."[55]

The jury reported its verdict of guilty a little more than a week later, after deliberating for an hour and five minutes. The courtroom burst into applause. Guiteau was silent at first, but as the jury members were polled he suddenly shrieked, "My blood be on the head of the jury, don't you forget it. That is my answer." He was manacled and led to the prison van, surrounded by a jeering crowd shouting, "All America is with you," and the like. He was shortly sentenced to hang.

Attempts to win a new trial were rejected, and the assassin's remaining hope rested with the President. A number of leading neurologists circulated a petition asking Arthur to appoint a commission of experts to inquire into Guiteau's mental condition. He received the document and three of its sponsors at the White House on June 22 and listened patiently to a twenty-minute appeal. Attorney General Brewster was asked for comment and replied with a lengthy defense of the trial. Furthermore, he warned, a stay of execution would "establish a dangerous precedent. It will shake the public confidence in the certainty and justice of the courts, by substituting your will for the judgment of law." Arthur heard a further plea on behalf of Guiteau's insanity but accepted Brewster's advice. When Guiteau heard of this he shouted, "Arthur has sealed his doom and the doom of this nation. He and his cabinet are possessed of the devil."

The condemned man was executed on June 30. The warden of the prison claimed to have received 20,000 requests for tickets. The captain of the guard sold guaranteed pieces of lining from Guiteau's coffin to spectators. The headline on the front page of the Chicago *Tribune* read "THE HYENA HANGS."[56]

The 47th Congress assembled on December 5, 1881, and on the following day listened to the President's first annual message. It was a frank, well-written document, revealing that Arthur had thoughtfully reviewed the broad range of subjects recently placed before him, and that despite the political handicap of being an "accidental" President he was inclined to aid Congress in its decision-making process with suggestions and advice. It also illustrated his dedication to the pursuit of popular policies businessmen called "sound" and showed his willingness to cooperate with reformers.

The message opened with a fairly detailed survey of American foreign relations, largely formulated by Blaine, and moved to the subject of national finances. Arthur approved Treasury Secretary Folger's recommendation for the early retirement of silver certificates and concurred in the proposal to abandon the compulsory coinage of a fixed amount of silver. Noting that the federal government was predicted to have a surplus of $130,000,000 in the current fiscal year, the President called for a reduction in revenues by the repeal of all internal revenue taxes, other than those on tobacco and distilled and fermented liquors, and the license fees needed to supervise their collection. "There seems to be a general sentiment in favor of this course," he noted. Arthur was reserved about the tariff, stating merely that it needed revision and that "important changes should be made with caution." He endorsed the recommendation, approved by the Senate and the Treasury Secretary, for a tariff commission to study the issue.

The President accepted Robert Lincoln's proposal to increase the army to its full strength of 30,000 men, largely to protect settlers and their property against Indians. At the same time, he called for legislation to prevent intrusion upon land set apart for Indians and outlined measures for helping them to become full citizens. "For the success of the efforts now making to introduce among the Indians the customs and pursuits of civilized life, and gradually to absorb them into the mass of our citizens, sharing their rights and holden to their responsibilities, there is imperative need for legislative action."

Arthur also requested measures for increasing the efficiency of the American navy. "I cannot too strongly urge upon you my conviction that every consideration of national safety, economy, and honor imperatively demands a thorough rehabilitation of our Navy." He deplored the decline of America's merchant marine and hoped that members of Congress would consider the matter, "with the suggestion that no question of greater magnitude or farther-reaching importance can engage their attention."

Among other things, the President asked for the creation of a government for the people of Alaska. He repeated earlier appeals for laws suppressing polygamy in the western territories. He called for federal aid to education, alluding specifically to the need to assist southern Negroes in their pursuit of literacy. He advised caution in the granting of pension claims to Union veterans and recommended an increase in the Pension Bureau staff to increase its efficiency. He requested construction of a building for the Library of Congress and called attention to proposals made for improvements within the District of Columbia. He also asked Congress to consider the weighty constitutional issues surrounding the collection and declaration of the Electoral College vote and the role of the Vice-President at the incapacitation of the Chief Executive.

In the section of the message devoted to the postal service, the subject of the star route trials quickly emerged. Arthur wrote: "I have enjoined upon the officials who are charged with the conduct of the cases on the part of the Government and upon the eminent counsel who, before my accession to the Presidency, were called to their assistance, my duty of prosecuting with the utmost vigor of the law all persons who may be found chargeable with frauds upon the postal service."

Highly sensitive to the groundswell of sympathy toward civil service reform since Garfield's death, Arthur devoted several pages of his message to the subject. He quoted from his address accepting the vice-presidential nomination, pointing to his acceptance of the principle that original appointments be based upon a candidate's fitness for a position, that tenure of office be stable, that promotions "so far as practicable" be filled by worthy and efficient employees, and that complaints be investigated promptly and punishments dealt swiftly. These views, he wrote, would govern his administration of the executive branch. "They are doubtless shared by all intelligent and patriotic citizens, however divergent in their opinions as to the best methods of putting them into practical operation." He objected, however, to the proposal that appointments be by competitive examination to the lower grades only, with promotions based on similar competition. This method was successful in Great Britain, he observed, but would not work here due to the absence of certain key features found within the English system, such as virtual lifetime tenure and a limitation on the maximum age at which an applicant could enter the civil service. Arthur made it clear that he distrusted tests that strictly equated book-learning with characteristics making for an honest and efficient civil servant, and he raised the specter of college youths monopolizing appointments. He suggested that certain nominations might be submitted to a central board of examiners, created to test the qualifications of applicants without resort to competitive examinations. Moreover, he thought that the introduction of outsiders into the middle ranks of the civil service from time to time was healthy. The entire subject of reform, he concluded, "is one of grave importance. The evils which are complained of cannot be eradicated at once; the work must be gradual." The English had taken fifteen years to develop their system. Still, "If Congress should deem it advisable at the present session to establish competitive tests for admission to the service, no doubts such as have been suggested shall deter me from giving the measure my earnest support." Should Congress fail to pass legislation covering the issue at this session, he urged the appropriation of $25,000 to reactivate the Civil Service Commission.[57]

Arthur's ambitious message was received favorably throughout the nation. Many observers noticed the absence of the usual Republican "paragraph about the South" and thought that at last the "bloody shirt" had been discarded. The portion devoted to the civil service drew special praise. Godkin thought it "very remarkable" for being "the first serious discussion of the 'British civil-service system' by a Stalwart politician. Hitherto the Stalwarts have never been able to refer to it with straight faces, and the fact that their spokesman has stopped laughing at it, and made an explicit announcement that it must be treated as a serious political question, is an encouraging sign of the times."[58]

The first several months of the new administration won considerable praise, even from the President's natural political enemies. Arthur made no serious mistakes and revealed a dignity and eagerness to please that many Americans had not expected. There were those, however, who remained wary, especially the students of New York politics intimately familiar with Arthur's past. Godkin noted that every administration enjoyed a honeymoon, adding that it seldom lasted long.[59]

CHAPTER FIFTEEN

A Veritable Chesterfield

For THE FIRST nearly three months of Arthur's presidency his private office was on the second floor of the Jones residence. Fred Phillips, his private secretary, and the clerical staff inherited from Garfield occupied almost the entire first floor of the elegant granite home. Messengers could be seen each day scurrying back and forth from the White House carrying mail and an assortment of documents to be examined and signed. During the Hayes Administration it had become apparent that the executive mansion was in need of repairs; its condition deteriorated rapidly when portions of it were later converted into a hospital. Arthur ordered renovations undertaken as soon as Mrs. Garfield moved out. Louis C. Tiffany of New York, son of the famous jeweler and one of the nation's foremost decorators, was requested to send designers to fashion the alterations. The President took special interest in the project, and almost every evening after dinner he strolled over to his future quarters to inspect the work in progress and make suggestions.[1]

Initially, much furniture and many carpets and drapes were replaced. Twenty-four wagonloads of furniture and household articles, dating back to the first Adams Administration, were cleared from the premises and sold at public auction.[2] Special attention was given to the President's private dining room on the first floor. The walls were covered with heavy gold paper in large designs and the windows and mantelpiece draped with hangings of pomegranate plush. An open fireplace and side-lights of crimson glass were suggested by Arthur. A sideboard was made to match an elaborate one ordered by Mrs. Hayes, and on both pieces could be seen specimens of Limoges china designed by Theodore Davis.[3]

In the fall of 1882, following failure of a proposal to construct a new presidential residence south of the White House, more extensive redecorating of the executive mansion was undertaken. The walls of the main corridor were tinted a pale olive and the large niches covered with squares of gold leaf. The frieze consisted of a narrow border of India brass-work backed with colors and geometric designs in pale tints and gold and silver. The ceiling was decorated in gold and silver broken by traceries in colors in which "U.S.A." was interwoven. The walls of the Red Room were tinted a dull Pomeranian red; its ceiling boasted circles of stars in gold, silver, and copper with a border of the national stripes studded with stars. The open fireplace was surrounded by a cherry mantelpiece, a jeweled glass screen, and panels of Japanese leather. The furniture was a subtle ruby. The Blue and East rooms received similar attention. A screen of jeweled glass, fifty feet long, fitted with imitation marble columns, was made in New York by Tiffany and used to replace old glass doors that formerly separated the main corridor from the north vestibule. The screen was a showpiece for twenty-one years before it was removed by Theodore Roosevelt during a far more thorough White House renovation.[4]

Arthur moved into the White House on December 7, 1881, and was soon joined by his youngest sister, Mary Arthur McElroy. Mrs. McElroy, a petite, dark-haired, dark-eyed woman of forty, had been educated at Emma Willard's famous seminary in Troy, New York, and in 1851 married John E. McElroy, an Albany insurance man. She had lived in Albany since her marriage and was the mother of four. Her brother persuaded her to come to Washington four months a year to serve as "Mistress of the White House," a position requiring her to assume most of the social duties usually performed by the First Lady. "When I went to it I was absolutely unfamiliar with the customs and formalities," she later recalled. She quickly learned and became popular for her grace and charm. She flattered Washington socialites by inviting them to receive with her at receptions. Her oldest daughter, May, and little Nell Arthur were usually on hand. "We stood in the blue room," Mrs. McElroy recalled, "and the gay girls always soon did away with any stiffness there might have been." With her brother's assistance, she developed a definite order of procedure at all social functions. The code, with slight modifications, was used for more than a generation by First Ladies.[5]

Several Presidents were known for their generous hospitality and elegant dinner parties—Washington, Jefferson, both Adamses, Buchanan, Grant. Chester Arthur had spent most of his adult years in an urban environment and, with his wife's encouragement, had learned to appreciate the pleasures and demands of upper-class society. He understood the art of entertaining with refinement and faultless taste. He enjoyed good liquors, excellent cuisine, and expensive cigars, and delighted in the formalities that accompanied them. An employee would recall, "he wanted the best of everything, and wanted it served in the best manner."[6] As Chief Executive he seemed eager to escape the drudgery and loneliness of an office he had not sought and anxious to free his mind of the tragedy that had stalked him within the past two years. Arthur initiated a series of personal and public entertainments that elevated White House social life to a peak it would rarely, if ever, reach again. In less than a full term the President gave some fifty state dinners and enjoyed innumerable private suppers with large and small groups of friends.[7]

Arthur's first state ceremony was an official reception at the White House on the second day of 1882. Members of the Cabinet were in attendance, as were members of the diplomatic corps, numerous foreign ministers, Justices of the Supreme Court and the district courts, a large number of Congressmen, military officers, and others. It was a subdued affair, for Washington was still officially in mourning.[8]

Three months later, at the first state dinner, given in honor of General and Mrs. Grant, the new administration's elegant approach to entertainment was first revealed. The East Room and dining room were profusely decorated with flowers. The table, set for thirty-four, featured an elaborate center decoration around which were crystal compotes and cut-glass decanters. Bouquets of roses sat at each lady's plate, tied with satin ribbons, and small boutonnieres awaited each gentleman. The cards were of heavy gilt-edged board, embossed with the national coat of arms in gold, below which were the names of guests. The Marine Band performed popular operatic selections. Dinner was served in fourteen courses, with which came eight varieties of wine, each variety having its appropriate glass. The lavishly dressed guests spent two hours at the table.[9]

At a subsequent state dinner the table centerpiece was called "The Swinging Garden of Babylon"—a floral piece four feet long and one and a half feet high, composed of red and white carnations, honeysuckles, and roses, topped with clusters of rare blossoms from the nunplant. Twenty-one courses were served.[10]

"I dined at the President's Wednesday," Mrs. Blaine wrote to her daughter. "The dinner was extremely elegant, hardly a trace of the old White House taint being perceptible anywhere, the flowers, the damask, the silver, the attendants, all showing the latest style and an abandon in expense and taste."[11]

On occasion Arthur gave musical entertainments. The Fisk Jubilee singers performed at the White House in February 1882, moving the President to tears. The opera company of Madame Adelina Patti appeared a year later, followed shortly by Madame Christine Nilsson, a friend of the President's late wife. Before Madame Nilsson performed, guests were invited to enter the state dining room. Covers were laid for fifty-four, and there were 378 glasses on the table.[12]

Rutherford B. Hayes read reports of these enjoyments and snarled, "Nothing like it ever before in the Executive Mansion—liquor, snobbery, and worse."[13]

Arthur's personal appearance prompted as much comment as his social accomplishments, for not since Franklin Pierce had Washington seen a President so devoted to fastidious attire. A shrewd reporter described Arthur in the spring of 1882 as "the 'city man,' the metropolitan gentleman, the member of clubs, the type that is represented by the well-bred and well-dressed New Yorker; the quiet man who wears a scarf and a pin and prefers a sack coat to the long tailored frock coat that pervades politics, and a derby hat to the slouch [hat] that seems to be regarded in some quarters of this Union as something no statesman should be without. This is a novel species of president."[14] Arthur's clothes were made by a well-known New York tailor whose high prices reflected the status of his customers. The President spent considerable time as well as money on his apparel; it was said that one day he tried on twenty pairs of trousers made to his measurements before selecting one to his taste. For business hours he wore the choicest tweeds. In the afternoon he put on a black frock coat, white or gray waistcoat, gray trousers, black tie, and silk hat. At dinner he wore a tuxedo. He was rarely seen at the theater, opera, or at an evening reception except in full evening habiliments. Alec Powell, Arthur's Negro friend from the Customhouse, served as the President's valet. Tom Platt later called Arthur "the beau-ideal of the American citizen."

> Six feet two in height, symmetrically built; a head adorned with silken, wavy hair, always carefully combed; whiskers of the Burnside variety, invariably trimmed to the perfection point; blue, kindly eyes, straight nose, ruddy cheeks—these and his polished manners gave him the address of a veritable Chesterfield.[15]

Washingtonians were also fascinated by Arthur's elaborate style of equipage. His handsome carriage, built in New York, was painted a dark green, relieved in red; its trimmings were of morocco and cloth, the cushions and doors faced with heavy lace. The dress blankets and lap robes bore the monogram "C.A.A." worked in silk. The two horses were magnificent bays with black points, matched almost perfectly. The harness, made by Wood Gibson of Fifth Avenue, was mounted with silver. Expensively dressed coachmen and a Negro driver, William Willis, accompanied the carriage everywhere. "The entire 'turn-out' is a model of quiet magnificence and good taste," wrote one observer.[16]

Before long, Arthur designed his own coat of arms, and a seal was made bearing its features. He also created a presidential flag, blue ground with white spread eagle and eighteen stars, displayed proudly on the presidential ship, the U.S.S. *Despatch.* An old Stalwart friend later remarked bitterly, "It was amusing to those who had known Arthur all his life to hear him talk about good blood, and heraldry, and all that sort of thing, after he became duly installed in the White House."[17]

Wherever he went, the President's impeccable manners were the subject of conversation. "It is not that he is handsome and agreeable— for he was both long ago," wrote an admirer, "but it is his ease, polish and perfect manner that make him the greatest society lion we have had in many years." The same writer noted Arthur's carefully manicured hands and thought they revealed his gentlemanly character. ". . . the President can open a door, restore a handkerchief, or hand a chair to a lady without exhibiting a colossal amount of clumsy dignity as did the eminent Rutherford B. Hayes; nor, on the other hand, does he effervesce with the effusive gallantry of men of distinction from the South."

While on vacation in Newport in the summer of 1882 Arthur was called upon by a number of young society leaders, including August Belmont Jr., eager to scrutinize the new President. "Of all critics," wrote the observer, "they are the most severe because the idol of their lives is 'form.' If a man is 'proper' they are in with him for all they are worth; but if he is not, their contempt is as insulting shown to a President as to a pauper." Arthur quickly won them over.

> It was an odd sight to see them in the Casino a few days ago, sur- rounding and talking to him with the upmost respect. They were in all the agony of morning toilet with a new wasp waist, English Prince Albert coats and trousers strapped under their varnished boots. They sucked the ends of their sticks and listened with respect to the fashion- ably dressed President standing erect among them with an expression of reticent good fellowship on his handsome face and an air of easy familiarity in his bearing.

"I find it impossible," the writer concluded, "to imagine these men talking to any other President than Chester A. Arthur."[18]

While walking or riding the streets of Washington, Arthur seemed pleased by salutations and invariably acknowledged them by lifting his hat and making an elaborate bow, without regard to the social status of the citizen involved. At his death a local newspaper would declare, "No president since the war has been so universally popular here."[19]

Arthur's conversation charmed many White House guests. Following a dinner with the President in early 1882, Timothy Howe wrote to his niece, "General Arthur is a much more accomplished man than I had supposed. He has more tact and more general culture than any man I have seen in the White House."[20] Mrs. Blaine, as might be expected, had a different impression. She thought the President worth little more than "a quotation from Thackeray or Dickens, or an old Joe Miller told with uninterfered-with particularity . . ." Unlike her husband, "All his ambition seems to center in the social aspect of the situation."[21]

Beyond the social obligations of the presidency, Arthur usually found the duties of his office distasteful. He arrived at his office late, about 10:00 A.M., and received Congressmen until noon. On Tuesdays and Fridays Cabinet meetings were held at 12:00 P.M. On Wednesdays, Thursdays, and Saturdays the President greeted the general public for an hour. After lunch he remained in his office until four or five o'clock, seeing callers by appointment. From five to seven thirty he read, rested, or rode horseback, and then dressed for dinner. Sundays and Mondays he reserved for himself.[22] Members of his staff often felt it necessary to urge the President to attend to matters at hand. A White House clerk recalled in 1925, "President Arthur never did today what he could put off until tomorrow." On one occasion he took a month to copy a letter of condolence prepared in the State Department for transmission to a European court. There was a tradition among the staff that he had a "property basket" filled with official-looking documents which he brought with him to appointments to create the appearance of industry. The annual messages to Congress, it was said, were written by Arthur's good friend Daniel G. Rollins, a talented thirty-five-year-old Yale graduate with solid political and legal experience.[23]

A man well placed within the administration said of the President, "He is a sensitive, almost a timid man, I mean with reference to his responsibilities. He is also a moody man." At dinners he is at his best, and chats with the men over cigars "with a zest that makes us feel he is kind of a boy." "But when you go into his office in the morning, there you see a man oppressed with either duties or the inversion of his natural hours, or staggering under a sense of responsibility which he does not like." As collector, Arthur could delegate most duties to subordinates. "But in the Presidency, he cannot delegate much, and the successive shocks of conflict over almost every office, and his desire not to offend either public opinion or the large personal influences which make up his party, keep him in a measure stunned, uncertain, and in any event moody, possibly unhappy."[24] Old Dr. Brodie Herndon stayed at the White House for several months in 1882 and described the President in his diary as deeply worried, unwell, and disconsolate. "Chester says with Solomon 'All is vanity & vexation of spirit; and His golden chain is but a chain at last.' "[25]

Arthur especially disliked the reception of general callers. He greeted these visitors in the White House library and stood throughout the three hours of light conversation, shifting back and forth on his feet to cut short importunate interviewers. At full-dress public receptions crowds of two and three thousand lined up to shake hands with the President.[26] Office-seekers engulfed the White House and occasionally broke past secretaries to reach Arthur. On one occasion an insurance agent eluded Fred Phillips, and it took thirty minutes to persuade him to leave.[27] Arthur became convinced that Presidents should be provided with a home separate from the executive offices. He told a reporter, "You have no idea how depressing and fatiguing it is to live in the same house where you work. The down-town business man in New York would feel quite differently if after the close of his day he were to sit down in the atmosphere of his office to find rest and recreation instead of going uptown to cut loose absolutely from everything connected with his work of the day."[28] During summers and whenever possible, Arthur resided in the presidential cottage in the grounds of Soldiers' Home on the outskirts of Washington, a handsome brick home covered with stucco. There he could often be seen sitting on the porch, smoking, drinking, and chatting with companions.[29]

More than ever, Arthur enjoyed late evening walks and suppers with his close friends, and he rarely retired before 2:00 A.M. In March 1882, he took a two-hour stroll through the streets of Washington with Steve French and Clint Wheeler that started at one in the morning. (At all times he refused the company of a bodyguard.) He called it the first relaxation he had had since becoming President. A few days later, with Wheeler and Tom Murphy, he set out at 3:00 A.M. for a forty-five-minute walk.[30] Major General William T. Sherman later recalled, "When he threw off the cares of office he seemed at his best. I have sat up with him till midnight, and then, when I excused myself, he would say, 'Oh, General, don't go; stay and let us have a good time.' "[31]

The President's political opponents, of course, eagerly seized upon reports of his work habits and after-hours entertainments and turned them against him. The Chicago *Tribune* editorialized, "Mr. Arthur's temperament is sluggish. He is indolent. It requires a great deal for him to get to his desk and begin the dispatch of business. Great questions of public policy bore him. No President was ever so much given to procrastination as he is."[32] A New York Half-Breed commented, "The only man who can do anything with Arthur is Grant. Arthur is so indolent and uncertain and timid and so under the weight of his office and his foolish hopes to get another nomination that he hardly ever makes a step but he puts his foot into it."[33] The editor of the Philadelphia *Times* assured his readers in March 1882, "That Arthurism is to share the same destiny of all the previous Presidential accidencies, no intelligent and unbiased observer of political events can doubt . . ."[34]

The President carefully shielded his children from both the public and the press. Since Jackson's time, Presidents' families had been the objects of popular scrutiny to a degree that would have startled European royalty; it was as though democracy had made them common property. But Arthur resolved from the start to draw a sharp line between the public and private life of the White House. He felt he had suffered humiliation and slander at the hands of journalists and gossips and was determined to protect his son and daughter from similar mistreatment. Then too, there was his well-developed sense of propriety. In a rare discourteous moment, he once snapped at a prying visitor, "Madam, I may be President of the United States, but my private life is nobody's damned business."[35]

Nell was not quite ten when her father became the Chief Executive, and she remained in New York with the household servants and her governess until late 1882, when the Lexington Avenue home was rented. She appeared at a few afternoon receptions late in the administration, she was sometimes seen with the President in his carriage, and she was permitted to become president of the Washington Children's Christmas Club, an organization created to provide a huge Christmas tree and dinners for children of the poor in the District of Columbia. But she was rarely photographed, and the public learned little about her.[36]

Alan entered Princeton shortly before his father moved into the White House. Tall, slender, and strikingly handsome in his late teens, he spent money freely on fine clothes and developed something of a reputation as a party-goer and lady-chaser. The President confided to a relative that he feared his son was wasting his youth on pleasures and indulgences belonging to maturer years.[37] Tom Murphy said, "He is not an even boy in his behavior. Still there is nothing alarming about him."[38] A scandalized friend of Rutherford B. Hayes wrote to the former President describing a chaperoned party at the White House following a performance by the Princeton Glee Club. "Two suppers were served, one at midnight and one at half past three and at both there was wine and at one of them champagne for these very young people. I have detailed accounts from more than one who was present. At a late hour there was a regular romp including a display of leaping by one of the young men who was quite an athlete in the east room."[39]

Arthur's children sometimes accompanied him on Sundays to St. John's Episcopal Church, across Lafayette Square. (In memory of his wife he gave a window to the church, where she had sung before their marriage. He ordered it placed on the south side of the building so that he could see it from his private quarters in the White House.) In April 1882, he took them to Annapolis to view the Herndon monument, erected in honor of their maternal grandfather. That summer they sailed with him on the U.S.S. *Despatch* to New York.[40]

From time to time, rumors floated through Washington of a presidential romance. One of Secretary Frelinghuysen's daughters was frequently mentioned, and there were several aspirants for Arthur's attentions. Mrs. Henry Adams sniggered in early 1882, "Our good king Arthur . . . all the pretty girls taken up to him and presented . . ."[41] Julia Sand chided, "Do you remember any other President as restless as yourself— who was rushing home every few weeks? If, as Washington gossip hints, you are engaged—& wish to see the lady without having her name dragged before the public—of course the end justifies the means."[42] Reporters learned that fresh flowers were brought daily to the White House and placed beside the photograph of a woman. Scandalmongers were silenced when it was learned that the photograph was of Arthur's late wife.[43]

CHAPTER SIXTEEN

Terribly to the Test

THE FIRST SESSION of the 47th Congress, which opened on December 5, 1881, and continued until August 8 of the following year, found Republicans with slim majorities in both branches. The margins were uncomfortable, however, and party leadership was weak. When the House organized itself, a fumbling Ohio Stalwart named J. Warren Kiefer was chosen Speaker. Responding to the self-satisfaction of the period, neither party was committed to a significant legislative program; indeed, few Congressmen seemed devoted to anything beyond the acquisition of favors for constituents.[1] A leading New York newspaper would call the session "the most disgraceful . . . ever held by the Congress of the United States."[2]

The President, of course, carried very little political weight in Congress, and he was not inclined to attempt a dramatic redefinition of the duties expected of a Chief Executive at the time. Arthur restricted his role in legislative affairs to annual messages and vetoes. His initial message was virtually ignored on Capitol Hill, but on three occasions during the session he formally disagreed with the wisdom of congressional actions.

The first was a bill calling for the restriction of immigration from China. As early as 1850, Californians had discriminated against Chinese laborers who entered the country to assist in railroad building and work in mines, and during the Depression of the 1870s a movement for their exclusion made headway. Objections centered around the foreigners' strange customs, their alleged filth and vice, and above all their willingness to work for low wages. Both national party platforms in 1876 criticized the principle of free immigration between China and the

United States, embodied in the Burlingame Treaty of 1868, and in early 1879, Congress passed a bill abrogating key portions of the treaty and severely limiting the number of Chinese who could enter the country. The bill was strongly favored on the Pacific Coast and was endorsed by many labor organizations. Many missionaries and businessmen, on the other hand, objected to it as a unilateral modification of a treaty, and feared serious retaliation by the Chinese. Several eastern Republicans, like George William Curtis, thought the suppression of free immigration undemocratic. Hayes vetoed the measure on the ground that it was an attempt to amend existing treaties by legislation.[3]

In 1880, all the parties, Republican, Democratic, and Greenback, condemned the unrestricted immigration of the Chinese. In November of that year a new treaty was negotiated allowing Congress to "regulate, limit, or suspend" the immigration of Chinese laborers if such immigration seemed to threaten public order.

The 47th Congress passed a bill suspending the importation of Chinese laborers for twenty years. It furthermore denied citizenship to Chinese; it required every Chinese already in the country to register himself at the United States Customhouse before departing our shores, should he wish to return; and it demanded that every Chinese citizen whose entrance into the country was not prohibited provide himself, before coming, with a passport written in English describing his person and intentions, countersigned by an American consular representative in China. The bill had powerful support: it passed the Senate 29 to 15, one short of a two-thirds vote; it was approved in the House 167 to 66, 18 more than two-thirds. Some of those who voted negatively declared that they would have favored the measure had the period of suspension been reduced to a decade, for there were fears that the bill violated the recent treaty with the Chinese.[4]

On March 30, a week after the bill sailed through the House, Edwin D. Morgan privately urged Arthur to use his veto, arguing that the twenty-year period was too lengthy.[5] Arthur had before him papers outlining the negotiations of the treaty with Peking, documents unavailable to Congress, as well as a memorandum from the Chinese minister at Washington protesting the bill. The Cabinet met in special session on April 3, and afterward it was learned that the President would return the bill to Congress but would be pleased to sign a similar measure suspending immigration for only ten years.[6]

In a lengthy and forceful veto message, Arthur described some of the history of the 1880 treaty and contended that signers envisioned merely a "reasonable" suspension of immigration. A period of twenty years, "nearly a generation," would be more like a prohibition. He regarded this provision of the act "a breach of our national faith" and said that "the honor of the country" constrained him to object. He accepted the view held by the majority in Congress that Chinese immigration should be restricted, he continued, but urged legislators to attempt "a shorter experiment." Arthur also observed that under the treaty the United States was bound to extend to Chinese within the country all the privileges, immunities, and exemptions accorded to citizens and subjects of the most favored nation. Provisions in the bill requiring personal registration and the taking out of passports were "undemocratic and hostile to the spirit of our institutions." "A nation like the United States, jealous of the liberties of its citizens, may well hesitate before it incorporates into its polity a system which is fast disappearing in Europe before the progress of liberal institutions." The message closed with a eulogy of Chinese contributions to American economic development and a warning that the bill in question "must have a direct tendency to repel Oriental nations from us and to drive their trade and commerce into more friendly hands."[7]

The veto received widespread support; *The New York Times*, for example, congratulated the President for his "firmness and wisdom."[8] Former Governor Morgan, an importer anxious to retain good relations with China, was delighted with his long-time friend: "Your reasons are unanswerable. They could not have been better."[9] Some proponents of the bill, however, who failed to read Arthur's message, leaped to the conclusion that he favored unrestricted immigration. Labor organizations in the East held huge rallies to condemn the President. The Chicago *Tribune* called the veto "another echo" from the "bulldog pistol of Charles J. Guiteau." In San Francisco flags were hung at half-mast; some merchants draped their stores in mourning.[10]

An attempt in the Senate to pass the bill over the veto failed, and anti-Chinese legislators designed another measure calling for the term of exclusion to be reduced to ten years. The other features of the original bill, to which Arthur objected, remained, including the denial of American citizenship to all Chinese. The legislation was backed, as before, by a coalition of Democrats and western Republicans, rendering its political overtones negligible. The vote was again lopsided: in the Senate the bill passed 32 to 15, and in the House 201 to 37. Arthur signed what is usually called the Chinese Exclusion Law on May 6, 1882. It marked a sharp departure from the national policy of offering a haven to the peoples of all countries.[11]

On July 1 Arthur vetoed a bill enacting safety and health standards for steamships bringing large numbers of immigrants to the United States. He did not disagree with the aim of the legislation; his objections involved serious technical mistakes in the bill's wording, errors he felt would bring financial losses to steamship companies and deter European immigration. Once again, Congress yielded to the President and passed a new measure tailored to his suggestions.[12]

The third Arthur veto prompted headlines all across the country. For years Congressmen had been criticized for securing appropriations for expenditures in their districts under the cover of "River and Harbor" bills. There was increasing belief that they constituted little more than thievery. The appropriation in 1870 had been under $4,000,000; by 1881 it had soared to $11,451,300. A year later, with a huge surplus in government coffers, a bill called for an unprecedented expenditure of almost $19,000,000.

Opposition to the new proposal began to mount in mid-May, when the House Commerce Committee made its recommendations. *The New York Times* forecast a presidential veto.[13] When the measure cleared the Senate in mid-July, the clamor for its defeat was intense. In New York the *Sun* editorialized, "What an opportunity for a shrewd and brave man! What an opportunity for CHESTER A. ARTHUR!"[14] *The Times* called the bill "a monstrous swindle" that "violates not only every principle of economy and prudence but every limitation of national authority applicable to internal improvements. . . . In short, it is in great part a scandalous misappropriation of public money for the advancement of local jobbery." The President "has an excellent opportunity to place himself on the side of economy and public decency by vetoing it."[15] The New York *Tribune*, the New York *World*, the Boston *Journal*, and newspapers and journals of both parties in all corners of the nation voiced similar sentiments. Roscoe Conkling, who, with Grant and most of the Stalwarts, had long frowned upon such legislation, told an audience in Utica, "The tendency is to spending largely, the tendency in Government is to profuse, perhaps lavish, appropriations of the public money. In the affairs of Government and in the affairs of business, unless I greatly mistake, the lesson, the need, and the admonition of the hour is frugality, foresight, and care."[16] New York business leaders were known to be solidly opposed to the bill. Surveying the climate of opinion, the Chicago *Tribune* flatly predicted a presidential veto. Nevertheless, Arthur received strong pressure from Congressmen to sign the measure.[17]

In his annual message, Arthur had left the question of internal improvements to the wisdom of Congress, suggesting merely the advisability of removing obstructions in the Mississippi River and improving the harbor lines on the Potomac. By special message in April he had endorsed a report from the Mississippi River Commission calling for large-scale improvements along the river.[18] Funds for these projects were included in the bill, but few thought they would persuade the President to accept the entire appropriation.[19]

On August 1, Arthur sent his veto of the River and Harbor bill to Congress. In his message he recognized the presence of his earlier recommendations, stating that he continued to consider them valuable. "It is not necessary that I say that when my signature would make the bill appropriating for these and other national objects a law it is with great reluctance and only under a sense of duty that I withhold it." His principle objection to the bill, he continued, was that it contained appropriations for purposes "not for the common defense or general welfare, and which do not promote commerce among the States." These grants were "entirely for the benefit of the particular localities in which it is proposed to make the improvements," and were therefore "beyond the powers given by the Constitution to Congress and the President." Such appropriations, furthermore, tended to increase in number and amount as localities vied with each other for federal funds. "Thus as the bill becomes more objectionable it secures more support." Lastly, Arthur wrote, the bill at hand contained appropriations "which in my opinion greatly exceed in amount the needs of the country for the present fiscal year." "The extravagant expenditure of public money is an evil not to be measured by the value of that money to the people who are taxed for it. They sustain a greater injury in the demoralizing effect produced upon those who are intrusted with official duty through all the ramifications of Government."

Arthur recommended that one half of the amount called for in the vetoed bill be appropriated, leaving the actual expenditure of funds in the hands of the President and Secretary of War. This proposal, similar to one made by Grant in 1870, would eliminate the "jobbery" intended by Congressmen.[20]

The message was warmly applauded, Senator George F. Hoar, a defender of the bill, conceded that "The press of the country, almost without exception, supported the President."[21] A large number of businessmen showered Arthur with congratulatory telegrams.[22] Old Simon Cameron crowed, "It was the act of a great statesman and all men say so."[23] Julia Sand wrote to Arthur, "How can I tell you how delighted I was at your veto of the Harbor Bill? Ah, if you only realized what a thrill of enthusiasm you awaken, every time you show the people plainly that you have the good of the whole country at heart . . ."[24]

Despite the popularity of Arthur's action, Congress passed the bill over his veto almost immediately. The responsibility was divided equally between Republicans and Democrats; chief support came from states along the Mississippi River and in the South. *The New York Times* declared that Congress was "generally condemned for its reckless viola-tion of the Constitution and its disregard for the wise counsel of the Executive."[25] Senator Hoar later recalled a "storm of indignation" over repassage of the bill. "A large number of the members of the House who had voted for it lost their seats. If the question of my reelection had come on within a few weeks thereafter, I doubt whether I should have got forty votes in the whole Legislature."[26]

This session of Congress concluded with little to its credit. A Bank Charter Extension Act was passed, but only after repeated appeals from the business community. Tariff revision was avoided by authorizing the President to appoint a committee to study the question. The issue of presidential succession was debated, but no conclusions were reached. Urgently needed legislation concerning bankruptcy and relief for the Supreme Court failed to win consideration. On the whole, Congressmen seemed largely committed to local rather than national goals, eager espe-cially to spend federal funds to reward friends and bolster their own chances for reelection. A week before adjournment so few Senators and Representatives remained in Washington that the transaction of new business was impossible.[27]

Shortly before Congress had completed its second week in session and while plans were being made for the White House Christmas decora-tions, disturbing headlines suddenly loomed in the press warning of scandal and crisis in the State Department. During the first days of 1882 Arthur was informed by Frederick Frelinghuysen that research in the department archives had uncovered evidence of recklessness and im-propriety in Blaine's diplomacy, and permission was requested to reverse the entire thrust of the Plumed Knight's Latin American foreign policy. Such a step, of course, would enrage Half-Breeds and deepen divisions within the GOP. It might also humiliate the President, who had bestowed his approval on at least the broad outline of Blaine's diplomatic objec-tives.

Foreign affairs were greeted for the most part with indifference and antipathy during the Gilded Age; Congress, the public, and the press sought consistently to avoid overseas entanglements. Rutherford B. Hayes's second Annual Message devoted almost as much space to the District of Columbia as to international concerns.[28] From Appomattox to the sinking of the *Maine* the nation was preoccupied with its own internal development.

The State Department's executive and clerical staff was small—only fifty-one under Evarts—and frequently inefficient. (At one point, a valuable book of records, missing for weeks, was discovered under a pillow on the second assistant secretary's chair, which had been too low for him.) The United States sent and received no ambassadors. In 1880 its diplomatic representatives consisted of twenty-five ministers and five chargés d'affaires. Some three hundred consulates were also maintained as well as a large number of commercial agencies. Most ministers were selected because of their political connections. They were badly paid and housed and had to possess independent incomes or go into debt to honor their appointments. In 1881 John Hay thought the Foreign Service "like the Catholic Church, calculated only for celibates."[29]

For all of the nation's disinterest in the world beyond its shores, however, forces were at work in the late nineteenth century that prompted at least a minimum of activity in foreign affairs and set the stage for more dramatic events at the turn of the century. Many Americans sought to enhance their country's prestige by enlarging its role in international questions. The country's booming productive capacity prompted business-men, farmers, and government officials to search for fertile overseas markets. More than a few American nationalists felt the Monroe Doctrine endangered by ruthless Europeans, and called for actions that would preserve Latin America exclusively for their own purposes.

Each Secretary of State after the war was affected by pressures to expand abroad, and each took steps to increase American political and economic influence. The boldest of them, William Henry Seward, pro-pounded a sweeping vision of American empire that would fascinate statesmen for more than a century. He purchased Alaska and the Midway Islands, sought a reciprocity treaty with Hawaii, and vigorously defended the open-door policy in Asia. He desired the purchase of the Dutch West Indies and Santo Domingo, spoke of an American-controlled isthmian canal, and looked forward to the time when Central America and Canada would enter the Union.

Hamilton Fish shared much of Grant's grandiose designs for the extension of American interests. He signed the first reciprocity treaty with Hawaii, opened Samoa to American shipping, and supported Grant's addition to the Monroe Doctrine, "that hereafter no territory on this continent shall be regarded as subject to transfer to a European power." When Venezuela erupted in revolution, Fish informed Germany that the United States would not tolerate concerted intervention, and he later offered American assistance to halt the use of Dutch force against the troubled nation.

William M. Evarts spoke aggressively of seeking foreign markets for surplus manufacturing goods, and pleased American businessmen by revitalizing the consular corps and initiating monthly consular re-ports that described overseas economies, customs, and governments. He was keenly sensitive to all European motions in the direction of Latin America and protested loudly against alleged British encroachment of Guatemala. When the Frenchman Ferdinand de Lesseps formulated plans for an isthmian canal, Evarts attempted to pressure Colombia into conceding that a treaty gave the United States "potential control" over any canal.[30]

Blaine had revealed little interest in foreign affairs as a Congressman, and few believed that his Cabinet appointment had anything to do with his grasp of international events. Foreign policy issues did not command the attention of Garfield or his Secretary of State during the first months of the administration, and during the summer of 1881, while Garfield lay dying, Blaine confined his activity to the routine duties of his office.

When Arthur became President, Blaine realized that he could not remain in the Cabinet serving the wishes of his long-time Stalwart opponent. And he also no doubt instantly saw himself as a prime contender for the White House in 1884. At first he wished to resign as early as possible. But when Arthur persuaded him to remain until the convening of Congress he set to work creating several bold new departures in foreign policy that had Washington buzzing. From the gloomy day in September when the nation went into mourning until his delayed departure from the State Department on December 19, Blaine labored furiously at his desk forging a record of achievement that would enhance his stature within the GOP and perhaps appeal to all voters once talk again turned to possible presidential candidates. Much of this sudden burst of energy was waged after his successor had accepted office. The extent to which Arthur understood or approved these activities during the first trauma-filled days of his administration is not entirely clear, but it seems certain that Blaine was given virtually a free hand and that the actual, if not the ultimate, responsibility for the extraordinary actions during this period rests squarely with the outgoing Secretary of State.[31]

Blaine's first diplomatic correspondence of consequence in late 1881 concerned the isthmian question, a topic of interest to Americans for decades. As early as 1846 the United States signed a treaty with New Granada (later Colombia) acquiring free transit across the isthmus in return for an American guarantee of Colombian sovereignty over the area and isthmian neutrality. Nicaragua soon appeared to possess a more feasible canal route, and rivalry between Britain and the United States over the site led to the Clayton-Bulwer Treaty of 1850, by which neither nation was permitted to build or operate a canal without the participation of the other.

Completion of the Suez Canal in 1869 sparked renewed interest in a similar New World project, and in 1871 President Grant appointed a commission to study the matter. Five years later the commission recommended a route across Nicaragua, and Secretary Fish attempted unsuccessfully to sign a treaty with Nicaraguan officials. When the French secured a concession from Colombia to dig a canal across the Isthmus of Panama, and de Lesseps, the builder of the Suez Canal, formed a company in 1879 to carry out the project, many Americans took alarm. President Hayes, in a special message to Congress, called for strict United States control over any canal project. Garfield expressed a similar demand in his inaugural address. Congress passed resolutions condemning all foreign-sponsored canals, and the House called for the abrogation of the Clayton-Bulwer Treaty.

Shortly after taking office, Blaine protested a proposal for European arbitration of an isthmian boundary dispute between Colombia and Costa Rica. In June he prepared a full policy statement on American rights in the Isthmus of Panama and sent it to each of the American legations in Europe for distribution. Based on an interpretation of the Monroe Doctrine favored by mid-century expansionists plus a somewhat strained version of the Treaty of 1846, the document stated flatly that the United States would be most unfriendly to European powers meddling in the affairs of Colombia.

That fall, with his days in the State Department numbered, Blaine went further than any of his predecessors by requesting an entire reconstruction of the Clayton-Bulwer Treaty, a critical obstacle to American aspirations in Nicaragua. In a letter of November 19 to our minister to London, James Russell Lowell, Blaine suggested, among other things, that the United States be permitted to fortify and control a Nicaragua canal. Ten days later he sent a note to Lowell containing arguments and evidence asserting that Britain and the United States had long considered abrogation and modification of the treaty.

Blaine surely realized that his proposal would be rebuffed, as indeed it was almost a month after he left office. The British saw no reason to surrender treaty rights in a significant area of the world on demand, and Blaine's shaky argumentation was rejected out of hand. Several observers, then and later, suggested that the Secretary's messages were "for the record"—that they not only enhanced his image as a statesman at the time but that in the event his successor chose to pursue a similar course of action, Blaine could claim much of the credit.[32]

While attempting to limit foreign involvement in the construction and operation of an inter-oceanic canal, Blaine also determined to prove the United States capable of leading Latin American nations to settlement of serious disputes among themselves. European powers appeared eager to intervene in such conflicts, in the hope of expanding their political and economic authority in the area, and numerous politicians and businessmen in the United States sought to close such doors by taking action to preserve peace and stability.

The most troublesome South American dispute underway at the time of Garfield's inauguration was the War of the Pacific, a struggle between Chile, Peru, and Bolivia that had erupted in 1879 over a strip of desert between the Andes and the Pacific Coast rich in deposits of guano and nitrates. Foreign interest in the war was high from the start, for Europeans had played a large role in the development of guano and nitrate industries and floated government loans in the region. British shipyards constructed warships for the Chilean navy, and British shipping did a lively business in the ports of Valparaiso and Santiago. In 1879 and 1880, Britain offered to mediate the conflict, and before long, France suggested joint mediation by France, England, and the United States. The State Department was quickly under pressure, especially from American business interests, to take steps on its own to end the war. An effort in that direction was made in October 1880. But by then Chile had enjoyed major military victories over Peru, capturing the guano beds, and her harsh terms were rejected by the Lima government.

In May 1881, Blaine appointed new ministers to Chile and Peru. Both men were unfortunate choices. General Hugh J. Kilpatrick, sent to Santiago, was related to the local archbishop and sympathized wholly with Chile's aspirations. He was soon stricken with Bright's disease and rendered unable to carry out his duties. Stephen J. Hurlbut, a former Blaine campaign manager, was reportedly given to drunkenness and had once been convicted of taking a bribe. Charges of corruption stuck to his every activity in Peru, and his brash and aggressively partisan tactics virtually committed the United States to Peruvian goals. By late September the War of the Pacific remained unsettled, and suspicion of American intentions in the struggle had become general.

Blaine exercised little leadership in the matter while Garfield lived. His instructions to the new ministers were general and mild. During the summer of 1881 he seemed to pay scant attention to dispatches from Chile and Peru. That fall, however, while serving under Arthur, he took a definite interest in the war.

With both Hurlbut and Kilpatrick under fire from the press, Blaine decided to send envoys to the belligerent nations to clarify and strengthen America's position. To head the mission he selected William Henry Trescot, an extremely able diplomat whose service in similar capacities stretched back to the 1850s. Walker Blaine, the secretary's son, then serving as third assistant secretary of state, was sent along.

Blaine's instructions to Trescot clearly revealed the bold new approach to the War of the Pacific. In late September Chile had seized the head of the Peruvian government, García Calderón, and soon whisked him off to Santiago. Calderón had been recognized by Blaine, following a Peruvian revolution, and was suspected by Chilean leaders of intriguing with Hurlbut. Trescot was asked to determine if the arrest was a deliberate insult to the United States. If so, the diplomat was to tell the Chilean government "that the President considers such a proceeding as an international and unwarranted offense . . . an act of such unfriendly import as to require the immediate suspension of all diplomatic intercourse." Moreover, if Chile was determined to establish a government in Peru that would favor her designs on conquered Peruvian territory prior to a peace conference, Trescot was to express "disappointment and dissatisfaction." Should Chile reject the good offices of the United States altogether, Washington "will hold itself free to appeal to the other republics of this continent to join it in an effort to avert consequences which cannot be confined to Chile and Peru, but which threaten with extremest danger the political institutions, the peaceful progress, and the liberal civilization of all America." The next day Trescot was told to visit Argentina and Brazil on his way home.[33]

A boundary dispute between Mexico and Guatemala also attracted Blaine's attention. The United States had close ties with both nations. Guatemalan dictator Justo Rufino Barrios was particularly friendly: he welcomed American capital, bestowed generous concessions, and offered to sell strategic islands to the Hayes Administration. In 1880, Barrios had announced plans to create a confederation of Guatemala, Honduras, and El Salvador, and take Nicaragua by force. Thereafter, he hinted, he would be ready for talks with the United States about a canal concession in Nicaragua. A Central American union interested Blaine, as it had Evarts. It might bring stability and prosperity to the quarrelsome, backward states of the region, forestall European entanglements, and yield valuable canal rights. Not long after taking office, Blaine told the Nicaraguan minister that he favored a canal across Nicaragua and instructed United States minister Cornelius A. Logan to work for a strong, unified government in Central America.

In May 1881, the Guatemalan minister to the United States believed his nation threatened by invasion over claims to the border province of Chiapas and appealed to the Secretary of State as "the natural protector of the integrity of the Central American territory" to restrain powerful Mexico. More than willing to play the role of protector, Blaine promptly offered the State Department's good offices. When Mexico scorned the overture and moved troops into the disputed area, Blaine warned its

leaders that the continuation of aggression would be deemed an unfriendly act by the United States. Privately, he expressed fear that
Guatemala might cede her rights in the disputed territory to a European
power.

In June, Guatemala asked for a loan of $2,000,000 to strengthen her
military. At the same time, her minister to Washington requested
American assistance in forming a Central American union, and proposed
an alliance between the emergent nation and the United States. The
picture was clear: if Blaine wished to see a united Central America he
would have to come to Guatemala's rescue. But to assist Guatemala in
any meaningful way would rupture relations with Mexico.

On November 28, during his last three weeks in office, Blaine
drafted a major policy statement on the issue—the first since the preceding spring. The American minister to Mexico was instructed to continue
to urge arbitration on Mexico, recognize her claim to Chiapas, and to
exert the maximum "moral influence" of the United States to settle the
dispute. He went on to warn the Mexican government that continued
hostility against Guatemala would not be "in harmony with the friendly
relations between us, and injurious to the best interests of all the republics of this continent."[34]

The next day Blaine sent out invitations to all the independent states
of Latin America (excluding Haiti) to attend a great inter-American
peace congress in Washington on November 22, 1882. This was the first
such proposal ever extended by the United States and was the crowning
touch to Blaine's extraordinarily aggressive foreign policy of late 1881.
The secretary based his invitations on the need "to seek a way of
permanently averting the horrors of cruel and bloody combat between
countries, oftenest of one blood and speech, or the even worse calamity
of internal commotion and civil strife." Perhaps to soothe Chile and
Mexico, he gave assurances that the congress would not take up existing
conflicts. "Its mission is higher. It is to provide for the interests of all in
the future, not to settle the individual differences of the present."

It seems clear, however, that current unsettled conditions in Latin
America were foremost on Blaine's mind when he called for a Pan-
American meeting. One scholar has called the move "a brilliant last-
minute effort to rescue his own spirited but rather ineffectual record as
secretary of state in the Garfield administration."[35] As he prepared to
leave the State Department, Blaine could look back over the preceding
nine and one-half months with little pleasure. Diplomatic relations with
Mexico were deteriorating rapidly, and the boundary dispute with
Guatemala was not approaching settlement. The War of the Pacific continued; Chile was angry over what it considered State Department

favoritism toward Peru, and scandal hovered over the conduct of the American minister to Peru. Colombia and Costa Rica were resentful and suspicious owing to the effort to block European arbitration of their differences. In short, Blaine's active assumption of responsibilities in Latin America had not proven fruitful and threatened to blacken his reputation as a leader and statesman.

Blaine hoped that the peace congress would bring pressure to bear on Mexico to arbitrate by making arbitration a Pan-American concern. It was also possible that the congress would create an inter-American arbitration treaty, thus decreasing the opportunities for European intervention in the New World. Moreover, Blaine counted on the summons to strengthen Trescot's hand and bring the War of the Pacific closer to a satisfactory solution. Invitations to the meeting were sent to neutral nations immediately, but Trescot was given charge of those to Chile, Peru, and Bolivia for use in his delicate talks with Chile.

Even if Mexico and Chile remained recalcitrant, however, Blaine's record now contained a dramatic and unprecedented proposal that would elevate his public status and turn attention away from the more bitter realities of recent American foreign policy. What Blaine could not predict as he cleared out his desk in Washington was the future of that clever proposal in the hands of Arthur and Frelinghuysen.[36]

Frederick Frelinghuysen and Blaine were very different sorts of men in background, temperament, and ambition. The new Secretary of State was the scion of a family long distinguished in political and legal affairs and was steeped by heritage and education in the obligation of responsible public service. He was quiet, conservative, reliable, at all times a proper gentleman; his methods were orthodox, his integrity unquestionable. Not driven by desires for high office or wealth, he sought merely to serve the President honorably, loyally, and to the best of his ability. One Stalwart newspaper heralded his arrival at the State Department by contrasting his "wise conservatism" to Blaine's penchant for "dramatic adventures."[37]

To assist him with his new duties, Frelinghuysen appointed J. C. Bancroft Davis first assistant secretary of state. Davis was a veteran diplomat of considerable talent who had worked closely with Hamilton Fish during the Grant years. Blaine recognized Davis's ability and had offered him a position earlier in 1881, but Davis was a Stalwart, and a conference with Conkling persuaded him to reject the overture.

Frelinghuysen came to work on December 20 and left three days later for the Christmas holiday. In his absence, Davis began to burrow through State Department files on the War of the Pacific to acquaint himself with the complex facts of the conflict and test mounting charges in the press that disreputable financial interests had attached themselves to United States diplomacy. A week later he was convinced that "we were on the highway to war for the benefit of about as nasty a set of people as ever gathered about a Washington Department." When Frelinghuysen returned at New Year's, Davis met him at the station and presented his evidence in the carriage on the way to the secretary's home. The documents bared suspicious relationships between the State Department's Peruvian policy, a French banking house, the Crédit Industriel, and an American organization called the Peruvian Company. They also revealed Trescot's harsh instructions, which indicated that Blaine was using the proposal for a peace congress to bring pressure upon Chile. After consultations with Senator George F. Edmunds and the President, Frelinghuysen decided to order what Davis called "an instant halt and about face."[38] The Arthur Administration sought no claim to the scandal brewing in Peru, and it did not intend to become sucked into the War of the Pacific or any other war.

Early in January the secretary revoked most of Trescot's instructions, making it clear that the United States had no wish to "dictate or make any authoritative utterance to either Peru or Chile as to the merits of the controversy existing between those republics" or the settlement.[39] He also temporarily suspended support of an inter-American peace convention.[40] Following another meeting with Senator Edmunds, Frelinghuysen decided that the State Department would make public all of its documents relating to the War of the Pacific. In this way the Secretary of State could wash his hands completely of his predecessor's actions, and at the same time, perhaps, ward off the inevitable contention that Blaine was being abused by Stalwarts out of political spite.

Davis privately advised Hamilton Fish of recent events and predicted, "A desperate fight is ahead." Not long after the first of the State Department documents was made public, Davis by chance met Mr. and Mrs. Blaine on a Washington street. "An iceberg was warm in comparison," he remarked later.[41]

At first, Blaine exercised what his wife called "the dignity of perfect silence."[42] In late January, however, he granted an interview in which he accused Frelinghuysen of sending Trescot on a "fool's errand" that threatened the "utter spoilation" of Peru.[43] A few days later he published a lengthy letter to the President. Blaine began by tracing the idea of a peace congress to the early months of his term and claiming that Garfield had "warmly approved" it (a contention few students of the subject have accepted). He went on to assert that Arthur had been fully apprised of the project and had personally ordered the invitations sent.

He accused Frelinghuysen of truckling to Europe in his revocation of Trescot's instructions, adding that "the voluntary humiliation of this government could not be more complete, unless we should petition the European governments for the privilege of holding the Congress." Finally, Blaine invoked a new appeal for support by declaring that his hopes for the congress had always included commercial advantages to the United States.[44]

Blaine was correct in stating that the President had approved the plan to convene a peace congress, but he did not reveal the extent to which the Chief Executive was privy to its short-term goals. The administration let it be known that Blaine did not show all of Trescot's instructions to the President before they were sent; mentioned specifically was the order to visit Argentina and Brazil on the way home—visits intended to intimidate the Chilean government.[45] The order in question, it will be recalled, was dispatched a day after the main body of Trescot's instructions. Arthur was also unacquainted with the Crédit Industriel and the Peruvian Company when he bestowed his blessing upon what he thought was a major step toward future peace in the Western Hemisphere.

The President, of course, must share some of the burden for the dubious activities of late 1881. He might have scrutinized Blaine's correspondence more carefully, asked sharper questions, taken nothing for granted. But during the trying and painful first months in the nation's highest office, Arthur was unquestionably pleased to be able to leave international matters in the strong hands of the incumbent Secretary of State. He had pled with Blaine to remain in office to give the new administration a sense of continuity, and he had little reason to question his motives for staying on. Blaine's assistance was greatly needed in constructing the foreign policy section of the first annual message; relevant paragraphs mirror in general terms Blaine's views of the world.[46] A reporter quoted friends of the President as concluding, "If any mistakes were made, they were the mistakes which any President might have made acting under advice of his Secretary of State, supposing him to be well informed and controlled by a desire to pursue the course calculated to strengthen abroad the influence of the Government of the United States."[47] To his credit, Arthur did not hesitate to turn administration policy sharply around when he discovered it necessary.

Public response to the shift closely followed partisan lines. The New York *Tribune* (with Blaine's encouragement) published scathing letters and editorials attacking the President for weakness and indecision. Stalwart newspapers fired back; Blaine's actions had brought us to the brink of war, the New York *Herald* trumpeted, "war in a bad cause, unnecessary and to us disgraceful." Independent organs, strongly isolationist, were pleased by the administration's new approach.[48]

Arthur and Frelinghuysen determined early in 1882 to submit the proposal for a Pan-American peace conference to Congress.[49] The idea, when divorced from current conflicts, had appealing long-range possibilities and was favored by many Latin American governments. Serious objections were raised at home, however, that called for consultation with Capitol Hill. Some critics contended that the President lacked constitutional authority to convene a peace congress. Others argued that the nation's treaty rights, concerning especially the Isthmus of Panama, might be endangered at such a meeting.

On April 18, Arthur sent a special message on the subject to Congress. In it he expressed a personal lack of enthusiasm for a November convention, pointing to the wide range of disputes continuing to plague Latin American republics. "It was hoped that these differences would disappear before the time fixed for the meeting of the congress. This hope has not been realized."[50] He argued convincingly, on the other hand, against the view that he was without the authority to summon a peace congress. The thorny issue of isthmian rights was raised without comment. The wisest course of action, Arthur concluded, was to refer to Congress the propriety of convening a conference in the fall. He submitted a copy of the earlier invitation to participate in an international meeting and promised to act in accordance with the wishes of the nation's legislators.[51]

The President's decision was considered prudent and proper at the time. His message, however, evoked only a feeble response from the 47th Congress. Two joint resolutions were introduced calling for a conference in November, but neither advanced beyond committee discussion. Twenty-four petitions supporting a peace congress were received on Capitol Hill, but they made little impression. Pan-Americanism was simply beyond the concerns of most Congressmen in 1882. On August 9, with no instructions from Congress and without a provision for the conference, Frelinghuysen formally canceled the invitations.[52]

Allegations of malfeasance in the nation's dealings with Chile and Peru interested many Congressmen, however, in large part because of the political overtones. The House Committee on Foreign Affairs investigated the matter from early March through the middle of June. Charges and countercharges occupied the front pages of newspapers even longer. At one point, testimony linked Blaine directly with an unscrupulous representative of the Peruvian Company, and in April the former Secretary of State took the stand for three days on his own behalf. The committee's final report, issued August 1, cleared all State

Department officials of charges of dishonest conduct. Several financial schemers were condemned, however, and Blaine's reputation was unquestionably battered by the fray. When the smoke had cleared, few citizens expressed regret over the significant shift in United States Latin American policy ordered early in the year.[53]

During the months in which Congress deliberated, much of the President's time was occupied with the distribution of patronage. His general approach to the extremely delicate matter, outside the South, was traditional and safe: he heeded the advice of Republican Senators and Representatives from the states and districts where appointments were to be made. Unlike many of his predecessors, he granted interviews to office-seekers only three days a week, and then only during stated hours.[54] He told one gentleman that he did not intend to appoint a single man to office unless his full record revealed fitness. Furthermore, he would make no removals except for cause, and not until the officer in question had received notice of the charges against him and had been given proper time to reply.[55] Had such standards been followed scrupulously, of course, Arthur would have been unique among Presidents. Still, his record on appointments and removals was better than anyone with the slightest knowledge of his history had anticipated.

Data is unavailable to determine exactly how equitably patronage was distributed among GOP factions. A few old Stalwart friends of the President were given posts: Thomas Acton,[56] John N. Knapp,[57] Adam Badeau,[58] and James Armstrong.[59] Conkling was permitted to name the postmaster at Utica.[60] Barney Biglin's brother was made an assistant appraiser in the New York Customhouse.[61] But in only two instances were Independents and Half-Breeds greatly upset by Arthur's appointments. Without consulting either of Massachusetts's Republican Senators, the President named Stalwart newspaper editor Roland Worthington collector of the port at Boston. (Both Senators Hoar and Dawes, administration sources wryly recalled, were prominent in insisting, when Robertson was named, that Garfield had exercised a privilege that could not properly be questioned.)[62] A short time later, Arthur selected two of John F. Smyth's favorites to fill federal posts in Albany.[63]

Though Independents constantly predicted a purge of federal officials, it never came about. By June 1882, only sixteen removals had been made in the Treasury Department, where thousands of jobs were potentially available.[64] In the summer of 1882 the administration released figures showing that out of 874 appointments made in the preceding nine months, only 49 were owing to removals, and it contended that most of those removals were for cause.[65]

Reformers thought they had a better case against the administration on the issue of political assessments. In December 1881, the New York Civil Service Reform Association demanded that Secretary Folger take action against General Newton M. Curtis, a special Treasury Department agent and treasurer of New York's Republican State Committee, for accepting funds in violation of the anti-assessment statute of 1876. This law prohibited government officials who were not appointed by the President and confirmed by the Senate from soliciting or receiving money or property for political purposes. The federal government decided to prosecute, but its first indictment was quashed on a technical error: the defendant's name was presented as "Nehemiah" rather than Newton. Arthur took most of the blame for the blunder. "Who is responsible for that mean little trick about 'Nehemiah M. Curtis?'" Julia Sand asked. "But why should I ask, when I know, as well as you do, that you are? The thing would not have been done without your approval."[66] The government appeared ready to drop the case until goaded into making a second effort by the New York association. Curtis was tried and convicted.

E. D. Morgan pled with his former protégé to pardon Curtis for doing "simply what the most of us have ourselves done."[67] The request must have pained Arthur to read, for fate had indeed forced him to condemn as criminal a practice he had dutifully performed and encouraged since entering politics, a practice he had failed to discuss in his speeches and messages containing references to the civil service. However he may have wished to assist Curtis, he refused, anticipating the public outcry that would greet his intervention—the acrid rehashing of his career as a spoilsman, more of the bitter lament about Guiteau's deed. Curtis was denied a new trial and fined $1,000 and expenses. The sum was paid by the New York Republican State Committee, at the suggestion of its new chairman, Clint Wheeler.[68]

Republican leaders were far from ready to abandon assessments, despite obviously growing animosity toward them across the country. In May 1882, Congressman Jay Hubbell, chairman of the Republican congressional campaign committee, mailed the regular assessment letters to officeholders, asking an average of 2 percent to assist with the important fall election campaigns. Reformers loudly protested the move. Arthur too suffered criticism, for the letters explained that the committee was "authorized to state that such voluntary contributions from persons employed in the service of the United States will not be objected to in any official quarter." The administration was scored again in July when the payment of Hubbell's circulars was aided by an opinion from Attorney General Brewster stating that the 1876 statute, by which Curtis was convicted, did not apply to Congressmen. The President declared that no one in the federal service who declined to pay assessments would be subjected to discharge or criticism. But reformers quickly noted that this was merely an affirmation of the contention in the circulars: assessments were voluntary contributions.[69]

Members of the House during the 47th Congress were less willing than the President to take steps in the direction of civil service reform. Congressmen from both parties voted to reject Arthur's plea for a $25,000 appropriation to reactivate the Civil Service Commission. When the figure was scaled down to $15,000, only five Republicans favored the proposal. Later, perhaps in response to much adverse press comment, the sum of $15,000 was passed in a bill appropriating more than $25,-000,000. Civil service reform was ridiculed at length on the floor of the House. And when Speaker Kiefer appointed members of the House Select Committee on Civil Service Reform he included an outspoken defender of the spoils system, a signer of assessment circulars, a Congressman elected through the efforts of an ex-Democratic boss, and Jay Hubbell. At the conclusion of six months' labor, the committee produced "a bill to enlarge the powers and duties of the Department of Agriculture."[70]

When Congress adjourned, Arthur left Washington almost immediately. With his children and some friends, he sailed to New York to relax before traveling to Newport as the guest of E. D. Morgan and going fishing with R. G. Dun. On August 21 a Cabinet meeting was convened at the President's home, the first such meeting in the state since the days of George Washington.[71] The day before, Arthur had decided to pay a quiet visit to his ardent admirer and self-appointed conscience, Julia Sand.

By this time the President had saved fifteen letters from the perceptive, intelligent, and sometimes scolding commentator. They offered political advice freely, revealing a political sympathy with the reform branch of the GOP. They urged Arthur to repudiate his past, ignore his Stalwart allies, and become a President known for integrity and courage. Miss Sand was convinced that Arthur had the intelligence and stamina to become a great Chief Executive. Did he have, she asked, the will and the fortitude?

> . . . it is by our opportunities that we will be judged. The Presidency puts a man terribly to the test. If he has fine qualities, they will shine with double brilliancy. If he is commonplace, it kills him. What has Grant been good for since—except to eat dinners? Will Hayes ever be heard of again—unless at a Sunday School festival?

But Julia Sand was no harridan. Her letters disclosed a deep personal concern for the President just shy of adoration ("as yet I have not met anybody who believes in you, as I do"). They also contained more than a little charm and wit, qualities Arthur was known to appreciate. She often referred to herself as the President's "little dwarf"—an allusion to the only member of a royal court who dared tell the king the truth.

Arthur could glean only small bits of information about his correspondent from her writing. She described herself as being young, "I feel exactly as if I were your mother—which you must own is generous, considering you are old enough to be mine." She revealed that she was unmarried and an invalid. For five years, she wrote, she had been "dead and buried," and hinted at spinal difficulties, lameness, and deafness. She could and did travel to fashionable Saratoga Springs and Newport, she read French, liked poetry, and was obviously a careful observer of politics. Miss Sand began to urge Arthur to visit her in a letter of November 8, 1881, and became irritated in subsequent letters over his failure to acknowledge her in any way. On the evening of August 20, 1882, a handsome carriage suddenly appeared in front of the Seventy-fourth Street residence owned by Miss Sand's brother, and out stepped the President.

According to Miss Sand, she was caught by surprise at the President's entrance: "[I] had disdained roast beef and scorned peach-pie, was on the lounge, vowing that I would never write another line to that horrid man, and at the same time wondering who that gentle-voiced Episcopal minister in the front parlor might be . . ." Although the President stayed for almost an hour, his thirty-two-year-old hostess was so flustered by his presence that afterward she could remember very little of what was said. (She did recall, somewhat bitterly, the presence of an excessively large number of relatives in the home during the visit.) The subject of politics did come up, and Arthur told Miss Sand that she ought not to believe all she read in newspapers, and that one day he would enlighten her about a number of matters. He even referred to a specific item she had raised in one of her letters, showing that the President had indeed paid attention to his dwarf.[72]

CHAPTER SEVENTEEN

Public Enemies

To win public confidence, administration leaders understood well that they would have to continue and even intensify the effort to bring the star route conspirators before the bar of justice. The number of convictions obtained would be a major test of their desire and ability to rise above politics in the service of the nation. *The New York Times*, which had done much of the work to expose the frauds, stated the issue succinctly: "This simple fact presents itself to the people of the United States, that the Administration of President Arthur has charged itself with bringing to justice a set of public plunderers whose operations will rank with those of the whiskey ring and the Tweed combination, and that either faltering or failure in that enterprise will react on the Administration and the party responsible for it."[1]

Many were skeptical about the administration's intentions. Would Republicans consent to put their national committee secretary behind bars? Hadn't Arthur worked closely with Dorsey and others named in the frauds during the campaign of 1880? And what about the infamous speech at Delmonico's? Stalwart newspapers, like Washington's *National Republican* and the *Critic*, had blasted the Garfield Administration for investigating star route matters. And hadn't Wayne MacVeagh resigned from Arthur's Cabinet muttering vaguely about the administration's lack of resolve in the star route cases? True, the President had declared repeatedly and unequivocally that he was devoted to the vigorous prosecution of the accused. But more than a few considered that political rhetoric and were convinced that the administration would find channels through which Dorsey and the others would escape. Two months after Arthur took office *The Times* contended it was the only prominent journal in the country that expected to see a single star route suspect sent to jail.[2]

Altogether there were 9,225 star routes in sparsely settled areas of the West and South. Congress was generous with its mail subsidies, and in 1879–80 the routes cost almost $6,000,000. Because of the sudden requirements occasioned by mining rushes, Indian wars, and the like, Congress had authorized the Post Office Department to alter the conditions and compensation of contracts with private mail carriers as circumstances warranted. That duty fell to Second Assistant Postmaster General Thomas J. Brady, a Grant appointee and Stalwart, and he and a number of friends profited handsomely. Star route contracts were awarded to politicians and their allies who made ridiculously low bids on the private understanding that their financial return would soon be increased. Many of the contracts were sublet or sold, and Brady associates made sizable profits for intermediary services.

The first investigations into the star routes had begun in the early 1870s. A congressional inquiry of 1878 first involved the names of prominent public servants, including Senator Dorsey. The Post Office Department began making requests for deficiency appropriations in 1877, and in 1880 asked Congress for an additional $2,000,000. Following a further investigation, Congress appropriated $1,100,000, and charges of lobbying and bribery soon swirled through Washington and into the press.

In April 1881, Postmaster General James presented Garfield with evidence of enormous star route frauds. He received the President's instructions to prosecute all guilty parties without consideration of political affiliations. Brady was soon removed from office. A clerk of Dorsey's, Montfort C. Rerdell, contacted James in early June and confessed to participation in the frauds, presenting evidence implicating Dorsey, his brother John, and three others. Shortly, Dorsey reached Rerdell and, with pleading and threats, exacted an affidavit from him renouncing his confession. The President urged James to accelerate the investigation.[3]

Attorney General MacVeagh was also looking into the question, and hired two Washington attorneys, A. M. Gibson and William A. Cook, to assist him. Both Gibson and Cook had shady reputations, and Garfield was angered by their employment. (MacVeagh told a friend that he was fully aware of Cook's background. "He said Mr. Cook was employed upon the theory of setting a thief to catch a thief.") But the President was unwilling to interfere with the work he had assigned to others and chose to respect his Attorney General's decision.[4]

Toward the end of August, with Garfield near death, MacVeagh decided to turn over the star route investigations to attorneys known to be friendly with the Vice-President. Benjamin Brewster, whose legal experience extended over more than forty years, was selected by the Attorney General. Thomas L. James suggested George Bliss, an old friend with a successful legal career that had begun more than twenty years earlier. When MacVeagh and James resigned, the government team handling the star route cases consisted of Attorney General Brewster, Bliss, P. H. Woodward (a highly competent postal inspector employed by James), Gibson, and Cook.[5]

Problems arose quickly, for Bliss and Woodward discovered that Gibson and Cook were undermining the government's cases and selling evidence to suspects. Moreover, Bliss soon learned that Washington District Attorney Corkhill was close to Brady and could not be trusted. Gibson and Cook resigned in early 1882, publicly contending that the administration was insincere in its desire to convict star route conspirators. Corkhill kept his position because the administration was afraid his dismissal would be linked to the Guiteau trial, but he was excluded from all participation in the government's plans.[6]

In January 1882, Brewster added William W. Ker to the government's staff. Ker was a distinguished Philadelphia attorney and an expert in drafting indictments. Two months later, in response to a suggestion by Senator George Edmunds, a powerful member of the Senate Judiciary Committee, Brewster employed Richard T. Merrick, a much-experienced Washington attorney. Both Ker and Merrick were Democrats, chosen in part by Brewster to disassociate the star route cases from political partisanship. Ker later recalled, "He [Brewster] told me that it was not a question of politics, but one of the administration of justice; that he was glad that I was a Democrat; that he knew the fact very well; that he was all the more confident that I would do my duty, and that there would be less reason to complain about any action that might be taken in the cases."[7]

Though the Attorney General left most of the work of preparing and arguing the cases to Bliss and his assistants, Brewster kept a keen eye on developments and reported frequently to the President. He later quoted Arthur as saying, "I want this work to be done as you are doing it, in the spirit in which you are doing it; I want it to be done earnestly and thoroughly. I desire that these people shall be prosecuted with the utmost vigor of the law. I will give you all the help I can. You can come to me whenever you wish to, and I will do all I can to aid you." Brewster added, "And he did so all the way through, without a moment's hesitation—always stood by me and strengthened me and gave me confidence."[8]

The odds are high that Arthur knew of the star route frauds before ascending to the presidency. He worked closely with Dorsey and Brady in the struggles of 1880, and surely had a solid understanding of the sources of Republican financial income. Dorsey, boiling with rage at the President for continuing the investigations, claimed publicly on several occasions that Arthur and many other GOP leaders were perfectly aware of his postal profits in 1880 and were not above asking him for $40,000.[9] Interestingly, Platt and Conkling wanted William Chandler to direct the star route cases, and he was the one Cabinet member reportedly opposed to the prosecutions.[10] At one point during the trials, Conkling gave legal advice to a subpoenaed witness, enabling him to avoid testimony.[11] Then too, Senator John P. Jones and Clint Wheeler were both Dorsey bondsmen.[12]

However that may be, Arthur acknowledged his duty as President and unhesitatingly (though no doubt sadly) threw the weight of his office behind the government attorneys. While they quarreled bitterly among themselves, not one of the lawyers denied receiving anything other than the full support of the Justice Department and the White House. When Dorsey requested a private interview with the President, he was refused.[13] Nine days after assuming office, the President ordered a number of removals of federal employees tainted with star route complicity. Three weeks later, First Assistant Postmaster James N. Tyner, labeled "Stalwart of the Stalwarts" by opponents, was asked to resign because of ties with Dorsey and Brady.[14]

Many continued to doubt the administration's earnestness, however, because of the *National Republican*, a Stalwart newspaper published in Washington that was widely thought to be an administration organ. Brady was its owner, and not unexpectedly the paper assailed all attempts to expose the star route frauds. To discontinue this opposition, a number of Arthur's friends purchased the newspaper in February 1882. (George Bliss held a one seventy-sixth interest.) The publication was not financially sound, and soon there was talk of selling. But funds were raised and economies made to keep the newspaper in friendly hands.[15]

Bliss and his three associates worked feverishly for several months gathering information and preparing legal documents with which to go before a grand jury. An enormous quantity of data was gathered from across the country, sorted, and analyzed. Bliss had studied the prosecution of the Tweed Ring and observed that attempts to convict ring members of individual acts had usually failed. After a careful scrutiny of federal criminal statutes, he determined to charge the star route plunderers with conspiracy to defraud the government. Conspiracy was difficult to prove conclusively in the absence of at least one confession, of course, but the prosecution found itself without alternatives.[16]

A formal presidential photograph, 1882

LEFT, *Arthur as Vice-President, 1881*

BELOW, *President Cleveland's inauguration, 1885*

RIGHT, *Thomas C. Platt (1833–1910), New York Stalwart leader who, together with Roscoe Conkling, resigned from the United States Senate to protest appointments made by President Garfield*

FAR RIGHT, *James G. Blaine (1830–1893), one of the most significant Republican politicians of the Gilded Age and Secretary of State under Garfield and Arthur*

CLOCKWISE FROM ABOVE

*Mary Arthur McElroy (1841–1917),
the twenty-first President's
younger sister, who served as First Lady
during the Arthur Administration*

Chester A. Arthur, taken in 1882

Julia Sand (1850–1933), Arthur's "dwarf"

On March 4, 1882, a grand jury indicted nine men, including Dorsey, Brady, and Rerdell. They were charged with conspiracy involving nineteen mail routes, routes for which compensation had been increased from $41,135 to $448,670.90.[17] One route in Dakota and Montana had been let at $2,350 and was boosted to $70,000 annually; on another, in Oregon, the hike was from $8,288 to $60,000 a year, and so on. The Dorsey-Brady case was selected for special emphasis by Bliss not only because of the notoriety of the accused but also because of the abundance of evidence pointing to the existence of conspiracy. Richard T. Merrick later said, "The evidence in this case satisfied me beyond all possible doubt of the guilt of all the parties, and I have seldom had occasion to try a case in court with the testimony in which I was more entirely satisfied."[18]

Several obstacles blocked the path to a speedy trial. Technical errors were discovered in the indictment. A battery of defense attorneys, most notably Dorsey's counsel, loquacious Robert Ingersoll, employed numerous stalling tactics. Dorsey's brother John, a co-defendant, disappeared temporarily. Many government witnesses, brought thousands of miles to testify, complained loudly of the delays. Finally, on June 1, the trial got under way. Critics noted that the Arthur Administration was almost nine months old.[19]

The judge hoped that the trial would be completed by Independence Day, but it lasted through the hot, steamy summer until September 15. Government attorneys presented ninety-eight witnesses whose testimony covered 3,286 printed pages, and they offered 2,300 documents in evidence. This took two months. The prosecution's case was highly detailed and complex, and there seems little reason to doubt that the average citizens on the jury were frequently confused. The eleven defense lawyers took every opportunity to disrupt testimony, question evidence, and raise objections.

The defense took the position that the increases in star route costs were made in response to population growth, needs of the army, and requests by Congressmen; in several instances they were said to be the result of honest mistakes. The leading defendants elected not to take the stand.

Interior Secretary Teller testified about his own requests as a Colorado Senator to increase mail service in the West. Some observers considered his appearance an adminisration blunder and worse, but it played no significant role in the course of the trial. More embarrassing to the President were three letters from early 1881, released to the press by Dorsey during the trial, in which the defendant appeared as an intimate friend and champion of Conkling and Arthur.[20] George Bliss also brought criticism upon the administration in mid-August when he was quoted by a New York *Herald* reporter as saying that the case against Dorsey was "the weakest of the lot." In a letter to the newspaper, the attorney clarified his statement: "I have only said that, owing to the exclusion of testimony by the court, the case proved was not as strong against Dorsey as against others." Attorney General Brewster was furious with Bliss.[21]

Brewster had followed the trial as closely as his broad duties permitted, and had offered advice on several occasions. Determined to make the administration's position as clear as possible, he prepared himself thoroughly and closed the arguments for the prosecution in person. Much of his almost two-day speech was devoted to the crimes of Dorsey.[22]

The verdict disappointed everyone. Rerdell and another minor defendant were convicted; one man was acquitted, and the jury could not agree about the Dorsey brothers, Brady, and one Harvey M. Vaile. Bliss later called the verdict "a solecism and an absurdity," for if the two were guilty so were the others with whom they conspired. Merrick made it known immediately that the government would seek a new trial.[23]

Shortly thereafter it was learned that the jury foreman had read an affidavit to his colleagues behind closed doors that charged that a government agent had attempted to bribe him. On September 15, the judge set aside the verdict and granted a retrial on grounds of the foreman's activity and of the general unreasonableness of the jury's findings. The new proceeding was set for the first Monday in December.[24]

In the interim, the attorneys for the government labored intensively to strengthen their case. To bolster public confidence in the prosecution's integrity, Bliss requested the removal of five federal officeholders for revealing sympathies with the star route defendants. The dismissals were carried out swiftly by the President. Included in the list was former Senator George E. Spencer of Nevada, the Stalwart who had sought Conkling's aid to escape an appearance at the recent trial.[25] In addition, Brewster made public a letter to the President in which he expressed his firm conviction that each of the defendants was guilty. "It was a condign act of infamous conspiracy, and as such deserves the severest punishment the law can inflict. Such men are traitors to social and official duty and they are public enemies, against whom the authority of the law must be exerted without hesitation or reluctance. The higher their past position the greater their sin—the sterner must be their punishment."[26] *The New York Times* applauded these moves but stressed the importance of winning convictions against the accused. "The case has reached a point where nothing but success in this regard will save the reputation of the

Administration, and the more clearly this fact is appreciated the better it will be for all concerned."[27]

When a new jury was selected, local citizens had to be found who could claim to have no firm opinions about the star route case. This was difficult, for Washington newspapers had devoted their strongest language to the issue for months. The government was permitted to use only three peremptory challenges; attorneys for the defense seemed determined to seek the least educated among the people interviewed. Merrick later called it "the worst jury I ever saw summoned to the box. . . . I think there were some men on that jury that could neither read nor write."[28]

The second trial began on December 7 and lasted until June 14, 1883, one of the longest trials on record. Bliss opened the government's argument with a blistering attack against Dorsey—countering charges that he had previously underemphasized Dorsey's role in the conspiracy. In mid-February Rerdell broke down and made a second confession, throwing himself on the mercy of the court. He was called to the stand, and his testimony led to the appearance of twenty-seven new witnesses. Altogether the prosecution examined 121 witnesses, and offered 2,761 documents in evidence; there were 4,481 pages of testimony in the 5,876 pages of record in the four-volume account of the trial! Post Office Inspector Woodward said later, ". . . the record will remain a permanent memorial of the thoroughness with which the case was prepared, and of the completeness with which the charges were proved."[29]

Defense attorneys again attempted to exhaust and confuse the jury, and numerous delays resulted. Ingersoll frequently injected sarcastic sneers against Bliss and Merrick into the proceedings, and outbursts of temper were common during the long months the trial ground on. On other occasions Ingersoll would fall into treacly pleas for his clients that left spectators in tears. Fearing the effectiveness of the government's case against them, the defendants testified on their own behalf and recruited more than a score of new witnesses to do likewise. While the trial was in progress, Dorsey resigned from the Republican National Committee, and in a letter released to the press wrote, "There was no act of mine in respect to the management of the [1880] campaign—either as to its general scope or as to any of its numberless details—that was not thoroughly known to our candidates for President and Vice-President, and by them and each of them fully approved both before and after the election."[30]

Merrick's closing argument to the jury was an impressive display of his oratorical ability and of the soundness of the case against the defendants; *The New York Times* remarked that it showed "how forcibly a great lawyer can present the salient points of a great mass of evidence and brush away the ingenious pleas by which skillful opponents have endeavored to obscure the facts."[31] For a second time the charge of the judge bore heavily against the defense. But on June 14, the jury voted to acquit each of the defendants.

The verdict thundered across the country in newspaper headlines, causing gasps of disbelief, alarm, and anger. Although two of the accused had previously been convicted (one of whom pled guilty during the second trial), and despite the weight of the government's evidence and the charge by the judge, not one of the men who grossed millions of dollars in star route profits now faced jail. George Bliss could only say, "I am astonished."[32] The President was reported to be "very deeply annoyed."[33] To a crowd of Negroes who serenaded him at his home, Dorsey said, "The trembling wires of intelligence that bore the message of acquittal to Berlin, Moscow, and Dublin, told the poor, the lowly, and the hopeless, that there were yet 12 men could be found who would deal justly by them; that there was not a Government large enough, that there was not a public treasury fruitful enough, that there were not leads of gold thick enough and there was not Executive power great enough to seduce the judgment of 12 honest men."[34]

There was, in fact, good reason to believe that the jury had been tampered with by the defense. Warrants were issued for the arrest of eight persons, but only one case was brought to trial, and all charges were later dropped by the Cleveland Administration.[35] Government attorneys ascribed their defeat to the jury's general lack of intelligence. *The New York Times* said sadly, "A great part of the evidence must have been beyond their comprehension. It was certainly unfortunate that in the greatest conspiracy case ever tried in this country the proof was laid before men who could not understand it because of their stupidity and lack of common education, who were fuddled with whiskey, or who yielded, unconsciously perhaps, to arguments not made in court."[36]

Democrats hooted at the verdict. The New York *Sun* asserted, ". . . reform is impossible so long as the Republicans are allowed to remain in power."[37] The New York *Herald* declared, "The Republican party has outlived not merely its usefulness but its moral sense. But it probably needed this result of the star route trials to break the back of the public's patience."[38] Everyone within the GOP was dissatisfied. Independents were wary of the administration's resolve; Half-Breeds chortled at its embarrassment; Stalwarts were angry with it for initiating the trials. Dorsey referred to the President scoffingly as "the stalled ox feeding at the rich trough of accident."[39]

Criminal conspiracy charges having failed, the administration proceeded to file twenty-four civil suits. Bliss was willing to lead the effort, but he was under fire for the legal fees he had already charged the government ($59,332), and Brewster thought it wise to look elsewhere. There was some delay as the Attorney General searched unsuccessfully for an appropriately inexpensive attorney. Finally, the cases were assigned to district attorneys in the areas where the mail routes in question were located. That strategy was abandoned in late 1884, and the cases were handed over to a special assistant attorney general. Several cases were lost at the hands of juries. Years later the government registered a victory when the Supreme Court ruled that errors of fact, as well as fraud, leading to excessive compensation was ground on which the government could demand restitution.[40] None of the defendants acquitted in 1883, however, was affected by the decision.

The Arthur Administration could boast that the star route trials had halted the postal frauds under scrutiny, saving the government some $2,000,000 annually. Benjamin Brewster told a congressional committee in 1884 that the swarms of dishonest jobbers who had haunted the halls of the Post Office Department had disappeared: "The wholesome terror of these trials has expelled them."[41]

Still, the administration paid a high price for the failure to convict Dorsey, Brady, and the others. Democrats were given the issue of "corruption in government" to employ in the congressional elections of 1882 (the first verdict was announced a few weeks before the polls opened), and in the presidential contest of 1884. The star route frauds were led by Republicans during Republican administrations; the perpetrators had slipped through Republican fingers. Then too, shadows were again cast on the narrow Republican victory of 1880, covering many Republicans including the Chief Executive. "Stalwart" had a more odious ring than ever. The influential Independent wing of the GOP was growing increasingly irritated and restless.

Arthur's personal image was unquestionably tarnished by the trials. To many he appeared ineffectual, even vaguely corrupt; perhaps he was still the man who was driven from the Customhouse. Stories appeared in the press claiming that Bliss had stalled in the case of Republican Senator William Pitt Kellogg, a Stalwart widely believed part of the Dorsey-Brady conspiracy, enabling him to escape.[42] If that was true, might not Bliss have sabotaged the prosecution in all the star route cases? And wasn't George Bliss a close friend of the President? They had both attended the dinner in Dorsey's honor at Delmonico's. One shrewd newspaper columnist reviewed recent events and concluded, "The Star Route trials were a dead failure, and Chester A. Arthur will go home at the end of his term."[43]

CHAPTER EIGHTEEN

Sick in Body and Soul

THE ELECTIONS of 1882 would reveal much about Republican strength throughout the nation and enable party leaders to weigh their chances for success in the presidential contest two years later. There were indications of trouble, not the least of which was the outcry raised by the Republican Congressional Committee's assessment circulars. Jay Hubbell's committee refused to heed the warnings of critics, and continued through the summer to pursue portions of government employees' salaries for the benefit of Republican Congressmen. Newspapers reported strong rumors of support for Hubbell in the executive departments at Washington, rumors that brought condemnation upon the administration in particular and the GOP in general.[1]

Moreover, the party continued to be deeply divided, exposing itself to defeat. In Pennsylvania, for example, Reformers were mounting an attack against Stalwart boss Don Cameron, preparing to run an Independent ticket that could mean a Democratic victory. In New York, Republicans appeared ready for a violent clash over the control of local machinery. Ironically, the President's attempt to distribute patronage equitably between factions in the larger states seemed to have exacerbated frictions. Stalwarts felt betrayed, and some swore revenge; Half-Breeds and Independents, on the other hand, interpreted every Stalwart appointment as evidence of the President's desire to turn the federal government over to Grant men. Should the GOP suffer sizable losses in the fall, as some observers predicted, few party leaders were likely to hesitate to point to the White House while assessing their misfortune.

The President was also condemned in some quarters for his methods designed to build Republican strength in the South. It was claimed that he had taken a bold new approach to the reconstructed states that had linked the GOP with debt repudiators and corrupt spoilsmen. Critics bore down most heavily on the administration's relations with General William H. Mahone, leader of the Virginia Readjusters. Wayne Mac-Veagh exclaimed publicly in April 1882, "You cannot pretend to be interested in the degrading spectacle of Mahoneism in Virginia; the deliberate prostitution of Government powers to aid repudiation of a State's obligations. If we could charge that upon the Bourbon Democrats it would be some relief, but, to our sorrow and humiliation, these things are done in the name of Abraham Lincoln. Instead of going forward, the Arthur Administration makes a retrograde movement."[2]

Throughout the 1870s political movements had risen in the South calling for the repudiation, scaling down, and adjustment of crushing state debts. In Virginia, where the liability threatened to bankrupt the state and impoverish most of its citizens, the Readjusters appeared, a faction seeking to shift a third of the debt to West Virginia (which had separated from its mother state during the war) and asking for a refunding of the remainder at low interest rates. The faction's stand on a number of other issues helped to rally a majority of Virginia's voters—black and white—to its support: it called for funds to improve public education and the humanitarian and charitable institutions of the state, honest elections ("a free ballot, a full vote, and a fair count"), an end to dueling, and the abolition of the poll tax and the whipping-post. In 1879, Readjusters captured 56 of the 100 seats in the Virginia House of Delegates and 24 of the 40 in the Senate. Later in the same year they elected a domineering ex-Confederate general and railroad entrepreneur, William H. Mahone, to the United States Senate. In 1881, the Readjusters retained control of both houses of the legislature and elected a governor and a second Senator. Bourbon Democrats were removed from virtually every significant public office in the state.

During the Hayes Administration several northern Republicans, especially among the Stalwarts, sensed that the Readjusters might be useful allies in cracking what had become by then a solidly Democratic South. Simon Cameron quietly visited Mahone in the fall of 1879, and several conferences between Republicans and Readjusters followed. President Hayes, however, wanted nothing to do with "Mahoneism." He remained hopeful that the southern Bourbons would deal with the Negro in a just and honorable way if left alone, and urged Virginia Republicans "to cooperate with the debt payers."

When Garfield came into office, he was besieged with appeals to strike a bargain with the Readjusters. Mahone corresponded regularly with George C. Gorham, editor of the Stalwart *National Republican*, and through him made overtures to leaders of the new administration. Senator Don Cameron of Pennsylvania worked hard to persuade the President of the value of a Republican-Readjuster alliance, claiming that Mahone could do more for the Negro and the GOP in the South than the federal government could do with a standing army. Like Hayes, Garfield objected to debt adjustments, and he feared that an open alliance with Mahone would alienate conservative eastern financial interests. Publicly and privately he expressed qualms about the Readjusters. But it was he, not his successor, who initially altered the Republican party's policy toward the South.

In March 1881, when Mahone traveled to Washington, he discovered that his vote would decide which of the major parties would control an almost evenly divided Senate. For his allegiance, Republicans awarded him valuable committee assignments, positions in the Senate bureaucracy, and federal patronage in his state. In addition, they promised to merge the Republican and Readjuster tickets in Virginia, an act carried out in August at a convention in Lynchburg. Northern Republicans raised and donated funds for the candidates. As might be expected, terms of the agreement were played down by the Republican press; several major newspapers claimed that Mahone's deed was based solidly on patriotism. After Garfield's death the image created of him by GOP orators eliminated the possibility of an alliance with repudiators, ex-Democrats, and rebels. The support given to Readjusters by Republicans in Washington, it would be claimed, originated with the twenty-first President rather than his venerated predecessor. Mahone himself thought otherwise. In April 1882, he told a reporter, "The only hope of success for the Readjuster cause was in a union, and the leading men in the movement saw it. The assistance rendered by President Garfield was exceedingly valuable. If he had not been shot the movement would have gathered strength much more rapidly than it did."[3]

The Arthur Administration's policy toward the South, however, moved significantly beyond the agreement nervously endorsed by Garfield, and the responsibility rested in large part upon Navy Secretary William E. Chandler. Chandler had done much to engineer the Republican presidential victory in 1877 and was a careful student of southern politics. By 1882 he, along with a good many other Republicans, despaired of their years of effort in the South, for it was painfully obvious that neither Reconstruction tactics nor conciliatory measures had won many converts to the GOP; the southern branch of the party had become, in H. Wayne Morgan's words, "a closed, ceremonial club for a handful of patronage brokers."[4] Chandler concluded that the best hope for Republicanism in the South now lay with men like Mahone. The general's victories in Virginia had spurred a growing number of independents throughout the South, and if they could be won over by the administration, he thought, it stood a chance of breaking the back of Bourbon democracy. As Chandler pondered the immediate future, he feared that a divided Republican party in the North was threatened with substantial setbacks in 1882. If true, this meant that the GOP would need numerous southern allies to retain its strength in Congress, and who better than the independents? The alternative to looking toward the Mahones of the South, he felt, was political disaster regionally and nationally. Partisan politics aside, Chandler admired the personal and social guarantees that Mahone and other independents were espousing. He explained his outlook to Blaine:

> The situation is bad in New York and Pennsylvania. It is important to carry the House, for the next Presidential election depends upon it. We cannot carry as many seats in the North as two years ago. We must increase our Southern representation by ten to twenty. That depends upon Republican support of the Democratic revolt in the South and the overthrow of the Bourbons there. . . . Every independent Democrat in the South pledges himself to a free vote, an honest count, the obliteration of race distinctions and popular education by the common school system. Shall we fail to follow our principles when they are vital? Our straight Republican and carpetbag and Negro governments cannot be revived. Without the aid of independent Democrats in the South we cannot carry enough seats there to save the next Presidential fight. Beyond that, the safety of the colored race at the polls depends upon it.[5]

The President was obviously of the same mind, for unlike Garfield he showed no qualms about turning over federal patronage in Virginia to Mahone: 200 offices in the Treasury, 1,700 in the Post Office, 70 in the federal courts, and many positions in the Norfolk navy yard. All employees, of course, received assessment letters on appropriate occasions to assist Readjuster campaigns. By April 1882, the Virginia Readjusters announced that they wished to be known thereafter as "Administration men."[6] In May, Mahone declared that the entire nation was moving toward peace and fraternity "under the guidance of a President whose policy toward the South is one of friendship."[7]

The administration moved quickly to forge coalitions between Republicans and independents in other parts of the South as well. In Alabama, Arkansas, Mississippi, North Carolina, South Carolina, Tennessee, and Texas, ex-Democrats won support from Washington. Several of the southern independent leaders were Greenbackers, and some sought unlimited coinage of silver.

The degree to which Chandler controlled the administration's posture toward the South is uncertain, but clearly his was the dominant voice. Vincent P. De Santis has speculated that "had it not been for Chandler, the administration might never have given a second thought to the Independents."[8] The pro-administration *National Republican* often pictured the President as encouraging southern Republicans to cooperate with independents, and there is no reason to doubt that he sincerely backed Chandler's southern strategy. John S. Wise, a Virginia Readjuster and a personal friend of Arthur's, recalled in 1906 that the President thought it useless to continue to placate Bourbon Democrats. "He had married in the South, and had been thrown [together] a great deal with the old Southern aristocracy. In a social way he liked them, and was glad to be kind and hospitable to them, but he had seen enough of them to know that it was just as impossible to make a Republican out of the average Southern Bourbon Democrat as it is for the leopard to change his spots." Wise remembered that once in the White House, after a session with a number of Democratic Congressmen, the President said to him, "What a pleasant lot of fellows they are. What a pity they have so little sense about politics. If they lived North the last one of them would be Republicans. But they cannot stop thinking or talking about negroes long enough to think or talk about anything else." Wise noted also that Arthur lacked faith in scalawags and thought it foolish to continue to work for an alliance with them. These southern Republicans, he said, were "mere birds of prey." "As well expect the song birds to come and roost on the trees with the hawks that have harried them," said the President, "as to think the Southern people will join a party under their leadership." "We must hunt for Republican leaders in the South, for the future, somewhere else than among the scalawags or the Bourbons. There must be other kinds of people there, and when I find them I want them."[9]

Several Negro leaders castigated the administration for backing independents, charging that it had abandoned southern blacks. T. Thomas Fortune, a militant New York newspaperman, was Arthur's harshest critic. From the pages of his New York *Globe,* he harangued the President for adopting a policy that satisfied "no one but Democrats and soap and water Republicans." "We have had enough of the Garfield type of man—nerveless, vacillating, always dodging. Away with President Arthur who combines the weakness of his predecessors without possessing their slim stock of virtues."[10] A few recent historians have echoed this viewpoint. One, Stanley Hirshson, asserted that Hayes and Arthur had the same objective toward the South. "Both Presidents attempted to foster Republicanism in the South by dropping the Negro-dominated factions and by appealing to discontented white Democrats." He contended that the administration was unconcerned about the civil rights of southern Negroes, and claimed to be able to document occasions on which Arthur criticized blacks.[11]

The case is not persuasive. By and large, the administration courted only those former Democrats who had the support of their state's Republicans, black and white. The glaring exception was Mississippi, where the GOP split along racial lines, whites winning administration recognition. But here Negro Republicans were accused of advocating the election of Democrats in order to win patronage from Democratic Senators. Bickering between black and white Republicans in Georgia prevented the administration from backing an independent movement in that state. In Louisiana, the administration rejected an overture from a would-be Mahone and cast its lot with carpetbagger William Pitt Kellogg, in part because Chandler was convinced that Negro leaders in the state were behind Kellogg.[12]

Chandler argued publicly and privately that the protection of Negro rights was an important consideration in the decision to support independents. He thought an alliance between independents and Republicans the only effective way to curb the violence waged against blacks by southern Democrats, and called the merger "a great struggle against Bourbon Democracy in favor of free speech, free education, free suffrage, and an honest counting of ballots." Mahone wanted "every man to vote, white or black, and I want him to vote as he pleases, and to be neither threatened beforehand nor ostracized afterwards for expressing his free opinion." The Readjusters repealed the poll tax and enfranchised about 20,000 Negroes; they established a Negro college and added $40,000,000 to the state budget for education, most of which was used to create Negro schools.

Almost every Negro newspaper in the country endorsed the administration's policy toward the South, and so did the most prominent Negro spokesmen, including Frederick Douglass, John Mercer Langston of Virginia, Robert Brown Elliott of South Carolina, ex-Senator Blanche K. Bruce of Mississippi, and John R. Lynch, Republican National Committeeman from Mississippi. In 1882, Douglass declared he was "just as heartily in favor of the Mahone movement in Virginia as any man now on the stump assisting that movement," and approved "of any decent movement looking to the abolition of the color line in American politics." Langston, serving as Arthur's minister to Haiti, agreed. "The success of the Mahone movement in Virginia means education, liberty, a free ballot, and a fair count for the colored man and the abolition of the whipping-post, and I am for it heart and soul, and not against it." Many white

Republicans held similar views. U. S. Grant believed that with Mahone, "The interests of all citizens will then become so great that no fear need be entertained of bad government, no matter which political party may have the ascendency." Senator John J. Ingalls proclaimed: "Were I a Virginian I should act with Mahone, believing that he represents the progressive elements, by whose supremacy race prejudice will be obliterated, the ballot made free and priceless, and the South regenerated through the beneficent energy of impartial justice and universal education."[13]

While Arthur may well have been unable to step out of the intellectual milieu of the Gilded Age to accept total Negro equality, the one-time abolitionist did continue to show sympathy toward blacks, and not only in the South, where the line between concern for Negroes and the desire for Republican strength was often blurred. The President privately contributed funds for a Negro church.[14] He personally awarded diplomas to graduates of a black high school in Washington.[15] The choir from Fisk University was invited to perform at the White House (and moved the President to tears).[16] Arthur appointed several Negroes to fairly important government positions. P. B. S. Pinchback, a newspaper owner and former acting governor of Louisiana, became surveyor of the port of New Orleans; H. C. C. Astwood, Pinchback's associate editor, was named consul to Trinidad; ex-Senator Blanche K. Bruce became an assistant United States commissioner general; Mifflin W. Gibbs was made receiver of monies at Litttle Rock, Arkansas.[17] In three of his annual messages to Congress, Arthur called for federal aid to Negro education, suggesting initially that proceeds from the public domain be channeled in that direction. And when the Supreme Court, in 1883, declared the Civil Rights Act of 1875 illegal, Arthur forcefully expressed his disagreement with the highly popular decision in a message to Congress:

> The fourteenth amendment of the Constitution confers the rights of citizenship upon all persons born or naturalized in the United States and subject to the jurisdictions thereof. It was the special purpose of this amendment to insure to members of the colored race the full enjoyment of civil and political rights. Certain statutory provisions intended to secure the enforcement of those rights have been recently declared unconstitutional by the Supreme Court.
>
> Any legislation whereby Congress may lawfully supplement the guaranties which the Constitution affords for the equal enjoyment by all the citizens of the United States by every right, privilege, and immunity of citizenship will receive my unhesitating approval.[18]

Despite its many endorsements, the Administration's southern policy was the target of repeated attacks by mid-1882. Many Republicans intensely disliked debt repudiation and soft money, and cringed at the thought of a union between the GOP and economic radicals. *The New York Times* commented in September, "It has from the first been questionable whether the break in the Democratic ranks made by Gen. Mahone, with all the advantages of free elections, was not purchased too dearly by the success of the repudiation which Gen. Mahone's party advocated."[19] Civil service reformers were angered by the patronage given to Mahone and by the wholesale removals in Virginia. Some observers considered Mahone a tyrant and a dictator, and thought him as bad as the Bourbons. Many veterans were enraged by the support given to ex-Confederates such as General James R. Chalmers of Mississippi, described by every "bloody shirt" orator as the villain of the "Fort Pillow massacre." Others rankled at the prospect of a large body of southern officeholders marching on the GOP's national convention in 1884 to back the nomination of the President. Blaine termed the Republican-Readjuster alliance a serious blunder, "the last degree of folly for the Republicans."[20]

Much attention was focused upon New York in 1882, for the election of that year in the Empire State was thought certain to gauge GOP strength in the North and forecast the party's opportunity to recapture the presidency two years later. New York belonged to neither major party. Republicans had won only a slight edge in the balloting over the past four years—an average plurality of 19,750 out of a total vote averaging about 950,000. In only one year, 1880, was there an absolute GOP majority, and that was but a little over 7,000 votes. In 1881, Republicans elected almost all of their state ticket and gained a plurality of 13,023, but Democrats controlled both branches of the state legislature. Moreover, a quarter of a million voters stayed home, and Independents were unusually quiescent.[21]

Republican leaders in New York remained bitterly divided, revealing no inclination to bury the past and unite behind a single party figure, least of all the President. Stalwarts were increasingly unenthusiastic about Arthur because of his unwillingness to remove Robertson from the Customhouse and lavish federal positions upon his friends. (An associate reported Conkling "just as rampant as he ever was, and you can spend the most disagreeable hour and a half with him if you happen to be his friend that you ever have in your life. He upbraids everyone, assails the course of events, regards himself as defrauded, duped, and sold out.")[22] Half-Breeds, of course, could never be Arthur partisans, and were already laying plans for a Blaine triumph at the national convention. The pages of Whitelaw Reid's New York *Tribune* contained a steady bombardment of the administration's every move; in 1881, Blaine men controlled the state convention and nearly reorganized the party in New York along lines that would have given them long-term power.[23] Independents were suspicious of both the President and the man from Maine.

Alonzo Cornell was up for reelection in 1882, and his candidacy was certain to exacerbate intraparty friction. He had been a popular governor; many Half-Breeds found him agreeable, while Independents lauded his administration for its efficiency and honesty. But Cornell was seriously estranged from the President and was disliked by most New York Stalwarts for his lukewarm support of Conkling's bid for reelection to the Senate and his stinginess with state patronage. (Conkling was said to be especially hostile to the governor, and sneeringly referred to him as "that lizard on the hill.")[24]

In early April newspapers reported that several New York Stalwarts intended to run Treasury Secretary Charles Folger for the gubernatorial nomination against Cornell. They were apparently as anxious to remove Folger as they were to replace Cornell. The secretary, in their judgment, had been unduly slow in distributing jobs to his own faction, especially in the New York Customhouse; he was "old fogishy," and "too cautious." With Folger in Albany, they hoped, a new secretary could be appointed who would have no qualms about handing out federal posts to the "right" people.[25] In late May, a careful observer of Washington politics wrote, "the old machine that Arthur brought up by hand is determined to have Folger out of the Treasury Department, and there is no way to get him out but to nominate him for Governor."[26]

In mid-June, the President let it be known that he sincerely wished to avoid factional bloodletting in New York, and asserted through a friend that the administration would not run a gubernatorial candidate.[27] Rumors subsided after that for about a month, but as the state convention neared, a charge was made that "Administration men" were planning some sort of scheme against Cornell.[28] Several New York newspapers envisioned a plot by Jay Gould and Conkling against the Governor.[29] According to one report, John J. O'Brien, chairman of the city's central committee, was organizing opposition to Cornell's nomination among officeholders, and claimed to represent the White House.[30] First Assistant Postmaster General Frank Hatton was said to have asked the President to approve up to forty changes in the New York Post Office to bolster the anti-Cornell movement.[31] By late August, Cornell was saying publicly that he was a marked man.[32] Anxious to be reelected, the governor turned to Blaine men for support, becoming virtually the Half-Breed candidate for the nomination. Blaine brought the New York *Tribune* to Cornell's side by telling Reid that "Conkling and Arthur [were] determined to kill him."[33]

Charles Folger indeed sought Cornell's office, and admitted it openly on August 30.[34] But he could not be sure of Arthur's support, despite the newspaper stories and the governor's trepidations. Presidential confidants such as Barney Biglin and Johnny O'Brien were encouraging, but Arthur himself said little. While in New York, on September 5, Folger wrote a personal letter to Arthur urging him to lend a hand while there was time.

> I have seen several people here who seem disturbed and irresolute, for the reason that they do not know, as they say, what it is that the administration wishes in regard to the nomination for Governor. There is an impression that Mr. Conkling, T. C. Platt and others of like position are for Clarence A. Seward. It is doubted whether or not you are in favor of him. It is represented as desirable that you let some one, as for instance Pierre C. Van Wyck, say what you wish.[35]

Folger heard nothing, and soon expressed the doubt that he was really the administration's candidate.[36]

Arthur must have agonized over the political situation in his home state. If he entered the contest in earnest—as he no doubt burned to do—he could greatly assist Folger and wreak revenge on Cornell, but the price would be his reputation as a high-minded President; direct intervention would bring scalding attacks from the press, branding him indelibly as the lowest form of political manipulator. Yet if he remained aloof from the fray, Folger, an old and dear friend, would be deeply offended. Then there were O'Brien, Biglin, and the others. Arthur wished at all cost to avert any break with these close friends—they called frequently and provided much companionship and relaxation. But he could not respond favorably to their constant pleas for federal jobs. He unquestionably knew of their desire to remove Folger, and perhaps led them to believe that the secretary was in part responsible for the lack of patronage channeled their way.[37] Since Folger wanted to be governor, and "the boys" sought his replacement in the Treasury Department, all might be well if Folger won the gubernatorial nomination, a victory that would also cripple Cornell's political future and strike a blow against the Half-Breeds. The Stalwart wing of the GOP in New York remained strong, but it was questionable whether or not it could withstand an assault by a cunning governor in league with powerful

Half-Breeds and Independents. Arthur's help would be useful and appreciated, but how could he extend it and fail to sully the high office he had acquired by assassination?

However much it may have pained him personally, Arthur decided against intervention in New York. Wishing to avoid giving offense, he extended encouragement to both Folger and the machine leaders; nevertheless, he did not take steps to help them. (Folger would later claim bitterly that the President failed to lift a finger on his behalf.)[38] To symbolize his disengagement, he left New York for Washington shortly before the state convention assembled.[39] Still, Cornell and his adherents loudly proclaimed that the administration was hard at work to thwart the will of the people. As they viewed the situation, the entire federal bureaucracy in New York had been mobilized by the President to elevate an administrative candidate over a responsible, well-liked, and generally nonpartisan governor. Their evidence was weak, but they could point to the presence of Sharpe, French, Smyth, Wheeler, and a number of other Arthur associates in the Folger camp to bolster their case. And since the President did not emphatically disassociate himself from the activities of his friends—in retrospect a serious mistake—the public quite naturally accepted the thesis that he was furtively pulling strings on behalf of his Cabinet member. One influential Republican from Cattaraugus County warned, "Mr. Arthur's veto of the River and Harbor bill has strengthened him considerably in this section. All this good feeling will count for nothing if he lends himself to defeating Gov. Cornell at Saratoga."[40]

The state convention opened in Saratoga on September 20. Prior to the first session, the state committee held a brief meeting to select a temporary chairman to preside over the convention proceedings. Factional lines were apparent immediately: Folger men nominated Edmund M. Madden, while Cornell supporters backed State Senator Edmund L. Pitts. Thirty-two votes were cast in person or by proxy, and Madden won 18 to 14. A few eyebrows were raised when Steve French announced that he held Collector Robertson's proxy and cast it for Madden. When the convention assembled, both sides demanded a show of hands from all the delegates on the temporary chairmanship. The office was insignificant, but the tally would serve as a barometer of factional strength. Madden won 251 votes to Pitts's 243. Later in the day, Folger won the gubernatorial nomination on the second ballot, collecting 257 votes to Cornell's 222. B. Platt Carpenter, a Folger supporter, was nominated for lieutenant governor.[41] Within a few days, Stalwarts sealed their victory by winning a majority on the state committee and by electing Smyth its chairman.[42]

Many observers were shocked by the revelation that Steve French's proxy, used in the state committee meeting prior to the formal opening of the convention, was a forgery. Whether French and his friends were responsible for the foul play or were the victims of a scheme to humiliate Folger supporters remains debatable.[43] But Cornell's forces grossly magnified the proxy's significance and were soon claiming that Folger had won the *nomination* by illicit means. *The New York Times* declared solemnly that "the vote cast on the selection of a temporary Chairman was the turning point in the struggle between the people and the Federal machine," and accused the administration of forcing its candidates upon the people by "bribery and forgery, and other means equally corrupt."[44] George William Curtis wrote that Folger's nomination "was procured by the combined power of fraud and patronage, and to support it at the polls would be to acquiesce in fraud and patronage as legitimate forces in a nominating convention."[45] The charges were echoed by gleeful Democrats, who nominated forty-five-year-old Grover Cleveland, the reform-minded mayor of Buffalo, to oppose the Treasury Secretary in the governor's race.

Early in October, a few days after Curtis published his attack against the administration, newspapers across the country carried an Associated Press dispatch emanating from Washington stating that the Surgeon General had examined the President during the past summer and discovered that he was suffering from Bright's disease, an almost inevitably fatal kidney affliction in adults. A specialist from New York was consulted, the report continued, and had confirmed the diagnosis. The only prescription the physicians were able to give for this still somewhat mysterious malady was rest and relaxation. Many readers began sending a variety of nostrums to the White House.[46]

Arthur did not comment directly on the report, but a friend denied it wholly "on the authority of the President himself" and asserted that Arthur had merely suffered a mild attack of malaria during the past summer and was fully recovered.[47] A friendly newspaper soon contended that reports linking the President with kidney disease were "pure fiction."[48]

Four separate accounts, written after Arthur's death, place his encounter with Bright's disease in 1883, but it seems likely that the President was informed of his condition, as the Associated Press reported, the year before.[49] In any case, it is now known that the symptoms of this malady may precede diagnosis by many years, producing spasmodic nausea, mental depression, and indolence. Perhaps Bright's disease was in part responsible for Arthur's early distaste for the presidency; surely it helps explain his reportedly lackadaisical approach to the details of his office. (While it is impossible to know precisely when Arthur began to suffer from the illness, it will be remembered that his conduct during the campaigns of 1879 and 1880 was described as vigorous by insiders.) By mid-1882 he was far from well. His cousin, Dr. Brodie Herndon, stayed in the White House from early May through the summer of that year and described Arthur to his private diary as discouraged, irritable, and often physically ill. On August 1, the elderly physician wrote, "The President sick in body and soul."[50] When Arthur left for a vacation in late September, there were numerous reports that he was unwell. On returning to Washington October 7, he termed his health "improved."[51] Two weeks later he retired to the presidential summer cottage weary and exhausted.[52] Persons close to the President, one New York newspaper reported that same month, said that Arthur had no intention of seeking the nomination in 1884.[53]

In January 1883, when the President paid a visit to New York, his physical appearance provoked comment. "He has grown thin and feeble looking," a reporter noted. "His cheeks are emaciated, and he has aged in appearance." It was said that Arthur had cut down on his private entertaining and feasting. "He does not work so hard as formerly, but the work seems to be more burdensome."[54] The President soon confided to his son, "I have been so ill since the adjournment [of Congress] that I have hardly been able to dispose of the accumulation of business still before me."[55] A little later, a friend was quoted as saying, "It is no secret whatever that the President's health is poor, that he chafes under the wear and tear of his office, and that he looks forward with intense longing to the day of his release from his irksome responsibilities." It was reported that, "He has repeatedly given his friends to know that under no conceivable circumstances would he again be President."[56]

Prospects for a GOP victory in New York were dim from the start of the campaign and faded steadily; enthusiasm for Folger was alarmingly low and few observers thought he could triumph over Cleveland. Many Republicans were convinced that Folger's nomination was a product of the crookedness that had plagued the party since Grant, of the "bossism" that condoned Jay Hubbell's fleecing of federal employees. Most Half-Breeds and Independents thought it part of a plan by the President to carry the party's national convention in 1884, and they gave their support, if at all, reluctantly. Said one newspaper columnist, "President Arthur has less moral backing than any President the United States ever had. . . . I can tell him from considerable intercourse with people in all directions that he is regarded as the first President whom nobody ever thought of in connection with his high office, and he has increased unconsciously the dignity of that office by his unworthiness to fill it, and coming to it in the way he did."[57] One newspaper called Republican defections "a wholesale revolt."[58] A Treasury Department officer wrote to Folger's campaign manager describing the "sad state of things" in New York, and adding, "Eternal wrath attend the man who invented the terms *Half-breed* (whatever they may be) and *Stalwartism,* (whatsoever that may mean) for the Democracy owes its good fortune & successes to that infamous invention more than to its own deserts and merits!"[59] One man observed Republicans betting against Folger's election, and told of a gentleman who could find no one to accept his wager of $10,000 to $8,000 that Cleveland would win by a 50,000-vote majority.[60] By late October, Folger and Arthur were reported depressed by what seemed certain defeat.[61]

Despite charges to the contrary, the President continued to refuse to assist Folger. He might have raised funds, sent speakers and strategists, even made personal appearances and appeals for party unity and Republican victory. But he stubbornly clung to his original position, determining not to embroil the presidency in partisan warfare as he had the vice-presidency a mere year and a half earlier.[62] Privately, Folger smarted over Arthur's attitude, and told a friend that he feared the President was displeased by his candidacy.[63] Of course, there was no way to persuade Republican opponents and Democrats of Arthur's uninvolvement; presidential "interference" was their campaign theme. When Arthur traveled to his New York home in early November to remove family belongings in preparation for the arrival of a tenant, stories of plots between the President and local Stalwarts stormed across the front pages of city newspapers. Old Thurlow Weed wrote in the New York *Tribune,* "General Arthur has been so long accustomed to party manipulations that he could not keep his hands off."[64]

Republicans suffered staggering losses at the polls. Cleveland defeated Folger by more than 190,000 votes—until then the greatest state election victory in American history. Democrats gained a commanding majority in the House of Representatives by winning sixty-two new seats, and rolled up important local victories in Ohio, Pennsylvania, Indiana, Connecticut, New Jersey, and Massachusetts. As Tom Platt was to write, "Not since the formation of the Republican party had such a disaster befallen it."[65]

Much of the blame fell on Arthur. Republicans of Kings County, New York, printed a pamphlet calling the fate of their state ticket "an emphatic rebuke to the National Administration for its unwarrantable interference in the political affairs of this State, and the deliberate condemnation of the fraud perpetrated at the Saratoga Convention, which resulted in the defeat of the candidate whose nomination was demanded by the people."[66] *The New York Times* editorialized, "The Republican Party's message to President Arthur reads something like this: 'Mind your own business, which is not that of interfering in the local politics of your own or any other state. Cease trying to be a ward politician and the Executive of the Nation at the same time.' "[67] Democrats published a lengthy poem entitled "Arthur and the Ghost," in which Garfield's spirit visited the President at midnight to excoriate him for the miserable condition of the party and the nation.[68] "It's the general impression around the country," the Chicago *Tribune* reported, "that Pres. Arthur was the worst-beaten man in the recent elections."[69]

Arthur made no reply, but George Bliss shared several thoughts with reporters about the election in New York, and his closeness to the President added weight to his observations. Bliss pointed to the strength Democrats traditionally enjoyed in the state when united and to the divisions within the GOP. He acknowledged too "a general feeling of dissatisfaction with what is sometimes called 'bossism,' which has been encouraged by the newspapers, and about which there has been said both a great deal of truth and a good deal of nonsense." He placed special emphasis upon the activities of New York Stalwart leaders, especially in the city machine, blasting those most responsible for Folger's candidacy as stupid and corrupt.[70]

Several city Stalwarts offered explanations of their own when approached by newsmen. Jake Hess attributed Folger's defeat largely to the internal struggles of the GOP and to the lack of newspaper support. Solon Smith put much of the blame on state committee Chairman Smyth, charging that his reputation was such that honest businessmen refused to contribute to the campaign; "the result was that the State Committee was bankrupt a week before election, and it did little or nothing for the organization in this County." Joel W. Mason expressed puzzlement over the origin of charges that the President had meddled in New York politics. "I have been his personal friend for 20 years, and had he dictated, suggested, or interfered in this campaign, I should have heard of it. He would have consulted me in some way, but I have seen French daily and received no communication from the President. I last saw Gen. Arthur last winter."[71]

Republicans gleaned at least two important lessons from the election debacle. In the first place, they had badly underestimated the appeal of civil service reform. Cleveland's warm endorsement of reform had been a potent weapon in his campaign; in Pennsylvania a reform Democrat, with the aid of Independents, captured the governor's chair, striking a powerful blow at Don Cameron's Stalwart machine. News of campaign assessments by the Republican Congressional Committee and an assortment of state and local committees provoked considerable public outrage. E. L. Godkin argued, "Never has the popular feeling against the demoralizing abuses of the spoils system been as definite, sincere, and strong as it is now. Never has the demand for the abolition of that system, and for a thorough reform of the civil service, been as loud and as general as it is to-day."[72]

The rank and file of the GOP appeared also to clamor for new leaders. They stayed away from the polls in droves in November or voted with the opposition to protest factional quarreling and express disgust at what they felt was corruption in high places. Godkin exclaimed, "The Republican party, utterly broken up by its crushing defeat, cannot and will not rally and reorganize its forces under the old leadership. That is out of the question."[73] The President, of course, was particularly vulnerable; there did not appear to be a single major state, including his own, that he could carry in 1884. George Bliss was of the opinion that intraparty animosities were so intense that Republicans might be forced to hand the nomination to a "neutral man with no color, of good character and little ability—some second Hayes . . ." Still, he predicted a Democratic victory.[74] Another Stalwart, New York City Police Justice Hugh Gardner, expressed the belief that the GOP was not permanently crippled by its recent losses. "A party which is composed of men intelligent enough and independent enough to rebuke its own leaders for their mistakes has a future before it."[75]

CHAPTER NINETEEN

Well-Informed Politicians

B_Y 1882, civil service reform was in the air. Reformers were organized on the state and national levels, their leadership was eloquent and aggressive, and their cause enjoyed support from the most influential and respectable elements of the business community and the press, particularly in the Northeast. Eager to profit from the popular trend, politicians increasingly announced their "conversion" to the principle. Almost all state party conventions of 1882 favored reform. Blaine endorsed a species of it in September.[1] Benjamin F. Butler of Massachusetts, one of the era's most blatant spoilsmen, declared in October that he was an advocate of competitive examinations for even the "highest" offices. "Integrity, capability, and efficiency in the incumbent," said Butler, "have always seemed to me to insure the occupant the best tenure of office. This in a public life of more than a score of years . . . has always been my guide."[2] The election results in November, especially from New York, appeared to confirm conclusively the view that public opinion had soured on the spoils system.

The lame duck session of the 47th Congress assembled in early December determined to pass some sort of civil service law. Both Republicans and Democrats were eager to take credit for the legislation, and each hoped to woo the votes of Independents. In addition, GOP Congressmen sought to protect the jobs of current officeholders in the all-too-likely event of defeat in 1884.

The President captured the mood of the day in his message to Congress. Earlier, in his letter accepting the vice-presidency and in his first congressional message, Arthur had expressed deep reservations about competitive examinations but had made it clear that he would sign reform legislation. Now he adopted a much more affirmative approach, contending that "the people of the country, apparently without distinction of party, have in various ways and upon frequent occasions given expression to their earnest wish for prompt and definite action." He also pointed out that the arduous task of supervising the appointment of the larger part of 100,000 federal employees diverted the time and attention of Presidents from more important duties.

Specifically, Arthur called for a stable tenure of office, unaffected by politician partisanship. For the first time, he acknowledged that political contributions by government employees were sometimes made out of fear of dismissal, and he urged that such assessments be prohibited by law. (Silas Burt winced when Arthur exclaimed, "I have always maintained and still maintain that a public officer should be as absolutely free as any other citizen to give or withhold a contribution for the aid of the political party of his choice.")[3] He also extended his support for the Pendleton bill, awaiting consideration by the Senate, which meant that he had abandoned his opposition to competitive examinations.[4]

Many observers were stunned by the President's new posture. The Chicago *Tribune* reflected, "In his message to Congress, President Arthur gives the order 'right about face' to the Stalwart army."[5] A New York reporter wrote, "One hears it said on the streets and in the hotels that the President has heard the verdict of the people and been guided by it."[6] E. L. Godkin smiled wryly; he had known Arthur for many years and continued to think of him as "an exceptionally well-informed politician."[7]

Senator George Hunt Pendleton, an Ohio Democrat, had introduced a civil service reform bill two years earlier that had been ignored by Congress. On the day of Arthur's initial message to Congress, Pendleton had tried again. The bill, drafted by New York reformer Dorman B. Eaton, called for the creation of a Civil Service Commission vested with the power to prescribe rules, investigate the progress of reform, and supervise examinations. Competitive examinations were to be given to all applicants for about 10,000 positions, a list of classified jobs that could be expanded by the President at his discretion. Entrance into the civil service was to be at the lowest grade. A period of probation was required to test fitness. Promotion was based on merit and competition. Officeholders would be free of the obligation to contribute time or money to political campaigns.

State reform associations, and the National Civil Service Reform League created in the summer of 1881, applied considerable pressure on Congress to take action, and newspapers and magazines were filled with articles calling for reform. But it took the election returns of 1882 to convince a majority of Congressmen that there was political gain in a partial surrender of the appointing power.

Debate over reform began soon after Congress convened. It followed partisan lines, as both parties vied to engineer specific portions of the impending legislation to their advantage. Three major amendments resulted, each of which weakened Pendleton's proposal. Democrats were successful in their bid to open all grades to competitive examination, a move designed to shorten the time required for an equal distribution of offices. (This was justified on the ground that certain offices demanded special skills that were not developed during the ascent from the lowest grades.) To please Senators from the West and South who feared that competitive examinations would favor the most educated and leave their regions underrepresented, appointments were to be parceled out to the various states according to population. And while the solicitation and acceptance of assessments were forbidden, federal officeholders retained the right to make "voluntary contributions." The political overtones of the debate were clear when ballots were cast on the latter amendment. Republicans, in power, favored the motion; Democrats opposed it, hoping to seal off an important avenue of their rivals' financial strength in 1884.[8]

The Pendleton bill passed the Senate 38 to 5, not a single Republican siding with the opposition. (Democrat Joseph Brown of Georgia suggested the title "a bill to perpetuate in office the Republicans who now control the patronage of the government.") The House soon concurred, following a thirty-minute debate, 155 to 47.[9] The measure became law on January 16, 1883. The irony of ex-Collector Arthur, the "Gentleman Boss," affixing his signature to the nation's first civil service reform legislation was not entirely overlooked.

At first the Act applied only to the federal departments in Washington and to the customhouses and post offices with more than fifty employees—about 10 percent of all federal jobs. The nation's 47,000 postmasters, for example, were not affected, neither were "old soldiers," "mere workmen," or those appointed by the President and confirmed by the Senate. The law's enforcement rested squarely with the Chief Executive. He might or might not appoint a three-man bipartisan commission; he could adopt or neglect to adopt regulations; he could extend, or not, the rules that were adopted. Senator Henry L. Dawes was correct in asserting that the Act "presupposes a friendly president."[10]

Arthur's selections for the commission were unanimously approved by reformers. The chairman, Dorman B. Eaton, had been chairman of Grant's Civil Service Commission, was a leader of the New York Civil Service Reform Association, and was the author of the Pendleton bill.

(During the campaign of 1880 he had been one of the few reformers who spoke highly of the Republican vice-presidential candidate.)[11] Educator John M. Gregory, a college friend of Arthur's, was described by Godkin as "a man of uncommon attainments" who held a "profound belief in civil-service reform." Leroy D. Thoman was a thirty-two-year-old Democratic judge from Ohio, recommended by Senator Pendleton, and thought to be, Godkin reported, "a firm friend to the cause he is called upon to serve."[12]

Reformers remained wary of the administration's sincerity toward reform, however. They had objected strongly in December when a Stalwart was nominated to be commissioner of the District of Columbia. (The nomination was withdrawn.)[13] They felt that the President had taken an unusually long time to name members of the Civil Service Commission, and suspected the darkest motives.[14] Above all, they were concerned about Arthur's intentions toward Silas Burt, whose commission as naval officer at the New York Customhouse expired February 4.

As far back as early December, rumors circulated among reformers that Burt was a major target of Arthur's Stalwart friends, and that the President, while resisting pressure to remove Collector Robertson and numerous other New York officeholders, had agreed to replace the naval officer.[15] By early February, Burt had received the endorsement of *The New York Times*, the New York *Tribune*, the New York *Evening Post, Harper's Weekly*, and *The Nation. The Times* warned that Burt's removal "would give the lie to the President's distinct professions in regard to the reform of the civil service, and would be so inexcusable and unnecessary a piece of foolishness and bad faith that neither his enemies nor his professed friends nor any one but himself could convince the country that he has even thought of it."[16] George William Curtis assured Burt, "I do not believe that you will be disturbed because the one fact of displacing you would totally discredit all that the President has said about a reasonable Service. Moreover all signs seem to show that he, at best, has learned something."[17] Edwin D. Morgan warned Arthur to resist the temptation to remove the prominent reformer. "As Mr. Burt has been an exceptionally good Officer, giving satisfaction to our merchants and importers, there is a general call from them for his re-appointment, and in this, I fully concur. Besides, it is the order of the day to retain all good officers, and it is on this account also that I earnestly hope he will be reappointed."[18] Burt wrote formal letters to the President and the Treasury Secretary requesting his renomination on the sole ground of faithful service.[19]

On March 1, Surveyor Charles K. Graham was nominated to succeed Burt, and the naval officer was named to be chief examiner of the Civil

Service Commission. Graham had solid credentials for his appointment and was not considered a political figure. Burt's presence on the commission staff could only strengthen the effectiveness of that body. The Stalwarts who were said to have attempted to influence the President were reported depressed.[20] Nevertheless, Burt thought the President's move insulting, and fired off a telegram to the White House declining the nomination. He informed reporters that he was being punished for his many years of advocating reform principles.[21]

Burt had earlier heard that the President described him as "radical," and that Arthur was not above retaliation for his long persistence in defying spoilsmen. In October, he had again denied a request by the New York Republican State Committee for a list of naval office employees and their salaries. Shortly thereafter, a Stalwart leader appeared, bearing subtle warnings. When Burt called on the President soon afterward, he was given a chilly, almost hostile, reception. Many reformers thought that Burt would be selected a member of the Civil Service Commission, and when others were named, the naval officer was discouraged but not surprised. When the President suddenly, without consulting a single reformer, proposed that he be removed from the Customhouse and given a post paying only $3,000 a year—$5,000 less than his current salary—Burt understood that Arthur had at last enjoyed his revenge. He later wrote, "The party-workers thought it an excellent joke and I can imagine that the President's sense of humor was excited by it." Arthur unquestionably knew in advance that the nomination would be refused.[22]

The tactic was clever: Burt was not "removed" from office, he was simply reassigned to another position for which he was qualified. But reformers were not taken in, and quickly and loudly decried the President's action. The executive committee of the National Civil Service Reform League declared, "We . . . regard his removal, however ingeniously devised, as a serious blow at the reform in its strongest hold, a grave embarrassment of the work of the Civil Service Commission, and a violation of those sound principles of administration which the country has approved, which the President has commended in two Messages to Congress, and which Congress has enacted into law."[23]

Stalwarts, as well, were unhappy with the President, for they had pled for the appointment of one of their own to the naval office. Of what use was it to remove Burt and fill his chair with an engineer? (They were further angered when Arthur later abandoned a nominee for chief examiner endorsed by Grant and Don Cameron, accusing the President of "truckling" to reformers.)[24]

Arthur's petty act of spite against a man he had known for thirty-five years did little more than add to his unpopularity. Godkin commented that "while President Arthur forfeited the confidence of the reform element by the ignoble trick employed to get rid of Mr. Burt, the most exemplary man in the service, he failed to attach to himself the Machine politicians." The editor questioned the good sense of Arthur's advisers. "It requires no prophet to predict that the President, if he continues to follow such mentors, will not have a political friend in the world by the time his administration comes to an end."[25]

Arthur surprised many reformers by administering the Pendleton Act efficiently and effectively. In early May, he adopted the civil service rules proposed by the commission, making only slight modifications. Other minor changes were made in November, earning congratulations from reformers.[26] George William Curtis complimented the President in an address before the National Civil Service Reform League, citing his "desire to give the reform system fair play."[27] For the remainder of its tenure, the administration, at all levels, evidenced a willingness to abide by the principles of reform.[28] Even William Mahone soon complained that the President was giving him a "cold shoulder," and seemed disinterested in his fate.[29]

The Civil Service Commission's first annual report glowed with optimism. It noted a drop in the volume of political assessments, and contained abundant testimony from federal employees favoring reform. In December 1883, Republican Senator Joseph Hawley, chairman of the Senate Committee on Civil Service and Retrenchment, declared reform successful, adding that he had not heard a single Congressman complain about it.[30]

A year later, Arthur expressed his deep satisfaction with the results of reform legislation, "in securing competent and faithful public servants and in protecting the appointing officers of the Government from the pressure of personal importunity and from the labor of examining the claims and pretensions of rival candidates for public employment."[31]

In early 1885, the Civil Service Commission reported that the enforcement of the Pendleton Act "has been found both practicable and effective for the accomplishment of its purpose." "The more important functions of the Commission are in their nature both judicial and legislative, requiring a careful regard to the practical effects of its action, firm resistance of solicitation, and an unflinching adherence to principle," it continued. "These functions cannot be successfully discharged without the constant, firm, and friendly support of the President. That support has never failed. The Commission has never asked advice or an exercise of authority on the part of the President which has been refused."[32]

CHAPTER TWENTY

Unleashing the Tariff

REPUBLICANS were under pressure to enact a further reform before surrendering their control of Congress. A revival in the economy after 1879 had caused a large increase in the customs revenues, and the Treasury bulged with a surplus that averaged over $100,000,000 annually. (Few things separate us so sharply from Arthur's era than his reference to "the bane of an overflowing treasury.") Increasingly, demands arose for cuts in the high tariff rates passed during the Civil War. The election returns in November were widely thought to include a public mandate for lower rates, as many citizens were convinced they would favorably affect the cost of living. Numerous businessmen argued that the government's surplus funds were needed by an expanding economy. GOP leaders were as eager to take credit for tariff revision as they were civil service reform. Moreover, once Democrats controlled the House, the slashes in rates would likely be deeper than most Republicans desired. Thus the lame duck session of late 1882, with only some fifty working days at its disposal, tackled the awesomely complex and politically volatile issue of tariff reduction. One political observer was amused by the turn of events. "It is somewhat ludicrous," he said, "to witness the new-born zeal of such dyed-in-the-wool protectionists as Senators Hoar, Frye, Dawes, and others of their class who are now clamoring for a reduction of the tariff. There seems to be a perfect race among these worthies to see who shall come in first and be enabled to put in his claim as a tariff reformer."[1]

Republicans had traditionally favored high tariffs, arguing that they promoted national economic self-sufficiency and encouraged prosperity for both business and labor. Historically, Democrats had come out for lower tariff rates. They contended that "excessive" protection favored manufacturing over agriculture, fostered monopolies, and increased prices. There were divisions in both parties on the issue, however. Several Republican Congressmen, particularly from the Midwest, were committed to rate reductions. Members of the reform wing of the GOP, influential far beyond their number, used their newspapers and magazines to call repeatedly for moderate but meaningful decreases. An average of about forty Democrats in the House of Representatives, on the other hand, were staunch protectionists and prevented serious tariff revision for more than a decade. (Free trade was preached by only a handful of theorists.) Regardless of party label, Congressmen were usually concerned foremost about the economic well-being of their own districts and states. In 1883, Democratic Senator Daniel W. Vorhees of Indiana declared during a clash with a southern colleague, "I am a protectionist for every interest which I am sent here by my constituents to protect."[2]

Tariff duties had long been entangled with the broader issue of federal revenue. When the Treasury was empty in 1842, Congress passed a high protective tariff. Fifteen years later, an overflowing revenue caused rates to be reduced. The Morrill tariff was passed in 1861 in part to counteract a deficit. A 10 percent reduction was enacted in 1872 and repealed in 1875 largely because of the flux and flow of federal income.[3]

Every year since 1866 the Treasury took in more money than it spent, and by Arthur's term the surplus had become embarrassing. For the fiscal year ending June 30, 1882, it amounted to more than $145,000,000. Congress might have reduced the surplus by repealing federal excise taxes on liquor and tobacco, but this was politically dangerous, for it would anger prohibitionists and crusaders against smoking and tobacco chewing. Funds could have been spent on massive public works projects. The thrust of public opinion at the time, however, was in the opposite direction, calling for more government efficiency, lower taxes, and less federal involvement. The surplus could have been used to reduce the national debt, and indeed was, causing it to fall from $2.8 billion in 1866 to $2 billion in 1881. But when the government purchased its bonds on the market before they reached maturity, the cost of the bonds skyrocketed at the expense of taxpayers. The only reasonable solution seemed obvious. Vermont's venerable protectionist Senator Justin S. Morrill sighed, "I suppose that if the Bible has to be revised from time to time, the tariff may have to be."[4]

Shortly after Arthur assumed office, both high-tariff men and reformers held conventions and passed resolutions in the hope of influencing the conduct of Congress. The President's position on the tariff was little in doubt. Stalwarts had traditionally favored high rates; Grant and E. D. Morgan were soon to become leaders of the New York Association for the Protection of American Industry.[5] In his first message to Congress, Arthur pointed to the mounting Treasury surplus and recommended the removal of all excise taxes with the exception of those on liquor and tobacco. He also contended that the tariff was in need of revision. He advised caution, however, and endorsed a suggestion recently approved by the Senate that a commission be created to study the tariff and report to Congress at its next session.[6] The chief proponents of a tariff commission were high protectionists like Morrill, head of the Senate Finance Committee, and the powerful chairman of the House Ways and Means Committee, William D. ("Pig-Iron") Kelley of Pennsylvania; sensing that tariff reform was inevitable, they were anxious to gain time to blunt its impact. The commission bill passed the House 151 to 83, all but about 30 of the affirmative votes coming from Republicans. The Senate passed the measure 35 to 19, again by a largely party vote. Arthur signed the bill into law on May 15, 1882.[7]

It was the President's responsibility to nominate members of the commission, and he was not long without advice. The names of some 200 applicants reportedly poured into the White House within two days of the bill's passage, nearly all of them representatives of special interests or industries.[8] On the recommendation of Senator Morrill (and after a personal appeal by the applicant to William Chandler), John L. Hayes was named. He was a Harvard-trained attorney, secretary of the National Association of Wool Manufacturers, and a well-known lobbyist against tariff reduction. He became the commission chairman when Arthur's first choice for the position, former Vice-President William Wheeler, declined the appointment. This selection was balanced with a representative of the wool growers, Austin M. Garland of Illinois, who was favored by Senators Logan and Davis. Henry M. Oliver Jr. of Pennsylvania was nominated to please the iron interests of his state, as well as the Cameron machine. Jacob Ambler of Ohio, an ex-member of Congress, was a strong protectionist who was said to owe his preferment to Representative William McKinley. Alexander R. Boteler of West Virginia was a railroad director and a conservative tariff man. Duncan F. Kenner of Louisiana was a moderate protectionist who represented sugar. John W. H. Underwood of Georgia was also a moderate. William H. McMahon of New York was chief clerk of the fifth division of the Customhouse and an authority on customs administration. Robert P. Porter was a tax expert and statistician.[9]

Republican leaders were pleased with the President; arch-protectionist John Sherman thought the nominees "well selected."[10] Four of the men were personally or officially connected with protected industries; free traders were without representation. To many, the commission appeared to reflect the intentions of those who wished to yield as little as possible to reformers. *The New York Times* lamented, "For any practical results likely to follow from its appointment, the Tariff Commission was dead before it was born . . . there is no reason to believe that its report will seriously disappoint the vested interests which have been chiefly consulted in its make-up."[11]

Defying such pessimism, commission members set out to make a thorough and conscientious study. Their task, Hayes told them at the first meeting in Washington, was to recommend a revision, not destruction, of existing tariff rates, a revision "on a scale of justice to all interests." He continued, "No special industry can have undue advantage; no private interest can be subserved; no duty promoting one industry, yet oppressing another, can be justified, and the relations of the industries to each other, no less than the special necessities of each, must be considered."[12]

The commission worked hard, traveling 6,000 miles from July 6 to October 16, hearing 604 volunteer witnesses and taking 2,625 pages of testimony. Its lengthy report, submitted in early December to the lame duck session of Congress, surprised many critics. Tariff cuts averaging between 20 and 25 percent were recommended; in certain cases reductions of 40 to 50 percent were suggested. The free list was considerably enlarged. A great many changes in the administration of the customs service were recommended. And the creation of a customs court was proposed, to take jurisdiction over cases arising out of conflicting interpretations of tariff laws. E. L. Godkin called the report "a much more impressive document than was generally looked for."[13] *The New York Times* commended the proposals to Congress, stating that their adoption "would be a very decided step in the direction of reform, and might well be the turning point in the fiscal policy of the country."[14] Many high protectionists were equally congratulatory. Senator Sherman termed the report "an admirable and harmonious plan," and later reflected that it "was by far the most comprehensive exposition of our customs laws and rates of duty that, so far as I know, had been published."[15]

In his second annual message, which reached Congress on the same day the commission report arrived, Arthur renewed his desire to have steps taken to decrease the Treasury surplus. He called for the abolition of all excise taxes, except those on distilled liquors; he recommended the repeal of numerous customs duties that yielded small returns; he urged Congress to simplify complex schedules of duties, particularly those of cotton, iron, and steel; and he appealed for a "substantial reduction" of rates on cotton, iron, steel, sugar, molasses, silk, wool, and woolen goods. The exact rates fixed for the hundreds of items involved would be settled by Congress, of course; Arthur found detailed recommendations "under present circumstances . . . quite unnecessary." He called attention to the new commission report (which he had not yet seen), trusting that it would provide valuable data and specific suggestions for legislative action.[16] "The President goes further in his recommendations for a reduction of revenue than members generally expected," *The New York Times* commented. "It may safely be said that the Message has taken many persons by surprise."[17]

Arthur's years of experience in the Customhouse were perhaps of assistance in framing this part of his message. (On the issue of excise taxes he clashed with Treasury Secretary Folger, who took a more conservative position.) But similar requests had been heard in Congress and read in the press for over a year. The overriding consideration behind the President's suggestions was political. Republicans wanted desperately to avoid a repeat of the disaster they had recently suffered, and tariff reform, like civil service reform, would make good campaign oratory in 1884. There was little opposition within the party on the general issue of reduction. Benjamin Harrison stated solemnly, "The creation of the Tariff Commission was a confession that the tariff needs reform."[18] But many problems appeared when legislators began to ponder the particulars of the commission's report. Few GOP Congressmen found themselves able to place the concerns of the party ahead of demands by powerful local supporters for favorable rates.

The House Ways and Means Committee was dominated by high protectionists; three of its members, including its chairman, were from tariff-conscious Pennsylvania. Rather than submit the Tariff Commission's recommendations directly to the House, the committee decided to frame a measure of its own, and began an item-by-item examination of the commission's proposals, often making revisions in an upward direction. A reporter soon observed, "it is frequently said that the Ways and Means Committee have apparently endeavored to see how near they could come to the existing tariff without creating an impression that they were opposed to any reduction of rates."[19] Not to be outdone, the Senate Finance Committee began designing another tariff bill, tacking it onto a House measure on excise taxes passed during the previous session. The once-celebrated Tariff Commission report was soon forgotten in the scuffle.

The House bill, yielding reductions averaging only about 10 percent, was reported on January 16. Debate quickly bogged down in a tangle of quarrels and petty amendments as Congressmen attempted to gain advantages for their own constituents. Lobbyists swarmed into Washington to apply pressure. High-tariff men, reformers, and free traders held rallies and signed petitions. Discouraged Republican leaders saw little hope of passing a bill before the brief session of Congress expired.

The Senate Finance Committee also reported a bill that proposed a high scale of duties, but on the floor of the Senate it was amended to more closely approximate the commission recommendations than its counterpart in the House. It passed easily on February 20 and was sent to the other end of the Capitol. It received a cold reception, for high protectionist sentiment was strong in the lower chamber. Iron and steel men objected strongly to the measure's low rates; "Pig-Iron" Kelley declared they would ruin Pennsylvania's economy and kill the Republican Party. Other Congressmen raised the constitutional objection against the origination of a tariff bill by the Senate.

Facing an impasse with only a few days remaining in the session, weary Republican strategists elected to turn the Senate bill over to a conference committee. High-tariff men had been urging similar action for weeks, as the customs of both houses required that members of the committee would be taken from the Finance and Ways and Means Committees. In a conference group of ten, the majority would probably be composed of such staunch protectionists as Morrill, Sherman, and Kelley. Representative Thomas B. Reed (later dubbed "Czar" for similar exploits) devised an unprecedented rule that authorized the appointment of a conference committee to deal with the Senate's bill. The rule was approved by the House on February 27, 120 to 22, a party vote with most Democrats refusing to answer the roll call in order to break the quorum. As predicted, strong protectionists dominated the new committee. When Senate Democrats boycotted the two seats allotted them, their places were given to a dependable Republican and William Mahone.

The conference committee assembled on March 1. A mere twenty-four hours later it issued a revised version of the Senate bill. Many rates were discovered increased, some to even higher levels than those proposed earlier in the House and Senate. Iron and steel duties had climbed almost to their current level. Their backs to the wall, Senate Republicans united almost to a man; the conference committee bill squeaked through 32 to 31 in the early hours of March 3. The House assembled at noon that day, the last full day of the 47th Congress. Opponents of the bill forced it to be read in its entirety, a delaying action that took two valuable hours. Debate then raged for more than three hours before a packed gallery eager to see the results of the voting. At 5:30 P.M. the bill passed, 152 to 116. There was some cross-over voting, chiefly by Congressmen from Ohio and Pennsylvania: the nineteen Democrats who voted affirmatively were high-tariff men; the twelve Republicans who voted no, one of whom was William McKinley, thought the bill insufficiently protective. But the new tariff was credited by everyone to the GOP. Arthur signed the measure shortly without comment.[20]

After struggling for weeks, the Republican-controlled Congress produced a law that reduced duties on the average of only 1.47 percent. Its many awkward compromises prompted critics to label it "the mongrel tariff." Its many confused sentences and grammatical errors caused lobbyist James M. Swank to call it an open invitation to fraud.[21] The GOP gained little for its effort. Many business interests expressed displeasure at what had happened. The wool manufacturers regretted that the Morrill tariff had been tinkered with. The wool growers of Ohio loudly assailed John Sherman when he returned home. (In 1895, Sherman would write, "The tariff act of 1883 laid the foundation of all the tariff complications since that time.")[22] The iron and steel manufacturers of Pittsburgh thought themselves in a "position of danger." Some high protectionists termed the bill a "surrender." "All concessions" made in the law "to the free trade sentiment," Pennsylvania's Joseph Wharton wrote to William Chandler, were "mistakes in party policy and injurious to the country."[23] At the same time, those who had cried for genuine tariff reform from Congress were disappointed and often resentful. E. L. Godkin called the new law "a game of grab played on a large scale."[24] If the Republican debacle at the polls a few months earlier rested in part upon a demand for meaningful tariff reduction, the elections of 1884 seemed further imperiled by the last-ditch labors of the lame duck session.

No one blamed the President directly for the "mongrel tariff." He had spoken out forcefully in his message to Congress for the sort of changes reformers were after. His selections for the Tariff Commission had proved wise. The commission's report would later be described by a knowledgeable scholar as "a scheme of a tariff law more scientific, based upon a broader conception of the respective rights of producer and consumer, and of conflicting industries, than any law which had been passed, up to that time."[25] Once the report was in the hands of Congress, Arthur was expected to leave the matter to the likes of Morrill and Kelley. During the heat of the tariff struggle in Congress, Godkin observed, "The Legislature is the fountain of government vigor. From it the Executive derives its force, activity, and efficiency. If the Legislature cannot command, the readiness of the Administration to obey, so valuable under ordinary circumstances, is of no value at all."[26] The aggressive, whip-cracking Chief Executive who badgered and browbeat Congress to do his will awaited the succeeding century. Even had Arthur wished to step beyond the restricted boundaries of the presidency in his time, his political influence over the lame duck session, convened a short time after the November elections, was at best minimal. (Indeed, in his second message, Arthur proposed an amendment to the Constitution giving the executive the authority to veto specific items in appropriation bills rather than being compelled to accept or reject the bills as a whole, a discretionary power enjoyed by the governors of fourteen states. Congress ignored the suggestion.)[27] The scores of Republican Congressmen who met defeat at the polls looked to Arthur primarily as a source of future employment. Timothy Howe confided to his niece, "The President is at his wits['] end to provide for all these members of Congress who were beaten last fall."[28]

The new tariff law had little effect on the economy. Customs receipts decreased slightly during the last two years of the Arthur Administration, but largely because it was a period of declining trade.[29] Slowly but unmistakably the country was sinking into another of its periodic depressions. The economic slump did not begin, as it had in 1837 and 1873 and would again in 1893 and 1929, with dramatic business failures, runs on banks, sharp drops in the stock exchange, and widespread public despair. The depression economic historians have charted from late 1882 into 1886 had manifestations that were, in the words of one expert, "small and cumulative, rather than intensive and acute."[30] Prices of commodities and stocks steadily declined. Business failures rose from 6,738 in 1883 to almost 10,000 for both 1884 and 1885. By one estimate, business activity fell 25 percent, and the production of durable goods experienced a similar drop. New railroad construction fell from 11,569 miles in 1882 to only 2,982 in 1885. The annual production of pig-iron declined by 649,000 tons between 1882 and 1885. Bank clearings in New York City fell from more than $46 billion in 1882 to about $25 billion in 1885, and in the nation as a whole from more than $61 billion to just short of $38 billion. Immigration dropped from nearly 750,000 in 1882 to less than 400,000 in 1885. A survey of the industrial situation in the Northeast published in October 1884, fixed the number of unemployed at 350,000, an average of about 13 percent of total employment. A study of Massachusetts during 1884–1885 concluded that nearly 30 percent of all employed persons had been unemployed an average of about four months during the preceding year. In 1885, a government report stated that a million Americans were unemployed, about 7½ percent of those working in industry, agriculture, and trade. Terence Powderly, of the Knights of Labor, thought the correct figure more like two million, explaining why "a deep rooted feeling of discontent pervades the masses. . . . the army of the discontented is gathering fresh recruits day by day. . . ." The total cost of charity in New York City alone was more than $5,000,000 by 1882.[31]

There was no adequate diagnosis of the problem and no reliable prescription for its solution; falling prices and the frequently fluctuating level of industrial activity baffled businessmen, economists, and politicians in the United States and Europe throughout the era. Carroll D. Wright, the first commissioner of labor, appointed in 1885, observed, "Clergymen and moralists largely incline to assert that social and moral influences . . . produce the industrial difficulties, . . . manufacturers incline to give industrial conditions, labor legislation, labor agitation, . . . overproduction . . . ; while the workingmen attribute industrial diseases to combinations of capital, long hours, low wages, machinery, and kindred causes."[32] The party in power could also be blamed, of course. Mindful of the "mongrel tariff" and of a growing unrest across the nation over the depression, many Democrats were convinced that the issue of prosperity would be among the strongest weapons in their arsenal during the next presidential contest.

A Seafaring People

T HE LAME DUCK SESSION of the 47th Congress acted not only on civil service and tariff reform but also took steps to rehabilitate the navy. The physical and intellectual foundations of the new navy date from the early 1880s. Once again, the President played a positive role in the passage of legislation for which there was considerable demand.

America's naval force deteriorated rapidly after the conclusion of the Civil War. In late 1864, the navy list included almost 700 vessels mounting nearly 5,000 guns. Six years later only 52 ships were in commission; they were in poor repair, and most of their some 500 guns were obsolete. By 1881, the United States Navy was inferior to those of all the major European nations and several Latin American states. Even its ability to stand up successfully against the Chinese fleet was in doubt. A British journal commented, "Never was there such a hopeless, broken-down, tattered, forlorn apology for a navy."[1]

In his first report as Secretary of the Navy, William Chandler noted that the United States owned only one first-rate ship (the *Tennessee*, of 4,840 tons displacement), fourteen second-raters (2,100 to 4,000 tons), and twenty-two third-raters (900 to 1,900 tons). At a time in which other nations were rapidly constructing steel navies, America's thirty-seven vessels were made of wood, except for four of the smallest ships which had iron hulls. The navy also possessed thirteen single-turreted monitors, shallow-draft ironclads built during the war for harbor defense, now much too slow and unseaworthy to be effective, and without modern artillery. On the subject of ordnance, Chandler called attention to the fact that the navy did not have a single modern high-powered cannon, and owned only eighty-seven guns worth retaining.

To man this puny fleet, there were 1,817 naval officers—59 to a ship, one for every five seamen. Many within this wholly disproportionate number owed their positions of high authority to political and social influence and were virtually immune to reprimand or dismissal. Several political pets were incompetent drunkards. More than a few of those with attractive commands were known to regard the ships under their control as private yachts.

Nine navy yards and five naval stations stood ready to repair the almost comic flotilla. They employed nearly 4,500 workmen and had cost the federal government more than $54,000,000 through mid-1882. Chandler complained of "extravagant expenditures" and vowed sharp reductions.

The merchant marine, like the navy, had fallen into dilapidation since the war. In 1866, over 75 percent of the foreign carrying trade of the United States was handled by American vessels; by 1882, the figure had dropped to 15.5 percent. Congressional stinginess accounted for much of the slump, but heavy duties on the iron and steel needed to modernize the merchant marine's obsolete ships were also to blame. Chandler argued that the navy and the merchant marine were mutually dependent, and that Congress should take measures to strengthen both. In critical periods the navy would be called upon to defend the nation's commercial marine. (The secretary clung to the popular Jeffersonian view that "The Protection of Commerce is the first object of a naval establishment.") So, too, in emergencies the merchant marine could provide the navy with ships and trained personnel. In peacetime, shipyards busy with the construction of commercial vessels could provide the navy with the requirements for rebuilding its own fleet. Above all, Chandler contended, an effective merchant marine was indispensable on economic grounds. Foreign competition hurt the balance of trade, deprived businessmen of profits and seafarers of employment. Other nations gave generous subsidies to their merchant marines. Shipping stood alone among the major American industries unprotected by the federal government.

"If the naval establishment is not to be made effective," Chandler concluded, "it should be discontinued, and the fifteen millions annually expended should be reserved to procure, in national emergencies, the assistance of foreign ships and guns." If steps were not taken immediately by the government to arrest the disappearance of American ships from the world's oceans, he warned, "we shall soon cease to be a seafaring people and shall not need to maintain a Navy of our own."[2]

There were several reasons for the decline of the navy in the immediate postwar years. Antimilitarism revived once the shooting stopped, affecting all branches of the defense establishment. In 1874, the army was reduced to 25,000 men, and remained that size until the Spanish-American War. Without foreign colonies to defend, and with wide oceans to protect them from potential enemies, many Americans saw little reason for maintaining a powerful naval force. Few spoke of building the navy to promote overseas trade. The settlement of the West, together with unrestricted immigration, created what appeared to be an insatiable home market for the factories growing under the protective wing of a high tariff. Neither major political party came out forcefully for the reconstruction of the navy during the first fifteen years after the war.

Creativity and innovation from within the navy were stifled by the Grant Administration's willingness to rely upon the judgment of senior line officers. This ultraconservative class of professionals, jealous of its prestige and position, was prejudiced against steam power and did much to frustrate postwar efforts by the engineer corps to modernize the service. A general order of 1869 required "full sail power" for all new vessels, another threatened serious penalties for burning coal except in emergencies. In 1872, the Navy Department requested authority to construct several wooden warships, already proven fatally vulnerable against ironclads equipped with shell-guns. In 1876, a prominent officer told a congressional committee that "few, if any, of the experienced officers of the Navy . . . would advocate . . . building . . . heavily iron-plated ships for cruising or fleet operations." The service remained committed to the "cut-and-run" single-ship strategy popular during the War of 1812. From the same era came the dominant theory that the principle function of the navy in time of war was the protection of American harbors. Few navy men considered it their responsibility to sail beyond sight of American soil during an armed conflict.

The navy also suffered from the low state of politics and business during the Grant years. Funds appropriated for the Navy Department for repairs largely benefited a corps of friendly contractors and a horde of political appointees who enjoyed make-work jobs and dutifully paid assessments. House Democrats probed into the administration of the Navy Department in 1876. Congress became aware that something was seriously wrong with the navy but responded merely by curtailing appropriations from an average of $20,000,000 a year for the period 1869–1877 to an average of $15,000,000 during the next four years. No funds were allocated for the construction of new ships.

The Hayes Administration paid little attention to naval affairs. Secretary of the Navy Richard W. Thompson of Indiana was so ignorant of these matters, or so it was said, he expressed surprise on learning that ships were hollow. Throughout his term of office he appeared oblivious to the state of technological development abroad, and in 1879 expressed doubt that European navies were superior to our own.[3]

By the time Arthur was summoned to the duties of Chief Executive, however, a number of factors had brought the United States to the threshold of a new era in maritime policy. Several newspapers, top naval officers, and more than a few Congressmen were calling for a new approach to America's navy. The most common arguments were based on fear. A few South American republics, it was discovered, had been acquiring warships and were said to pose a threat to the nation's security. Rear Admiral John Rogers declared that within three weeks after a declaration of war Chile could control Pacific commerce and attack San Francisco without effective resistance from American warships. It was rumored that the major European powers were contemplating joint control of a canal across the Isthmus of Panama. In the last analysis, warned the Washington *Post*, the integrity of the Monroe Doctrine rested on force. Secretary of State Blaine's often aggressive pronouncements lent support to the campaign for a revitalized naval fortress.

Appeals to national pride were also common. Representative Washington C. Whitthorne of Tennessee, sometime chairman of the House Naval Affairs Committee, contended that the greatest nations, from Phoenicia to Great Britain, had always enjoyed powerful navies. An American minister to Germany warned, "We cannot rely solely upon the moral sense of mankind for respect for our treaty rights, or the safety of our citizens."

The nation's anemic merchant marine drew increasing attention. Businessmen clamored for federal subsidies and reduced rates on raw materials vital to domestic shipbuilders. The nation's exports increased more than 200 percent between 1870 and 1880, and many thought this just the beginning of commercial expansion. Representative William Ward of Pennsylvania spoke of a "new world" within American reach. Some naval leaders went a step farther, reflecting an early attraction to imperialism. Commodore Robert W. Shufeldt, a harbinger of many of the ideas of Captain Alfred Thayer Mahan, trumpeted, "The man-of-war precedes the merchantman and impresses rude people with the sense of the power of the flag. . . . I believe that our merchant marine and our Navy are joint apostles, destined to carry over the world the creed upon which its institutions are founded."[4]

Garfield's Navy Secretary, William H. Hunt, took a strong interest in rebuilding the navy. He surrounded himself with able advisers, entertained the naval affairs committees, and lobbied in Congress. On his own he appointed a board of naval officers to formulate future plans. Following heated deliberations reflecting the controversy within the navy over technological progress, a majority report, issued on November 7, 1881, recommended a sharp increase in naval vessels, including the construction of a large number of steel ships. Though more expensive than wood and iron, steel was the preferred building material because of its light weight and endurance.[5]

Arthur strongly endorsed the development of naval strength in his first message to Congress. While recognizing that the recent recommendations called for sizable expenditures, he was convinced that the funds would constitute a sound investment in the nation's future security, prosperity, and honor. "We must be ready to defend our harbors against aggression; to protect, by the distribution of our ships of war over the highways of commerce, the varied interests of our foreign trade and the persons and property of our citizens abroad; to maintain everywhere the honor of our flag and the distinguished position which he may rightfully claim among the nations of the world."[6]

The House Committee on Naval Affairs soon made a lengthy study of the subject and concluded that "the time for wise and energetic action has come." It added, "To longer delay action looking to the building up of our Navy would . . . be not only folly but even crime."[7] Congress proceeded with extreme caution, however. By an act of August 5, 1882, it compromised between the past and future by authorizing construction of two steel cruisers carrying full sail power. No funds were appropriated, and the project was subject to the approval of a second advisory board with complete authority to plan and supervise construction of the new vessels.[8] Members of the board were to be selected by Hunt's successor.

Chandler had long known his way around the Navy Department. At the beginning of Lincoln's second administration he was named its solicitor and judge-advocate, and since 1868 he had walked its halls as the principal lobbyist for shipbuilder John Roach. Chandler and Roach were close personal friends as well as business associates, and more than a few observers smirked when the new Navy Secretary expressed an intense interest in maritime expansion.[9]

To head the Naval Advisory Board Chandler selected Commodore Robert Shufeldt. The appointment was a sop to Stalwart Aaron Sargent of California and was not particularly advantageous, for Shufeldt was far more experienced in diplomatic than technical matters. The four other naval officers named to the board, while qualified to serve, were likewise undistinguished for outstanding achievements in the fields of naval architecture or marine engineering. Two civilian experts were also appointed.[10]

The United States was far behind other nations in naval architecture, and Congress might have done well to purchase ships from foreign sources. It was the general feeling, however, that a powerful American fleet would benefit from American design; in the long run the acquisition of domestic expertise in planning and constructing would outweigh the inevitable errors encountered in the initial effort at building steel ships. So experimental was the nature of its task that the advisory board was required by Congress to advertise publicly for plans, models, designs, and suggestions.

In his December report, Chandler assured Congress that the board's work was proceeding "with care and caution," and that it was his determination as well as the board's "to design and complete the two best ships which can possibly be constructed in this country."[11] Arthur supported Chandler and the board in his second message, calling the reconstruction of the navy "of the upmost importance to the national welfare."[12]

The advisory board was frustrated by a lack of proposals submitted for its scrutiny, and took upon itself the responsibility for planning the nucleus of the new navy. On December 20, it recommended that instead of beginning with the two large vessels approved in August, funds should be appropriated to construct three steel cruisers and a dispatch boat or "clipper." It also recommended completion of four partially constructed double-turreted monitors.

The lame duck session of the 47th Congress looked kindly on the report, and on March 3, 1883, Arthur signed a bill into law that marked the legislative origin of the new navy. Funds were provided for a 4,300-ton cruiser with two-thirds sail power, two 3,000-ton cruisers with two-thirds sail power, and a dispatch vessel. The building material was to be steel. Funds were also included to install machinery in the monitors. At Chandler's urging, the law contained a clause prohibiting the repair of any vessel if the expense exceeded 20 percent of its original cost, a provision that aroused anger from politicians with a selfish interest in navy yards and insured the early retirement of many aging and obsolete ships. Years later Chandler said, "I think that I did my best work in destroying the old Navy, although I did build four new ships."[13]

The proposed 3,000-ton cruisers were later dubbed the *Atlanta* and *Boston*, the largest cruiser *Chicago*, and the dispatch vessel *Dolphin*. They became popularly known as "the ABCD ships."

Anxious to get the ships into production, Chandler submitted the advisory board's basic designs to the navy's bureau chiefs for criticism. The move backfired, for the chiefs were jealous of the board's power and took to quarreling over details. In order to quell the controversy, Chandler agreed to share the board's ultimate authority over the ships with the haughty chiefs, a step that caused delay and confusion.[14]

By late April, Chandler thought the blueprints sufficiently completed to begin construction. Only private shipyards were equipped to perform the work, and in conformity with the 1883 law, the secretary advertised for public bids. He may have been overly eager, for the hull design of the *Dolphin* was approved only one hour before the bids were opened on July 2, and specifications for the machinery and boilers of the other ships were agreed upon later.

Some forty people gathered in Chandler's office on July 2 to view the opening of eight sealed bids. When the last had been read aloud, the lowest bidder on each of the ships was John Roach. An unsuccessful competitor jumped to his feet, his face flushed with rage, and cried, "Mr. Secretary, are you going to give all these contracts to one man?" Chandler nervously replied, "I don't see how I can help it." The gentleman who raised the question soon complained bitterly to a reporter about what he termed "the Chandler-Roach combination."[15]

Sixty-seven-year-old John Roach, stocky, broad-shouldered, with a massive head and smooth-shaven face, was the leader of the shipbuilding industry and no stranger to controversy. He had emigrated from Ireland, penniless and barely literate, in 1832. His first steady job was as a hod carrier in an iron works for twenty-five cents a day. Through hard work, cunning, and some luck he became a wealthy iron maker during the next quarter century, and by the end of the Civil War was one of the nation's foremost builders of steam engines. Two years later he assembled the finest marine-engine works in the country and became a power in the tool manufacturing business. Roach was one of the first to see a bright future for iron steamers, and in the early 1870s began to assemble what developed into the most modern shipyard in the United States, equipped to handle every stage of ship construction "from the ore up," excepting only the laying of carpets and the furnishing of utensils. By mid-1882 he employed 1,800 men at his huge yard in Chester, Pennsylvania. Between 1872 and 1887, more than 100 vessels were built in the yard and launched into the Delaware River, perhaps more ships than were produced by all of his competitors combined. The quality of his products was consistently excellent.

Roach's business dealings with the Navy Department began in 1862, and before long the federal government was one of his major customers. He employed Chandler in 1868 to wheedle contracts, favors, and subsidies. At times he entered into Navy Department politics to get his way. He became a generous GOP donor and struck up friendships with Hayes, Conkling, Blaine, Garfield, and other party leaders. Blaine, with his strong interest in American mercantile expansion and his friendship with

Chandler, was a particularly vocal supporter. Roach's tactics for gaining advantage were, of course, exactly those of his competitors.

As might be expected, Roach did not want for enemies. Many Democrats thought him anathema because of his Republican ties. Roach had been a favorite of Grant's corrupt Naval Secretary George M. Robeson, and while no evidence emerged linking the shipbuilder with illegal activities, Democratic newspapers ran "Roach, Robeson, Robber" headlines for years. Business rivals, as well, worked incessantly to blacken Roach's reputation. Because of his belief in high tariffs and a subsidized merchant marine, he was the symbol of great wrong to advocates of free trade and free ships.[16]

Intense controversy emerged from the news that Roach had won the contracts for all of the ABCD ships. Charges of collusion and fraud were hurled with abandon. Predictably, a *Puck* cartoon portrayed Roach and Robeson as pirates dancing with joy over the bold caption, "The Old Partners in the New Navy job." But, in fact, careful research into the matter indicates that Roach had not sought favors from Chandler during his tenure as Navy Secretary and that the shipbuilder won the contracts fairly. Roach based his bids on the estimated cost of material and labor plus 5 percent profit, and his success was founded on the superiority of his well-established shipbuilding complex. His bids totaled $2,440,000, more than $744,000 under the advisory board's estimate and $315,000 less than the next lowest bids. Privately, Roach assured Chandler in his broken English, "I pledge my selfe to you that every precaution in my power to see that there is no extra bills and that you can proudly say when the work is done that no private Endevidual garded his own interest with more vegilence and care than you have in this instance garded the interest of your department." An unsuccessful bidder confided to Chandler, "Your whole course in asking for bids, and opening the same was most fair & honorable, and I do not see how you could have done differently from what you did and certainly there was not a bidder there who had cause to object to your action, or complain of Mr. Roach because he determined to bid very low." Still, it was unquestionably embarrassing to Chandler to turn over all of the large contracts to his friend and former employer, and politically it was damaging. Few observers thought that the transaction contributed positively to the public's trust in the administration.[17]

Construction of the ABCD ships assumed heavily partisan overtones. Democrats charged the administration with seeking a strong navy in order to stir up international turmoil. In his third message to Congress, Arthur responded, "It is no part of our policy to create and maintain a Navy able to cope with that of the other great powers of the world," adding, "We have no wish for foreign conquest, and the peace which we have long enjoyed is in no danger of interruption."[18] The Naval Advisory Board's plans for the vessels were soon under attack, and the Senate Naval Affairs Committee held public hearings to air the complaints. Democrats took delight in publicizing hostile opinions, and at every turn branded the designers incompetent and the builder corrupt. In the first session of the 48th Congress the Democratically controlled House stymied a proposal to construct seven additional steel vessels.[19] By early 1884, with a presidential contest in the offing, Roach (through his secretary) wrote to Chandler, "When the ships are finished, no matter how good they are, there will be a disposition to find fault, and if the Democratic Party should succeed, which I hope they will not, in order to vindicate their own charges they would actually aid in destroying the character of the vessels and they would find plenty of men in the Construction and Engineers Corps to aid them. I want and must have the vessels finished in your time."[20]

Numerous delays plagued Roach's good intentions. The production of adequate steel took much longer than anticipated to manufacture when a subcontractor failed to meet rigid navy specifications. Bad weather hampered construction work. A fire destroyed valuable shipyard equipment. Worst of all, the advisory board's plans contained numerous errors that required extensive attention. The board ordered fifty changes or additions to the plans for the *Dolphin* alone; twenty-three involved ripping out completed work. When the *Dolphin* finally made a trial run in November 1884, a shaft snapped, demanding several months of additional labor. The delays forced Roach to the brink of financial ruin. By March 1885, eighteen months after the contracts for the ABCD ships were signed, only the dispatch vessel was completed, and it had not been formally accepted by the contractor.[21]

Chandler made it known early in his term that he would be an active, forceful Navy Secretary. Many of his predecessors had been content to "let the admirals run the navy," but because of his temperament and long experience with maritime affairs, he quickly became the administration's most aggressive Cabinet member. He lacked the support of jealous bureau chiefs and might have accomplished more with their backing.[22] Still, his aspirations and achievements rank him among the most significant public servants of the period.

On his own initiative, and in defiance of the bureau chiefs, Chandler ordered the establishment of the Naval War College on October 6, 1884, a project doggedly advocated since 1877 by Commodore Stephen B. Luce.[23] The Office of Naval Intelligence was set up during this period.

On the recommendation of the Gun Foundry Board, created by Congress in 1883 and appointed by the President, plans were laid for the nation's first ordnance plants.[24] When Congress authorized a commission on navy yards in the bill of August 1882, Chandler named Commodore Luce its chairman and complied with its recommendations by closing down the yards at Pensacola and New London. He reduced the force in several other shipyards, repeatedly lashed out against waste, and was the first Navy Secretary to condemn patronage among navy yard personnel.[25]

Chandler, of course, well understood the political uses of shipyards. Early in the Arthur Administration, Mahone had been given a free hand in the Norfolk Yard, and during the campaign of 1882 it was widely believed that all of the yards were major sources of assessment income. After the shock of the 1882 elections and passage of the Pendleton Act, however, Chandler, like the President, became an advocate of honesty and efficiency in government service. In his report of 1883 he declared that the navy yards needed to "be thoroughly reorganized in such a way as to exclude all political considerations from their management, otherwise bad and expensive work will be the result. We cannot afford to destroy the speed of our naval engines in order to make votes for a political party."[26] Throughout his term, GOP leaders bombarded Chandler with requests for jobs and make-work projects; most came away empty-handed. Even Mahone was obliged to promise the secretary in mid-1883 not to seek favors at the expense of the government. Chandler put into effect the law calling for an eight-hour day in the yards. Commandants of the yards were held to strict accountability for their funds and were not permitted to overspend their budgets. During the campaign of 1884 the secretary was particularly unresponsive to efforts at obtaining assessments.

Perhaps if Chandler had enjoyed absolute authority he might have gone further toward the efficiency and nonpartisanship he advocated in his annual reports. Congress alone had the power to take radical action, and its inclinations lay in the opposite direction. But then, as his biographer suggests, Chandler surely could have done more on his own.[27] Politics continued to be a force in the shipyards to the end of the administration, and Chandler's successor, William C. Whitney, introduced political and economic reforms on a broader scale.[28]

Chandler was intent on reducing the surplus of commissioned naval officers. By the Act of August 5, 1882, no future appointments were to be given to Naval Academy graduates except to fill vacancies; those who were unsuccessful would receive a year's salary and an honorable discharge. The law also called for leaving several high-ranking vacancies unfilled. In his annual reports the secretary urged Congress to take more drastic steps to decrease the number of officers. In 1883, he recommended mandatory retirement at sixty-two. He sought a board with authority to create a list of competent officers of all grades qualified for promotion, and a similar list of those who were "an incubus upon the establishment" and would be encouraged to retire. He repeated an earlier request for the abolition of the grade of commodore. And he sought a fixed amount of sea service in each grade as a condition of promotion.[29] Congress paid little attention, in large part because of the political ties enjoyed by many high-ranking officers, to whom Chandler was a menace.

In each of his annual reports Chandler expressed irritation over the power of naval officers with congressional connections. In one he complained that "the practice has prevailed of soliciting and procuring favoritism for officers, by such devices and with such pertinacity and influence as to create a system resistance to which may make unenviable the position of the head of the department."[30] He was particularly disturbed by the number of officers who were restored to active duty through political favor after having been dismissed for misconduct or incompetence. He wrote to the chairman of the Senate Naval Committee in 1884, "Charity toward an officer who had done his duty in the war has no place here. If his services were of such value that he should be supported at public expense, that is one story, but he should not be entrusted with ships where his drunkenness or inefficiency will endanger property or life."[31]

Chandler made a significant revision in the administrative mechanics of the department that shifted responsibility in the direction of his office. All other than routine orders, including those given to cruising vessels, were required to receive the approval and signature of the secretary and should be presented to him only after having been passed upon by three navy officers. This curtailment of the independent authority of top officers caused friction. Chandler stirred even greater resentment within high naval circles by an order of July 5, 1883, requiring officers to leave their families at fixed places of residence on penalty of removal from duty. This was an attempt to curtail the practice of congregating ships in attractive ports such as Yokohama, Rio, and Villefranche for the benefit of officers' wives. The order was generally ignored.[32]

In two instances Chandler's clashes with defiant officers reached the public, drawing severe criticism from Independent and Democratic journalists. The first involved Commander Henry H. Gorringe, an engineer known for his efficiency in transporting the Central Park obelisk from Egypt in 1880. Gorringe drew a reprimand from Chandler for publishing an article in the *North American Review* attacking naval administration.[33] The commander then published an interview in the

New York *Post* advocating the principle of free ships. Chandler flew into a rage at such insolence, accusing Gorringe of "vituperating" him and of being "in British pay." "This is the old Bill Chandler of the stump and the caucus all over," E. L. Godkin smirked.[34] Gorringe came to Washington and demanded proof of the secretary's allegation that he was in foreign employ. Chandler backed down, saying merely that he was now satisfied there was no truth in the charge. Gorringe promptly submitted his resignation to the President, the letter containing angry references to the Navy Secretary's probity.[35]

Commander Robley D. Evans was also a publicity-conscious officer known to have close friends in Congress. "Fighting Bob," as intimates called him, could boast of a brilliant service record and was a major force in Secretary Hunt's Naval Advisory Board. Evans had been loaned to the Treasury Department and was serving as naval inspector of the Fifth Lighthouse District in Virginia in July 1884, when he was suddenly removed from his post by Chandler. Neither man made a public statement, but news of the matter was soon in the press. Evans's congressional allies took action promptly to win the commander's reinstatement, one of them appealing directly to the President. Social pressure was applied to Mrs. Chandler. Democratic newspapers condemned the secretary, charging that the removal was an act of vengeance against the commander for his resistance to moves by the Mahone machine.

Chandler stood steadfast and continued to refrain from public comment. For the efforts of Evans's friends, he canceled a leave the commander had wangled and placed him on "waiting orders" at reduced pay. The issue in Chandler's mind was the authority of his office. In a letter to the President of January 20, 1885, he declared that if Evans could question his order, "when no reasons are assigned or intended to be assigned, military administration is at an end."

The incident lay dormant until 1901 when Evans published his autobiography. In it he contended that his removal had been due to his refusal to appoint "disreputable men" at the request of bosses "quite as disreputable." But then, he sniffed, "I had felt the stings of insects before in my life and did not consider them of much importance."

Chandler demanded that proper action be taken against Evans. (The Navy Department sent him a stiff note of censure.) He then prepared a memorandum explaining the facts of the case as he recalled them. Treasury Secretary Folger had requested Evans's removal because of the officer's overbearing attitude toward subordinates and his occasional use of profanity. Chandler had resisted the request at first, due to the turmoil it would inevitably elicit from officers who "were very largely self-governing." Folger eventually buckled under the ensuing furor and asked that

Evans be reinstated. Chandler refused, stating that once he had given the order, the matter passed beyond the boundaries of Treasury Department business. It became a question "whether the Secretary of the Navy, in his discretion, issued orders to naval officers, or whether the officers devised and controlled their own orders."

It is impossible to determine with confidence whose version of the story is correct. Evans's imperiousness cannot be questioned, but neither can the partisanship of Folger and Chandler. However that may be, the secretary's view of naval discipline did not falter during his term. Letters poured into his office following Evans's dismissal congratulating him for his courage. Some expressed delight that "Fighting Bob" had at last encountered a combatant as formidable as himself.[36]

The President appeared particularly interested in seeing the construction of a modern navy under way during his term. Each of his annual messages to Congress, and a special message of March 26, 1884, contained strong appeals for funds to build ships. Defense seemed foremost among his considerations. In his last message he wrote, "As the long peace that has lulled us into a sense of fancied security may at any time be disturbed, it is plain that the policy of strengthening this arm of the service is dictated by considerations of wise economy, of just regard for our future tranquillity, and of true appreciation of the dignity and honor of the Republic."[37] After its initial support, a divided Congress paid little attention until early 1885 when both parties voted for a bill appropriating $1,895,000 for two cruisers and two gunboats. Arthur signed the bill into law on his last day in office.[38]

A week later, the *Dolphin* steamed into Long Island Sound for a further trial run. William Whitney, intent on embarrassing his predecessor and the GOP in general, attempted at length to discredit the ship and its builder. Before long, he drove Roach into receivership and seized the Chester, Pennsylvania, shipyard. Roach died heartbroken in 1887. "A meaner, more ignoble and more partisan persecution has never been known in American politics," said Whitelaw Reid in the New York *Tribune*.[39]

The *Dolphin* proved eventually to be superbly constructed. In 1888 and 1889, it traveled 58,000 miles around the world, requiring only a single engine adjustment that took less than two hours. Secretary of the Navy Benjamin F. Tracy (a Republican) declared, "This performance is probably without a parallel in the history of naval vessels, and bears conclusive testimony to the high skill of American artisans and the excellence of their work." The dispatch ship continued to perform admirably until scrapped in 1922.[40]

By 1889, all of the ABCD ships had joined the fleet and were organized into the "Squadron of Evolution." They were not large and powerful by European standards. Some nations owned battleships displacing from 6,000 to 15,000 tons, carrying rifles as large as seventeen inches in caliber. The *Chicago*, largest of the new American ships, displaced only 4,500 tons and mounted four eight-inch rifled guns. Many foreign cruisers had twice the tonnage and firepower of the *Chicago*. Several transatlantic steamers were much faster. Moreover, the new vessels did not have side armor; their guns were impeded by sailing gear; their boilers were perched atop old-fashioned brick fireboxes, incapable of creating steam rapidly.[41]

But the United States lacked the desire, the technology, and the facilities to build ships in the early 1880s that would rival the finest in Europe. In order to match the speed of the fastest transatlantic steamers, for example, a ship of at least 11,000 tons costing $4,000,000 would have to be constructed, and such a vessel lay far beyond the intentions of Congress.[42]

While Chandler had consistently sought more in the way of naval progress than Congress would fund, he was nevertheless proud of the four ships in his charge. In 1884, he wrote of the three cruisers, "No armed merchant steamer could withstand them, and they are capable of overtaking ninety-six per cent of the merchant steamers of the world." They were "of moderate size and cost, well protected, handy, and heavily armed—useful and important parts of a modern naval force."[43]

The ships that were financed, planned, and partially constructed with the administration's encouragement would later be called "tangible evidence of the physical rebirth of American naval power."[44] The first painful steps in the transition from wood to steel ships paved the way for more impressive efforts in the near future. During the next four years alone, thirty new vessels were authorized with an aggregate displacement of nearly 100,000 tons.

It would be many decades, however, before the Arthur Administration would receive the applause historians now bestow. The publicity generated by Chandler and the ABCD ships was largely negative. Democrats and Independents were relentless in their charges of extravagance and corruption. In early 1884, the Chicago *Tribune* published a nine-column "exposé" of what it described as "Our useless Navy" and "Our Pinafore Navy." Wayne MacVeagh declared in *Century Magazine* that if a good President were elected in 1884, "His Secretary of the Navy would cleanse that Department of its rottenness . . ."[45] Not one of the five men who gave speeches on behalf of Arthur's nomination at the Republican National Convention alluded to the new navy.

Hail to the Chief

DURING 1883 and 1884, references to the President in the press did not always focus upon politics and affairs of state. Arthur continued to preside over the pleasures of the winter social seasons, hosting one lavish banquet, reception, and ball after another that won the adulation of all who attended. He and his sister were considered successful at arranging both large and small festivities. Public receptions were especially popular. At one the throng was so huge that General Sheridan and his wife had to enter the White House through a window. To get to the Blue Room the President had to work his way through some 3,000 lady admirers.[1] The composition of the crowds on such occasions was unpredictable. Six Flathead Indian chiefs in full native costume made an appearance in February 1884, and were observed busily fanning themselves with feathered headdresses.[2]

The President's state banquets were frequently in the news, even those of a more intimate nature. In early 1884, he set a precedent by giving a dinner for thirty-seven Congressmen who were bachelors or widowers or who were living in Washington for a time unaccompanied by their wives.[3] *The New York Times* editorialized a few days later, "The art of dining and party-giving has made so much progress of late years that it might fairly be said that nothing festal in the older times could at all compare with the beauty and brilliancy of the entertainments given in the Executive Mansion during the past Winter." It concluded, "What we may call the official hospitality of President Arthur's Administration is without a flaw."[4]

The Chief Executive's attendance at an opera could not go unnoticed. During one performance of *La Traviata* Arthur entered midway through the first act, accompanied by his daughter and a niece, May McElroy. Mme. Patti, the leading lady, abruptly stopped singing, gave a nod to the conductor, and the orchestra broke into "Hail to the Chief." Moments later the hall was filled with applause. Arthur rose, bowing graciously to the artists and to the audience. All thought it a splendid scene.[5]

The President's appearance at a wedding, of course, gave great prestige to the event and always drew attention. Blaine's eldest daughter, Alice, was married on February 6, 1883, and Arthur and his entire Cabinet were present. The service and the banquet that followed were fashionably gaudy and sumptuous, the source of great pride to Mrs. Blaine. Arthur was the first to salute the bride, and he personally escorted her to the dining room. One observer would recall that "the wedding surpassed any similar festal scene ever witnessed at Washington . . ."[6] That evening, Arthur, his children, the McElroys, members of the Cabinet, Justices of the Supreme Court, and other dignitaries attended the wedding of Benjamin Brewster's stepdaughter.[7]

A few weeks later Arthur attended the wedding of Colorado Senator Horace A. W. Tabor and Elizabeth Nellis McCourt Doe of Oshkosh, Wisconsin. Fifty-two-year-old "Hod" Tabor had been a grocer during the Colorado silver rush of the 1870s, and, by grubstaking two prospectors, had acquired an interest in a fabulously rich mine in Leadville. Once a millionaire, Tabor lost interest in his austere New England wife and struck up an affair with a beautiful divorcee in her late twenties known as "Baby Doe." Tabor secured a divorce secretly, and in September 1882, he and his paramour were quietly married in a civil ceremony conducted by a friend in St. Louis.

Tabor was politically ambitious, and largely because of his wealth was named to fill out the remaining thirty days of a vacant senatorial term. On the day he took the oath of office he vowed to his new wife that they would enjoy a proper religious marriage ceremony before his term expired. "If all goes well," he wrote, "you'll have both a priest and a president at your ceremony."

The Roman Catholic service was held in Washington's Willard Hotel on March 1, 1883. The President, Interior Secretary Teller, ten Senators, and six Representatives were in attendance. No wives were present, as word of the previous marriage ceremony had leaked out. (Teller later wrote to a friend, "I humiliated myself to attend [Tabor's] wedding because he was a Senator from Colorado . . .") The enormous room was decorated for supper. The centerpiece was six feet high, featuring a wedding bell of white roses, topped by a heart of red roses pierced by an arrow of violets that was contained in a Cupid's bow of heliotrope.

At either end of the long table stood a colossal four-leaf clover made of roses, camellias, and violets, garlanded with smilax. Baby Doe wore a $7,000 gown of virginal white and carried a bouquet of white roses. (Tabor had ordered her a $75,000 diamond necklace, reportedly part of the jewels pawned by Queen Isabella to outfit Columbus for his voyage to the New World. It failed to arrive on time.) Her relatives, mourning a deceased member of the family, arrived in black. Tabor embellished their drab apparel with elaborate diamond and onyx ornaments.

At the conclusion of the nuptial mass, the President stepped forth to offer his felicitations. "I have never seen a more beautiful bride," he said, taking the young woman's hand. "May I not beg a rose from your bouquet?"

The next day the officiating priest, pastor of one of the city's wealthiest churches, was shocked to learn of the divorces and the St. Louis wedding, and stated publicly that he had been duped by Baby Doe's father. *The New York Times* observed in a front-page story, "The prominence and great wealth of the bridegroom, the fact that President Arthur was present during the ceremony, and the character of St. Matthew's Church have made the matter one of the sensations of the day." Secretary Teller soon confided to an intimate, "Tabor has gone home, I thank God he was not elected for six years; thirty days nearly killed us . . ."[8]

The gaiety of the administration's first full social season was sobered by the death of Edwin D. Morgan on February 14, 1883. Arthur had been his close friend for more than twenty years, and despite the disappointment over Morgan's refusal to serve in the Cabinet, he had continued to revere the wartime governor and pay his respects whenever possible.[9]

Postmaster General Timothy Howe died unexpectedly on March 25 at the age of sixty-seven. The President was acutely grieved by the loss of his good friend. "Poor Arthur," Mrs. Blaine wrote privately, "he will find the Presidency more grewsome with a favorite cabinet minister gone!" Following a visit to Mrs. Haynesworth, she reported, "The White House itself is an abode of gloom."[10]

Howe's portfolio was accepted by fifty-one-year-old Walter Q. Gresham, a federal judge from Indiana with a highly distinguished Civil War record. Benjamin Harrison had wired the President asking that his state be awarded the Cabinet post. Arthur shocked Indiana Republicans by naming Gresham, a man of somewhat independent mind who had spurned two powerful political positions offered by President Grant and had supported Benjamin Bristow for the GOP presidential nomination in 1876. The selection was based on Arthur's personal admiration for Gresham and was well received by reformers.[11]

Another long-time confidant and political ally, Treasury Secretary Charles Folger, died on September 4, 1884. Since his humiliating defeat nearly two years earlier, Folger had become something of a recluse, was frequently ill, and suffered spells of severe depression. A friend would remember him in his last years as "one of the most sadly degenerated men I ever saw."[12]

Folger's post, late in the life of the administration, did not appeal to many ambitious men, and Arthur had difficulty finding a suitable candidate. While awaiting a reply to one offer, he was compelled by law to name someone, and he selected Gresham, already determined to leave the Cabinet for a seat on the United States Circuit Court.[13] Within a few weeks Gresham again became a judge and the Treasury position was given to seventy-five-year-old Hugh McColloch of Maryland, a former comptroller of the currency and Secretary of the Treasury from 1865 to 1869.[14] The Postmaster General's portfolio devolved upon thirty-eight-year-old Frank Hatton of Iowa, the aggressive Stalwart who had served for three years as first assistant postmaster general. Hatton's stop-gap appointment made him the youngest Cabinet member since the days of Alexander Hamilton.[15]

Perhaps as painful to Arthur as the demise of his Stalwart colleagues was the break, in March 1883, with Congressman Richard Crowley, a close friend since the war. Crowley had introduced a bill in Congress in December 1881, calling for permission to construct a cantilever railroad bridge across the Niagara River to Canada. The bill, backed by William H. Vanderbilt, failed to pass, and Crowley turned to Arthur for assistance, as the Canadian government requested consent by either Congress or the President. At first, Arthur was agreeable, and promised to bestow his approval. But when Attorney General Brewster advised against the move, he changed his mind. Crowley was furious and demanded an interview with the President. He called four times in one day at the White House but without success. Within a short time, Arthur attempted to patch up the friendship, but the damage was beyond repair. The New York Congressman permanently severed relations with the President.[16] Crowley was the last of the Stalwart leaders to believe that Arthur could be used. Roscoe Conkling was said to have sneered, "I have but one annoyance with the Administration of President Arthur, and that is that, in contrast with it, the Administration of Hayes becomes respectable, if not heroic."[17]

By March 1883, the President's physical condition was deteriorating seriously. From a statement made three years later by a personal physician, it seems clear that Arthur was suffering from hypertensive heart disease brought on by the high blood pressure associated with his kidney ailment. Moreover, the nausea produced by what is now called glomerulonephritis left him at times weak and enervated.[18] Arthur made occasional fishing trips and enjoyed brief excursions on the presidential steamer to improve his health. Almost daily he took short horseback rides and walks to shed the tensions of his office. But at the conclusion of the congressional session and the social season of 1883, he decided to seek peace and quiet outside the nation's capital, and announced plans for a vacation trip to central Florida. The White House officially described the President as suffering from a cold.[19]

By the early 1880s a winter visit to Florida had become almost as fashionable for wealthy New Yorkers as a summer trip to Europe. One newspaper editor returned from an excursion to the area in 1883 and reported it swarming with opulent northerners.[20] Several northern entrepreneurs were buying land and constructing plantations and cities in Florida, and invitations from a few such men first interested the President in a journey to the state.

The President's entourage included Navy Secretary Chandler, a guide to southern politicians, Charles E. Miller, a friend from New York City, and his personal secretary, chef, and valet. Four reporters were reluctantly given permission to tag along. The party left Washington on April 5 by fast mail train. Arthur's private car, placed at his disposal by the Pennsylvania Railroad Company, contained a richly furnished parlor, dining room, state room, pantry, and small kitchen.[21] Three of his late wife's favorite cousins, Mr. and Mrs. Henry T. Botts and Captain George A. Mercer, boarded the train at Savannah before it sped toward Jacksonville.

The trip was hot and dusty, and by the time the party reached Waycross, Georgia, M. Cupplinger, the French chef Arthur had brought with him to the White House from New York, was covered with grime. "Dis is a tretful drip," he complained to an amused reporter. "I have poot on tree shirts dees tay. Ven I poot on vun, in fife minute it look like I sweep de shimney." When the passengers stepped off the train at Folkston, a short time later, it was noticed that Secretary Chandler was darkened by layers of Georgia soil. Minor delays added to the discomfort of the journey. At one point a broken coupling left the President's car stranded for two hours in the countryside.

A cheering crowd and sweltering ninety-degree weather welcomed the train at Jacksonville on the evening of April 6. The mayor and a Republican Congressman from Florida were on hand to extend greetings. The Jacksonville Light Infantry, the Florida Light Artillery, and the Negro Infantry were in formation and fired a twenty-one-gun salute. Arthur gave a brief speech of appreciation in which he said, "I recognize, in this demonstration your respect for the chief magistrate of the Nation and your loyalty to the Federal authority which he represents." A Negro representative greeted him not only as chief magistrate but as a "life long friend."

The party hastily boarded a steamer which headed south up the beautiful St. Johns River. At times the shores were lit with fireworks displays and bonfires; cannons fired salutes welcoming the travelers. At Green Cove Springs, Arthur chatted with Daniel G. Tyler, his private secretary during the war. At Palatka, Mrs. George A. Mercer and two young girls joined the party. Arthur slept aboard ship, trying unsuccessfully to fit his six-foot-two-inch frame comfortably into a five-foot-eight-inch berth.

At noon the next day the ship docked at Enterprise. Scores of Negroes streamed to the dock to catch a glimpse of Arthur. One made his way on board carrying a young eagle he had brought thirty-five miles as a gift for the President. When Arthur was assured it would grow up to have a bald head and white tail, he suggested smilingly that it be put in the charge of the Navy Secretary as a reminder of the national emblem.

A short time later the ship anchored at Sanford, and the party took carriages to the Belaire orange plantation owned by Henry S. Sanford, a former minister to Belgium. En route, Chandler could not resist the temptation to scamper up a tree to pick prize examples of the local fruit. At the Sanford House six Negro boys entertained the guests with singing and dancing. In a little room off the hall M. Cupplinger packed traps to be taken shortly up the Kissimmee River. Already shocked by the sight of an alligator on the St. Johns, he now pondered stories he had heard of insects and vicious Seminole Indians. "I vish tomorrow it may rain all tay like it do now," he said. "Den de boss he not go. I like not dem inseck. I vish I vas pack at de Vite House."

Arthur too was beginning to doubt the wisdom of his journey. He was exhausted from the travel and prostrated by the intense heat. His health was worse than it had been in Washington. He grew increasingly irritable on Sunday, April 8, and by Monday was described by a reporter as "savage and dangerous."

On Monday morning the party left Sanford for Kissimmee City. A stop was made at Maitland, and the travelers went by buckboard to

Winter Park. Chandler and a lady seated beside him were thrown out backward when the buckboard hit a dip in the road. The lady was unhurt, but Chandler was stunned momentarily and severely wrenched his back. He soon made light of the incident, saying that as he had no backbone to spare it was unfortunate that an accident should occur to it. At Winter Park the party boarded a train bound for Orlando. It was another intensely hot day. Arrangements had been made to welcome the President in Orlando, but Arthur, ill and irritable, had seen enough of crowds and agreed only to appear on the platform. When the train stopped instead of merely slowing down, Arthur quickly reentered his car with a look of "intense" anger.

The travelers reached the tiny hamlet of Kissimmee at noon, and the President and his male companions boarded the *Okeechobee* and steamed into Lake Tohopekaliga. Camp was soon set up on the Kissimmee River, twenty miles south of the town and the nearest telegraph office. Arthur quickly caught five ten-pound trout, and Fred Phillips shot an alligator. Chandler's diary entry for the day reported "Fishing—mosquitos." The area swarmed with insects to such an extent that the party decided to cut the visit short. At one point in his journey, perhaps here along the Kissimmee, Arthur became infected with malaria, a disease that would compound his physical misery during the few remaining years of his life.[22]

That evening the campers visited nearby Fort Gardiner, where they unexpectedly met Tom Tigertail, a gaily dressed sub-chief of the Seminoles, accompanied by his mother, two wives, and a child. Arthur shook hands with the chief and offered him a cigar. Tigertail eagerly accepted the gift, lighting it with a burning cigar snatched from the President's mouth. Arthur gave the child a quarter, and Chandler made a present of his pocketknife to the chief. The Seminoles promised the Chief Executive a special tribal dance if he would journey farther south, but the offer was politely declined. Reporters had already described the President as having "reached the end of civilization."

On Friday the travelers departed down the St. Johns to Tocol, where they took a train to nearby St. Augustine. The reception committee at the station was headed by General Fred Dent, Grant's brother-in-law. Arthur decided to relax a few days in the historic city and then travel to Savannah by ship and return North by rail. The four days in St. Augustine were the most pleasant of the trip. The weather was cool and the pace of life slow. Arthur enjoyed a large amount of personal freedom, and strolled the streets alone studying buildings and looking in shop windows. That Sunday he attended services in an Episcopal church, the old Spanish cathedral, and a Negro Methodist church.

Early Wednesday morning the President and his party boarded the *Tallapoosa*. After a rough voyage the ship docked the next morning at Savannah. Arthur took a long drive in the hot sun in an open carriage and stopped at a park to attend a rifle-shooting contest. Lunch was "Savannah shrimp salad," and Arthur ate heartily. Returning to the city, he was again exposed to the sun. A long reception followed, during which he shook hundreds of hands. After dinner that evening at the home of Mr. Botts, Arthur and his party returned to the *Tallapoosa* about midnight.[23]

About 2:30 A.M. the guard at the President's cabin heard a cry for a servant. Alec Powell was hastily summoned and discovered the President in agony. Dr. Black, the ship's surgeon, was routed out of bed and soon feared the Chief Executive near death. Between his paroxysms of pain, Arthur confessed to the physician "something which no one but himself and one or two of his immediate friends had any knowledge of." Dr. Black recalled many years later, "Then he said that certainly functional and probably organic disease of the kidneys had attacked him. I was satisfied that this statement was correct, for some of the symptoms of the acute indigestion were those that are frequently observed when attacks of that kind are associated with Bright's Disease."[24] Two hours later, after constant application of hot towels to his body, Arthur began to show slight improvement and was given a mild sedative to enable him to rest.

By noon the next day Arthur was still unable to swallow coffee. That evening he managed to dress and appear on deck, and a reporter thought him "washed out" and looking "far from well." He spent a bad night and was said to be extremely weak. Further sea travel was out of the question, and Arthur expressed the desire to return to Washington immediately.[25]

News of the President's misery exploded across the nation's front pages. *The New York Times* described the illness as "sudden and violent," and stated that at one point it "gave the Secretary of the Navy and the other members of the party serious concern." Dr. Black, sworn to secrecy about his patient's kidney ailment, told reporters that the President was suffering from overexposure to the sun and indigestion caused by seasickness. This explanation seemed reasonable in light of Arthur's recent movements, and reporters found it acceptable. Their concern remained intense, however, for when the President appeared at the Savannah railroad station on Saturday morning, April 21, to start the journey home, he appeared "feeble," "very ill," "feverish and irritable."[26]

While awaiting his private car at the station, Arthur was angered to learn for the first time that his illness had become public knowledge.

Upon inquiry, Chandler admitted that he had given reporters the information. The President then learned that Fred Phillips had failed to tell him of numerous telegrams inquiring anxiously about his physical condition.[27]

Arthur was firmly intent on concealing the facts of his deteriorating health, and only a very few intimates were ever taken into his confidence while he inhabited the White House. Even later, when bedridden and approaching death, he would talk optimistically about his recovery and chat with guests about future plans. The explanation lies in his extraordinary pride and fortitude. To Arthur it was undignified and unmanly to burden others with one's personal pain; adversity was to be suffered privately. He refused to be the object of sympathy or pity. As one account put it later, "He could not bear to have his friends or the public know that the strong man whom they knew in health was slowly fading away, and even after the first reports of his serious illness had been published there were many who failed to realize its solemn import, so difficult was it to get any confirmation of the sad news."[28]

The President arrived in Washington on the evening of April 22 and was greeted by his son, Attorney General Brewster, a battery of reporters, and a crowd of several hundred. He appeared healthy, and told a friend, "I am feeling perfectly well, as well as ever, in fact. I have not been sick at all." He had suffered a slight indisposition that lasted only a few hours, he said, and it was nothing worth mentioning.[29] On reaching the White House steps, he exclaimed, "I was never better in my life." He was also heard to complain about the elastic imaginations of newspapermen.[30]

When interviewed by reporters, Chandler vigorously denied reports of the President's severe illness. He criticized "sensational dispatches," and echoed Arthur's reference to a "slight indisposition," which he attributed to "a long ride in the hot sun." Fred Phillips said reports of the President's ill health were greatly exaggerated by journalists. The Chief Executive had been bothered by a slight attack of indigestion on Thursday evening, he stated, and no one was aware of it until the next morning.[31]

A month later Arthur traveled to New York City for the opening of the Brooklyn Bridge. It was a day local residents had eagerly awaited for fourteen years, and hundreds of thousands turned out in lovely weather to see and cheer the dignitaries, military regiments, and marching bands. So many ships appeared in the East River that a reporter called it "an aqueous Broadway." Some 900 city policemen were on hand to handle the crowds, and 150 of them surrounded the Fifth Avenue Hotel following the arrival of the President, his son, Secretaries Frelinghuysen, Folger, Chandler, and Gresham, and Governor Grover Cleveland.

According to the New York *Herald,* Arthur suffered a stomach disorder on the morning of the ceremony, which gave "an unaccustomed pallor to his lips and cheeks." But he was in good spirits and appeared delighted by the warm reception he received. He told a friend, "There's no place like New York." The hostility that had surrounded his journey to the state shortly before the Folger-Cleveland election seemed to have evaporated.

The President and New York City Mayor Franklin Edson emerged from the hotel arm in arm in the early afternoon of May 24 and entered the first of twenty-five carriages lined up for the procession to the bridge. From the open carriage Arthur tipped his tall black beaver hat repeatedly to acknowledge the thunderous cheering of the throng. The carriages stopped at City Hall, and the dignitaries, led by the President, walked to the bridge and started across. At the New York tower, cannons were fired from Governor's Island. When the Brooklyn tower was reached, Mayor Seth Low greeted the party and shook Arthur's hand. Ships in the East River fired guns, blew whistles, and jangled chimes, while a band blared "Hail to the Chief" and thousands of spectators roared their approval. Speeches were given in a nearby Brooklyn railway station, and then the President paid his respects to Washington A. Roebling, the engineer who had supervised the construction of the mammoth suspension bridge, and whose father had drawn its plans. That evening the electric lights across the bridge were turned off, and the public was treated to a gigantic display of fireworks. "The middle of the bridge looked like the crator of a belching volcano," wrote a spectator.[32]

Arthur remained in the Fifth Avenue Hotel for a week to recover his strength. After returning to Washington he retired to the Soldiers' Home for further rest. He began to delay his appearances at the White House until noon. On Cabinet days he would not arrive until 1:00 P.M. Anti-administration newspapers began to complain regularly of "the shadow of repose that has come over the Government business."[33]

In early July, Arthur returned briefly to New York. He gave orders before leaving Washington that he would receive no callers. When the train arrived at Jersey City, he professed himself too fatigued to talk with anyone, and hurried to a waiting carriage.[34]

On July 23, Arthur and his daughter spent the day at the resort city of Cape May, New Jersey. There was little opportunity for relaxation, however, as crowds, troops, bands, and reporters hovered close to the President wherever he turned. Newspapers were full of stories of an unprecedented presidential visit to Yellowstone National Park, and

Democrats had blasted the move as entailing extravagant costs and exemplifying Arthur's inattention to duty. A reporter asked, "Will your Western trip form a portion of your vacation?" Not quite himself, Arthur snapped, "Vacation, eh? That is the way all the newspapers talk. They speak of my journeys as junketings. I need a holiday as much as the poorest of my fellow citizens; but it is generally supposed that we people at Washington do not want any rest."[35]

Since 1870, when the area was explored extensively, Yellowstone had welcomed many travelers. Into its splendors had come, among others, Secretary of War W. W. Belknap, Generals William T. Sherman and O. O. Howard, and Carl Schurz. General Philip H. Sheridan, whose military jurisdiction encompassed the park, led sizable parties through the area in 1881 and 1882. And in late July 1883, Roscoe Conkling and a party of friends were scheduled to leave for a tour of the Yellowstone country. The completion of the Northern Pacific Railroad to Bozeman now opened the area to the world, and the future of the nation's first national park was the cause of widespread concern.

In a much-publicized report to the War Department in late 1882, General Sheridan had warned against the leasing of park lands to private corporations, eager to grab game, minerals, and grazing land, and to reap profits from the anticipated swell of tourists. Governor John Schuyler Crosby of Montana urged shortly that the park be made into "an asylum for the great game of the Northwest." In early 1883, George Bird Grinnell, editor of the journal *Forest and Stream*, began a barrage of editorials calling for the preservation and expansion of the park exclusively for the public. A struggle of considerable significance to the American people was building in Congress over the future of Yellowstone, and conservationists were noting the presence of an unusually vigorous and wealthy band of lobbyists for special interests.

Senator George G. Vest of Missouri waged a tireless campaign to preserve the park. In March 1883, he successfully defended amendments to the Sundry Civil Appropriation Bill which increased funds for the park's protection and improvement, and sharply restricted leasing rights. Still at issue, however, were General Sheridan's suspicions about incompetence and corruption within the park's civil administration, and a proposal to enlarge the preserve. Few believed that corporate greed had been entirely quelled by Senator Vest's recent efforts.

As early as January 22, Senator Vest had suggested that he and General Sheridan conduct a tour that summer through Yellowstone for a party of dignitaries, including President Arthur. It is highly probable that he sought to generate support for his vision of the park's protection.

As his friend Grinnell editorialized, "The important point of the excursion will be that members of the Government, whose influence should be strongest in shaping legislation on this important subject, will be able to see for themselves a part of the needs of the Nation in respect to the Yellowstone Park."[36]

The administration had shown a lively interest in the West. Interior Secretary Teller repeatedly called for repeal of the timber culture and preemption laws and urged revision of the homestead laws to protect settlers from speculators. He often overruled decisions by the land commissioner in cases where he felt settlers had not received justice. He opposed the fencing of public lands by cattlemen—a common practice in Colorado—and publicly advised homesteaders to cut such barriers when they were encountered. Arthur was especially interested in preserving the forests on the public domain, and in three messages called for appropriate legislation. In 1882, he wrote, "The condition of the forests of the country and the wasteful manner in which their destruction is taking place give cause for serious apprehension."[37]

The administration's approach to what was often called the "Indian Problem" was generally well received. Since 1880, public sentiment had taken a sharp turn in favor of justice toward the nation's quarter of a million Indians. In part this was due to the fiery personality of Carl Schurz, Hayes's reform-minded Secretary of the Interior. Americans were becoming increasingly concerned about frauds against the Indian and encroachment upon his land, and the dramatic story of the Ponca Indian removal touched the hearts of thousands. Organizations like the Women's National Indian Association and the Indian Rights Association began to prosper during the Arthur years and make their views known in Congress. Beyond simple justice, reformers sought Indian assimilation, the transformation of savage warriors into civilized, peaceable farmers tilling their own soil. This meant, of course, the abandonment of Indian culture and the destruction of tribal land ownership, but at the time such steps were thought benevolent and enlightened. On the whole, the Arthur Administration's position on the subject reflected the "best" public opinion, although Secretary Teller, being a westerner, held a less kindly attitude toward Indians than did the President. Arthur wrote in his first message to Congress, "For the success of the efforts now making to introduce among the Indians the customs and pursuit of civilized life and gradually to absorb them into the mass of our citizens, sharing their rights and holden to their responsibilities, there is imperative need for legislative action."

Arthur and Teller strongly stressed the need for more Indian schools. Teller was more concerned with vocational education than the President and proposed that graduates of manual labor schools be given livestock and farm equipment. He sought to create a permanent school fund out of proceeds from the sale of public lands, and submitted a plan by which five or six million dollars a year would be devoted to the purpose annually. While unwilling to go that far, Congress boosted appropriations for Indian education considerably. By 1884, the federal government operated eighty-one boarding schools, seventy-six day schools, and six industrial schools. Greater strides in this direction would be taken as the century progressed.

Teller did not accept the currently popular principle of allotment in severalty, but Arthur saw wisdom in it and called repeatedly for a law permitting individual land ownership by Indians. "Many of them realize the fact that their hunting days are over and that it is now for their best interests to conform their manner of life to the new order of things. By no greater inducement than the assurance of permanent title to the soil can they be led to engage in the occupation of tilling it." Both political parties had already supported a bill extending severalty to the Utes of Colorado, and in Cleveland's first term the Dawes Severalty Act would divide tribal land and attempt, with tragic results, to force Indians to "conform."

Both the President and the secretary sought an oft-requested act extending state and territorial laws to Indian reservations. "The Indian should receive the protection of the law," wrote Arthur. "He should be allowed to maintain in court his rights of person and property. He has repeatedly begged for this privilege." Teller created an interesting piece of legal machinery called the Court of Indian Offenses, by which Indians themselves handled breaches of rules connected with certain "heathen" tribal ceremonies and customs.

The administration made several attempts to protect Indian land from encroachment. It resisted pressure from Congress to open up portions of Indian Territory to settlers, and Arthur and Teller requested an increased penalty for those convicted of intruding in the area. An executive order preserved Zuni land from relatives of Senator Logan. But in early 1885, the President was severely criticized by reformers for opening the Crow Creek Reservation in Dakota Territory to settlement. Teller, always eager to see surplus Indian soil available to homesteaders, had persuaded Arthur that the tribe did not hold title to the land. An investigation proved the secretary wrong, and the order was revoked by Cleveland shortly after he took office.

Some church groups were critical of Teller for appointing Indian agents without regard for their religious affiliations, ending the questionable practice of naming missionaries. Others found fault in what they called the secretary's "absurd policy" toward leases of surplus land in Indian Territory by cattlemen. Teller thought the rental rates too low and sought power to regulate them. When he failed to receive such authority from Congress, he declared that the department would not recognize or enforce the leasing agreements, and threatened to terminate them under certain circumstances. The result was chaos.

Still, the administration's western policies had more defenders than detractors. Senator Hoar thought Teller's first annual report the best of its kind in over two decades. Helen Hunt Jackson, whose books *A Century of Dishonor* (1881) and *Ramona* (1884) vividly portrayed injustices suffered by Indians, was Teller's close friend and supporter.[38]

However concerned Arthur may have been with the administration's western record, his major reason for accepting the invitation to travel to Yellowstone was the poor condition of his health. Plans for the trip, drawn up almost entirely by General Sheridan, were designed to assure the President a maximum of the rest and relaxation he desperately needed to recover a measure of his strength.

The framework of the plans was shared with Senator Vest in early April. A party of ten would start out from Chicago on August 1 and travel to Rawlins, Wyoming, and from there go by spring wagons to Fort Washakie, on the Shoshone Reservation. Thereafter, for 350 miles, the participants would travel by horseback. The distance to the Upper Geyser Basin, wrote Sheridan, "will be made in easy marches and we will encamp on a trout stream every day, and those who want to hunt, after two or three days out, will find plenty of game. This will probably be the most interesting part of the trip. From the Upper Geyser Basin we will go to the Lower Geyser Basin, and then to Fort Ellis, returning home by the Northern Pacific Railroad." The trip would be semi-official, several duties in connection with Indian affairs being pursued during and after the excursion. But the emphasis would be on pleasure: the President and his party were to enjoy Yellowstone as thoroughly as possible. "On your return, my dear Senator," Sheridan wrote to Vest, "I am sure you will feel as if your longevity has been increased 20 years."

Sheridan sought to limit the party to ten for reasons of supply and transportation. Arthur invited an old friend, Daniel G. Rollins, surrogate of New York; Sheridan selected his brother, Lieutenant Colonel Michael V. Sheridan, Lieutenant Colonel James F. Gregory, Captain Philo Clark of the Second Cavalry, and Brigadier General Anson Stager, a late replacement for Senator John A. Logan. Also included were Secretary of War Lincoln, Montana Governor Crosby, and Senator Vest. Traveling with the party was a physician, Major W. H. Forwood, and a photographer, Frank Jay Haynes. Several newspapers vied to send representatives, but no reporters were allowed at the private request of the President. Most of the Associated Press accounts of the trip were written by Lieutenant Colonels Sheridan and Gregory, and all were approved prior to release by Arthur.

Sheridan ordered seventy-five men from Troop G, Fifth Cavalry, to accompany the travelers. From Cheyenne Depot, Wyoming, and Fort Custer a total of 175 pack animals was ordered to Fort Washakie, later prompting the historian Hiram Chittenden to call it "one of the most complete pack trains ever organized in this or any other country." An elaborate courier system was devised to enable the President to keep in touch with the outside world.[39]

Arthur left Washington for the West on the morning of July 30. Two days later, in Louisville, Kentucky, he participated in ceremonies opening the Southern Cotton Exposition. The crowds were huge and enthusiastic, and attempts at seclusion proved fruitless. A correspondent noted, "The President is wearied with too much welcome, and says he will be glad when he gets into the mountains, although his visit here has been one of pleasure."[40]

The next morning the train headed across Indiana. Its engine was decorated with flags and bore a huge picture of the President. Arthur and his party enjoyed the luxury of George Pullman's private car. Several stops were made along the way. At Greencastle Arthur shook hands with a few spectators, and the rush to reach the President became so great that the welcoming platform collapsed. At Lafayette he kissed a baby thrust at him by a persistent mother and received a handsome gift from the Negro citizens of the city bearing a plaque thanking him for his devotion to "justice to an oppressed people."[41]

In Chicago a reporter thought him thinner, grayer, and somewhat older than he had seemed at the Republican National Convention. His voice was described as "mellifluous," and his courtesy and tact drew detailed attention. Both Arthur and Secretary Lincoln were annoyed by aggressive Chicago newspapermen. Arthur spoke with them briefly on an assortment of topics, but protested at one point, "Ah, you really must excuse me. I make it a habit not to talk politics with you gentlemen of the press. When I have anything to say to the country I shall probably say it in black and white. By the way, I hope you are not interviewing me—I believe that is the word—or intending to quote what I have been saying. Do you know, I dislike very much to open a newspaper in the morning and find a column or so of a conversation in which I have taken part the day before." His words appeared the next morning in the Chicago *Tribune* under the headline "A Chat with Chet." Just before the party was set to leave, a reporter complained to Robert Lincoln, "It is easier for a man to get a post-office in Indiana than it is for a reporter to get on that train." Lincoln replied, "If one does get on he will be dropped through the trestle-work of the first bridge we reach."[42]

On the evening of August 4, the presidential train arrived at Cheyenne, Wyoming, where the President, Secretary Lincoln, and Senator Vest said a few words of greeting. The party reached Green River the following morning and spent the remainder of the Sunday relaxing aboard the train.

The next day, three mule-drawn spring wagons took the party to the banks of the Sweetwater. During the last forty-five miles of the trip the President moved outside next to the driver.

Fort Washakie was reached the following day, where the party prepared for the long journey by horseback. Shoshone and Arapahoe chiefs called upon the President, and shortly some 500 warriors staged a sham battle for his pleasure. Chief Washakie of the Shoshones and Black Coal, Chief of the Arapahoes, then responded to a presidential greeting with thanks and avowals to live in peace with the whites, "adopting as fully and as rapidly as possible their customs and manners of life." Arthur was then presented with a pony for his daughter, a war dance followed, and the festivities were concluded with an exhibition drill by troops from the Fifth Cavalry, who had met the party at the fort.

At 7:00 A.M. on August 9 the party started out on horseback, the escort and pack mules following, northwest into the Wind River Valley. For the next three weeks the President and his companions enjoyed the sparkling air, clear streams, and magnificent scenery of the Yellowstone country. The Continental Divide was crossed three times, and camp was set up once at a point 9,000 feet above sea level. Temperatures often fell below freezing during the night. The daily regimen of the travelers prompted Arthur to alter his habits considerably. The men arose at five and at six were in the saddle. They rode until afternoon and then camped beside a stream, hiking, hunting, and fishing for the remainder of the day. Arthur proved to be an able horseman and retained his reputation as a skilled angler. On the 23rd, at the edge of the National Park, he and Vest caught 105 pounds of fish! The young newspaper columnist Eugene Field soon published a playful poem in which a frustrated Shoshone chief vowed to move farther west to escape Presidents who threatened to spoil the local fishing.[43]

The end of the 350-mile march was reached on August 31, when the party arrived at the park hotel at Mammoth Hot Springs. The President was in high spirits; one reporter quoted him as calling the journey "better than anything I ever tried before."[44] He professed annoyance, however, at stories of the trip fabricated by the Chicago *Tribune*. Among other things, the *Tribune* reported a rendezvous between Arthur and Secretary Teller, and it spent several days describing details of a plot by cowboys to kidnap the President and hold him for ransom.[45]

On September 1, Arthur traveled by spring coach seven miles to the train that would take him to Livingston, on the main line of the Northern Pacific. Two days later he appeared with General Grant and other dignitaries at festivities in St. Paul celebrating the completion of the Northern Pacific's east-west hookup.[46] On September 4, he was again in Chicago, where a reporter observed, "He is looking better even than when he passed through this City en route to the West. His face is tanned, and he says he feels invigorated."[47]

At a public reception the following evening, some 10,000 people paid their respects to the Chief Executive. The pace was terrific: 350 filed by him in five minutes. On his feet for hours, shaking thousands of hands and bowing when the strength in his arms failed, Arthur was soon totally exhausted.[48] Vacations to the Everglades, the Grand Tetons, even to the Soldiers' Home were ephemeral flights offering illusory benefits. The presidency, he could not fail to realize, was hastening his end. The highest office in the land, a position men like Blaine would give almost anything to possess, was his curse.

Arthur might have called a halt to public receptions and banquets and gone into seclusion when he returned to the nation's capital. But this would have constituted a public confession of his illness and signaled his inability to handle the tasks assumed at Garfield's death. Washington would again go into mourning, lamenting the tragedies that followed Republican victory in 1880. The twenty-first President would be remembered merely as a sickly caretaker of the White House, a pitiable misfortune to his party and country. And all to add, at best, a very few years to a life already darkened by the death of his wife and the loss of almost every close friend. The alternative was to carry on as before, filling the executive mansion with lights and laughter and presenting evidence that the Chief Executive was a strong, worthy administrator who deserved the confidence and respect of the American people.

When Arthur arrived in Washington on September 7 he publicly described himself in perfect health. Privately he summoned a personal physician. The doctor found him in great pain, and his badly swollen legs pointed again to the presence of Bright's disease. With treatment the pain subsided and the swelling decreased. But both men understood that the treatment was temporary.[49]

His Turn Has Come

During THE SUMMER of 1883, with Washington quiet and the news relatively uneventful, several newspapers began to poll Republicans about their choices for party standard-bearer in the forthcoming presidential election. In July *The New York Times* published the results of letters sent to over 400 points in the United States. Of forty-three possible candidates mentioned, Blaine led with 103 preferences, Arthur was a poor second with 64, and Senator George Edmunds received 57½. The administration, commented *The Times,* "has unquestionably been more satisfactory to the party in all parts of the Union than was expected." But Arthur's strength stemmed largely from southern officeholders, meaning that his opportunity for winning the election if nominated was exceedingly slim. Of the votes received from all-important New York, Edmunds received 17, Blaine 16, and Arthur 4.[1]

The President's popularity with a broad range of opinion-makers was asserted shortly by the Chicago *Daily News.* To welcome the Chief Executive on his way to Yellowstone, the newspaper devoted fifteen columns to letters received from distinguished men in all sections of the nation evaluating the conduct of the administration. Henry Ward Beecher wrote, "In my opinion President Arthur has proved himself to be a safe man in the administration of government, prudent in counsel, felicitous in all that he has written, wise in the selection of men for office, with remarkable capacity for silence, and yet frank when he speaks. I can hardly imagine how he could have done better, in the very trying circumstances which surrounded his administration." George William Curtis thought that Arthur's "pacific and temperate administration has gained the general approval of the country." Mark Twain added, "I am but one in the 55,000,000; still, in the opinion of this one-fifty-five millionth of the country's population, it would be hard indeed to better President Arthur's administration. But don't decide till you hear from the rest."[2]

Twain's caution was well advised, for as the year wore on, it became increasingly unlikely that the President could muster the necessary votes in the national convention. A poll of Republican newspaper editors in Wisconsin showed Arthur winning only 11 of 76 votes, trailing a favorite son and Blaine.[3] A prominent New Jersey Republican thought GOP strength had declined 30 percent since 1881, stating, "People look upon this Administration as a sort of summer holiday—a kind of lapse between one man who was elected and another who is going to be elected."[4] In the fall elections, Stalwarts suffered defeat in Ohio, and a careful observer wrote, "The best friends of the President have now but little faith in his selection."[5] Arthur's southern support sagged at the same time, for the Virginia Readjusters were crushed in November following a campaign that featured a bloody race riot in Danville.[6] E. L. Godkin noted that the result in Virginia could "scarcely be said to have added to the President's popular strength." "It is perfectly apparent that the Republican candidate who will be most likely to win next year will be the one who can command the support of the independent voters not only in New York, but in other parts of the country. There has never been any evidence that President Arthur would be that kind of a candidate."[7] In December, a poll taken in New York contended that Arthur could not secure more than half of the state's delegates to the national convention. Tom Platt stated that if Arthur was the GOP candidate he would lose New York by 100,000 votes.[8] A short time later, a poll taken by the Erie, Pennsylvania, *Dispatch* of voters in 400 counties in the states of New York, Pennsylvania, Ohio, Indiana, and Illinois showed Blaine leading Arthur 151 to 20. In New York, Blaine was preferred in 21 counties to Arthur's 8. The President, in fact, was regarded with less favor in New York than in any other state except Pennsylvania.[9]

Blaine had chosen to remain in the public spotlight after leaving the State Department. Instead of returning to Maine, he moved into a plush new home in northwest Washington and entertained frequently. He often expressed his views on domestic and international affairs in the press and before Congress.

Outwardly Blaine and Arthur remained cordial. They tipped hats and smiled when encountering each other at social events, and from time to time they exchanged visits. But a great many observers were convinced that these two cagy, experienced, political professionals were biding their time, waiting for the right moment to dispatch each other into political oblivion. Chauncey Depew said in March 1882, "It is of course perfectly apparent that there is a game of chess being played now for the nomination of 1884." He thought the odds were with Arthur. "He is an adroit, farseeing, and eminently tactful man and with plenty of resources for emergencies. He will make none of those dangerous small mistakes, and he knows better than almost any New York politician how to fight a man politically and keep on good terms with him personally."[10] The Philadelphia *Times* took a different view: "neither time nor circumstance can avert the conflict or change the result. It will overthrow Arthur, and Republicanism must be overthrown to overthrow Blaine."[11]

Blaine was often publicly critical of the administration, attacking especially its course of action in Latin America, the southern strategy, and its tariff policy. He planted stories in the New York *Tribune* denouncing the President in the strongest terms. But there was no response from the White House. Mrs. Blaine (who may have expressed her husband's point of view) looked at Arthur with contempt, writing him off as a boob, a dandy interested merely in fine wines and flowers. As election year approached, many pro-administration men began to have similar thoughts. How could one explain Arthur's curious silence and his unwillingness to employ the powers of his office for personal advantage? The Gresham appointment, for example, was not designed to win friends in Indiana. On his way to Yellowstone, the President avoided many opportunities to reap political gain from his travel across key states.[12]

Stephen Dorsey, on the other hand, remembered Chester Arthur from his days as the "Gentleman Boss" and expressed confidence that he knew what he was doing. Dorsey predicted a virtual sweep of New York delegates to the convention. "One thing is certain, that there will be nothing left undone on the part of himself and friends to secure a solid delegation, and those who underrate his power and his active management will be left behind in the race."[13]

Arthur decided not to bow out of the contest for the Republican nomination, knowing that such a retreat would raise suspicion about his health, cast doubt upon his competence to handle the burdens of the presidency, and carry with it the implication of cowardice—of a record as President that could not bear scrutiny, of a personal fear of defeat at the convention or at the polls.[14] Through a friend, Arthur took the official position that he would welcome the role as standard-bearer and that he hoped to establish a record worthy of the honor.[15] But he realized, along with many other political appraisers, that there was little chance the GOP would turn to him.

In early 1884, Arthur was virtually a President without a party. Each of the GOP's warring factions found him objectionable. As Robert D. Marcus has noted, "The usual ground for coalition in American presidential politics is not a common policy, but a common enemy."[16] Opposition to the Arthur Administration at the time dominated the thoughts of Republican strategists, with results that could not have been predicted four years earlier.

Half-Breeds, of course, were implacable opponents of the President. They had enjoyed a minimum of patronage since Garfield's death and felt they owed Arthur nothing for his willingness to retain Collector Robertson. They were already powerful in New York and Pennsylvania, and their influence was increasing in Illinois and Ohio.

Very few Stalwarts might be counted on to back their former leader; a second Arthur Administration would merely preside over the continuation of their ill fortune. Grant came out for John Logan in late March, and soon described the Arthur Administration as "ad interim," one that had "fewer positively hearty friends than any except Hayes possibly."[17] Tom Platt declared for Blaine, finding Conkling "struck speechless" by the decision.[18] The lordly Roscoe expressed disinterest in politics. Tom Murphy, unemployed and facing bankruptcy, told a reporter sadly that the President had never even invited him to the White House for dinner.[19]

Ironically, Independents distrusted Arthur and were never completely convinced of his sincerity toward civil service reform. Some of them pointed to Silas Burt, others to Jay Hubbell and Mahone. Every presidential appointment was greeted with suspicion. As early as March 1883, Carl Schurz observed that Arthur had failed to please either the machine politicians or their critics. "He literally sat down between two chairs."[20] A year later, E. L. Godkin agreed, writing that the President "has sought to conciliate the bosses and reformers by turns, and has fallen between two stools."[21]

Many Independents were seriously alienated from the administration because of its failure to convict the star route conspirators. Wayne MacVeagh remained convinced that the President bore personal responsibility for the jury verdicts, and in a much-publicized open letter in May he bitterly assailed Arthur's record in state and national politics.[22] *The New York Times* declared, "The Republican Party might as well nominate Dorsey himself at Chicago as to nominate the President to whose complacent toleration of the studied and deliberate mismanagement of the star route trials the men who plundered the Treasury of millions owe their immunity from the punishment they so richly deserved."[23]

As early as February 1884, Independents were buzzing about the candidacy of Vermont's taciturn Senator George Edmunds, thought of by some as a Half-Breed and by others as a Stalwart.[24]

Republicans of all persuasions recalled the landslide defeats of 1882 and doubted that the President was sufficiently popular to reverse them. Arthur's home state was a case in point. *The New York Times* analyzed state voting returns from 1876 through 1882 by counties and concluded, "Mr. Folger was stronger than Mr. Arthur would be."[25] In April, *The Nation* reported, "All the newspapers are devoting much space to demonstrations of the actual strength of the various boom candidates, and all of them agree that Blaine is far in advance of all others . . ."[26]

Despite his popularity and the eagerness of supporters to work on his behalf, Blaine appeared disinterested in the presidential nomination in early 1884. He refused to work for delegates, and asked friends not to make pledges or raise money on his behalf. Perhaps he thought that no Republican could win that year—that the nomination would be a barren honor. His wife believed at one point that he wished only to be Secretary of State again. In May, he urged General William T. Sherman to seek the nomination, suggesting that he sought to be the power behind the throne of another Garfield. On the other hand, Blaine may have been playing coy; followers like Whitelaw Reid were worried that his candidacy might be put forward too early for maximum effect. One could never be entirely certain about the Man from Maine. On February 22, he wrote, "I do not desire or expect the nomination, but I don't intend that man in the White House shall have it." That same month newspapers carried extracts of his forthcoming book *Twenty Years of Congress,* prompting Godkin to regard the advance publication as designed to "fix attention upon Blaine's person and name." A few weeks before the convention, Blaine remarked, "I do not think I shall be nominated, but I am disturbing the calculations of others at an astonishing rate."[27]

Because of the vagueness of Blaine's intentions, his supporters were poorly organized prior to the convention. Half-Breeds writing to Reid for advice and assistance received only encouraging generalities. Nevertheless, Blaine's popularity—and the President's unpopularity—resulted in important gains for Half-Breeds at state conventions in the spring. In Pennsylvania, they won a majority of the delegation.[28] In New York, Arthur men had to strike a bargain with Independents to prevent a Blaine victory, and Half-Breeds came out of the contest with a large minority of the delegates. Stalwart leaders were said to be "mortified" at the President's showing in his own state.[29] In Ohio, Half-Breeds claimed about one half of the delegates. And by mid-May, Logan backers in Illinois were sidling toward Blaine.[30]

On May 22, Blaine authorized forty-three-year-old Stephen B. Elkins to represent him in all matters at the convention. "Steve" Elkins was a somewhat controversial figure who had made a fortune in law, lobbying, railroads, and mining. He had served on the Republican National Committee and in Congress as the territorial representative from New Mexico. He enjoyed political and financial ties with a wide range of Republicans and was considered a skilled wire-puller.[31]

Blaine thus entered the national convention the overwhelming favorite, leading in the polls and commanding solid delegate strength from key states. His forces could boast able, if uninspiring, leadership. The odds were heavy that he could win within six ballots, and his most ardent backers were predicting victory within two.

Almost the only sign of enthusiasm for Blaine's closest rival, the President, came from business leaders. Many of them were attracted by Arthur's conservatism, especially in fiscal matters and foreign policy, and at the same time were concerned about Blaine's "restless, aggressive disposition."[32] A giant rally was held in New York City on May 20, and nearly all of the area's principal merchants, bankers, and professional men were reported solidly behind the President.[33] A delegation of one hundred city businessmen would soon travel to the national convention to lobby for Arthur, prompting opponents to label him the "Wall Street candidate."[34] Chicago business leaders also gave strong evidence of their support.[35] George F. Hoar recalled later that in Massachusetts, "The business men liked Arthur. They thought their interests were safe with him."[36]

Southern officeholders could also be counted on to back the Chief Executive. But GOP politicians were puzzled by Arthur's apparent disregard for this source of strength. In a meeting of the Republican National Committee in January 1883, William Chandler attempted unsuccessfully to push through a new plan of representation in the national convention that would have decreased the relative strength of southern delegations. One veteran observer could only conclude that Chandler, while in Arthur's Cabinet, was somehow an advocate of Blaine.[37] When Mahone went down to defeat that fall he complained bitterly to newsmen, "We got worse than no aid from the Administration."[38]

Arthur, of course, had no intention of making a serious effort for the nomination. Privately, he asked each of his Cabinet members to stay away from the national convention. (Frelinghuysen had been told of the President's physical condition by Arthur's Washington physician and was probably the only Cabinet member at the time who shared the secret.)[39] This dictum included Chandler, who might have been of inestimable assistance. When Chandler was told that he was not to appear in Chicago, he said later, "I was aghast." "Why, Mr. President," he exclaimed, "if you don't let me go as a delegate to the convention you will not have anyone there with practical leadership in national politics to direct the delegates who have been elected to support you. You know enough about politics to know what that would mean." Arthur assured him that he did, adding merely that he did not want to partake of political manipulation—a response that left Chandler "mentally sick."[40]

In late May, Arthur asked to see Frank B. Conger, a young assistant postmaster of Washington, D.C., the son of a Stalwart United States Senator, and an avid Arthur delegate. Conger was requested by the President to abandon efforts on his behalf and to persuade his colleagues to do likewise. "I do not want to be re-elected," Arthur said. "Go to your friends and get them to stop their activities." Conger thought the President excessively modest and politely refused. Arthur invited him to return to the White House after the convention for a chat.[41]

A few days before the convention assembled, Arthur quietly refused an offer of eighteen delegates in return for the Postmaster General's portfolio.[42] One insider was positive that John Logan was eager to make a last-minute deal with the President, but the Illinois Senator got nowhere with his overture.[43] A New Yorker arrived in Chicago with $100,000 in currency, the gift of a single donor to the Arthur campaign. When the President learned of it, he wired instructions to a friend requesting that the money be returned. Arthur men at the convention found themselves with barely enough funds to pay hotel expenses.[44]

The President permitted a few minor gestures on his behalf. His private secretary went to New York to gauge administration support prior to the state convention and traveled to Chicago to distribute campaign literature.[45] The meeting of New York businessmen had administration involvement, and a favorable newspaper account of the rally was mailed to each national convention delegate.[46] But this was hardly the sort of activity Dorsey had predicted.

Frank Hatton and Frank Conger assumed command of the Arthur delegates as they congregated in Chicago. The President quietly created an advisory committee, consisting of three veteran United States Senators, to assist them.[47] Elihu Root, Silas Dutcher, Johnny O'Brien, Steve French, and several other "boys" from what remained of Conkling's city machine were also on hand. But it was quickly obvious that the Arthur leadership was woefully inadequate. Hatton, from a state without a single delegate pledged to the President, seemed particularly inept. Walter Q. Gresham soon wrote, "An army without [an] efficient commander will straggle. Hatton will do for some things, but he was out of place at Chicago; the undertaking was too big for him."[48] Conger was one of two representatives from Washington, D.C.; he quarreled openly with his black colleague and drew derisive laughter from delegates. "The Arthur forces are practically without a good leader, and they sorely need one," a reporter observed. "There is not much good leadership on the Blaine side, but there is not such great need of it."[49]

Despite organizational and financial difficulties of their own, Blaine supporters remained extremely confident. Several leading Stalwarts were in their camp. Independents committed themselves to Edmunds, and seemed unlikely to forge an alliance with administration men. George F. Hoar, the powerful Senator from Massachusetts, announced that he and many of his state's delegates would not vote for the President because of the River and Harbor veto of 1882 and an unsatisfactory appointment in the Boston Customhouse; Hoar backed Edmunds but said he preferred Blaine to Arthur.[50] Newspaper polls of convention delegates showed the Plumed Knight comfortably ahead from the start. A reporter on the scene reflected, "Whatever may happen, it is clear enough that Arthur is beaten." Almost prophetically, a special train from New York bearing Arthur delegates had a minor accident on its way to Chicago, tearing off a portion of a huge sign on the front car reading "Chester A. Arthur for President."[51]

The eighth national convention of the Republican Party opened on June 3 in the same Chicago Exposition Building where Garfield and Arthur had been nominated four years before. The huge structure was packed with 1,600 delegates and alternates and more than 6,000 spectators. Bands played; banners swayed; applause rippled through the crowd as George William Curtis and William Mahone strode in at the head of their delegations.

The first test of delegate strength concerned General Powell Clayton of Arkansas, a former Arthur backer who had hastily converted to Blaine a few days earlier when the President refused to trade a Cabinet seat for convention votes. The national committee, dominated by Blaine men, named Clayton temporary chairman of the convention. It was a silly move that angered many delegates committed to Blaine, for while Clayton's "empty sleeve" drew sympathy from veterans, he was widely reputed to have been an accomplice in the star route frauds. When Clayton's nomination came before the convention, Edmunds supporters, led by Henry Cabot Lodge, expressed opposition and moved to substitute the name of John R. Lynch, a Negro Republican from Mississippi. Lynch's candidacy was supported by a speech from "an active, nervous, light-haired, gray-eyed" young man named Theodore Roosevelt, "who had just thrown off a straw hat and scrambled to his perch in the chair, with juvenile activity." Lynch won the vote 424 to 384, and some delegates were convinced that Blaine's popularity had been exaggerated. That evening the Arthur forces hired a glee club to sing the praises of the President all night through the lobbies of the Grand Pacific Hotel. But the temporary chairmanship was of little significance, and Clayton's cause could not be equated with Blaine's. If the newspaper assessments of delegate sentiment were accurate, the Man from Maine remained the favorite and could be stopped only by a coalition involving several other candidates.[52]

A second blunder by Blaine men occurred the next day when a Half-Breed from Tennessee revived Roscoe Conkling's proposal of 1880 that no delegate should be entitled to hold his seat who would not pledge his support to the convention's choice. The motion was an obvious response to rumors from within Independent circles of a party bolt should Blaine be named to head the national ticket. Immediate objection erupted from the Edmunds delegates, and George William Curtis spoke out eloquently against the proposal. "A Republican and a free man I came to this convention," he said, "and by the Grace of God a Republican and a free man I will go out of it." The motion was withdrawn. Blaine leaders suffered yet a third setback when their nominee for permanent chairman was defeated in committee.

General John B. Henderson of Missouri, an Edmunds man, was elected permanent chairman of the convention, and in a short speech he paid compliments to each of the candidates; "our embarrassment is not in the want but in the multiplicity of Presidential material." He drew loud applause on alluding to Arthur. "New York has her true and tried statesman, upon whose administration the fierce and even unfriendly light of public scrutiny has been turned, and the universal verdict is: 'Well done, thou good and faithful servant.' "[53]

That evening, leaders of the Arthur and Edmunds forces talked for hours behind closed doors in the Grand Pacific trying to thrash out some sort of agreement that would prevent Blaine's nomination. But in the end the effort was futile. Arthur's delegates could not be transferred to another candidate; they were largely southern officeholders and under no discipline, and many of them were rumored ready to declare for Blaine if Arthur's column broke. The Arthur leadership, in Stalwart fashion, wound up committed to the President to the bitter end. The Independents could not bring themselves to support Arthur, and after a brief flirtation with John Sherman's managers, they appeared resigned to defeat.[54]

The following morning, the day fixed for presenting nominations,

President Andrew D. White of Cornell University entered the convention building and noticed that the portraits of Washington and Lincoln had been removed from the platform to protect them from demonstrations. He mentioned this to George William Curtis, who replied, "Yes, I have noticed it, and I am glad of it. Those weary eyes of Lincoln have been upon us here during our whole stay, and I am glad that they are not to see the work that is to be done here to-day."[55]

The roll call of states began during the evening session. When Connecticut was reached, Augustus Brandegee placed the name of favorite son General Joseph R. Hawley in nomination. His effusive oration drew attention largely because of its thinly veiled references to the party's major candidates. Blaine men scowled when Brandegee said, "General Hawley believes in the morality of practical politics. He is a reformer. . . . His public record is without a flaw. There is nothing to apologize for; there is nothing to conceal; there is nothing to extenuate and naught to offend." New York City delegates squirmed in their seats as the speaker railed against the "machine" and "political bummers."[56]

When Illinois was reached, Shelby M. Collum nominated his senatorial colleague General John A. Logan. The emphasis of his oration was predominantly on Logan's military record. "He never lost a battle; I repeat again, Mr. President and fellow-citizens, he never lost a battle in all the struggles of the war."[57]

When the state of Maine was called, pandemonium broke loose in the huge auditorium. The body of delegates "cheered and yelled and shouted as if it was mad. The stamping of feet produced a sound resembling the roll of distant thunder." Collector Robertson was seen among the wildly cheering Blaine men in the New York delegation standing on a chair waving a tall white hat in the air, perspiration rolling down his face. The shouting and applause lasted a full ten minutes, and before it concluded, Judge William H. West, the famous "Blind Orator" of Ohio, was led to the platform. His impassioned panegyric impressed everyone and was interrupted repeatedly by outbursts of approval. "Through all the conflicts of its progress, from the baptism of blood on the plains of Kansas to the fall of the immortal Garfield, whenever humanity needs succor, or freedom needed protection, or country a champion, whenever blows fell thickest and fastest, there in the forefront of the battle, was seen to wave the white plume of James G. Blaine, our Henry of Navarre." Several times West jabbed at the President's candidacy. "The odds of the Solid South are against us. Not an electoral gun can be expected from that section." At one point he bellowed, nominate " 'the Wall street candidate,' and the hand of resurrection would not fathom his November grave."[58]

As the speaker was helped from the stage, the audience cheered itself into a frenzy. "The applause rose and fell like the breakers rushing up on the sands," an observer wrote. "Again and again it subsided only to burst forth again with increased strength." Flags, banners, and shields were ripped from the stage and galleries and paraded through the aisles. One delegate rushed to the platform waving a flagstaff on which was perched a garlanded helmet with a snow-white plume; the spectators roared. Andrew D. White later referred to the crowd reaction as "absolutely unworthy of a convention of any party, a disgrace to decency, and a blot upon the reputation of our country."[59]

When order was restored, Cushman K. Davis of Minnesota opened his seconding speech with a sentence that won more applause: "In the face of the demonstration which we have seen and heard, it would seem scarcely necessary to second a nomination which appears already to be a foregone conclusion."

The third such speech was delivered by Tom Platt. With his old friends in the New York delegation glaring at him scornfully, he said with an air of pride: "I rise with pleasure to second the nomination of James G. Blaine. I second this nomination, believing, as I do, that his turn has come; believing, as I do, that expediency and justice demand it; believing, as I do, that the Republican people of the Republican States that must give the Republican majorities want him; believing, as I do, that he is the representative of that strong, stern, stalwart Republicanism which will surely command success; believing, as I do, that with him for our standard-bearer success is surely assured; believing, in my inmost heart, that with him as our standard-bearer success is assured in the great State of New York." Platt's comments won only faint applause from the exhausted audience. Several New York delegates shouted, "Conkling! Conkling! Now, let us hear from Roscoe Conkling."[60]

When the roll call reached New York it was the occasion for the President's name to be placed in nomination. The bumbling leadership of the Arthur camp had failed to name a principal convention speaker until the proceedings were under way. The task fell to Martin I. Townsend, an elderly district attorney from Troy, New York. As might be expected, Townsend's speech was poorly prepared—he later called it "extemporaneous from necessity." It quoted from orations delivered earlier in the evening, rambled on about the virtues of the Bible, and wound up pleading that Arthur not be "struck down and cast into oblivion." Townsend managed to refer to the Pendleton Act, and to illustrate the President's devotion to nonpartisan government by pointing to the enmity of Platt and Conkling and the presence of Collector Robertson on the convention floor. But these were the only redeeming features of the dismal performance. At least twice there were loud hisses from the audience; conversations became so audible that the chairman had to bang his gavel to restore order.[61]

Congressman Harry H. Bingham of Pennsylvania gave the initial seconding speech for Arthur. He had a fine stage presence and spoke convincingly. A graceful allusion to Curtis was warmly applauded. The President was praised for his courage and dignity following Garfield's death and congratulated for what was portrayed as an outstanding record in office. "Read the vetoes of Chester A. Arthur, and you will find him courageous to rebuke extravagance, even when his own party has formulated the legislation. The foreign relations of the country bring us only love and respect, and the State Department is quiet, and at peace with all the world. Our home conditions mark a people prosperous, happy and contented, capital employed, labor protected, a fair day's living wages for a fair day's work. The manufacturing interests will find the name of Chester A. Arthur signed to the legislation of the Forty-seventh Congress, side by side with that of William D. Kelley, of Pennsylvania; McKinley, of Ohio; Morrill, of Vermont; and Aldrich, of Rhode Island. Commerce finds in him a familiar defender, agriculture an advocate, and labor a devoted champion. The men of the South will eloquently tell how true he has been to their cause, to liberty, and the right."

John R. Lynch of Mississippi followed with a brief, apologetic exhortation. By this time the delegates were getting restless, and several left the building while Lynch was speaking. Patrick H. Winston of North Carolina stepped to the platform a few minutes later and delivered a terse, pointless collection of generalities that irritated listeners. When he had finished, a motion to adjourn was made by a delegate from California: "it is now past eleven o'clock, and these people are tired." The motion lost.

The last speech for Arthur was delivered by P. G. S. Pinchback of Louisiana, who dwelled upon the integrity of southern Negro delegates. "I want to demonstrate, by our fealty to this chosen chief of ours, that we are as pure, as incorruptible, when holding public trust, as the whitest man that may sit beneath this roof."[62]

The convention seemed relieved as the last of the Arthur men sat down. If their speeches had any effect on delegates, it was no doubt negative. When J. B. Foraker placed John Sherman's name in nomination, the audience came alive again. A favorable allusion to Blaine triggered another ten-minute demonstration. Foraker took a swipe at the Plumed Knight by calling for a candidate who possessed a record "so clear, so bright as not only to defy criticism, but at the same time to make him the representative of all the highest and purest ambitions of the great Republican Party." But Sherman's popularity could not approach that enjoyed by the front-runner.

At midnight, former Governor John D. Long of Massachusetts nominated George F. Edmunds. The Vermonter had served in the Senate since 1866 and was currently its president *pro tem*. He was highly respected in GOP circles and had been chosen chairman of a joint caucus of Republican Senators and Representatives summoned to plan for the coming election. Long called attention to his "tested service" and "tried incorruptibility" and described him as a candidate who would appeal to all factions of the party. Curtis added eloquent commentary, and after a wrangle over adjournment the weary delegates dragged themselves back to their hotels.[63]

Nine hours later, on the morning of June 6, the convention was again called to order. The delegates were tense with excitement, for it was at last time to select the national ticket. There were 820 delegates accredited at the convention, and 411 votes were needed to win.

The first ballot went virtually as predicted. Blaine collected $334\frac{1}{2}$ votes, Arthur 278, Edmunds 93, Logan $63\frac{1}{2}$, Sherman 30, and Hawley, Robert Lincoln, and William T. Sherman divided the remainder. The hopelessness of the President's position was obvious. Of his 278 votes, all but about 100 came from the South. He received no votes from Ohio, 1 of 44 from Illinois, 9 of 30 from Indiana, and 11 of 60 from Pennsylvania. He carried only 31 of the 71 votes cast from his own state. And there was no likelihood that his strength would increase as the balloting continued. It was impossible to win support from Blaine backers, an attempted alliance with the Edmunds men had already failed, and Logan was expected to declare for the Man from Maine at any time.

There was a slight shift to Blaine on the second ballot. His total inched ahead to 349, while Arthur claimed 276 votes and Edmunds 85. On the third ballot Blaine moved to 375, aided largely by defections among Edmunds men. Arthur's vote remained steady at 274. Seeing Blaine near the winning mark, members of the opposition combined to support a motion to recess. It was defeated 458 to 356, and the contest was over.

Logan handed over almost all of his votes to Blaine on the fourth ballot; 67 Arthur men and 28 Edmunds backers also jumped aboard the bandwagon. Blaine's total soared to 541, Arthur received 207 votes, and Edmunds wound up with only 41. As Blaine went over the top, Carl Schurz looked at his pocket watch, apparently oblivious to the jubilant chaos around him, and said sadly, "From this hour dates the death of the Republican party." William McKinley elbowed his way through the crowd to the New York delegation and requested speeches from

Roosevelt and Curtis. Roosevelt refused. Curtis simply shook his head slowly. That evening, Logan was selected as Blaine's running mate.[64]

Blaine received word of his nomination at his home in Augusta, Maine, and his joy rendered him practically incoherent. He soon wrote Elkins:

> I want you to come here. I can write nothing. I must speak. I want to express to you now all the gratuitive admiration obligation [sic] which the human heart can feel. For myself I want to speak of my hopes for us, perturbations, confidences and distrusts. It is idle to open the subject on papers, I must see you face to face.
>
> I postpone everything till I see you.[65]

The news reached Arthur at the White House, where he had followed the convention proceedings by wire. He immediately sent a telegram expressing his "earnest and cordial support." He then ordered a carriage and was quickly lost from sight.[66]

Two weeks later, Frank B. Conger called at the White House, as the President had requested before the convention. After a few words of appreciation, Arthur "greatly astonished and terribly shocked" his young visitor by telling him confidentially that he suffered from an advanced case of Bright's disease and was probably destined for only a few months or at best a couple of years of life. For this reason, Conger learned, he had been asked not to work actively as an Arthur delegate.[67]

While Republicans met in Chicago, the first session of the 48th Congress continued its work in Washington. This being a presidential election year, the postures and machinations of Senators and Representatives won special attention from the press and public. Even before the session had convened, Democrats earned headlines from a heated struggle over organization of the House, where they enjoyed a majority of 77. The contest for Speaker was between Pennsylvania's Samuel J. Randall, long identified with high-tariff sentiment in the party, and John G. Carlisle of Kentucky, who stood for moderate tariff reduction. Carlisle carried the caucus by a margin of two to one, indicating that tariff reform would be a central issue in the forthcoming campaign. The new Speaker appointed Congressmen of similar persuasion to valuable committee posts. William R. Morrison of Illinois, whose desire for across-the-board tariff reductions earned him the name "Horizontal Bill," was named chairman of the Committee on Ways and Means and charged with the responsibility of formulating appropriate legislation.[68]

In early May, a coalition of protectionist Democrats and Republicans in the House killed a bill that would have lowered most tariff schedules 20 percent. The defeat reopened a serious split among Democrats and reinforced the conviction of Republicans that their opponents were unfit for national authority. "There is something the matter with the Democratic side," thought Theodore Lyman. "There are some able and very many honest men over there, but they have no unity of action, nor ruling ideas."[69]

Both parties united in the desire to spend money cautiously, despite the huge surplus of federal funds, and this view was given teeth by the presence of Randall ("the watch-dog of the Treasury") as chairman of the powerful House Committee on Appropriations. The most costly measure proceeding from the committee was a Rivers and Harbors bill calling for expenditures totaling almost $14,000,000. This was less than half the sum recommended by the War Department and was the first such bill signed by a President in three years.[70] Congress also granted $1,000,000, in the form of a loan, to the directors of the World's Industrial and Cotton Centennial Exposition at New Orleans, coupled with an appropriation of $300,000 for a United States building on the site. (On December 16, 1884, the President would press a telegraph key at the White House, officially opening the Exposition.)[71]

The session resulted in several significant pieces of legislation. Following persistent pleas by the President, civil government was extended to the Territory of Alaska.[72] A National Bureau of Labor was created as an adjunct of the Interior Department, designed to collect data on the condition of labor in the country.[73] A Bureau of Animal Industry was established, charged primarily with the suppression of communicable diseases among livestock.[74] A bill was passed to make the Chinese exclusion law more effective.[75] A shipping bill removed several burdens from the American shipping trade.[76]

Still, when the session adjourned on July 7, few were entirely satisfied with its record. The tariff stood unaltered. Though debated at length, the law of presidential succession went unchanged. Legislation to provide for the settlement of disputes over electoral votes sailed through the Republican-controlled Senate but got nowhere in the Democratic House. Forest conservation was discussed, but to no positive end. And too much time, it was felt, had been spent by both houses on the celebrated case of Fitz John Porter.

Major General Porter, a West Point graduate, had been tried and convicted by a general court-martial for disobeying orders at the second Battle of Bull Run. The sentence, approved by President Lincoln in early 1863, cashiered Porter from the service and forever disqualified him from holding an office of trust or profit under the federal government. During the Grant years, Porter repeatedly requested a retrial, but the President, convinced of Porter's guilt, would hear nothing of it. President Hayes relented, however, and appointed a board of army officers to examine new evidence in the case. In March 1879, the board issued a report exonerating Porter completely and requesting the President to annul the sixteen-year-old verdict, set aside the sentence, and restore Porter to his rank in the army. Hayes believed himself without sufficient legal authority to take such action, and submitted the matter to Congress.

In 1880, a bill of relief was debated at length in the Senate. The case had already assumed partisan overtones. Porter was a Democrat, and many of his supporters in Congress had served the Confederacy. Porter's conviction had been sanctioned by Lincoln and Grant; James A. Garfield had been a member of the original court-martial and was an outspoken opponent of Porter's claims; "Black Jack" Logan was a vituperative enemy of the bill, and was one of the few members of the Senate who could claim to have mastered the complex facts of the case. The bill passed the Senate in December 38–20, but it was permitted to die in the House—at the request of President-elect Garfield.

While Garfield lived, Porter was without hope. But when Arthur assumed the presidency, the former officer and his friends resumed the struggle. Their cause was advanced considerably by the sudden conversion of Grant. In a letter to Arthur of December 22, 1881, Grant informed the President that he had spent three full days studying the subject, at Porter's request, and had changed his mind. "The reading has thoroughly convinced me that for these nineteen years I have been doing a gallant and efficient soldier a very great injustice." He continued, "What I would ask in General Porter's behalf from you is that you give the subject the same study that I have given it." The following day, Porter wrote to the President asking for an annulment of the verdict against him and the restoration of his army rank.

During the next few months Grant wrote letters to prominent Congressmen for Porter and again appealed to Arthur by letter and in person. The President, mindful of Hayes's reservations about the authority of his office in the matter, consulted the Attorney General. It was Brewster's opinion that Hayes had been correct: the Chief Executive could not review the proceedings of a legally competent court-martial and annul its sentence. The most the President could do was to remit—or pardon— the unexpired penalty imposed on Porter disqualifying him from holding federal office. Porter formally requested such action, and on May 4, 1882, following two Cabinet sessions devoted to the question, the President issued an order granting the plea. Arthur expressed no opinion about Porter's guilt or innocence, but based his action upon doubts raised by Hayes's review board.

Porter promptly sent a new appeal to Congress requesting the restoration of his rank. Several months later, Grant published an article in the *North American Review* entitled "An Undeserved Stigma," which rallied many Americans to Porter's cause. After another bitter debate in Congress, a Porter bill was again allowed to die in the House.

When the new Congress convened in December 1883, Porter's friends were ready with new legislation. Despite all the previous oratory expended on Porter, the House devoted two weeks to a relief bill, finally passing it 184–78. In mid-March the Senate approved the still highly controversial bill 36–25.

The bill reached Arthur in mid-June, and on July 2 he vetoed it, again heeding advice from Attorney General Brewster. The first objection was wholly constitutional. The bill requested the President to award Porter the rank of colonel in the United States Army. Congress was thus creating an office that could be filled only by a particular individual, which, Arthur wrote, was an encroachment upon executive authority. The President had the right to nominate, and the Senate's duty was to consent or dissent; the legislative branch had no constitutional power to restrict the choice of the Chief Executive in making an appointment. If the bill should be regarded merely as an enactment of advice and counsel, it served no useful purpose on the statute books. *The New York Times* thought this argument "simply unanswerable" and "of unassailable strength."

Secondly, Arthur contended that neither the President nor Congress had the authority to set aside the decision of a legal court-martial. This was an extension of the view held earlier by Hayes. The bill before him, he noted, assumed that the findings made during the war had been discovered erroneous. But he reminded Congressmen that the review board of the late 1870s did not have the power to compel the attendance of witnesses and did not have access to much of the evidence used during the court-martial proceedings. Moreover, the board was not established in pursuance of any statutory authority and could not produce a lawfully enforceable judgment. It was one thing, he wrote, to pardon continuing penalties imposed upon a convicted man, and quite another to set aside the verdict of a legal tribunal.

The veto was overriden in the House on the following day 168–78, but was sustained by the Senate 27 to 27. It was strictly a party vote.[77]

Porter's backers, especially Grant, were crushed by the turn of events. "Were Job alive," the Philadelphia *Times* remarked, "he would send a cablegram to patient Fitz John Porter."[78] Predictably, they vowed to persist. (Two years later, Grover Cleveland would sign a similar bill restoring Porter to a rank in the army and placing him on the retirement list.) But other observers paid tribute to Arthur's strict interpretation of constitutional powers and his unwillingness to disturb the authority of courts of law. Collector Robertson told a reporter, "The veto was an able document, creditable to the patriotism and the statesmanship of the President. When the present generation shall have passed away I do not believe that there will be anybody to question its soundness."[79] *The New York Times* commented, "Had the salutary principles of military discipline been fully enforced [Porter] would not have lived to persist in his effort to have the sanctions of a military tribunal subverted and the principles of the Constitution set aside for a vindication which he does not deserve."[80]

The Democratic National Convention opened on July 8 at Exposition Hall in Chicago. Over the last four years the party had suffered from acute disorder and internal dissension; despite the victories of 1882 it had lost the last six presidential elections and was again without effective national leadership. Erratic Ben Butler of Massachusetts coveted the role of standard-bearer but was taken seriously by only a few. Randall of Pennsylvania had shown an interest before his defeat in the Speaker's race of 1883. Wealthy Roswell Pettibone Flower of New York was mentioned by some as a possibility. Favorite sons, such as Ohio's Henry B. Payne and Allen Granberry Thurman, were touted by friends. Tilden had been considered again, but in mid-June he declared for the governor of New York, a man who was slowly gaining nationwide attention.

Grover Cleveland was aloof, stolid, virtually without wit or imagination, and never a personally popular man. But his blunt honesty, his willingness to work hard, and his devotion to economy and efficiency in government won him many admirers. He had not publicly sought national office, and was even known to wince at the mention of the presidency. But several of his managers had quietly toured parts of the nation on his behalf for months, and by mid-1884 they had drummed up considerable interest in their man. Cleveland, they argued, was a proven vote-getter: who could forget his margin of victory over the President and his henchmen? And with Tilden's endorsement, the governor could carry the Empire State again. He was a symbol of clean government and could attract Independent votes, a factor that could be critical in November. He could appeal to all sections of the country. No one else, they claimed persuasively, had a better chance against Blaine.

Cleveland's victory was secured easily on the second ballot. Vituperative opposition from Tammany Hall no doubt hastened the triumph.

The ticket was completed with Indiana's elderly spoilsman Thomas A. Hendricks, who had run with Tilden eight years earlier.

The Democratic presidential candidate had no national record and was unknown to millions of voters. His achievements in Albany had been largely negative, stressing limited government and opposition to the spoils system; he was best known for his vetoes. Republicans were at first without a plan of attack. An initial volley by the New York *Tribune* labeled the rotund Governor "a small man everywhere but on the hay scales."[81]

Even before the Democrats met in Chicago, Republican Independents, occasionally called Mugwumps, bolted their party in large numbers. Men like Curtis, Godkin, and Schurz had opposed Blaine's presidential aspirations since 1876, considering the Plumed Knight the incarnation of political wickedness. They had bombarded him with abuse all spring in editorials, articles, letters, and cartoons, and now that he was to lead the party, they were compelled, as they had been in 1872, to go outside the GOP for a suitable candidate. They found that candidate in Cleveland, "a synonymn of political courage and honesty and of administrative reform," and announced they would vote for the man, not his party. Mugwumps were largely from Massachusetts and New York, and in the latter state they had a real opportunity of effecting the outcome of the election. Their influence on the press was especially significant: seven New York City journals that had supported Garfield in 1880, with a combined circulation of 500,000, now declared for Cleveland.[82]

Early in the campaign, Blaine stressed the need for a high tariff. He employed the theme to win over protection-conscious businessmen, to explain away the Mugwump revolt, to appeal to the Irish, to win over the "New South," and to attract workingmen in every section. (Recommendations by the President and his Tariff Commission were ignored.) Cleveland remained silent on the subject because it divided his party, and the issue failed to win much public attention. Soon more emotionally charged questions dominated the contest.

In late July, a Buffalo newspaper revealed the fact that Cleveland had fathered an illegitimate child. Before long, Republicans everywhere were chanting, "Ma, Ma, where's my Pa? Going to the White House, ha! ha! ha!" The New York *Sun* called Cleveland "a coarse debauchee who might bring his harlots to the White House." (Depressed Mugwumps spent months explaining the vital distinction between private and public morality.) The Democratic nominee was said to have hired a convict as a "substitute" in the Civil War. He was supposed to have enjoyed hanging two criminals while sheriff of Erie County.

The opposition also traded in such currency. A new series of "Mulligan letters" was published, linking the former Speaker of the House with railroad corruption. Gleeful Cleveland supporters sang:

Blaine, Blaine, James G. Blaine,
Continental Liar from the State of Maine!

Harper's Weekly and *Puck* ran vitriolic cartoons of a Blaine steeped in corruption and shame. One pictured the candidate at a piano singing:

I know not what the way may be—
I know not how I'll get that seat.
I'll have to use chicanery—
I'll have to lie and bribe and cheat.

From Indianapolis came a widely circulated (and false) charge that Mrs. Blaine had been pregnant when married. Blaine was said to be a Know-Nothing, a persecutor of the foreign-born, an anti-Catholic demagogue (even though his mother had been a Catholic and a sister was a nun).[83] "The public is angry and abusive," Henry Adams wrote a friend. "Every one takes a part. We are all swearing at each other like demons."[84] Andrew D. White wrote of "the vilest political campaign ever waged."[85]

Democrats were well financed throughout the contest, but Republicans found themselves perilously short of funds. Gloom hovered over the GOP's national headquarters; "Money is coming in *very* slowly," Jay Gould was informed in October.[86] Frantic appeals were sent to railroads, banks, and wealthy entrepreneurs.

The administration was in part responsible for the party's poor financial situation. Nothing approaching Arthur's previous efforts to wring money out of government workers was attempted in 1884. (The vast majority of federal, state, and local officeholders remained unprotected by civil service legislation.) Gresham refused to permit meekly worded circulars from the national committee to be distributed in postal buildings. The Civil Service Commission reported very few and only minor violations of law concerning assessments, and declared that only about one fourth to one half of the average campaign haul was raised.[87]

The President and his Cabinet played virtually no role in the contest. Arthur would not meet with the national committee; the committee's chairman said that he knew of only one speech given by a Cabinet member on behalf of the national ticket.[88] Blaine was later bitterly critical of the administration for its lack of support.[89] In all-important New York, Stalwarts gave Blaine only perfunctory assistance. The state committee, led by Arthur men, concentrated much of its energy on local candidates.[90] Conkling worked quietly for Blaine's defeat and predicted a Democratic victory. When asked to enter the campaign for the Republican standard-bearer, he snapped, "No, thank you, I don't engage in criminal practice."[91]

Because of the critical shortage of money in New York, Blaine reluctantly agreed to appear in the state at the end of an extraordinary six-week speaking tour through the Midwest. The decision probably doomed his bid for the presidency. On October 29, Reverend Samuel D. Burchard, pastor of Murray Hill Presbyterian Church, stood near Blaine before an audience of ministers and reporters and gave a brief speech in which he referred to Democrats as the party of "rum, Romanism and rebellion." Blaine apparently did not hear the alliteration when it was first uttered. He soon denounced it, but by then Democrats had distributed leaflets bearing the abusive words at the doors of thousands of Catholic churches across the country.

On the evening of that same fateful day, Blaine attended a fund-raising dinner at Delmonico's restaurant. Two hundred of the city's wealthiest men, including Jay Gould, Russell Sage, Cyrus W. Field, John Jacob Astor, Andrew Carnegie, and Levi P. Morton, were in attendance, along with a few clergymen, lawyers, and judges. Blaine's speech glorified American wealth. The next morning, Democratic newspapers lashed out at the dinner with blazing headlines: "Mammon's Homage," "Belshazzar's Feast," "The Boodle Banquet." One cartoon in Joseph Pulitzer's sensationalistic New York *World* depicted a starving worker's family begging crumbs from the lavish table. "Burchard lost us thousands, the Delmonico dinner hundreds of voters," groaned Alonzo B. Cornell.[92]

The election was the closest in American history. With almost 10,000,000 people casting ballots, Cleveland won a plurality of only about 30,000 votes. His electoral majority of 37 was achieved by carrying New York, Indiana, Connecticut, New Jersey, and the Solid South. New York gave Democrats the victory margin, and the state was won by only 1,149 votes: slightly less than .1 percent of the votes cast. If 600 New Yorkers had switched from Cleveland to Blaine, the Man from Maine would have been President.

Despite his narrow defeat, Blaine ran a strong campaign. In the Empire State he virtually eliminated the huge majority Cleveland had won two years earlier, and city Republicans claimed the largest percentage of the vote they had received since the Civil War. Nationally, the GOP gained 22 seats in the House and would control the Senate 41–34.[93]

Still, for the first time in almost a quarter century, Republicans were to vacate the White House and surrender the treasury of patronage it commanded. New York had again been the pivotal state, and party workers spent months arguing over what had gone wrong. Some pointed to the Mugwumps, who were eager to take credit. The Prohibition ticket had won 25,000 votes, far more than enough to put Blaine over the top. The events of October 29 were often mentioned. "If Blaine had eaten a few more swell dinners, and had a few more ministers call on him," John Logan remarked sourly, "we should not have carried a northern state."[94] Blaine himself wrote bitterly of "an ass in the shape of a preacher" but thought rainy weather on election day equally to blame.[95] Many noticed that Conkling's home county, which had gone for Garfield and Arthur by 1,946 votes, was won by Cleveland by a margin of 100, a defection that alone might have cost Blaine victory. The New York *Sun* concluded, "It was a handful of unforgiving Stalwarts that did it."[96]

After the election, Arthur was said to have expressed deep regret over the party's loss but could find little personal sympathy for Blaine. The story was told of how Blaine had reacted two years earlier to the suggestion that Arthur might be the GOP candidate in 1884. Tossing his thumb in the direction of the President, he scoffed, "What, this man? This man? Why, he will no more be the candidate than I will fly across the Potomac."[97]

A Bolder Diplomatist

O NCE IT WAS OFFICIAL that the President could not succeed himself, most politicians expected little from the administration before it faded into memory in March 1885. It could summon only meager support on Capitol Hill and could not anticipate much activity from the lame duck session of the 48th Congress scheduled to open in December. There was no discernible mandate for action from the public. After the defeat in Chicago, newspapers increasingly applauded Arthur's courage and propriety at a time of national crisis and called attention to his administration's modest achievements and freedom from corruption. But nothing extraordinary was anticipated during the remaining months of the twenty-first President's term of office. Chester A. Arthur, like Charles J. Folger, Roscoe Conkling, and the word "Stalwart" itself, would soon be consigned to the musty world of historians.

Instead of choosing to be inert, however, the Arthur Administration surprised critics and admirers alike by using its last nine months to attempt to create a formidable record in foreign affairs. The White House and State Department exerted both energy and audacity in the hope of developing an expansionist foreign policy more aggressive, in some respects, than Blaine had envisioned during his controversial service as Secretary of State. Reaction to this gritty effort varied considerably. At one point, *The New York Times* editorialized, "It is in no sense a partisan and much less a personal policy, but it is national and patriotic in its purpose and elevated in its spirit. It is in these regards true to the traditions of the best American diplomacy, and should be so acknowledged."[1] A powerful Congressman, on the other hand, thought the policy "worse than useless," one that could be "a source of great embarrassment to the incoming Administration."[2] Decades later, scholars would see moves by Arthur and Frelinghuysen as significant links in the development of modern American foreign policy.

For more than a year after he took over the State Department, Frelinghuysen attended largely to problems inherited from his predecessor. At the top of the agenda was the restoration of peace in Latin America. The administration was eager for resolution of the clashes between Chile and Peru, Mexico and Guatemala; they invited European intervention and threatened United States economic and political strength in the hemisphere. But Arthur and Frelinghuysen were determined to eschew Blaine's unpopular and unproductive approach to these conflicts and calm the waters with a diplomacy characterized by tact, restraint, and caution.

In Chile and Peru the new posture resulted initially in confusion. William H. Trescot, the special envoy sent to the trouble spot bearing Blaine's inflammatory instructions, learned of the administration's altered plans at the Chilean foreign office; his revised instructions, made public by the State Department, reached the press before they arrived at his desk. Moreover, the Chilean government made much use of American newspaper attacks against Blaine's foreign policy. Trescot and his colleague Walker Blaine departed for Washington in May, frustrated and angry.

Frelinghuysen dispatched two seasoned diplomats to replace them. One, Dr. Cornelius A. Logan, minister to Central America, went to Santiago with instructions to carry out impartial mediation. The secretary declared that it was hoped Peru would cede at least some territory lost in battle and that Chile would accept a reasonable indemnity for war expenses and moderate its demands for conquered soil.

Logan's efforts dragged on for months. Chile, in command of the entire coast of Peru including its capital, refused to lower its high price for a treaty, and Peru continued to hope for a gesture of United States favoritism. On December 4, in his second annual message, President Arthur deplored Chile's harsh peace terms but made it clear for the first time that Peru could not anticipate American intervention on its behalf. A dictated peace, he wrote, "would need to be supplemented by the armies and navies of the United States. Such interference would almost inevitably lead to the establishment of a protectorate—a result utterly at odds with our past policy, injurious to our present interests, and full of embarrassments for the future."[3] This frank statement, in Logan's judgment, improved the prospects for peace.

American diplomats played only a minor role in the negotiations during 1883. García Calderón, president of Peru, was discovered to be president of a nitrate company owning a large concession in the disputed territory. A revolt in his beleaguered country enabled a new government to sign a peace protocol in May. In October, the War of the Pacific was concluded by the Treaty of Ancón.

In a letter to our Peruvian minister, Frelinghuysen wrote the epitaph of our awkward and unhappy involvement in the conflict by declining comment on terms of the treaty. The United States

> respects the independence of Peru as a commonwealth entitled to settle its own affairs in its own way. It recognizes too keenly the calamities of protracted strife, or the alternative calamity of prolonged military occupation by an enemy's forces, to seek, by anything it may say or do, to influence an adverse decision of the popular representatives of Peru. And a due respect for their sovereign independence forbids the United States from seeming to exert any positive or indirect pressure upon these representatives to influence their course.[4]

The administration approached the boundary dispute between Mexico and Guatemala in the same way. Guatemalan officials had been delighted by Blaine's warning to Mexico not to attack her weaker neighbor, and warmly approved the proposal for an inter-American conference. They approached Frelinghuysen several times bearing proposals for close relations with the United States. The secretary made it clear from the beginning, however, that his predecessor's policy was not his own.

In March 1882, Frelinghuysen told the Mexican minister to Washington that the State Department would not force its mediation on either party to the dispute; America's good offices were available but only at the invitation of both nations. To further test the administration's intentions, the Mexican official asked Grant to confer directly with the President on the subject. Arthur gave his old chieftain solemn assurances that he had abandoned Blaine's interventionist goals. When the president of Guatemala traveled to Washington in July seeking aid, he too was informed that at most the United States would serve as arbiter and only at the request of his own and the Mexican government.

With the possibility of American intervention out of the picture, leaders of Mexico and Guatemala soon settled their dispute. On September 27, a treaty was signed calling for direct negotiation without assistance from the United States. The administration, of course, could claim no great diplomatic triumph; predictably, Half-Breeds jeered. But its quiet, friendly, and impartial policy again contributed to the creation of peace and avoided a foreign imbroglio the American people did not seek and would not have approved.[5]

In several matters appearing to offer sizable economic advantages to the United States, Frelinghuysen was more assertive and venturesome than Blaine had been. Much of the secretary's bolder activity occurred after the Republican National Convention, when he was a lame duck, and critics contended that he was as guilty as Blaine in late 1881 of tying his successor to a controversial foreign policy that could be abandoned only at the cost of embarrassment and confusion. The charge was especially potent after November 4 when it was realized that the next Secretary of State would be a Democrat.

The perennial question of the site for an inter-oceanic route, however, concerned Frelinghuysen from the start. Arthur had endorsed Blaine's effort to revise the Clayton-Bulwer Treaty, asserting that the canal issue was "of grave national importance."[6] Western farmers and businessmen continued to lust for the vast profits available when European and Atlantic coast markets were brought nearer. Many eastern manufacturers spoke of great fortunes to be won in Asia and along the west coast of South America. Nationalists, aware of the excavations in Panama by the Frenchman de Lesseps, repeatedly appealed in the name of the Monroe Doctrine for action against European imperialists.

Much public attention was being paid to promoters of two rival transit projects seeking financial assistance from Congress. The Maritime Canal Company, which enjoyed Grant's public support and held a concession in Nicaragua, claimed that a canal across Nicaragua's natural sea-level waterways would cost less than a third of the project under way in Panama and offer superior commercial and political benefits.[7] James B. Eads, a renowned engineer who had constructed jetties at the mouth of the Mississippi River, toured the country selling the idea of a ship-railway across an isthmus in southern Mexico.[8] While the merits of each proposal continued to be debated. Frelinghuysen determined to do something about the Clayton-Bulwer Treaty, which barred construction and operation of a canal solely by the United States.

On May 8, 1882, the secretary sent a letter to London urging, for the first time, the treaty's total abrogation. Among his arguments was the contention that the canal provisions of the 1850 document referred to a specific Nicaraguan project then under way and had no bearing on the present. Another objective of the treaty, he claimed, was to dispossess Great Britain of settlements in Central America; the subsequent appearance of the crown colony of British Honduras rendered the treaty voidable.[9]

While awaiting a reply from Lord Granville, the British foreign secretary, Frelinghuysen coolly began to explore the possibility of an American-owned canal in Nicaragua. He had gradually come to think this desirable; the Maritime Canal Company's concession did not, in his view, adequately safeguard the nation's authority over the proposed transit route. In September, Navy Captain Seth L. Phelps (president of the company) was sent to Nicaragua to seek coaling stations at a point midway across the proposed canal route. The special mission failed when a local anti-American newspaper got wind of what was going on and published a shrill attack against its objective. But the idea of a marine highway across the isthmus belonging exclusively to the United States continued to interest Frelinghuysen.[10]

In December, Lord Granville rejected the secretary's arguments of May 8, declaring that the Clayton-Bulwer Treaty had been intended to establish general principles applicable to all inter-oceanic routes, and denying that Britain had created a Central American colony illegally. Frelinghuysen restated his case in letters of May 5 and November 22, 1883; these later messages contained more pointed references to the Monroe Doctrine. Granville's position, however, remained unaltered; the treaty would continue in full force and effect indefinitely.[11] The State Department's two-year exercise in persuasion had been in vain.

By early 1884, Frelinghuysen was deeply concerned over the nation's inability to throw its weight behind an inter-oceanic transit project. British intransigence was only part of the picture. Congress was dead-locked in its debate between supporters of the Maritime Canal Company and the Eads ship-railway, and showed no signs of reaching a conclusion in the near future. The Canal Company urgently needed federal financial support because its concession extended only to September, and unless excavations were begun by then the Nicaraguan government would probably permit the concession to expire. Rumors of increased pressures by Britain, France, and Germany on Central America reached the State Department regularly, and in January, Frelinghuysen heard that the Canal Company was about to seek capital in Europe.

To reverse the frustrating trend of events, the secretary decided to take the initiative in Nicaragua. He first looked into the opportunity to purchase rights held by the Canal Company. Then the government at Managua was approached directly to see if it would permit the United States to build a canal. At first President Adán Cárdenas was delighted to learn of the renewed interest in an American canal. But negotiations quickly broke down over terms of an agreement. In March, Frelinghuysen was willing to offer up to $5,000,000 for political jurisdiction over a five-mile strip of land on either side of the canal. Bargaining and bickering continued, however, and in May, American diplomats decided to suspend negotiations temporarily.

The following month Frelinghuysen appeared before congressional committees to defend a request, originating in the Senate, for the sum of $250,000. Word of the secret request had leaked to the press, and charges appeared that a "slush fund" was about to be created with which to buy expiring rights from the financially troubled Maritime Canal Company and bribe Nicaraguan officials. The American minister to Central America was informed by Frelinghuysen that the money was intended for the purchase of private claims along the canal route and for future publicity purposes. Whatever the case, Congressmen were determined to avoid controversy during an election campaign, and the appropriation was defeated.[12]

Negotiations between Washington and Managua continued through the summer and fall and were concluded after Cleveland's election. The Frelinghuysen-Zavala Treaty was signed on December 1. Its terms revealed numerous compromises by both parties. The canal was to be built by the United States but ownership would be shared with Nicaragua. The host nation would supply facilities and appropriate tax exemptions; construction was to begin within two years of the treaty's ratification and reach completion within the following decade. Profits of the venture were to be divided, two thirds going to the United States and one third to Nicaragua. A six-man board of directors would operate the canal, each nation having three representatives. The project would be fortified by the United States as part of a defensive alliance with Nicaragua. Joint ownership of a two-and-one-half-mile canal strip was planned, but only Nicaragua's peacetime rights in the area were specified. Near the treaty's conclusion was an article requiring the United States to loan Nicaragua $4,000,000 for internal improvements affecting business of the canal, the sum to be repaid from canal receipts.

Accompanying the document to the Senate was a message from the President urging prompt ratification. The treaty was negotiated, Arthur wrote, "under a conviction that it was imperatively demanded by the present and future political and material interests of the United States." He continued, "For all maritime purposes the States upon the Pacific are more distant than those upon the Atlantic than if separated by either ocean alone. Europe and Africa are nearer to New York, and Asia is nearer to California, than are these two great States to each other by sea. . . . A nation like ours can not rest satisfied with such a separation of its mutually dependent members." The political effect of an interoceanic canal in Nicaragua would be "to knit closer the States now depending upon railway corporations for all commercial and personal intercourse, and it will not only cheapen the cost of transportation, but will free individuals from the possibility of unjust discriminations." Economically, "By piercing the Isthmus the heretofore insuperable obstacles of time and sea distance disappear, and our vessels and productions will enter upon the world's competitive field with a decided advantage, of which they will avail themselves." Arthur was confident that the canal would be immediately profitable and lead to the speedy repayment of the Nicaraguan loan. He stressed the treaty's respect for Nicaraguan rights, and denied that the United States sought territorial acquisition or political control beyond the nation's present borders. "The two Governments unite in framing this scheme as the sole means by which the work, as indispensable to the one as to the other, can be accomplished under such circumstances as to prevent alike the possibility of conflict between them and of interference from without."[13]

The public first learned of the Frelinghuysen-Zavala Treaty from a brief announcement in Arthur's fourth annual message to Congress.[14] Various versions of the accord appeared in newspapers shortly after it was signed, and the complete document, much to Frelinghuysen's irritation, appeared in the December 18 New York *Tribune*. A storm of controversy arose almost immediately over the lame duck administration's startling proposal. The Springfield *Republican* called the treaty "the boldest feat of American diplomacy since the acquisition of Texas or the purchase of Louisiana."[15] *The Nation* gasped, "The undertaking is on the whole the most formidable one of a peaceful nature which this Government has ever entered on. In fact, it has entered on none at all approaching it in magnitude except the suppression of the Southern Rebellion."[16]

Supporters of the treaty, like the expansion-minded New York *Herald*, believed with the President that an American-sponsored canal would bind the nation more closely together and greatly stimulate its sagging economy. Some thought it would revitalize the Monroe Doctrine and contribute to the development of a modern navy.

Forces opposed to ratification, however, had a longer list of arguments. Independent journals asserted repeatedly that the Frelinghuysen accord violated the Clayton-Bulwer Treaty. Some critics shuddered at its military responsibilities and wondered how they could be met with our meager fleet. Many businessmen thought the enterprise too expensive (the estimated cost of construction was between $100,000,000 and $150,000,000) and doubted that it would yield a steady profit. Several— like Blaine, writing anonymously in the New York *Tribune*—recalled the "slush fund" and thought the proposed loan to Nicaragua a "corruption fund." *The New York Times* expressed the thoughts of many when it suggested a project of such gravity required extensive deliberation. "It might be the height of folly to rush through, with merely superficial examination, a treaty involving a change in policy on the part of the United States of the most momentous character, and the adoption of a position absolutely novel. Moreover, a new administration is coming in. It will unquestionably deal with this subject, if left to it, in the national interest and not from a narrow partisan point of view. There is no danger in leaving it open, and there is every reason why this should be done."[17]

While Frelinghuysen conducted negotiations with Nicaragua during 1884, he and the President were actively engaged in constructing a system of reciprocity treaties in Latin America that would prove equally controversial. When the full scope of the design was realized later in the year, many expressed astonishment at the administration's daring. One newspaper reported, "The men about Washington who have been in the habit of expressing admiration for Blaine as a man with a brilliant foreign policy are amazed to discover in President Arthur a diplomatist much bolder and more comprehensive than their defeated favorite."[18]

Debate over the wisdom of granting special tariff privileges antedated the war and was a feature of virtually every session of Congress throughout the Gilded Age. Certain statesmen, businessmen, and tariff reformers favored reciprocity agreements from time to time as tools for opening new markets, disposing of the nation's dollar surplus, and expanding American political influence. They seemed especially appealing to many in the latter part of the Arthur Administration because of declining prosperity, the failure of meaningful tariff reform, and a growing surplus of American manufactured products. (Congressman Abraham Hewitt agreed with an estimate that the United States was producing in six months all it could consume in a year.)[19] The often formidable opposition to such treaties consisted of a mélange of strict protectionists, uncompromising tariff reductionists, ultranationalists, and interests adversely affected by adjusted schedules. Up to Arthur's time, struggles in Congress over reciprocity had been closely fought. In 1876 and 1880, House committees favored reviving the Elgin-Marcy Treaty with Canada, but no action resulted. Treaties with Hawaii were defeated in 1855 and 1867; in 1875, a measure squeaked through only to be attacked a few years later as it approached renewal.

In the early 1880s, reciprocity advocates turned their attention increasingly to Latin America. Europeans were expanding their financial and commercial prowess there at a rate that shocked some Americans; by 1883, they did four times as much business as the United States.[20] Lack of shipping was a major reason for our lackluster performance, but the nation's high tariff was equally to blame. Blaine later claimed that the Garfield Administration had plans for increasing commercial relations with Latin American countries; in fact, the task was first assumed by Arthur and Frelinghuysen.

The administration's earliest negotiations were with Mexico, where American investments already totaled several million dollars. In November 1881, a fifty-year-old commercial treaty between the United States and Mexico was permitted to expire, in part, perhaps, because of Blaine's officious manner in the boundary dispute with Guatemala. The following August, Frelinghuysen appointed former President Grant and William Henry Trescot to serve as commissioners to work out a new agreement. A treaty, described by the New York *Tribune* as "the most important convention negotiated by the United States government in many years," was signed in early 1883, placing more than 100 categories of products on the free list.

Congress did not get around to discussing the reciprocity agreement until a year later when it emerged from the Senate Foreign Relations Committee without amendment. On the Senate floor it failed to win a two-thirds majority by a single vote. The State Department quickly obtained a six-month extension from Mexico, and the administration intensified its effort to round up the necessary support. On March 11, 1884, the treaty was ratified by a slim margin. To gain this victory, however, pro-administration Senators had to agree to an amendment requiring implementing legislation; the treaty could not be legally in force until appropriate action was taken by the House. The Ways and Means Committee reported favorably on a bill in June, but it failed to come to a vote before the lower chamber. The fate of the Mexican treaty, the administration assumed, would be decided by the short session of the 48th Congress. In his last annual message Arthur expressed the hope to Congressmen that the necessary legislation would be "among the first measures to claim your attention."[21]

In February 1883, about a month after the Mexican treaty was signed, the administration sent diplomat John W. Foster to Madrid to explore similar negotiations covering Cuba and Puerto Rico. The tariff imposed by Spain on these islands was designed to favor Spanish shipping; American commerce was burdened with exorbitant duties, arbitrary fines, and high consular fees. In return, the United States collected a special 10 percent tax on Cuban products in Spanish vessels, as well as a general tariff duty on sugar. Despite these obstacles, Cuba did almost seven times more business with its northern neighbor in 1881 than with Spain; four fifths of that trade consisted of Cuban exports. To invigorate the island's steadily deteriorating economy, Cuban members of the Spanish legislature petitioned the government in Madrid for a commercial treaty with the United States. Spain was eager to see America's 10 percent retaliatory tax dropped, and in mid-1882, it authorized a general tariff reform. Several months of talks convinced Foster that Cuba and Puerto Rico were excellent targets for a reciprocity agreement. In early 1884, he informed Frelinghuysen that a few concessions and lower duties on sugar might lead to "such a treaty with Spain as will secure to us almost the complete monopoly or control of the rich commerce of these islands."

Foster's serious negotiations with Spanish officials began shortly after Republicans concluded their national convention in Chicago. He brought with him a copy of the Mexican treaty and informed his somewhat reticent auditors of American plans for reciprocity agreements with other Caribbean countries. The talks promised to be lengthy; Foster observed wryly, "the Spanish temperament does not admit of celerity in the dispatch of public business." At times the American diplomat grew pessimistic, and at one point he wrote to Walter Q. Gresham, "If we fail in this treaty, I am pretty sure President Arthur will be disposed to 'growl' a little . . ."

On November 18, a treaty was signed calling for significant reductions in duties by both Spain and the United States and extending the free list to embrace eighty-eight categories. Foster was delighted by the result of his long labor, and at his suggestion he was recalled to Washington to observe the debate over ratification. On arriving at the nation's capital, the diplomat was shocked to read the full text of the treaty on the front page of *The New York Times*. The newspaper had purchased it for $2,000 from a Spanish official and rushed it into print before the new session of Congress could receive it from the President. The document was the sudden focus of immense controversy on Capitol Hill. "The question of its ratification or rejection," *The Times* stated proudly, "is by all odds the most important one now under discussion in Washington."[22]

A few days earlier Frelinghuysen had bestowed his signature on yet another reciprocity treaty, this time with the Dominican Republic. The original suggestion for such an agreement occurred in early 1883 when an American consul discussed reciprocity with the Dominican President, hoping to undercut French economic and political influence. Before long the nation's foreign minister proposed a treaty with the United States, and negotiations began in June 1884. Terms of the signed agreement were highly pleasing to the State Department; sixty-eight American products were placed on the free list, the tariff on such items as cotton and linen textiles was sharply lowered, and the dollar was made the Dominican Republic's unit of currency in international trade.

In the late fall the British initiated discussions in Washington for a reciprocity treaty with its Caribbean colonies. Proposals for similar treaties were received from three or four other Latin American nations eager to be part of a new commercial system.[23]

At the same time, Frelinghuysen was negotiating with the Hawaiian government for a lengthy extension of its reciprocity treaty. The document was signed on December 6, a few days after Congress assembled. It guaranteed controversy, for the original convention had been under fire in the Senate for more than three years. When Arthur asked Senators in June for advice on the matter, action upon the request was postponed.[24]

Lawmakers convening in Washington were thus faced during the short session not only with the Nicaraguan canal agreement but with four completed reciprocity treaties. Political observers marveled at the State Department's activity, but many questioned the willingness—even the ability—of Congress to agree to all the measures suddenly facing it.

By late 1884, concern was building in Congress and in the press about another administration venture in foreign affairs viewed by some to be extremely dangerous. In the spring of the year the United States had been the first nation to extend recognition to a state in Central Africa promoted by the controversial king of Belgium. In mid-November America's minister to Germany participated officially in a conference of European powers called to determine the future of the Congo Valley. Those who thought the traditional isolation of the United States threatened by a canal agreement and reciprocity treaties looked upon our interest in the heart of Africa with alarm and near disbelief.

Eight years earlier, Leopold II of Belgium had become intrigued with the prospect of creating a colony north of Portuguese Angola along the Congo. To mask his exploitive aspirations he created the African International Association and proclaimed its dedication to the highest scientific and humanitarian goals. He then sent an American agent, Colonel Henry S. Sanford, to employ the famous explorer Henry M. Stanley to negotiate treaties with natives. By the time Arthur became President, the association's flag flew over twenty-two stations in the lower Congo region. When France and Portugal made claims to adjacent areas, and Portugal appealed to Britain to recognize its alleged territorial rights, Leopold decided to seek recognition for his stations from the United States.

The king anticipated American friendship for several reasons. Sanford was a wealthy Republican with good connections in Washington. Stanley was very popular in the United States, still remembered for his rendezvous in 1871 with Dr. Livingstone. The administration's desire for trade was intense and did not seem inhibited by distance (a commercial treaty with Korea was signed in 1882).[25] Humanitarian and perhaps commercial aims had led the nation into a close relationship with Liberia.[26] Some Americans clung to the hope of exporting Negroes to Africa. Sanford even claimed that Americans would be wooed by the analogy between the association's stations and the American colonies in their struggle for international recognition.[27]

In April 1883, Sanford entertained Arthur at his Florida mansion during the President's southern vacation. In June, he and Leopold II sent letters to the White House suggesting that the United States recognize the neutrality of the Congo stations and promising in return to admit American products duty-free. That November, Sanford traveled to Washington to wage a direct campaign on Leopold's behalf, and he presented his case to the President and Secretary of State. Frelinghuysen wondered if the stations were self-sustaining and could qualify as a nation. He declined to extend recognition on the basis of evidence at hand and suggested that Sanford draft a description of the association's undertaking for further consideration. Arthur was obviously sympathetic with Sanford, and incorporated his claims into the annual message.

> The rich and populous valley of the Kongo is being opened to commerce by a society called the International African Association, of which the King of the Belgians is the president and a citizen of the United States the chief executive officer. Large tracts of territory have been ceded to the association by native chiefs, roads have been opened, steamboats placed on the river, and the nuclei of states established at twenty-two stations under one flag which offers freedom to commerce and prohibits the slave trade. The objects of the society are philanthropic. It does not aim at permanent political control, but seeks the neutrality of the valley. The United States can not be indifferent to this work nor to the interests of their citizens involved in it. It may become advisable for us to cooperate with other commercial powers in promoting the rights of trade and residence in the Kongo Valley free from the interference or political control of any one nation.[28]

During the first three months of 1884, Sanford proceeded to wage an intensive and expensive campaign to generate support for Leopold's project. He gave lavish dinners, made speeches, paid newspapers to run flattering articles and editorials, and appeared frequently at the State Department. He persuaded the New York chamber of commerce to come out for recognition and distributed thousands of reprints of the resolutions. He won over powerful Senator John T. Morgan of Alabama— who thought the Congolese "states" would welcome southern textiles and Negroes. The Senate Foreign Relations Committee, of which Morgan was a member, became a champion of the association's request. On April 10, with Senate backing, the President approved the extension of formal recognition.

Philanthropy, despite Sanford's propaganda and Arthur's message, was almost as insignificant to the American supporters of recognition as it was to Leopold. The great appeal in Washington and New York was the prospect of free trade, the hope of creating an open door in the Congo Valley for American products. Morgan told the Senate Foreign Relations Committee that trade in the Congo region already totaled two million pounds a year. In September, responding to action taken by Morgan, Frelinghuysen appointed a commercial agent for the area, instructing him to avoid political entanglements and spend his time seeking markets. "Both the people and the Government of the United States will be much better satisfied with the early extension and increase of our commerce there than by any other result of your mission," the secretary wrote.

While Leopold's stations were fairly secure by the spring of 1884, European powers continued to quarrel over adjacent territory for months. In the fall, German Chancellor Bismarck called a general conference to discuss free trade and navigation, and establish rules for creating new colonies. The meeting was scheduled for mid-November in Berlin, and invitations were sent to the United States and all interested European countries.

At the time, German-American relations were somewhat strained due to Berlin's ban on the importation of American pork products. The move was part of a broader European effort to protect domestic markets but was disguised in Germany as a health measure. (Arthur invited the German government to examine American packing plants. Ignored, he appointed a special commission to undertake an inspection.) Subsequent friction between American minister Aaron A. Sargent and the Iron Chancellor had led to Sargent's resignation in April 1884.[29] The new minister to Berlin, John A. Kasson, was a Stalwart, an expansionist, and a personal friend of Sanford; on the way to his post he stopped in Brussels for a chat with Leopold II. Not unexpectedly, Kasson assured Frelinghuysen that attendance at Bismarck's conference was desirable; he pointed to the presence on the program of significant commercial and humanitarian issues and noted that each participating government reserved the right to adopt or reject conference conclusions. The secretary accepted the invitation, instructing the minister to avoid action that would conflict with our venerable policy of noninterference and to work for unrestricted freedom of trade in the region.

Frelinghuysen soon approved a request by Kasson that Sanford and Stanley be permitted to join him on the American delegation to provide expertise. Both men continued in Leopold's employ and during the convention were at times in England and France working on behalf of the association. United States representation at the Berlin Congo Conference appeared thoroughly committed to the interests of the king of Belgium.

Kasson took an active part in the fourteen-nation conference when discussion centered upon free trade, and he and Stanley were instrumental in securing a strong statement on the subject. With Leopold's backing, he tried to win a guarantee of neutrality for the entire Congo Basin. He argued forcefully on behalf of machinery to settle international disputes stemming from the region. He spoke out against the interior slave trade and the liquor traffic with natives.

On February 25, the conference held its final session and extended formal recognition to the association's stations as the Congo Free State. (One scholar would call Leopold II the "real winner" at the conference.) Delegates signed a general act that supported free trade, free navigation, a conditional recognition of neutrality, religious freedom, and the suppression of the slave trade. One article required belligerent signatories to seek arbitration from a third party before going to war. Kasson and his colleagues were understandably pleased with the act and sent it immediately to Washington.[30]

American participation in the Berlin Conference drew a mixed reaction from the nation's press, with the more influential eastern newspapers and journals standing in opposition. Free trade lured many proponents, while others praised the humanitarian declarations in the general act. Critics, of course, condemned American diplomatic involvement with Europeans over matters they considered far too remote from our immediate interests. Blaine asked Sir Lionel Sackville-West, "How can we maintain the Monroe Doctrine when we take part in conferences on the internal affairs of other continents? We shall either be told some day to mind our own business or else be forced to admit governments to participation in the questions affecting America."[31] Even the New York *Herald* observed, "Some fine morning we may wake up to find a Berlin, London, Paris, or Madrid conference—to which we may not be invited as one among fifteen—sitting in solemn conclave and settling the internal affairs and local administration of Mexico, Panama, or Nicaragua."[32] Some opponents feared being dragged into a war over Africa. Several questioned Leopold's motives. A few wondered precisely what American products would be purchased by Central African natives.

The administration had evidence of support from the 48th Congress for its vision of commercial expansion. The Senate Foreign Relations Committee was cordial to a spirited and aggressive foreign policy; chairman John F. Miller led a bipartisan coalition that backed the Arthur-Frelinghuysen efforts almost without dissent. The Senate had voted to recognize the International Association of the Congo. The Mexican treaty had been ratified by two thirds of the Senate. In July, lawmakers approved funds for a three-man commission to sound out Latin American nations on the subject of greater hemispheric unity through reciprocity treaties and the development of an international silver coin.[33] Still, there were several good reasons for predicting that the second session of the 48th Congress would be a burial ground for most if not all of the outgoing administration's hopes.

The session had only three months in which to cope with four reciprocity treaties, the Nicaraguan canal treaty, and the general act of the Berlin Congo Conference. Congressional leadership at the time was weak; the first session's pace had been notoriously slow. Moreover, the proposals were complex and extremely controversial. The canal treaty contained unprecedented political and financial commitments in Latin America and appeared to violate a thirty-four-year pact with Great Britain. The reciprocity agreements threatened to reopen the entire debate over tariff reform. The general act could reverse a long tradition of isolation from European diplomacy. Each of the measures called for nothing less than a reassessment of the Monroe Doctrine.

Then too, the recent elections undoubtedly cost the administration a number of votes in the Senate. Half-Breeds, irritated by Frelinghuysen's abandonment of Blaine's foreign policy, bitterly resented what they considered Arthur's apathy during the recent contest. The Democratic minority, which controlled more than a third of the votes, was content to await the wishes of the next President. The House, faced with voting an appropriation for the loan to Nicaragua, enforcing the Mexican treaty, and implementing the reciprocity treaties, was controlled by Democrats, who had nothing to gain from an alliance with the administration. Perry Belmont, a trade-minded Democrat who sat on the House Foreign Affairs Committee, said in early December, "Even if it were possible to pass upon the merits of these treaties, I would consider it a duty to wait until Mr. Cleveland had outlined the policy which he and his Cabinet intend to pursue."[34]

Undaunted by the odds facing them, Arthur and Frelinghuysen were determined to persuade Congress to see things their way. They seemed especially anxious for the success of the Nicaraguan agreement. On the day he submitted his lengthy message to the Senate accompanying the treaty, the President ordered Navy Secretary Chandler to send a surveying party to Nicaragua. When this action was challenged by Senator G. G. Vest of Missouri, a backer of the Eads ship-railway, Chandler calmly referred to the power of his department under the Chief Executive to issue such orders to naval officers as may be deemed in the public interest.[35] When an intense dispute arose after the text of the treaty mysteriously appeared in the New York *Tribune*, Arthur and Freling-huysen huddled privately with the Senate Foreign Relations Committee. The President, apparently, did much of the talking, defending the earlier "slush fund" request and the loan to Nicaragua. He appointed Chairman Miller and Senators George F. Edmunds and E. G. Lapham to serve as a special subcommittee to work for ratification. Reports soon circulated that the Foreign Relations Committee had supported the treaty with only a single negative vote.[36]

On January 14, Frelinghuysen supplied Senator Miller with a lengthy defense of the pact, no doubt to be used by members of the subcommittee in dealings with colleagues. He went over the ground covered earlier by the President in detail and enclosed documents supporting administration contentions. On the sticky subject of our relations with the British, he repeated his earlier belief that the Clayton-Bulwer Treaty had lapsed; it "was a contract not obligatory upon one of the parties in case of default or violation of its provisions by the other." The canal accord, he emphasized, bore numerous rewards.

> It tends to prevent alien control or encroachment upon this continent, without interfering in any way with the free and independent sovereignty of Nicaragua, and without discriminating against any other nation. It knits our own country more closely together . . . ; it opens the markets of Asia and the West Coast of South America to the manufacturers of the Atlantic seaboard, and the Gulf ports and Europe to the producers of the Pacific Coast; it provides a new field for our coasting trade, and incidentally tends to the increase of American steam merchant marine and to the building of a class of steamers which, while profitable in peace will in time of war add largely to our effective naval force; . . .

The secretary acknowledged criticism of the administration for presenting to Congress such delicate and significant measures as the canal treaty and the reciprocity agreements at a late date. He asserted, however, that the policy undergirding them, which he described as "conservative and tending to the continuance of that amity and friendship which it is our duty to cultivate with all nations," was developed years earlier, shortly after Arthur took office. Correspondence about the Clayton-Bulwer Treaty prepared the way for an agreement with Nicaragua, with whom talks had long been under way; the Mexican treaty, which had roots going back to the summer of 1882, was the first step in the direction of new reciprocity agreements. "Treaties so important as these cannot be quickly concluded; much preliminary study is necessary before direct negotiations can begin, and after agreement upon general principles there is necessarily delay and discussion upon details. These treaties are all in the line of the same policy which aims to peacefully knit together the nations of this continent by bringing them into intimate commercial relations."[37]

The canal treaty came before the Senate in executive session on January 29. The first vote taken was on a motion to postpone consideration of the agreement until after March 4. The motion failed by a narrow margin of 25 to 22, and it was clear that the treaty as it stood could not win the two-thirds majority necessary for ratification. Treaty proponents then voted for an amendment offered by John Sherman, which passed by a large majority, requiring negotiations with Great Britain to secure the abrogation or major alteration of the Clayton-Bulwer Treaty. They realized that the amendment could delay construction of a canal indefinitely, given Britain's attitude toward the 1850 accord, but they hoped their concession might avert total defeat. Senator Edmunds and his colleagues from the Foreign Relations Committee worked all afternoon and into the evening to drum up votes, but in the end the amended treaty passed 32 to 23, five votes short of a two-thirds majority. The final ballot was a partisan response: only one Democrat outside the Foreign Relations Committee voted for the measure; the leader of the opposition was Thomas F. Bayard, soon to be Frelinghuysen's successor at the helm of the State Department.[38]

During the session's last week, Frelinghuysen forwarded dispatches to the Senate describing French and German interest in Central America, and he urged the Foreign Relations Committee to bring the canal treaty to another vote. It could not be done, and one of the administration's fondest hopes expired a few days later.[39]

Within several weeks of entering the White House, Grover Cleveland withdrew the Nicaragua treaty for "reexamination" and it was not resubmitted to the Senate. In his first annual message, the new President paid homage to "that irresistible tide of commercial expansion" and favored the general principle of an inter-oceanic waterway. But he thought the nation wiser to seek a neutralized canal, "a trust for mankind, to be removed from the chance of domination by any single power, nor become a point of invitation for hostilities or a prize for warlike ambitions."[40] On Bayard's advice, the United States detached itself from Central American affairs. The return to a more aggressive and nationalistic canal policy awaited other Republican Presidents at the turn of the century.

The reciprocity treaty with Spain fell under fire immediately after its public disclosure by *The New York Times*. Even before the treaty was officially submitted to Congress several tariff reformers joined with such ultra-protectionists as "Pig-Iron" Kelley in denouncing the document; a poll of the House Ways and Means Committee showed twelve of its fifteen members unequivocally opposed; Professor William Graham Sumner of Yale warned, "This treaty will have the effect to break up the protective tariff system." Within a few weeks, opposition was voiced by Samuel Gompers of the cigarmakers' union, the National Association of Wool Manufacturers, the Louisiana sugar planters, and business groups in more than twenty states. Blaine, as usual, did what he could to rally admirers against the administration.[41]

The Spanish treaty reached Capitol Hill on December 10, and like the canal accord was accompanied by a message from the President. It was a brief, uninspiring statement that described a bit of the document's history and goals and concluded with a personal commendation.[42] The administration launched its full offensive a few days later when newspapers carried a lengthy letter by Frelinghuysen explaining the treaty article by article and pointing out numerous economic advantages to the United States. "I cannot doubt," he wrote, "that the convention will work immediate benefit to our citizens, our trade, and our vessels." The tariff schedules attached to the treaty were published in the *Congressional Record* and in the press.[43]

The next day John W. Foster appeared at the offices of the New York chamber of commerce to defend the treaty before an audience of prominent businessmen and reporters. He stressed the value of obtaining free sugar in exchange for the opening of a new market for surplus American products, and he predicted a wide range of similar agreements. "This treaty must be promptly acted upon," he stated. "It cannot wait. It is the forerunner of others."[44]

On December 26, Frelinghuysen wrote a public letter to Senator Miller, at the request of the sympathetic Foreign Relations Committee chairman, replying to charges made against the Spanish treaty in Congress and in the press. The secretary emphatically denied rumors that the administration anticipated the annexation of Cuba and Puerto Rico. "Such action would be unwise . . . for, even could it be accomplished by general consent, our institutions would be endangered by this beginning of a colonial system, or by an incorporation into our body politic of a large population not in entire sympathy with our Government aims and methods." Still, by building a strong economic bridge between the United States and the islands the treaty "confers upon us and upon them all benefits which would result from annexation were that possible."

The treaty in question, he explained, was "one of a series of international engagements" involving reciprocity agreements with Mexico, Santo Domingo, Central America, and Colombia as well as the canal treaty with Nicaragua which "while bringing the most distant parts of our own country into closer relations opens the markets of the West Coast of South America to our trade and gives us at our doors a customer able to absorb a large portion of those articles which we produce in return for products which we cannot profitably raise." The letter concluded with responses to other arguments employed by treaty opponents: that it seriously reduced our tariff revenue, that it endangered our own sugar and tobacco industries, and that it was one of a class of agreements that infringed upon the constitutional rights of Congress.[45]

The effectiveness of the administration's campaign to this point was questionable; a great many observers predicted a dim future for the treaty. Some critics saw their most poignant argument standing outside the debate over the treaty's merits. E. L. Godkin wrote of "the rule which forbids a man retiring from an office to lay down lines of policy or create responsibilities unnecessarily for his successor." The editor was not above adding, "About the observance of this rule President Arthur ought to have been more than usually sensitive, seeing that he was not elected President, and that he never would, had the matter been submitted to the people, have been charged with the great powers which he is now exercising."[46]

Even though the text of the treaty with Spain was public knowledge and the press had covered much of the controversy surrounding it, the Senate discussed the reciprocity agreement behind closed doors during the first month of the session. On January 7, arch-protectionist Justin S. Morrill, chairman of the Senate Finance Committee, decided to bring his case against reciprocity out in the open by delivering a long speech on the Senate floor that was subsequently published in the *Congressional Record*. In the course of his address, the powerful Vermont Senator offered a resolution that read: "That so-called reciprocity treaties, having no possible basis of reciprocity with nations of inferior population and wealth, involving the surrender of enormously unequal sums of revenue, involving the surrender of immensely larger volumes of home trade than are offered to us in return, and involving constitutional questions of the gravest character, are untimely and should everywhere be regarded with disfavor." He singled out the Mexican accord as a case in point and submitted nine reasons why it should be discarded.[47]

Senator Lapham of the Foreign Relations Committee responded the next day, denying that reciprocity agreements encroached upon the constitutional power of the House to initiate money bills. Frelinghuysen took more than a month to reply. In a well-documented, carefully prepared letter to Senator Miller, the secretary countered the main thrust of the Senate resolution by arguing that reciprocity treaties were most effective when extended to the very nations Morrill labeled "inferior"—countries rich in raw materials and in need of the manufactures of other lands.

> The resources of the countries with which such treaties may be concluded are practically without limit, and their governments and people are fully alive to this fact. It follows that the superior nation which aids in such development can monopolize the greater portion of the import trade of each and all. . . . To attain such a consummation some revenue will have to be surrendered, and, perhaps, some home trade displaced; but for every dollar of revenue surrendered, and for every dollar's worth of home trade displaced, we will receive equivalent in our enlarged exports, and the impetus given to our various industries from the field to the factory and from the foundry to the ship-yard.[48]

The impact of the letter is unknown, for the Senate discussed it in executive session. By mid-February, however, it was clear to the administration that the Spanish treaty was in deep trouble. On February 24, the letter to Miller was made public, and two days later the President amended the treaty, extending the time limit for implementing legislation. On March 2, as a last-ditch effort to spur the Senate into action, Arthur sent four additional articles to Capitol Hill, worked out with Spain, designed to placate the domestic tobacco and sugar industries. But nothing happened; the treaty was not ratified. Cleveland withdrew it shortly and it permanently entered the State Department archives. The treaty with Santo Domingo was also permitted to die.[49]

The Mexican reciprocity treaty, already ratified, required action by the House. Abraham Hewitt of New York, a low-tariff Democrat, tried three times in late January to win consideration of an appropriate bill, but his motions were defeated by large majorities. Congressmen appeared indifferent to the treaty and were preoccupied with local questions, such as pensions for constituents. On February 27, Hewitt made a lengthy emotional appeal on behalf of the treaty, describing the need to secure foreign markets and lauding the Arthur Administration for its "very enlightened and conservative views." But the speech was ignored, and the House took no action before adjourning.[50] The reciprocity bill would be buried by a bipartisan vote a little more than a year later.

Difficulty was anticipated with the extension of the Hawaiian reciprocity treaty. The original agreement of 1875, which among other things placed sugar on the free list, was pushed through Congress over the angry objections of protectionists, eastern refiners, and southern sugar and rice planters only by an appeal to the strategic value of the islands. The battle resumed as the treaty approached termination. From the earliest months of the Arthur Administration, Congress was bombarded by petitions, resolutions, and propaganda. The Senate Committee on Finance, under the influence of Senator Morrill, criticized the treaty on both economic and political grounds. The Senate and House Committees on Foreign Relations, on the other hand, supported renewal. A deadlock ensued and had not been resolved when Frelinghuysen and the Hawaiian minister signed a new treaty on December 6.

For commercial reasons the administration looked favorably on the treaty from the start; Arthur endorsed extension in three annual messages. Proponents could point to a dramatic growth of Hawaiian sugar production and to a sharp rise in the American share of Hawaiian imports. Capital from the United States had poured into the islands, and by 1883 the Hawaiian economy was dominated by American businessmen. West Coast supporters pointed with pride to Claus Spreckels's gigantic sugar refinery, to a stimulated shipbuilding industry, and to the protection afforded them by the friendly islands. Expansionists gloried in the extension of American influence; the Hawaiian Islands, stated the Senate Committee on Foreign Relations, "may be said to be properly within the area of the physical and political geography of the United States. They are nearer to us than to any other great power." George S. Boutwell, lobbying for the treaty, warned that Great Britain was prepared to negotiate a similar agreement immediately should the American accord be abrogated.

Those who took exception to these arguments claimed that the treaty severely handicapped domestic planters and refiners, that it lacked genuine reciprocity and drained our treasury, and that it served as a cover to import sugars not within the scope of the agreement. Anti-imperialists feared that annexation was in the minds of too many supporters; the Senate Finance Committee denied the need for colonial possessions "so long as one-third of our acreage of lands remains uncultivated, and so long as the country is able annually to absorb and Americanize a million of foreign immigrants."

The second session of the 48th Congress was unable to iron out the intense differences of opinion about the new treaty with Hawaii. Even the Foreign Relations Committee fell into bickering over the contents of the document, some members seeking to add a naval station to the bargain. Senators packed their bags for home without taking action on the agreement. Two years later, Secretary of State Bayard, working with Senators Miller and Morgan, obtained an extension of the treaty with an amendment calling for a naval base at Pearl Harbor.[51]

The administration laid the groundwork for the general act of the Berlin Congo Conference many weeks before its contents were fully known. In his last annual message, Arthur wrote of "the rich prospective trade of the Kongo Valley" and advised Congress of Kasson's participation.[52] Frelinghuysen soon supplied the Senate Foreign Relations Committee with a preliminary report on the conference, and a few weeks later, upon request, submitted two full reports to the House covering the background and proceedings of the Berlin meeting. The House Foreign Affairs Committee sharply disapproved of American participation. Republicans on the committee reported a resolution that began, "no prospect of commercial advantage warrants a departure from the traditional policy of this Government which forbids all entangling alliances with the nations of the Old World . . ." The debate was moot, however, for the general act of the conference did not reach the Senate Foreign Relations Committee until a few days before the session ended, and no effort was made to present it on the floor of the Senate.[53]

Cleveland quickly disassociated the United States from the general act, declaring that the government did not consider its freedom of action in the Congo at all impaired, and adding that "an engagement to share in the obligation of enforcing neutrality in the remote valley of the Kongo would be an alliance whose responsibilities we are not in a position to assume . . ."[54] Frelinghuysen's commercial agent for the Congo, who had earlier transmitted reports that "the Congo Valley surpasses in wealth the valley of the Amazon," traveled to Central Africa and wrote letters to Bayard in 1885 and 1886 strongly discouraging American involvement in the region. A personal survey of the Free State's geography, climate, economy, population, government, and transportation facilities convinced him that the Arthur Administration had been badly misled by the glowing promises of Leopold II and his minions.[55]

Only the reciprocity treaty with Hawaii survived of the precipitous measures proposed in the winter of 1884–1885, and it was really the product of an earlier decade and was ratified after Arthur's death. Frelinghuysen returned to New Jersey following Cleveland's inauguration, discouraged and mortally ill. (He died of hepatitis on May 20.) All of his private papers and much of his public correspondence disappeared. He was quickly forgotten in Washington. The Arthur Administration's foreign policy, aside from its peace-keeping activities, appeared to most contemporaries to be without consequence, and it would earn little attention from historians until well into the next century.[56]

The Angel of Sorrow

ARTHUR ANTICIPATED his retirement from public life with great pleasure during the last months of his term. When George Bliss asked about his future plans, he replied with a smile, "Well, there doesn't seem anything else for an ex-President to do but to go into the country and raise big pumpkins."[1] He was financially comfortable. Much, if not most, of his annual $50,000 salary had been spent for personal and official expenses while in the White House, and there was no pension for a former Chief Executive to fall back on. But he had some stock and more than several thousand dollars in cash at hand, and over the years he had purchased and inherited a number of valuable pieces of property in New York City and in Long Branch, New Jersey. He knew too that he could command a good yearly income by rejoining his law firm. (His total worth a few years later approached $161,000.)[2] Arthur needed rest and quiet, and intended to return to his Lexington Avenue home and live out the remainder of his life with his children. He would, of course, keep an eye on local politics: Stalwarts were still a force in the city and state Republican machinery; Johnny O'Brien was chairman of the city's central committee. But his consistently declining health, if not the keen sense of propriety attained with the presidency, would preclude any active involvement in the partisan warfare that had occupied most of his life.

Unaware of the President's physical condition and his desire to become and remain a private citizen, a number of loyal New York Stalwarts met in an Albany hotel on December 3, 1884, to discuss Arthur's candidacy for the United States Senate. Conkling's old seat, held since mid-1881 by Elbridge G. Lapham, would soon be up for grabs, and

Steve French, George Sharpe, and Jim Warren, among others, concluded that their former boss would be the ideal candidate. They knew that Arthur had flirted with the thought of a senatorship before seeking the vice-presidency. And they were naïvely confident that Republicans of all persuasions in the legislature would rally behind the Chief Executive once he declared for the office.[3]

Arthur was approached by his friends on December 4 and declined their overture. For several days the appeals continued, but without result. The Stalwarts refused to concede defeat at the outset, and newspapers were left free to speculate about the President's intentions. Half-Breeds throughout New York quickly swore their opposition to Arthur's candidacy; the New York *Tribune* carried numerous attacks upon the administration's conduct during the recent national election. Conjecture was concluded on December 14 when presidential secretary Fred Phillips stated unequivocally that Arthur was not and had never been a candidate for the Senate seat.[4]

The race soon became a contest between Levi P. Morton and William M. Evarts. Cornell, Platt, Payn, Dutcher, and other anti-Arthur Stalwarts were behind Morton. This was undoubtedly a factor in persuading almost all of the Arthur men to support Evarts. George Bliss, Johnny O'Brien, and Jim Warren found themselves working side by side with the young reformer Theodore Roosevelt and veteran Blaine campaigner Senator Warner Miller. Such was the total wreck of GOP factions produced by the dizzying events of recent years. On January 19, the Republican caucus gave Evarts the nod by a lopsided vote of 61 to 28. Roosevelt crowed, "It is a victory for clean halfbreeds, clean stalwarts, and the independent wing of the party."[5]

The public had several opportunities to view the twenty-first President during his final months in office. On December 20, he appeared at Dupont Circle in Washington to dedicate a huge statue of the late Rear-Admiral Samuel Francis Dupont. William Chandler, one of four Cabinet members present, made brief remarks, and Senator Thomas Bayard followed with an oration devoted to the controversial navy hero.[6]

Two months later Arthur read a terse and eloquent speech at the dedication of the Washington National Monument. The cornerstone of the 555-foot column had been laid on July 4, 1848. Funds ran out in a few years, and the unfinished structure, an unsightly pile with a derrick atop its summit, loomed over the nation's capital for nearly a quarter century. In 1876, Congress finally took steps toward its completion, and on December 6, 1884, the 3,300-pound capstone was put in place while cannons roared their approval below.

Snow lay on the ground on George Washington's Birthday and the weather was cold and blustery. At the base of the majestic shaft 800 people shivered in the grandstand, applauding speeches by Senator John Sherman, chairman of the Joint Congressional Committee, W. W. Corcoran of the Washington National Monument Society (which had paid $300,000 of the $1,187,710 cost), and Colonel Thomas L. Casey of the United States Engineer Corps. The President was greeted with cheers, and his eulogy of Washington won the crowd's attention and respect. A grand procession to the Capitol followed under the marshalship of General Sheridan. In front of the east main entrance Arthur, surrounded by dignitaries and a crowd of 3,000, reviewed waves of troops. The President, his Cabinet, and General Sheridan and his staff then proceeded to the House of Representatives where they were joined by members of Congress, the Supreme Court, the diplomatic corps, the judiciary of the District, and a packed gallery. Representative John D. Long of Massachusetts read an address given thirty-seven years earlier at the laying of the cornerstone by Robert C. Winthrop of Boston. A florid oration by Governor John W. Daniel of Virginia concluded the ceremonies of the historic day. "Encompassed by the inviolate seas stands to-day the American Republic which he founded—a free Greater Britain—uplifted above the powers and principalities of the earth, even as his monument is uplifted over roof and dome and spire of the multitudinous city."[7]

That evening Arthur hosted his last public reception. Some 3,000 people poured into the White House to pay their respects and shake hands with the President. To conserve Arthur's strength, guests were hurried through the receiving line three and four abreast.[8]

On February 28, Mrs. McElroy's final reception drew another crowd of 3,000. Forty-eight young ladies, daughters of officials and Washington society people, were on hand to assist the President's sister. Another of Arthur's sisters, Mrs. Malvina Haynesworth, was also present; over the past three and one half years she had appeared from time to time at the White House to take care of Nell and participate in social events. Reporters described in rich detail the costly attire of the most prominent figures in attendance. Someone noticed the arctic explorer Lieutenant Adolphus Washington Greely discussing cremation with one wide-eyed lady, a topic apparently suggested by his recent harrowing experiences in the frigid zone.[9]

Arthur's last official act was the signing of a message to the Senate nominating U. S. Grant to be placed on the army retired list with the rank and full pay of general. The sixty-two-year-old former President, bankrupt, dying, desperately trying to complete his war memoirs, found himself again in the highest public favor, and efforts were made in

Congress to reward him for his long service to the nation. When he refused to accept a pension, Arthur sent a special message to Congress on February 3, 1885, urging passage of legislation that would authorize the President to nominate Grant as a general on the retired list.[10]

Democratic floor leader Samuel Randall brought a Grant bill before the House with less than three hours remaining to the 48th Congress. It passed 198 to 78, and Congressmen cheered until they were hoarse. The bill was sent to the Senate where it was received with more cheering and approved by a unanimous vote. The clock was set back six minutes to give the President, seated nearby in the Vice-President's room, sufficient time to sign the bill and hastily write a message complying with its mandate. When Fred Phillips rushed into the Senate chamber with the message in his hand, he was greeted with a burst of elated shouts and applause. The Senate confirmed the nomination unanimously in open session and resumed the demonstration. These last-minute proceedings in the upper house were observed by members of the diplomatic corps, who had entered in full court dress to participate in the ceremonies inaugurating the twenty-second President.[11]

Arthur and Cleveland had ridden side by side from the White House to the Capitol in the rear seat of a handsome barouche drawn by spanking bays. Pennsylvania Avenue was splendidly decorated with flags and banners, and thousands of people turned out in warm, clear weather to see the spectacular procession of troops, bands, and officials. Democrats had streamed into Washington, eager to catch a look at their party's first President since Buchanan; windows along the route were leased at from $6 to $25 according to the height above the street; many rooms were let for $200 apiece. Cleveland graciously acknowledged the deafening clamor of the crowd with bows, his hat in hand; in the following carriage Thomas A. Hendricks, Cleveland's running mate, similarly welcomed the boisterous cheering—and occasional rebel yells.

With the work of the 48th Congress concluded, the Senate chamber filled with diplomats, Supreme Court justices, Congressmen, Cabinet members, generals, admirals, governors, and scores of others who could wangle seats to the ceremony at which the Vice-President-elect and a number of newly elected Senators took their oath of office. (Henry Teller was sworn in as a Senator from Colorado.) Arthur and Cleveland made separate entrances, each drawing loud ovations from the standing audience.

A throng estimated at from 30,000 to 50,000 roared with delight when the dignitaries filed out onto the huge platform at the east front. The new and outgoing Presidents were seated beside each other in the first row, opposite Chief Justice Waite. On Arthur's right sat a long-time admirer, the silver-bearded historian George Bancroft. The inaugural address contained a predictable quantity of bland historical allusions and pious pronouncements, and was well received. To allay fears about his backing from the Solid South, Cleveland stressed the need for national unity and expressed his concern for the rights of southern Negroes. He committed himself to frugality with public funds and promised to enforce civil service reform. The only faint reference to the work of the Arthur Administration occurred when he called for a strictly isolationist foreign policy, "rejecting any share in foreign broils and ambitions upon other continents and repelling their intrusion here."[12]

After Cleveland was sworn in, he and Arthur returned to the White House and reviewed a procession containing some 25,000 men. The ex-President then gave a luncheon for his successor. Arthur had been quiet and dignified throughout the pomp and pageantry of the long day and revealed nothing of his thoughts to the crowds or to the few with whom he briefly chatted. He was obviously emotional, however, when he said good-bye to the White House staff that afternoon.[13] His personal belongings were crated, ready for shipment to 123 Lexington Avenue. He was to spend the next few days at the Frelinghuysen residence.

That evening the massive new Pension Building was the site of a lavish inaugural ball. Arthur, accompanied by members of his Cabinet and their wives, arrived at the ballroom at 10:45, and Cleveland and his party appeared a few minutes later. The two Chief Executives stood at either end of a huge semicircle shaking hands for over an hour with hundreds of well-wishers. Arthur received a great many compliments during this his last public ceremonial at the nation's capital. At some point during the flow of adulation he might have thought back to that day of anguish, not four years earlier, when he stepped off the steamer from Albany to learn that the President had been gunned down in his name and that he was the target of nationwide contempt.[14]

Arthur had announced in mid-January that he would resume the practice of law in New York City and devote his entire time to it. He wished to head his old firm, but his health was such that he could serve only as counsel. A handsome suite was provided on the fourth floor of the Mutual Life Building; a life-size painting of Grant hung behind Arthur's personal desk, and in the outer office were pictures of E. D. Morgan and William Evarts. The former President was paid a salary of $1,000 a month, but his duties were restricted to office matters of little consequence, and he was frequently too ill to leave home.[15]

During the last six weeks of his residence in the White House Arthur's physical condition had caused personal friends much concern;

one later described it as "deplorable."[16] He was soon receiving almost daily massage treatments, and physicians paid frequent visits.[17] At times he felt stronger, but relapses were sudden and inevitable. He attended Frelinghuysen's funeral and Alan's graduation from Princeton in the spring of 1885.[18] His last public appearance was on December 30 of that year when he presided over a meeting held at the Court of Common Pleas in New York City honoring retiring Chief Justice Charles P. Daly.[19]

The following February, Arthur's health took a sharp turn for the worse, and news of his encounter with Bright's disease leaked into the press. By March, Arthur's condition was at times critical, and he made out his will. Only milk and pepsin would stay in his stomach, and the advanced heart disease linked with his kidney ailment became apparent. Mrs. Regina Caw and Mrs. Mary McElroy left their families to be with their brother, and Alan and Nell rarely left the house. In April, Arthur caught cold and it was feared the end was near. In June, he rallied slightly, and his family took him to a cottage in New London, Connecticut, for quiet relaxation. When they returned to New York on October 1, Arthur remained an invalid, spending most of his time in bed or propped up in a reclining chair in his bedroom.[20] When Chief Justice Waite and former President Hayes called shortly, Arthur could rise only on one elbow to greet them, and was later described by Hayes as "thin and feeble."[21]

Though he had known for years of his fatal disease, and while his condition was now obviously grave, Arthur persisted in exuding optimism to callers, correspondents, even his sisters. Walter Q. Gresham was assured in August, "My progress in recovering my health is slow and tedious, but I have strong hope that ere the summer is past I shall be as good as new."[22] In a letter to William Chandler dictated the day before his fifty-seven birthday, Arthur said, "I think I am getting better—but very slowly."[23] He told Mary McElroy of his vacation plans for the following summer and spoke about future real estate transactions he had in mind.[24] Every effort was made to honor his wish that word of his illness should not reach the press. His private physician would later recall, "he was a brave, strong man to the last, and few men deserved better to live."[25]

On November 16, Arthur had a mild resurgence of strength. He received visitors, dictated several letters, and was able to sign some legal documents. He told his doctor, "I haven't felt better in six months."[26] At his father's request, Alan brought an old Customhouse friend named Jimmy Smith to the Arthur home, and Smith was asked by the former President to destroy virtually all of his personal and official papers. While Alan watched, three large garbage cans were filled repeatedly and their contents burned.[27] Arthur had told a Cabinet member during his stay at New London that there were many things in his political career he wished had been different.[28] He sternly advised his son never to go into politics; the price demanded of him for his office had been far too high.[29]

At 8:00 A.M. on November 17, Arthur was found unconscious by his male nurse, the victim of a massive cerebral hemorrhage. At 5:00 A.M. the next morning he was dead.

Washington clothed itself in black and lowered its flags to half-mast. Executive departments closed on November 22 and a cannon boomed at half-hour intervals. Numerous organizations quickly assembled to pass resolutions honoring the memory of the twenty-first President. Newspapers of every persuasion heaped praise upon Arthur for his services in the White House; the Democratic New York *Sun* proclaimed, "it is not too much to say that he was one of the most successful and meritorious in our whole list of Presidents."[30] Very few thought it proper to talk about the "Gentleman Boss." When a reporter approached Carl Schurz for a comment on Arthur's career, he politely declined, saying that he had met the deceased only four or five times and had no personal reminiscences.[31]

Private funeral services were held on Monday, November 22, at the Church of the Heavenly Rest, Mrs. Arthur's former parish. A thousand policemen and six companies of United States artillery kept a huge crowd at a distance of several blocks as more than a hundred carriages slowly made their way in the rain to Fifth Avenue and Forty-fifth Street. Inside, the cloth-covered oak coffin was placed lengthwise in the aisle on a low catafalque. To its right sat Arthur's children, his five sisters and their husbands, and several other relatives. (William Arthur Jr. was stationed in San Antonio, Texas.) In the pews on the left were the pallbearers: Walter Q. Gresham, Robert T. Lincoln, William E. Chandler, Frank Hatton, Benjamin H. Brewster, General Philip H. Sheridan, Dr. Cornelius R. Agnew, Cornelius N. Bliss, Robert G. Dun, George H. Sharpe, Charles L. Tiffany, and Cornelius Vanderbilt. Behind them sat President Cleveland and his Cabinet and former President Hayes. Benjamin F. Butler was in the adjoining pew. Chief Justice Waite and Supreme Court Justices Blatchford and Harlan were next, and in a side pew could be seen the now snow-white Hyperion curl of Roscoe Conkling. Behind the judges sat Blaine. Many Senators, Representatives, and local officials were on hand, as were diplomats, military figures, delegations from clubs, organizations, the press, and financial institutions, and hundreds of others.

The coffin was taken to Albany in Cornelius Vanderbilt's private car and was buried in the Arthur family plot at the Rural Cemetery. Three years later a large black marble monument was erected on the spot. A bronze, life-size Angel of Sorrow lays a palm branch on top of a black granite sarcophagus.[32]

In 1899, a seventeen-foot-eight-inch, full-length bronze statue of Arthur was unveiled in the northeast corner of Madison Square, a few blocks from his former Lexington Avenue residence and opposite the building that once housed the Union League Club. The $25,000 asked by sculptor George E. Bissell was raised by friends. Mary McElroy and two or three hundred invited guests were present for the ceremony, as were several thousand spectators. Elihu Root, within a month of being named Secretary of War by President McKinley, gave the presentation speech. He dwelt at length on the anguish he had observed Arthur suffer during the summer and fall of 1881.

> Surely no more lonely and pathetic figure was ever seen assuming the powers of government. He had no people behind him, for Garfield, not he, was the people's choice. He had no party behind him, for the dominant faction of his party hated his name, were enraged by his advancement, and distrusted his motives. He had not even his own faction behind him; for he already knew that the just discharge of his duties would not accord with the ardent desires of their partisanship, and that disappointment and estrangement lay before him there. He was alone. He was bowed down by the weight of fearful responsibility and crushed to the earth by the feeling, exaggerated but not unfounded, that he took up his heavy burden, surrounded by dislike, suspicion, distrust, and condemnation as an enemy of the martyred Garfield and the beneficiary of his murder.

Root went on to praise Arthur for his ability to overcome these handicaps and create a creditable record as Chief Executive. "He was wise in statesmanship and firm and effective in administration. Honesty in national finance, purity and effectiveness in the civil service, the promotion of commerce, the re-creation of the American navy, reconciliation between North and South and honorable friendship with foreign nations received his active support. Good causes found in him a friend and bad measures met in him an unyielding opponent."[33]

Visitors today might notice that the statue looks toward the southeast corner of the small park where another fine bronze statue ponders human vanity. It is of Roscoe Conkling.

Conclusion

MUCH TRUTH lies within Elihu Root's panegyric. Arthur deserves praise for his desire and ability to overcome the extremely negative image he presented to the nation during the spring and summer of 1881; the abrupt but nonetheless genuine transformation from a spoils-hungry, no-holds-barred Conkling henchman into a restrained, dignified Chief Executive who commanded the admiration of the American people was recognized and appreciated by a great many of his contemporaries. Alexander K. McClure exaggerated excusably when he wrote, "No man ever entered the Presidency so profoundly and widely distrusted as Chester Alan Arthur, and no one ever retired from the highest civil trust of the world more generally respected, alike by political friend and foe."[1] Ironically, he might have been better remembered by future generations if he had conducted himself in the White House as his most fervid detractors predicted. Albert K. Weinberg once correctly observed, "Had Arthur only fulfilled the sensational pessimism of his initial critics—that is, proved a bad President—he doubtless would have had greater fame."[2]

Root alluded to the President's most commendable achievements. His appointments, if unspectacular, were unusually sound; the corruption and scandal that dominated the business and politics of the period did not tarnish his administration. The pursuit of the star route plunderers was honorable. The veto of the Rivers and Harbors bill was long considered courageous. Arthur played a positive role in the passage of the Pendleton Act and won plaudits for his enforcement of civil service reform. His selections for the Tariff Commission proved wise. He contributed in no small way to the beginnings of the new navy. And the reversal of Blaine's meretricious Latin American foreign policy was popular at the time.

More than anything, the public sought from Chester A. Arthur an end to the chaos and tension that surrounded the struggle for the New York Customhouse and Garfield's murder; he was asked to restore calm and confidence. His success with that deceptively simple request was acknowledged by most observers. During the Progressive Era, when Presidents were expected to be dramatic and demanding and the federal government was seen as a powerful public benefactor, William Chandler undertook the difficult task of explaining what had been expected of Arthur a mere generation earlier. "If his conduct of affairs be criticized as lacking aggressiveness," he wrote, "it may confidently be replied that aggressiveness would have been unfortunate, if not disastrous. Rarely has there been a time when an indiscreet president could have wrought more mischief. It was not a time for showy exploits of brilliant experimentation. Above all else, the people needed rest from the strain and excitement into which the assassination of their president had plunged them. The course chosen by President Arthur was the wisest and most desirable that was possible."[3] Indeed, Arthur was most frequently and loudly criticized for the assertiveness he chose to display during his brief term. Steps taken to bolster the navy, construct an inter-oceanic canal, open the Congo to American products, and create reciprocity treaties with other nations of the hemisphere appeared unnecessary and even dangerous on Capitol Hill. A great majority of the often extraordinarily farseeing requests made by Arthur in his annual messages were ignored by Congress. The message of 1883, for example, contained eight important recommendations, including federal aid for education, a presidential succession law, regulation of interstate commerce, and forest preservation. Congress responded to only one of the eight, territorial government for Alaska, and that was endorsed probably with the thought of eventual votes, offices, and patronage.[4]

The calming effect Arthur had on the country, especially after the elections of 1882, contributed to his great popularity with East Coast business leaders. (Historian Matthew Josephson observed of Arthur, "In some ways he impressed himself upon the minds of important businessmen as the most effective President since Lincoln." The assessment is plausible.)[5] At a giant rally of business moguls in New York on May 20, 1884, convened to boost Arthur's nomination, Henry Ward Beecher proclaimed, "I hold that the business part of the community represents in many respects the best interests of our whole country, and business men perhaps more than others require stable government."[6] Of course, Arthur was also appreciated for his conservative views on currency, banking, the tariff, taxation, and the role of government. Two days after he left office he was unanimously elected an honorary member of the New York chamber of commerce. A prominent official of the chamber orated, "Mr. Arthur has . . . by his prudent and conservative course and by the ability of his administration of the executive branch of the Government, earned the confidence and respect of men of all parties. He has always been ready to listen with intelligent appreciation to the representatives of business men, and his recommendations to Congress relating to commercial and financial affairs have been especially sound."[7] In the 1880s— and long after—few if any honors could be considered equal to such praise.

Still, there was no evidence in 1884 of a significant public outcry for a second term. Arthur badly trailed Blaine in the polls taken prior to the Republican National Convention, and the Plumed Knight's personality and political ties comprise only a partial explanation. The President, while quite popular by every available indicator, did not inspire great numbers of men to rally behind him. However grateful the American people were to Arthur for his dignified and responsible handling of the nation's highest office at a time of crisis, they appeared perfectly willing to see him retire on March 4, 1885.

Arthur was unable to overcome completely the memories of his background as a machine spoilsman. For one thing, there was too little time: he was actively pursuing Stalwart interests until the day Garfield was shot. Charges—almost all of them false—encircling Conkling's Supreme Court nomination, the alliance with Mahone, the disastrous elections of 1882, the humiliation of Silas Burt, the awarding of ship contracts to John Roach, and the star route trials convinced many that the President, however well intentioned he might be, was a victim of his past. The cloud of Grantism that hovered over the White House during the fall of 1881 was never entirely dispelled.

Then too, most of Arthur's finest efforts had no immediate positive impact. Dorsey and his friends escaped jail; the Rivers and Harbors veto was overridden; the Tariff Commission's recommendations were dismissed by Congress; the rejuvenation of the navy was barely begun.

In retrospect it is impossible to avoid the conclusion that Arthur might have made an even more attractive impression on his contemporaries (and for posterity) by communicating more regularly and openly with the public. The administration sustained many wounds because no one at the White House would firmly and officially set the record straight, and that was the President's fault. Arthur had no regular dealings with the press and granted very few interviews. When he did encounter newspapermen, he consistently refused to answer questions dealing with personal or political affairs.[8] For information, reporters turned to the President's friends and visitors. (Cabinet members were also tight-lipped.) They very frequently resorted to rumors—often started by Arthur's enemies. A later student of the subject called the administration "one of the really arid spots in the long history of Presidential relations with the press."[9]

Throughout his entire political career Arthur was extremely sensitive to newspaper criticism. Silas Burt noted this as early as 1866.[10] In 1883, a New York Stalwart spoke of "the mental fear" the President had of newspapers.[11] Before entering the White House Arthur had no doubt wished to keep the details of his occupation private; spoilsmen worked most effectively behind closed doors. He was also touchy about his reputation. He never forgave the press for the coverage given to his speech at Delmonico's, for the roasting he took while traveling to Albany as Vice-President, or for the insinuations by some journalists that he was in league with Guiteau. As President he was unable to overcome this prejudice, and every burning cartoon in *Puck* or biting editorial in the New York *Tribune* only caused him to withdraw further from reporters. Then, too, Arthur cherished what privacy he could retain in the White House and strove to shield his children from the corruptions of fame. He also affected a degree of aristocratic disdain for the public; he felt it undignified to share his thoughts through any other channel than formal presidential messages and an occasional dedicatory speech.[12]

Of course, there were two important secrets Arthur was intent on keeping from the prying pens of the press during his last years of the administration: his mortal illness and the decision not to make an effort for the 1884 nomination. These above all, perhaps, explain his unwillingness to become more friendly and open with the public. He was not running for office; indeed, he had never sought the presidency and gave every indication of disliking it intensely. He was without the need to rally men to his banner, and he chose not to try.

Given Arthur's political background, the traumatic and unprecedented circumstances of his elevation to the White House, his fractured party, the divided and slothful Congresses he faced, the severe restraints upon the presidency at the time, and the burden of his poor health, his record as Chief Executive is both respectable and admirable. He was a good President at a period in our history when the American people neither expected nor sought great Presidents.[13] The New York *World* concluded in 1886, "No duty was neglected in his administration, and no adventurous project alarmed the nation. There was no scandal to make us ashamed while he was in office and none to be ripped up when he went out of it. He earned and deserved the honest fame he possesses."[14] Those who had known Arthur as a young man—as a student, teacher, fledgling attorney, and military officer—were surely not surprised by his able performance. Most of those who had known only the "Gentleman Boss" were astonished and pleased.

SELECTIVE BIBLIOGRAPHY

MANUSCRIPT COLLECTIONS

Arthur, Chester A.: Papers, Library of Congress
Arthur, Chester A.: Papers, New-York Historical Society
Arthur, Chester A.: Personnel File, General Records of the Treasury Department, National Archives
Arthur Family Papers, Library of Congress
Blaine, James G.: Papers, Library of Congress
Bliss, George: Papers, New-York Historical Society
Bristow, Benjamin: Papers, Library of Congress
Burt, Silas: Papers, New-York Historical Society
Burt, Silas: Papers, New York Public Library
Chandler, William E.: Papers, Library of Congress
Chandler, William E.: Papers, New Hampshire State Historical Society
Cleveland, Grover: Papers, Library of Congress
Conkling, Roscoe: Papers, Library of Congress
Cornell, Alonzo B.: Cornell University
Davis, David: Papers, Chicago Historical Society
Depew, Chauncey M.: Papers, Yale University
Evarts, William M.: Papers, Library of Congress
Folger, Charles J.: Papers, New York Public Library
Frelinghuysen, Frederick T.: Papers, Library of Congress
Garfield, James A.: Papers, Library of Congress
Grant, U. S.: Papers, Library of Congress
Greene, Augustus Porter: Papers, New-York Historical Society
Gresham, Walter Q.: Papers, Library of Congress
Hampton, Vernon B.: Papers, Staten Island, New York
Harrison, Benjamin: Papers, Library of Congress
Hayes, Rutherford B.: Papers, Rutherford B. Hayes Library, Fremont, Ohio
Herndon, Brodie: Papers, University of Virginia
Howe, Timothy O.: Papers, State Historical Society of Wisconsin
Jay Commission: Papers, National Archives

Joline, Adrian Hoffman: Collection, Henry E. Huntington Library, San Marino, California
Jonas, Harold J.: Collection, New York Public Library
McCulloch, Hugh: Papers, Library of Congress
Morgan, Edwin D.: Papers, New York State Library
Morton, Levi P.: Papers, New York Public Library
Pinkerton, Charles: Collection, Library of Congress
Porter, Fitz John: Papers, Library of Congress
Reeves, Thomas C.: Collection, Library of Congress
Sherman, John: Papers, Library of Congress
Spicka, Mrs. Charles: Collection, Microfilm, Wyoming State Historical Society
Strouse, Norman H. and Charlotte A.: Collection, Free Library of Philadelphia
Teller, Henry M.: Papers, Colorado State Historical Society
White, Andrew D.: Papers, Cornell University

NEWSPAPERS

Albany *Evening Journal*
Albany *Examiner*
Albany, *The Knickerbocker Press*
Albany *Morning Express*
Atlanta *Constitution*
Baltimore *Sun*
Boston *Herald*
Boston *Transcript*
Boston *Weekly Journal*
Buffalo *Commercial Advertiser*
Chicago *Evening News*
Chicago *Herald*
Chicago *Inter Ocean*
Chicago *Times*
Chicago *Tribune*
Cincinnati *Enquirer*
Cleveland *Leader*
Frederick Douglass' Paper
Harper's Weekly
Hartford *Evening Post*
Indianapolis *Journal*
Johnstown (New York) *Daily Republican*
Lansingburgh (New York) *Democrat*

Lansingburgh (New York) *Semi-Weekly Chronicle*
Manchester (New Hampshire) *Union*
The Nation
New York *Commercial Advertiser*
New York *Daily News*
New York *Dispatch*
New York *Evening Post*
New York *Journal*
New York *Mail and Express*
New York *Sun*
New York Times, The
New York *Tribune*
New York *Truth*
New York *World*
Philadelphia *Press*
Philadelphia *Times*
Rochester *Sunday Morning Herald*
Schenectady *Gazette*
Troy (New York) *Light and Life*
Troy (New York) *Northern Budget*
Troy (New York) *Record*
Washington *Commercial Advertiser*
Washington, *The National Republican*

Washington *Post*

OTHER PUBLICATIONS

Adams, Henry: *Letters of Henry Adams, 1858–1891.* Edited by Worthington Chauncey Ford. Boston, 1930.
Adams, Henry, Mrs.: *The Letters of Mrs. Henry Adams, 1865–1883.* Edited by Ward Thoron. Boston, 1937.

Alden, John D.: *The American Steel Navy.* New York, 1972.

Alexander, De Alva Stanwood: *A Political History of the State of New York.* New York, 1909. 4 vols.

Arthur, William: *An Etymological Dictionary of Family and Christian Names, with an Essay on their Derivation and Import.* New York, 1857.

Arthur, William, ed.: *The Antiquarian, and General Review.* Schenectady and Lansingburgh, New York, 1845–1849. 4 vols.

Badeau, Adam: *Grant in Peace, From Appomattox to Mount McGregor.* Hartford, 1887.

Bancroft, Caroline: *Silver Queen, the Fabulous Story of Baby Doe Tabor.* Boulder, 1950.

Barnard, Harry: *Rutherford B. Hayes and His America.* Indianapolis, 1954.

Barnes, James A.: *John G. Carlisle, Financial Statesman.* New York, 1931.

Barnes, Thurlow Weed: *Memoir of Thurlow Weed.* Boston, 1884.

Barrows, Chester Leonard: *William M. Evarts, Lawyer, Diplomat, Statesman.* Chapel Hill, 1941.

Barry, David S.: *Forty Years in Washington.* Boston, 1924.

Bastert, Russell H.: "Diplomatic Reversal: Frelinghuysen's Opposition to Blaine's Pan-American Policy in 1882," *Mississippi Valley Historical Review,* XLII (1956), 653–671.

————: "A New Approach to the Origins of Blaine's Pan-American Policy," *Hispanic American Historical Review,* XXXIX (1959), 375-412.

Belden, Thomas Graham and Marva Robins: *So Fell the Angels.* Boston, 1956.

Belmont, Perry: *An American Democrat, the Recollections of Perry Belmont.* New York, 1940.

Binkley, Wilfred E.: *The President and Congress.* New York, 1947.

Blaine, Mrs. James G.: *The Letters of Mrs. James G. Blaine.* Edited by Harriet Stanwood Blaine Beale. New York, 1908. 2 vols.

Boutwell, George S.: *Reminiscences of Sixty Years in Public Affairs.* New York, 1902. 2 vols.

Bradley, Hugh: *Such Was Saratoga.* New York, 1940.

Brisbin, James S.: *From the Tow-Path to the White House.* Philadelphia, 1880.

Bronner, Frederick L.: "Chester A. Arthur, His College Years," in *Chester Alan Arthur Class of 1848.* Schenectady, 1948.

Brown, Philip Marshall: "Frederick T. Frelinghuysen," in Samuel Flagg Bemis, ed.: *The American Secretaries of State and Their Diplomacy.* New York, 1927–1929. 10 vols.

Brummer, Sidney D.: *Political History of New York State During the Period of the Civil War.* New York, 1911.

Burt, Silas: *My Memories of the Military History of the State of New York During the War for the Union, 1861–65.* Albany, 1902.

Callow, Alexander B., Jr.: *The Tweed Ring.* New York, 1966.

Carpenter, Francis, ed.: *Carp's Washington.* New York, 1960.

Chandler, William E.: "Chester A. Arthur," in James Grant Wilson, ed.: *The Presidents of the United States.* New York, 1914. 4 vols.

Chidsey, Donald Barr: *The Gentleman from New York, a Life of Roscoe Conkling.* New Haven, 1935.

Clancy, Herbert J.: *The Presidential Election of 1880.* Chicago, 1958.

Clews, Henry: *Fifty Years in Wall Street.* New York, 1908.

Coffin, Charles Carleton: *The Life of James A. Garfield with a Sketch of the Life of Chester A. Arthur.* Boston, 1880.

Colman, Edna M.: *Seventy-Five Years of White House Gossip from Washington to Lincoln.* Garden City, New York, 1925.

Conkling, Alfred R.: *The Life and Letters of Roscoe Conkling, Orator, Statesman, Advocate.* New York, 1889.

Connelley, William Elsey: *The Life of Preston B. Plumb 1837–1891.* Chicago, 1913.

Connery, T. B.: "Secret History of the Garfield-Conkling Tragedy," *Cosmopolitan Magazine,* XXIII (1897), 145–162.

Cortissoz, Royal: *The Life of Whitelaw Reid.* New York, 1921.

Crocker, Henry: *History of Baptists in Vermont.* Bellows Falls, Vermont, 1913.

Crook, William H.: *Memories of the White House: The Home Life of Our Presidents from Lincoln to Roosevelt, Being Personal Recollections of Colonel W. H. Crook.* Edited by Henry Rood. Boston, 1911.

———: *Through Five Administrations: Reminiscences of Colonel William H. Crook.* Edited by Margarita Spalding Gerry. New York, 1900.

Crowley, Richard, Mrs.: *Echoes from Niagara: Historical, Political, Personal.* Buffalo, 1890.

Curtis, George William: *Orations and Addresses of George William Curtis.* Edited by Charles Eliot Norton. New York, 1894. 3 vols.

Davison, Kenneth E.: *The Presidency of Rutherford B. Hayes,* Westport, Connecticut, 1972.

Dawes, H. L.: "Garfield and Conkling," *Century Magazine,* XLVII (1894), 341–344.

Dawson, George: *Pleasures of Angling with Rod and Reel for Trout and Salmon.* New York, 1876.

Depew, Chauncey M.: *My Memories of Eighty Years.* New York, 1922.

De Santis, Vincent P.: *Republicans Face the Southern Question: The New Departure Years, 1877–1897.* Baltimore, 1959.

Dobson, John M.: *Politics in the Gilded Age, a New Perspective on Reform.* New York, 1972.

Documents Issued by the Union Republican Congressional Committee, Presidential Campaign of 1880. Washington, 1880.

Doyle, Burton T. and Homer H. Swaney: *Lives of James A. Garfield and Chester A. Arthur. . . .* Washington, 1881.

Dozer, Donald Marquand: "The Opposition to Hawaiian Reciprocity, 1876–1888," *Pacific Historical Review,* XIV (1945), 157–183.

Dyer, Brainerd: *The Public Career of William M. Evarts.* Berkeley, 1933.

Eidson, William G.: "Who Were the Stalwarts?," *Mid-America,* 52 (1970), 235–261.

Eisenschiml, Otto: *The Celebrated Case of Fitz John Porter, an American Dreyfus Affair.* Indianapolis, 1950.

Ellis, Elmer: *Henry Moore Teller, Defender of the West.* Caldwell, Idaho, 1941.

Evarts, William Maxwell: *Arguments and Speeches of William Maxwell Evarts.* Edited by Sherman Evarts. New York, 1919. 3 vols.

Falk, E. A.: *Fighting Bob Evans.* New York, 1931.

Feuss, Claude M.: *Carl Schurz, Reformer.* New York, 1932.

Foraker, Julia B.: *I Would Live It Again.* New York, 1932.

Foster, John W.: *Diplomatic Memoirs*. Boston, 1909. 2 vols.

Fowler, Dorothy Ganfield: *The Cabinet Politician: The Postmasters General, 1829–1909*. New York, 1943.

Garraty, John A.: *The New Commonwealth, 1877–1890*. New York, 1969.

Gignilliat, John L.: "Pigs, Politics, and Protection: The European Boycott of American Pork, 1871–1891," *Agricultural History*, XXXV (1961), 3–12.

Goff, John S.: *Robert Todd Lincoln, a Man in His Own Right*. Norman, 1968.

Gorringe, Henry H.: "The Navy," *North American Review*, CXXXIV (1882), 486–506.

Goulding, Lawrence G.: *Arthur and the Ghost, with a Synopsis of the Great Battle of November 7, 1882*. New York, 1883.

Gresham, Matilda: *Life of Walter Quintin Gresham, 1832–1895*. Chicago, 1919.

Hamilton, Gail [Mary Abigail Dodge]: *Biography of James G. Blaine*. Norwich, Connecticut, 1895.

Hartman, William J.: "Politics and Patronage: The New York Custom House, 1852–1902." Unpublished doctoral dissertation, Columbia University, 1952.

Hayes, Rutherford B.: *Diary and Letters of Rutherford Birchard Hayes*. Edited by Charles Richard Williams. Columbus, Ohio, 1922–1926. 5 vols.

———: *Hayes: The Diary of a President*. Edited by T. Harry Williams. New York, 1964.

Henry, Sam: "The Ulster Background of Chester Alan Arthur Twenty-First President of the United States," in *Ulster-Irish Society Year Book, 1939*. Rutland, Vermont, 1939.

Herrick, Walter R., Jr.: *The American Naval Revolution*. Baton Rouge, 1966.

Hesseltine, William B.: *Ulysses S. Grant Politician*. New York, 1935.

Hinman, Arthur P.: *How a British Subject Became President of the United States*. New York, 1884.

Hirsch, Mark D.: *William C. Whitney, Modern Warwick*, New York, 1948.

Hislop, Codman: *Eliphalet Nott*. Middletown, Connecticut, 1971.

Hoar, George F.: *Autobiography of Seventy Years*. New York, 1903. 2 vols.

Hoogenboom, Ari: *Outlawing the Spoils: A History of the Civil Service Reform Movement, 1865–1883*. Urbana, Illinois, 1961.

Howe, George F.: *Chester A. Arthur, a Quarter-Century of Machine Politics*. New York, 1934.

Hudson, William C.: *Random Recollections of an Old Political Reporter*. New York, 1911.

Ingalls, John James: *A Collection of the Writings of John James Ingalls: Essays, Addresses, and Orations*. Edited by William Elsey Connelley. Kansas City, Missouri, 1902.

Ingraham, C. A.: *Elmer E. Ellsworth and the Zouaves of '61*. Chicago, 1925.

Ivins, William Mills: *Machine Politics and Money in Elections in New York City*. New York, 1887.

Johnson, Robert Underwood: *Remembered Yesterdays*. Boston, 1923.

Jordan, David M.: *Roscoe Conkling of New York, Voice in the Senate*. Ithaca, New York, 1971.

Josephson, Matthew: *The Politicos, 1865–1896*. New York, 1938.

Kirkland, Edward C.: *Industry Comes of Age: Business, Labor and Public Policy, 1860–1897*. New York, 1961.

Klotsche, J. Martin: "The Star Route Cases," *Mississippi Valley Historical Review*, XXII (1935), 407–418.

La Feber, Walter: *The New Empire, an Interpretation of American Expansion, 1860–1898.* Ithaca, New York, 1963.

Lambert, Oscar Doane: *Stephen Benton Elkins.* Pittsburgh, 1955.

Lowitt, Richard: *A Merchant Prince of the Nineteenth Century: William E. Dodge.* New York, 1954.

Marcus, Robert D.: *Grand Old Party: Political Structure in the Gilded Age 1880–1896.* New York, 1971.

McClure, Alexander K.: *Our Presidents and How We Make Them.* New York, 1900.

————: *Recollections of Half a Century.* Salem, Massachusetts, 1902.

McCulloch, Hugh: *Men and Measures of Half a Century.* New York, 1888.

McElroy, Robert: *Levi Parsons Morton: Banker, Diplomat and Statesman.* New York, 1930.

Merritt, Edwin Atkins: *Recollections, 1828–1911.* Albany, 1911.

Miller, William: "The Realm of Wealth," in John Higham, ed.: *The Reconstruction of American History.* New York, 1962.

Millington, Herbert: *American Diplomacy and the War of the Pacific.* New York, 1948.

Morgan, H. Wayne: *From Hayes to McKinley: National Party Politics, 1877–1896.* Syracuse, 1969.

————, ed.: *The Gilded Age: A Reappraisal.* Syracuse, 1963.

Murlin, E. L.: "The Life of Chester A. Arthur of New York," in E. V. Smalley, ed.: *The Republican Manual.* New York, 1880.

Muzzey, David Saville: *James G. Blaine, a Political Idol of Other Days.* New York, 1934.

Nevins, Allan: *Grover Cleveland, a Study in Courage.* New York, 1933.

————: *Hamilton Fish: The Inner History of the Grant Administration.* New York, 1936.

Nichols, Jeannette Paddock: "Rutherford B. Hayes and John Sherman," *Ohio History,* 77 (1968), 125–134.

Oberholtzer, Ellis Paxson: *A History of the United States Since the Civil War.* New York, 1917–1937. 5 vols.

Pennanen, Gary: "Public Opinion and the Chinese Question, 1876–1879," *Ohio History,* 77 (1968), 139–148.

Platt, Thomas Collier: *The Autobiography of Thomas Collier Platt.* Edited by Louis J. Lang. New York, 1910.

Plesur, Milton: *America's Outward Thrust, Approaches to Foreign Affairs, 1865–1890.* Dekalb, Illinois, 1971.

Pletcher, David M.: *The Awkward Years: American Foreign Relations Under Garfield and Arthur.* Columbia, Missouri, 1962.

Pollard, James E.: *The Presidents and the Press.* New York, 1947.

Poore, Ben Perley: *Perley's Reminiscences of Sixty Years in the National Metropolis.* Philadelphia, 1886.

Priest, Loring Benson: *Uncle Sam's Stepchildren, the Reformation of United States Indian Policy, 1865–1887.* New Brunswick, New Jersey, 1942.

Proceedings of the Eighth Republican National Convention Held at Chicago, Illinois, June 3, 4, 5 and 6, 1884. Chicago, 1884.

Proceedings of the Fifth Annual Meeting of the Baptist Convention of the State of Vermont. . . . Brandon, Vermont, 1830.

Proceedings of the Republican National Convnetion Held in Chicago, Illinois, June 2–8, 1880. Chicago, 1881.

Putnam, George Haven: *Memories of a Publisher, 1865–1915.* New York, 1915.

Rawley, James A.: *Edwin D. Morgan 1811–1883, Merchant in Politics.* New York, 1955.

Reeves, Thomas C.: "Chester A. Arthur and Campaign Assessments in the Election of 1880," *The Historian,* XXXI (1969), 573–582.

————: "Chester A. Arthur and the Campaign of 1880," *Political Science Quarterly,* LXXXIV (1969), 628–637.

————: "The Diaries of Malvina Arthur: Windows into the Past of Our 21st President," *Vermont History,* XXXVIII (1970), 177–188.

————: "The Mystery of Chester Alan Arthur's Birthplace," *Vermont History,* XXXVIII (1970), 291–304.

————: "President Arthur in Yellowstone National Park," *Montana, the Magazine of Western History,* XIX (1969), 18–29.

————: "The President's Dwarf: The Letters of Julia Sand to Chester A. Arthur," *New York History,* LII (1971), 73–83.

————: "The Search for the Chester A. Arthur Papers," *The Wisconsin Magazine of History,* 55 (1972), 310–319.

The Republican Text-Book for the Campaign of 1880. New York, 1880.

Rezneck, Samuel: *Business Depressions and Financial Panics, Essays in American Business and Economic History.* New York, 1968.

Richardson, James D.: *A Compilation of the Messages and Papers of the Presidents.* Washington, 1896–1927. 20 vols.

Richardson, Joe M.: "The Florida Excursion of President Chester A. Arthur," *Tequesta,* 24 (1964), 41–47.

Richardson, Leon B.: *William E. Chandler, Republican.* New York, 1940.

Rogers, Emma: "Chester A. Arthur Man and President." Unpublished master's thesis, University of Wisconsin, 1921.

Rosenberg, Charles E.: *The Trial of the Assassin Guiteau: Psychiatry and Law in the Gilded Age.* Chicago, 1968.

Ross, Ishbel: *Proud Kate.* New York, 1953.

Rothman, David J.: *Politics and Power, the United States Senate, 1869–1901.* Cambridge, Massachusetts, 1966.

Russell, William H.: "Timothy O. Howe, Stalwart Republican," *The Wisconsin Magazine of History,* XXXV (1951), 90–99.

Sage, Leland L.: *William Boyd Allison, a Study in Practical Politics.* Iowa City, 1956.

Savidge, Eugene Coleman: *Life of Benjamin Harris Brewster, with Discourses and Addresses.* Philadelphia, 1891.

Schurz, Carl: *Speeches, Correspondence and Political Papers of Carl Schurz.* Edited by Frederick Bancroft. New York, 1913. 6 vols.

Seager, Robert, II: "Ten Years Before Mahan: The Unofficial Case for the New Navy, 1880–1890," *Mississippi Valley Historical Review,* XL (1953), 491–512.

Sherman, John: *Recollections of Forty Years in the House, Senate and Cabinet: An Autobiography.* Chicago, 1895. 2 vols.

Shores, Venila Lovina: *The Hayes-Conkling Controversy, 1877–1879.* New York, 1919.

Singleton, Esther: *The Story of the White House.* New York, 1907. 2 vols.

Smalley, E. V.: "The White House," *Century Magazine,* XXVII (1884), 806–815.

Smith, Charles Emory: "How Conkling Missed Nominating Blaine," *Saturday Evening Post,* 172 (1901), 2–3.

Smith, Theodore Clarke: *The Life and Letters of James Abram Garfield.* New Haven, 1925. 2 vols.

Snyder, Louis L.: "The American-German Pork Dispute, 1879–1891," *Journal of Modern History,* XVII (1945), 16–28.

Sproat, John G.: *"The Best Men," Liberal Reformers in the Gilded Age.* New York, 1968.

Sprout, Harold and Margaret: *The Rise of American Naval Power, 1776–1918.* Princeton, 1939.

Stanwood, Edward: *American Tariff Controversies in the Nineteenth Century.* Boston, 1903. 2 vols.

Statements of the Special Committee of the Chamber of Commerce of the State of New York, on Customs Revenue Reform. New York, 1877.

Stewart, William M.: *Reminiscences of Senator William M. Stewart of Nevada.* Edited by George Rothwell Brown. New York, 1908.

Stoddard, Henry L.: *As I Knew Them: Presidents and Politics from Grant to Coolidge.* New York, 1927.

Stoddard, William O.: *The Lives of the Presidents: Rutherford Birchard Hayes, James Abram Garfield, and Chester Alan Arthur.* New York, 1889.

Stone, Melville E.: *Fifty Years a Journalist.* London, 1922.

Swann, Leonard Alexander, Jr.: *John Roach Maritime Entrepreneur, the Years as Naval Contractor, 1862–1886.* Annapolis, Maryland, 1965.

Taussig, F. W.: *The Tariff History of the United States.* 5th edition, New York, 1910.

Terrill, Tom E.: *The Tariff, Politics, and American Foreign Policy, 1874–1901.* Westport, Connecticut, 1973.

Thayer, William Roscoe: *The Life and Letters of John Hay.* Boston, 1908. 2 vols.

Trefousse, Hans L.: "Ben Butler and the New York Election of 1884," *New York History,* 37 (1956), 185–196.

Tyler, Alice Felt: *The Foreign Policy of James G. Blaine.* Minneapolis, 1927.

Van Deusen, Glyndon G.: *Thurlow Weed, Wizard of the Lobby.* Boston, 1947.

Welch, Richard E., Jr.: "George Edmunds of Vermont: Republican Half-Breed," *Vermont History,* XXXVI (1968), 64–73.

White, Andrew D.: *Autobiography of Andrew Dickson White.* New York, 1905. 2 vols.

White, Leonard D.: *The Republican Era: A Study in Administrative History.* New York, 1958.

Wilgus, A. Curtis: "James G. Blaine and the Pan-American Movement," *Hispanic American Historical Review,* V (1922), 662–708.

Wise, John S.: *Recollections of Thirteen Presidents.* New York, 1906.

Wolf, Simon: *The Presidents I Have Known from 1860–1918.* Washington, 1918.

Younger, Edward: *John A. Kasson, Politics and Diplomacy from Lincoln to McKinley.* Iowa City, 1955.

Zink, Harold: *City Bosses in the United States: A Study of Twenty Municipal Bosses.* Durham, North Carolina, 1930.

UNITED STATES GOVERNMENT DOCUMENTS

Congressional Globe
Congressional Record
Department of State: *Papers Relating to the Foreign Relations of the United States.* Washington, [1862———].
43d Congress, 1st Session, House of Representatives, Miscellaneous Document No. 264.
45th Congress, 1st Session, House of Representatives, Executive Document No. 8.
45th Congress, 2d Session, House of Representatives, Executive Document No. 25.
48th Congress, 1st Session, House of Representatives, Miscellaneous Document No. 38, Part 2.
48th Congress, 2d Session, House of Representatives, Executive Documents Nos. 156, 247.
48th Congress, 2d Session, Senate, Executive Document No. 11.
49th Congress, 1st Session, House of Representatives, Executive Document No. 50.
49th Congress, 1st Session, Senate Executive Document No. 99.

ADDITIONAL SOURCES

Arthur, Chester A.: folder, Chicago Historical Society.
Arthur, Chester A.: folder, Office of the Curator, The White House.
Arthur, Chester A.: folder, Rutherford B. Hayes Library.
Arthur, Chester A.: Scrapbooks, Columbia University.
Arthur, Chester A., II: Scrapbook, Dr. Manning E. Grimes, St. Louis, Missouri.
Arthur family Bible: Library of Congress.

NOTES

CHAPTER ONE · ZACK

1. Sam Henry, "The Ulster Background of Chester Alan Arthur Twenty-First President of the United States," in *Ulster-Irish Society Year Book, 1939* (Rutland, Vt., 1939), pp. 38–46; Arthur family Bible, Library of Congress (hereafter cited as L.C.); Ulster-Scot Historical Society, *The Scotch-Irish and Ulster* (Belfast, 1965), p. 18. The homestead has been refurbished and is now an Ulster tourist attraction.
2. Letter of July 12, 1822, signed by Charles C. Cotton and trustees of the Free School, Charles Pinkerton Collection, L.C.; Arthur family Bible; Arthur P. Hinman, *How a British Subject Became President of the United States* (New York, 1884), pp. 39, 41, 69.
3. Arthur family Bible; interview with Chester A. Arthur III, December 30, 1970.
4. Materials on the Stone family are in the Chester A. Arthur Papers, L.C. Family tradition regarding Judith Stevens is from an interview with Chester A. Arthur III, July 26, 1969.
5. The dates and places of birth of the Arthur children are as follows:
   1. Regina Malvina, March 8, 1822, Dunham, Lower Canada.
   2. Jane, March 14, 1824, Burlington, Vermont (died April 15, 1842).
   3. Almeda Malvina, December 22, 1825, Jericho, Vermont.
   4. Ann Eliza, January 1, 1828, Waterville, Vermont.
   5. Chester Alan, October 5, 1829, Fairfield, Vermont.
   6. Malvina Almeda, April 5, 1832, Fairfield, Vermont.
   7. William, May 28, 1834, Hinesburgh, Vermont.
   8. George, May 24, 1836, Perry, New York (died March 8, 1838).
   9. Mary, July 5, 1841, Greenwich, New York.
   From the Arthur family Bible.
6. Certificate of November 8, 1827, signed by the clerk of the Baptist church of Waterville, Vermont, Charles Pinkerton Collection; Hinman, *How a British Subject Became President*, pp. 45, 47, 49, 51; "A Chapter of Unpublished History," Boston *Weekly Journal*, August 11, 1893; Frank Grant

Lewis to Vernon B. Hampton, November 27, 1931, Vernon B. Hampton Papers, Staten Island, New York.

7. "Population of Vermont 1790–1940," mss., Vermont State Library, Montpelier; *Proceedings of the Fifth Annual Meeting of the Baptist Convention of the State of Vermont* . . . (Brandon, Vt., 1830), p. 28.

8. Reverend Henry Crocker, *History of Baptists in Vermont* (Bellows Falls, Vt., 1913), p. 371; Hinman, *How a British Subject Became President,* p. 72.

9. See the letter by "a resident of Saratoga" in P. C. Headley, *Public Men of To-Day* . . . (Hartford, Conn., 1882), p. 50. The issue is discussed in detail in Thomas C. Reeves, "The Mystery of Chester Alan Arthur's Birthplace," *Vermont History,* XXXVIII (1970), 291–304.

10. See *ibid.*

11. "Gen. Arthur's Birthplace," New York *Sun,* September 21, 1881.

12. The President's grandfather, Alan, was known as "Screeghy" because of his high voice and fiery temper. Henry, "The Ulster Background of Chester Alan Arthur," p. 38.

13. Hinman, *How a British Subject Became President,* p. 69; "The President's Father," Boston *Transcript,* September 22, 1881. See also "Incidents in the Life of President Arthur's Father," *Light and Life* (Troy, N.Y.) May 1882; "Pencilings by the Rambler," Manchester (N.H.) *Union,* November 27, 1886; articles on pp. 21 and 26 of Volume one, "Current Comment," Chester Arthur Scrapbooks, Columbia University.

14. "President Arthur's Father," Cincinnati *Enquirer,* October 12, 1881; William E. Chandler, "Chester A. Arthur," in James Grant Wilson (ed.), *The Presidents of the United States* (New York, 1914), III, 198–199, and William O. Stoddard, *The Lives of the Presidents: Rutherford Birchard Hayes, James Abram Garfield, and Chester Alan Arthur* (New York, 1889), p. 3; George E. Finlay to Vernon B. Hampton, November 6, 1931, Hampton Papers.

15. See the relevant correspondence in the Hampton Papers. See also Zadock Thompson, *History of Vermont, Naval, Civil and Statistical* (Burlington, Vt., 1842), p. 90, and "Accident to Sister of Deceased President [Ann Eliza]," Johnstown (N.Y.) *Daily Republican,* May 25, 1910.

16. See William Arthur (ed.), *The Antiquarian, and General Review* (4 vols., Schenectady and Lansingburgh, N.Y., 1845–1849), IV, 39–40. One of Arthur's strongest interests was the study of names, and in 1857 he published in New York City *An Etymological Dictionary of Family and Christian Names, with an Essay on Their Derivation and Import.* Another book, *Tongue of Fire,* was translated into French. Lansingburgh *Semi-Weekly Chronicle,* November 12, 1864.

17. See *The Antiquarian,* IV, 81–85; Jane S. Lord, *et al., Lansingburgh New York 1771–1971* (Lansingburgh, N.Y., 1971), pp. 22–23.

18. See "Gen. Arthur at School," *The New York Times,* July 28, 1880; "Chester Arthur: A Reminiscence," Schenectady *Gazette,* October 20, 1911.

19. Two editions of this semimonthly paper are in the Schaffer Library at Union College. An undated school paper from this period entitled "The Influence of the press" is in the Chester A. Arthur Papers, New-York Historical Society (hereafter cited as N.Y.H.S.).

20. "Chester A. Arthur," Boston *Herald,* June 13, 1880.

21. Dixon Ryan Fox, *Dr. Eliphalet Nott (1773–1866)—and the American Spirit* (Princeton, N.J., 1944), pp. 8–13; Codman Hislop, *Eliphalet Nott*

(Middletown, Conn., 1971), pp. 229–230, 244, 249–250 *et passim*; Silas Burt, "My Personal Reminiscences," I, 134–135, Silas Burt Papers, N.Y.H.S.

22. See the interview with Arthur H. Masten, November 25, 1931, Hampton Papers.

23. Frederick L. Bronner, "Chester A. Arthur: His College Years," in *Chester Alan Arthur Class of 1848* (Schenectady, N.Y., 1948), p. 8; Silas Burt, "Ms. of a history of N.Y. politics . . . ," p. 4, Silas Burt Papers, New York Public Library (hereafter cited as Silas Burt Biography).

24. Bronner, "Chester A. Arthur," pp. 8–10; Burt, "My Personal Reminiscences," I, 139–140. See the comments of Arthur's fraternity brothers in Arthur Papers, N.Y.H.S., and see Albert Poole Jacobs, *The Psi Upsilon Epitome* (Boston, 1884), pp. 8, 11, 12, 19, 85, 87, 107, 108, 123, 124, 132, 133, 147. See also Frederick W. Seward, *Reminiscences of a War-Time Statesman and Diplomat 1830–1915* (New York, 1916), pp. 447–448; and Emma Rogers, "Chester A. Arthur Man and President," unpublished master's thesis, University of Wisconsin, 1921, p. 3.

25. The three items are in the Arthur Papers, N.Y.H.S.

26. See "Hoosick Woman Recalls President Arthur's Life as Resident of Hoosick County," Troy (N.Y.) *Record*, May 28, 1932; Nathaniel Bartlett Sylvester, *History of Saratoga County, New York 1609–1878* (Philadelphia, 1878), pp. 234–235, and *History of Rensselaer Co., New York* (Philadelphia, 1880), pp. 312, 314; articles in the Lansingburgh *Democrat*, January 20, May 25, November 30, 1848. The one-room schoolhouse in Schaghticoke was still standing 123 years later. See Warren F. Broderick, "President Arthur's Father Lived in Area," *The Record Newspapers* (Troy, N.Y.), October 16, 1971.

27. "Arthur as a Poet," Chicago *Herald* clipping from mid-April 1883, Chester A. Arthur Scrapbook, 1883, Arthur Family Papers, L.C.; "A Poem by Chester A. Arthur," *The New York Times*, December 17, 1882.

28. See "Current Comment," II, 9–10, Chester A. Arthur Scrapbooks; "The Nation's Sorrow," New York *Journal*, November 20, 1886. See also Thomas C. Reeves, "The Diaries of Malvina Arthur: Windows into the Past of Our 21st President," *Vermont History*, XXXVIII (1970), 177–188.

29. Ten of the letters are in the Chester A. Arthur Papers, L.C. Another, dated August 20, 1853, is in the Henry A. Wallace Papers, University of Iowa. A twelfth such letter, of April 7, 1853, is in the Norman H. and Charlotte A. Strouse Collection, the Free Library of Philadelphia.

30. E. L. Murlin, "The Life of Chester A. Arthur of New York," in E. V. Smalley (ed.), *The Republican Manual* (New York, 1880), p. 304. This is the most accurate of the 1880 campaign biographies, edited by a friend of Garfield, a New York *Tribune* reporter.

31. See the the interview with George W. Parker in "Preparing for the Burial," New York *World*, November 20, 1886.

32. See Vernon B. Hampton's interview with Chester A. Arthur II, December 5, 1931, Hampton Papers.

33. See copies of Chester A. Arthur to Ann Arthur, March 11, 1855, and Chester Arthur to Mrs. William Arthur, March 29, 1855, Arthur Family Papers.

34. Quoted in Philip S. Foner, *Business and Slavery: The New York Merchants and the Irrepressible Conflict* (Chapel Hill, N.C., 1941), p. 62.

35. See 5 Sanford, 681; 26 Barbour, 270; 20 New York Court of Appeals

Reports, 562. On Evarts's role, see Brainerd Dyer, *The Public Career of William M. Evarts* (Berkeley, 1933), pp. 34–39; Sherman Evarts (ed.), *Arguments and Speeches of William Maxwell Evarts* (New York, 1919), I, 3–90.

36. "Lives of the Candidates," *The New York Times*, June 9, 1880; Murlin, "Life of Chester A. Arthur," in Smalley (ed.), *The Republican Manual*, p. 305; "Notes of a sketch of President Arthur corrected by him April 8, 1884," Chester A. Arthur folder, Chicago Historical Society. See Alexander K. McClure, *Recollections of Half a Century* (Salem, Mass., 1902), p. 116.

37. See, for example, James S. Brisbin, *From the Tow-path to the White House* (Philadelphia, 1880), p. 543; Charles Carleton Coffin, *The Life of James A. Garfield with a Sketch of the Life of Chester A. Arthur* (Boston, 1880), pp. 368–369; "Chester A. Arthur Dead," New York *Daily News*, November 19, 1886; Chandler, "Chester A. Arthur," in Wilson (ed.), *The Presidents of the United States*, III, 200. A. G. Riddle, *The Life, Character and Public Services of Jas. A. Garfield* (Cleveland, 1880), claimed that Arthur "prepared all the papers in the case . . ."

38. Chester A. Arthur to William Arthur, March 23, 1858, copy in "Arthur Family Notes & Letters," Arthur Family Papers.

39. *N.Y. Court of Appeals, Report Of The Lemmon Slave Case . . .* (New York, 1860), p. 15; "Arthur, Chester A. 9 Checkbooks with stubs 1858–1869," Arthur Papers, N.Y.H.S.

40. See "Outrage upon Colored Persons," *Frederick Douglass' Paper*, July 28, 1854; "Legal Rights Vindicated," *ibid.*, March 2, 1855; "City Items," New York *Tribune*, February 23, 1855; Murlin, "Life of Chester A. Arthur," in Smalley (ed.), *The Republican Manual*, pp. 306–307; "Notes of a sketch of President Arthur corrected by him April 8, 1884," Chester A. Arthur folder, Chicago Historical Society.

41. Chester A. Arthur to Nell Herndon, August 30, 1857, Arthur Papers, L.C.

42. *The Champion* (Atchison, Kans.), April 23, 1882; clipping in Chester A. Arthur Scrapbook, 1883, p. 49. The former article also appears in *The New York Times*, May 7, 1882, under the title "Gen. Arthur in Kansas."

43. Interview with George W. Parker in "Preparing for the Burial," New York *World*, November 20, 1886.

44. See "Gath," Cincinnati *Enquirer*, September 5, 1881; A. N. Cole to Chester A. Arthur II, November 18, 1886, Arthur Family Papers; DeAlva S. Alexander, *A Political History of the State of New York* (New York, 1909), II, 194.

45. Murlin, "Life of Chester A. Arthur," in Smalley (ed.), *The Republican Manual*, pp. 307–308.

46. "Chester A. Arthur," Boston *Herald*, June 13, 1880. The reporter quoted Arthur "substantially."

47. See Glyndon G. Van Deusen, *Thurlow Weed, Wizard of the Lobby* (Boston, 1947), pp. 105–106; Sidney D. Brummer, *Political History of New York State During the Period of the Civil War* (New York, 1911), pp. 20–24.

48. James A. Rawley, *Edwin D. Morgan 1811–1883, Merchant in Politics* (New York, 1955), pp. 12–22, 45–59, 72–83, 122; Alexander, *A Political History of the State of New York*, III, 54–55; John B. Huyck (Chief, Bureau of War Records, State of New York) to the author, December 17, 1969. Arthur received his commission in the militia on February 3, 1858.

49. Silas Burt Biography, p. 8; E. D. Morgan to U. S. Grant, December 1, 1871, Personnel File, Chester A. Arthur, General Records of the Treasury Department, National Archives. See also Seward, *Reminiscences of a War-Time Statesman and Diplomat*, p. 448.

50. [John W. Herndon], "Ellen Lewis Herndon . . . ," Arthur Papers, L.C.; John W. Herndon to Chester A. Arthur III, January 28, February 10, 15, 1947, Arthur Family Papers; interview with Chester A. Arthur III, July 26, 1969; "Mrs. Herndon," New York *Herald*, May 11, 1878; comments by George W. Parker in "Preparing for the Burial," New York *World*, November 20, 1886. For more on the Herndon ancestry, see John G. Herndon, *The Herndon Family of Virginia* (2 vols. [the second with the title *The Herndons of the American Revolution*], n.p., 1947–1952); interview between Vernon B. Hampton and George Barton French, November 25, 1932, Hampton Papers.

51. Chester A. Arthur to Nell Herndon, August 30, 1857, Arthur Papers, L.C. Chester A. Arthur II once took his son to the porch of the United States Hotel in Saratoga to show him where his father proposed to Ellen Herndon. Interview with Chester A. Arthur III, March 16, 1970.

52. See "Loss of the Central America," *The New York Times*, September 21, 1857.

53. Hundreds of pertinent receipts, bills, and checks are in the Arthur materials at the Library of Congress.

54. The slave living with Mrs. Herndon and the Arthurs in 1860 appeared in the census taken that year. New York State Census of 1860, Third Division, 18th Ward, p. 203.

55. Diary of Brodie Herndon, February 26, 1858, Brodie Herndon Papers, University of Virginia.

56. Arthur family Bible; "Married," *The New York Times*, October 29, 1859.

CHAPTER TWO · WITHOUT GOLD AND SILVER

1. See Chester A. Arthur to M. R. Patrick, June 10, 1861, Edwin B. Janes Collection, Henry E. Huntington Library; broadside (undated) calling for infantry volunteers, in the author's possession.

2. "The Autobiography Of George Bliss," pp. 148–149, George Bliss Papers, N.Y.H.S.

3. Murlin, "Life of Chester A. Arthur," in Smalley (ed.), *The Republican Manual,* p. 312; Burt, "My Personal Reminiscences," p. 31, Burt Papers, N.Y.H.S.; John Meredith Read, Jr., "Military Affairs of New York State in 1861, Some Personal Experiences and Impressions," *Magazine of American History*, XIV (1886), 288. See also Silas W. Burt, *My Memories of the Military History of the State of New York During the War for the Union, 1861–65* (Albany, 1902), p. 102. The full story of Morgan's leadership in New York during the war is in Rawley, *Edwin D. Morgan*, pp. 120–185.

4. Silas Burt Biography, pp. 12, 15. Only once was Arthur indirectly involved with controversy: four New York gentlemen he appointed to inspect uniforms somehow overlooked the fact that Brooks Brothers was furnishing the state with shoddy materials. Burt, *My Memoirs of the Military History*, pp. 20–21; Rawley, *Edwin D. Morgan*, p. 154.

5. John B. Huyck to the author, December 17, 1969; J. C. Reed to William Chandler, June 17, 1886, Arthur Papers, L.C.
6. Burt, *My Memories of the Military History of the State of New York*, p. 31.
7. In 1880, Arthur said of this often-cited event in his career: "Billy Wilson had a very bad reputation indeed as a fighter; but, as I remember our encounter, it amounted to nothing. I was physically powerful then, and he made hardly any resistance." "Chester A. Arthur," Boston *Herald*, June 13, 1880.
8. See the relevant correspondence and clippings in the Mrs. Charles Spicka Collection, on microfilm at the Wyoming State Historical Society.
9. Murlin, "The Life of Chester A. Arthur," in Smalley (ed.), *The Republican Manual*, pp. 313–315; "In Time of War and Peace," *The New York Times*, January 1, 1880; C. A. Ingraham, *Elmer E. Ellsworth and the Zouaves of '61* (Chicago, 1925), pp. 127–135. The special voucher Arthur made in order to get supplies aboard the ship, dated April 29, 1861, is in the Edwin D. Morgan Papers, New York State Library. See also C. A. Arthur to John H. Linsly, May 31, 1861, *ibid.*
10. S. H. Roberts to Alan and Ellen Arthur, December 30, 1886, Arthur Family Papers; Murlin, "Life of Chester A. Arthur," in Smalley (ed.), *The Republican Manual*, p. 315. A camp on Staten Island was called "Camp Herndon" in honor of Arthur's father-in-law by another group of grateful volunteers. See the "Autobiography of Major Augustus Porter Greene," pp. 41–42, 49–51, 87, 93–94, Augustus Porter Greene Papers, N.Y.H.S.
11. Burt, *My Memories of the Military History of the State of New York*, p. 145; Silas Burt Biography, pp. 10, 14; Murlin, "Life of Chester A. Arthur," in Smalley (ed.), *The Republican Manual*, p. 316.
12. *Ibid.*, pp. 319–320; "The Defenses of the Harbor of New York," *The New York Times*, January 16, 1871; Burt, *My Memories of the Military History of the State of New York*, p. 72; E. D. Morgan to Thurlow Weed, January 11, 1862, Thurlow Weed Papers, L.C.; "Papers relating to Board of Engineers upon N.Y. Harbor," Mrs. Charles Spicka Collection; W. H. Talcott to Silas Burt, July 2, 9, 1862, *ibid.*
13. Order of March 13, 1862, by Adjutant General William Hillhouse, *ibid.*; editorial, New York *Herald*, January 25, 1861.
14. "In Time of War and Peace," *The New York Times*, January 1, 1880.
15. Burt, *My Memories of the Military History of the State of New York*, p. 87.
16. "In Time of War and Peace," *The New York Times*, January 1, 1880; "The Autobiography of George Bliss," pp. 150–151, Bliss Papers; Rawley, *Edwin D. Morgan*, p. 122; Murlin, "Life of Chester A. Arthur," in Smalley (ed.), *The Republican Manual*, pp. 318–319.
17. Vernon B. Hampton interview with George Barton French, November 25, 1932, Hampton Papers. French mentioned Burnside, leader of the second Battle of Fredericksburg, fought on December 13, 1862. Nevertheless, the substance of the recollection could well be authentic. See William Arthur Jr. to Regina Caw, May 29, 1862, Arthur Family Papers. General Arthur was in Fort Corcoran, Virginia, at this time, headed for Baltimore.
18. See "The Ex-President's Life," *The New York Times*, November 19, 1886; Chandler, "Chester A. Arthur," in Wilson (ed.), *The Presidents of the United States*, II, 202; *Annual Report of the Quartermaster General State of New York, December 31, 1862, New York Assembly Documents*, 1863, p. 10.

19. See *ibid.*, pp. 11–20; printed request of July 5, 1862, signed by Adjutant General William Hillhouse, Mrs. Charles Spicka Collection; Burt, *My Memories of the Military History of the State of New York*, pp. 102–103; Murlin, "Life of Chester A. Arthur," in Smalley (ed.), *The Republican Manual*, pp. 323–324; Rawley, *Edwin D. Morgan*, pp. 180–181.

20. *Report State of New York: Quartermaster General's Department, New York, December 31, 1862, New York Assembly Documents*, 1863, p. 26.

21. See "Military Matters in the City," *The New York Times*, July 27, 1862; Burt, *My Memories of the Military History of the State of New York*, p. 145; E. D. Morgan to U. S. Grant, December 1, 1871, Personnel File, Chester A. Arthur, General Records of the Treasury Department, National Archives. See also Marsena R. Patrick to Silas W. Burt, December 1, 1864, Arthur Papers, N.Y.H.S.

22. *Annual Report of the Quartermaster General State of New York, December 31st, 1863, New York Assembly Documents*, 1864, VI, 3.

23. Vernon B. Hampton interview with Chester A. Arthur II, December 5, 1931, Hampton Papers.

24. Brodie Herndon Diary, entry of June 2, 1861, Herndon Papers.

25. Copy, Lucy Herndon to Mrs. [Elizabeth Herndon] Botts, August 30, 1863, Pinkerton Collection.

26. *Ibid.*; entries of "August" and November 25, 1863, Brodie Herndon Diaries, Herndon Papers.

27. Entry of "June" 1861, *ibid.*

28. Entry of "June" 1862, *ibid.*

29. Vernon B. Hampton interview with George Barton French, November 25, 1932, Hampton Papers.

30. See [Herndon], "Ellen Lewis Herndon," Arthur Papers, L.C.; "Ex-President Arthur," Boston *Sunday Herald*, November 28, 1886; Silas Burt Biography, pp. 20–21.

31. See [Herndon], "Ellen Lewis Herndon," Arthur Papers, L.C. No evidence exists to support the claim that Arthur twice secured the release of Dabney Herndon from Union prisons. George F. Howe, *Chester A. Arthur: A Quarter-Century of Machine Politics* (New York, 1934), pp. 26, 29.

32. William Arthur Jr. to Regina Caw, February 26, 1854, Arthur Family Papers. See Chester A. Arthur to Regina Caw, January 26 [1854], *ibid.* Another Arthur sister, Ann Eliza, taught school in South Carolina before and after the war. Her most famous pupil was Benjamin Tillman. See "Sister of Deceased President," Johnstown (N.Y.) *Daily Republican*, May 25, 1910.

33. See copy, Malvina Stone Arthur to William Arthur Jr., January 26, 1863, Arthur Family Papers; Malvina Haynesworth to William Arthur Jr., July 25, 1864, George F. Howe transcripts, L.C.; copy, Malvina Haynesworth to William Arthur Jr., August 2, 1864, Arthur Family Papers.

34. Regina Caw to William Arthur Jr., May 19, 1864, Howe transcripts, L.C. Cf. E. D. Morgan to J. Bell, January 30, 1863, Morgan Papers.

35. Silas Burt Biography, pp. 22–23.

36. Burt, *My Memories of the Military History of the State of New York*, pp. 144–145.

37. Silas Burt Biography, pp. 17–18.

38. Copy, Chester A. Arthur to William Arthur Jr., June 12, 1864, Arthur Family Papers.

39. "Gath," Cincinnati *Enquirer*, September 5, 1881. See "Day Book of Arthur & Gardiner 1858–1872," Arthur Papers, N.Y.H.S.
40. Letter by Owen A. Sheffield, December 11, 1958; copy, R. G. Dun to R. Douglass, August 6, 1862, Arthur Papers, L.C.
41. E.g., Chester A. Arthur to Regina Caw, January 29, 1862, Arthur Papers, L.C.
42. Regina Caw to William Arthur Jr., April 19, 1864, Howe transcripts.
43. Copy, Malvina Arthur to William Arthur Jr., January 26, 1863, Arthur Family Papers.
44. Copy, William Arthur to William Arthur Jr., October 1, 1862, *ibid*.
45. Copy, Chester A. Arthur to William Arthur Jr., July 9 [1863], *ibid*. The boy was born on December 10, 1860. Arthur family Bible.
46. Interview with Chester A. Arthur III, July 26, 1969.
47. Copy, Malvina Haynesworth to William Arthur Jr., August 2, 1864, Arthur Family Papers; Regina Caw to William Arthur Jr., August 10, 1864, Howe transcripts. Mr. Caw's obituary is in the Cohoes (N.Y.) *Cataract*, August 6, 1864.
48. Regina also inherited her father's literary interests. See Francis P. Cowell, "Mrs. Regina M. Caw—A Memoir," Albany *Examiner*, December 8, 1910.
49. See William Arthur [Jr.] to James B. Fry, December 4, 1864, Arthur Family Papers, and [Chester A. Arthur] to Edwin M. Stanton, n.d., *ibid*.
50. Copy, Chester A. Arthur to Mary McElroy, August 30, 1864, Hampton Papers.
51. See copy of a letter from E. D. Morgan to James B. Fray (in Chester A. Arthur's handwriting), July 11, 1865, Arthur Family Papers, and John I. Davenport to Chester A. Arthur, December 13, 1865, *ibid*. Despite his handicap, William Arthur remained in the army until he retired, a major and a paymaster, in 1898.

CHAPTER THREE · A GOOD APPOINTMENT

1. See "Arthur's Tranquil End," New York *Herald*, November 19, 1886.
2. See William Mitchell to Chester A. Arthur, November 12, 1861, Mrs. Charles Spicka Collection; assessment circular of October 7, 1862, *ibid*.
3. See "Day Book of Arthur & Gardiner 1858–1872," "9 Checkbooks with stubs 1858–1869," Arthur Papers, N.Y.H.S. In March 1872, Murphy claimed to have known Arthur "ten or twelve years." Senate Report, 42d Cong., 2d Sess., III, 432.
4. "Chester A. Arthur," Boston *Herald*, June 13, 1880. Cf. "In Time of War and Peace," *The New York Times*, January 1, 1880. See also George H. Mayer, *The Republican Party 1854–1966* (New York, 1967), pp. 118–119.
5. Rawley, *Edwin D. Morgan*, pp. 199–200; Silas Burt Biography, p. 26.
6. Edna M. Colman, *Seventy-Five Years of White House Gossip from Washington to Lincoln* (Garden City, N.Y., 1925), p. 268.
7. "Gath," Cincinnati *Enquirer*, August 14, 1883.
8. Copy, [Regina Caw] to Ann Arthur, September 26, 1865, Arthur Family Papers.
9. When Senator Morgan voted to sustain President Johnson's veto of the Freedmen's Bureau bill, Arthur sent his congratulations. See *Congressional Globe*, 39th Cong., 1st Sess., 917.

10. Silas Burt Biography, pp. 16, 27–30. Burt's conversation with Arthur no doubt occurred two or three months later than the "January or February 1866" he remembered twenty years later. For more on the close wartime relationship between Arthur and Burt, see Chester A. Arthur to Silas W. Burt, July 21, 1862, Norman H. and Charlotte A. Strouse Collection.

11. Chester Arthur to Edwin D. Morgan, January 24, 1866, Morgan Papers.

12. Edwin D. Morgan to T. C. Acton, June 25, 1866, *ibid.*

13. Silas Burt Biography, pp. 30–33.

14. See *ibid.*, p. 32.

15. Mrs. Richard Crowley, *Echoes from Niagara: Historical, Political, Personal* (Buffalo, N.Y., 1890), p. 150.

16. Silas Burt Biography, p. 35.

17. "Ex-President Arthur," Boston *Sunday Herald*, November 28, 1886. At one point in his life Arthur was elected to the Burns Society for being able to recite "Tam o' Shanter" from memory. See the interview with Auditor Treichel in "General Arthur Dead," New York *Commercial Advertiser*, November 18, 1886. Few of the urban bosses studied by Harold Zink were readers of books, and some even ignored newspapers. Harold Zink, *City Bosses in the United States: A Study of Twenty Municipal Bosses* (Durham, N.C., 1930), p. 22.

18. "The Lordly Roscoe," New York *Commercial Gazette*, June 18, 1883.

19. Andrew D. White, *Autobiography of Andrew Dickson White* (New York, 1905), I, 188.

20. Quoted in Donald Barr Chidsey, *The Gentleman from New York, a Life of Roscoe Conkling* (New Haven, 1935), p. 148.

21. William Elsey Connelley (ed.), *A Collection of the Writings of John James Ingalls: Essays, Addresses, and Orations* (Kansas City, Mo., 1902), p. 355.

22. George S. Boutwell, *Reminiscences of Sixty Years in Public Affairs* (New York, 1902), II, 264. For a summary of the origins of the dispute, see David M. Jordan, *Roscoe Conkling of New York: Voice in the Senate* (Ithaca, N.Y., 1971), pp. 67–69, 72–81.

23. Gideon Welles, *Diary of Gideon Welles, Secretary of the Navy Under Lincoln and Johnson* (Boston, 1911), III, 16. Conkling was a moderate Radical, much closer to Edwin D. Morgan and Abraham Lincoln than Thaddeus Stevens on the issues of abolition and Reconstruction. See Jordan, *Roscoe Conkling of New York*, pp. 44–46, 64–68, 90–92, 128–130.

24. Quoted in Chidsey, *The Gentleman from New York*, p. 115.

25. Quoted in Alexander, *A Political History of the State of New York*, III, 172.

26. E.g., Ari Hoogenboom, "Spoilsmen and Reformers: Civil Service Reform and Public Morality," in H. Wayne Morgan (ed.), *The Gilded Age: A Reappraisal* (Syracuse, N.Y., 1963), pp. 70–73. For a useful synthesis of this issue, see William Miller, "The Realm of Wealth," in John Higham (ed.), *The Reconstruction of American History* (New York, 1962), pp. 137–156.

27. William Mills Ivins, *Machine Politics and Money in Elections in New York City* (New York, 1887), pp. 11–12.

28. Alexander B. Callow Jr., *The Tweed Ring* (New York, 1966), pp. 5–6.

29. For a full discussion of this point, see Seymour Martin Lipset (ed.), Moisei Ostrogorski, *Democracy and the Organization of Political Parties* (New York, 1964), pp. 179–227. Especially useful on political bosses and machines are

the essays in *Annals of American Academy of Political and Social Sciences,* 353 (May 1964).

30. Silas Burt Biography, p. 40; "The Ex-President's Life," *The New York Times,* November 19, 1886. See E. J. Edwards, "New News of Yesterday," New York *Evening Mail,* January 12, 1911.
31. See Alexander, *A Political History of the State of New York,* III, 221–222; Jordan, *Roscoe Conkling of New York,* pp. 113–115.
32. Silas Burt Biography, p. 40. See also letterpress copy, Chester A. Arthur to A. D. Shaw, October 2, 1868, Arthur Papers, N.Y.H.S.
33. Letterpress copy, Chester A. Arthur to E. D. Morgan, October 12, 1868, *ibid.*
34. "Gath," Cincinnati *Enquirer,* September 2, 1883. See also Crowley, *Echoes from Niagara,* p. 155.
35. "Day Book of Arthur & Gardiner 1858–1872," Arthur Papers, N.Y.H.S.
36. See Senate Report, 42d Cong., 2d Sess., III, 437–440. See also George Alfred Townsend, "Chester Alan Arthur," New York *Sun,* September 6, 1881; Callow, *The Tweed Ring,* pp. 22–23, 80–81, 214–221, 229–230. In 1877, Tweed allegedly named Charles Folger and Richard Crowley as recipients of Ring bribes. See "Tweed's 'Confession,' " *The New York Times,* April 18, 1877, "W. M. Tweed's Confession," *ibid.,* April 25, 1877.
37. Arthur apparently had close dealings with Smith. See letterpress copy, Chester A. Arthur to Henry Smith, June 11, 1870, Arthur Papers, N.Y.H.S.
38. See "Gath," Cincinnati *Enquirer,* September 2, November 22, 1883; Crowley, *Echoes from Niagara,* p. 155; Silas Burt Biography, p. 37. (Burt noted that Arthur was also employed at the time by New York City internal revenue collectors to study bonds rendered by liquor manufacturers.) Cf. Senate Report, 42d Cong., 2d Sess., III, 424, 442–443, 464; "Mr. Murphy Resigns," *The New York Times,* November 21, 1871; and Howe, *Chester A. Arthur,* p. 42.
39. "United States Internal Revenue Receipt for Income Tax," May 28, 1873, in Chester A. Arthur II Scrapbook, owned by Dr. Manning E. Grimes of St. Joseph, Missouri.
40. Malvina Arthur Diary, January 17, 1869, Arthur Family Papers.
41. Brodie Herndon Diary, "May 1869," Herndon Papers.
42. Copy, Chester A. Arthur to William Arthur Jr., May 27, 1869, Arthur Family Papers.
43. Interview with Samuel Blatchford in "Chester Arthur Dead," New York *Commercial Advertiser,* November 18, 1886.
44. Zink, *City Bosses in the United States,* p. 25.
45. Edwin Atkins Merritt, *Recollections, 1828–1911* (Albany, 1911), p. 79; George Rothwell Brown (ed.), *Reminiscences of Senator William M. Stewart of Nevada* (New York, 1908), p. 255. As early as May 24, R. G. Dun wrote his brother-in-law, Senator Zachariah Chandler, urging support for Murphy as collector. "Murphy is an old friend of Dr. Chalmers & a very particular friend of my good friend Genl. Arthur." Copy, R. G. Dun to Zachariah Chandler, May 24, 1870, Arthur Papers, L.C.
46. See William B. Hesseltine, *Ulysses S. Grant, Politician* (New York, 1935), p. 212.
47. See Brown (ed.), *Reminiscences of Senator William M. Stewart,* p. 255.
48. "The Interests of the Party," *The Nation,* XI (July 7, 1870), 4. See also "The Week" in the same issue.

49. Brown (ed.), *Reminiscences of Senator William M. Stewart*, p. 255; Alfred R. Conkling, *The Life and Letters of Roscoe Conkling, Orator, Statesman, Advocate* (New York, 1889), p. 374. Prior to his Senate speech, Conkling paid a quiet visit to Secretary of State Hamilton Fish, an old friend, to persuade him to relax his opposition to Murphy. Fish reluctantly acquiesced, but later informed the President of his doubts about Murphy's integrity. Grant said that Murphy had told him he had made his money in real estate. Alan Nevins, *Hamilton Fish: The Inner History of the Grant Administration* (New York, 1936), pp. 368, 595.

50. Senate Report, 42d Cong., 2d Sess., III, 402–404, 452–457.

51. Alexander, *A Political History of the State of New York*, III, 235–238; Ari Hoogenboom, *Outlawing the Spoils: A History of the Civil Service Reform Movement 1865–1883* (Urbana, Ill., 1961), p. 77.

52. Silas Burt Biography, pp. 41–44.

53. Hoogenboom, *Outlawing the Spoils*, pp. 85–92.

54. *Ibid.*, pp. 89–90.

55. Horace Porter to Thomas Murphy, July 13, 1870, U. S. Grant Papers, L.C.

56. Silas Burt Biography, pp. 44–46; William J. Hartman, "Politics and Patronage: The New York Custom House, 1852–1902" (unpublished doctoral dissertation, Columbia University, 1952), pp. 160–162.

57. See Jordan, *Roscoe Conkling of New York*, pp. 154–156.

58. *Ibid.*, pp. 156–159; Alexander, *A Political History of the State of New York*, III, 250–264; Hoogenboom, *Outlawing the Spoils*, pp. 97–98.

59. "Shoddy as a Means of Making Republican Leaders," New York *Tribune*, September 22, 1871.

60. "The Week," *The Nation*, XIII (September 28, 1871), 201.

61. See Murphy's testimony in Senate Report, 42d Cong., 2d Sess., III, 372–432. Solid summaries of the investigation are in Hartman, "Politics and Patronage," pp. 166–179, and in Hoogenboom, *Outlawing the Spoils*, pp. 102–105.

62. "The Week," *The Nation*, XIII (November 23, 1871), 329; "Local Affairs," *The New York Times*, December 27, 1871; Senate Report, 42d Cong., 2d Sess., III, 432.

63. See Personnel File, Chester A. Arthur, General Records of the Treasury Department, National Archives; George Alfred Townsend, "Chester Alan Arthur," New York *Sun*, September 6, 1891. Cf. Burton T. Doyle and Homer H. Swaney, *Lives of James A. Garfield and Chester A. Arthur . . .* (Washington, 1881), p. 188; Howe, *Chester A. Arthur*, p. 47.

64. "A Day of Resignations," New York *Tribune*, November 21, 1871. See also "Our New Collector," *ibid.*, November 22, 1871.

65. "The Week," *The Nation*, XIII (November 23, 1871), 329.

66. "Mr. Murphy's Resignation," *The New York Times*, November 21, 1871.

67. Thurlow Weed to Hamilton Fish, November 23, 1871, Hamilton Fish Papers, L.C.

CHAPTER FOUR · THOSE DERISIVE SMILES

1. Hartman, "Politics and Patronage," pp. 18–19.

2. See *ibid.*, pp. 10-31; Hoogenboom, *Outlawing the Spoils*, p. 131.

3. "The Week," *The Nation*, XXII (May 11, 1876), 302.

4. As George William Curtis put it: "In plain words and in general, civil service reform means filling the subordinate offices of the government by men of tested capacity and fitness for the duties, without regard to their political views, and removing them for incapacity. dishonesty, or unfitness, and not because of their party preferences." "The Demand for Reform," *Harper's Weekly*, XX (December 2, 1876), 966.

5. "The Primaries and Civil-Service Reform," *The New York Times*, August 20, 1876. See also "Government by the Best," *ibid.*, September 21, 1876.

6. Dorman B. Eaton, "Parties and Independents," *North Ameican Review*, CXLIV (1887), 550.

7. John G. Sproat, *"The Best Men," Liberal Reformers in the Gilded Age* (New York, 1968), pp. 9–10. Sproat goes so far (p. 271) as to argue that "All of the liberal proposals for reforming politics, including civil service reform, rested essentially on the proposition that the American people as a whole were unworthy of self-government. Restriction, not reform, was the basic ingredient in their view of democracy." See also H. Wayne Morgan, *From Hayes to McKinley: National Party Politics 1877–1896* (Syracuse, N.Y., 1969), pp. 28–31.

8. Hoogenboom, *Outlawing the Spoils*, p. ix. Hoogenboom was a student of David Donald, one of the status theory's most ardent proponents. For the thesis in its most sophisticated form, see Geoffrey Blodgett's brilliant *The Gentle Reformers: Massachusetts Democracy in the Cleveland Era* (Cambridge, Mass., 1966), especially pp. 19–47.

9. For a stimulating discussion of this issue, see Gerald Sorin, *The New York Abolitionists* (Westport, Conn., 1971), pp. 3–17, 119–123. But see also Seymour Martin Lipset and Earl Raab, *The Politics of Unreason: Right-Wing Extremism in America, 1790–1970* (New York, 1970), esp. pp. 24–31, 61–67, 117–118.

10. The most balanced analyses of the civil service reformers are in John A. Garraty, *The New Commonwealth 1877–1890* (New York, 1969), pp. 251–258, and in Leonard D. White, *The Republican Era: A Study in Administrative History* (New York, 1958), pp. 278–302.

11. Quoted in Hoogenboom, *Outlawing the Spoils*, p. 108. See also White, *The Republican Era*, pp. 278–283.

12. Roscoe Conkling to Andrew D. White, January 31, 1872, Andrew Dickson White Papers, Cornell University.

13. Hartman, "Politics and Patronage," pp. 97–99.

14. See *ibid.*, p. 186; and copy, R. G. Dun to Zachariah Chandler, October 24, 1877, Arthur Papers, L.C.

15. See "General Arthur's Proposed Custom Reform," *The New York Times*, December 24, 1871, and "The General Order Business," *ibid.*, February 27, 1872.

16. "The End of the General Order Extortions," New York *Evening Post*, March 11, 1872.

17. Letterpress copy, Arthur to Conkling, May 5, 1874, Arthur Papers, N.Y.H.S.

18. Letterpress copy, Arthur to Babcock, June 6, 1874, *ibid.*

19. Letterpress copy, Arthur to T. C. Platt, December 23, 1874, *ibid.*

20. See B. H. Bristow to Arthur, December 6, 31, 1874, January 12, 1875, Ben-

jamin Bristow Papers, L.C.; letterpress copy, Arthur to Bristow, "Private," January 16, 1875, Arthur Papers, N.Y.H.S.

21. Statement by Joel B. Erhardt in "General Arthur Dead," New York *Commercial Advertiser,* November 18, 1886; statement by Chief Clerk of Customs Treloar in "Preparing for the Burial," New York *World*, November 20, 1886. Silas Burt recalled, "It was painful for him to remove for any other cause than political contumacy . . ." Silas Burt Biography, p. 48.

22. See Hartman, "Politics and Patronage," pp. 183–184. See also the excellent editorial by George William Curtis, "Collector Arthur's Letter," *Harper's Weekly,* XXII (January 26, 1878), 66.

23. "Mr. Bliss's Reply," *The Nation,* XXII (September 7, 1876), 151.

24. Silas Burt Biography, pp. 74–80.

25. Letterpress copy, Fred Phillips to George H. Washburn, April 24, 1874, Arthur Papers, N.Y.H.S.

26. "General Arthur Dead," New York *Commercial Advertiser,* November 18, 1886; Chauncey M. Depew, *My Memories of Eighty Years* (New York, 1922), p. 117.

27. "Gath," Cincinnati *Enquirer,* March 28, 1882; Silas Burt Biography, pp. 63–65.

28. Interview with Chester A. Arthur III, July 26, 1969.

29. Correspondence in the Arthur Papers, N.Y.H.S.; Levi P. Luckey to Arthur, December 30, 1875, U. S. Grant to Arthur, January 22, 1876, U. S. Grant Papers, L.C. Arthur informed Morgan of his election. "You see we have not consulted your individual wishes in the matter, but have thought only of strengthening our cause & promoting the success of the party." Letterpress copy, Arthur to Morgan, August 1, 1871, Arthur Papers, N.Y.H.S.

30. Letterpress copy, Arthur to Blaine, April 18, 1873, *ibid.* See also Blaine to Arthur, December 9, 1871, Adrian Hoffman Joline Collection, Henry E. Huntington Library.

31. Letterpress copy, Arthur to Grant, November 21, 1874, Arthur Papers, N.Y.H.S. The President received fifty-five cases.

32. In 1872 Arthur became part of the firm of Arthur, Phelps, Knevals and Ransom. Phelps died in 1880 and the firm was reorganized as Arthur, Knevals and Ransom and remained that way until Arthur took the presidential oath. While collector, according to a partner, Arthur paid very little attention to his law practice. Interview with Rastus Ransom in "Preparing for the Burial," New York *World,* November 20, 1886. The favor, noted above, was for Sherman W. Knevals. Phelps was the district attorney.

33. Correspondence in the Arthur Papers, N.Y.H.S.

34. See letterpress copy, Arthur to Babcock, "Personal," December 6, 1872, *ibid.*

35. Nevins, *Hamilton Fish,* p. 659.

36. "The City Republicans," *The New York Times,* January 11, 1879.

37. Silas Burt Biography, pp. 64–65.

38. For insights into Republican-Tammany bargains of 1876, see the editorial "Our Local Political Problem," *The New York Times,* May 4, 1879; the statement by A. J. Dittenhoefer in "Opinions of Politicians," *ibid.,* May 21, 1879; and James R. Angel to President Hayes, July 13, 1877, Personnel

File, Chester A. Arthur, General Records of the Treasury Department, National Archives. See as well the editorials of April 14, 20, 1877, in *The New York Times*.

39. See the relevant letterpress copies, Arthur Papers, N.Y.H.S.
40. "The Utica Convention," New York *Tribune*, September 24, 1874.
41. "The Utica Convention," *ibid.*, August 22, 1872.
42. Henry Clews, *Fifty Years in Wall Street* (New York, 1908), pp. 297–312.
43. Frederic Bancroft (ed.), *Speeches, Correspondence, and Political Papers of Carl Schurz* (New York, 1913), II, 405.
44. See Earle Dudley Ross, *The Liberal Republican Movement* (Ithaca, N.Y., 1910), pp. 184–188; Rawley, *Edwin D. Morgan*, pp. 238–245; Hesseltine, *Ulysses S. Grant, Politician*, pp. 269–281.
45. Silas Burt Biography, p. 54.
46. See Dorman B. Eaton, "Political Assessments," *North American Review* (September 1882), p. 198; Hartman, "Politics and Patronage," p. 178. Seven checks from Arthur to state party leaders, written during the campaign, exist in the Arthur Papers, L.C. Averaging about $1,000 each, they were made out to George Bliss, James M. Boyd, Bernard Biglin, and A. B. Cornell, and probably represent a distribution of funds raised from Customhouse assessments.
47. Editorial, *The New York Times*, October 4, 1872. A few months earlier, Greeley's *Tribune* had charged accurately: "The Post-Offices and Customhouses are remorselessly worked by committeemen, to the full extent of their capacity. Not only are contributions in money extorted, but the paid servants of the Government are openly set to doing the work of partisan committees." "Reform Impossible with Grant," New York *Tribune*, August 24, 1872.
48. Silas Burt Biography, pp. 54–57.
49. Letterpress copy, Arthur to Curtis, October 11, 1872, Arthur Papers, N.Y.H.S.
50. Arthur to Morgan, July 12, 1872, William E. Chandler Papers, New Hampshire State Historical Society.
51. Alexander, *A Political History of the State of New York*, III, 306.
52. "The Utica Convention," New York *Tribune*, September 25, 1873. A reporter on the scene said that "Federal office-holders largely predominate."
53. "The State Canvass," September 19, 1874, "The Utica Convention," September 24, 1874, in *ibid.* See the *Tribune's* editorial gasp at Murphy's selection in the September 24 issue.
54. A. B. Paine, *Thomas Nast: His Period and His Pictures* (New York, 1904), p. 326.
55. Hesseltine, *Ulysses S. Grant, Politician*, pp. 380–381.
56. Nevins, *Hamilton Fish*, pp. 781–783, 834–835.
57. See John McDonald, *Secrets of the Great Whiskey Ring* (St. Louis, 1880), p. 51: Rawley, *Edwin D. Morgan*, p. 241.
58. "The Week," *The Nation*, XXII (March 2, 1876), 137.
59. "Washington," New York *Tribune*, March 4, 1876; Sister Mary Karl George, *Zachariah Chandler: A Political Biography* (East Lansing, Mich., 1969), p. 201. For a sound account of the Whiskey Ring, see Ross A. Webb, *Benjamin Helm Bristow: Border State Politician* (Lexington, Ky.,

1969), pp. 187–212. The assertion by Ellis Paxon Oberholtzer that Arthur was a contributor to the Babcock fund is unsubstantiated. See his *A History of the United States Since the Civil War* (New York, 1937), III, 156.

60. See U.S. Congress, House of Representatives, 43d Cong., 1st Sess., Misc. Docs. No. 264, May 2, 1874; Richard Lowitt, *A Merchant Prince of the Nineteenth Century: William E. Dodge* (New York, 1954), pp. 275–281.

61. Nevins, *Hamilton Fish*, p. 726. While a Senate committee debated the bill, Arthur privately offered the services of an assistant collector for testimony. Letterpress copy, Arthur to Conkling, June 3, 1874, Arthur Papers, N.Y.H.S.

62. See Hoogenboom, *Outlawing the Spoils*, p. 131. The annual salaries of the surveyor and naval officer were set at $8,000 apiece.

By 1875, Arthur would write to a friend, "I am hard pressed for money for current expenses." This appears to have been due in large part to the payment of taxes on his land holdings. See letterpress copy, Arthur to Hon. William Fullerton, December 15, 1875, Arthur Papers, N.Y.H.S. In December 1876, Arthur heard a rumor that he was to be appointed U.S. Attorney. He declined the opportunity, writing to Conkling: "I am aware that any friends who urge my appointment think they are doing what would be to my pecuniary advantage but *I* know that it would not be so." Letterpress copy, Arthur to Conkling, December 15, 1876, "Confidential," *ibid.*

63. See "Arthur Family Expense Book, 1873–1876," Arthur Papers, L.C. For examples of their attendance at social gatherings, see Ishbel Ross, *Proud Kate* (New York, 1953), pp. 236–237; "The Union League Club," *The New York Times,* January 25, 1877; Brodie Herndon Diary, October 3, 1873, Herndon Papers.

64. Ellen Lewis Herndon Arthur Address Book, Arthur Papers, L.C.

65. "Arthur's Bower," dispatch of September 16, 1883, in Chester A. Arthur Scrapbook, 1883, p. 155.

66. "Gath," Cincinnati *Enquirer,* September 2, 1883.

67. "Mrs. Arthur's Grave," in Chester A. Arthur Scrapbook, 1883, p. 168.

68. "The Bee," Cincinnati *Enquirer,* November 22, 1883.

69. In New York *Mail,* August 8, 1878.

70. Brodie Herndon Diary, April 19, 1871, Herndon Papers.

71. Silas Burt Biography, p. 61.

72. "Personal Intercourse with the Vice Presidential Candidate," Boston *Herald,* June 13, 1880.

73. See the many family bills and receipts in the Arthur Papers, L.C.

74. See George Dawson, *Pleasures of Angling with Rod and Reel for Trout and Salmon* (New York, 1876), pp. 101–104, 130–131, 139–142, 164–165, 176–179; copy, R. G. Dun to J. A. Dun, September 10, 1873; R. G. Dun to Edward Russell, June 23, 1875, in Arthur Papers, L.C.; "A Sportsmen's Paradise," *The New York Times,* June 8, 1880; a statement by Arthur's son-in-law, in Calvin Dill Wilson, "Our Presidents Out of Doors," *Century,* LV (March 1909), 709.

75. Interview with Chester A. Arthur III, December 29, 1970; William Arthur will (drawn up by his eldest son), Arthur Papers, L.C.

76. Copy, Regina Caw to William and Alice Arthur, November 2, 1875, Arthur Family Papers.

77. Silas Burt Biography, p. 71.

78. Cornell to Grant, November 29, 1875, Personnel File, Chester A. Arthur, General Records of the Treasury Department, National Archives.

79. "Collector Arthur," New York *Dispatch*, April 12, 1874.

80. David J. Rothman, *Politics and Power: The United States Senate, 1869–1901* (Cambridge, Mass., 1966), p. 28.

81. Editorial, *The New York Times*, December 14, 1875. See also "Term of Office," New York *Evening Express*, December 17, 1875, and "The Collector of the Port of New York," Albany *Evening Journal*, December 17, 1875.

82. "The Reappointment of Collector Arthur," Troy (N.Y.) *Northern Budget*, December 20, 1875.

83. "Personal," *Harper's Weekly*, XX (January 8, 1876), 23.

84. See "State Politics" and the editorial "The Saratoga Convention" in *The New York Times*, September 9, 1875.

85. "The Campaign of 1876," *ibid.*, March 10, 1876.

86. "The Conkling Machine," *The Nation*, XXII (March 23, 1876), 188–189.

87. "The Work of the Convention," *The New York Times*, March 23, 1876.

88. See "The Conkling Machine," *The Nation*, XXII (March 23, 1876), 188–189. See also Louis J. Lang (ed.), Thomas Collier Platt, *The Autobiography of Thomas Collier Platt* (New York, 1910), p. 72.

89. "Determination of Conkling's Friends to Control the Convention," *The New York Times*, March 21, 1876.

90. "New-York Republicans," *ibid.*, March 23, 1876.

91. "The Conkling Machine," *The Nation*, XXII (March 23, 1876), 188–189.

92. "The National Campaign," *The New York Times*, June 9, 1876; "The Republican Campaign," *ibid.*, June 10, 1876.

93. Quoted in Alexander, *A Political History of the State of New York*, III, 333.

94. See "The National Convention," *The New York Times*, June 12, 1876; "The National Convention," *ibid.*, June 13, 1876; "The Republican Convention," *The Nation*, XXII (June 22, 1876), 392; "The Few Necessary First Steps to Civil-Service Reform," *ibid.*, XXII (June 29, 1876), 407.

95. See "The Week," *ibid.*, XXII (May 4, 1876), 286; (May 18, 1876), 313.

96. "The National Convention," *The New York Times*, June 13, 1876.

97. Editorial, *ibid.*, June 14, 1876.

98. "The Party in Council," New York *Tribune*, June 15, 1876.

99. See Hamilton J. Eckenrode, *Rutherford B. Hayes: Statesman of Reunion* (New York, 1930), 135; George F. Hoar, *Autobiography of Seventy Years* (New York, 1903), I, 243. The familiar story of the convention is described especially well in Kenneth E. Davison, "The Nomination of Rutherford Hayes for the Presidency," *Ohio History*, 77 (1968), 96–110; and Harry Barnard, *Rutherford B. Hayes and His America* (Indianapolis, 1954), pp. 284–294.

100. "Hayes and Wheeler," "Response of the Country," *The New York Times*, June 17, 1876. According to Tom Platt, Conkling "took his defeat much to heart." See Lang (ed.), *The Autobiography of Thomas Collier Platt*, pp. 75–76.

CHAPTER FIVE · HAND-OVER STREET

1. Henry Adams to Charles Milnes Gaskell, June 14, 1876, in Worthington Chauncey Ford (ed.), *Letters of Henry Adams (1858–1891)* (Boston, 1930), p. 288; "The Republican Platform and Nominations," *The Nation*, XXII (June 22, 1876), 390.
2. See "The Democratic Nomination," *ibid.*, XXIII (July 6, 1876), 4.
3. "The Republican Campaign," *The New York Times*, July 10, 1876.
4. See "Gen. Hayes' Letter of Acceptance," *ibid.*; "The Republican Campaign," *ibid.*, July 11, 1876; Hoogenboom, *Outlawing the Spoils*, p. 143.
5. "The Republican Rally," *The New York Times*, July 13, 1876; "Opening the Campaign," New York *Tribune*, June 13, 1876.
6. Letterpress copy, Arthur to Conkling, July 11, 1876, Arthur Papers, N.Y.H.S.
7. See Alexander, *A Political History of the State of New York*, p. 339; Howe, *Chester A. Arthur*, pp. 58–59.
8. With a straight face, George Bliss used Cornell's defeat to illustrate the independence of federal officeholders from Senator Conkling. See "Mr. Bliss's Reply," *The Nation*, XXIII (September 7, 1876), 151.
9. "The Week," *ibid.*, XXIII (August 31, 1876), 126. Godkin portrayed the Conkling machine as completely behind Cornell, for "Should Cornell be defeated, Mr. Conkling's prestige will be gone, and he will be relegated to that limbo of politicians—a 'back seat in the rear car.' " He was able, however, to allude to but a single incident of machine support for the candidacy—by a customs weigher in Newburgh! See "The Week," *ibid.*, XXII (August 17, 1876), 98.
10. For the story of the Saratoga Convention, see "The Campaign of 1876," *The New York Times*, August 21, 1876; "The State Republicans," *ibid.*, August 22, 1876; "Progress at Saratoga," *ibid.*, August 23, 1876; "The State Republicans," *ibid.*, August 24, 1876.
11. Silas Burt Biography, pp. 86–88.
12. Canceled checks in the Arthur Papers, L.C.
13. *Ibid.*; letterpress copy, Arthur to Chandler, November 27, 1876, January 4, 1877, Arthur Papers, N.Y.H.S.
14. See Rawley, *Edwin D. Morgan*, p. 257.
15. "Things for Mr. Hayes's Consideration," *The Nation*, XXIII (July 20, 1876), 36.
16. Schurz to Hayes, July 14, 1876, in Bancroft (ed.), *Speeches, Correspondence and Political Papers of Carl Schurz*, III, 260.
17. See Dorothy Ganfield Fowler, *The Cabinet Politician: The Postmasters General 1829–1909* (New York, 1943), p. 159. Assessments for the campaign had first appeared a year earlier when a circular was sent out by the secretary of the congressional committee to postmasters throughout the country.
18. In *ibid.*
19. In *ibid.*, p. 157.
20. Robert D. Marcus, *Grand Old Party: Political Structure in the Gilded Age 1880–1896* (New York, 1971), p. 13.

21. Hayes to Schurz, September 15, 1876, in Bancroft (ed.), *Speeches, Correspondence and Political Papers of Carl Schurz,* III, 339.
22. "The Fundamental Reform," *The New York Times,* September 30, 1876.
23. "The Work in this State," *ibid.,* October 6, 1876.
24. Jordan, *Roscoe Conkling of New York,* p. 245; "Mr. Conkling at Utica," *The New York Times,* October 4, 1876.
25. Stalwarts were conspicuously absent from party rallies featuring Blaine, Schurz, and Evarts. See "Mr. Blaine in New-York," *The New York Times,* October 17, 1876; "Reception to Mr. Schurz," *ibid.,* October 22, 1876; "Mr. Evarts' Great Speech," *ibid.,* November 2, 1876.
26. "Republican Primaries," *ibid.,* October 21, 1876; "Republican County Convention," *ibid.,* October 26, 1876.
27. "Local Politics," *ibid.,* October 28, 1876; "Gen. Arthur and Mr. E. B. Hart," *ibid.,* October 29, 1876.
28. "The County Republicans" *ibid.,* November 1, 1876.
29. "Along Fifth Avenue," *ibid.,* November 4, 1876. Earlier, Arthur appeared with Thurlow Weed, Morgan, Cornell, William Lloyd Garrison, and others at the unveiling of the Seward statue in Madison Park—several yards from the spot on which his own statue would be erected twenty-three years later. "In memory of Mr. Seward," *ibid.,* September 28, 1876.
30. Harry Barnard, *Rutherford B. Hayes and His America* (Indianapolis, 1954), p. 301.
31. Modern scholarship has concluded that Hayes lost Florida but probably won South Carolina and Louisiana, thus losing in the electoral count 181 to 188. See *ibid.,* pp. 307–393; C. Vann Woodward, *Reunion and Reaction: The Compromise of 1877 and the End of Reconstruction* (Boston, 1951). Cf. Allan Peskin, "Was There a Compromise of 1877?," *Journal of American History,* LX (June 1973), 63–75.
32. Chandler, "Chester A. Arthur," in Wilson (ed.), *The Presidents of the United States,* III, 205. See Keith Ian Polakoff, *The Politics of Inertia, the Election of 1876 and the End of Reconstruction* (Baton Rouge, La., 1973), p. 202.
33. See George, *Zachariah Chandler,* p. 256.
34. Letterpress copy, Arthur to Gould, December 4, 1876, Arthur Papers, N.Y.H.S.
35. The best account of Conkling's activities throughout the election crisis is in Chidsey, *The Gentleman from New York,* pp. 220–234. See also editorial, *The New York Times,* January 26, 1877.
36. "Sudden Removal from Office," and editorial, *ibid.,* March 3, 1877.
37. See Schurz to Hayes, January 25, 1877, in Bancroft (ed.), *Speeches, Correspondence and Political Papers of Carl Schurz,* III, 367–374.
38. "A Look into the Senate Chamber," "President Hayes' Inaugural," *The New York Times,* March 6, 1877.
39. See Jeannette Paddock Nichols, "Rutherford B. Hayes and John Sherman," *Ohio History,* 77 (Winter, Spring, and Summer 1968), 125–134.
40. "Washington," "Examination of Custom-House," New York *Tribune,* April 9, 1877.

CHAPTER SIX · EXCITING THE WHOLE TOWN

1. T. Harry Williams (ed.), *Hayes: The Diary of a President 1875–1881* (New York, 1964), p. xvi; Barnard, *Rutherford B. Hayes and His America,* pp. 456–457.
2. *Ibid.,* pp. 450–452; Nichols, "Rutherford B. Hayes and John Sherman," pp. 136, 200; John Sherman, *Recollections of Forty Years in the House, Senate and Cabinet: An Autobiography* (Chicago, 1895), II, 677.
3. Letterpress copies, Arthur to Sherman, April 16, 17, 20, 1877, Arthur Papers, N.Y.H.S.; Sherman to Hayes, January 31, 1879, Personnel File, Chester A. Arthur, General Records of the Treasury Department, National Archives. Cf. Howe, *Chester A. Arthur,* p. 63.
4. "Examination of Custom-Houses," New York *Tribune,* April 9, 1877; "Custom-House Irregularities," *ibid.,* April 10, 1877; *Statements of the Special Committee of the Chamber of Commerce of the State of New York, on Customs Revenue Reform* (New York, 1877), p. 5; editorial, *The New York Times,* April 17, 1877.
5. "The New-York Custom-House," *ibid.,* April 18, 1877; "Local Miscellany," *ibid.,* April 27, 1877. Excerpts of Arthur's testimony were released later. See "Local Miscellany," *ibid.,* May 26, 1877.
6. The following references to the commission hearings, unless otherwise stated, are based on *The New York Times* stories appearing almost daily from May 1 through June 9, 1877. See also John Jay's "Civil Service Reform," *North American Review,* CXXXVII (1878), 273–287. A small and relatively insignificant collection of Jay Commission papers is in the National Archives.
7. "Commissions to Examine Certain Custom-Houses of the United States," House Executive Docs., 45th Cong., 1st Sess., I, 44–47.
8. Letterpress copy, Arthur to Jay, May 21, 1877, Arthur Papers, N.Y.H.S.
9. "Commissions to Examine Certain Custom-Houses of the United States," House Executive Docs., 45th Cong., 1st Sess., I, 14–17.
10. See *ibid.,* I, 26, and "The Custom House Inquiry," *The New York Times,* June 8, 1877.
11. See Arthur to Sherman, March 21, 1877; Sherman to Arthur, May 9, 1877, John Sherman Papers, L.C.
12. "Commissions to Examine Certain Custom-Houses of the United States," House Executive Docs., 45th Cong., 1st Sess., I, 17–20.
13. *Statements of the Special Committee, passim;* "Customs Review Reform," *The New York Times,* June 5, 1877.
14. "The Custom-House Inquiry," *ibid.,* June 6, 1877; letterpress copy, Arthur to Jay, June 13, 1877, Arthur Papers, N.Y.H.S.
15. "New York Custom-House," *The New York Times,* June 7, 1877.
16. For the recollections of a participant, see Richard Grant White, "The Business of Office-Seeking," *North American Review,* CXXXV (October 1882), 46–47. There is no evidence to support rumors of a purge of anti-Conkling personnel. See letterpress copy, Arthur to Jay Commission, June 12, 1877, Arthur Papers, N.Y.H.S.
17. "The New-York Custom-House," *The New York Times,* June 11, 1877.
18. "Washington," *ibid.,* June 26, 1877.

19. See "Commissions to Examine Certain Custom-Houses of the United States," House Executive Docs., 45th Cong., 1st Sess., I, 36–42.

20. Norton to Hayes, July 22, 1877, Rutherford B. Hayes Papers, Rutherford B. Hayes Library. On Evarts, see Sherman to Hayes, March 8, 1881, *ibid.;* "Washington," *The New York Times,* August 30, 1877; and Dyer, *The Public Career of William M. Evarts,* pp. 190–192.

21. Sherman to Hayes, July 5, 1877, Hayes Papers.

22. See "Commissions to Examine Certain Custom-Houses of the United States," House Executive Docs., 45th Cong., 1st Sess., I, 50–71. Cf. the booklet *Answer of the Weighers of the Port of New York to the Report of the Commission to Investigate the New York Custom House,* in the Arthur Papers, L.C.

23. "New York Republicans," *The New York Times,* August 29, 1877. Appraiser Dutcher was also present. This tactic was probably ordered by Conkling, who had returned from a European vacation on August 10. See the editorial quoting Conkling comments to the Oswego (N.Y.) *Palladium, ibid.,* September 9, 1877.

24. "The National Capital," *ibid.,* September 1, 1877; "The Civil Service Order," *ibid.,* August 31, 1877. Scores of Customhouse workers soon began resigning from Republican organizations. E.g., "Local Political Affairs," *ibid.,* September 5, 1877; "The President's Order," *ibid.,* September 6, 1877; "The Civil Service Order," *ibid.,* September 7, 1877; "The Civil Service Order," *ibid.,* November 11, 1877.

25. See Sherman, *Recollections,* II, 679–681; "New York Custom-House," *The New York Times,* September 7, 1877; letterpress copy, Arthur to Sherman, September 7, 1877, Arthur Papers, N.Y.H.S.

26. *Ibid.;* McCormick to Sherman, September 7, 1877, Sherman Papers.

27. Cf. Sherman to Hayes, January 31, 1879, in the booklet *Message of the President of the United States and Letter of the Secretary of the Treasury . . .* in Personnel File, Chester A. Arthur, General Records of the Treasury Department, National Archives, and Arthur to Conkling, February 1, 1879, in "The Long Contest Ended," *The New York Times,* February 4, 1879.

28. See "Republicans in Council," *ibid.,* September 25, 1877; "New-York Republicans," *ibid.,* September 26, 1877; "The State Republicans," *ibid.,* September 27, 1877; Conkling, *The Life and Letters of Roscoe Conkling,* pp. 536–549.

29. Quoted in Edward Cary, *George William Curtis* (Boston, 1894), pp. 257–258.

30. "The State Republicans," *The New York Times,* September 27, 1877.

31. Sherman to Arthur, October 15, 1877, in Sherman, *Recollections,* pp. 681–682.

32. "The New-York Custom-House," *The New York Times,* October 8, 1877; "Nominations to Office," *ibid.,* October 13, 1877.

33. At a proadministration rally in New York City on October 10 featuring George William Curtis, Roosevelt sat on the platform. "The President Sustained," *ibid.,* October 11, 1877.

34. "The New-York Custom-House," *ibid.,* October 20, 1877.

35. Cf. Hoogenboom, *Outlawing the Spoils,* p. 161.

36. Sherman to Arthur, October 15, 1877, in Sherman, *Recollections,* II, 681–

682; telegram, Sherman to Arthur, October 19, 1877, Hayes Papers; letterpress copy, Arthur to Sherman, October 19, 1877, Arthur Papers, N.Y.H.S.

37. Williams (ed.), *Hayes: The Diary of a President*, p. 100.

38. Barnard, *Rutherford B. Hayes*, p. 455.

39. Conkling to Hayes, November 15, 1877, Hayes Papers; "New York and Chicago Officials," *The New York Times*, November 16, 1877.

40. "The New-York Appointments," *ibid.*, November 20, 1877.

41. Copy, Dun to Chandler, November 22, 1877, Arthur Papers, L.C.; letterpress copy, Arthur to Conkling, November 24, 1877, Arthur Papers, N.Y.H.S.

42. Letterpress copy, Arthur to Conkling, November 27, 1877, *ibid.*

43. See House Executive Docs, 45th Cong., 2d Sess., pp. 7–16. George Bliss may well have had a hand in writing the letter. See "Arthur," Cincinnati *Enquirer*, September 25, 1881.

44. "Collector Arthur's Letter," *Harper's Weekly*, XXII (January 26, 1878), 66. Cf. his evaluation of a few months later in Charles Eliot Norton (ed.), *Orations and Addresses of George William Curtis* (New York, 1894), II, 128–130.

45. Earlier, Morgan had privately appealed to Hayes to abandon his attack against Arthur. "He is strong and popular with the merchants and businessmen of both parties. He is an able lawyer, an excellent man of business, kind and generous to all, and liberal in furnishing the 'sinews of war.'" Morgan to Hayes, October 6, 1877, Hayes Papers. The President may not have fully appreciated the reference to assessments.

46. "Paying Political Assessments," *The New York Times*, October 30, 1877. See also Hoogenboom, *Outlawing the Spoils*, pp. 163–164. Arthur remained aloof from the campaigns, which saw Democrats win majorities in the city, county, and state. Cornell appeared only at state committee offices to view election returns. "Election Day Incidents," *The New York Times*, November 7, 1877.

47. Venila Lovina Shores, *The Hayes-Conkling Controversy, 1877–1879* (New York, 1919), p. 242.

48. "Mr. Hayes and the Senate," *The New York Times*, December 7, 1877.

49. Williams (ed.), *Hayes: The Diary of a President*, p. 107; "Washington," *The New York Times*, December 6, 1877.

50. "Mr. Hayes and the Senate," and editorial, *ibid.*, December 7, 1877.

51. "Washington," *ibid.*, December 12, 1877; "The New-York Custom-House," *ibid.*, December 13, 1877.

52. Williams (ed.), *Hayes: The Diary of a President*, p. 107.

53. Letterpress copy, Arthur to Conkling, December 13, 1877, Arthur Papers, N.Y.H.S.

54. "Receiving the President," *The New York Times*, December 22, 1877.

CHAPTER SEVEN · THE KEYS TO THE CUSTOMHOUSE

1. Editorial, *The New York Times*, January 5, 1878; Williams (ed.), *Hayes: The Diary of a President*, p. 101. See also E. L. Godkin's poignant evaluation in "After One Year of President Hayes," *The Nation*, XXVI (March 7, 1878), 164–165.

2. See "The Custom-House Inquiry," *The New York Times*, January 9, 1878; Sherman to Arthur, January 7, 18, February 5, 25, 1878, Sherman Papers.

3. See Arthur to Sherman, March 2, 1878, *ibid.;* Arthur to Sherman, January 28, February 27, 1878, Arthur Papers, L.C.

4. See editorial, *The New York Times*, December 12, 1877; "The University Regents," "Fairchild's Defeat," and editorial, *ibid.*, January 16, 1878; editorial, *ibid.*, January 18, 1878.

5. "Mr. Smyth Declines a Hearing" and editorial, *ibid.*, February 21, 1878; "State Affairs at Albany," *ibid.*, February 22, 1878; "Supt. Smyth's Trial Begun" and editorial, *ibid.*, March 8, 1878; "The Case of Supt. Smyth," *ibid.*, March 9, 1878; "Smyth's Trial Concluded" and editorial, *ibid.*, March 22, 1878; "Smyth and the Senate," *ibid.*, March 25, 1878; "Supt. Smyth Acquitted," *ibid.*, March 28, 1878; "The Insurance Bargain," *ibid.*, April 4, 1878; "Smyth and the Bargain," *ibid.*, April 7, 1878; "Fish Wants to Drop It," *ibid.*, April 17, 1878; Hilton to Hayes, March 6, April 6, 1878, Hayes Papers.

6. "Mr. Howe and the Administration," "Results of Conciliation," *The New York Times*, March 26, 1878.

7. "Republican Campaign" and editorial, *ibid.*, April 11, 1878; "President Hayes' Policy," *ibid.*, April 17, 1878.

8. Editorial, *ibid.*, June 25, 1878; editorial, *ibid.*, April 25, 1878; Hoogenboom, *Outlawing the Spoils*, p. 166. See also comments by Senator Dorsey in "Congress and Politics," *The New York Times*, May 4, 1878.

9. "Claims for Customs Drawbacks," *ibid.*, April 21, 1878; "Custom House Business," *ibid.*, April 23, 1878.

10. "Custom-House Methods," *ibid.*, May 16, 1878; "The Customs Commission," *ibid.*, May 17, 18, 1878; "The Importers' Complaint," *ibid.*, May 29, 1878.

11. Copy, Sherman to William A. Wheeler, January 15, 1879, in Personnel File, Chester A. Arthur, General Records of the Treasury Department, National Archives. Portions of the report leaked to the press. See "The Custom-House Report," *The New York Times*, September 26, 1878.

12. See the undated manuscript by Schurz in the Hayes Papers; Sherman to Hayes, July 10, 1878, *ibid.*; "Gen. Arthur's Removal," *The New York Times*, July 12, 1878.

13. "The Custom-House Changes," *ibid.*, July 15, 1878; "Sherman's Great Exploit," *ibid.*, July 17, 1878; editorial, *ibid.*, July 20, 1878. Affecting indifference toward the matter, Arthur told Burt that neither he nor Merritt could be confirmed by the Senate. Silas Burt Biography p. 97.

14. See Hayes, to Curtis, August 22, 1878, Hayes Papers. Cf. Hoogenboom, *Outlawing the Spoils*, pp. 168–169.

15. Quoted in Shores, *The Hayes-Conkling Controversy*, p. 254.

16. "The Republican Campaign," *The New York Times*, September 25, 1878; "A Patriotic Convention," *ibid.*, September 27, 1878.

17. "Republican City Canvass," *ibid.*, October 12, 1878; "The Contest in This City," *ibid.*, October 18, 1878; "Hon. Thomas Murphy for Senator," *ibid.*, October 19, 1878; "The Battle in New-York," *ibid.*, October 20, 1878; "A Ticket to Beat Tammany," *ibid.*, October 22, 1878. See also "The Week," *The Nation*, XVII (October 24, 1878), 247.

18. "Victorious Republicans" and editorial, *The New York Times,* November 6, 1878; "A Word for 'Barney' Biglin," *ibid.,* October 31, 1878; "Biglin's Demonstration," and editorial, *ibid.,* November 20, 1878; "The XVIIIth District," *ibid.,* December 10, 1878.

19. See "The New Customs Investigation," *ibid.,* September 3, 1878; "The Custom-House Guillotine," *ibid.,* October 1, 1878; editorial, *ibid.,* October 11, 1878; "Gen. Merritt's Tenure," *ibid.,* December 2, 1878.

20. Theodore Clarke Smith, *The Life and Letters of James Abram Garfield* (New Haven, 1925), II, 664; Sherman, *Recollections,* II, 683.

21. Williams (ed.), *Hayes: The Diary of a President,* p. 176.

22. "The City Republicans," *The New York Times,* January 11, 1879.

23. "Gen. Arthur's Suspension," *ibid.,* January 17, 1879.

24. Copy, Sherman to William A. Wheeler; January 15, 1879, in Personnel File, Chester A. Arthur, General Records of the Treasury Department, National Archives.

25. "The Custom-House Battle," *The New York Times,* January 16, 1879; Shores, *The Hayes-Conkling Controversy,* p. 258.

26. Conkling to Arthur, January 15, 1879, Arthur Papers, L.C.

27. "Gen. Arthur's Suspension," *The New York Times,* January 17, 1879.

28. "New-York's Next Senator," *ibid.,* January 21, 1879; "The Week," *The Nation,* XXVIII (February 6, 1879), 93.

29. "Affairs of the Nation," "Republican Central Committee," *The New York Times,* January 22, 1879. While Arthur was in Albany, George Bliss kept him informed of developments in Washington concerning the nominations. Two telegrams, Bliss to Arthur, January 20, 1879, Arthur Papers, L.C.

30. "The Custom-House Issue," *The New York Times,* January 18, 1879.

31. *Ibid.;* "Gen. Arthur's Vindication," "Mr. Cornell's Reply," *ibid.,* January 28, 1879.

32. "The Collectorship War," *ibid.,* January 30, 1879.

33. Conkling to Arthur, January 29, 1879, Arthur Papers, L.C.; editorial, *The New York Times,* January 30, 1879. Merritt may well have had a hand in garnering signatures for the Albany petition. See Sherman to Merritt, January 18, 1879, and telegram, Merritt to Sherman, January 28, 1879, Sherman Papers. Democratic Senator Kernan sided with Conkling.

34. The pamphlet is in the Personnel File, Chester A. Arthur, General Records of the Treasury Department, National Archives.

35. "Mr. Sherman's Rejoinder," *The New York Times,* February 1, 1879; "The News in Albany," *ibid.,* February 4, 1879.

36. See "The New-York Collectorship," *ibid.,* February 3, 1879; Sherman, *Recollections,* II, 684.

37. Williams (ed.), *Hayes: The Diary of a President,* p. 184.

38. "The Long Contest Ended," *The New York Times,* February 4, 1879; "The Sherman-Arthur Correspondence," *ibid.,* February 7, 1879; "Affairs of the Nation," *ibid.,* February 12, 1879.

39. Cf. Hoogenboom, *Outlawing the Spoils,* p. 171, and Shores, *The Hayes-Conkling Controversy,* pp. 262–266. See editorial, *The New York Times,* February 4, 1879. When pairs are included, Merritt's nomination was confirmed 40–30, twenty-five Republicans and fifteen Democrats voting affirmatively.

40. "Who Is Responsible for the Custom-House?," *The Nation*, XXVIII (February 6, 1879), 96.
41. Hayes to Curtis, "Private," February 5, 1879; Hayes to Merritt, February 4, 1879, Hayes Papers. See also Conkling to Arthur, February 6, 1879, Arthur Papers, L.C. While a complex of strict civil service regulations was formulated and enforced under his leadership, Merritt removed several Arthur henchmen, including Alexander Powell. See "Civil Service Methods," *The New York Times*, April 2, 3, 1879. For more on the post-Arthur Customhouse see Hartman, "Politics and Patronage," pp. 221–228.

CHAPTER EIGHT · ON THE BATTLEFIELD

1. "The Candidates of 1880," *The New York Times*, April 10, 1879.
2. "Gath," Cincinnati *Enquirer*, October 17, 1880.
3. "The City Republicans," *The New York Times*, February 19, March 19, 1879.
4. See "The Police Commission," *ibid.*, March 21, April 6, 1879; "Our Local Political Problem," *ibid.*, May 4, 1879; "The Department Vacancies," "An Anxious Commissioner," *ibid.*, May 6, 1879; "Nominations by the Mayor," "The Mayor and the Politicians," *ibid.*, May 7, 1879.
5. "Anti-Tammany Surprised," *ibid.*, May 21, 1879; Bliss to Kelly, March 19, 1879, Arthur Papers, L.C.; "Gath," Cincinnati *Enquirer*, September 2, 1883.
6. "The Republican General Committee," "Opinions of Politicians," *The New York Times*, May 21, 1879. Arthur reportedly sided with Kelly again when the city was reapportioned. See "The New Apportionment," *ibid.*, June 10, 1879; "Anti-Tammany Indignant," "The New Apportionment," *ibid.*, June 18, 1879.
7. "A Police Investigation," editorial, *ibid.*, July 31, 1879; "The Mayor Restrained," editorial, *ibid.*, August 5, 1879; "Mr. De Witt C. Wheeler's Shoes," editorial, *ibid.*, December 3, 1879. Wheeler paid some of the money back. "Miscellaneous City News," *ibid.*, September 6, 1879.
8. See "Mr. Conkling's Invective," *ibid.*, June 20, 1879; David S. Barry, *Forty Years in Washington* (Boston, 1924), pp. 71–74; Connelley (ed.), *A Collection of the Writings of John James Ingalls: Essays, Addresses, and Orations*, pp. 348–355; Edward Mayes, *Lucius Q. C. Lamar: His Life, Times, and Speeches* (Nashville, Tenn., 1896), p. 386.
9. See Ross, *Proud Kate*, pp. 231–260, and Thomas Graham Belden and Marva Robins Belden, *So Fell the Angels* (Boston, 1956), pp. 287–319.
10. Williams (ed.), *Hayes: The Diary of a President*, p. 243.
11. "Cornell Losing Support," *The New York Times*, September 3, 1879.
12. Curtis to Hayes, September 5, 1879, Hayes Papers. One reporter estimated the presence of at least 100 delegates who were "the direct creatures of Federal office-holders . . ." "Federal Office-Holders at Work," *The New York Times*, September 1, 1879.
13. See "The Republican Campaign," "The Evening Session," "Mr. Conkling's Victory," *ibid.*, September 4, 1879; Junius [Dorman B. Eaton], *The Independent Movement in New York as an Element in the Next Elections and a Problem in Party Government* (New York, 1880), pp. 35–38.
14. See E. McClung Fleming, "The Young Scratcher Campaign of 1879: The

Birth of the Mugwumps," *New York History*, XXIII (1942), 323–325; "Geo. Wm. Curtis Resigns," *The New York Times*, October 12, 1879. Cf. Curtis to Burt, "Private," September 30, 1879, Silas Burt Papers, N.Y.H.S.

15. "Gath," Cincinnati *Enquirer*, September 2, 1883.
16. See "A Field for Independent Effort," *The New York Times*, September 21, 1879; "Miscellaneous City News," *ibid.*, October 6, 1879. See also *The Times*' editorials of September 21, 23, October 1, 7, 11, 1879.
17. See "Gath," Cincinnati *Enquirer*, October 17, 1880; "On the Eve of Election," *The New York Times*, November 3, 1879.
18. See Arthur to Schurz, September 25, 1879, Schurz to Arthur, October 10, 1879, Carl Schurz Papers, L.C.; Arthur to Sherman, September 25, 1879, Sherman to Arthur, September 29, 1879, Sherman Papers; Evarts to Arthur, September 28, 1879, William Evarts Papers, L.C. Benjamin Bristow also sent his regrets. Bristow to Arthur, September 24, Bristow Papers.
19. "Issues of the Campaign," *The New York Times*, October 22, 1879; Chester Leonard Barrows, *William M. Evarts, Lawyer, Diplomat, Statesman* (Chapel Hill, N.C., 1941), pp. 331–332.
20. "The Republican Canvass," *The New York Times*, October 24, 1879.
21. "Cornell as a Candidate," *ibid.*, October 29, 1879; Sherman to Jay, October 4, 1879, in Sherman, *Recollections*, p. 748.
22. "Sound Republican Words," *The New York Times*, October 28, 1879.
23. "The City Republicans," *ibid.*, October 4, 1879.
24. "Progress of the Canvass," *ibid.*, October 22, 1879.
25. See Hamilton Fish to Arthur, October 24, 1879, Fish Papers. One colleague recalled: "Almost all the Republican bankers and merchants approved of Hayes's administration, but they felt some little pity for Arthur, being turned out of his office, and therefore gave him money for political ends with the less reluctance." "Gath," Cincinnati *Enquirer*, September 2, 1883.
26. "Voluntary Contributions," *Harper's Weekly*, XXIII (November 22, 1879), 918. See also "The Administration and the New York Election," *The Nation*, XXIX (October 23, 1879), 271.
27. See "The General Political News," *The New York Times*, December 13, 1879.
28. "Close of the County Canvass," *ibid.*, November 22, 1879. Elihu Root lost his bid to become justice of the common pleas.
29. "Political Organization," *ibid.*, November 26, 1879.
30. "The Speakership Contest," *ibid.*, January 4, 1880; "The Assembly Organization," *ibid.*, January 6, 1880.
31. "Dangerous Illness of Mrs. Gen. Arthur," *ibid.*, January 11, 1880; Howe, *Chester A. Arthur*, p. 98.
32. See [Herndon], "Ellen Lewis Herndon. . . ," Arthur Papers, L.C., and John W. Herndon to Mrs. V. T. Dunn, April 22, 1932, *ibid.* See also "Death of Mrs. Chester A. Arthur," Albany *Evening Journal*, January 13, 1880.
33. The physician in attendance told a cousin that Mrs. Arthur died of heart disease accompanied by double pneumonia. Brodie Herndon Diary, entry of February 24, 1880, Herndon Papers.
34. "The Last Rites," Albany *Morning Express*, January 16, 1880; "Mrs. Arthur's Funeral," *The New York Times*, January 16, 1880.
35. Copy, Dun to M. A. Smith, January 11, 1880, Arthur Papers, L.C.; "The

Bee," Cincinnati *Enquirer,* November 22, 1883; Brodie Herndon Diary, entry of February 14, 1880, Herndon Papers.

36. [Herndon], "Ellen Lewis Herndon . . . ," Arthur Papers, L.C.

CHAPTER NINE · A TIME TO DO BATTLE

1. Hesseltine, *Ulysses S. Grant, Politician,* p. 434.
2. Cameron to Howe, February 19, 1880, Timothy O. Howe Papers, State Historical Society of Wisconsin.
3. George Francis Dawson, *Life and Services of Gen. John A. Logan as Soldier and Statesman* (Chicago, 1887), p. 285.
4. "Our Albany Legislators," *The New York Times,* January 30, 1880; "The State Government," *ibid.,* February 18, 1880. Public pressure forced the withdrawal of Smyth's renomination as superintendent of the insurance department. Editorial, *ibid.,* March 3, 1880. The law firm handling the business of the department in New York City during at least the last months of Smyth's regime was Arthur, Phelps, Knevals, and Ransom. See "Superintendent Smyth's Last," editorial, *ibid.,* April 28, 1880.
5. "The Choice of New-York," *ibid.,* February 24, 1880; "Grant Triumphs at Utica," "The Utica Convention," *ibid.,* February 26, 1880.
6. Smith, *The Life and Letters of James Abram Garfield,* II, 957.
7. See Rothman, *Politics and Power, The United States Senate 1869–1901,* pp. 31–32. Cf. William G. Eidson, "Who Were the Stalwarts?", *Mid-America,* 52 (October 1970), 235–261.
8. See Gail Hamilton [Mary Abigail Dodge], *Biography of James G. Blaine* (Norwich, Conn., 1895), pp. 481–483; David Saville Muzzey, *James G. Blaine, a Political Idol of Other Days* (New York, 1934), pp. 164–166; Smith, *The Life and Letters of James Abram Garfield,* II, 957.
9. "A Disgraceful Scheme," *The New York Times,* May 10, 1880; Herbert J. Clancy, S.J., *The Presidential Election of 1880* (Chicago, 1958), pp. 28–31, 38–42; Oberholtzer, *A History of the United States,* IV, 77 f.2.
10. See Smith, *The Life and Letters of James Abram Garfield,* II, 945–957.
11. See "To Secure an Honest Count," *The New York Times,* April 30, 1880; editorial, *ibid.,* May 1, 1880; "The Proposed New Charter," "Convivial Legislation," *ibid.,* May 2, 1880; "Miscellaneous City News," *ibid.,* May 3, 1880; "An Honest New-York Election," *ibid.,* May 5, 1880; "The Republican Caucus," editorial, *ibid.,* May 6, 1880.
12. Platt to Cornell, March 3, 1880, Alonzo B. Cornell Papers, Cornell University.
13. "The Trouble in Albany," *The New York Times,* May 7, 1880; "The Work of the Caucus," editorial, *ibid.,* May 8, 1880; "Mr. Wheeler's Successor," *ibid.,* May 26, 1880.
14. "Senator Robertson's Decision," *ibid.,* May 7, 1880; "The Leaders in the Bolt," *ibid.,* May 8, 1880.
15. "To Abide by Instructions," *ibid.;* "Grant's Friends and Foes," *ibid.,* May 28, 1880; "The Contest at Chicago," *ibid.,* May 29, 1880.
16. "Incidents of the Struggle," *ibid.,* May 30, 1880.
17. Smith, *The Life and Letters of James Abram Garfield,* II, 958–959.
18. "The Eve of the Contest," *The New York Times,* June 2, 1880.

19. See Smith, *The Life and Letters of James Abram Garfield*, II, 963–964; Clancy, *The Presidential Election of 1880*, pp. 86–87; Hoar, *Autobiography of Seventy Years*, I, 389–393. William Chandler later claimed that Arthur dissuaded some colleagues from betraying the bargain giving Hoar his office. See Chandler, "Chester A. Arthur," in Wilson (ed.), *The Presidents of the United States*, III, 209.

20. "The New-York Delegation," "Confident of Grant's Success," *The New York Times*, June 2, 1880.

21. "Some of the Incidents," *ibid.*

22. "The National Convention," *ibid.*, June 3, 1880.

23. "The Convention and Its Work," *ibid.*; Melville E. Stone, *Fifty Years a Journalist* (London, 1922), p. 103.

24. See editorial, *The New York Times*, June 3, 1880. Unless otherwise stated, accounts of convention business are based on *Proceedings of the Republican National Convention Held in Chicago, Illinois, June 2–8, 1880* (Chicago, 1881).

25. "Enthusiastic Grant Caucus," *The New York Times*, June 3, 1880; William Elsey Connelley, *The Life of Preston B. Plumb 1837–1891* (Chicago, 1913), p. 246.

26. Editorial, *The New York Times*, June 4, 1880.

27. See Lang (ed.), *The Autobiography of Thomas Collier Platt*, p. 102; Clancy, *The Presidential Election of 1880*, p. 92.

28. Williams (ed.), *Hayes: the Diary of a President*, p. 277.

29. Hoar, *Autobiography of Seventy Years*, I, 393.

30. Lang (ed.), *The Autobiography of Thomas Collier Platt*, pp. 104–111; Conkling, *The Life and Letters of Roscoe Conkling*, pp. 596–603; "Progress of the Contest," *The New York Times*, June 6, 1880.

31. Smith, *The Life and Letters of James Abram Garfield*, II, 974; Boutwell, *Reminiscences of Seventy Years in Public Affairs*, II, 268.

32. See Smith, *The Life and Letters of James Abram Garfield*, II, 975–976.

33. On the seventeenth ballot one more New York delegate switched from Grant to Blaine. See Chidsey, *The Gentleman from New York*, pp. 290–291.

34. "Grant's Foes Alarmed," *The New York Times*, June 8, 1880; Lang (ed.), *The Autobiography of Thomas Collier Platt*, p. 103.

35. See Charles Emory Smith, "How Conkling Missed Nominating Blaine," *Saturday Evening Post*, 172 (June 9, 1901), 2–3.

36. "Garfield and Arthur," *The New York Times*, June 9, 1880.

37. Lang (ed.), *The Autobiography of Thomas Collier Platt*, p. 116.

38. Robert McElroy, *Levi Parsons Morton: Banker, Diplomat and Statesman* (New York, 1930), pp. 102–103. For a recollection of Arthur's preconvention views, see E. J. Edwards, "New News of Yesterday," New York *Evening Mail*, September 9, 1911.

39. The best contemporary accounts of this series of events are: "Garfield and Arthur," *The New York Times*, June 9, 1880; New York *World* dispatch of June 10 in "More of Gov. Dennison's Foolishness," Cleveland *Leader*, June 21, 1880; William Henry Smith to Rutherford B. Hayes, June 15, 1880, in Charles Richard Williams (ed.), *Diary and Letters of Rutherford Birchard Hayes* (Columbus, Ohio, 1924), III, 605. Tom Murphy's story is in "Gath," Cincinnati *Enquirer*, August 14, 1883. The eyewitness account of the confrontation between Arthur and Conkling is in William C. Hudson, *Random*

Recollections of an Old Political Reporter (New York, 1911), pp. 96–99. For more on Conkling's response to Arthur's decision see the interview with Stephen Dorsey in "Washington," Cincinnati *Enquirer*, September 27, 1882, and George Alfred Townshend, "Chester Alan Arthur," New York *Sun*, September 6, 1891. Morton's story is in a letter of 1908 in McElroy, *Levi Parsons Morton*, pp. 105–106. For Depew's account see Depew to A. B. Samford, June 3, 1920, Chauncey M. Depew Papers, Yale University. Cf. Henry L. Stoddard, *As I Knew Them: Presidents and Politics from Grant to Coolidge* (New York, 1927), pp. 118–120. See also Alexander K. McClure, *Our Presidents and How We Make Them* (New York, 1900), p. 274, and his *Recollections of Half a Century*, pp. 110, 118–119; Alexander, *A Political History of the State of New York*, III, 442–444. Cf. White, *Autobiography of Andrew Dickson White*, I, 192–194.

40. Henry R. James, a bolter, presented Wheeler's name, but the nomination was withdrawn, without dissent, by a machine regular. "Garfield and Arthur," *The New York Times*, June 9, 1880. The exact mechanics of the call for a caucus are obscure.
41. Hudson, *Random Recollections of an Old Political Reporter*, p. 105.
42. "Gen. Arthur at Home," *The New York Times*, June 12, 1880.
43. "The Nation's Sorrow," New York *Herald*, November 20, 1886.
44. "After the Nominations," *The New York Times*, June 9, 1880; William E. Curtis to Morton, July 20, 1880, Levi P. Morton Papers, New York Public Library.
45. "Gov. Foster Speaks for Ohio," *The New York Times*, June 11, 1880.
46. "What Thurlow Weed Says," *ibid.*, June 9, 1880. Of the civil service plank, Weed growled: "Civil service reform was a humbug always, and is doubly a humbug now . . ."
47. Claude M. Feuss, *Carl Schurz, Reformer* (New York, 1932), pp. 272–273.
48. "The Week," *The Nation*, XXXI (June 17, 1880), 445.
49. Sherman to Warner M. Bateman, June 9, 1880; Sherman to James M. Hoyt, June 12, 1880, Sherman Papers.
50. Burt to Hayes, June 9, 1880, Hayes Papers.
51. Quoted in Clancy, *The Presidential Election of 1880*, p. 118.
52. "Garfield and Arthur," New York *Herald*, June 9, 1880.
53. "Gen. Arthur at Home," *The New York Times*, June 12, 1880.
54. "Gen. Arthur Serenaded," *ibid.*, June 13, 1880.
55. Williams (ed.), *Hayes: The Diary of a President*, p. 278.

CHAPTER TEN · PUSHING THINGS

1. See Marcus, *Grand Old Party*, pp. 5–11; Garraty, *The New Commonwealth*, pp. 236–241.
2. See Clancy, *The Presidential Election of 1880*, pp. 52–81, 122–156; Morgan, *From Hayes to McKinley*, pp. 82–84, 97–101.
3. Sherman, *Recollections*, II, 807.
4. In Smith, *The Life and Letters of James Abram Garfield*, II, 996.
5. *Ibid.*, 996–1000; Richardson, *William E. Chandler*, pp. 258–259; Sarah Forbes Hughes (ed.), *Letters and Recollections of John Murray Forbes* (Boston, 1899), II, 196–198.

6. Arthur offered no advice. See telegram, Arthur to Garfield, July 11, 1880, James A. Garfield Papers, L.C.

7. Smith, *The Life and Letters of James Abram Garfield*, II, 1002–1003.

8. In Clancy, *The Presidential Election of 1880*, p. 182.

9. "Gen. Arthur's Acceptance," *The New York Times*, July 19, 1880.

10. Editorial, "Gen. Arthur's Acceptance," *ibid.*

11. "The Week," *The Nation*, XXXI (July 22, 1880), 54.

12. Curtis to Burt, July 22, 1880, Burt Papers, N.Y.H.S.

13. Copy, Regina Caw to Alice [Mrs. William] Arthur, June 11, 1880, Arthur Family Papers.

14. "Chester A. Arthur," Boston *Herald*, June 12, 1880.

15. "Notes of the Campaign," *The New York Times*, July 16, 1880; "The Contest of Parties," *ibid.*, July 21, 1880; Conkling to Morton, August 1, 1880, Morton Papers.

16. See telegrams, Arthur to Garfield, June 28, 30, 1880, Garfield Papers; Smith, *The Life and Letters of James Abram Garfield*, II, 998.

17. See *ibid.*, 1007–1011; telegram, Dorsey to Garfield, July 24, 1880, Garfield Papers.

18. "Gen. Garfield Welcomed," "The Greeting in This City," *The New York Times*, August 5, 1880.

19. "Greetings for Garfield," *ibid.*, August 3, 1880.

20. Smith, *The Life and Letters of James Abram Garfield*, II, 1012.

21. Lang (ed.), *The Autobiography of Thomas Collier Platt*, pp. 127–128.

22. *Ibid.*, pp. 126–127; Conkling, *The Life and Letters of Roscoe Conkling*, pp. 611–613.

23. Royal Cortissoz, *The Life of Whitelaw Reid* (New York, 1921), II, 37–38.

24. Lang (ed.), *The Autobiography of Thomas Collier Platt*, p. 128, and "Leaders in Consultation," *The New York Times*, August 6, 1880, make it clear that the traditional date of the meeting between Garfield and Conkling's lieutenants, August 6, is incorrect. The error stems from a misleading entry in Garfield's diary.

25. Lang (ed.), *The Autobiography of Thomas Collier Platt*, pp. 130–132. For the creation of the secret fund, see McElroy, *Levi Parsons Morton*, pp. 109–111. Platt's account closely resembles one given by Stephen Dorsey in 1883. See "The Pledges of Garfield," New York *Sun*, July 16, 1883.

26. "Among the Political Workers," *The New York Times*, August 10, 1880.

27. T. B. Connery, "Secret History of the Garfield-Conkling Tragedy," *Cosmopolitan Magazine*, XXIII (June 1897), 150.

28. Smith, *The Life and Letters of James Abram Garfield*, II, 1015.

29. On Dorsey's leadership of the national committee, see Hughes (ed.), *Letters and Recollections of John Murray Forbes*, II, 197–198. After the November election, Dorsey served as the committee spokesman. "Summing up the Victory," *The New York Times*, November 8, 1880.

30. *Garfield and Arthur Campaign Song Book* (Philadelphia, 1880), p. 22. See also the *Garfield and Arthur Campaign Songster* (New York, 1880).

31. See "New Publications," *The New York Times*, August 23, 1880.

32. See Clancy, *The Presidential Election of 1880*, pp. 222–231; Smith, *The Life and Letters of James Abram Garfield*, II, 1027.

33. *Ibid.*, 1928. For replies to charges against Garfield, see *Documents Issued by the Union Republican Congressional Committee, Presidential Campaign of*

1880 (Washington, 1880); *The Republican Text-Book for the Campaign of 1880* (New York, 1880), pp. 170–193.

34. Smith, *The Life and Letters of James Abram Garfield*, II, 1026; "Maine's Fusion Majority," *The New York Times*, September 15, 1880.
35. See C. E. Henry to Garfield, July 27, 1880, in James D. Norris and Arthur H. Shaffer (eds.), *Politics and Patronage in the Gilded Age: The Correspondence of James A. Garfield and Charles E. Henry* (Madison, Wis., 1970), p. 285.
36. See "The 'Old Guard' in Line," *The New York Times*, September 12, 1880; Thomas C. Reeves, "Chester A. Arthur and the Campaign of 1880," *Political Science Quarterly*, LXXXIV (December 1969), 630–631. The state committee also sent speakers into New Jersey, Connecticut, "and other States." "The State Committee," *The New York Times*, October 30, 1880.
37. "A Grand Republican Plea," "Union Boys Again in Line," *ibid.*, September 18, 1880.
38. Reeves, "Chester A. Arthur and the Campaign of 1880," 631; telegrams from Arthur to Garfield, September 11, 13, 14, 17, 1880, Garfield Papers; Smith, *The Life and Letters of James Abram Garfield*, II, 1031–1032. See also Garfield to Conkling, September 27, 1880, Roscoe Conkling Papers, L.C.
39. Smith, *The Life and Letters of James Abram Garfield*, II, 1032.
40. See *ibid.*, 1033–1034; Lang (ed.), *The Autobiography of Thomas Collier Platt*, pp. 134–135; Conkling, *The Life and Letters of Roscoe Conkling*, pp. 622–624. Conkling cited Garfield's renewed pledge at Mentor in an appearance before a caucus of Republican Senators on April 27, 1881. "The New-York Nominees," *The New York Times*, May 2, 1881.
41. Conkling, *The Life and Letters of Roscoe Conkling*, p. 626.
42. "Sixty Thousand in Line," *The New York Times*, October 12, 1880.
43. Reeves, "Chester A. Arthur and the Campaign of 1880," 632. Conkling's nephew reported that the Senator made about twenty speeches on behalf of the national ticket and sacrificed $29,000 in legal fees to hit the campaign trail. Conkling, *The Life and Letters of Roscoe Conkling*, pp. 614–615, 626–627.
44. Silas Burt Biography, pp. 101–102. Burt again refused to pay.
45. For the full story of the state committee's fund-raising efforts, see Reeves, "Chester A. Arthur and the Campaign of 1880," 633–635; Thomas C. Reeves, "Chester A. Arthur and Campaign Assessments in the Election of 1880," *The Historian*, XXXI (August 1969), 573–582.
46. See "The Ex-President's Life," *The New York Times*, November 19, 1886; "Gath," Cincinnati *Enquirer*, March 28, 1882; "The Pledges of Garfield," New York *Sun*, July 16, 1883. See also "Vigorous Campaign Work," *The New York Times*, September 30, 1880.
47. E.g., "The Knavery in Indiana," *ibid.*, September 15, 1880.
48. George W. Marston to Chandler, September 15, 1880, Chandler Papers, New Hampshire State Historical Society.
49. See "The Pledges of Garfield," New York *Sun*, July 16, 1883; Marcus, *Grand Old Party*, p. 56; James Ford Rhodes, *History of the United States from Hayes to McKinley: 1877–1896* (New York, 1919), p. 135.
50. Smith, *The Life and Letters of James Abram Garfield*, II, 1034; Leland L. Sage, *William Boyd Allison, a Study in Practical Politics* (Iowa City, 1956), pp. 164–165.

51. See Fowler, *The Cabinet Politician*, pp. 172, 174–175. The congressional campaign committee reportedly raised about $100,000. See Frederick W. Whitridge, "Political Assessments," in John J. Lalor (ed.), *Cyclopaedia of Political Science* . . . (New York, 1890–1893), I, 152–155. Senator Allison claimed in 1882 that out of 100,000 employees asked to contribute to the congressional committee favorable responses were received from only 11,514.

52. "Pushing the Campaign," *ibid.*, October 15, 1880; "Republicans Rejoicing," *ibid.*, October 16, 1880. Conkling congratulated Morton on the victory. Conkling to Morton, October 14, 1880, Morton Papers.

53. "Pushing the Campaign," *The New York Times*, October 15, 1880.

54. See "The Week," *The Nation*, XXXI (August 19, 1880), 123.

55. Clancy, *The Presidential Election of 1880*, pp. 233–237.

56. Morgan, *From Hayes to McKinley*, p. 114.

57. *The New York Times*, October 30, 1880; "William Dowd for Mayor," *ibid.*, October 23, 1880. The Republican machine also nominated Daniel G. Rollins for recorder and Jacob Hess for register.

58. Clancy, *The Presidential Election of 1880*, p. 239.

59. Account Book, "Campaign of 1880, Deposit book and checques special a/c, Closed Oct. 3, 1881." Arthur Papers, L.C. Many of the checks are in *ibid.* A total of $47,528 was raised by November 10, leaving the committee with a surplus of $7,082. The account book reveals that a single corporation, Hitchcock Darling and Company, contributed $10,000.

60. See *Harper's Weekly*, XXVIII (November 15, 1884), 748. William Barnum, chairman of the Democratic National Committee, and John Kelly charged that at least 20,000 illegal Republican votes were cast in New York. See Clancy, *The Presidential Election of 1880*, pp. 243–245.

61. *Ibid.*, p. 242.

62. See *ibid.*, pp. 246–247; Alexander, *A Political History of the State of New York*, III, 462–463. All of New York City's local races were won by Democrats.

63. Editorial, *The New York Times*, November 3, 1880.

64. Lang (ed.), *The Autobiography of Thomas Collier Platt*, p. 132.

CHAPTER ELEVEN · WITH A FEATHER

1. "Gen. Arthur Congratulated," *The New York Times*, November 4, 1880.

2. Smith, *The Life and Letters of James Abram Garfield*, II, 1047. See McElroy, *Levi Parsons Morton*, p. 121; "High Office Politics," *The New York Times*, January 2, 1881.

3. Smith, *The Life and Letters of James Abram Garfield*, II, 1053–1055.

4. *Ibid.*, 1049, 1052, 1055.

5. Depew, *My Memories of Eighty Years*, p. 112.

6. Cortissoz, *The Life of Whitelaw Reid*, II, 45, 47.

7. Smith, *The Life and Letters of James Abram Garfield*, II, 1056–1057. See "Gen. Garfield's Neutrality," *The New York Times*, January 12, 1881.

8. Connery, "Secret History of the Garfield-Conkling Tragedy," 150.

9. Boutwell, *Reminiscences of Sixty Years in Public Affairs*, II, 273.

10. "Gen. Sharpe the Speaker," *The New York Times*, January 4, 1881.

11. "New-York in the Senate," *ibid.*, January 12, 1881.

12. "The New-York Contest," *ibid.*, January 13, 1881.
13. In McElroy, *Levi Parsons Morton*, p. 123.
14. "The New-York Contest," *The New York Times*, January 13, 1881.
15. "Results of the Caucus," *ibid.*, January 15, 1881; "Senator Thomas C. Platt," *ibid.*, January 14, 1881. See Crowley, *Echoes from Niagara*, pp. 195–202.
16. Depew, *My Memories of Eighty Years*, p. 112; Alexander, *A Political History of the State of New York*, III, 468; Cortissoz, *The Life of Whitelaw Reid*, p. 50.
17. *Ibid.*, p. 51. Platt makes no mention of this bargain in his autobiography and asserts that he was a reluctant candidate. Lang (ed.), *The Autobiography of Thomas Collier Platt*, pp. 139–141.
18. Smith, *The Life and Letters of James Abram Garfield*, II, 1058–1059.
19. McElroy, *Levi Parsons Morton*, pp. 124–125.
20. Smith, *The Life and Letters of James Abram Garfield*, II, 1074.
21. Blaine to Garfield, December 16, 1880, Garfield Papers.
22. Smith, *The Life and Letters of James Abram Garfield*, II, 1059–1060, 1074.
23. *Ibid.*, 1075–1078.
24. Conkling to Howe, January 19, 1881, Howe Papers.
25. Sprague to Arthur, "Strictly Confidential," January 18, 1881, Arthur Papers, L.C.
26. "Gen. Arthur in Washington," *The New York Times*, February 20, 1881.
27. "Gen. Arthur Visits the Senate," *ibid.*, February 24, 1881; "Gath," Cincinnati *Enquirer*, September 2, 1883.
28. "Indiana October Vote," *The New York Times*, February 12, 1881. Arthur later claimed, or so said an uncritical admirer, that the speech was invented by an unfriendly reporter. Stone, *Fifty Years a Journalist*, p. 148.
29. "The Week," *The Nation*, XXXII (February 24, 1881), 122.
30. Richardson, *William E. Chandler*, pp. 266–267.
31. Blaine to Garfield, February 13, 1881, Garfield Papers.
32. Smith, *The Life and Letters of James Abram Garfield*, II, 1082–1087; Connery, "Secret History of the Garfield-Conkling Tragedy," 150.
33. *Ibid.*, 152–153; Cortissoz, *The Life of Whitelaw Reid*, p. 55; Morton to Conkling, "Private," March 2, 1881, Morton Papers. Cf. McElroy, *Levi Parsons Morton*, pp. 129–130.
34. Cortissoz, *The Life of Whitelaw Reid*, p. 55.
35. *Ibid.*, pp. 55–56; Fowler, *The Cabinet Politician*, p. 176.
36. See Smith, *The Life and Letters of James Abram Garfield*, II, 1093–1094.
37. Dorsey to Garfield, March 4, 1881, Garfield Papers.
38. Smith, *The Life and Letters of James Abram Garfield*, II, 1098.
39. Grant to Conkling, March 5, 1881, Conkling Papers.

CHAPTER TWELVE · THE CRISIS OF HIS FATE

1. Ben: Perley Poore, *Perley's Reminiscences of Sixty Years in the National Metropolis* (Philadelphia, 1886), II, 390–398; "The New Chief Magistrate," *The New York Times*, March 5, 1881. Cabinet officers and a few other appointees were confirmed prior to the tussle over organization.
2. "Mahone's Deciding Vote," *ibid.*, March 12, 1881; "Republicans in Control," *ibid.*, March 15, 1881; Vincent P. De Santis, *Republicans Face the Southern*

Question: The New Departure Years, 1877–1897 (Baltimore, 1959), pp. 142–146; Rothman, *Politics and Power*, pp. 32–33.

3. See "The Republican Senate," *The New York Times*, March 19, 1881; *Congressional Record*, 47th Cong., Special Session of the Senate.

4. See the editorial "The End of the Extra Session," *The New York Times*, May 21, 1881.

5. "The Federal Appointees," *ibid.*, March 29, 1881; Smith, *The Life and Letters of James Abram Garfield*, II, 1104; Boutwell, *Reminiscences of Sixty Years*, II, 273.

6. Smith, *The Life and Letters of James Abram Garfield*, II, 1105; "New-York Offices Filled," "What Is Said at Albany," *The New York Times*, March 23, 1881; Merritt, *Recollections, 1828–1911*, p. 136. Garfield's private secretary told Merritt that Blaine had "insisted upon" Robertson's appointment.

7. See Poore, *Perley's Reminiscences of Sixty Years in the National Metropolis*, II, 402; Muzzey, *James G. Blaine*, pp. 190–191.

8. "A Sketch of the Nominee," New York *Herald*, March 24, 1881.

9. "The Week," *The Nation*, XXXII (April 7, 1881), 231–232. See the editorial "Political Pretenses," *The New York Times*, March 30, 1881.

10. Smith, *The Life and Letters of James Abram Garfield*, II, 1106; editorial "Yesterday's Appointments," New York *Tribune*, March 24, 1881. A leading Stalwart newspaper reported that Arthur men were particularly irate over the Robertson appointment and made no attempt to conceal their anger. "A Presidential Bomb," New York *Herald*, March 24, 1881.

11. Smith, *The Life and Letters of James Abram Garfield*, II, 1109.

12. "State Capital Methods," *The New York Times*, March 24, 1881; "The Assembly Reconsiders," *ibid.*, March 29, 1881.

13. "Voice of the Press," Albany *Evening Journal*, April 4, 1881.

14. Smith, *The Life and Letters of James Abram Garfield*, II, 1111–1112.

15. *Ibid.*, 1112–1115; Lang (ed.), *The Autobiography of Thomas Collier Platt*, p. 155; Cortissoz, *The Life of Whitelaw Reid*, II, 60–61.

16. " 'Stalwarts' in Conference," New York *Herald*, April 4, 1881; "Views of Prominent Men," New York *Tribune*, April 4, 1881.

17. Smith, *The Life and Letters of James Abram Garfield*, II, 1117–1118.

18. Editorial "Conkling and Street-Cleaning," New York *World*, April 8, 1881; "The New-York Custom-House," *The New York Times*, April 6, 1881.

19. Editorial, *ibid.*, April 15, 1881.

20. Editorial, Chicago *Evening Journal*, April 8, 1881.

21. Cortissoz, *The Life of Whitelaw Reid*, II, 64–65.

22. "Mr. Conkling on Mahone," *The New York Times*, April 11, 1881.

23. "The New-York Nominees," *ibid.*, May 2, 1881; H. L. Dawes, "Garfield and Conkling," *Century Magazine*, XLVII (January 1894), 343.

24. "The New-York Nominees," *The New York Times*, May 2, 1881; Smith, *The Life and Letters of James Abram Garfield*, II, 1122.

25. Dawes, "Garfield and Conkling," 344.

26. "Troubles of the Senate," *The New York Times*, May 3, 1881; "The Senatorial Caucus," *ibid.*, May 4, 1881.

27. "The Senate Goes to Work," "Brady's Harmless Boast," *ibid.*, May 5, 1881.

28. Smith, *The Life and Letters of James Abram Garfield*, II, 1125–1126. Grant, who had privately rebuked the President for his hostility to New York's

Stalwarts, attributed the tactic entirely to the Secretary of State. He wrote to Adam Badeau, "Garfield has shown that he is not possessed of the backbone of an angle-worm." In Adam Badeau, *Grant in Peace: From Appomattox to Mount McGregor* (Hartford, Conn., 1887), p. 534.

29. "The Views of State Legislators," *The New York Times*, May 7, 1881.
30. Editorial "The New-York Nominations," *ibid.*, May 6, 1881.
31. Smith, *The Life and Letters of James Abram Garfield*, II, 1126–1127.
32. See Connery, "Secret History of the Garfield-Conkling Tragedy," 145–162. Connery was quoting Arthur "in so many words."
33. See Smith, *The Life and Letters of James Abram Garfield*, II, 1129–1132.
34. "Mr. Conkling's Grievances," *The New York Times*, May 10, 1881; "The Republican Caucus," *ibid.*, May 11, 1881; "The Robertson Contest," *ibid.*, May 14, 1881.
35. "The President's Choice," *ibid.*, May 15, 1881.
36. Lang (ed.), *The Autobiography of Thomas Collier Platt*, pp. 150–159; Tom Murphy's account in "The Bee," Cincinnati *Enquirer*, November 22, 1883; Depew, *My Memories of Eighty Years*, p. 113.
37. "A Sensation in Politics," "The Letter of Resignation," *The New York Times*, May 17, 1881.
38. "Differing Views in This City," editorial, *ibid.*; "Comments of the Press," "Mr. Beecher on the Situation," *ibid.*, May 18, 1881.
39. Smith, *The Life and Letters of James Abram Garfield*, II, 1134–1135.
40. In William Roscoe Thayer, *The Life and Letters of John Hay* (Boston, 1908), I, 451–452.
41. "The Protesting Senators," *The New York Times*, May 18, 1881; "Mr. Robertson Confirmed," *ibid.*, May 19, 1881.
42. "The Fight Begun at Albany," *ibid.*, May 17, 1881; "Conkling's Hopes Fading," *ibid.*, May 19, 1881; statement by George Sharpe in "Lessons," Cincinnati *Enquirer*, June 12, 1882. Cf. Hudson, *Random Recollections of an Old Political Reporter*, pp. 116–118. See Whitelaw Reid's unconvincing report to Garfield of an earlier conversation with Payn, obviously designed to bolster the President's resolve. In Cortissoz, *The Life of Whitelaw Reid*, II, 64–65. Garfield renominated three of the five major Stalwarts for federal office after the resignations, Payn being one of the two men dropped.
43. "Conkling's Poor Chances," *The New York Times*, May 20, 1881.
44. "The Deadlock at Albany," *ibid.*, June 13, 1881. See editorial, *ibid.*, June 3, 1882.
45. "The New-York Senators," "An Outside View," *ibid.*, May 23, 1881.
46. Depew, *My Memories of Eighty Years*, p. 114.
47. Quoted in Rothman, *Politics and Power*, p. 179.
48. "Beginning the Contest," *The New York Times*, May 25, 1881.
49. "Strength of the Opposition," editorial, *ibid.*
50. "The Situation Last Night," *ibid.*, May 26, 1881.
51. "Conkling Losing Ground," *ibid.*, May 27, 1881.
52. Editorial "A Public Scandal," New York *Tribune*, May 26, 1881.
53. "The Week," *The Nation*, XXXII (June 9, 1881), 397.
54. See Albert B. Paine, *Thomas Nast: His Period and His Pictures* (New York, 1904), pp. 449, 486–487.
55. See "The Situation Last Night," *The New York Times*, May 26, 1881; "Mr. Conkling Returns to Albany," editorial, *ibid.*, May 30, 1881.

56. "Conkling's Cause Lost," editorial, *ibid.*, May 31, 1881.
57. "Naming the Candidates," editorial, *ibid.*, June 1, 1881; Smith, *The Life and Letters of James Abram Garfield*, II, 1137.
58. "The Ex-President on Conkling," *The New York Times*, June 2, 1881. See Platt quoted in "A View Through Stalwart Eyes," *ibid.*, June 5, 1881.
59. Taken from daily accounts of the voting in *ibid.*
60. Harold F. Gosnell, *Boss Platt and His New York Machine* (Chicago, 1924), p. 28.
61. "The Tragedy in the Depot," *The New York Times*, July 3, 1881; Charles E. Rosenberg, *The Trial of the Assassin Guiteau: Psychiatry and Law in the Gilded Age* (Chicago, 1968), pp. 2–3.

CHAPTER THIRTEEN · ON THE ANNALS OF HISTORY

1. See "Gen. Arthur's Later Years," *The New York Times*, November 19, 1886; "The Scenes in Wall-Street," *ibid.*, July 3, 1881.
2. "Gen. Arthur's Movements," *ibid.* Two drafts of telegrams to Arthur are in the James G. Blaine Papers, L.C.
3. The wire calling Arthur to Washington is in the Arthur Papers, L.C. See "Gen. Arthur's Movements," *The New York Times*, July 3, 1881.
4. Rosenberg, *The Trial of the Assassin Guiteau*, pp. 3–4; Smith, *The Life and Letters of James Abram Garfield*, II, 1195.
5. Rosenberg, *The Trial of the Assassin Guiteau*, pp. 32–36.
6. "The Candidates Honored," *The New York Times*, August 7, 1880; "Local Political Work," *ibid.*, August 22, 1880.
7. Rosenberg, *The Trial of the Assassin Guiteau*, pp. 37–42. For a fascinating recollection of Guiteau as an office-seeker, see Margarita Spalding Gerry (ed.), *Through Five Administrations: Reminiscences of Colonel William H. Crook* (New York, 1900), pp. 266–269.
8. "A Great Nation in Grief," *The New York Times*, July 3, 1881.
9. Editorial "The Civil Service," *The National Republican*, July 18, 1881.
10. Editorial "The Public Sentiment," Rochester (N.Y.) *Sunday Morning Herald*, July 17, 1881.
11. Editorial "The Tide of Reform," New York *Evening Mail*, August 1, 1881. See Hoogenboom, *Outlawing the Spoils*, pp. 209–213.
12. Editorial "To Whom It May Concern," *The New York Times*, July 3, 1881. See "Opinions of the Press," *ibid.*
13. "The Week," *The Nation*, XXXIII (July 7, 1881), 1.
14. White, *Autobiography of Andrew Dickson White*, I, 193.
15. "The Scenes in Wall-Street," "Thunderbolt at Albany," *The New York Times*, July 3, 1881.
16. Williams (ed.), *Diary and Letters of Rutherford Birchard Hayes*, IV, 23.
17. Bancroft (ed.), *Speeches, Correspondence and Political Papers of Carl Schurz* (New York, 1913), IV, 147.
18. "Senator Harrison on Arthur," *The New York Times*, November 19, 1886.
19. "Vice-President Arthur," *ibid.*, July 5, 1881. Adam Badeau recalled, "At one time in the crisis he entered the room of an intimate friend in an agony of anxiety, flung himself on a couch and burst into tears." "Ex-President Arthur," Boston *Sunday Herald*, November 28, 1886.

20. Poore, *Perley's Reminiscences of Sixty Years in the National Metropolis*, II, 427–428.
21. "Blaine and Arthur Closeted," *The New York Times*, July 7, 1881.
22. See Harriet S. Blaine Beale (ed.), *Letters of Mrs. James G. Blaine* (New York, 1908), I, 230, 236–237.
23. "Blaine and Arthur Closeted," *The New York Times*, July 7, 1881.
24. "The Danger Line Passed," "The Vice-President in the City," *The New York Times*, July 14, 1881.
25. Copy, Conkling to Alexander T. Brown, July 9, 1881, Conkling letters, Harold J. Jonas Collection, New York Public Library.
26. "Conkling's Curious Position," *The New York Times*, July 9, 1881.
27. "The Choice of a Caucus," *ibid.*
28. "Conkling's Ranks Broken," *ibid.*, July 17, 1881.
29. "Roscoe Conkling Beaten," *ibid.*, July 23, 1881.
30. "Conkling to His Followers," *ibid.*
31. *Ibid.* Conkling soon left for Utica. He wrote to a friend from his home, "Here sorting, packing, and burning the sediment of twenty years' stewardship . . ." Conkling to Ben: Perley Poore, July 30, 1881, Miscellaneous Papers, Henry E. Huntington Library.
32. ". . . this was remarked as very queer conduct for Gen. Arthur to display under the circumstances." "Conkling and His Friends," *The New York Times*, July 24, 1881.
33. "The President Very Low," *ibid.*, August 16, 1881.
34. According to his son, Arthur never left the house during these weeks, being highly sensitive to the attacks made upon him. See notes of an interview of December 5, 1931, between Chester A. Arthur II and Vernon Hampton, Hampton Papers.
35. "Vice-President Arthur," *The New York Times*, August 17, 1881.
36. *Ibid.*
37. Williams (ed.), *Diary and Letters of Rutherford Birchard Hayes*, IV, 115; "Postmaster-General James's Visit," *The New York Times*, August 28, 1881; "Vice-President Arthur," *ibid.*, August 29, 1881; "Death of Gen. Arthur," New York *Star*, November 19, 1886.
38. "A Talk with Gov. Foster," *The New York Times*, July 3, 1881.
39. The letter and a larger envelope addressed in Arthur's hand are in the Arthur Papers, L.C.
40. Both MacVeagh letters are in *ibid.*
41. John S. Wise, *Recollections of Thirteen Presidents* (New York, 1906), p. 150.
42. "Giving Voice to Sorrow," *The New York Times*, November 21, 1886.
43. "The Oath Administered," "Preparation for the Funeral," *ibid.*, September 20, 1881; the recollections of Judge Brady in "Arthur's Tranquil End," New York *Herald*, November 19, 1886; "Chester A. Arthur . . . A Sketch of His Life," New York *Daily News*, November 18, 1886.
44. See the statement by George Bliss in "Giving Voice to Sorrow," *The New York Times*, November 21, 1886.
45. See the transcript of a letter from Reed to "My Lord" [Tennyson], November 27, 1886, Hampton Papers.
46. See Beale (ed.), *Letters of Mrs. James G. Blaine*, II, 52–53; Smith, *The Life and Letters of James Abram Garfield*, II, 1201.

47. James D. Richardson, *A Compilation of the Messages and Papers of the Presidents, 1789–1902* (Washington, 1907), VIII, 34.
48. See Poore, *Perley's Reminiscences of Sixty Years in the National Metropolis,* II, 429.
49. Richardson, *Messages and Papers of the Presidents,* VIII, 33–34.
50. Editorial "President Arthur," *The New York Times,* September 21, 1881.
51. Quoted in Howe, *Chester A. Arthur,* p. 156.
52. Quoted in Philip Kinsley, *The Chicago Tribune: Its First Hundred Years* (Chicago, 1946), III, 27.
53. "The Week," *The Nation,* XXXIII (September 29, 1881), 241.
54. Quoted in Cortissoz, *The Life of Whitelaw Reid,* II, 72.

CHAPTER FOURTEEN · ENCOURAGING SIGNS

1. Hoar, *Autobiography of Seventy Years,* II, 46.
2. "The President's Plans," "The President Warned," *The New York Times,* October 1, 1881.
3. See Poore, *Perley's Reminiscences of Sixty Years in the National Metropolis,* II, 432–435.
4. See Seward, *Reminiscences of a War-Time Statesman and Diplomat,* pp. 449–453; Richardson, *Messages and Papers of the Presidents,* VIII, 37.
5. Cortissoz, *The Life of Whitelaw Reid,* II, 76.
6. Morgan to Arthur, August 22, 1881, Arthur Papers, L.C.
7. Sand to Arthur, September 28, 1881, *ibid.*
8. See Blaine to Arthur, October 13, 1881, *ibid.* The draft is in the Blaine Papers.
9. Grant to Arthur, October 8, 1881, Arthur Papers, L.C.
10. Arthur to Morgan, October 21, 1881, Morgan Papers. Morgan's acceptance, Arthur added, "would enable us to carry the State."
11. Weed to Arthur, October 25, 1881, Arthur Papers, L.C. Weed may have originally suggested Morgan's name for the position. See Weed to Arthur, October 19, 1881, in Thurlow Weed Barnes, *Memoir of Thurlow Weed* (Boston, 1884), p. 566.
12. Morgan to Arthur, October 25, 1881, Morgan Papers; "Talk About the Cabinet," *The New York Times,* October 26, 1881. See Morgan to Rutherford B. Hayes, October 3, 1881, Hayes Papers.
13. "Judge Folger Appointed," *The New York Times,* October 28, 1881; "Summary of the Week's News—Domestic," *The Nation,* XXXIII (November 3, 1881), 346.
14. Draft, Arthur to MacVeagh, November 7, 1881, Arthur Papers, L.C.
15. See MacVeagh to Arthur, November 8, 14, 1881, *ibid.* Cf. Robert Underwood Johnson, *Remembered Yesterdays* (Boston, 1923), pp. 368–369 and "Mr. MacVeagh's Retirement," *The New York Times,* November 30, 1882.
16. See Brewster to Arthur, November 1, 1881, Arthur Papers, L.C.
17. See Frederick Frelinghuysen to Arthur, December 2, 1881, *ibid;* "Making a New Cabinet," editorial, *The New York Times,* December 17, 1881. Eugene Coleman Savidge, *Life of Benjamin Harris Brewster, with Discourses and Addresses* (Philadelphia, 1891) is a treacly biography.
18. Beale (ed.), *Letters of Mrs. James G. Blaine,* I, 268–269.

19. See Blaine to Arthur, October 13, 1881, Arthur Papers, L.C.

20. Cortissoz, *The Life of Whitelaw Reid*, II, 77.

21. Ward Thoron (ed.), *The Letters of Mrs. Henry Adams, 1865–1883* (Boston, 1937), p. 297.

22. Crowley, *Echoes from Niagara*, p. 228. See Stoddard, *As I Knew Them*, p. 121.

23. "The Bee," Cincinnati *Enquirer*, November 22, 1883.

24. See Sprague to S. G. Pomeroy, October 15, 1881, Arthur Papers, L.C.; Sprague to Arthur, October 21, 1881, *ibid*. Mrs. Sprague hoped that Conkling would be appointed Secretary of the Treasury.

25. See "The News at Washington," *The New York Times*, December 13, 1881. Earlier, Frelinghuysen had declined to become Attorney General because of poor health. See Frelinghuysen to Arthur, November 1, 19, 1881, Arthur Papers, L.C.

26. Whitelaw Reid called Frelinghuysen "an abject worshipper of Grant, [with] a timid flunkey's distrust of everybody on the other side." See David M. Pletcher's superb *The Awkward Years: American Foreign Relations Under Garfield and Arthur* (Columbia, Mo., 1962), pp. 61–62.

27. Frelinghuysen to Arthur, November 19, 1881, Arthur Papers, L.C.

28. See "President Arthur on 'Punishment,'" *The Nation*, XXXIII (November 3, 1881), 348; copy, Howe to "My dear Grace" [Grace T. Howe of Kenosha], January 6, 1882, Howe Papers.

29. See "Talk About the Cabinet," *The New York Times*, October 26, 1881; Judge Folger Appointed," *ibid.*, October 28, 1881.

30. James to Arthur, December 12, 1881, Arthur Papers, L.C.

31. See the Howe Papers.

32. See "Mr. MacVeagh's Retirement," *The New York Times*, November 30, 1882; Thoron (ed.), *The Letters of Mrs. Henry Adams*, pp. 300–301.

33. See William H. Russell, "Timothy O. Howe, Stalwart Republican," *The Wisconsin Magazine of History*, XXXV (1951), 90–99.

34. Poore, *Perley's Reminiscences of Sixty Years in the National Metropolis*, II, 479; Samuel B. French to Arthur, May 26, 1884, Arthur Papers, L.C.

35. Blaine to Chandler, January 12, 1882, Chandler Papers, New Hampshire State Historical Society.

36. See "New Cabinet Officers," *The New York Times*, April 7, 1882; "William E. Chandler Confirmed," *ibid.*, April 13, 1882; E. D. Morgan to Arthur, January 14, 1882, Morgan Papers.

37. See Dan Elbert Clark, *Samuel Jordan Kirkwood* (Iowa City, 1917), pp. 363–371.

38. See "New Cabinet Officers," *The New York Times*, April 7, 1882; "The Week," *The Nation*, XXXIV (April 13, 1882), 304; Elmer Ellis, *Henry Moore Teller, Defender of the West* (Caldwell, Idaho, 1941), esp. pp. 112–113, 120–121, 132–135.

39. John S. Goff, *Robert Todd Lincoln, a Man in His Own Right* (Norman, Okla., 1968), pp. 122–123.

40. "Gath," Cincinnati *Enquirer*, April 11, 1882.

41. Howe to "My dear Grace," [January] 1882, Howe Papers. Howe was also the source of some sport for the President. "When I met him last night he said to gentlemen and ladies standing around—'Don't he look sweet?' Last Friday I went to the Cabinet meeting with my black travelling suit on. It had

just been pressed. He asked gentlemen to note 'how elegantly the Postmaster General was dressed.' Some three weeks ago, when I left the Council Chamber he *kissed* his hand to me."

42. Crowley, *Echoes from Niagara*, p. 228.
43. "Gath," Cincinnati *Enquirer*, November 22, 1883.
44. *Ibid.*, September 2, 1883.
45. Crowley, *Echoes from Niagara*, p. 227. According to Elihu Root, when Arthur was asked about giving patronage to his Stalwart friends, he said, "I will not consent to basing a revolution upon the assassination of the President of the United States." Interview between Vernon Hampton and Elihu Root, November 15, 1930, Hampton Papers.
46. Crowley, *Echoes from Niagara*, p. 231; Lang (ed.), *The Autobiography of Thomas Collier Platt*, pp. 180–181; Hudson, *Random Recollections of an Old Political Reporter*, p. 127.
47. Hugh J. Hastings to Arthur, "Confidential," January 23, 1882, Arthur Papers, L.C.
48. "Important Nominations," *The New York Times*, December 20, 1881.
49. Copy, Howe to "My dear Grace," February 22, 1882, Howe Papers.
50. "Mr. Conkling Confirmed," *The New York Times*, March 3, 1882.
51. "Mr. Conkling's Nomination," *The Nation*, XXXIV (March 2, 1882), 180.
52. See "The Nomination of Conkling," *The New York Times*, March 4, 1882.
53. "The Vacant Judgeship," editorial, *ibid.*, March 14, 1882.
54. Editorial "Guiteau's Trial," *ibid.*, November 14, 1881.
55. Guiteau to Arthur, January 14, 1882, Arthur Papers, L.C. Scoville attempted to summon Arthur to the trial as a witness. Scoville to Arthur, October 8, December 6, 1881, *ibid.*
56. For the full story, see Rosenberg, *The Trial of the Assassin Guiteau*, an excellent study on which this account is largely based. See also copy, Howe to "My dear Grace," June 28, 1882, Howe Papers.
57. Richardson, *Messages and Papers of the Presidents*, VIII, 37–65.
58. "The Week," *The Nation*, XXXIII (December 8, 1881), 441.
59. "The Next Stage of the Administration," *ibid.*, XXXIII (December 29, 1881), 506.

CHAPTER FIFTEEN · A VERITABLE CHESTERFIELD

1. Henry Rood (ed.), *Memories of the White House: The Home Life of Our Presidents from Lincoln to Roosevelt, Being Personal Recollections of Colonel W. H. Crook* (Boston, 1911), pp. 159–160.
2. See Esther Singleton, *The Story of the White House* (New York, 1907), II, 179–180. This was the first such sale since the Buchanan Administration and netted about $6,000. Arthur preserved bust portraits of John Adams and Martin Van Buren from the garret and had them placed in the parlor of the Red Room. "The White House," New York *Herald*, October 2, 1883.
3. "A Banquet at the White House," *The New York Times*, March 9, 1882.
4. See "New White House Decorations," *ibid.*, December 20, 1882; "The White House," New York *Herald*, October 2, 1883; E. V. Smalley, "The White House," *Century Magazine*, XXVII (April 1884), 806–815. See also *Cong. Record*, 47th Cong., 1st Sess., pp. 5126–5128. Funds for refurbishing

the White House appear to have come exclusively from congressional appropriations. The glass partition cost taxpayers $3,380. See the records of the Office of Public Buildings and Grounds, National Archives. The first White House elevator was installed during Arthur's term, but contracts were let prior to Garfield's death.

5. "Albany Woman Tells of Her Reign as White House Mistress," *The Knickerbocker Press* (Albany), March 16, 1913; "Notes from the Capitol, President Arthur's Youngest Sister," *The Nation*, CIV (February 8, 1917), 169–170. See also "Mrs. John E. McElroy," New York *Evening Post*, January 9, 1917.

6. Rood (ed.), *Memories of the White House*, p. 163.

7. "Albany Woman Tells of Her Reign," *The Knickerbocker Press*, March 16, 1913.

8. "A White House Reception," *The New York Times*, January 3, 1882.

9. Poore, *Perley's Reminiscences of Sixty Years in the National Metropolis*, II, 459–462.

10. See *ibid.*, pp. 184–186; "Brilliant Social Life Marks Half Century," Washington *Post*, December 6, 1927. White House expenses, paid by the first steward, were sizable for the time. In 1882, they totaled $11,000.39; in 1883, $11,136.79; in 1884, $15,250.56. These sums included funds for food, liquor, and cigars, all livery and stable costs, the head coachman's salary, cooks' salaries, and valet expenses. Arthur account books, Arthur Papers, L.C. Cf. Kenneth E. Davison, *The Presidency of Rutherford B. Hayes* (Westport, Conn., 1972), pp. 79–82. One observer later contended that Arthur "usually served at least fourteen courses, at a cost of more than ten dollars a plate, and since there were always about forty guests, each dinner cost him up to five hundred dollars." See Francis Carpenter (ed.), *Carp's Washington* (New York, 1960), pp. 55, 57–58.

11. Beale (ed.), *Letters of Mrs. James G. Blaine*, II, 4–5.

12. "Jubilee Singers in the White House," New York *Tribune*, February 19, 1882; unidentified clipping in the Arthur H. Masten folder, Arthur Family Papers.

13. Eckenrode, *Rutherford B. Hayes: Statesman of Reunion*, p. 335.

14. "President Arthur—Life in the White House," New York *Tribune*, April 16, 1882.

15. "How Presidents Dress," p. 40 of the 1883 Arthur Scrapbook; Lang (ed.), *The Autobiography of Thomas Collier Platt*, p. 182.

16. See "The President's Carriage," *The New York Times*, December 20, 1881. The White House stables housed twenty-three horses during Arthur's term, along with three carriages. Statement in the handwriting of Chester A. Arthur II, Arthur Family Papers.

17. Crowley, *Echoes from Niagara*, p. 229.

18. See "Mr. Arthur in Society," an undated New York dispatch to the San Francisco *Argonaut*, Chester A. Arthur presidential folder, Hayes Library; "Entertaining the President," *The New York Times*, September 23, 1883. See also Simon Wolf, *The Presidents I Have Known from 1860–1918* (Washington, 1918), p. 133.

19. "Arthur's Popularity," Washington *Commercial Advertiser*, November 19, 1886.

20. Copy, Howe to "My dear Grace," January 15, 1882, Howe Papers.
21. Beale (ed.), *Letters of Mrs. James G. Blaine*, II, 8.
22. Singleton, *The Story of the White House*, II, 176–177.
23. Memorandum, "Mr. C. M. Hendley's association with President Arthur," April 22, 1925, Arthur Papers, L.C.; Gerry (ed.), *Through Five Administrations*, pp. 277–278.
24. "Gath," Cincinnati *Enquirer*, in "Personal," II, 150, Chester A. Arthur Scrapbooks.
25. See Brodie Herndon diaries, entries of May 24, 26, June 8, August 1, 1882, Herndon Papers.
26. E.g., "Reception at the White House," *The New York Times*, January 31, 1883; "The President's Public Levee," *ibid*., February 6, 1884.
27. "Our Washington Letter," Buffalo *Commercial Advertiser*, March 9, 1882.
28. "Washington Gossip," New York *World*, December 14, 1884.
29. See Barry, *Forty Years in Washington*, p. 84; "Arthur's Bower," New York *Dispatch*, October 19, 1882. Arthur was the last President to reside in the cottage.
30. "Our Washington Letter," Buffalo *Commercial Advertiser*, March 9, 1882; "Gath," Cincinnati *Enquirer*, March 28, 1882.
31. "Giving Voice to Sorrow," *The New York Times*, November 21, 1886.
32. Editorial "Arthur's Policy," Chicago *Tribune*, March 2, 1882.
33. "Gath," Cincinnati *Enquirer*, April 11, 1882.
34. "Arthur's Coming Contest," Philadelphia *Times*, March 16, 1882.
35. Hugh Bradley, *Such Was Saratoga* (New York, 1940), p. 200.
36. See Gerry (ed.), *Through Five Administrations*, p. 276.
37. Brodie Herndon diaries, entry of May 24, 1882, Herndon Papers. Alan and the crown prince of Siam once became intoxicated and were arrested for swimming nude in a White House fountain. Interview with Chester A. Arthur III, July 26, 1969.
38. "The Bee," Cincinnati *Enquirer*, November 22, 1883.
39. Austine Snead to Hayes, May 11, 1883, Hayes Papers. For more on Alan, see the interview between Vernon Hampton and George Barton French, November 25, 1932, Hampton Papers, and Alan's Scrapbook for the White House years in the Arthur Family Papers.
40. "The President at Annapolis," *The New York Times*, April 20, 1882; "President Arthur at Home," *ibid*., August 13, 1882.
41. Thoron, *The Letters of Mrs. Henry Adams*, p. 356.
42. Sand to Arthur, January 7, 1882, Arthur Papers, L.C.
43. See George W. Parker's statement in "Preparing for the Burial," New York *World*, November 20, 1886; Gerry (ed.), *Through Five Administrations*, p. 276.

CHAPTER SIXTEEN · TERRIBLY TO THE TEST

1. See William A. Robinson, *Thomas B. Reed Parliamentarian* (New York, 1930), pp. 79–81.
2. Editorial "The Worst Session of Congress," New York *World*, August 9, 1882.

3. For an up-to-date survey of these familiar events, see Gary Pennanen, "Public Opinion and the Chinese Question, 1876–1879," *Ohio History*, 77 (Winter, Spring, and Summer 1968), 139–148.

4. See "The Chinese Bill Passed," *The New York Times*, March 24, 1882.

5. Morgan to Arthur, March 30, 1882, Morgan Papers.

6. "The Chinese Bill to Be Vetoed," *The New York Times*, April 4, 1882.

7. Richardson, *Messages and Papers of the Presidents*, VIII, 112–118.

8. Editorial "The President's Veto," *The New York Times*, April 5, 1882.

9. Morgan to Arthur, April 8, 1882, Morgan Papers.

10. See Oberholtzer, *A History of the United States Since the Civil War*, IV, 303–304.

11. See *Cong. Record*, 47th Cong., 1st Sess., pp. 2617, 2967–2974, 3404–3412. The law required numerous supplementary bills, one of which was signed by Arthur. See also Pletcher, *The Awkward Years*, p. 201.

12. See *Cong. Record*, 47th Cong., 1st Sess., p. 5068; Richardson, *Messages and Papers of the Presidents*, VIII, 118–120.

13. "The River and Harbor Job," *The New York Times*, June 8, 1882.

14. Editorial "Use the Veto," New York *Sun*, July 14, 1882.

15. Editorial "The River and Harbor Job," *The New York Times*, July 27, 1882.

16. "An Ex-Senator at Home," *ibid.*, July 12, 1882.

17. See editorial "Pending Veto of the River and Harbor Bill," Chicago *Tribune*, July 29, 1882; editorial "A Timely Veto," *The New York Times*, August 2, 1882; "Arthur as a Candidate," New York *Sun*, April 22, 1883.

18. Richardson, *Messages and Papers of the Presidents*, VIII, 95–96.

19. The Cabinet discussed the issue at length. See the William E. Chandler diaries, entries for July 25, 28, August 1, 1882, Chandler Papers, New Hampshire State Historical Society. Reportedly, members of the Cabinet "were practically a unit in agreeing that the bill should not be approved." "The Great Steal Vetoed," *The New York Times*, August 2, 1882.

20. Richardson, *Messages and Papers of the Presidents*, VIII, 120–122.

21. Hoar, *Autobiography of Seventy Years*, II, 113.

22. See "Approval of the Veto," *The New York Times*, August 3, 1882.

23. Cameron to Benjamin Brewster, August 3, 1882, Arthur Papers, L.C.

24. Sand to Arthur, August 2, 1882, *ibid.*

25. Editorial "The Responsibility," *The New York Times*, August 4, 1882. See *Cong. Record*, 47th Cong., 1st Sess., pp. 5058–5065, 5936–5950, 6444–6447, 6524–6526, 6770–6771, 6800–6804.

26. Hoar, *Autobiography of Seventy Years*, II, 113–115. See editorial "River and Harbor Bill Congressmen," *The New York Times*, November 10, 1882.

27. See "The Work of Congress," *The Nation*, XXXV (August 3, 1882), 86.

28. Seymour H. Fersh, *The View from the White House, a Study of the Presidential State of the Union Message* (Washington, 1961), pp. 54–55.

29. Pletcher, *The Awkward Years*, pp. 18–19.

30. For a good summary, see Walter La Feber, *The New Empire, an Interpretation of American Expansion 1860–1898* (Ithaca, N.Y., 1963), pp. 24–46.

31. See Pletcher, *The Awkward Years*, pp. 13–16, 62–63.

32. See *ibid.*, pp. 22–33, 64–67; Muzzey, *James G. Blaine*, pp. 197–201.

33. Herbert Millington, *American Diplomacy and the War of the Pacific* (New York, 1948), pp. 53–96; Pletcher, *The Awkward Years*, pp. 40–58, 71–75.

34. *Ibid.*, pp. 33–39, 75–76; Alice Felt Tyler, *The Foreign Policy of James G. Blaine* (Minneapolis, 1927), pp. 46–50.
35. Russell H. Bastert, "Diplomatic Reversal: Frelinghuysen's Opposition to Blaine's Pan-American Policy in 1882," *Mississippi Valley Historical Review*, XLII (March 1956), 655.
36. See Russell H. Bastert, "A New Approach to the Origins of Blaine's Pan-American Policy," *Hispanic American Historical Review*, XXXIX (August 1959), 375–412.
37. Quoted in Bastert, "Diplomatic Reversal," 658.
38. See *ibid.*, 660–661.
39. See Pletcher, *The Awkward Years*, p. 80.
40. *Foreign Relations of the United States, 1882*, pp. 57–58.
41. Bastert, "Diplomatic Reversal," 660–661.
42. Quoted in Hamilton, *Biography of James G. Blaine*, p. 553.
43. "What Mr. Blaine Says," *The New York Times*, January 30, 1882.
44. "Blaine to the President," *ibid.*, February 4, 1882. The original letter is in the Arthur Papers, L.C.
45. "The President's Position," *The New York Times*, February 4, 1883; "Mr. Blaine's Controversy," *ibid.*, February 5, 1882.
46. Richardson, *Messages and Papers of the Presidents*, VIII, 40–43.
47. "Mr. Blaine's Controversy," *The New York Times*, February 5, 1883.
48. See Pletcher, *The Awkward Years*, pp. 82–83.
49. "Mr. Blaine's Controversy," *The New York Times*, February 5, 1883.
50. Arthur opened the second paragraph with, "In giving this invitation I was not unaware that there existed differences between several of the Republics of South America which would militate against the happy results which might otherwise be expected from such an assemblage." The author of the first important scholarly article on this subject misquoted the sentence, and had Arthur state that he was "not aware" of the differences. The President by this account, of course, was a fool. A. Curtis Wilgus, "James G. Blaine and the Pan-American Movement," *Hispanic American Historical Review*, V (1922), 675. The error and the erroneous conclusion were incorporated into Russell H. Bastert's influential "Diplomatic Reversal," 663–664, 667.
51. Richardson, *Messages and Papers of the Presidents*, VIII, 97–98.
52. Bastert, "Diplomatic Reversal," 667–669. On July 24, Frelinghuysen sent a letter to the chairman of the Senate Foreign Relations Committee in which he discouraged plans for a November meeting. He pointed to continuing disturbances in Latin America and objected to participation in an international conference in which the United States would have only a single vote. See Pletcher, *The Awkward Years*, pp. 85–86.
53. See Muzzey, *James G. Blaine*, pp. 242–251.
54. See "President Arthur on 'Punishment,' " *The Nation*, XXXIII (November 3, 1881), 348.
55. "News from the Capital," *The New York Times*, November 19, 1881.
56. Assistant Treasurer in New York City. "Important Nominations," *ibid.*, December 20, 1881.
57. Collector of Internal Revenue in the 24th District, New York, "A Stalwart Nomination," *ibid.*, June 15, 1882.
58. Consul General at Havana. "Diplomatic Offices Filled," *ibid.*, April 21, 1882.

59. Collector of Internal Revenue in the 21st District, New York. Armstrong was an Assemblyman from Utica, one of the first to espouse the cause of Conkling and Platt when they sought reelection to the Senate. "Offices for Conkling's Friend," *ibid.*, June 28, 1882.

60. "Politics in Post Offices," *ibid.*, July 30, 1882; Conkling to Fred Phillips, July 10, 1882, Arthur Papers, L.C.

61. Silas Burt Biography, p. 153. Alec Powell's wife and three friends of the President's late wife were given minor places in the Interior Department. Chester Alan Arthur [II] to Grover Cleveland, January 12, 1887, Grover Cleveland Papers, L.C.

62. "The Boston Nomination," *The New York Times,* April 9, 1882. Worthington was confirmed in the Senate 38 to 14. *The Times* commented, "It will be observed that 'courtesy of the Senate,' for which Mr. Conkling suffered martyrdom and which Vice-President Arthur struggled hard to vindicate, has received a fatal blow at the hands of President Arthur." See "The Boston Collectorship," editorial, *ibid.,* May 16, 1882. See also Hoar, *Autobiography of Seventy Years*, I, 406; Richardson, *William E. Chandler,* p. 342.

63. Collector of Internal Revenue and Surveyor of Customs. "The New York Patronage," *The New York Times,* May 26, 1882. Other minor favors shown to friends of Smythe, Platt, William Mahone, Robert Lincoln, and Richard Crowley may be viewed in letters by James B. Butler, the Treasury Department's chief of Appointment Division, Charles J. Folger Papers, New York Public Library. See also "Rewarding Faithful Friends," editorial, *The New York Times,* January 24, 1885; "Notes from Washington," *ibid.,* February 27, 1885.

64. "The Truth about Removals," New York *Commercial Advertiser,* June 10, 1882.

65. See "The Week," *The Nation,* XXXV (July 13, 1882), 22. Of the remainder, 428 were reappointments and 446 were appointments to fill vacancies caused by death, disability, or the expiration of the term of office. Reformers claimed that by refusing to reappoint officeholders Arthur was able to replace them with partisans. George William Curtis said, "He has found it necessary to dismiss nearly fifty per cent of the officers whose terms had expired." Norton (ed.), *Orations and Addresses of George William Curtis,* II, 208. But reformers revealed no evidence stating who the replacements were or the brand of politics they espoused. Their unusual quiescence while hundreds of jobs were being filled weakens their case in retrospect. See also Fowler, *The Cabinet Politician,* pp. 181–182.

66. Sand to Arthur, "April," 1882, Arthur Papers, L.C.

67. Morgan to Arthur, June 9, 1882, *ibid.*

68. See Hoogenboom. *Outlawing the Spoils,* p. 227; "Gen. Curtis Sentenced," editorial, *The New York Times,* August 3, 1882. Veteran Conklingite Stewart Woodford was the United States Attorney during the appeal and moved for sentence of the prisoner.

69. See "The Cabinet on Assessments," *ibid.,* July 26, 1882; Hoogenboom, *Outlawing the Spoils,* pp. 227–229.

70. See *ibid.,* pp. 223–224; Norton (ed.), *Orations and Addresses of George William Curtis,* II, 211–212.

71. "The President's Advisers," *The New York Times,* August 22, 1882.

72. Arthur saved twenty-three letters from Miss Sand, the last dated September

15, 1883. She died in 1933, a spinster, at the age of eighty-three. A nephew, who was present during the President's visit, told Chester A. Arthur III in 1938: "Every one, especially Aunt Julia, was interested in politics. It was all civil service. The Tariff—do you ever hear anything about that now? I was brought up on it." See Thomas C. Reeves, "The President's Dwarf: The Letters of Julia Sand to Chester A. Arthur," *New York History*, LII (January 1971), 73–83.

CHAPTER SEVENTEEN · PUBLIC ENEMIES

1. Editorial "The Presidential 'Legacy,'" *The New York Times*, November 20, 1881.
2. *Ibid.*
3. House of Representatives, 48th Cong., 1st Sess., Misc. Doc. 38, Part 2, "Testimony Relating to Expenditures in the Department of Justice. The Star-Route Cases," pp. 1–7. This document will hereafter be cited as Springer Committee Hearings.
4. *Ibid.*, pp. 336, 805–809.
5. *Ibid.*, pp. 8–9, 22, 334.
6. *Ibid.*, pp. 161–167, 195–203, 340–346, 533, 846–847. MacVeagh had been angered by Arthur's refusal to dismiss Corkhill, and thought it evidence of the President's insincerity toward the prosecution of the suspects. *Ibid.*, pp. 32–34.
7. *Ibid.*, pp. 532, 847–848.
8. *Ibid.*, pp. 846–847.
9. E.g., "The Pledges of Garfield," New York *Sun*, July 16, 1883. See Dorsey to Arthur, March 8, 1882, Arthur Papers, L.C.
10. See W. H. Painter to Chandler, November 10, 1881, William E. Chandler Papers, L.C.; "The Star Route Verdict," *The New York Times*, June 16, 1883.
11. Springer Committee Hearings, p. 57.
12. *Ibid.*, p. 231; "Senator Jones's Star Route Bond," *The New York Times*, August 4, 1881.
13. Springer Committee Hearings, p. 682; Dorsey to Arthur, September 26, 1881, Arthur Papers, L.C. See a Dorsey telegram to Arthur of October 6, 1881, in *ibid.*
14. "Gen. Tyner Requested to Resign," *The New York Times*, October 18, 1881.
15. Springer Committee Hearings, pp. 696–697; "Brady Sells Out to Bliss," New York *Sun*, February 4, 1882; Philip C. Jessup, *Elihu Root*, I, 135; Leon B. Richardson, *William E. Chandler, Republican* (New York, 1940), pp. 343–344; W. A. Paton to George Bliss, "Private," May 16, 1882, Arthur Papers, L.C. Critics incorrectly claimed that Bliss was Brady's attorney in a transaction with others. Brady continued to own the *Critic*, which repeatedly attacked Bliss.
16. Springer Committee Hearings, pp. 159–160, 534; editorial "The Star Route Trial," *The New York Times*, July 15, 1882.
17. The full accounts of the trials is in *Proceedings in the First and Second Trials in the Case of the United States vs. John W. Dorsey, John R. Miner, John M. Peck, Stephen W. Dorsey, Harvey M. Vaile, Montfort C. Rerdell, Thomas J. Brady and Wm. H. Turner* (Washington, 1882, 3 vols.; 1883, 4 vols.),

hereafter referred to as *Star Route Trials*. See *Star Route Trials*, 1882, III, 2575.

18. Springer Committee Hearings, p. 597. Bliss attempted to settle several weaker cases out of court to win the return of funds to federal coffers. The proposal was dropped when Brewster questioned its legality. *Ibid.*, pp. 177–179, 382–387.

19. *Ibid.*, pp. 186, 536–537, 540; "A Fugitive Conspirator," *The New York Times*, May 5, 1882.

20. "Dorsey's 'Frozen Facts,'" *ibid.*, August 13, 1882; "Disinterested Dorsey," *ibid.*, August 20, 1882.

21. Springer Committee Hearings, pp. 546–547, 879.

22. See *ibid.*, pp. 549, 652, 865–866.

23. *Star Route Trials*, 1882, p. 3236. See Springer Committee Hearings, pp. 186, 601. The jury voted 8–4 on its first informal ballot to convict all of the defendants. Twelve ballots were taken. "Voting in the Jury-Room," *The New York Times*, September 12, 1882.

24. Editorial "A New Star Route Trial," *ibid.*, September 16, 1882. Jurors were not confined during the trial. Government agents followed some of them during the fourteen weeks to insure their fidelity. Springer Committee Hearings, p. 208. Ker said later, "The first jury would have convicted if it had not been for the foreman." *Ibid.*, p. 553.

25. *Ibid.*, pp. 643–644, 669–670, 679–680. Senator O. H. Platt of Connecticut said shortly of Arthur: "He has been the subject of strong factional pressure, yet I think he has avoided it to a greater extent than he has been given credit with doing. As a case in point, no man has been more intimate at the White House than ex-Senator George E. Spencer, yet, when there was cause for it, the President did not hesitate to 'cut off his head' officially, and for such an act I believe him entitled to the credit which the newspaper writers, for instance, will not give him." "The Party's Present Duty," *The New York Times*, November 30, 1882.

26. "A Star Route Bomb-Shell," *ibid.*, November 26, 1882. See "Col. Ingersoll's Views," *ibid.*, November 27, 1882.

27. Editorial "The Government and the Star Route Trial," *ibid.*

28. See Springer Committee Hearings, pp. 553, 615–616. The judge again refused to confine the jury.

29. *Ibid.*, pp. 349, 553, 663.

30. "Mr. Dorsey Resigns," *The New York Times*, January 17, 1883.

31. Editorial, *ibid.*, June 9, 1883. Cf. "Poor Bliss," New York *Truth*, June 15, 1883.

32. "Not Guilty as Indicted," *The New York Times*, June 15, 1883.

33. Editorial, *ibid.*, June 17, 1883.

34. "The Star Route Verdict," *ibid.*, June 16, 1883.

35. J. Martin Klotsche, "The Star Route Cases," *Mississippi Valley Historical Review*, XXII (December 1935), 416-417; Howe, *Chester A. Arthur*, p. 190.

36. Editorial "Justice Defeated," *The New York Times*, June 15, 1883. Three of the jurors were black, and there were racial overtones in such charges. For a more charitable view of the jury, see "The Star-route Verdict," *The Nation*, XXXVI (June 21, 1883), 524.

37. Quoted in the editorial "Turn the Rascals Out," *The New York Times,* June 15, 1883.
38. Quoted in Klotsche, "The Star Route Cases," 417.
39. "Ex-Senator Dorsey's Revenge," Baltimore *Sun,* June 22, 1883.
40. Springer Committee Hearings, pp. 870-871; Howe, *Chester A. Arthur,* pp. 191–192.
41. Springer Committee Hearings, p. 887.
42. There is good evidence suggesting that Bliss was unenthusiastic about seeking an indictment of Kellogg. This apparent reluctance caused considerable dissention between Bliss and Democrats Ker and Merrick. Ker and Merrick, however, alleged at no time that Brewster and Arthur were unsympathetic to Kellogg's prosecution. Brewster, in fact, prodded Bliss hard in the matter. so hard that Bliss almost resigned. A jury failed to indict Kellogg in the summer of 1882, and the following spring the court ruled that the statute of limitations had run out on the charge against him. See Springer Committee Hearings, pp. 208–210, 421–431, 544, 565–571, 621–634, 643, 685, 761–765, 849–854, 864, 880–883.
43. "Gath," Cincinnati *Enquirer,* June 16, 1883.

CHAPTER EIGHTEEN · SICK IN BODY AND SOUL

1. E.g., editorial "The Assessment Business," *The New York Times,* August 22, 1882.
2. "Wayne MacVeagh's Lament," *ibid.,* April 14, 1882. See also William L. Royall, *The President's Relations with Senator Mahone and Repudiation, An Attempt to Subvert the Supreme Court of the United States* (New York, 1882), *passim.*
3. "In and Out of Congress," *The New York Times,* April 11, 1882. See also C. Vann Woodward, *Origins of the New South 1877–1913* (Baton Rouge, La., 1951), pp. 92–101; Nelson Morehouse Blake, *William Mahone of Virginia, Soldier and Political Insurgent* (Richmond, Va., 1935), pp. 182–220; De Santis, *Republicans Face the Southern Question: The New Departure Years, 1877–1897,* pp. 133–150; Stanley P. Hirshson, *Farewell to the Bloody Shirt, Northern Republicans and The Southern Negro, 1877–1893* (Bloomington, Ind., 1962), pp. 111–112; Rothman, *Politics and Power,* pp. 32–33.
4. Morgan, *From Hayes to McKinley,* p. 175.
5. See Richardson, *William E. Chandler,* pp. 221–222, 344–347.
6. Editorial, *The New York Times,* April 11, 1882.
7. Editorial, *ibid.,* May 19, 1882.
8. De Santis, *Republicans Face the Southern Question,* p. 167.
9. Wise, *Recollections of Thirteen Presidents,* pp. 160–163.
10. Quoted in De Santis, *Republicans Face the Southern Question,* p. 174.
11. Hirshson, *Farewell to the Bloody Shirt,* pp. 106–107. Hirshson's indictment is based on meager evidence. Two examples of Arthur's alleged indifference toward civil rights come from materials found in the Attorney General's files at the National Archives. In one instance, Brewster apparently took no action

toward a complaint; in another, he argued convincingly that the issue in question was outside federal jurisdiction. The President played no direct role in either matter. (In a South Carolina case cited by Hirshson, Brewster tried diligently to enforce election laws, only to be frustrated by local Democrats.) Hirshson points to three examples of the President's "criticism" of Negroes. One quotation has Arthur mildly chiding blacks for failing to retain the power handed them during Reconstruction, and then portrays him as urging Negroes "to unite with the men who can give you success." The other two quotations appeared originally in T. Thomas Fortune's New York *Globe*, and are suspicious at best.

12. See De Santis, *Republicans Face the Southern Question*, pp. 160–166.
13. See Hirshson, *Farewell to the Bloody Shirt*, pp. 108–109, 113–114, 116–118.
14. Entry of July 25, 1882, Presidential Check Book, 1882–1884, Arthur Papers, L.C.
15. "The Miner Normal School," *National Republican*, June 12, 1883.
16. "Jubilee Singers in the White House," New York *Tribune*, February 19, 1882.
17. Rayford W. Logan, *The Negro in American Life and Thought, the Nadir 1877–1901* (New York, 1954), p. 45.
18. Richardson, *Messages and Papers of the Presidents*, VIII, 58, 143–144, 184, 188.
19. Editorial "The South and the Administration," *The New York Times*, September 4, 1882.
20. Quoted in De Santis, *Republicans Face the Southern Question*, p. 155.
21. "Presidential Babble," *The New York Times*, August 31, 1882; "Power of the Shifting Vote," *ibid.*, November 23, 1883.
22. "Gath," Cincinnati *Enquirer*, May 13, 1882.
23. See "The Week," *The Nation*, XXXV (September 28, 1882), 251.
24. "Folger's Ardent Friends," *The New York Times*, April 3, 1882.
25. *Ibid.*
26. "Dry Rot," Cincinnati *Enquirer*, June 1, 1882.
27. "The New-York Governorship," *The New York Times*, June 15, 1882.
28. "The Coming Governor," *ibid.*, July 19, 1882.
29. Editorial "Gould and Conkling," *ibid.*, August 18, 1882.
30. "Trying to Beat Cornell," *ibid.*, August 21, 1882.
31. "The News at Washington," *ibid.*, August 22, 1882.
32. Editorial "Gov. Cornell and His Traducers," *ibid.*, August 26, 1882.
33. See Marcus, *Grand Old Party*, p. 76.
34. "Active Campaign Work," *The New York Times*, August 31, 1882.
35. Folger to Arthur, September 5, 1882, Arthur Papers, L.C. See also Folger to Fred Phillips, August 14, 1882, *ibid.*
36. "Who Is the Dark Horse?" *The New York Times*, September 14, 1882. Folger confided to his campaign manager, "You have no idea of the bitterness in this region [New York] toward all Stalwarts and persons supposed to be in harmony with the Admt. Old personal friends & clients of mine declare that they will not vote for me if nominated, not, they say, that they dislike me, but those behind me." Folger to James B. Butler, "Private," September 11, 1882, Folger Papers.
37. See James B. Butler to Folger, October 1, 1882, *ibid.*
38. See Crowley, *Echoes from Niagara*, p. 231. Roscoe Conkling said later of

Folger, "I was not one of those who coaxed him to become a candidate for the Governorship of this State and then stabbed him, defeated him, broke his heart, and drove him to the grave." "Roscoe Conkling Indignant," *The New York Times,* February 4, 1885.

39. "The President in Washington," *ibid.,* September 20, 1882.
40. "Feeling in the State," *ibid.,* September 18, 1882.
41. "End of a Great Struggle," *ibid.,* September 21, 1880; "Completing the Ticket," *ibid.,* September 22, 1880. The city machine had much to do with the strong showing by Madden and Folger, for its delegates were hand-picked and always voted as a bloc. E. L. Godkin claimed that four fifths of the Republican voters of New York City were thus disfranchised at Saratoga. "The Week," *The Nation,* XXXV (September 28, 1882), 251.
42. "The State Committee," *The New York Times,* September 27, 1882. Smyth received 16 votes; his nearest competitor won 7.
43. See Lang (ed.), *The Autobiography of Thomas Collier Platt,* pp. 170–176; "Gov. Cornell Leading," *The New York Times,* September 17, 1882; "Mr. French's Authority," *ibid.,* September 22, 1882; editorial "Forgery in Politics," *ibid.,* September 27, 1882.
44. "Completing the Ticket," *ibid.,* September 22, 1882.
45. "Mr. Curtis's Emphatic Protest," *ibid.,* October 4, 1882.
46. E.g., "Arthur's Health," Indianapolis *Journal,* October 9, 1882; "Personal Intelligence," Atlanta *Constitution,* October 10, 1882.
47. "Points about Folger and Arthur," New York *Tribune,* October 10, 1882.
48. "President Arthur's Health," New York *Herald,* October 21, 1882.
49. See "Dead Among His Kindred," *The New York Times,* November 19, 1886; "Twice Critically Ill," *ibid.,* December 13, 1886; "Chester A. Arthur Dead," New York *Sun,* November 19, 1886; E. J. Edwards, "A Presidential Tragedy the Nation Narrowly Escaped," New York *Evening Mail,* January 12, 1911. Chester A. Arthur II told his son that the President knew of his fatal disease before the Republican National Convention of 1884. Interview with Chester A. Arthur III, July 26, 1969.
50. See Brodie Herndon Diary, entries of May 23, 26, June 8, August 1, 1882, Herndon Papers.
51. "The President Coming Home," *The New York Times,* October 8, 1882.
52. "Arthur's Bower," New York *Dispatch,* October 19, 1882.
53. "Why Arthur Is Absent from Washington," New York *Sun,* October 3, 1882.
54. "President Arthur in Town," New York *World,* January 23, 1883.
55. Arthur to Alan [Chester A. Arthur II], March 11, 1883, Arthur Papers, L.C. See "The President Not Well," *The New York Times,* April 5, 1883.
56. "The President's Ambition," Hartford (Conn.) *Evening Post,* May 23, 1883.
57. "Gath," Cincinnati *Enquirer,* October 27, 1882.
58. Editorial "The Lesson in New York," Chicago *Tribune,* November 2, 1882.
59. W. P. Robins to James B. Butler, October 13, 1882, Folger Papers.
60. "Gath," Cincinnati *Enquirer,* October 27, 1882.
61. "Judge Folger Depressed," New York *Sun,* October 28, 1882.
62. James B. Butler, the Treasury Department's chief of Appointment Division, sent a few federal employees to work in the campaign, however, and put some twenty minor jobs at Folger's disposal. Butler to Folger, October 7, 11, 1882; P. H. Eaton to Butler, December 9, 1882, Folger Papers. See also

George Bliss's comment in "Oiling a New Machine," *The New York Times*, November 11, 1882.

63. "Arthur's Record," New York *Herald*, December 25, 1882.
64. "Thurlow Weed on the Campaign," New York *Tribune*, September 20, 1882. See also "Arthur's Record," New York *Herald*, December 25, 1882.
65. Lang (ed.), *The Autobiography of Thomas Collier Platt*, pp. 176–177. The only good news came from the South, where six Virginia Readjusters and one independent from Mississippi and North Carolina were elected to the House, nearly doubling the size of proadministration Congressmen from that region. De Santis, *Republicans Face the Southern Question*, p. 178.
66. See "Re" folder, Folger Papers.
67. Editorial, *The New York Times*, November 8, 1882.
68. Lawrence G. Goulding, *Arthur and the Ghost, with a Synopsis of the Great Battle of November 7, 1882* (New York, 1883).
69. Editorial "Fixing the Responsibility for Defeat," Chicago *Tribune*, November 12, 1882.
70. "Oiling a New Machine," *The New York Times*, November 11, 1882.
71. "Other Interviews," *ibid.*
72. "The November Elections," *The Nation*, XXXV (November 16, 1882), 416.
73. *Ibid.*
74. "Oiling a New Machine," *The New York Times*, November 11, 1882.
75. "Other Interviews," *ibid.*

CHAPTER NINETEEN · WELL-INFORMED POLITICIANS

1. See editorial "Mr. Blaine on Reform," *The New York Times*, September 10, 1882.
2. See "General Butler's Acceptance," *The Nation*, XXXV (October 12, 1882), 300.
3. Silas Burt Biography, pp. 128–130.
4. Richardson, *Messages and Papers of the Presidents*, VIII, 145–147. Arthur included data showing that his administration had been extremely prudent in its removals.
5. Editorial, Chicago *Tribune*, December 7, 1882.
6. "The Message and Documents," *The New York Times*, December 5, 1882.
7. "The President's Message," *The Nation*, XXXV (December 7, 1882), 480.
8. See Hoogenboom, *Outlawing the Spoils*, pp. 217–220, 236–252.
9. For solid analyses of the voting, see *ibid.*, pp. 246–251; "The Reform Bill Passes the Senate," *The New York Times*, December 28, 1882; editorial "The Triumph of Reform," *ibid.*, January 5, 1883.
10. Quoted in Morgan, *From Hayes to McKinley*, p. 164.
11. "A Tribute to Gen. Arthur," *The New York Times*, June 16, 1880. Silas Burt called Eaton "an open admirer of the President" and contended that Arthur consulted the reformer before writing his second message to Congress. Silas Burt Biography, p. 127. Nevertheless, Eaton endorsed Arthur's removal from the New York Customhouse. See his article "Civil Service Reform," in

John J. Lalor (ed.), *Cyclopedia of Political Science* . . . (New York, 1890), I, 484–485.

12. "The Week," *The Nation*, XXXVI (February 22, 1883), 159.

13. See "Olmstead's Washington Career," *The New York Times*, December 24, 1882; "Gossip of the Capital," *ibid.*, January 16, 1883. Cf. editorial, *ibid.*, January 3, 1883.

14. "A Clear Alternative," *The Nation*, XXXVI (February 15, 1883), 140. Cf. Dorman B. Eaton to Rutherford B. Hayes, February 19, 1883, Hayes Papers.

15. "New York Office Seekers," *The New York Times*, December 11, 1882.

16. Editorial "The New-York Offices," *ibid.*, February 4, 1883.

17. George William Curtis to Silas Burt, December 25, 1882, Burt Papers, N.Y.H.S.

18. Copy, Edwin D. Morgan to Chester A. Arthur, December 7, 1882, *ibid.*

19. Silas Burt Biography, p. 133.

20. "New-York Offices Filled," *The New York Times*, March 2, 1883. Young Elihu Root was appointed to his first public office at this same time. He was named United States Attorney for the Southern District of New York, replacing Stewart L. Woodford, who had clashed with Attorney General Brewster. *Ibid.*

21. "Mr. Burt Will Not Accept," *ibid.*; entry of March 2, 1883, White House Telegram Book, Charles Pinkerton Collection.

22. See Silas Burt Biography, pp. 122–143. Dorman Eaton tried unsuccessfully to persuade Burt to accept the President's nomination, in part because Arthur's "cordial support" of reform "is absolutely essential." See Eaton to Burt, "Confidential," March 13, 1883; "March" 1883, Burt Papers, N.Y.H.S.; Silas Burt Biography, pp. 141–143.

23. "Not Civil Service Reform," *The New York Times*, March 9, 1883.

24. "Mr. Keim Without Hope," *ibid.*, May 10, 1883. The office went to Charles Lyman, who was supported by reformers. Editorial, *ibid.*, May 10, 1883; "The Week," *The Nation*, XXXVI (May 17, 1883), 413. Burt soon accepted Grover Cleveland's offer to become the chief examiner of New York State's Civil Service Commission. See "Civil Service Reform Work," *The New York Times*, June 1, 1883.

25. "The Week," *The Nation*, XXXVI (April 5, 1883), 285.

26. Editorial, *The New York Times*, May 8, November 9, 1883.

27. Norton (ed.), *Orations and Addresses of George William Curtis*, II, 236.

28. E.g., Thomas C. Platt to William Chandler, December 3, 1883, Chandler Papers, L.C.; James B. Butler to J. D. Cameron, January 17, 1883, Folger Papers; Folger to W. O. Chesbro, October 9, 1883, *ibid.* Occasional exceptions occurred. E.g., A. P. Ketchum to James B. Butler, July 7, 1883, *ibid.*; "The Week," *The Nation*, XXXVI (April 19, 1883), 329.

29. See *ibid.*, XXXVI (May 24, 1883), 435; editorial "Mahone on the Result," *The New York Times*, November 9, 1883.

30. See Hoogenboom, *Outlawing the Spoils*, p. 255. The following year, however, reformers would be defeated in an attempt to pass legislation to extend reform principles to some 3,500 of the most important and highly paid civil servants. See *ibid.*, p. 259.

31. Richardson, *Messages and Papers of the Presidents*, VIII, 252.
32. *Second Annual Report of the United States Civil Service Commission* (Washington, 1885), pp. 7, 55.

CHAPTER TWENTY · UNLEASHING THE TARIFF

1. "Reforming The Tariff," *The New York Times*, December 5, 1882.
2. Quoted in Garraty, *The New Commonwealth*, p. 246. The basic alignment on the tariff question was one of economic interests. See Edward C. Kirkland, *Industry Comes of Age: Business, Labor and Public Policy, 1860–1897* (New York, 1961), pp. 188–189; Tom E. Terrill, *The Tariff, Politics, and American Foreign Policy, 1874–1901* (Westport, Conn., 1973), pp. 3–36.
3. F. W. Taussig, *The Tariff History of the United States* (5th ed., New York, 1910), pp. 230–231.
4. Quoted in Morgan, *From Hayes to McKinley*, p. 171.
5. "In Favor of Protection," *The New York Times*, February 2, 1883.
6. Richardson, *Messages and Papers of the Presidents*, VIII, 49.
7. See Edward S. Bradley, *Henry Charles Lea, A Biography* (Philadelphia, 1931), pp. 213–214; James A. Barnes, *John G. Carlisle, Financial Statesman* (New York, 1931), pp. 52–53; editorial "The Democrats and the Tariff Commission," *The New York Times*, June 9, 1882.
8. "The Tariff Commission," *ibid.*, May 18, 1882.
9. See Edward Stanwood, *American Tariff Controversies in the Nineteenth Century* (Boston, 1903), II, 202–203; Pletcher, *The Awkward Years*, p. 152; Richardson, *William E. Chandler*, p. 337; "The Tariff Commission," *The New York Times*, June 8, 1882; "Chosen by the President," *ibid.*, June 17, 1882. See also Ida M. Tarbell, *The Tariff in Our Times* (New York, 1911), pp. 101–103.
10. Sherman, *Recollections of Forty Years*, II, 843.
11. Editorial, *The New York Times*, June 17, 1882.
12. Quoted in Stanwood, *American Tariff Controversies*, II, 204–205.
13. "The Week," *The Nation*, XXXV (December 7, 1882), 475.
14. Editorial "The Tariff Commission's Report," The *New York Times*, December 6, 1882.
15. Sherman, *Recollections of Forty Years*, II, 851, 854. See the two-volume report, House Misc. Doc. No. 6, 47th Cong., 2d Sess., esp. I, 1–10.
16. Richardson, *Messages and Papers of the Presidents*, VIII, 134–136; "Gossip of the Capital," *The New York Times*, December 3, 1882.
17. "The Message and Documents," *ibid*, December 5, 1882.
18. "Congress and the Tariff," *ibid*, December 4, 1882.
19. "The Rival Tariff Measures," *ibid.*, January 5, 1883.
20. See Stanwood, *American Tariff Controversies*, II, 209–219; Barnes, *John G. Carlisle*, pp. 57–63; N. M. Stephenson, *Nelson W. Aldrich, a Leader in American Politics* (New York, 1930), pp. 49–52; "A Report on the Tariff," *The New York Times*, March 3, 1883; "The Tariff Bill Passed," "The Tariff Bill a Law," *ibid.*, March 4, 1883.
21. Pletcher, *The Awkward Years*, pp. 155–156.
22. Sherman, *Recollections of Forty Years*, II, 852, 855.

23. See Oberholtzer, *A History of the United States Since the Civil War,* IV, 158. Cf. "Criticizing the Tariff," *The New York Times,* March 6, 1883; "Opinions on the Tariff," *ibid.,* March 7, 1883. Several excise taxes were removed by the bill, but the tax was retained on liquor and tobacco.

24. "The Week," *The Nation,* XXXVI (March 8, 1883), 199.

25. Stanwood, *American Tariff Controversies,* II, 204.

26. "Congressional Paralysis," *The Nation,* XXXVI (February 22, 1883), 164. Cf. Howe, *Chester A. Arthur,* p. 222.

27. Richardson, *Messages and Papers of the Presidents,* VIII, 138–139; editorial "Drift of Work in the Senate," *The New York Times,* December 6, 1882.

28. Timothy O. Howe to "My Dear" [Grace T. Howe], January 24, 1883, Howe Papers.

29. Stanwood, *American Tariff Controversies,* II, 218–219.

30. Samuel Rezneck, *Business Depressions and Financial Panics, Essays in American Business and Economic History* (New York, 1968), p. 152.

31. See *ibid.,* pp. 152–155; Kirkland, *Industry Comes of Age,* pp. 6–8.

32. Quoted in Rezneck, *Business Depressions and Financial Panics,* p. 156.

CHAPTER TWENTY-ONE · A SEAFARING PEOPLE

1. Quoted in Foster Rhea Dulles, *Prelude to World Power, American Diplomatic History, 1860–1900* (New York, 1965), p. 124.

2. See *Report, Secretary of the Navy, 1882,* pp. 5–12, 31–34, 40; Richardson, *William E. Chandler,* pp. 286–287.

3. Harold and Margaret Sprout, *The Rise of American Naval Power, 1776–1918* (Princeton, 1939), pp. 165–182.

4. *Ibid.,* pp. 183–186; Pletcher, *The Awkward Years,* pp. 119–120; Milton Plesur, *America's Outward Thrust, Approaches to Foreign Affairs, 1865–1890* (Dekalb, Ill., 1971), pp. 93–95; Robert Seager II, "Ten Years Before Mahan: The Unofficial Case for the New Navy, 1880–1890," *Mississippi Valley Historical Review,* XL (1953), 496–497.

5. See Leonard Alexander Swann Jr., *John Roach Maritime Entrepreneur, the Years as Naval Contractor, 1862–1886* (Annapolis, Md., 1965), pp. 154–161.

6. Richardson, *Messages and Papers of the Presidents,* VIII, 51–52.

7. "Ships for a New Navy," *The New York Times,* March 8, 1882.

8. See Swann, *John Roach,* pp. 168–170.

9. Roach recommended Chandler for the post of Navy Secretary, but his letter was one of the least significant received by Arthur on the subject. See *ibid.,* p. 272.

10. *Ibid.,* pp. 171–173.

11. *Report, Secretary of the Navy, 1882,* p. 22.

12. Richardson, *Messages and Papers of the Presidents,* VIII, 140–141.

13. Richardson, *William E. Chandler,* pp. 291–292.

14. Swann, *John Roach,* pp. 176–177.

15. *Ibid.,* pp. 178–180.

16. *Ibid., passim.*

17. *Ibid.,* pp. 178–182; Richardson, *William E. Chandler,* pp. 295–296.

18. Richardson, *Messages and Papers of the Presidents,* VIII, 181–182.
19. Richardson, *William E. Chandler,* pp. 296–302.
20. In *ibid.,* p. 302.
21. Swann, *John Roach,* pp. 191–208.
22. See Charles O. Paullin, "A Half Century of Naval Administration," U.S. *Naval Revolution* (Baton Rouge, La., 1966), p. 34.
23. John A. S. Grenville and George Berkeley Young, *Politics, Strategy, and American Diplomacy, Studies in Foreign Policy, 1873–1917* (New Haven, 1966), pp. 16–18. Luce's protégé Alfred T. Mahan was an early fixture at the War College.
24. Congress endorsed the recommendation in 1885, marking the beginning of the American armament industry. See Walter R. Herrick Jr., *The American Naval Revolution* (Baton Rouge, La., 1966), p. 34.
25. Richardson, *William E. Chandler,* pp. 308–309.
26. *Report, Secretary of the Navy, 1883,* p. 18.
27. Richardson, *William E. Chandler,* pp. 308–309.
28. See Mark D. Hirsch, *William C. Whitney, Modern Warwick* (New York, 1948), pp. 258–263, 292. During the presidential campaign of 1888, however, over 1,000 men were reported temporarily employed at the New York navy yard. White, *The Republican Era,* pp. 173–174.
29. *Report, Secretary of the Navy, 1883,* pp. 11–12.
30. *Report, Secretary of the Navy, 1882,* p. 9.
31. See Richardson, *William E. Chandler,* p. 306; *Report, Secretary of the Navy, 1884,* p. 42.
32. Richardson, *William E. Chandler,* pp. 321, 323.
33. Henry H. Gorringe, "The Navy," *North American Review,* CXXXIV (May 1882), 486–506.
34. "The Week," *The Nation,* XXXVI (March 1, 1883), 180–181.
35. Richardson, *William E. Chandler,* p. 317.
36. See *ibid.,* pp. 317–321; Swann, *John Roach,* pp. 214–215. Cf. E. A. Falk, *Fighting Bob Evans* (New York, 1931), pp. 135–139.
37. Richardson, *Messages and Papers of the Presidents,* VIII, 248.
38. Arthur also gave his backing annually to increased armament for the nation's seacoast defense. In a special message of April 11, 1884, he requested $1,500,000. Congress appropriated $700,000 in July. In his last message to Congress Arthur recommended an appropriation of $6,000,000. *Ibid.,* 211, 246. He repeatedly supported the report of the Gun Foundry Board.
39. See Swann, *John Roach,* pp. 209–234.
40. The *Atlanta* was sold in 1912. The *Chicago* lasted until 1936. The *Boston* was sunk in 1946. John D. Alden, *The American Steel Navy* (New York, 1972), p. 16.
41. See Herrick, *The American Naval Revolution,* p. 36.
42. *Report, Secretary of the Navy, 1884,* pp. 7–8.
43. *Ibid.*
44. Sprout, *The Rise of American Naval Power,* pp. 188–189.
45. Hirsch, *William C. Whitney,* pp. 258–259.

CHAPTER TWENTY-TWO · HAIL TO THE CHIEF

1. "Albany Woman Tells of Her Reign as White House Mistress," *The Knicker-bocker Press* (Albany), March 16, 1913.
2. "The President's Public Levee," *The New York Times,* February 6, 1884.
3. "Another State Banquet," *ibid.,* March 6, 1884.
4. Editorial "White House Hospitality," *ibid.,* March 9, 1884.
5. "Hospitalities at the Capital," *ibid.,* February 25, 1883.
6. Beale (ed.), *Letters of Mrs. James G. Blaine,* II, 83–86; Poore, *Perley's Reminiscences of Sixty Years,* II, 463–465.
7. The presidential carriage suffered minor accidents traveling to and from the Brewster wedding, forcing Arthur and Nell to walk several blocks alone in a downpour to reach the White House. "The occurrence created some excitement," a reporter noted, "and gave rise to a number of alarming rumors as to the President's safety." "Weddings at the Capital," *The New York Times,* February 7, 1883.
8. Caroline Bancroft, *Silver Queen, The Fabulous Story of Baby Doe Tabor* (Boulder, Col., 1950), pp. 51–53 and *passim*; "Senator Tabor's Marriage," *The New York Times,* March 4, 1883; "Senator Tabor's Two Weddings," *ibid.,* March 5, 1883; Henry Teller to Thomas F. Dawson, March 6, 1883, Henry Teller Papers, Colorado State Historical Society. The Washington wedding scene, complete with the President, was re-created by Douglas Moore in his opera *The Ballad of Baby Doe,* produced in 1956.
9. See editorial "Edwin D. Morgan," *The New York Times,* February 15, 1883.
10. Beale (ed.), *Letters of Mrs. James G. Blaine,* II, 93.
11. Telegram, Chester A. Arthur to Benjamin Harrison, April 3, 1883, Benjamin Harrison Papers, L.C.; telegram, Walter Q. Gresham to Chester A. Arthur, April 4, 1883, White House Telegram Book, Charles Pinkerton Collection; editorial "A New Cabinet Minister," *The New York Times,* April 5, 1883; Matilda Gresham, *Life of Walter Quintin Gresham, 1832–1895* (Chicago, 1919), II, 489. Cf. Fowler, *The Cabinet Politician,* pp. 183–184.
12. See Crowley, *Echoes from Niagara,* pp. 148, 231; Gresham, *Life of Walter Quintin Gresham,* pp. 499–500.
13. "Sworn in at Midnight," *The New York Times,* September 26, 1884.
14. See Hugh McColloch, *Men and Measures of Half a Century* (New York, 1888), pp 31, 482–485.
15. See "The Sad News in Washington," *The New York Times,* March 26, 1883; Fowler, *The Cabinet Politician,* p. 181; Lowell Joseph Ragatz, "Frank Hatton," in Dumas Malone (ed.), *Dictionary of American Biography* (New York, 1932), VIII, 397–398.
16. Crowley, *Echoes from Niagara,* pp. 261–264; "Crowley and the President," New York *Sun,* April 10, 1883; telegrams from Crowley to Fred J. Phillips, March 20, 22, 24, 26, 1883, White House Telegram Book, Charles Pinkerton Collection.
17. Quoted in Howe, *Chester A. Arthur,* p. 244.
18. "Chester A. Arthur Dead," New York *Sun,* November 19, 1886. See also "Arthur Dead," New York *Mail and Express,* November 18, 1886.

19. "The President Not Well," *The New York Times*, March 11, 1883; "Officials on the Sick List," *ibid.*, March 25, 1883.

20. Joe M. Richardson, "The Florida Excursion of President Chester A. Arthur," *Tequesta*, no. 24 (1964), p. 41.

21. "The President's Florida Trip," *The New York Times*, April 5, 1883.

22. See "General Arthur Dead," New York *Commercial Advertiser*, November 18, 1886; "Preparing for the Burial," New York *World*, November 20, 1886.

23. The account of the Florida trip was based on *The New York Times* articles of April 11, 13, 17, and 20, as well as Richardson's "The Florida Excursion of President Chester A. Arthur." See also "The President's Health," New York *Sun*, April 22, 1883.

24. E. J. Edwards, "A Presidential Tragedy the Nation Narrowly Escaped," New York *Evening Mail*, January 12, 1911. Elisha Jay Edwards (1847–1924) was the Washington correspondent of the New York *Sun* during the Garfield and Arthur administrations.

25. "The President Taken Ill," *The New York Times*, April 21, 1883.

26. *Ibid.;* "The President's Illness," *ibid.*, April 22, 1883.

27. *Ibid.*

28. "Dead Among His Kindred," *ibid.*, November 19, 1886.

29. "News from Washington," New York *Tribune*, April 23, 1883.

30. "Washington," New York *Evening Post*, April 23, 1883.

31. See "News from Washington," New York *Tribune*, April 23, 24, 1883.

32. See "The Big Bridge Open," New York *Sun*, May 25, 1883; "Crowned," New York *Truth*, May 25, 1883.

33. See "Movements of the President," *The New York Times*, May 26, 1883; "The President's Leisure," Philadelphia *Times*, June 25, 1883; "Ramsdell's Letter," Philadelphia *Press*, July 15, 1883.

34. "The President in Town," New York *Herald*, July 3, 1883.

35. "President Arthur," *ibid.*, July 24, 1883.

36. Thomas C. Reeves, "President Arthur in Yellowstone National Park," *Montana, the Magazine of Western History*, XIX (Summer 1969), 18–19.

37. Ellis, *Henry Moore Teller*, pp. 144–146; Richardson, *Messages and Papers of the Presidents*, VIII, 144–145, 183, 185–186, 250, 253.

38. *Ibid.*, 50, 54–58, 143, 183, 250, 266–268, 277–278, 305–307; Ellis, *Henry Moore Teller*, pp. 139–144; *Annual Report, Secretary of the Interior, 1882*, pp. 3–17; *ibid.*, *1883*, pp. iii–xxix; *ibid.*, *1884*, pp. 3–14; editorial "The Zuni Indians Protected," *The New York Times*, May 7, 1883; editorial, *ibid.*, July 6, 1884; Allan Nevins, *Grover Cleveland, A Study in Courage* (New York, 1933), p. 228; Loring Benson Priest, *Uncle Sam's Stepchildren, the Reformation Of United States Indian Policy, 1865–1887* (New Brunswick, N.J., 1942), *passim.* Arthur spoke out sharply in his first message against Mormon polygamy and requested legislation to quash it. Congress responded with the Edmunds Act of March 22, 1882. See Oberholtzer, *A History of the United States Since the Civil War*, IV, 668–669. The Utah Commission, authorized by the same act, studied the government of the territory. Its reports prompted the President to recommend that Congress assume political control of the area and govern it through a commission. See *ibid.*, IV, 676; Richardson, *Messages and Papers of the Presidents*, VIII, 57–58, 144, 184, 250.

39. Reeves, "President Arthur in Yellowstone National Park," 19–23.
40. "The President," Chicago *Tribune*, August 2, 1883.
41. "The President in Indiana," Indianapolis *Journal*, August 3, 1883.
42. "The President," Chicago *Tribune*, August 3, 4, 1883.
43. For more on the journey, see Reeves, "President Arthur in Yellowstone National Park," 24–29.
44. "The 'Passing of Arthur,'" Chicago *Inter Ocean*, September 5, 1883.
45. See the *Tribune* columns titled "The President" published during the trip.
46. "St. Paul's Gala Day," *Daily Minnesota Tribune*, September 5, 1883.
47. "The President in Chicago," *The New York Times*, September 5, 1883. In December 1883, Grinnell wrote, "The trip . . . is already, as we predicted last summer would be the case, resulting in action for the proper preservation of the Park." See "The Yellowstone Park," *Forest and Stream*, XXI (December 20, 1883), 401; "Yellowstone Park Matters," and "The Yellowstone Park Bill," *ibid.*, XXII (March 13, 1884), 121, 124–125. Cf. Oberholtzer, *A History of the United States Since the Civil War*, IV, 680. See also Richardson, *Messages and Papers of the Presidents*, VIII, 186.
48. "A Popular President," Chicago *Inter Ocean*, September 6, 1883.
49. "Twice Critically Ill," *The New York Times*, December 13, 1886.

CHAPTER TWENTY-THREE · HIS TURN HAS COME

1. See "The Presidential Race," *The New York Times*, July 17, 1883.
2. See the Chicago *Daily News* issue of August 3, 1883.
3. "Voice of the Press," *Wisconsin State Journal*, August 3, 1883.
4. "Gath," Cincinnati *Enquirer*, August 14, 1883.
5. "Booms," *ibid.*, November 1, 1883.
6. "Mahone on the Result," *The New York Times*, November 9, 1883.
7. "The Week," *The Nation*, XXXVII (November 15, 1883), 403.
8. "The Presidency," Chicago *Tribune*, December 16, 1883.
9. "Arthur's Little Army," *The New York Times*, February 27, 1884.
10. "A Tact Tack," Chicago *Times*, March 27, 1882.
11. "Arthur's Coming Contest," Philadelphia *Times*, March 16, 1882.
12. E.g., "Booming Arthur in Chicago," *The New York Times*, September 4, 1883.
13. "Dorsey Discourses," *Rocky Mountain News*, January 20, 1884.
14. See interview of September 9, 1933, between Vernon Hampton and Frank B. Conger, Hampton Papers.
15. "The Presidential Race," *The New York Times*, July 17, 1883.
16. Marcus, *Grand Old Party*, p 67.
17. Badeau, *Grant in Peace*, p. 558. When the firm of Grant and Ward went bankrupt in May, leaving Grant hard-pressed for funds, he was reported willing to declare for Arthur if the President would persuade influential congressional Republicans to pass a retirement bill on his behalf. See Samuel B. French to Arthur, May 26, 1884; G. H. S. [George H. Sharpe] to Arthur, May 26, 1884, Arthur Papers, L.C. Arthur refrained from taking such action before the convention.
18. Lang (ed.), *The Autobiography of Thomas Collier Platt*, p. 81.

19. "Gath," Cincinnati *Enquirer,* August 14, 1883.
20. "Arthur's Friends," New York *Commercial Gazette,* March 31, 1883.
21. "The Boom Candidates," *The Nation,* XXXVIII (April 17, 1884), 334–335.
22. "Wayne MacVeagh Speaks," *The New York Times,* May, 20, 1884.
23. "Placing the Responsibility," *ibid.,* May 27, 1884.
24. See "Must Arthur Be the Man," *ibid.,* February 19, 1884; Richard E. Welch Jr., "George Edmunds of Vermont: Republican Half-Breed," *Vermont History,* XXXVI (Spring 1968), 64–73.
25. Editorial "Arthur's Weakness in New York," *The New York Times,* June 1, 1884.
26. "The Boom Candidates," *The Nation,* XXXVIII (April 17, 1884), 334.
27. See Muzzey, *James G. Blaine,* pp. 254, 268–269, 271–274. See also copy, Walter Q. Gresham to David Davis, March 7, 1884, David Davis Papers, Chicago Historical Society.
28. Marcus, *Grand Old Party,* pp. 62–64, 72–74.
29. "Arthur's Barren Victory," *The New York Times,* April 24, 1884.
30. As early as 1882, rumors floated of a deal between Blaine and Logan. See Marcus, *Grand Old Party,* pp. 68–69, 78–80.
31. See *ibid.,* pp. 64–66; Oscar Doane Lambert, *Stephen Benton Elkins* (Pittsburgh, 1955), pp. 37–38, 90–91.
32. See "Receiving the News Here," *The New York Times,* June 7, 1884.
33. "Enthusiasm for Arthur," Washington *Post,* May 21, 1884.
34. See J. C. Reed to Arthur, May 26, 1884, Arthur Papers, L.C.; "To Urge Arthur's Claims," *The New York Times,* May 29, 1884.
35. Stone, *Fifty Years a Journalist,* p. 147.
36. Hoar, *Autobiography of Seventy Years,* I, 406.
37. "Rules for Republicans," *The New York Times,* January 18, 1883.
38. "Mahone on the Result," *ibid.,* November 9, 1883. Mahone led a Virginia delegation to the national convention in support of Arthur, however. Twenty-one of the state's twenty-four votes were cast for the President on the first ballot.
39. "Dead Among His Kindred," *ibid.,* November 19, 1886.
40. E. J. Edwards, "How Arthur Helped to Defeat Himself," clipping in Charles Pinkerton Collection. See "Anecdotes of Mr. Arthur," New York *Sun,* November 28, 1886; memorandum "Mr. C. M. Hendley's association with President Arthur," April 22, 1925, Arthur Papers, L.C. See the annotated state-by-state list of southern delegates signed by "W. C." in *ibid.*
41. See the interview of September 9, 1933, between Vernon Hampton and Frank B. Conger, Hampton Papers. See also "Minor Gossip of the Capital," *The New York Times,* February 3, 1883; E. J. Edwards, "New News of Yesterday," New York *Evening Mail,* April 12, 1912.
42. Stone, *Fifty Years a Journalist,* pp. 149–150.
43 Arthur "made significantly little effort to obtain the nomination in 1884. I suppose he was under the impression that his administration might speak for him; there was something almost haughty in the way he disregarded some of the powerful politicians, with their following." Gerry (ed.), *Through Five Administrations,* p. 280.

44. "Anecdotes of Mr. Arthur," New York *Sun,* November 28, 1886.
45. See J. C. Reed to Fred Phillips, April 9, 1884; J. C. Reed to Arthur, May 26, 1884, Arthur Papers, L.C.
46. Walter Q. Gresham to Benjamin H. Bristow, May 15, 1884, Walter Q. Gresham Papers, L.C.; J. C. Reed to Arthur, May 26, 1884, Arthur Papers, L.C.
47. Interview of September 9, 1933, between Vernon Hampton and Frank B. Conger, Hampton Papers.
48. Quoted in Fowler, *The Cabinet Politician,* p. 186. David Davis called the Arthur campaign managers "idiotic." Copy, Davis to Walter Q. Gresham, June 25, 1884, Davis Papers.
49. See "Arthur Losing Ground," "A Canvass of the Delegates," "Arthur Practically Beaten," *The New York Times,* June 2, 1884. Conger also held a seat on the national committee.
50. Hoar, *Autobiography of Seventy Years,* I, 405–406.
51. "Arthur Practically Beaten," *The New York Times,* June 2, 1884.
52. "The Outlook for To-Day," "The Convention's First Work," *ibid.,* June 4, 1884; *Proceedings of the Eighth Republican National Convention Held at Chicago, Illinois, June 3, 4, 5 and 6, 1884* (Chicago, 1884), pp. 6–23.
53. *Ibid.,* pp. 37–38, 43; "The Story of the Convention," *The New York Times,* June 5, 1884.
54. "Combining to Beat Blaine," "The Blaine and Arthur Booms," *ibid.* See Marcus, *Grand Old Party,* pp. 82–84; "The Week," *The Nation,* XXXVIII (June 12, 1884), 495.
55. White, *Autobiography of Andrew Dickson White,* I, 203–204.
56. See "The Presentation Speeches," *The New York Times,* June 6, 1884.
57. *Proceedings,* pp. 101–103.
58. *Ibid.,* pp. 104–106; "The Presentation Speeches," *The New York Times,* June 6, 1884.
59. *Ibid.;* White, *The Autobiography of Andrew Dickson White,* I, 204–205.
60. *Proceedings,* pp. 104–109; "The Presentation Speeches," *The New York Times,* June 6, 1884.
61. *Ibid.; Proceedings,* pp. 110–114. See Martin I. Townsend to Arthur, June 13, 1884, Arthur Papers, L.C.
62. *Proceedings,* pp. 114–120; "The Presentation Speeches," *The New York Times,* June 6, 1884.
63. See *ibid.; Proceedings,* pp. 120–127; Julia B. Foraker, *I Would Live It Again* (New York, 1932), pp. 79–80. See also "Congressmen in Caucus," *The New York Times,* January 17, 1884.
64. *Proceedings,* pp. 141–142, 146–147, 149–150, 162–163; Marcus, *Grand Old Party,* p. 85; John W. Foster, *Diplomatic Memoirs* (Boston, 1909), II, 267; "The Convention's Closing Work," "Logan for Vice President," *The New York Times,* June 7, 1884. See copy, Leonard Swett to David Davis, June 10, 1884, Davis Papers.
65. Quoted in Marcus, *Grand Old Party,* p. 85.
66. "The News in Washington," *The New York Times,* June 7, 1884.
67. Interview of September 9, 1933, between Vernon Hampton and Frank B. Conger, Hampton Papers. The President confided to his son about the same

time that he had only approximately two years to live. Interview with Chester A. Arthur III, July 26, 1969. See also Walter Q. Gresham to W. P. Fishback, June 10, 1884, Gresham Papers.

68. See "Carlisle to Be Speaker," *The New York Times*, December 2, 1883; editorial "Mr. Carlisle's Committees," *ibid.*, December 25, 1883.

69. Quoted in Morgan, *From Hayes to McKinley*, p. 185.

70. See editorial "River and Harbor Appropriations," *The New York Times*, July 8, 1884.

71. "The Exposition Opened," "The Ceremonies in Washington," *The New York Times*, December 17, 1884.

72. See Oberholtzer, *A History of the United States Since the Civil War*, IV, 690–692.

73. See editorial "The National Labor Bureau," *The New York Times*, July 1, 1884.

74. See White, *The Republican Era*, pp. 246–247.

75. See Oberholtzer, *A History of the United States Since the Civil War*, IV, 307–308.

76. For an able summary of the congressional session, see the editorial "Congress," *The New York Times*, July 8, 1884.

77. For an adequate survey, see Otto Eisenschiml, *The Celebrated Case of Fitz John Porter, an American Dreyfus Affair* (Indianapolis, 1950), *passim*. Letters from Grant to Arthur, dated December 22, 1881, and April 10, 1882, are in the Fitz John Porter Papers, L.C., as is Robert T. Lincoln to Porter, April 15, 1882. A copy of the veto, in Arthur's handwriting, is in the Arthur Papers, L.C. For the formal statement, see Richardson, *Messages and Papers of the Presidents*, VIII, 221–223. For an interesting but questionable recollection, see Henry Watterson, *"Marse Henry" An Autobiography* (New York, 1919), I, 216–218. See also *The New York Times* stories of April 16, 17, 18, May 6, 7, June 1, 1882; January 20, February 2, July 3, 4, 1884.

78. Quoted in Eisenschiml, *The Celebrated Case of Fitz John Porter*, pp. 296–297.

79. "Fitz John Porter's Case," *The New York Times*, July 4, 1884.

80. Editorial "The Fitz John Porter Veto," *ibid.*, July 4, 1884.

81. Quoted in Morgan, *From Hayes to McKinley*, p. 208.

82. See Mark D. Hirsch, "The New York Times and the Election of 1884," *New York History*, XXIX (July 1948), 306; John M. Dobson, *Politics in the Gilded Age, a New Perspective on Reform* (New York, 1972), p. 150.

83. See Morgan, *From Hayes to McKinley*, pp. 214–217.

84. Ford (ed.), *Letters of Henry Adams, 1858–1891*, p. 360.

85. White, *Autobiography of Andrew Dickson White*, I, 209.

86. Quoted in Marcus, *Grand Old Party*, p. 94.

87. Fowler, *The Cabinet Politician*, pp. 184–186. Whitelaw Reid later contended, "There has never been a National election when the Federal officeholders were less active than this year." Editorial "Campaign Funds," New York *Tribune*, November 15, 1884. See also "Gath," Cincinnati *Enquirer*, November 19, 1884. Independents and Democrats claimed that W. W. Dudley, head of the U.S. Pensions Bureau, led a band of civil servants into West Virginia and Indiana dealing out bribes and propaganda. A House committee later probed the alleged abuses. See "National Capital Topics," *The New York Times*, February 26, 27, 1885.

88. Frelinghuysen refused to travel a few miles from his country home to attend

a Blaine rally. Pletcher, *The Awkward Years*, p. 270. The most active Cabinet member was William Chandler, involved in the Republican subsidization of Ben Butler's presidential campaign. It was hoped that Butler would capture a significant number of New York Irish Catholic votes from Cleveland. See Hans L. Trefousse, "Ben Butler and the New York Election of 1884," *New York History*, 37 (April 1956), 185–196. For more on the administration and the campaign, see "The Week," *The Nation*, XXXIX (December 25, 1884), 534; "The Mournful Past," *ibid.*, XL (January 8, 1885), 26–27; "Hawley Defends Arthur," *The New York Times*, January 5, 1885.

89. Oberholtzer, *A History of the United States Since the Civil War*, IV, 210; "Blaine and the Stalwarts," *The New York Times*, November 10, 1884; Pletcher, *The Awkward Years*, p. 270.

90. Marcus, *Grand Old Party*, p. 96. See J. C. Reed to Frederick J. Phillips, July 9, 1884, Arthur Papers, L.C. Stalwarts later claimed that Elkins and the national committee starved the state committee of campaign funds. "Blaine and the Stalwarts," *The New York Times*, November 10, 1884.

91. Muzzey, *James G. Blaine*, pp. 307–308. See "Talk About Conkling," New York *Tribune*, November 17, 1884.

92. Quoted in Muzzey, *James G. Blaine*, p. 320. The dinner also failed to produce badly needed election-day funds. See Marcus, *Grand Old Party*, p. 99.

93. See the editorial "Some Plain Facts," New York *Tribune*, November 14, 1884.

94. Quoted in Morgan, *From Hayes to McKinley*, p. 232. Robert D. Marcus concluded that Blaine would have narrowly succeeded in New York had it not been for Burchard. *Grand Old Party*, p. 99.

95. Quoted in Muzzey, *James G. Blaine*, p. 322.

96. Quoted in Morgan, *From Hayes to McKinley*, p. 233. Morgan agreed: "If Conkling had instructed followers to vote or campaign for Blaine, he could have made him president. . . . Conkling had his revenge."

97. "Blaine and the Stalwarts," *The New York Times*, November 10, 1884.

CHAPTER TWENTY-FOUR · A BOLDER DIPLOMATIST

1. Editorial "Mr. Arthur's Trade Treaties," *The New York Times*, December 15, 1884.

2. "Talk about the Treaty," *ibid.*, December 11, 1884.

3. Richardson, *Messages and Papers of the Presidents*, VIII, 130–131.

4. Pletcher, *The Awkward Years*, pp. 89–101; Philip Marshall Brown, "Frederick T. Frelinghuysen," in Samuel Flagg Bemis (ed.), *The American Secretaries of State and Their Diplomacy* (New York, 1927–1929), VIII, 9–17. See Millington, *American Diplomacy and the War of the Pacific*, pp. 121–143.

5. Pletcher, *The Awkward Years*, pp. 106–111.

6. Richardson, *Messages and Papers of the Presidents*, VIII, 41.

7. See Ulysses S. Grant, "The Nicaraguan Canal," *North American Review*, CXXXII (February 1881), 107–116.

8. See Estill McHenry (ed.), *Addresses and Papers of James B. Eads, Together With a Biographical Sketch* (St. Louis, 1884).

9. *U.S. Foreign Relations*, 1882, pp. 271–283.

10. Pletcher, *The Awkward Years*, pp. 112–114.
11. *U.S. Foreign Relations, 1883*, pp. 418–421, 477–478, 484–490, 529–532.
12. Pletcher, *The Awkward Years*, pp. 271–276; "News from Washington," *The New York Times*, June 17, 1884.
13. Richardson, *Messages and Papers of the Presidents*, VIII, 256–260.
14. *Ibid.*, VIII, 238.
15. Quoted in Pletcher, *The Awkward Years*, p. 279.
16. "The Nicaraguan Canal," *The Nation*, XXXIX (December 18, 1884), 516.
17. See articles in *ibid.*, December 11, 18, and 25, 1884; Pletcher, *The Awkward Years*, pp. 278–283; editorial "The Nicaragua Treaty," *The New York Times*, February 20, 1885.
18. "Gen. Arthur's Diplomacy," *ibid.*, December 19, 1884.
19. See *Congressional Record*, 48th Cong., 2d Sess., Appendix, pp. 168–176. With the year 1899 as the standard, the output of American manufactured goods increased from an index of 30 in 1877, to 42 in 1880, to 50 in 1883. The downturn of 1884–1885 produced a temporary drop of only three points. Some important manufactures—steel, tobacco, processed foods—were never subject to a decline during the late nineteenth century. See Garraty, *The New Commonwealth, 1877–1890*, p. 80.
20. Pletcher, *The Awkward Years*, p. 178.
21. See *ibid.*, pp. 180–191; Richardson, *Messages and Papers of the Presidents*, VIII, 238.
22. Pletcher, *The Awkward Years*, pp. 287–297; Foster, *Diplomatic Memoirs*, I, 239–259; editorial "Our West Indies Trade," *The New York Times*, December 8, 1884. See also *Congressional Record*, 48th Cong., 2d Sess., pp. 148–156.
23. Pletcher, *The Awkward Years*, pp. 297–301.
24. Donald Marquand Dozer, "The Opposition to Hawaiian Reciprocity, 1876–1888," *Pacific Historical Review*, XIV (June 1945), 172.
25. Arthur took a keen interest in trade with the Hermit Kingdom, believing that "it needs the implements and products which the United States are ready to supply." Richardson, *Messages and Papers of the Presidents*, VIII, 174. On the treaty itself, see Charles O. Paullin, *Diplomatic Negotiations of American Naval Officers, 1778–1883* (Baltimore, 1912), pp. 282–328.
26. See Pletcher, *The Awkward Years*, pp. 225–227.
27. In 1877, Senator Conkling had urged the appointment of a commission to hold talks with other nations about the possibility of a trans-African railroad. A year later, Commodore Robert W. Shufeldt, on his way to the Orient, visited West Africa, calling it the "great commercial prize of the world" and recommending an American consular service on the coast. The American Colonization Society called for an American survey of the West African coast. See Plesur, *America's Outward Thrust*, pp. 147–148.
28. Richardson, *Messages and Papers of the Presidents*, VIII, 175–176.
29. See Louis L. Snyder, "The American-German Pork Dispute, 1879–1891," *Journal of Modern History*, XVII (1945), 16–28; John L. Gignilliat, "Pigs, Politics, and Protection: The European Boycott of American Pork, 1871–1891," *Agricultural History*, XXXV (January 1961), 3–12.
30. Pletcher, *The Awkward Years*, pp. 308–320; Edward Younger, *John A. Kasson, Politics and Diplomacy from Lincoln to McKinley* (Iowa City, 1955), pp. 322–336.

31. Muzzey, *James G. Blaine*, p. 425.
32. Quoted in Pletcher, *The Awkward Years*, pp. 323–324.
33. See Richardson, *Messages and Papers of the Presidents*, VIII, 239–240; U.S. Congress, House, 49th Cong., 1st Sess., House Executive Doc. 50. One of the three commissioners appointed by Arthur was his good friend George H. Sharpe. See "Nominations by the President," *The New York Times*, July 8, 1884.
34. "Talk about the Treaty," *ibid.*, December 11, 1884.
35. "Congress and the Canal," *ibid.*, December 18, 1884; "Considering the Treaty," *ibid.*, December 21, 1884. See U.S. Congress, Senate, 48th Cong., 2d Sess., Senate Executive Doc. 11; U.S. Congress, Senate, 49th Cong., 1st Sess., Senate Executive Doc. 99.
36. Pletcher, *The Awkward Years*, p. 330; "Secrets of the Senate," *The New York Times*, January 9, 1885.
37. "The Nicaragua Treaty," *ibid.*, March 2, 1885.
38. "Voting Against the Canal," *ibid.*, January 30, 1885; Pletcher, *The Awkward Years*, p. 331.
39. *Ibid.*
40. Richardson, *Messages and Papers of the Presidents*, VIII, 327.
41. "Against the Treaty," "Prof. Sumner's Views," *The New York Times*, December 10, 1884; "Against Home Interests," *ibid.*, December 14, 1884; Foster, *Diplomatic Memoirs*, I, 260.
42. Richardson, *Messages and Papers of the Presidents*, VIII, 255–256.
43. "An Analysis of the Treaty," "The Schedules of the Treaty," *The New York Times*, December 12, 1884.
44. A special committee of the chamber soon issued a report favoring ratification. "Explaining the Treaty," *ibid.*, December 13, 1884; "No Such Treaty Wanted," *ibid.*, December 23, 1884.
45. "Explaining the Treaties," *ibid.*, December 27, 1884.
46. "The Administration and the Treaties," *The Nation*, XXXIX (December 25, 1884), 538.
47. *Congressional Record*, 48th Cong., 2d Sess., pp. 506–513.
48. *Ibid.*, pp. 548–551, Senate Misc. Doc. 45.
49. "The Reciprocity Policy," *The New York Times*, February 25, 1885; Pletcher, *The Awkward Years*, p. 337; Richardson, *Messages and Papers of the Presidents*, VIII, 279. Foster later recalled, "While there were Democratic Senators who were warm advocates of the Cuban treaty, the influence of the incoming Administration was thrown against it. Foster, *Diplomatic Memoirs*, I, 259–260. The Dominican treaty had been withheld temporarily by the Arthur Administration pending approval of the treaty with Spain.
50. See *Congressional Record*, 48th Cong., 2d Sess., pp. 1042–1043, 1059–1060; *ibid.*, Appendix, pp. 168–176; "The Mexican Treaty," *The New York Times*, January 29, 1885; Richardson, *Messages and Papers of the Presidents*, VIII, 279. On the final vote by the House see *Congressional Record*, 49th Cong., 1st Sess., p. 7341.
51. Dozer, "The Opposition to Hawaiian Reciprocity, 1876–1888"; Pletcher, *The Awkward Years*, pp. 173–177, 339–340.
52. Richardson, *Messages and Papers of the Presidents*, VIII, 236.
53. Pletcher, *The Awkward Years*, pp. 342–343; U.S. Congress, House, 48th Cong., 2d Sess., 1885, House Executive Docs. 156, 247; Perry Belmont, *An*

American Democrat, the Recollections of Perry Belmont (New York, 1940), pp. 311–334.

54. Richardson, *Messages and Papers of the Presidents*, VIII, 330.
55. *U.S. Foreign Relations, 1885*, pp. 285–289, 294–315.
56. In 1882, the United States participated for the first time in the convention of the International Red Cross. That same year, Americans attended an international conference on the protection of submarine cables. A conference of nations, initiated by the United States, met in Washington in late 1884 and established the international prime meridian of Greenwich.

CHAPTER TWENTY-FIVE · THE ANGEL OF SORROW

1. "Arthur's Tranquil End," New York *Herald*, November 19, 1886.
2. "Statement, Charles E. Miller and Daniel G. Rollins as Executors and Trustees under the last Will and Testament of Chester A. Arthur, deceased, July 24, 1888," Arthur Family Papers.
3. "New-York in the Senate," *The New York Times*, December 5, 1884; "The Senatorial Problem," *ibid.*, December 6, 1884.
4. "Washington Gossip," New York *World*, December 14, 1884.
5. "Morton Already Beaten," *The New York Times*, January 19, 1885; "Mr. Evarts to Be Senator," *ibid.*, January 20, 1885.
6. "The Dupont Statue Unveiled," *ibid.*, December 21, 1884.
7. "Marking a People's Love," *ibid.*, February 22, 1885; Poore, *Perley's Reminiscences of Sixty Years in the National Metropolis*, II, 472–477.
8. "The President's Guests," *The New York Times*, February 22, 1885.
9. "Mrs. McElroy's Last Reception," *ibid.*, March 1, 1885. For more on Greely, see A. L. Todd, *Abandoned: The Story of the Greely Arctic Expedition, 1881–1884* (New York, 1961); Richardson, *Messages and Papers of the Presidents*, VIII, 248.
10. *Ibid.*, VIII, 270–271.
11. "Last Labors in the House," "Gen. Grant's Retirement," *The New York Times*, March 5, 1885; Richardson, *Messages and Papers of the Presidents*, VIII, 280.
12. See *ibid.*, VIII, 299–303. For responses from across the country, see "The Inaugural Address," *The New York Times*, March 6, 1885.
13. Gerry (ed.), *Through Five Administrations*, p. 280.
14. See the solid accounts of the inaugural ceremonies in *The New York Times*, March 5, 1885. See also Barnes, *John G. Carlisle*, p. 91.
15. "Mr. Arthur's Plans," *The New York Times*, January 24, 1885; "Preparing for the Burial," New York *World*, November 20, 1886; "Death of Gen. Arthur," Washington *Star*, November 19, 1886.
16. "Arthur Dead," New York *Mail and Express*, November 18, 1886. See the interview between Vernon Hampton and Arthur H. Masten, November 25, 1931, Hampton Papers.
17. See checks and medical receipts in the Arthur Papers, L.C. One check dated June 15, 1886, was for $1,420; another of January 10, 1887, amounted to $1,560.
18. See "Mr. Brewster's Tribute," *The New York Times*, November 19, 1886.
19. "In Honor of Justice Daly," New York *Tribune*, December 31, 1885.

20. "Arthur Dead," New York *Mail and Express*, November 18, 1886; "Chester A. Arthur Dead," New York *Sun*, November 19, 1886.
21. Williams (ed.), *Diary and Letters of Rutherford Birchard Hayes*, IV, 294.
22. Arthur to Gresham, "Personal," August 1886, Gresham Papers.
23. Arthur to Chandler, October 4, 1886, Chandler Papers, New Hampshire State Historical Society.
24. "Chester A. Arthur Dead," New York *Daily News*, November 18, 1886.
25. "General Arthur Dead," New York *Commercial Advertiser*, November 18, 1886.
26. "General Arthur Dead," Philadelphia *Press*, November 19, 1886.
27. "Chester A. Arthur Dead," New York *Daily News*, November 18, 1886; interview with Chester A. Arthur III, July 26, 1969; interviews between Chester A. Arthur III and Vernon B. Hampton, 1937–1938, Hampton Papers; Library of Congress, *Index to the Chester A. Arthur Papers* (Washington, 1961), v. Smith called on Arthur's son-in-law, Charles Pinkerton, during the Progressive Era and described his deed. Charles Pinkerton to the author, April 1, 14, 1970, Thomas C. Reeves Collection, L.C.
28. "Ex-President Arthur," New York *Evening Post*, November 19, 1886.
29. Chester A. Arthur III to Carey McWilliams, October 22, 1946, Arthur Family Papers. Years later when Alan had the opportunity to be named a United States Senator from Colorado he recalled his father's admonition and flatly refused the offer. Interview with Chester A. Arthur III, July 26, 1969.
30. Editorial, New York *Sun*, November 19, 1886.
31. "Preparing for the Burial," New York *World*, November 20, 1886.
32. "Buried Near His Wife," New York *Sun*, November 23, 1886. Relevant materials are in the Arthur Papers, L.C.
33. "Arthur Statue Unveiled," New York *Sun*, *The New York Times*, June 14, 1899.

CHAPTER TWENTY-SIX · CONCLUSION

1. McClure, *Recollections of Half a Century*, p. 115.
2. Albert K. Weinberg, "Our Least-Remembered President," Baltimore *Sun*, October 5, 1930.
3. Chandler, "Chester Alan Arthur," in Wilson (ed.), *The Presidents of the United States 1789–1914*, III, 235.
4. See Wilfred E. Binkley, *The President and Congress* (New York, 1947), pp. 176–177.
5. Matthew Josephson, *The Politicos, 1865–1896* (New York, 1938), p. 323. On the other hand, Josephson's account of Arthur's career is one of the least accurate in print. The opening quotation of the chapter covering the years 1881–1884 (p. 319) is a distorted and misleading sentence from Howe's *Chester A. Arthur* (p. 206).
6. "Enthusiasm for Arthur," Washington *Post*, May 21, 1884.
7. "Complimenting Arthur," *The New York Times*, March 6, 1885.
8. See "President Arthur," Chicago *Inter Ocean*, August 3, 1883.
9. James E. Pollard, *The Presidents and the Press* (New York, 1947), pp. 491–492.
10. Silas Burt Biography, pp. 32–34.

11. "The Bee," Cincinnati *Enquirer*, November 22, 1883.

12. See George Haven Putnam, *Memories of a Publisher, 1865–1915* (New York, 1915), pp. 86–89; Cortissoz, *The Life of Whitelaw Reid*, II, 79; "Washington Gossip," New York *World*, December 14, 1884.

13. I have chosen to avoid the essentially antihistorical game of "President-ranking." For a good survey of these ratings, see Joseph E. Kallenbach, *The American Chief Executive, the Presidency and the Governorship* (New York, 1966), pp. 267–271.

14. Editorial "Ex-President Arthur," New York *World*, November 20, 1886.

INDEX

A Note on the Type

The text of this book was set on the Linotype in Garamond No. 3,
a modern rendering of the type
first cut by Claude Garamond (1510–1561).
Garamond was a pupil of Geoffroy Troy and is believed
to have based his letters on the Venetian models,
although he introduced a number of important differences,
and it is to him we owe the letter which we know as old-style.
He gave to his letters a certain elegance
and a feeling of movement that won for their creator
an immediate reputation and the patronage of Francis I of France.